D0345674

The **AA** **KEY**Guide
Britain

Contents

KEY TO SYMBOLS

- Map reference
- Address
- Telephone number
- Opening times
- Admission prices
- Bus number
- Train station
- Ferry/boat
- Driving directions
- Tourist office
- Tours
- Guidebook
- Restaurant
- AA rosette (▷ 333)
- Café
- Shop
- Bar
- Toilets
- Number of rooms
- Parking
- No smoking
- Air conditioning
- Swimming pool
- Gym
- Other useful information
- Shopping
- Entertainment
- Nightlife
- Sports
- Activities
- Health and beauty
- For Children
- ▷ Cross reference
- ★ Walk/tour start point

HOW TO USE THIS BOOK

Understanding Britain is an introduction to the country, its geography, economy and people. **Living Britain** gives an insight into Britain today, while **The Story of Britain** takes you through the country's past.

For detailed advice on getting to Britain—and getting around once you are there—turn to **On the Move**. For useful practical information, from weather forecasts to emergency services, turn to **Planning**.

Out and About gives you the chance to explore Britain through walks and drives.

The **Sights**, **What to Do** and **Eating and Staying** sections are divided into seven regions, which are shown on the map on the inside front cover. These regions always appear in the same order. Towns and places of interest are listed alphabetically within each region.

Map references for the **Sights** refer to the atlas section at the end of this book or to individual town plans. For example, Manchester has the reference ✚ 434 G14, indicating the page on which the map is found (434) and the grid square in which Manchester sits (G14).

UNDERSTANDING BRITAIN

On a map of the world Britain looks surprisingly small.
But don't assume that you can see the whole country in just a week or two.
Unrivalled variety, from world-class culture in dynamic cities to a beautiful,
subtle patchwork of landscapes shaped by thousands of years of history,
is concentrated in this densely populated island. Britain's inhabitants
can be contradictory. They can prize both order and individuality, and value
tradition but look forward rather than back. They've made their mark on
their island with prehistoric monuments, castles, stately homes and
elegant abbeys, all playing a part in Britain's dramatic history.
And they've changed the world with the English language, the
Industrial Revolution... and the gin and tonic.

Left: a cottage in the English countryside. Middle: rugby union is the national sport of Wales. Right: Scottish clans identify themselves by wearing different tartans

WHAT IS BRITAIN?

Even to those who live there, the word 'Britain' is a source of confusion. It covers England, Wales and Scotland. Britain plus Northern Ireland equals the United Kingdom, the political entity that is governed from the capital city, London. The Republic of Ireland is a separate country, but the islands of Ireland and Britain plus the Channel Islands make up the British Isles. A government survey in 2001 found that fewer than half of Britons thought of themselves as British; they much preferred to describe themselves as English, Welsh or Scottish.

At 50,331sq miles (130,357sq km) England is the largest nation in Britain, followed by Scotland at 30,405sq miles (77,080sq km), then Wales at 8,188sq miles (20,758sq km).

In a country where every hillside and woodland is named, it isn't surprising that Britain's regions have a proliferation of names. England, Wales and Scotland consist of areas of local government known as counties. Most counties have very long histories, have distinct characters and attract fierce loyalties. We've divided Britain into seven regions based on county boundaries; see the map on page 7.

THE ECONOMY

In the 19th century, Britain was the world's superpower and its empire stretched across one quarter of the world's surface. Two world wars diminished the country's strength and influence considerably. Today the UK is one of the top three European economies and a member of the G8 group of leading industrialized nations. Services and the financial sector are superseding manufacturing and industry as the basis of the economy. Unemployment is low when compared to some European countries, but there are pockets of deprivation in most cities, and rural economies are increasingly threadbare as the younger generation relocate to the cities to find work.

POLITICS

Despite being one of the first countries to develop a parliamentary democracy, Britain retains a monarch, currently Queen Elizabeth II. Decisions are made in two debating chambers: the House of Lords and the House of Commons. The Commons, where ultimate legislative power rests, consists of 646 Members of Parliament (MPs) who each represent a constituency in the UK. There are three main political parties: Labour, Liberal Democrat and Conservative (Tory). Britain's 'first past the post' electoral system, in which the MP who wins the most votes in their constituency then represents their party in Parliament, generally means that one party is in overall control and forms the government. Since 1997 the official Opposition has been the Conservatives (the Tories), with the Liberal Democrats also wielding considerable influence. The current Labour government is led by Prime

Minister Tony Blair. One of the first policies to be put into effect by his government was to devolve power to Scotland, Wales and Northern Ireland. The Welsh Assembly in Cardiff has 60 members and Scotland's new Parliament has 129 MSPs (Members of the Scottish Parliament). These bodies make decisions about their respective countries' domestic issues such as health and education.

Britain is a member of the European Union (EU) and the North Atlantic Treaty Organization (NATO), and is one of the five permanent members of the United Nations Security Council. Relations with other European nations are usually good, if complex, and Britain often acts as a transatlantic intermediary between the United States and the rest of Europe.

HERITAGE

Look beyond the modern veneer of Britain and you find links to the past everywhere. Many British cities and towns have Roman origins: place names ending with 'caster' or 'chester', for example, come from the Roman word *castrum*, meaning a military base. So unruly were the locals that Britain was the only province in the Roman Empire to have a permanent garrison of soldiers, and walls were erected to protect many towns. Those of York, Chester and Conwy remain intact.

By early medieval times most of today's settlements were already on the map. Their names are not far removed from the originals. The suffixes -ham, -ton and -ing suggest Saxon origins; Vikings from Scandinavia settled in eastern England in places that carry the suffix -by (such as Whitby).

For many centuries, Britain's most impressive buildings were castles, stately homes and places of worship. Castles were erected to defend coasts, towns and borders. Many were deliberately 'slighted' (rendered unusable) by invaders notably during the Civil War in the 17th century—and now stand as jagged ruins. Kenilworth Castle is one of the finest of these. The opulent stately homes of Britain's landed gentry can also be hugely impressive, and today many are open to the public.

Religious buildings provide another key to the country's past. While Saxon church architecture is rare, the Normans introduced a huge scheme of church building. Their rounded arches gave way in turn to elaborate Gothic flourishes. Meanwhile, monasteries were among the richest landowners of medieval Britain. Their dissolution in the 1530s by Henry VIII

ended a centuries-old way of life. Most became roofless ruins; many stand today as poignant landmarks.

Britain's countryside has been shaped by its people. Over the centuries, settlers have largely removed Britain's ancient forest, leaving tracts of moorland on higher ground, consisting of heather, bogs and bracken. At lower levels, fields are bounded by hedges and dry-stone walls.

Pre-Roman settlers left numerous reminders of their existence. The early farming communities of the Neolithic period and Bronze Age erected ceremonial sites, such as stone circles, standing stones and burial mounds. You can find some of Britain's richest concentrations of such prehistoric sites in western Cornwall, Dartmoor (in Devon), Wiltshire and the Orkney Islands in Scotland.

LANGUAGE

English owes its roots to a mixture of Teutonic and Latin languages, reflecting waves of invasion

Sunrise at Stonehenge: The summer solstice draws many people to this ancient monument

during the early medieval period. Through Britain's vast colonial expansion it has become the first language of 300 million people, and is understood by many more.

Traditional English dialects have been steadily eroded over the past century. Where there are differences, they tend to be minor. But somehow accents have survived to a surprising degree. The Scottish accent is unmistakable; the West Coast accent (especially around Glasgow) can be incomprehensible to outsiders. Speakers in Yorkshire and Lancashire tend to use broad vowel sounds, and there are subtle local variations. Liverpudlian has been immortalized by the Beatles, Brummy is the key signature of the West Midlands, South Wales has a singsong quality and the West Country has a distinct burr. In the South East the differences have blurred, with 'Estuary English' gaining ground over the crisp Home Counties accent.

Welsh, an old Celtic language that the Iron Age peoples spoke before the Romans arrived, is still spoken by around a quarter of the population of Wales. Banned by Henry VIII when Wales was officially united with England in 1535, it survived and is now taught in schools, and appears on bilingual signs. In Scotland, Gaelic is another ancient Celtic language, but it is less widely spoken than Welsh.

The West Country Cornwall, Devon, Dorset, Wiltshire, Somerset and Gloucestershire. *Main cities: Bristol, Plymouth.* The West Country is Britain's most popular tourist area. It has beautiful, long beaches along an extraordinarily varied coastline. Many prehistoric sites punctuate a largely rural landscape.

The South East and East Anglia Counties surrounding London–Hertfordshire, Essex, Buckinghamshire, Surrey–are called the Home Counties. Sussex (West and East), Berkshire, the Isle of Wight and Hampshire don't neighbour London but are considered part of the South East. *Main city: London.* The South East is densely populated, yet has large areas of surprisingly deep countryside–much of it a prosperous commuterdom known as the 'stockbroker belt', with property prices to match. East Anglia comprises Norfolk, Suffolk, Cambridgeshire and northern Essex. *Main cities: Cambridge, Peterborough, Norwich.* Mainly flat, fertile farmland towards England's east coast, East Anglia is dominated by fields of crops, watery landscapes of reedy marshes and coastal dunes (including important bird reserves), country estates and historic villages and small towns, many with imposing churches and varied architecture.

London Greater London includes vast suburbs that stretch out to the M25 motorway. Inner, or central, London is the political and economic heart of Britain.

The Midlands Ill-defined, but includes the central English 'shires', including Warwickshire, Shropshire, Herefordshire, Staffordshire, Derbyshire, Leicestershire, Rutland, Oxfordshire,

Left: fishing boats at Whitby harbour. Whitby was a Viking settlement; today visitors can take boat trips with fishermen. Middle: Tower Bridge in London by night. Right: the Old Man of Coniston in the Lake District, seen from Brantwood, home of Victorian critic John Ruskin

Worcestershire, Nottinghamshire and Northamptonshire–and arguably Cheshire, Lincolnshire, Gloucestershire and Bedfordshire. *Main cities: Birmingham, Coventry, Nottingham, Derby, Leicester, Oxford.* Britain's industrial heartland is in the Midlands, notably around the second city of Birmingham and the surrounding 'Black Country', with some of the world's earliest Industrial Revolution sites. Scenically a mixed bag, with the Peak District among the most prized landscapes.

Wales *Main cities: Cardiff, Swansea.* Wales is an ancient kingdom, separate from England until 1535, and with its own Assembly since 1999. It's largely rural, with most of the population living in the south. The Marches share the borderland with England. South Wales includes the industrial valleys north of Cardiff–now that coal mining has virtually halted these are economic backwaters and many skilled workers have moved away. In mid-Wales sheep greatly outnumber people and even the main roads are almost deserted. North Wales includes Snowdonia, the highest mountain area in Wales and England, and the low-lying Isle of Anglesey. Pembrokeshire, in the west, is known for its unspoiled coast.

The North Yorkshire, Lancashire, Cumbria, Durham and Northumberland. *Main cities: Leeds, Bradford, Manchester, Liverpool, Sheffield, Newcastle.* England's highest land, including the Pennine Hills that roughly divide the region in two, the North spans the mountains of the Lake District and the heathery plateaux of the North York Moors. It is densely populated in the south, with a chain of industrial towns and cities, but much emptier farther north, beyond York and west of Newcastle, and towards central and northern Northumberland.

Scotland *Main cities: Glasgow, Edinburgh, Aberdeen.* Natural features divide Scotland far more distinctively than its administrative districts. The mountainous Western Highlands feature the Trossachs; Wester Ross, among the most spectacular of all highland scenery, in the far northwest; the Cairngorm Mountains; the islands and archipelagos, including the Western Isles or Outer Hebrides (Lewis and Harris, North Uist, South Uist and Barra), the Inner Hebrides (Skye, Arran, Mull, Bute and smaller islands), and the isles of Orkney and Shetland. Lowlands are everything south of the Highland Fault, including Glasgow and Edinburgh, the Southern Uplands, and the green hills and ruined abbeys of the Borders.

BRITAIN'S REGIONS AT A GLANCE

ORKNEY ISLANDS

SHETLAND ISLANDS

WESTERN ISLES

MORAY

HIGHLAND

ABERDEEN-SHIRE

ABERDEEN

PERTH & KINROSS

ANGUS

ARGYLL & BUTE

STIRLING

FIFE

EAST LOTHIAN

NORTH AYRSHIRE

SOUTH LANARKSHIRE

BORDERS

EAST AYRSHIRE

SOUTH AYRSHIRE

DUMFRIES & GALLOWAY

NORTHUMBERLAND

TYNE & WEAR

DURHAM

CUMBRIA

ISLE OF MAN

NORTH YORKSHIRE

LANCASHIRE

WEST YORKSHIRE

EAST RIDING OF YORKSHIRE

ISLE OF ANGLESEY

MERSEYSIDE

GREATER MANCHESTER

SOUTH YORKSHIRE

CONWY

CHESHIRE

DERBY-SHIRE

LINCOLNSHIRE

GWYNEDD

NOTTINGHAM-SHIRE

STAFFORD-SHIRE

LEICESTERSHIRE

RUTLAND

NORFOLK

SHROPSHIRE

WEST MIDLANDS

NORTHAMPTON-SHIRE

CAMBRIDGE-SHIRE

SUFFOLK

CEREDIGION

POWYS

WORCESTER-SHIRE

WARWICK-SHIRE

BEDFORD-SHIRE

PEMBROKESHIRE

HEREFORD-SHIRE

GLOUCESTER-SHIRE

BUCKINGHAM-SHIRE

HERTFORD-SHIRE

ESSEX

CARMARTHEN-SHIRE

OXFORD-SHIRE

GREATER LONDON

BERKSHIRE

WILTSHIRE

SURREY

KENT

SOMERSET

HAMPSHIRE

WEST SUSSEX

EAST SUSSEX

DEVON

DORSET

ISLE OF WIGHT

CORNWALL

ISLES OF SCILLY

1	BLAENAU GWENT
2	BRIDGEND
3	BRISTOL
4	CAERPHILLY
5	CARDIFF
6	CLACKMANNANSHIRE
7	DENBIGHSHIRE
8	EAST DUNBARTONSHIRE
9	EAST RENFREWSHIRE
10	EDINBURGH
11	FALKIRK
12	FLINTSHIRE
13	GLASGOW
14	INVERCLYDE
15	MERTHYR TYDFIL
16	MIDLOTHIAN
17	MONMOUTHSHIRE
18	NEATH PORT TALBOT
19	NEWPORT
20	NORTH LANARKSHIRE
21	RENFREWSHIRE
22	RONDDA CYNON TAFF
23	SWANSEA
24	TORFAEN
25	VALE OF GLAMORGAN
26	WEST DUNBARTONSHIRE
27	WEST LOTHIAN
28	WREXHAM

BEST PLACES TO STAY

Gleneagles, Auchterarder (▷ 364) Two convincing reasons to stay at Scotland's top hotel: the golf and Andrew Fairlie's sublime cooking in the restaurant.

Hazelwood, York (▷ 397) An elegant and useful bed-and-breakfast in the heart of York.

Lavenham Priory, Lavenham (▷ 379) This luxurious bed-and-breakfast occupies a half-timbered medieval house.

Linthwaite House, Windermere (▷ 397) A delightful hilltop hotel in the Lake District with a fishing lake.

The Hotel Portmeirion, Portmeirion (▷ 388) Like a surreal filmset with views over the sea and mountains.

A Scottish pipe band at Gleneagles

BEST PLACES TO EAT

Le Champignon Sauvage, Cheltenham (▷ 335) David Everitt-Matthias' innovative, exciting cooking contrasts with the Regency elegance of this Cotswolds town.

Hibiscus, Ludlow (▷ 356) Claude Bosi cooks up French-influenced fare for gastronomic pilgrims to this small Shropshire town.

Midsummer House, Cambridge (▷ 341) Step off Cambridge's tourist trail and enjoy adventurous French cuisine at the city's finest restaurant.

Restaurant Gordon Ramsay, London (▷ 348) Flawless cooking from the chef with the biggest reputation in London—lunch is a bargain.

Restaurant Martin Wishart, Edinburgh (▷ 365) Eye-catching flair at this restaurant on Leith's fashionable waterfront.

Food for thought: British cuisine is improving

BEST RUINS

Bignor Roman Villa, West Sussex (▷ 93) Bignor's second-century owners commissioned breathtaking mosaics for their house, which survive today.

Hadrian's Wall, Northumberland (▷ 168) One Roman emperor's attempt to keep northern barbarians out is now Britain's most spectacular Roman ruin.

Lindisfarne Priory, Northumberland (▷ 174) Founded in AD635, Lindisfarne was an early crucible of English Christianity and remains a place of pilgrimage.

Maes Howe, Orkney (▷ 205) This burial chamber dates from 2800BC and may be the only World Heritage Site with Viking graffiti.

Rievaulx Abbey, Yorkshire (▷ 177) Perhaps the most beautiful and moving of England's ruined monasteries.

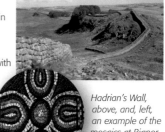

Hadrian's Wall, above, and, left, an example of the mosaics at Bignor Roman Villa

BEST GALLERIES AND MUSEUMS

Baltic Centre for Contemporary Art, Newcastle upon Tyne (▷ 175) An art gallery leading the way in a city's regeneration.

British Museum, London (▷ 122–123) Nothing less than an anthology of civilization; highlights include the Egyptian Room and the treasures from Sutton Hoo in Suffolk.

Burrell Collection, Glasgow (▷ 198) An outstanding collection of art, textiles and objects from around the world.

Tate Modern, London (▷ 129) You'll either love the art or not, but there's no disputing the triumphant building.

Weald and Downland Open Air Museum, West Sussex (▷ 115) More than 40 historic buildings, from medieval homes to a Victorian school, all in the fresh air.

The view from Tate Modern across the Millennium Bridge

THE BEST OF BRITAIN

BEST CASTLES

Caernarfon Castle, Gwynedd (▷ 135) Dwarfing the town, this harbourside castle was built by Edward I in 1283.
Dover Castle, Kent (▷ 99) From the Iron Age to the Cold War, this fortress has defended Britain's shores; exhibitions and reconstructions tell its story.
Eilean Donan Castle, Highlands (▷ 195) Imagine a classic Scottish castle beside a misty loch, it's probably Eilean Donan that you're thinking of.
Warwick Castle, Warwickshire (▷ 160) A slickly run showpiece castle, with lots of holiday events.
Windsor Castle (▷ 112) Have a look around the Queen's principal residence and the largest occupied castle in the world.

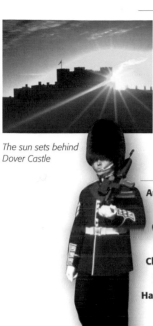

The sun sets behind Dover Castle

BEST STATELY HOUSES

Audley End, Essex (▷ 92) Adults can ponder how much one of England's greatest Jacobean houses would fetch today—Charles II paid £50,000 in 1668.
Castle Howard, Yorkshire (▷ 166) The drive through the estate is a dramatic prelude to this grand 18th-century house, still the home of the Howard family.
Chatsworth House, Derbyshire (▷ 152) A palatial 17th-century house in the country with plenty of stories to tell.
Hampton Court Palace, Surrey (▷ 100) Once a home to British monarchs, this Tudor palace on the Thames has magnificent interiors, gardens and a tricky maze.
Petworth House, West Sussex (▷ 110) Inside is the National Trust's finest art collection, with oil paintings by Van Dyck, Turner, Reynolds and Titian.

A Scots Guard on parade at Windsor Castle and, right, Hampton Court Palace

BEST GARDENS

Bodnant Garden, Conwy (▷ 135) With blazing flower displays in a gorgeous location in Wales, Bodnant is one of Britain's most popular gardens.
Inverewe Gardens, Highlands (▷ 197) Plants from the Himalayas, the Antipodes and South America flourish in this remote Scottish garden.
Lost Gardens of Heligan, Cornwall (▷ 82) Thankfully found and being restored, there are exotic plants, summer houses, pools and a grotto to discover at this fantastic estate.
Royal Botanic Gardens, Kew, Surrey (▷ 126) Awarded World Heritage status in 2003, Kew's Royal Botanic Gardens have an unparalleled collection of plants.
Westonbirt Arboretum, Gloucestershire (▷ 90) 18,000 trees, including many rare species, in one of Europe's most diverse collections.

Inverewe Gardens, above, and the standing stones at Avebury, below

BEST PREHISTORIC SITES

Avebury, Wiltshire (▷ 67) Surrounded by prehistoric barrows, Avebury is home to Britain's largest stone circle.
Calanais Standing Stones, Isle of Lewis (▷ 204) Pre-dating Egypt's pyramids by a millennium, there's mystery and breathtaking beauty in these standing stones.
Castlerigg Stone Circle, Cumbria (▷ 172) At the heart of the Lake District, this megalithic monument has a more scenic location than Stonehenge (▷ 87).

TOP 20 EXPERIENCES

Step back 800 years and walk around York's medieval walls, then explore the narrow lanes inside (▷ 181–183).

Take a trip on a steam train The North Yorkshire Moors Railway is one of the most scenic (▷ 309).

Harrods in London, and if you miss the sales (January and July), content yourself with a tour of the amazing food halls (▷ 235).

Have a cream tea, a refreshing afternoon tradition at any time of the year (▷ 331).

Go clubbing at Fabric in London, where Britain's best DJs play cutting-edge dance music (▷ 239).

Rent a bicycle and explore some of England's lanes or go mountain biking in Wales (▷ 246).

Take a ride on the British Airways London Eye for a bird's-eye view of the capital (▷ 120). Try to pick a clear day for views as far as the Thames Barrier.

Relax at a restored spa Harrogate (▷ 170) and Bath (▷ 68–71, 222; due to open 2006) have stunning new spas, based on the Roman originals.

People-watch at a Season event such as Royal Ascot (▷ 229) or the Royal Academy's Summer Exhibition (▷ 128) each year in June.

See a Shakespeare play in Stratford-upon-Avon (▷ 158), his home town, or at the Globe Theatre (▷ 128) in London, a re-creation of a 16th-century theatre.

Go punting in Oxford to see the spires of this university city from its waterways (▷ 104–107).

Watch the sun set from a deserted Pembrokeshire beach (▷ 144), but don't forget to bring a sweater.

Sing along at a rugby match in Wales, preferably one in which the national side is playing (▷ 243).

Climb a Munro in Scotland Buachaille Etive Beag, in the middle of Glen Coe, is a relatively easy and accessible introduction to the Scottish hills (▷ 196, 260).

Sample a pint or two of real ale, but choose your pub carefully; free houses often stock interesting beers from independent local breweries.

Pack a picnic for a day out in the Lake District (▷ 172).

See a city from the top deck of a double-decker bus London has red double-deckers as part of the public transport system; London, Oxford, Cambridge, Bath and York have special sightseeing tours by double-decker bus (▷ 57).

Party at a festival for free at Hogmanay in Edinburgh (▷ 266) or the Notting Hill Carnival in London (▷ 242).

Put on a pair of walking boots and explore a national park on foot (▷ 268–328).

Watch a traditional ceremony Changing the Guard is the most famous daily event in London (▷ 242).

You can still travel by steam engine in Britain (above). The classic cream tea (left)

The BA London Eye (above) and punting in Oxford (below)

Ye Olde Cheshire Cheese (below), a traditional London pub

A day at the races during Royal Ascot (left)

Notting Hill Carnival (below)

Living
Britain

Where's that ball? Not everyone can afford to play polo

Art imitates life: Lucian Freud's controversial 2002 portrait of Queen Elizabeth II

Prince Harry and Prince William at the Queen's Golden Jubilee

Society and Royalty

Picture this

Lucian Freud's portrait of Queen Elizabeth II was unveiled in 2002. Considered unflattering by some, including, the newspapers say, the subject herself, it testifies to the importance of the portrait in British society. It is difficult to tour a stately home without the great and the good looking down upon you. The tradition follows the fashion for genealogy among the aristocracy, and the Reformation in the 16th century, when religious imagery was proscribed. The best assortment of famous faces is in the National Portrait Gallery in London, whose marvellous collection ranges from a 1505 painting of Henry VII by an unknown artist, right up to a 1983 picture of Paul McCartney by Humphrey Ocean—a painted pageant of British characters.

Is Britain a classless society? True, there is more of a meritocracy with high-profile jobs no longer awarded on the basis of your school tie, and celebrities replacing high society. But the Establishment is alive and well, if less obvious. You won't find it at the traditional gatherings—Royal Ascot horse racing in June, Cowes Week yachting in August—which now seek corporate guests, nor between the pages of the society bible, *Tatler* magazine. Instead think of grouse shoots on Scottish estates and magazines like *Country Life* and *The Field*. But for those who still judge by manners, Debrett's etiquette guides continue to be required reading. The monarchy may be a limited and expensive institution, but many believe that it still has a role, not least to attract visitors to Britain with spectacular occasions such as Trooping the Colour in London in June, and royal properties such as Windsor Castle and Buckingham Palace.

Professional party-goer, and minor aristocrat, Tara Palmer-Tompkinson

Kylie Minogue, the Queen of Pop, and the Prince of Wales: Are celebrities more popular than royalty in Britain today?

Are you in it? *Debrett's People of Today* lists notable Britons while *Debrett's Peerage and Baronetage* is a guide to Britain's aristocracy

Frock on! Ladies' Day at Royal Ascot and all eyes are on the extravagant hats, rather than the horse racing

Victoria Beckham may have been a successful pop star, but it is her husband, the footballer David Beckham, who is a national hero in England

Royal warrant

Keep your eyes open and you'll spot royal warrants everywhere in Britain. Companies and individuals appointed to provide goods and services to the royal family can display a royal coat of arms for five years. The practice, which began in the 15th century, gives an insight into the royal lifestyle—look no further than a royal mole controller and a chimney sweep. No fewer than six champagne houses have royal warrants, and several chocolatiers—including Cadburys for the staff, and Prestat or Bendicks for the royals. The sporty monarchy has four official gunmakers, providers of riding breeches and fishing tackle, and a busy royal taxidermist.

Season hamper

Once just Britain's social elite laid out rugs and prepared picnics at the summer events such as race meetings and open-air operas that made up 'The Season'. Today you're more likely to find corporate hospitality tents. But that doesn't mean that the picnic-goer shouldn't make an effort for the sake of tradition. But since the picnic hamper sends out subtle signals to others, there are certain things you should specify. Smoked salmon, for example, should be wild not farmed. And strawberries should be English rather than Spanish. Scots may prefer to include some specialities from north of the border such as cullen skink soup or oatcakes. There are simple rules for drinks too. Cans must be avoided. Pimms—a deceptive, sweet, alcoholic drink first created in 1823—is traditional, but chilled champagne is preferred.

Rock's squirearchy

In the 1990s the pop group Blur satirized the British aspiration to buy 'a very big house in the country'. In spite of their lyrics, country homes are now the choice of celebrity 'new money'. Wiltshire is popular with a number of showbiz musical types: Nick Mason of Pink Floyd lives in Middlewick House in Wiltshire, while Madonna and her husband Guy Ritchie own Ashcombe House, not too far from Sting at Lake House, near Amesbury. Elsewhere, Jamiroquai's flamboyant Jay Kay resides at Horsenden Manor, Buckinghamshire, close to Oasis' Noel Gallagher in Chalfont St. Giles. And so it goes on. In rural Britain celebrities try to blend into the background. There are no Hollywood-style 'Homes of the Stars' tours, but that magnificent stately home you see from the car is more likely to house a collection of guitars than the family silver.

Marriage of the decade

It's a sign of how times have changed in Britain over the last 20 years that one of the first big marriages of the 21st century was not even a marriage in the traditional sense of the word. Rock legend Elton John and his partner David Furnish celebrated their civil partnership in December 2005, the first time such relationships have been recognized in the UK. The venue was Windsor's venerable old Guildhall, where Prince Charles and Camilla Parker-Bowles had also tied the knot just six months previously. Guests at the party that followed the formal ceremony included Sarah Ferguson, Hugh Grant, Sharon Stone, Rod Stewart and Victoria Beckham.

Vilified when it was completed in 1986, Richard Rodgers' Lloyds building is now a landmark in London's financial sector

The exit is this way: Reform of the House of Lords saw 659 unelected hereditary peers lose their seats, to be replaced by life peers appointed by an independent commission

Not all houses in London have a police guard: This is Number 10 Downing Street, the residence of the Prime Minister

Politics and Economy

A visitor poses with a member of the Household Cavalry, which consists of the oldest regiments in the British Army

Over the last 1,500 years political power moved gradually from Britain's regions to London. Now it is making the return journey: Scotland has a new Parliament in Edinburgh, permitted to make decisions on core issues such as health and education; the National Assembly of Wales began work in 1999. Further reforms, spearheaded by Prime Minister Tony Blair, touched the House of Lords, the unelected counterpart to the House of Commons.

General elections are held every four to five years in the UK, with candidates fighting to represent their constituency (one of 646) in the House of Commons as Members of Parliament (MPs). Although Britain has a monarchy, the Queen's role is largely symbolic.

Britain's economy is one of the strongest in Europe.

House of Lords

Historically, the most reliable way of gaining a seat in the House of Lords, Parliament's second chamber, was to inherit it. But in 1999 Labour government reforms threw out all but 92 of the hereditary peers. So how can you join the Lords today? You should be British—some aspiring members have had to renounce their birth citizenship to qualify. Senior figures in the military and the judiciary have an advantage, and Britain's 24 bishops are guaranteed a seat for now. Former politicians, including former prime minister Baroness Thatcher, and businessmen, such as supermarket boss Lord Sainsbury, aren't uncommon. And you needn't be old: Lord Freyberg is the youngest of the present House—born in 1970. You can even be nominated one of 15 People's Peers. But, with eminent scientist Dr. Susan Greenfield among them, they're hardly average either.

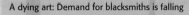
A dying art: Demand for blacksmiths is falling

Property prices in the capital are many times those elsewhere in Britain

Quality not quantity: the elegant Morgan car

Risk analysis: A trader checks prices on the London Stock Exchange

FINANCIAL TIMES

Classic cars

Almost 100 years ago the son of a clergyman started a company in Malvern, Worcestershire. He called it Morgan, and despite the decline of Britain's manufacturing industries, which saw the demise of many glamorous names in motoring, it still builds elegant sports cars today. Esteemed by Prince Charles, Aston Martin, like Jaguar, is now owned by Ford. BMW and Volkswagen took over Rolls-Royce and Bentley. Britain's car firms of the future will be, like their cars, small but tenacious. Morgan now employs 160 people, producing 14 cars per week. Waiting time has slipped below one year. To the north, in Blackpool, is TVR, manufacturers of the attention-grabbing Tuscan, while Surrey-based Caterham has been making speedy Caterham 7s for almost 50 years.

It's a lottery

The launch of the National Lottery in 1994 gripped the nation. It created a fund to benefit charitable and cultural projects—and offered a great opportunity to gamble. Since then, lottery money has helped fund a great variety of projects, some renowned—Tate Modern, the Eden Project—others less so. But one lasting effect has been to stimulate cultural tourism in deprived areas. The Lowry Centre in Manchester's Salford Quays is typical. Celebrating the life and work of local artist L. S. Lowry, it attracts thousands of visitors a year, most of whom would never have come to Manchester before. The lottery now sells fewer tickets, despite huge advertising campaigns and a relaunch as Lotto. The museum-building boom has slowed down, but the eagerness for a flutter has bequeathed Britain many new visitor attractions.

Property boom or bust

No longer is the weather the chief British talking point: It is now house prices. Since the property booms of the 1980s and 1990s, housing 'equity' is the nation's biggest source of inherited wealth. Britain has long had higher rates of home ownership than the rest of Europe. Margaret Thatcher's government promoted home ownership in the 1980s, chiefly by lowering interest rates. House prices spiralled again in the late 1990s, this time under a Labour government. But not everyone is rejoicing. The average price of a London property is now over £300,000, 13 times the average national salary. In contrast, the average price in Wales is just £145,000. The market that has benefited many is pitiless to first-time buyers, who have little chance of affording their own home.

A politician's word

As if being part of the world's oldest parliamentary democracy doesn't keep them busy enough, dozens of members of parliament (MPs) supplement their £59,095 salaries with second jobs. Many are directors of companies, or highly paid consultants, some pulling in several hundred thousand pounds a year. The most intriguing moonlighters are the novelists. In the 1990s the Conservative MP Edwina Currie began writing racy novels—with titles such as A Parliamentary Affair—in her spare time, while fellow Conservative Ann Widdecombe was advanced £100,000 for two restrained novels. Not surprisingly, a recent analysis of MPs' attendance records revealed that on average those with second jobs turned up to 30 per cent fewer Commons votes than those without.

The Punch and Judy show: old-fashioned entertainment on the beach

A schoolboy at Eton College, Britain's most exclusive public school

Regulars in a rural pub: Wearing tweed is not compulsory

The British

The Town Crier would announce the day's news to the community

The 57.1 million inhabitants of mainland Britain (a further 1.7 million live in Northern Ireland) represent one of the most ethnically diverse and vibrant nations in the world. Besides the Scots, English and Welsh, 270 ethnic groups call Britain home. Britain has long been an immigrant nation, colonized by Angles and Saxons from northern Europe, Celts from Ireland and Vikings from Scandinavia. In recent centuries the British Empire opened the way for people to arrive from Africa, Asia and the Caribbean. But if there is no such thing as a typical Briton, national characteristics do exist. Some say that the British are reserved, although this is less so the farther north you travel. Others think the British are belligerent, defining themselves by battles won—from Waterloo in 1815 against the French to the World Cup in 1966 when the English soccer team beat the Germans. Any 'bulldog spirit', however, is balanced by a self-deprecating sense of humour and an instinct for compromise.

Rise and fall

Unbelievably, at the beginning of the 20th century the British Empire comprised a quarter of the world's land surface and over a quarter of its population. It was the largest empire in the world's history. This colonial heritage can now be appreciated at the British Empire and Commonwealth Museum in Bristol (www.empiremuseum.co.uk). Housed in engineer Isambard Kingdom Brunel's Temple Meads train terminus, the BECM embodies the grandeur (and, some would argue, vanity) of the British Empire. Having started with a trading outpost in Newfoundland in 1497, the empire withered after World War II when many colonies gained independence in the 1950s and 1960s and the Commonwealth of Nations was formed. Several former colonies will soon celebrate a half-century of self-rule—Ghana will be one of the first in 2007.

Patriotism comes in various forms, some more eccentric than others

A dancer at Leicester's Caribbean Carnival

Choristers at King's College in Cambridge

It's true: From time to time it rains in Britain. Right. A performer at the Japanese Festival in London

People are strange

The British have long tolerated eccentrics. Cambridge University's Trinity College, for example, once permitted one of its students, the poet Lord Byron (1788–1824), to keep a bear in his rooms. That tradition of cherishing individuality is embodied today by the occupant of the vast Longleat estate, Alexander Thynne, the seventh Marquess of Bath. His spectacular Elizabethan mansion, set within parkland landscaped by Capability Brown and open to the public since 1949, has latterly been accompanied by a safari park. Lord Bath has painted vivid murals of his mistresses (he prefers the term 'wifelet') and of his 150 noble ancestors, and hung them throughout the west wing of the house.

Good sense of humour?

The Edinburgh Fringe Festival is the world's largest open arts festival, attracting a million people to 20,000 individual performances. This gives the festival's most prestigious award, the Perrier Award for the best comedy act, the stamp of authority. The list of nominees reads like a who's who of British comedy scene. The first winners were the Cambridge Footlights in 1981, including Stephen Fry and Emma Thompson. Al Murray, Dave Gorman, Johnny Vegas, the League of Gentlemen, Dylan Moran, Bill Bailey, Alan Davies, Steve Coogan, Frank Skinner, Eddie Izzard, Jack Dee – these past winners are British TV regulars. And typically white males too, fuelling critics' claims that the award is now more mainstream than fringe.

Sikh heritage

The largest Sikh temple outside India is in Havelock Road, Southall—a London suburb with a predominantly Asian population. Second in size only to the Golden Temple at Amritsar, in northern India, the London temple opened in 2003. It cost £17 million to construct, a sum raised by the local community. They hope that the building—which has capacity for 3,000 worshippers and can provide 20,000 meals over a festival weekend— will become a tourist attraction. However, some are less happy about an unfortunate coincidence: Havelock Road is named after Major-General Sir Henry Havelock. Sir Henry earned his knighthood crushing the Indian Mutiny of 1857 which challenged British rule in India. But, in a final twist, Sikhs remained loyal to the British colonialists in 1857 and many served in Havelock's forces.

Flying the flag

Each year the Proms— the annual series of classical music concerts sponsored by the BBC— heralds much singing of patriotic hymns and flying of flags: both the red, white and blue Union Flag of the United Kingdom and the red-on-white St. George's Cross of England. A few years ago this patriotic display was criticized within the BBC, on the grounds that these flags are often employed by right-wing political groups like the National Front. Now ordinary people have reclaimed the flag, the St. George's Cross in particular, first flown in 1189. The watershed was 2002, when the World Cup and the Queen's Golden Jubilee carpeted the nation with flags, particularly the St. George's Cross, given a new lease of life by the devolution of Scotland and Wales. Faint hearts still find it vulgar, but flying the flag is no longer the mark of a bigot.

Harvest time: Britain is the most intensively farmed country in Europe

Wharfedale is one of the most beautiful areas in the Yorkshire Dales National Park

THE NATIONAL TRUST
THE LOE POOL

Urban and Rural

Britain's urban tribes can be identified by their uniforms

The most densely populated country in Europe, Britain's population of about 57.1 million is spread across 88,375sq miles (228,800sq km) with 660 people per square mile. France, with a similar population, has just 285 people per square mile. Yet despite the claustrophobic statistics, breathing space is easily found, and often surprisingly close to Britain's cities, such as in the Peak District National Park between Manchester and Sheffield. Britain has been inhabited for thousands of years, and even on the remote Scottish islands you cannot escape evidence of the generations that have shaped the landscape. The lot of the rural dweller includes a number of grievances, from restrictions on hunting to rural poverty, and a crisis-hit farming industry. A central complaint is that decisions are made by urbanites with little understanding of the countryside. Meanwhile Britain's cities thrive, with exciting new arts venues, retail districts and nightlife. Revitalized Birmingham, Cardiff, Manchester and Newcastle upon Tyne are on the up, but with the caveat of a changing job market and higher property prices.

The National Trust

In 2002 Tyntesfield—a Victorian Gothic Revival mansion near Bristol—was put up for sale, its future unclear. Mercifully, because the house retained many of its original contents, the National Trust stepped in to save it for the nation, and it is now open to the public on a limited basis. This is a time of confidence for the NT. Founded in 1895 by Victorian philanthropists, it aims 'to preserve places of historic interest or natural beauty permanently for the nation to enjoy'. In response, membership has hit three million, more than all the political parties together. Stately homes are the Trust's most visible assets, though the NT has also rescued industrial and 20th-century buildings, including the modest childhood homes of former Beatles John Lennon and Sir Paul McCartney in Liverpool. Heritage is no longer stuck in the past.

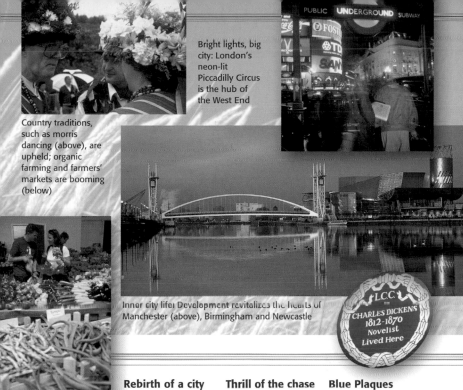

Bright lights, big city: London's neon-lit Piccadilly Circus is the hub of the West End

Country traditions, such as morris dancing (above), are upheld; organic farming and farmers' markets are booming (below)

Inner city life: Development revitalizes the hearts of Manchester (above), Birmingham and Newcastle

CHARLES DICKENS 1812-1870 Novelist Lived Here

Organic farming

Whether due to an awakening of environmental awareness, an increased interest in personal health, or canny marketing, demand for organically produced food is booming in Britain. One of the people meeting this demand is the Prince of Wales. In 1990 Prince Charles formed Duchy Originals, a company producing organic foods, from biscuits to bacon to beer. The project germinated at the Prince's Highgrove home in Gloucestershire and now extends across his estates, from the Duchy of Cornwall—allocated to each heir to the throne since the 14th century—to land in Lincolnshire. Duchy Originals is a successful and profitable enterprise (the profits go to the Prince's charities), and the amount of land converted to organic production doubles every year.

Rebirth of a city

To the buzzing guitars of rock band Oasis, the city of Manchester redefined itself at the end of the nineties. Always famous for music (it boasts the superb Hallé Orchestra), the city found a new cultural dynamism with several new museums and regenerated urban areas such as the Northern Quarter. Warehouses were converted to loft apartments, attracting new city-centre residents, essential for urban vitality. But despite the investment, Manchester remains a community of independents and individuals: bars, record labels, shops and the Mancunians themselves. Nowhere is this better demonstrated than by the rise and rise of FC United. This new football team was formed by disaffected fans of the city's biggest club, Manchester United. Now they are climbing through the divisions and already attracting crowds that would do justice to any League Two outfit.

Thrill of the chase

Hunting foxes with hounds has been part of British country life for generations and is synonymous with the sight of scarlet-clad horse-back riders. Some people think it was the stereo-type of fox hunting being a sport for "toffs" that led first the Scottish (in 2002) and then the Westminster parliament (in 2005) to make hunt-ing foxes with dogs illegal. Needless to say, the decision was unpopular with the hunting fraternity, and many saw it as an unjust swipe at a country-dwelling minority by city-based liberals. But has the ban made a difference? Many hunts continue to meet, to exercise their horses and their dogs. Fox numbers appear unchanged—they are mostly controlled by rifles and roadkill anyway. Governments north and south of the border have suggested enforcement of the ban is not a priority. Perhaps only a handful of foxes can tell the difference.

Blue Plaques

Imagine the rock guitarist Jimi Hendrix (1942–70) and the classical composer George Frideric Handel (1685–1759) discussing chords, tough crowds and flammable instruments. Apart from time (the small matter of over 200 years), this unlikely pair did have a brick wall in common. Hendrix stayed at No. 23 Brook Street in London's Mayfair from 1968 to 1969, entertaining, among others, The Beatles. George Frideric lived next door at No. 25 (now the Handel House Museum) for much of his life. This coincidence is commemorated by a Blue Plaque, one of 800 dished out by English Heritage to mark the homes of notable (dead) residents. Look hard enough and you'll spot one almost anywhere in London, especially in Bloomsbury and the Royal Borough of Kensington and Chelsea. The scheme has been gradually extended across the country.

Mountain biking is popular, with world-class trails in Wales, Scotland and northern England

Many people go boating on the canals built during the Industrial Revolution (above); Football fans in harmony (below)

The sedate sport of bowls (lawn bowling), popularized by Sir Francis Drake in 1588

Sport and Leisure

Shop till you drop

'The English are a nation of shopkeepers': Napoleon's famous jibe (originally coined in 1775 by economist Adam Smith) is no longer very apt. Nowadays, the British are a nation of shoppers. Every month shoppers spend at least £20 billion—approximately the annual gross domestic product of Morocco—on Britain's preferred leisure activity. And not just in city streets. Since Britain's first out-of-town shopping mall opened in 1976, more than 500 'retail parks' have mushroomed. Every week 500,000 consumers visit Lakeside in Essex or lose themselves among the 330 shops of Bluewater in Kent. Besides identical shops, these places provide important jobs behind the tills.

It doesn't take a genius to guess Britain's national sport. Even during the summer months when the football (soccer) season is over, newspapers speculate about player transfers. Most interest is in the English Premier League, but football is taken equally seriously in the provincial towns and local parks. Ironically, the English national rugby team enjoys greater success than the footballers, often ranking number one in the world. The Scots and Welsh are also keen rugby players, and matches against England are eagerly anticipated. If you cannot get a ticket, then watch the big TV screen with a pint of beer in the local pub. Others prefer the peace of the British countryside, usually explored on foot, but also by mountain bike or on horseback. Public footpaths and bridleways lace the land, linking towns and villages, although most of the land in Britain is privately owned. Meanwhile, two out of three people are gardeners, a group that spends £3.5 billion a year on the hobby. But the number-one leisure activity—in the country with the longest working hours in Europe—is shopping.

Spend, spend, spend: Shopping is Britain's preferred leisure activity

A tennis tan makes his patriotism obvious

Gardeners strive for the flawless English rose (below)

Howzat! Cricket is an essential summer experience in Britain

It's not cricket

English cricket is going through a radical change. Where once you might have found only the elderly gentlemen of the Marylebone Cricket Club politely applauding, you may now find international matches supported by a much more vocal crowd. Much of this new-found fervour stems from 2005, when England finally wrested the Ashes trophy off the previously all-conquering Australians. But some is due in part to the enthusiasm for the game spreading from Britain's ethnically diverse urban communities, from Pakistan, India, Bangladesh and the West Indies. Cricket can still be found on village greens, but is also strong on urban playing fields, and innovations like floodlit 20-20 games, where each side bats for only 20 overs, have dramatically altered the previously plodding nature of the sport.

Time gentlemen, please!

British bars and pubs continue to seem very restricted in their opening hours. You will still hear the traditional landlord's cry of "Time, please!" as he announces that the bar is closing and you have 15 minutes to finish your drinks and leave, but this no longer has to be at 11pm. In Scotland the system of extending licensing hours had been commonplace, so in 2005 England and Wales adopted a more flexible approach, allowing bars to apply for 24-hour opening. Many pubs, however, opted to retain their 11–11 hours, while others chose later closing times, especially at the weekend. Scottish laws are now changing to coincide with those south of the border, but with each pub licensed for different hours, it's as well to check your closing times before you get the drinks in.

Plucky losers?

The British sports fan has become increasingly accustomed to tearful failure. Despite creating many of the world's sports, the country sometimes seems to have forgotten how to win them. England's 1966 victory in the soccer World Cup has assumed a hallowed status in English sporting folklore. On the cricket pitch, England's celebrated victory over Australia to win the Ashes trophy in 2005 felt like the exception that proves the rule. The Wimbledon tennis tournament each June brings an outpouring of patriotism shortly followed by resigned expectations of doing better next time. The British still excel at snooker and darts— perhaps because they're pub games.

The future is rosy

The most-visited National Trust property in Britain is Wakehurst Place, an Elizabethan house near Ardingly. This Sussex outpost of the Royal Botanical Society, which also runs world-renowned Kew Gardens in London, is famous for its extensive gardens. But while most of Britain's army of avid gardeners are content to nurture their prize rose bushes, the Royal Botanical Society has grander ambitions. Housed next door to Wakehurst is the Millennium Seed Bank. This international project aims to collect and conserve the seeds of 24,000 (or 10 per cent) of the world's plants, safeguarding species that may be at risk of extinction. Already the seeds of 97 per cent of Britain's native flora have been collected in a unique act of preservation. Interactive exhibitions in the Millennium Seed Bank building are open to the public.

ALEXANDER MCQUEEN

The biggest name in British fashion is Alexander McQueen's, but the designer works in Paris not London

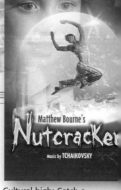

Vertical Rhythms by Terry Frost (1915–2003) at the Royal Academy's Summer Exhibition

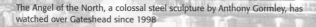

The Angel of the North, a colossal steel sculpture by Anthony Gormley, has watched over Gateshead since 1998

Matthew Bourne's **Nutcracker**
Music by TCHAIKOVSKY

Arts, Media and Culture

Fashion

The Alexander McQueen success story goes from the East End of London to the fashion houses of Paris. Born in 1969, the son of a London taxi driver, McQueen left school at 16 more interested in couture than cab driving. Following his apprenticeship on Savile Row, London, he completed an MA at St. Martin's School of Art. After a celebrated collection for his final exams, fashion's enfant terrible left London for Paris, working for Givenchy then Gucci. By 2001 the three-time British Designer of the Year had a reputation for being brilliant but difficult, once turning down an invitation from the Queen. During the biannual London Fashion Week (February and September), alumni of Britain's art colleges aspire to follow in his footsteps.

Britain's journalists and paparazzi work hard to feed a media industry desperate for stories. There are more than 20 national newspapers, from brash, populist tabloids to stimulating broadsheets. Governments are anxious to maintain positive relations with the more influential papers. There is also an immense appetite for magazines, unaffected by high levels of internet access; newsagents can cater to the most obscure interests. Broadcasting is less partisan than the papers, with the BBC indebted to television viewers who pay a compulsory annual fee. Britain's film industry is erratic. Underfunded, it can still produce well-made costume romps (such as adaptations of Jane Austen novels) and low-budget successes such as *Four Weddings and a Funeral* (1994). Occasionally a homegrown actor will cross over to Hollywood (and back). Theatre is in better shape, with a hit-packed West End, and the government-funded Royal Shakespeare Company and the National Theatre. Lower ticket prices for concerts, ballets and operas aim to increase accessibility.

Cultural high: Catch a hit show, above, or, below, visit a world-famous art gallery

Costume dramas: Colin Firth and Jennifer Ehle in the BBC's adaptation of *Pride and Prejudice* by Jane Austen

Engineering as art: The Gateshead Millennium Bridge over the River Tyne is a tourist attraction in its own right

The Eden Project: The world's most unusual music venue is in a greenhouse

A modern take on traditional English folk music: Eliza Carthy's *Anglicana* album was nominated for the Mercury Music Prize in 2003

Coldplay: Britpop's new generation of bands are a more thoughtful bunch

British pop—a revolution?

The fame of British pop music is due to a formula that took an established sound—typically American—and put a fresh spin on it. In the early 1960s the Beatles and the Rolling Stones updated R&B and blues and sold it back to the States. Punk, reggae and electronic dance music were equally invigorated in the 1970s and 1980s. This talent for reinvention, if a little threadbare during the Britpop years in the 1990s, is still strong. A homespun variation is the work of Eliza Carthy, daughter of Norma Waterson and Martin Carthy—key figures in centuries-old British folk music. While her body piercings and vividly dyed hair are anything but conventional, the accomplished singer and fiddler takes traditional British folk songs and forms such as reels, jigs and square dances, and subtly modernizes them with electronic flourishes.

Potter power

J. K. Rowling (born 1965) is a publishing sensation. The author of the Harry Potter series of children's books is the latest in a tradition of British writers—among them Roald Dahl (1916–90) and C. S. Lewis (1898–1963)—whose work appeals to both adults and children. Yet Rowling's success is unparalleled. Although paid an advance of just £2,500 for the first book, *Harry Potter and the Philosopher's Stone* (2000), her earnings exploded to about £28 million per year, making her one of the richest (and most charitable) women in the country. The film of the first book banked more than £600 million. It was shot (like its sequels) at historic locations around the country, including the Bodleian Library and Christ Church college in Oxford, Alnwick Castle in Northumberland and Gloucester Cathedral.

A matter of taste

Since the 1990s one man has dominated the British art scene. Charles Saatchi (born 1948) made his fortune founding two advertising agencies with his brother Maurice, and invests it in contemporary British art by artists such as Damien Hirst and Tracey Emin. Having bankrolled the Brit Art movement, in April 2003 he opened the Saatchi Gallery in County Hall on London's South Bank, although the gallery has now moved out and will be opening in a new location in Chelsea in 2007. Not everyone is impressed by the young British artists. Saatchi took his Sensation exhibition, including *The Holy Virgin Mary* by Chris Ofili—which featured his trademark use of elephant dung—to New York's Brooklyn Museum of Art in 1999. The then mayor Rudy Giuliani was so outraged he threatened to cut the museum's subsidy.

Global architecture

You have to travel a long way to escape the work of Norman Foster, born in 1935. Farther than Bilbao in Spain, where the top British architect has redesigned much of the metro system; and past Berlin, where his renovation of the Reichstag won the Pritzker Architecture Prize. On the far side of the world in Hong Kong, you pass through Lord Foster's Chep Lap Kok international airport, built on a man-made island. Closer to home, London's Canary Wharf Tube station and the Great Court in the British Museum are among the most distinctive buildings in Britain, all designed by the ubiquitous Foster and Associates. The newest addition to London's skyline, the environmentally friendly, 40-floor Swiss-Re headquarters (known as 'the Gherkin'), embodies layers of 'sky gardens' inside a largely self-ventilating structure.

Easy listening: Trevor Baylis's clockwork radio is used all over the world

Dolly the sheep: The world's first cloned animal died in 2003 and is now a museum exhibit

Human DNA is being unravelled by Britain's non-profit-making Sanger Institute
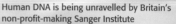

Technology and
Science

Since the 1970s Britain has developed from a manufacturing-based economy to a high-tech, knowledge-based economy. Scientific research is concentrated in areas such as the 'Silicon Fen' around Cambridge. Probably the most ground-breaking research programme is the Human Genome Project, which aims to decode the human genome; it is hoped the information will contribute to the cure of many illnesses. High levels of personal computer ownership, internet access and the numerous websites hosted in the country reflect the new skill trends. Hardly surprising when you consider that the inventor of the World Wide Web is a Briton, Tim Berners-Lee.

Dolly the sheep

Dead sheep rarely get pride of place in a national museum. But Dolly wasn't just any sheep. Produced in 1996 by scientists at the Roslin Institute in Scotland, Dolly was the world's first animal to be cloned from an adult cell, and was hailed as a scientific sensation. The subsequent debate about cloning was fuelled by her premature death. After the post-mortem Dolly (named after country singer Dolly Parton) was stuffed, and she is now on display in Edinburgh's National Museum of Scotland.

The clockwork wireless

Having come up with a number of the world's most useful inventions, including the train, the television and the gin and tonic, Britons seemed to have run out of steam. But inventors, such as Trevor Baylis, onetime escapologist with the Berlin State Circus, continue to tinker in garden sheds. Watching a documentary about AIDS in Africa, he realized that advice about the disease could be communicated more widely if radios were more readily obtainable. His solution was the wind-up radio—batteries not required—which was both cheap and practical in areas with patchy electricity. After a battle to get his invention produced, Trevor's radios are now distributed in the world's poorest countries and are a trendy accessory in the West.

Johnson and MacArthur

Seldom has second place overshadowed first so much. In 2001 Ellen MacArthur sailed *Kingfisher*, a state-of-the-art yacht, solo around the world in the Vendée Globe 2000 race. She didn't win, but the 25-year-old completed the fastest solo circumnavigation by a woman. In 2005 she broke the record for the fastest solo effort by anyone. Her record-breaking achievement mirrors those of another British woman, Amy Johnson. In 1930, at the age of 26, Johnson became the first woman to fly solo from Britain to Darwin, Australia; the 10,000-mile (16,000km) route took 20 days, three days short of the record. Born in Hull in 1903, Johnson took up flying in 1928. She went on to achieve many record flights in the 1930s. Her plane, a de Havilland Gypsy Moth named *Jason*, is displayed in the Science Museum in London.

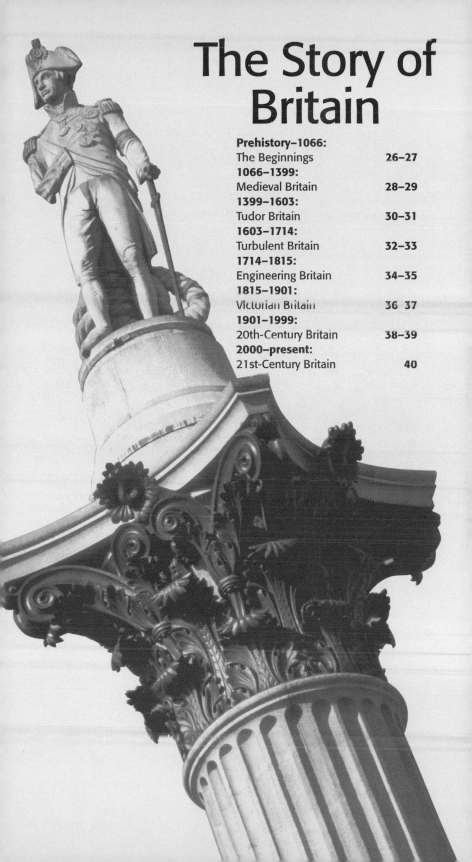

The Story of Britain

Prehistory–1066
Britain

Stone monuments, earth mounds, shattered pottery, tools and the occasional skeleton provide scattered clues to prehistoric life in Britain—tribal societies that had developed over millennia before work began on Stonehenge in the third millennium BC. From about 600BC Celtic influences with strong traditions in art, music and war arrived from central Europe. The Druidic elite that oversaw spiritual life confronted Julius Caesar's troops during the first Roman invasion in 55–54BC.

A century later, in AD43, Emperor Claudius started the job of conquest proper, and for 400 years southern Britain was a Roman province, adopting its gods, fashions, laws and language. Saxon raids tested an overstretched empire in the fifth century, and in AD410 the Romans pulled out, leaving southern Britain to split into petty kingdoms.

Christian missionaries arrived from Rome in AD597 to convert the kingdoms. By the eighth century pagan Vikings were raiding the eastern coast, soon settling in northern England. The treaty of AD871 between the Danes and Alfred, king of Wessex, was the basis of the kingdom of England. When the last Anglo-Saxon king, Edward the Confessor, died in 1066, a power struggle ensued between his successor Harold, William, Duke of Normandy and King Harald of Norway.

The face of Medusa on a floor mosaic at the Roman villa at Bignor, West Sussex (left); model for a theatrical mask found at the Roman baths in Bath (right)

The last hours of Pete Marsh

One day in the first century BC a man now nicknamed Pete Marsh marvelled at visions induced by his final meal of mistletoe and herbs. Behind him a Druid raised his club. Having smashed Pete's skull the priest garrotted him and then threw him into the sacred bog water of Lindow Moss, gateway to the gods. The remarkably preserved corpse was recovered from the Cheshire peat bog in 1984. According to archaeologists, Pete was one more victim of the Druidic human sacrifices described by Roman historians. The theory fits his bodily injuries and the mistletoe grains found in his stomach. Alternatively, this may just have been a prehistoric mugging. Whatever the case, Pete Marsh—now a permanent resident of the British Museum—and other similarly mutilated 'bog bodies' provide testimony to the grim but common social rituals of their age.

Prehistory

Remains of a house at Chysauster Iron Age village, Cornwall

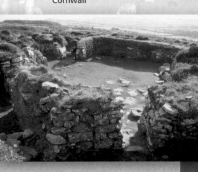

A stand against Rome

When Emperor Claudius decided to finish his predecessor Julius Caesar's job and conquer Britain in AD43, he faced stiff opposition from King Caratacus (Caradoc) who, with his brother Togodumnus, ruled the powerful Catuvellauni tribe. They met the Romans in force at the River Thames, but Togodumnus was cut down and Caratacus fled to the west. Five years later he was back, turning the tide of invaders from the western part of Britain now called Wales. His success was short-lived and he escaped again, only to be betrayed by Catimandua, queen of the Brigantes. Taken to Rome in chains, Caratacus so impressed Emperor Claudius that he and his family were pardoned, and lived the rest of their days in Italy.

Vortigern's leap

Deserted by Rome, fifth-century Britain descended into civil war. Vortigern (Gwrtheyrn), king of Powys in Wales, was in dispute with the Picts of Scotland, and invited Saxon mercenaries from Germany to strengthen his position; in return for their help the Saxons received land. But having established a foothold, they wanted more. Hundreds of their fellow countrymen poured in, expanding their territories while (according to sixth-century historian Gildas) massacring the British and destroying their towns. According to later legend, Vortigern, reviled by his people for letting in the enemy, escaped to the Lleyn Peninsula in northern Wales. Here he leaped—or perhaps was pushed—from a clifftop called Nant Gwrtheyrn (Vortigern's Stream), and was smashed on the rocks below.

St. Augustine's mission

In AD597 Abbot Augustine and a group of nervous monks from Rome landed in Thanet, Kent. They were greeted by the equally wary King Aethelbert of Kent, who cautiously met them out in the open. But the meeting was no accident: The delegation had been sent by Pope Gregory to spread the Christian word in a land of many tribes and beliefs; and Aethelbert's Christian wife had probably paved their way. Sixth century Britain was an uneasy, often violent place and en route the reluctant missionaries sent Augustine back to talk the Pope out of the whole idea—to no avail. In the event, Aethelbert was converted and, with his support, Augustine established an episcopal base in Canterbury. The kingdom of Kent now had the backing of Rome.

Escape from Lindisfarne

The east coast of Britain was a dangerous place in the eighth and ninth centuries. Plagued by Scandinavian raids, monasteries with their religious bullion were especially hard hit. After Danish attacks in 875, the monks of Lindisfarne island fled, taking the holy, illuminated Lindisfarne Gospels with them. The Latin text had been produced in about 720; an Anglo-Saxon translation was added in about 960. The Gospel Book was probably produced to highlight the cult of former bishop-monk St. Cuthbert (634–87). His relics too were carried to safety: By 995 they were enshrined in Durham. When the cathedral was pillaged during the 16th-century Reformation the Gospels were taken to London, eventually to be housed in the British Library.

St. John the Evangelist from the Lindisfarne Gospels, made around AD720

Alfred the Great, 849–99

Edward the Confessor, 1042–66

1066

The earth mound has long gone from the 5,000-year-old chamber tomb of Pentre Ifan, Pembrokeshire, Wales

Vortigern's deal with the Saxons goes wrong

A high cross on Iona, Scotland (above). The late Saxon church at Bradford-on-Avon, Wiltshire (left)

Medieval Britain

After King Harold's defeat at Hastings in 1066 the Norman conquest began in earnest. William I's followers snapped up parcels of land and built castles and new cathedrals; by 1086 England was secure enough to be surveyed in the Domesday Book. The main Norman dynasty itself died out following the civil war of King Stephen's reign (1135–54). Rule passed to a grandson, Henry II, who inherited an 'empire' that extended from central France to northern England.

His son, Richard I, neglected the English kingdom, preferring the glory of the Third Crusade. His successor, brother John, lost the French lands and battled with his English barons. The authority of the English Crown was further challenged in the 13th century by Simon de Montfort, whose rebellion was crushed at Evesham in 1265.

Welsh defiance in the 1270s was met with full-scale invasion by the all-powerful Edward I. His intervention in the Scottish power struggle between King John de Balliol and Robert the Bruce backfired in Edward II's reign with the rout of the English at Bannockburn. Edward III instead reclaimed French territories and triggered the Hundred Years' War.

The fatal arrow?

Arrows fly across the Hastings battle scene on the 11th-century Bayeux Tapestry; corpses litter the ground. Above the confusion are embroidered the words: 'Harold Rex Interfectus Est'; King Harold is dead. William, Duke of Normandy won the day at the Battle of Hastings on 14 October 1066. But is it King Harold shown gripping an arrow in his eye? Eyewitness William of Poitiers notes merely that Harold's face was unrecognizable after the battle, and he was identified by marks on his body. However Harold died, his mother, Gytha, wanted to give him a decent burial, and offered the Normans his body's weight in gold for the privilege. William refused, adding that too many lay unburied due to Harold's greed for power. But one legend claims the body was found and buried at Waltham, Essex.

Despite the shield wall, Harold II (left) was mortally wounded at the Battle of Hastings in 1066; Harlech Castle (below) was part of Edward I's ring around Wales

1066

A statue of Robert the Bruce on the site of the Battle of Bannockburn, 1314, where the Scots fought off English domination

Founding of Oxford University

A royal quarrel led to the foundation of the world's first English-speaking university. Henry II was at loggerheads with Philip Augustus of France, and in 1167 banned English students from attending Paris University. Some teaching had taken place in Oxford since the late 11th century, but now the scholars moved in. In 1188 the historian and cleric Gerald of Wales (Giraldus Cambrensis) lectured to a gathering of dons, and in 1190 the first foreign student, Emo of Friesland, was admitted. As student numbers grew, so did friction with the townspeople—in 1209 the first of many 'town versus gown' riots broke out. After this a group of disgruntled clerks packed their bags and headed east to establish Cambridge University.

The turbulent priest

Thomas Becket (1118–70), son of a Norman merchant, rose from banker's clerk to royal chancellor. He won Henry II's confidence and was appointed Archbishop of Canterbury in 1162. At once, Becket opposed the king on matters of Church rights. Angry and betrayed, Henry ordered his arrest and Becket fled to France. Attempts at reconciliation failed. Events came to a head when Becket returned to suspend the Archbishop of York for usurping his archiepiscopal rights. His rival complained to the king, whose irritated response—'will no one rid me of this turbulent priest?'—was overheard by four knights. They murdered Becket inside Canterbury Cathedral—an act greeted with disgust. Becket was canonized two years later; Henry did public penance.

Magna Carta

On 15 June 1215 peace negotiations at Runnymede between King John and his rebel barons were concluded with the sealing of the Magna Carta—the Great Charter. This charter of 'rights' was a significant development in the English constitution, setting limits on royal authority within the rule of law (typically set by the Crown): 'No free man shall be arrested or imprisoned…or victimized in any other way…except by the lawful judgement of his peers or by the law of the land' (Article 39). In the 13th century 'free man' applied to a powerful minority. John, however, was merely playing for time—civil war broke out within months. Nevertheless, a principle of law was established that would, over the centuries, be regarded as the bedrock of democracy.

The iron ring

Edward I consolidated his conquest of Wales with an iron ring of fortresses. Work began on his castle-palace at Caernarfon in 1283, as building got under way in Harlech and Conwy. The chief mason in charge of all these schemes—as well as several other sites—was Master James of St. George (c1235–1308), from Savoy. An army of craftsmen and workers came from all over England to realize his figure of eight design at Caernarfon, whose walls incorporated bands of different-coloured stone, symbolic of Constantinople's imperial defences. Practical features included a gatehouse with six fortified portcullises, massive towers and a town wall punctuated with eight watchtowers and two gateways. The ring of Edwardian castles is now a Unesco World Heritage Site.

Richard I got to within 12 miles (19km) of Jerusalem on the Third Crusade (1191)

Thomas Becket, archbishop of Canterbury

Geoffrey Chaucer's (c1340–1400) *Canterbury Tales* illustrated ordinary life in the Middle Ages

1399

King John reluctantly grants the Magna Carta in 1215 (left); the 1348 Black Death killed a third of the population

Tudor Britain

When Welsh landowner Owain Glyndwr took up arms against Henry IV, his countrymen readily followed. Welsh independence came within reach, but superior royal forces crushed the campaign in 1413. The Hundred Years' War rumbled on in France, with a major English triumph at Agincourt, but at home conflict over the throne plunged the country into 30 years of civil war. The rival houses of Lancaster and York were reconciled only when Lancastrian Henry VII married Elizabeth of York in 1485 and established the Tudor dynasty.

The Tudor age brought religious upheaval, overseas exploration and invasion threats. Henry VIII married six times in his bid to secure the dynasty, rejecting papal authority in the process. After Henry's only son's brief, staunchly Protestant reign, Mary Tudor failed to force a return to Catholicism. Her half-sister Elizabeth attempted a middle way, but incurred the wrath of Catholic Spain with the execution of Mary, Queen of Scots for conspiracy. The failure of Spain's subsequent invasion attempt sealed Elizabeth's popularity. During her long reign composers such as William Byrd and writers such as William Shakespeare led a cultural renaissance; and Sir Francis Drake and Sir Walter Raleigh sailed to a New World.

Uncle Jasper's risky career

Jasper Tudor (1431–95) was a key player during the Wars of the Roses. The Tudor family had married into the Lancastrian dynasty. Jasper's royal cause was stalled in 1461, when Lancastrian Henry VI was deposed by the Yorkist Edward IV. But Jasper had high hopes for his nephew Henry, Earl of Richmond, who had a claim to the throne. Slipping in and out of the country, Jasper maintained the rebels' momentum, before smuggling Henry to safety in Brittany in 1471. Fourteen years later the Tudors landed at Milford Haven and marched to Bosworth, where Richard III and the Yorkist cause were defeated. As king, Henry VII made his uncle Duke of Bedford and Lieutenant of Wales and the Marches in gratitude.

A Scottish invasion by James IV was defeated by the English at the Battle of Flodden Field, Northumberland, on 9 September 1513

Henry V (1387–1422), victor at the Battle of Agincourt in 1415 during the Hundred Years' War

1399

Sir Francis Drake circumnavigated the world in 1577–80 in the *Golden Hind*

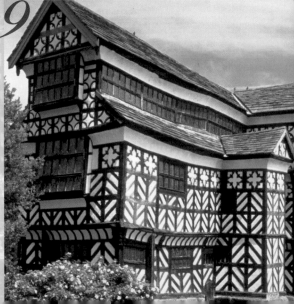

The printing press

Thirty years after Johannes Gutenberg's invention of movable type in 1440, the printing industry had yet to take off in Britain. A Kent merchant, William Caxton (1422–91), who learned the skill in Cologne, anticipated the demand for printed books. He tested the waters by producing the first printed book in English—Caxton's own translation of a history of Troy—from Bruges in about 1474. It was a great success. Three years later he and his apprentice Wynkyn de Worde had a press in Westminster, printing works by writers such as Chaucer, the poet and monk John Lydgate, and Sir Thomas Malory, as well as translations of works about religion, ethics and chivalry. The press quickly gained influence, helping to create a flowering of English literature.

Slashes and ruffs

The wedding of Henry VII's sister to the king of France was an opportunity for English aristocrats to note the latest fashions of the French court. Strangest of these was a style copied from German and Swiss troops and dating from the Battle of Grandson in 1476—when soldiers had plundered supplies of silk and cut it up to patch their clothes. Soon every Tudor trend-follower was ordering 'slashed' doublets, breeches and sleeves, with outer materials cut into slits and the lining—in contrasting textures and colours—pulled through. Meanwhile, necklines plunged, leaving under-shirts (or chemises) showing. The chemise was drawn together at the neck with a string, producing a concertina effect that over the years evolved into the full-blown, chin-tickling ruff.

Breaking with Rome

After more than 20 years of marriage to Catherine of Aragon, Henry VIII had no male heir. His eye was caught by lady-in-waiting Anne Boleyn, whom he determined to marry. In 1527 Cardinal Wolsey, his Lord Chancellor and, as the head of the English Church, the next most powerful man in Britain, tried to persuade the Pope to annul the marriage—without success. Wolsey was dismissed by the frustrated king in 1529 and he turned instead to theologian Thomas Cranmer, who engineered the 1534 Act of Supremacy, acknowledging Henry as head of the Church of England and severing the link with Rome. Having married his mistress, Henry then plundered church funds by dissolving and looting the country's monasteries.

Shipshape

From the day of her accession in 1558, Elizabeth I faced a constant threat of war from Catholic Spain. In 1588, provoked by the execution of Mary, Queen of Scots, and by raids on Spanish treasure ships, Philip II of Spain finally despatched an invasion armada. Elizabeth had inherited a poorly funded and depleted navy, and in 1569 persuaded explorer John Hawkins to restore it. Hawkins was determined to replace unwieldy 'floating fortresses' with faster, more flexible galleons that relied on broadside guns. Overcoming naval opposition, he designed *The Revenge*, which served as Sir Francis Drake's flagship against the Spanish. By 1588 a new, manoeuvrable and well-run fleet was ready to repel the Spanish Armada—with a little help from the weather.

Elizabethan adventurers: Sir Francis Drake (left) and Sir Walter Raleigh (right)

Religious unrest under Catholic Mary, Queen of Scots, led to her execution by Elizabeth I

1603

Henry VIII and his six wives (left); Elizabeth I (below) was the only child of Henry's second wife, Anne Boleyn

William Shakespeare (1564–1616), the Stratford playwright and poet

Timber-framed Little Moreton Hall, Cheshire, dating from the late 15th century, has the latest Elizabethan fashion of a long gallery

Turbulent Britain

Elizabeth I died unmarried and heirless. James VI of Scotland, son of Mary, Queen of Scots, acceded to the English throne as James I in 1603. Within two years he was nearly blown away when Guy Fawkes attempted to blow up the Houses of Parliament in protest at anti-Catholic measures. Money was another worry: James spent extravagantly on the arts and on buildings such as the Banqueting House in Whitehall, architect Inigo Jones' Renaissance showpiece. Costly foreign wars lingered into the reign of Charles I, provoking complaints from the English Parliament, already suspicious of royal 'papist' tendencies. Mutual distrust escalated into civil war, which ended with the king's execution. Radicals looked to the victorious Puritan general Oliver Cromwell for far-reaching reforms, but without success; Parliament was dismissed again, and Cromwell ruled as Lord Protector until his death in 1658.

The monarchy was restored in 1660 upon Charles II's return from exile. Smouldering religious enmities found expression through a burgeoning party political system. From the ashes of the 1666 Great Fire of London emerged Sir Christopher Wren's new capital, a hub of international finance and colonial trade. By the time Scotland was incorporated within the union in 1707, a constitutional, Protestant royal succession had been established.

The *Mayflower* Pilgrims

Suspicious of James I and his tolerance of Catholicism, some Protestants broke away from the Church altogether. Unable to practise their faith openly, about 125 Puritans from Scrooby in Nottinghamshire emigrated to the tolerant Netherlands. Fearing the advance of Catholic Spain, the community accepted an offer of land in the New World colony of Virginia. Lacking adequate funds, about 50 'Pilgrims' struck a deal with other emigrants and investors, and in September 1620 set sail from Plymouth in the *Mayflower*. After a stormy voyage the ship reached Cape Cod Bay in Massachusetts. Several weeks on, the Puritans founded the New Plymouth settlement.

Catholic conspirator Guy Fawkes plotted the attack on James I in 1605 (right)

1603

Puritan and royalty: Oliver Cromwell (above) and Charles I (right)

Drawing a blank

John Poyer, mayor of Pembroke, entered the Civil War as a staunch Parliamentarian. But he and his comrades, Colonel Powell and Rowland Laugharne—impatient with their meagre pay and obliged to fund their soldiers with their own money—threw in their lot with the Royalists. When Oliver Cromwell (1599–1658) arrived with an army in 1648, demanding Pembroke Castle, Poyer opened fire, killing 16 men. The turncoats held their ground for six weeks but eventually surrendered and were convicted of treason. Cromwell decided to spare two of them, and sent three pieces of paper to their cell: one was blank, the others read 'Life granted by God'. Poyer drew the blank, and was duly shot in 1649.

Robert Catesby

Sir Isaac Newton

The 17th century was a time of renewed intellectual activity, called by some a 'scientific revolution'. Among the greatest thinkers of the age was Sir Isaac Newton (1642–1727). As a student he was sent home from Cambridge in 1665 to escape the plague, and spent his unexpected leisure time figuring out differential calculus and gravity. Among other interests he also studied alchemy, and used astronomy to interpret the chronology of the Bible. His ground-breaking work on optics showed that light is composed of all colours; in the same vein he invented a reflecting telescope in 1668. Today, though, his best-known work is *Principia* (1687), setting out the theory of space, time and planetary motion that revolutionised our understanding of the universe.

Thomas Winter

The career of Aphra Behn

With the return of the monarchy in 1660 theatres reopened their doors and enjoyed a boom in 'Restoration' plays by a new generation of dramatists. Most remarkable among them was Aphra Behn (1640–89), the first female professional writer. She gained access to Charles II's court through her husband, a Dutch merchant. When he died Behn was sent to the Netherlands as a royal spy. Of her plays the most popular was *The Rover* (1678), tracing a cavalier's adventures. She also wrote poetry and novels, including *Oroonoko* (1688), an indictment of slavery based on her travels to Surinam. Behn often published anonymously to conceal her sex, but was admired by her contemporaries. She is buried in Westminster Abbey.

The Act of Union

Although Scotland and England shared a monarch from 1603, they were still independent states at the beginning of the 18th century. In 1688 the Catholic James II was removed from the throne and replaced by Protestant William of Orange. The new king was keen to unite the two nations and end the enmity; James and his heirs, however, had strong Scottish support. Met with hostility or indifference, William's attempt failed—as did another in 1702 when Anne, James' daughter, came to the throne. In 1705 the Scottish Parliament alarmed Westminster by claiming the right to choose its own monarch after Anne's death. Negotiations were stepped up: On 12 May 1707 the Scottish Parliament was abolished and its MPs and peers moved to London.

Sir Isaac Newton: as London went up in flames, he was thinking about gravitation

Aphra Behn—poet, playwright, novelist and spy—the first professional English female writer

1714

The Pilgrim Fathers prepare for the New World (left); William of Orange looks to his new country (right)

A spark from the house of the king's baker in Pudding Lane started the Great Fire of London on 2 September 1666

Engineering Britain

George, Elector of Hanover, was invited to take the British crown in 1714—the Georgian period was under way. It began inauspiciously with a Jacobite uprising and ran into financial scandal with the collapse in 1720 of the South Sea Company, whose investors ranged from ministers to maids.

This was a century of naval triumphs and territorial acquisition, of innovation and revolution. Agriculture produced new breeding and planting techniques, and land tenants were obliged to make way for cattle and crops. Inventions such as Sir Richard Arkwright's spinning jenny, a yarn-spinning machine, threatened jobs and provoked riots. In 1769 James Watt patented the steam engine while new smelting methods made iron production easier. Britain earned from her colonies and spent on wars, but in the 1760s American colonists began to protest against 'taxation without representation'. Concepts of rights framed during their successful independence struggle influenced radicals at home and revolutionary thinkers in France; as French heads fell, Britain's government clamped down hard on any suspected dissidence. Napoleon's march through Europe made popular heroes of his adversaries Nelson and Wellington. Pressure for reform continued, finally rewarded with a partial extension of the vote in 1832.

Ironbridge Gorge (left); George Stephenson's 1829 *Rocket* (right); Sir Richard Arkwright's 1775 yarn machine (below left)

Josiah Wedgwood

Wedgwood (1730–95) was a true person of his times—the Industrial Revolution. Born into a family of Staffordshire potters, he developed a distinctive style of fine blue china with white cameo designs, which flourished in the 1760s. This was also the age of the canal, and the Trent and Mersey Canal linked the Wedgwood works to the international market. An active reformer, in 1769 Wedgwood designed Etruria, a new pottery works that included a factory village for the workers, and also lobbied hard for road improvement. In 1705 he formed the General Chamber of Manufacturers of Great Britain, bringing industrialists together as a single, increasingly powerful voice in British politics.

1714

ARKWRIGHT'S MACHINE.

The peelers

It was Sir Robert Peel (1788–1850) who created Britain's first effective police force. The first 'peelers' or 'bobbies' were nicknamed after the Tory home secretary (later prime minister) and in 1829 stepped on to London's streets in blue uniforms and top hats. Their Whitehall head-quarters was off Scotland Yard. Many of them were ex-soldiers—'blue devils' was another nickname for them. Londoners prized their freedom and at first the badly paid constables faced suspicion and hostility. They were attacked, beaten up, even stoned. When one was killed by rioters in 1831, the coroner's jury recorded a verdict of justifiable homicide. Gradually, however, under their Irish chief Richard 'King' Mayne, who ran the force until his death in 1868, they won public trust and affection.

Edinburgh's New Town

Advances in medical science were partly responsible for the huge growth in Britain's population during the late 18th century. In Scotland alone the population trebled between 1750 and 1800. Edinburgh, the medieval capital, was bursting at the seams. In 1767 James Craig (d 1795) was given permission to design an area of neoclassical buildings set on a grid of wide streets to the north of the city. The town council decreed that each pavement should be 3m (10ft) wide and no more than 0.3m (1ft) above the street. Also, tenants of the new houses should be allowed to set up links to the common sewer, thereby improving general hygiene and ending the practice of emptying chamber pots out of the window.

Mad King George

In 1788 Britain had lost control of the American colonies and trouble was brewing across the English Channel. King George III (1738–1820) had appointed William Pitt as his prime minister in the face of political hostility. At this uneasy time the king began to show signs of bizarre behaviour, attacking his son and talking incessant gibberish. Dr. Francis Willis was summoned and prescribed a harsh regime involving straitjackets and fierce poultices. The king recovered—probably in spite of this treatment—though the condition re-emerged in 1810, when he declined into mental instability, made worse by deafness and blindness. Prince George, heir to the throne, was established as Prince Regent. It's now believed that George suffered from porphyria, a metabolic disorder.

The Battle of Waterloo

In 1815, back from exile on Elba, the French emperor Napoleon Bonaparte (1769–1821) advanced into Belgium. After fending him off at Quatre Bras, the Duke of Wellington's army sheltered behind a ridge near Waterloo. His Prussian allies had retreated, chased by the French, who fought them at Wavre and turned back—convinced that they had seen them off. Back at Waterloo on 18 June, wave after wave of Napoleon's troops was repelled, but eventually a farmhouse guarding the ridge was taken—Wellington's position looked bleak. Then the Prussians reappeared. Napoleon dithered over his next move and the French were routed. Surveying the carnage, Wellington remarked that the worst sight apart from a battle lost was a battle won.

The Duke of Wellington, victor over Napoleon at the Battle of Waterloo, Belgium, in 1815

The Elector of Hanover was the first of the Georgians in 1714

1815

As prime minister, William Pitt (1708–78), promoted the expansion of trade (left); English troops defeated the Jacobites in 1746 (below)

THE BATTLE OF CULLODEN WAS FOUGHT ON THIS MOOR 16TH APRIL 1746.

THE GRAVES OF THE GALLANT HIGHLANDERS WHO FOUGHT FOR SCOTLAND & PRINCE CHARLIE ARE MARKED BY THE NAMES OF THEIR CLANS

Viscount Nelson, on board HMS *Victory* at the Battle of Trafalgar (1805), receives a fatal wound from a French musket shot

Victorian Britain

Victorian Britain was confident and ambitious. Its empire spread across the globe, and industries led the way to a modern, machine age. Mass production and mass communication changed lives and expectations; steam power and the telegraph reduced time and travel, and towns sprang up as people flocked to work in factories, mines and mills. There was big money to be made, and industry created a new high society.

At the same time, those left at the bottom of the heap faced poverty and squalor; disease was rife in the overcrowded city slums. Calls for reform gathered pace, and by the end of the 19th century a string of new laws had been passed to meet the needs of industrial society, with attempts to tackle the worst abuses of child exploitation and an emphasis on wider education. Public lending libraries appeared, housed in typically grand civic buildings, as did public baths and a network of schools. Funds from the 1851 Great Exhibition were used to set up the Victoria & Albert Museum, to inspire and educate with the best of British design. By the turn of the century consumers were being tempted by the media of photography, recorded music and moving pictures, and a different kind of horsepower made its debut on the road.

A shapely sex: Bodices and bustles were all the rage in the 1870s

Isambard Kingdom Brunel, engineer of bridges, ships, docks and railways

Isambard Kingdom Brunel

As a young man Isambard Kingdom Brunel (1806–59) nearly drowned when water flooded into his father's pioneering project, the Thames Tunnel. Brunel recovered in Bristol, where he designed the Clifton Suspension Bridge in 1831—still the city's most famous landmark—and was engineer to the Great Western Railway. He was also responsible for three innovative transatlantic ships: the *Great Western*, the massive *Great Eastern*, and the first large screw-propelled iron ship, the *Great Britain*, now moored at Bristol. Unusually, Brunel received an academic education rather than training as an apprentice, and retained his faith in scientific principles. His excessive workload probably contributed to his early death.

1815

Saltaire workers' town, near Bradford, founded by manufacturer Sir Titus Salt (1803–76)

Back to basics

By the mid-19th century Britain was an industrial nation. As work became more mechanized, some mourned the loss of craftsmanship and individual dignity. Artist and socialist William Morris (1834–96) was among those who tried to redress the balance. As a leading light of the Arts and Crafts Movement, Morris harked back to the Middle Ages, as a time when art and life were inextricably linked, and sought to restore beauty to manufactured goods. His firm produced romanticized medieval designs for wallpaper, fabrics, tapestries and stained glass; the Kelmscott Press, which he founded in 1896, printed exquisitely decorated books. The Arts and Crafts style was showcased by his own home near London, Red House, designed by his partner Philip Webb.

Hard times

Victorians loved the railways—none more so than Charles Dickens (1812–70), who wrote a breathless account of the speedy journey to the south coast. Making the most of the new express trains, he took his mistress, actress Ellen Ternan, and her mother to France in 1865. But on the way back disaster struck. The train from Folkestone to London was derailed on a viaduct at Staplehurst: several carriages fell on the bridge and many people were killed or injured. One, containing Dickens and his companions, was left balancing on the edge. Having climbed free, Dickens rescued his companions and retrieved the final instalment of his last novel, *Our Mutual Friend*. The author never recovered from the shock of the incident, and his health declined until his death in 1870.

The wilderness years

When her husband Prince Albert died of typhoid fever in 1861, Queen Victoria wrote that 'the world is gone for me'. She duly retreated into seclusion. Despite continuing to work at her house at Balmoral, Victoria refused to appear in public. Her prolonged absence led to mockery by some, who nicknamed her 'Mrs Brown' for her dependence on Scottish manservant John Brown. Benjamin Disraeli (1804–81), who became prime minister in 1874, set about winning her over with flattery and gestures, such as the title Empress of India in 1876. Gradually Victoria re-emerged: During her Golden Jubilee of 1887 and Diamond Jubilee of 1897 she was cheered by a public whose suspicion had given way to affection and respect.

Doctors as heroes

In the 19th century the Scottish universities gave Britain its medical elite, notably the chief medical officers of health in the 1850s. Edinburgh's Henry Littlejohn and Glasgow's William Russell ensured the cities were adequately drained and supplied with clean water, in great projects such as Glasgow's Loch Katrine pipeline (1859). Medical missionaries such as David Livingstone (1813–73) and researchers such as Ronald Ross (1857–1932), who conquered the malaria-bearing mosquito, and Sir Robert Philip (1857–1939), who did the same for tuberculosis, became role models. Robert Knox, who employed bodysnatchers Burke and Hare in the 1820s to supply corpses for his Edinburgh dissection room, did not. Author Arthur Conan Doyle (1859–1930) studied medicine at Edinburgh University. He modelled Sherlock Holmes on his professor, Joseph Bell, who could deduce a scenario from the tiniest details.

Benjamin Disraeli, author and Conservative prime minister 1874–80

From 1836 to 1865, Charles Dickens' published works characterized the early Victorian period

1901

Monuments of the Victorian age: the neo-Gothic Manchester Town Hall (1868) and the former Birmingham Grand Central Station (1854)

Queen Victoria's gilt memorial of her husband, Prince Albert, in Kensington Gardens, London

In black and white: Queen Victoria was the first monarch to be captured by the camera

20th-Century Britain

In 1903 the American Wright brothers, Orville and Wilbur, completed the first successful powered flight. Several years later air forces took to the sky as the world went to war. Many of those who survived the horrors of World War I returned to unemployment or meagre pay. Wage disputes almost paralyzed Britain during the General Strike of 1926, and depression hit hard after the Wall Street Crash in 1929. In 1936 shipbuilders marched from Jarrow in the northeast to London to voice their desperation.

Television first appeared in the 1930s, but it was the wireless radio that dominated interwar entertainment. Millions tuned in to hear war declared on Nazi Germany in 1939. World War II left Britain weary and ready for change: A new welfare state promised health, education and security for all. Even as the empire was dissolving, its colonies demanding independence, immigration was encouraged to make up the workforce.

The first motorway, bypassing Preston, was opened in 1958. A year later the Mini was introduced. In the 1960s designer Mary Quant and The Beatles set the pace in fashion and pop. Heavy industry declined in the 1970s and 1980s amid conflict and strikes. By the century's end power had devolved from Westminster to Scotland and Wales, and peace in Northern Ireland inched closer.

In 1936 the 200-strong Jarrow Crusade marched 300 miles (480km) to London to petition for jobs and relief from poverty

The frontline suffragette

Emmeline Pankhurst (1858–1928) was the leading light of the campaign for women's suffrage—the right to vote. With her daughter Christabel (1880–1958), she founded the Women's Social and Political Union in 1903, promoting militant tactics. In 1908 she received the first of a series of prison sentences, including one for a bomb attack on a property belonging to the Chancellor of the Exchequer. Under the 'Cat and Mouse Act' she was released to regain her health and then re-arrested 12 times. With the outbreak of war in 1914, Emmeline turned her campaigning energies to recruiting troops to fight Germany. Women over 30 finally got to vote in 1918, with equal voting rights following ten years later.

Winston Churchill led Britons through the Blitz of 1940–41

1901

Suffragettes fought the law... and the suffragettes won

The Blitz

In September 1940 Germany began a series of night bombardments, described by the British press as Blitz (German for lightning) attacks. Between 7 September and 2 November, London suffered nightly raids. Later the focus shifted to other British cities and ports, and heavy strikes on Birmingham continued until 16 May 1941; intermittent air attacks continued through the remainder of the war. Over 3.5 million houses were destroyed and about 30,000 people killed—just over half were Londoners. There were 57 bombing raids on the capital alone, using 13,561 tonnes of explosive. By the war's end Allied pilots flying over Germany would drop more bombs in a single week than the total tonnage of bombs that hit London during the darkness of 1940–41.

The Welfare State

A month after the end of the war in Europe Britain went to the polls. Having led the country to victory, Conservative leader Sir Winston Churchill (1874–1965) hoped to take the helm in peacetime, but the electorate was hungry for change. Labour gained power with a landslide vote, promising to provide basic care for everyone, from cradle to grave: the Welfare State. Three years of legislation introduced an extended National Insurance scheme to fund pensions and pay during illness and unemployment, and free health care for all with the founding of the National Health Service in 1946. The school-leaving age was raised to 15 and free secondary education was ensured. Homelessness, exacerbated by war, was tackled with a massive state house-building programme.

Eurotunnel

Plans for an underwater tunnel to link Britain with the European continent were first mooted in 1802, envisaging horse-drawn transport and stables. In the 1880s work began on train tunnels on each side of the English Channel, only to be halted by Queen Victoria amid fears that British security would be breached. In the 1960s, and with Britain's entry into the European Economic Community in 1973, further plans were made but abandoned due to government crises and the rise in world oil prices. Digging finally began again in 1987 and, after years of delays and funding problems, the French and British tunnels were joined up in December 1990. In November 1994 trains carried their first passengers along the 31 miles (50km) of the Channel Tunnel.

Castaway choice

Like all the best ideas, the longest-running radio show in the world is exceptionally simple. It is the British Broadcasting Corporation's (BBC) *Desert Island Discs*. It was first aired in 1942 and continues to be broadcast on the Radio 4 channel. Each week a guest is 'stranded' on an imaginary desert island: They are permitted to take eight favourite pieces of music, one book and a luxury item. The Bible and Shakespeare's complete works are already on the island. Castaways have included royalty and five prime ministers. Over the years musical trends have fluctuated but the most recent lists show that Beethoven's Symphony No. 9 is the most requested piece of classical music, followed by Schubert's Quintet in C and *Soave sia il vento* from Mozart's *Cosi Fan Tutte*. The Beatles dominate the pop chart.

The face that launched the '60s look—Mary Quant

Diana, Princess of Wales (1961–97), at her wedding in 1981

1999

Please Please Me: Post-war Britain looked forward to new homes and the music of the Beatles

The Eurostar in London: Next stop Paris, Brussels, Lille, Avignon…

21st-Century Britain

Britain entered the new millennium with not so much a bang as a fizzle when a fireworks show failed to turn the Thames into a spectacular 'river of fire'. Things picked up with a successful, if rain-sodden, Commonwealth Games hosted by Manchester in 2002. The monarchy recovered from a few rocky years after the death of Princess Diana, with the Queen celebrating her Golden Jubilee in 2002. As well as the question of closer integration with Europe, Britain now faces the same issues as other countries around the world: a volatile world economy and global security.

Quids in

In the 1990s the euro, the single European currency, was at the root of a serious dissent within the ruling Conservative Party. In the early 2000s the Labour government struggled to sell the idea to a sceptical Britain. By 2005, with the issue of a constitution for the European Union finding disfavour among many member states, the prospect of Britain adopting the euro seemed further away than ever. Despite the growing strength of the euro, it may be some years before Britain sees the end of the quid (pound).

Goodbye, hello

Half a million people waited for up to 12 hours to file past the Queen Mother's coffin in Westminster Hall before her funeral in 2002. Westminster Abbey's tenor bell tolled for 101 minutes, one for each year of her life. Born Elizabeth Bowes-Lyon, she married the Duke of York in 1923 and he became King George VI in 1936. An estimated 300 million people watched on television as a carriage carried her coffin to the abbey, followed by the solemn

Bob Geldof and Annie Lennox at the Live 8 concert in Hyde Park, 2005 (right)

entourage of royals and political leaders. In contrast, the marriage of her grandson, Charles, to Camilla Parker-Bowles on 9 April 2005 was a rather subdued affair. The Prince, who divorced Diana, Princess of Wales nine years before, and the newly created Duchess of Cornwall, took their vows in a small civil ceremony at the Guildhall in Windsor.

Gig of the century

It was royalty of a different kind that drew huge crowds in 2005. This time it was the kings and queens of pop and rock who gathered in Hyde Park, in London, and at the Eden Project in Cornwall to attract the attention of the G8 summit leaders to global poverty. Led by maverick musician and campaigner Sir Bob Geldof, even the legendary Pink Floyd were persuaded to reunite alongside Paul McCartney, U2, Coldplay, Elton John, The Who, Madonna, Mariah Carey, REM and many others. The concert was broadcast on giant screens in cities all over Britain, and coincided with concerts around the globe. Over 200,000 attended the Hyde Park event, with another 50,000 packing into Murrayfield Stadium in Edinburgh for a follow-up gig a week later.

Campaigning to keep the pound (below)

Prince Charles married Camilla Parker-Bowles in Windsor, 2005 (right)

On the Move

ARRIVING

Arriving by Air

This is the most common method of entering the UK, and London, Britain's principal gateway, has air connections to all major world cities. Most long-haul flights arrive at either Heathrow or Gatwick, while the capital's three other airports—Stansted, Luton and London City—serve mainly short-haul destinations.

All airports have information desks, shops, banks, restaurants, car-rental companies, hotel reservation desks and left-luggage facilities. If departing from Heathrow or Gatwick make sure you know which terminal you need. Taxis are usually available outside the terminals.

A number of airports in other parts of the country also accept international flights. These include Birmingham International, Edinburgh, Glasgow (International and Prestwick), Manchester, Southampton and Leeds Bradford.

See also Some Low-cost and Domestic Airlines (▷ 59).

London Heathrow (LHR)

The world's busiest airport lies 12 miles (19km) west of central London. It has four terminals: 1, 2 and 3 in the main complex, and 4 on the south side of the airport. All terminals are linked to the London Underground (one station serves Terminals 1, 2 and 3, another serves Terminal 4), reached by moving walkways and elevators.

For general information about Heathrow tel: 0870 000 0123; www.heathrowairport.com. **Terminal 1** serves all domestic flights, most UK airline flights to Europe, and El Al and South African Airways flights. **Terminal 2** serves non-UK carriers' flights to Europe and some long-haul destinations. **Terminal 3** serves North American, South American, Asian and Asia Pacific airlines, plus most African carriers. **Terminal 4** serves British Airways (BA) long-haul flights, plus BA flights to Amsterdam, Basel, Brussels, Paris and Tel Aviv. KLM and Qantas also use Terminal 4. A fifth terminal, designed to deal

ON THE MOVE

Britain's major regional and international airports

Kirkwall
Orkney Islands
Wick
Stornoway
Sumburgh
Shetland Islands
Western Isles
Inverness Dalcross
Benbecula
Barra
Aberdeen
Tiree
Dundee
Islay
Edinburgh
Glasgow
Prestwick
Newcastle
Isle of Man
Ronaldsway
Durham Tees Valley
Blackpool
Leeds/ Bradford
Liverpool John Lennon
Humberside
Anglesey
Manchester
Robin Hood Doncaster Sheffield
East Midlands
Norwich
Birmingham
Coventry
London Luton
London Stansted
Cardiff
Bristol
London City
Southampton
London Heathrow
Exeter
London Gatwick
Plymouth
Bournemouth
Isle of Wight
Newquay
Penzance Heliport
Isles of Scilly
St Mary's Tresco Heliport

FROM	TAXI
Heathrow	1 hour, £45. Terminal 1: 020 8745 7487 Terminal 2: 020 8745 5408 Terminal 3: 020 8745 4655 Terminal 4: 020 8745 7302
Gatwick	60–75 min, £85 Checker Cars, tel: 01293 568800
Stansted	1–2 hours, £88 Stansted Airport Carz: 01279 662444
Luton	45 min–1hr, £55 Cabco: 01582 736666 Dial-a-Cab: 01582 595555
London City	20–30 min, £30 Taxi rank outside terminal

with new Airbus A380s, should open in 2008.

London Gatwick (LGW)
Britain's second-largest airport is 30 miles (48km) south of central London. Its two terminals, North and South, are linked by Gatwick Transit, an efficient, free monorail. Trains run every 3–4 minutes from each terminal, with a journey time of just under two minutes. South Terminal handles the bulk of Gatwick's traffic domestic, international and charter flights. For more information tel: 0870 000 2468; or visit **www.gatwickairport.com**.

London Stansted (STN)
Stansted, in Essex, is 35 miles (56km) northeast of London, not far from Cambridge. Its large, modern terminal (1991) was

designed by Norman Foster. Rapid transit trains shuttle between this and the airport's two other buildings. London's fastest-growing airport is a base for low-cost airlines such as Ryanair and

London Stansted, now a busy base for budget airlines

easyJet. There are no black taxis at Stansted. Tel: 0870 000 0303 or visit **www.stanstedairport.com**.

GETTING TO CENTRAL LONDON FROM THE AIRPORT

TRAIN	UNDERGROUND	BUS	CAR
Heathrow Express to Paddington, 15–20 min. Daily 5.10am–11.20pm, £14 (one way).	Piccadilly Line takes 1 hour. Mon–Sat 5.10am–11.50pm, Sun 5.57am–11.30pm, £3.80.	National Express No. 412 or 035 to Victoria Coach Station, 45 min. Every 30 min, £15 (return).	East along M4 from junction 3 or 4.
Gatwick Express to Victoria, 30 min. Every 15 min 5.15am–12.30am, hourly 1.30am–4.30am, £21.50. Thameslink to King's Cross, City, Farringdon, Blackfriars and London Bridge, 40 min, from £9.80.	N/A	National Express to Victoria Coach Station, 1 hour 15 min. Every hour, £11 (return).	North along M23 from junction 9.
Stansted Express to Liverpool Street, 40 min. Mon–Sat 5am–12am, £23 (return).	N/A	A6 Airbus to Victoria Coach Station, 90 min. Every 30 min, £15 (return). Terravision 1–2 per hour to Liverpool Street Station or Victoria Coach Station (£13.50 return).	South along M11 from junction 8.
Free shuttle bus to Luton Airport Parkway Station for Thameslink to King's Cross, Farringdon, City, Blackfriars and London Bridge, 35 min, daily 7am–10pm, £10. Some night services.	N/A	Greenline Bus No. 757 to Victoria Coach Station, 90 min. Every 30–60 min, £12.50 (return). easyBus runs minibuses to Baker Street in central London every hour. From £2	South along M1 from junction 10A.
N/A	DLR takes 22 mins. Mon–Sat 5.30am–12.30am Sun 7am–10.30pm every 10–16 mins, £2.80	Shuttle Bus to Liverpool Street Station, 25 min. Daily 6am–10pm, £13 (return).	N/A

REGIONAL AIRPORT TO CITY LINKS	
AIRPORT	**LINK**
Birmingham Off A45	Free Air Rail link to station (90 seconds) for trains to Birmingham New Street (15 min, £2.70) and London Euston (1 hour 35 min, £33.90)
Cardiff West of central Cardiff, off A4226	Shuttle bus to Cardiff Central train and bus station £4 Train 37 min (£2.70)
Edinburgh West of city, off A8	Bus to Waverley train station in city, £3.30 single, £5 return, 25 min; taxi £10–£20
Glasgow Near Paisley	Taxi, 20 min (£14). Bus to Paisley Gilmour Street Station for trains to Glasgow Central, 11 min (get a through ticket to include this fare). Bus to Glasgow
Glasgow Prestwick Off A77, southwest of central Glasgow	Drive, 35 min. AirTrain to Glasgow Central, 50 min (£5)
Manchester South of city, near M56 junction 5	Trains to Manchester Piccadilly, 15 min (£2.55); National Express and other buses to numerous destinations

Heathrow Express
Tel: 0845 600 1515;
www.heathrowexpress.co.uk
London City
Tel: 020 7646 0000;
www.londoncityairport.com. For
shuttle bus tel: 020 7646 0000
National Express Tel: 0870 808
080; www.nationalexpress.com
Stansted Express
Tel: 0845 850 0150;
www.stanstedexpress.co.uk
Thameslink Tel: 0845 330
6333; www.thameslink.co.uk

Arriving by Rail

Eurostar trains from France (Paris, Avignon and Lille) and Belgium (Brussels) speed to Waterloo International Station in under three hours. In 2007 this is due to change to the new St. Pancras International Station. Passports are required for travel and, on arrival, you must also clear customs. There are escalators and elevators to the main Waterloo complex and signs to the Underground (Northern, Bakerloo, Jubilee, and Waterloo and City lines) and buses. A taxi stand is outside the station on the left.

Trains from other parts of Britain arrive at one of London's main terminals, all of which have Underground and bus links (▷ 52–55).

Arriving by Coach

If you travel to Britain by coach (long-distance bus) you will probably arrive at London's

London Luton (LTN)
Luton airport occupies an ugly array of buildings 32 miles (52km) north of central London. A new passenger terminal opened in 1999, along with Luton Parkway train station, from where there are frequent trains to King's Cross. Luton caters mainly to low-cost charter flights, plus scheduled easyJet services. Tel: 01582 405100 or check www.london-luton.co.uk for information.

London City (LCA)
The capital's smallest (and newest) airport, set in the regenerated Docklands area 6 miles (10km) from central London, is especially popular with visitors on business. Flights operate to over 20 European destinations and British towns and cities.
Tel: 020 7646 0088;
www.londoncityairport.com

Gatwick's coach terminal: sign-posting is good in British airports

Glasgow Airport (GLA)
The busiest of Scotland's three international airports, Glasgow Airport is 8 miles (13km) west of the city. It receives flights from 35 destinations in Britain, Europe and North America. Tel: 0141 887 1111; www.glasgowairport.com

Manchester Airport (MAN)
Manchester Airport is the principal airport in the north of England and has flights to every continent from its three terminals. The airport is 10 miles (16km) south of the city. Tel: 0161 489 3000; www.manchesterairport.co.uk

Useful contacts
Gatwick Express Tel: 0845 850 1530; www.gatwickexpress.co.uk
Greenline Tel: 0870 608 7261; www.greenline.co.uk

LEAVING LONDON BY TRAIN			
LONDON TERMINAL	MAIN ROUTES	TRAIN OPERATORS	UNDERGROUND LINES
Charing Cross (via London Bridge)	Southeast England	South Eastern, Southern	Northern, Bakerloo
Euston	Midlands, northwest England, Scotland	Virgin Trains, First ScotRail, Silverlink	Northern, Victoria, Hammersmith and City, Metropolitan
Fenchurch Street (Tower Hill Underground)	Thames estuary, Essex	c2c	Circle, District
King's Cross	East Midlands, Yorkshire, Northeast, Scotland	GNER, Hull Trains, 'one' Great Northern, Thameslink (to 2007)	Northern, Piccadilly, Victoria, Hammersmith and City, Circle, Metropolitan
Liverpool Street	East Anglia, Essex	'one' Great Northern, Stansted Express	Hammersmith and City, Circle, Metropolitan, Central
London Bridge	Southeast England	Thameslink, Southern	Jubilee, Northern
Marylebone	Midlands	Chiltern Railways	Bakerloo
Paddington	South and West Midlands, West Country, Wales	First Great Western, Heathrow Express	District, Circle, Hammersmith and City, Bakerloo
St. Pancras	Midlands, France	Midland Mainline, Thameslink (from 2007), Eurostar	Victoria, Northern, Piccadilly, Hammersmith and City, Circle, Metropolitan
Victoria	Southern England	Gatwick Express, Southern	Victoria, District, Circle
Waterloo	Southwest England, Wales, France	South West Trains, Southern, South Eastern, Eurostar	Northern, Bakerloo, Jubilee, Waterloo and City

Victoria Coach Station (VCS), a ten-minute walk from Victoria Station. There is a taxi stand outside the coach station. The main coach company is National Express, but Greenline coaches also connect local cities and airports to London.
● **Victoria Coach Station**
164 Buckingham Palace Road, London SW1W 9TP
Tel: 020 7730 3466
● **National Express**
Tel: 08705 808080;
www.nationalexpress.com
● **Greenline**
4a Fountain Square, 123–151 Buckingham Palace Road, London SW1W 0SR, tel. 0870 608 7261; **www.**greenline.co.uk

Arriving by Car

Eurotunnel operates the train service for cars, caravans and motorcycles through the Channel Tunnel. The journey from Calais to Folkestone takes 20 minutes, and drivers and passengers remain in their vehicles. At Folkestone, the terminal joins the M20 north, at junction 11a and the drive to London takes about 1 hour 30 minutes.

Arriving by Ferry

Ferries now face stiff competition from Eurostar and Eurotunnel, so they can be a relatively inexpensive way of crossing the Channel. Various companies operate passenger and vehicle

services between Britain and Europe. Trains run from ports on the south coast—Dover, Folkestone, Ramsgate and Newhaven—to London Victoria. The train operator 'one' runs a service from Harwich to Liverpool Street. Along with regular ferry services, certain ports, such as Calais, operate faster Seacat and Superseacat vessels (▷ 58).

City links from ferry ports
● **Dover** Shuttle bus to Dover Priory Station, then train to London Charing Cross, 1 hour 45 min–2 hours
● **Fishguard** Train to Swansea, 3 hours 30 min
● **Folkestone** M20 to London, 1 hour 30 min–2 hours
● **Harwich** Train to London Liverpool Street, 1 hour 30 min
● **Holyhead** Train to Crewe (2 hours) via Chester (1 hour 40 min)
● **Newcastle** Bus to city centre and train station (20 min)
● **Newhaven** Train to London Victoria, from 1 hour 15 min
● **Portsmouth** Train to London Waterloo, 1 hour 35 min

A ferry crossing the Channel

GETTING AROUND

Crossing London

ON THE MOVE

You'll need to tackle the public transport system to cross London. The Underground train network (known as the Tube), the world's oldest, is quicker than taking a bus, but it can be hot and stuffy. Buses can be a pleasant alternative, offering views from the top deck. Riverboats run from quays along the River Thames to certain attractions, while taxis are a convenient but expensive option. Or you could walk—many Tube stations are actually very close to each other.

THE UNDERGROUND

London Underground operates nearly 500 trains between 260 stations. Twelve colour-coded lines make up the Greater London Underground system, each with its own name.
● Trains run Mon–Sat 5.30am– midnight (Sun 7am–11pm).
● Try to avoid the rush hours (7–9.30am, 4.30–7pm).
● If you cannot produce a valid ticket you will be fined £25.
● Space is limited so don't take too much luggage; fold buggies when you get on the train.
● Watch out for pickpockets. Ensure that your bags are closed and avoid carrying valuables in back pockets or rucksacks.
● Most stations have electronic ticket gates. If your ticket does not work, find a member of staff. You

will need your ticket to leave the station; don't discard it.
● Mobile phones won't work under ground.

BUSES

London's iconic red double-decker buses are a good way to make short journeys.
● Main bus stops (red circle on a white background) have timetables and route information. Buses stop automatically.
● At request stops (white circle on a red background) you must hail buses.
● At night treat all stops as request stops. Night buses (number preceded by 'N') run 11pm–6am on main routes.
● Each route is identified by a number on the front of the bus.
● In central London you must buy a ticket from a roadside machine before boarding.
● The Riverside service links the South Bank to the West End, with 40 attractions along the route.

BUS STOP
Marble Arch
towards
Oxford Circus

6	12	15
23	94	159
N3	N6	N12
N15	N16	N36
	N23	N98

TIPS
● Download Tube information in French, German, Spanish, Italian or Portuguese from www.tfl.gov.uk/tube/tourists. Check that trains are running in the update section or use the journey planner.
● For up-to-date news and information tel: 020 7222 1234, or go to www.tfl.gov.uk
● It is cheaper to travel after 9.30am and at weekends.

● A single adult fare on most routes within Greater London is £1.50. Children under 14 travel free. 14–15 year olds may travel free if they have photo ID.

RIVERBOATS

Most services start from Westminster Pier and run 6.30am–9.30pm. The route runs as fas as Hampton Court Palace to the west and the Thames Barrier to the east.

MAKING IT EASY—TICKETS

You can buy tickets for all forms of public transport at most Underground stations, train stations, information offices and many other outlets. Carry small change so you can use ticket machines instead of queuing at a ticket office. You can buy individual tickets for all types of transport, but the best option is a Travelcard. These are valid for the entire network in selected zones and give unlimited travel in the paid-for zone.

Central London occupies Zone 1, with Zones 2–6 following in progressively wider concentric rings, which are colour-coded on Tube maps. It is sensible to pay a little extra to allow travel in more zones.

Day Travelcard No photocard required *
Class   Ticket type   Price   Issue date
STD OFF-PEAK   £1   3810
Status   Valid on   Number
23 AUG   0020*05544001
Between   Zones   Valid
ALTON   T2S6 ZONES ONEDAY
Route/also available at
Valid within zone(s) indicated
Valid as advertised
Not for resale

One-Day Travelcard
Zones 1 and 2: adult £6.20/4.90 (peak/off-peak), child £3.10
Zones 1–4, adult £8.40/5.40, child £4.20

Three-Day Travelcard
Zones 1 and 2: adult £15.40, child £7.70

Family Travel
A £1 off-peak Child Day Travelcard is available for up to four under-16s accompanied by adult Travelcard holders.

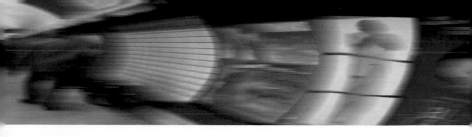

On The Move

HOW TO USE THE UNDERGROUND

- Stand on the right on escalators so that people in a hurry can walk on the left.
- If you have bulky items, buggies or folding bicycles you can go through the special wide gates. A member of staff will let you through.
- Stand clear of the train's closing doors. Obstructing them causes delays.
- Mind the gap between the platform and the train.

- Let passengers off the train before you get on.
- Note that there is no air-conditioning on the Underground and delays are not uncommon so it can get very hot, especially in summer.
- Stand behind the yellow line on the platform when waiting for a train.
- Threats and violent behaviour should be reported to members of staff.

TRAINS AND TRAMS

London is not the only British city to have an underground train system. Glasgow's is called the Subway and it runs daily to 15 stations on a circular route around the city. A single adult fare costs from £1 and a one-day pass costs £1.90. Trains run at intervals of between 5 and 8 minutes. Newcastle upon Tyne has called its underground the Metro, and it runs daily to 50 stations throughout Tyne and Wear. A single adult fare costs between £1.30 and £2.40.

Birmingham's tram network is also known as the Metro. It connects Wolverhampton with Birmingham via 23 stops. A single fare costs from 60p. And Manchester's tram service is the Metrolink, running to 37 stops with single fares costing from 60p.

UNDERSTANDING THE UNDERGROUND MAP

TUBE STATION
A simple dash indicates a station with no interchanges.

MAIN LINE STATION
This symbol indicates a connection with a main line station.

COLOUR-CODED LINES
Each line is colour-coded to make navigation easy.

STATION WITH INTERCHANGE
Interchanges with other Underground lines and with suburban rail are marked with a white circle. Two white circles show more than one line interchange.

© Transport for London Reg. user No. 02/3702

You will see a map like the section above in the train. Follow your journey, count the stops and watch for the names of stations so you know where to get off.

INTERCHANGING LINES
These symbols (left) show stations with connecting lines and their relevant colours.

GETTING AROUND **47**

Driving

One of the best ways of seeing Britain is by car. On the whole, motorists drive safely, roads are good, if busy, and signposting is efficient. In some parts of Britain, it is the only way of getting around, as local transport can be limited. The network of narrow, crooked lanes between small towns and villages makes a delightful opportunity to see the country, while the fast motorways link major towns and cities. Note that you must drive on the left-hand side of the road.

CAR RENTAL

Arranging to rent a car through your travel agent before arriving can save money and allows you to find out about deposits, drop-off charges, cancellation penalties and insurance costs in advance. However, the usual established car rental companies have offices throughout Britain. Smaller, local companies and online agents may offer better deals; check the *Yellow Pages*.

● You must have a valid driver's licence. An International Driving Permit may be useful if your licence is not in English.

● Most rental firms require the driver to be at least 23 years old and with at least 12 months' driving experience.

● Rental rates usually include free unlimited mileage.

● It is important to ensure that you have some form of personal insurance along with Collision Damage Waiver (CDW). Many companies also offer Damage Excess Reduction (DER) and Theft Protection for an additional premium. You will also have to pay more for additional drivers.

● Find out what equipment is standard: air-conditioning is not always available.

● Most cars use unleaded fuel; make sure you know what's required (unleaded or diesel) before filling the tank.

● Although reputable companies operate new fleets and service them to a high standard, make your own checks before accepting

a rental car, including checking for tyre wear. Insist on a different vehicle if you are unhappy with this. Check that rear seat belts are fitted and arrange for child car seats if you have small children.

THE LAW

● Drive on the left.

● The wearing of seat belts is obligatory, including in the back.

● Motorcyclists must wear helmets at all times.

● The speed limit in built-up areas is 30mph (48kph); outside built-up areas it is 60mph (97kph) on single carriageways and 70mph (113kph) on dual carriageways and motorways, unless a sign indicates otherwise.

● There are tough laws against drinking and driving. The best advice is not to drink alcohol at all if you are driving.

● Red routes are priority routes controlled by the police where no stopping is allowed at any time.

● Cars are banned from using bus lanes—look for signs.

CAR RENTAL FIRMS		
NAME	**TELEPHONE**	**WEBSITE**
Alamo	0870 599 3000	www.alamo.co.uk
Avis	0870 010 0287	www.avis.co.uk
Budget	01344 484100	www.budget.com
Easycar	0906 33 33 33 3	www.easycar.com
Europcar	0870 607 5000	www.europcar.com
Hertz	0870 599 6699	www.hertz.co.uk
National	0870 400 4579	www.nationalcar.co.uk
Practical	0121 772 8599	www.practical.co.uk
Sixt Kenning	01246 506218	www.e-sixt.com
Thrifty	01494 751 500	www.thrifty.co.uk

MAKING IT EASY AT ROUNDABOUTS

Give way to traffic on your right. Use the left-hand lane (if there is one) to turn left. Use mini roundabouts in the same way.

When approaching a roundabout, give priority to traffic on your right, unless directed otherwise by signs, road markings or traffic lights. Look forward before moving off to make sure traffic in front has moved. Watch out for vehicles already on the roundabout; be aware that they may not be signalling correctly, or at all.

● Give way to the right at roundabouts (see diagram, ▷ 48).

FUEL
● All large garages (gas stations) are self-service and sell higher-octane unleaded petrol (gas), unleaded 95 octane fuel and diesel. Note that leaded four-star fuel has been phased out. Higher octane is the most expensive. Prices vary slightly across the country.

CONGESTION CHARGE
● A congestion charge operates in central London. It costs £8 per car per day Monday to Friday 7am–6.30pm, excluding public holidays. You can pay online (www.cclondon.com), by phone 24 hours a day

(tel: 0845 900 1234), in person at outlets such as petrol stations and shops, or by credit or debit card at self-service machines at parking areas inside the zone and at other locations. You need to pay in advance or on the day, prior to 10pm. The charge rises to £10 if you pay after 10pm. Digital cameras check number plates; those in breach of regulations are fined £50.

PARKING
● Street parking in major cities is limited and for short periods.
● Check signs for any restrictions to certain vehicles or at certain time periods.

Never park
● if you cannot comply with or don't understand the regulations;

● on a pedestrian crossing or area marked with zigzags;
● at the side of a road that has a central double white line;
● on a clearway during operational times;
● on a cycle or bus lane or a tramway;
● in bays reserved for doctors, ambulances or disabled drivers.

Meters
● Meter parking is charged by the hour and charges vary.
● The maximum stay at a meter is usually two hours and usually you cannot return to the same parking spot within an hour.
● Generally, meter parking is free Monday to Friday after 6.30pm, Saturday from 1.30pm and Sunday all day, but there are exceptions.

ROAD SIGNS AND DRIVING TIPS

Classes of signs Plates below signs qualify their message			Circles order and prohibit	Triangles warn		Rectangles provide information	
Junctions and roundabouts	Give way to traffic on major road	Stop and give way	Crossroads	Roundabout	Mini roundabout (roundabout circulation)	No through road	
Traffic behaviour	No stopping (clearway)	National speed limit applies	Maximum speed limit applies	One-way traffic	No overtaking	No entry for vehicular traffic	
The road ahead	Two lanes merge into one	Double bend	Two-way traffic ahead	Cycle route ahead	Road works	Slippery road	
Motorways	Start of motorway and point from which motorway regulations apply	Temporary maximum speed limit	Reduced visibility ahead	End of restriction	Do not proceed further in this lane		

On-street pay and display

- If you park in a 'pay and display' area you must buy a ticket from the machine and display it clearly inside your vehicle as it will be checked.
- Some machines require you to type in the first three numbers of your vehicle number plate.

Parking restrictions

- A single yellow line indicates that parking restrictions apply; a notice should explain exactly what these are.
- No parking is allowed at any time on a double yellow line.
- A broken yellow line indicates limited restrictions.
- A single red line indicates that stopping is not permitted.
- Many streets in inner cities are reserved for permit-holding residents only.

Car parks (parking lots)

- The biggest car park operator is National Car Parks (NCP, tel: 0870 606 7050, www.ncp.co.uk). Rates are high.

TRAFFIC WARDENS/FINES

- Traffic wardens patrol streets in all major cities.
- The Fixed Penalty Notice for parking offences is £60.
- If you get a parking ticket, don't ignore it. Many fines carry a discount if paid within 14 days.

STOPPING

- You may pick up and drop off passengers in restricted areas but not on clearways–red routes in London.
- Continuous loading/unloading is permitted except where kerb markings indicate a loading ban, or on clearways.
- Check for notices on posts or walls to see when restricted hours apply.

CLAMPING AND TOWING AWAY

- If your car is parked illegally it may be clamped; the notice posted on your windscreen explains how to get it released.

Left: Britain's road network. Use the chart opposite to gauge the distance in miles (green) and duration in hours and minutes (blue) of a car journey

- Vehicles are usually released within one hour of payment.
- If your vehicle is removed it will cost at least £125 to get it back.
- Vehicles must be collected in person and you must produce at least one form of identification, such as your driver's licence.

CAR BREAKDOWN AND ACCIDENTS

- Several organizations in the UK can assist you in the event of breakdown. Check whether membership in your home country entitles you to reciprocal assistance from a British organization.

At the scene of an accident

- If, as a driver, you are involved in a road traffic accident, stop and remain at the scene and give your vehicle registration number, your name and address, and that of the vehicle owner, to anyone with reasonable grounds for asking for those details.
- If you do not exchange those details at the scene, you must report the accident at a police station or to a police officer within 24 hours.

MOTORWAYS

Britain has a vast network of motorways serving all parts of the country. The major arteries are the M1 north, M2 to the southeast, M3 south, M4 west, M5 southwest, the M6/M74 to Scotland, the M62 across the Pennines and the M8 across Scotland's central belt. The M6 has an alternative toll section that avoids a notorious

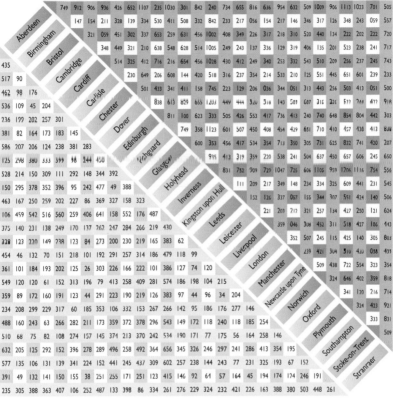

Distance chart (distances in kilometres — upper figures; distances in miles — lower figures)

Kilometres (reading from each origin across to the cities listed):

From \ To	Bir	Bri	Cam	Car	Carl	Che	Dov	Edi	Fis	Gla	Hol	Inv	Hull	Lee	Lei	Liv	Lon	Man	New	Nor	Oxf	Ply	Sou	Sto	Str
Aberdeen	749	912	906	936	426	652	1107	235	1030	301	842	240	734	655	816	636	954	632	509	1009	906	1113	1023	701	505
Birmingham		147	154	211	328	139	334	530	411	508	332	842	233	217	056	154	217	146	346	317	126	348	243	059	557
Bristol			321	059	451	302	337	653	259	631	456	1002	408	349	226	317	218	310	520	440	134	222	202	222	720
Cambridge				348	449	321	210	638	548	628	514	1005	249	243	137	336	129	319	406	135	201	523	238	241	717
Cardiff					514	325	412	216	654	1028	430	412	249	340	253	332	543	510	209	256	237	245	743		
Carlisle						230	649	206	608	144	420	518	316	237	354	214	533	210	125	551	445	651	601	239	500
Chester							501	433	341	411	158	745	223	129	206	036	344	051	313	443	256	503	413	051	500
Dover								838	613	829	655	1203	449	444	320	318	143	507	607	316	220	577	741	477	918
Edinburgh									811	100	623	333	505	426	553	417	736	413	240	740	648	804	442	303	
Fishguard										749	358	1123	601	507	450	408	454	429	651	710	410	457	438	413	818
Glasgow											600	353	456	417	534	354	713	350	305	731	625	832	741	420	207
Holyhead												935	413	319	359	220	538	241	504	637	450	657	606	245	650
Inverness													831	752	909	729	1047	725	606	1105	959	1206	1116	754	556
Kingston upon Hull														111	209	217	349	148	234	334	325	609	441	231	545
Leeds															152	126	337	067	155	344	307	551	424	140	506
Leicester																221	203	212	321	257	134	427	250	121	624
Liverpool																	359	046	308	452	311	518	427	106	443
London																		352	507	245	115	425	140	305	803
Manchester																			239	421	304	310	420	038	437
Newcastle upon Tyne																				509	438	722	554	323	354
Norwich																					324	646	402	359	818
Oxford																						341	120	216	714
Plymouth																							324	423	921
Southampton																								333	831
Stoke-on-Trent																									509

Miles (reading from each origin across to the cities listed):

From \ To	Abe	Bir	Bri	Cam	Car	Carl	Che	Dov	Edi	Fis	Gla	Hol	Inv	Hull	Lee	Lei	Liv	Lon	Man	New	Nor	Oxf	Ply	Sou	Sto
Birmingham	435																								
Bristol	517	90																							
Cambridge	462	98	176																						
Cardiff	536	109	45	204																					
Carlisle	236	199	202	257	301																				
Chester	381	82	164	173	183	145																			
Dover	586	207	206	124	238	381	283																		
Edinburgh	125	298	380	333	399	98	244	450																	
Fishguard	528	214	150	309	111	292	148	344	392																
Glasgow	150	295	378	352	396	95	242	477	49	388															
Holyhead	463	167	250	259	202	227	86	369	327	158	323														
Inverness	106	459	542	516	560	259	406	641	158	552	176	487													
Kingston upon Hull	375	140	231	138	249	170	137	262	247	284	266	219	430												
Leeds	328	123	220	149	238	123	84	273	200	230	219	165	383	62											
Leicester	454	46	132	70	151	218	101	192	291	314	186	479	118	99											
Liverpool	361	101	184	193	202	125	26	303	226	166	222	101	386	127	74	120									
London	549	120	120	61	52	313	196	79	413	258	409	281	574	186	198	104	215								
Manchester	359	89	172	160	191	123	44	291	223	190	219	126	383	97	44	96	34	204							
Newcastle upon Tyne	234	208	299	229	317	60	185	353	106	332	153	267	266	142	95	186	176	277	146						
Norwich	488	160	243	63	266	282	211	173	359	372	378	296	543	149	172	118	240	118	185	254					
Oxford	510	68	75	82	108	274	157	145	374	213	370	242	534	190	171	77	175	56	164	258	146				
Plymouth	632	205	125	292	152	396	278	289	496	258	492	364	656	345	326	246	297	241	286	413	354	195			
Southampton	577	135	106	131	139	341	224	152	441	245	437	309	602	257	238	144	243	77	231	325	193	67	152		
Stoke-on-Trent	391	49	132	141	150	155	38	251	255	171	251	123	415	146	92	61	57	164	45	194	174	124	246	191	
Stranraer	235	305	388	363	407	106	252	487	133	398	86	334	261	276	229	324	232	421	226	163	388	380	503	448	261

congested area, between junctions 4 and 11 around Birmingham. Cars pay £3.50 (or £2.50 between 11pm and 6am).

• Many motorways are fitted with electronic information panels that can be clearly seen from a distance and inform motorists of situations ahead on the road, such as accidents, fog or other problems.

• When joining the motorway from a slip road, give priority to traffic already on the motorway

• Do not overtake on the inside—this is against the law—except where traffic is stationary and the lane you are in is moving faster than the outer lanes, or where a slip road is indicated off the motorway by a short dotted line.

• Keep a safe distance from the vehicle in front.

• Do not exceed the 70mph (113kph) speed limit.

• Do not drive on the hard shoulder except in an emergency or if you are directed to do so.

BREAKDOWN ORGANIZATIONS

The Automobile Association (AA) 119–121 Cannon Street, London EC4N 5AT, tel: 0870 600 0371 (information) or 0800 444999 (new members), www.theaa.com; open daily 24 hours. You can become a member on the spot but it will cost you more than if you join beforehand.

The AA website (www.theaa.com) provides advice on what to do in the event of breakdown; a 'Route Planner', with maps and directions; traffic news and online road status reports. AA Roadwatch, tel: 0870 600 0371, has the latest on traffic jams. Calls cost up to 75p per minute from landlines. Mobile costs may vary.

The Environmental Transport Association (ETA)
Freepost, KT4021, Weybridge, Surrey KT13 8RS, tel: 0800 212 810. The ETA can be contacted Mon–Fri 8–6, Sat 9–4, closed Sunday. The breakdown number is supplied on joining and the service operates 24 hours (www.eta.co.uk).

The Royal Automobile Club (RAC)
RAC House, 1 Forest Road, Feltham TW13 7RR, tel: 0870 572 2722 for membership enquiries Mon–Fri 8am–9pm, Sat 9–5 and Sun 10–4. For breakdown assistance tel: 0800 828282 24 hours (www.rac.co.uk).

Trains

The railway is a British invention and, unfortunately for passengers, much of the 19th-century network is still in operation. However, the services generally work fairly efficiently and are not oppressively crowded outside peak periods. Following denationalization and the breakup of the British Rail network, over 20 different companies now operate the trains. This can lead to differing facilities and some curious price anomalies as each company determines its own fare structure. In some cases it is worth checking whether another company serving the same region can offer an alternative route or lower price.

Train services can be notoriously unreliable in hot weather (warped tracks), cold weather (icy tracks) and in autumn (leaves on the line), so always leave plenty of time for your journey, especially if you have to change trains.

Essential engineering work, usually carried out at weekends and public holidays, can severely disrupt services, with buses sometimes replacing trains in certain areas. Details are displayed at relevant stations, or check in advance with National Rail (www.nationalrail.co.uk) or national rail enquiries.

TRAIN INFORMATION
● Detailed information for the whole network—including operating companies, timetables, fares and restrictions—is available from National Rail Enquiries. Tel: 08457 484950; minicom: 0845 605 0600; www.nationalrail.co.uk.

Their useful free map and guide to using the national rail network is available from stations.

Eurostar has linked London with France and Belgium since 1994

● Staffed stations usually have free timetables of local services, and almost all stations display timetables. Note that there are different services for weekdays and Saturday and Sunday that are more limited.
● There are two classes of train travel: first and standard. First class is much more expensive but does guarantee you a seat on trains as well as complimentary drinks and newspapers. Standard class is acceptable and you can reserve a seat for longer journeys if you book your ticket in advance.
● Sleeping compartments can be reserved with First Scotrail on some overnight services to and from Scotland (tel: 0845 755 0033).

OTHER USEFUL CONTACTS
Eurostar Tel: 08705 186186 (UK), 0033 8 92 35 35 39 (France), 0032 25 28 28 28 (Belgium); www.eurostar.com
Eurotunnel Tel: 08705 35 35 35; www.eurotunnel.com

TIPS
● Research your route in advance and check for engineering works or other problems.
● Ask advice about the best fares or buy online; try www.thetrainline.com or www.qjump.co.uk.
● Buy combined Underground/rail tickets if you're going across London. Also look out for good-value combined rail journey and entrance tickets to some tourist attractions, such as Hampton Court and Legoland Windsor.
● Carry change and banknotes for ticket machines to avoid having to wait to pay.
● Arrange assistance in advance if needed.
● Avoid weekday rush hours (7–9.30am and 4.30–7pm) if possible. Note that the evening rush hour often starts earlier on Friday, especially before public holidays.
● Allow plenty of time, especially to make connections.

HOW TO BUY TICKETS
You must always buy a valid ticket for your journey before you board the train or you may be liable to a fixed fine. You can buy a ticket in person for any destination served by any company from any rail station, from the ticket office. Many stations have automated machines selling tickets for shorter journeys. Most London Underground stations also sell rail tickets, as do travel agents. Credit and debit cards are accepted. Station staff are obliged to inform you of the cheapest available fare.

● Standard ticket machines accept larger-denomination coins and £5 and £10 notes (not too crumpled) and will give change unless they indicate otherwise. An increasing number of automated ticket machines, especially on commuter routes, also accept debit and credit cards.

● You can also buy tickets online through www.thetrainline.com or www.qjump.co.uk, both of which give prices and fast booking for different types of tickets for any journey.

● Smaller, unstaffed stations often have ticket machines or machines that issue a 'permit to travel': insert any amount of money and this will be deducted from the fare when a member of staff issues your ticket later in the journey. If there is no means of purchasing a ticket in advance, you will be sold one on the train.

● Seat reservations are not usually necessary, but are advisable at peak times and are compulsory for certain services, in which case there is no extra charge.

TYPES OF TICKET

Rail travel is expensive and with so many different ticket options available, it pays to do some research in advance to find the best bargains. For some discounted fares you will need to buy tickets a week or more in advance.

● Unless you ask for first class, tickets issued will be for standard class travel.

● A cheap day return is the best option for a day out, but you can buy and use it only after 9.30am. Day return tickets usually consist of two separate tickets ('out' and 'return'), so make sure you keep both and use the correct one.

● Except for certain 'rover' or 'open' tickets, your journey(s) must be on the date(s) shown on the ticket and you cannot break the journey. This means you cannot get off en route and join a later train—if you get off before your original destination, you must then buy another ticket.

● At staffed stations you can buy tickets for travel on a specific date.

● If you change your plans you can get a refund, provided you have not started your journey.

● Tickets for journeys between London terminus stations will normally include travel on the Underground, but check your ticket before you set out.

Britain's main railway lines. Services are run by individual companies

MAIN TICKET OPTIONS		
TICKET TYPE	**RESTRICTIONS**	**VALIDITY**
Open single	None	On the date shown, or on either of the two following days
Day single/day return	None	Date shown; return same day
Saver return	Peak travel restrictions	Return within one calendar month
SuperSaver return	Not available for travel before 9.30am, on Fri, summer Sat and peak holidays	Return within one calendar month
Network AwayBreak	Not before 9.30am	London and South East only; return within five days
Cheap day return	Not before 9.30am	Return the same day
In approximately descending order of price.		

Other tickets

Apex This term refers to various options for certain long-distance journeys, bought three or more days in advance. The earlier you reserve, the more you save on the normal fare.

Plusbus A rail ticket with one day's unlimited bus travel on services at either end of the journey. Available for participating stations only (www.plusbus.info).

Concessions and passes

● Children under 5 travel free and 5- to 15-year-olds pay half price for most tickets, but check as there are exceptions.

● **Britrail Pass** This gives unlimited rail travel in Britain and Northern Ireland for non-UK residents only, but can only be purchased abroad. The BritRail Consecutive Pass gives freedom of travel over 4, 8, 15 or 22 consecutive days or a calendar month, and the BritRail FlexiPass covers any 4, 8 or 15 days of travel in a two-month period. Also available are Party Passes (50 per cent discount for third and fourth passengers); Family Passes (free travel for an accompanying child aged 5–15) and regional passes (days out from London, Scotland and Wales). For information visit www.britrail.com.

● **Regional passes** Available for Scotland, Wales and regions of England.

● **Railcards** For extensive use of services in southeast England it may be worth buying a railcard, valid for a year. It costs £20 and gives 33 per cent off fares to stations in the region. A Young Person's Railcard (16–25 year olds and mature students in

full-time education) costs £20 and is valid across the country. You'll need a passport-size photograph and proof of eligibility to buy one railcard.

AT THE STATION

Most train stations have electronic information displays showing departure times, station stops, platform numbers and estimated time of arrival. Larger stations are more like airport terminals, showing departures and arrivals for each platform. Information for visitors with a disability or with children is given later in this chapter (▷ 63–64).

London has 10 main termini, each serving a different region of the country, as well as providing cross-city services (see Arriving and rail network map, ▷ 44 and 53). Services from London can reach most parts of Britain in a day—Intercity trains on major routes travel at 140mph (225kph), so journeys from one end of the country to the other can take just a few hours.

Large main stations can be disorienting, but staff will help

Conversely, some trains stop at every station, and going even a relatively short distance can seem interminable.

● Keep your ticket with you at all times, or you may be liable to a penalty fare (£10, or the single fare to the next scheduled stop, whichever is the greater) and have to buy a ticket at the full fare.

● Most urban stations have automatic barriers. Put your ticket into the slot on one side. If you have a return ticket it then pops back out at the top: remember to collect it. The barrier will then open for you to pass. If you have a disability, luggage, children, or just need help, go instead to the staffed gate at the side of the barrier. The barriers retain used tickets at the end of a journey.

● Check the displays and listen to announcements to find out which platform (track) you need.

TYPES OF RAILCARD			
RAILCARD	**ELIGIBILITY**	**PRICE**	**INFORMATION**
Disabled Person's	Holder plus adult companion	£14	www.disabledpersons-railcard.co.uk
Family	Up to 4 adults and 4 children	£20	www.family-railcard.co.uk
Network	Over 16s for travel in London, South East	£20	www.railcard.co.uk/network
Senior	Ages 60 and over	£20	www.senior-railcard.co.uk
Young Person's	Ages 16–25, and full-time students of any age	£20	www.youngpersons-railcard.co.uk

- Changing trains can be tricky if your connection time is tight. So, if in doubt, ask the station staff. It is worth checking the train's destination with a guard as you board the train, especially if you are in a hurry or if services are experiencing problems, as platforms can be changed at short notice.
- Make sure you board the correct section of the train, as on some services carriages are added or detached during the journey. Note that some platforms can be very long, and you may need to walk some distance to find your carriage. If time is short get on at any door and walk through the train so you don't miss it.
- Dedicated indoor waiting areas are uncommon, but many stations have a café where you can wait. Major stations have facilities in varying degrees, ranging from newsstands and cafés to specialist shops, mini supermarkets, travel offices, restaurants, dry-cleaners, bureaux de change and pubs. Small or rural stations are usually devoid of facilities.
- Many (but by no means all) stations have toilets, but these are often closed when you need them most. Larger stations may charge for their use (usually 20p), and will have facilities for those with disabilities and for baby-changing.
- Smoking is generally allowed on station platforms (except the London Underground where smoking is not permitted

anywhere) and concourses, but not in shops.
- Few stations have left-luggage facilities, for security reasons, but King's Cross Station in London provides a good, if expensive, facility.

ON THE TRAIN

With so many different train operators running services on the national network, the facilities and conditions on board trains can vary enormously depending on the route. The rolling stock ranges from ancient 'slam-door' carriages (cars) to basic but comfortable commuter trains to sleek, modern carriages with sliding doors, access for visitors with disabilities, telephones and acceptable catering.
- With the exception of journeys at peak holiday times and on certain (usually long-distance) routes, seat reservations are not necessary. If you have reserved a seat, however, look for your numbered carriage and seat, which will display a tag. With a standard-class ticket you can sit anywhere—including a reserved seat outside the part of the journey covered by the reservation—but not in a first-class carriage (clearly marked with a '1' on the outside). Holders of first-class tickets may sit anywhere in the train.
- Generally, all trains should have toilet facilities, ranging from the basic to larger, wheelchair-accessible booths with baby-changing facilities.

Not all trains take bicycles; those that do may have limited space

- Most trains have an at-seat trolley service providing refreshments, and some longer routes also have buffet cars where you can buy drinks, sandwiches and other snacks. Prices are relatively high.
- Smoking is now banned on all trains in England, Scotland and Wales.
- Telephones are available on some longer routes, and some long-distance services have 'quiet carriages' where the use of mobile phones and personal stereos is prohibited.
- Sleeper services are available for journeys between London and Scotland and London and southwest England.
- Luggage can be stowed in overhead racks, behind the seats, in compartments at the end of some carriages or, in the case of larger items or bicycles, in the guard's van. Take care not to block the aisles or the doors with luggage.
- For lost property contact the train company or the relevant station.
- Safety information is clearly displayed throughout all trains, and the on-board guard or conductor can also offer help and advice.

The Heathrow Express: a fast, convenient but expensive link between central London and London Heathrow

Coaches

Coaches (long-distance buses) run from London's Victoria Coach Station (VCS) to all parts of the country and are a slower but much less expensive alternative to train travel. The main operator in Britain is National Express, whose routes cover the whole country. Journey times can be long (with some changes necessary), but coaches are comfortable, with air-conditioning, toilets and sometimes refreshments.

At Victoria Coach Station you can buy or reserve airport coach tickets, tours and excursions, London travelcards, theatre and concert tickets, domestic and European rail tickets, ferry and hovercraft tickets and travel insurance. The travel office can also arrange Western Union money transfer and organize car rental and hotel accommodation.

ON THE MOVE

TIPS

- It is cheaper to reserve in advance and travel midweek.
- You can get advance purchase coach tickets until two hours before departure, and for some journeys, tickets are also available from the driver.
- You can reserve by phone, online at sites such as www.nationalexpress.com, at travel agents and from Victoria Coach Station and other stations.
- Victoria Coach Station ticket hall is open daily 6am–11.30pm for tickets to UK and European destinations. Telephone Sales (tel: 020 7730 3499) are open Mon–Sat 8.30am–7pm.
- Ticket types include standard single or return, plus various saver tickets bookable in advance.
- Luggage allowances are two medium-size suitcases and one item of hand luggage per person, with no guarantee that any excess will be carried. Properly folded and covered bicycles are acceptable, as are assistance dogs.

 NationalExpress

USEFUL CONTACTS
- **Victoria Coach Station** 164 Buckingham Palace Road, London SW1W 9TP. The travel counter is open Monday to Friday 8am–7pm, Saturday 8.30am–4pm and Sunday 8am–3pm.
- **National Express** Tel: 08705 808080 (bookings, daily 8am–10pm); www.nationalexpress.com. For detailed information, routes, timetables and bookings.
- Other booking services include www.A2bTravel.com and Traveline (tel: 0870 608 2608;

www.traveline.org.uk) or www.coachtourismcouncil. co.uk
- Scottish **Citylink** connects 200 towns and cities in Scotland and beyond. Tel: 08705 505050; www.citylink.co.uk
- **Green Line Travel Office** 4a Fountain Square, 123–151 Buckingham Palace Road, London SW1W 0SR; tel: 0870 608 7261; www.greenline.co.uk. Services between London and local cities and airports.

Coaches can be economical alternatives to travel by train

COMPARATIVE JOURNEYS AND FARES BY TRAIN AND COACH		
DESTINATION	**BY TRAIN**	**BY COACH** (from Victoria Coach Station)
Bath	1 hour 25 min (Paddington), £29.50	3 hours, £16.50
Cambridge	45 min (King's Cross), £20	2 hours, £10.20
Oxford	1 hour (Paddington), £32.50	1 hour 40 min, £12
Stratford-upon-Avon	2 hours 20 min (Paddington), £25	3 hours 16 min, £14
Windsor	50 min (Waterloo), £12.60; 35 min (Paddington, change at Slough), £7.70	1 hour, £10
York	2 hours (King's Cross), £52	5 hours 24 min, £23

Prices are based on adult day-return tickets from London.

Buses

Buses often make a pleasant alternative to trains. Major towns and cities usually have frequent buses, but services can be erratic elsewhere, especially in rural areas. Some night services (buses have an 'N' prefix) are available in major towns and cities. Tourist information offices can provide information and timetables, but these can be complicated, so check carefully for services that run only on certain days or are otherwise restricted. In rural areas such as much of Wales and Scotland, the Lake District and Cornwall, the Royal Mail Postbus (tel: 0845 774 0740) also carries passengers.

Several competing bus companies may operate in urban areas. In some cases the services may overlap, but tickets are not valid on rival company buses.

ON THE MOVE

BUYING TICKETS
● Tickets are usually bought from the driver as you board.
● Children under 5 travel free, and those aged 5–15 travel for half fare. Card concessions for students and seniors are also available.
● You can buy single (one way) or return tickets (except in London). There are also a number of saver tickets available, especially in tourist areas, often in the form of 'rover' tickets that allow unlimited travel for set periods, usually ranging from one day to a week. However, where there are competing bus companies, your ticket will not be valid on services run by a rival operator.
● If you are using the London Underground as well, it's best to buy a Travelcard (▷ 46).

BUS STOPS
Bus stops are usually a sign on a pole giving the number(s) of the buses serving that stop, its location and the destination (direction of travel), sometimes accompanied by sheltered seats.

Newer stops in towns and cities often have displays showing the destinations and expected times of the buses. In contrast, rural bus stops may be difficult to spot and won't have much information.
● Buses will stop at main bus stops if passengers are waiting to get on or off. At a 'request stop' (usually intermediate stops and rural stops), stick out your arm to hail the bus. Check the number and destination on the front of the bus before you get on, as the stop may serve different routes.

ON BOARD
● Driver-only buses often have two doors: one at the front, where you board, and one midway, where you get off. London Routemaster buses (which now operate only on a few 'heritage' routes) have an open platform at the back where you get on and off, with a conductor to sell tickets and check passes.
● Show your pass or have change ready to pay the driver when you board. Drivers and conductors prefer the exact fare and in many cities no change is given.

● On all buses, press the red button once to get off (or pull the cord at the side of the cabin on Routemasters) and the bus will stop at the next stop.
● Keep your ticket until the end of the journey as inspectors may board buses to check tickets.

AIRPORT BUSES
These useful services run to Heathrow, Stansted, Luton, East Midlands, Birmingham and Manchester airports. Tell the driver which terminal you require when stowing your bags. Booking is not necessary, and timetables and tickets are available from relevant stations and on board. Stations with coach links to Heathrow include Feltham, Oxford, Reading, Swindon, Watford and Woking.

SIGHTSEEING TOURS
Major towns and cities can offer sightseeing tours on open-top buses. There may also be a commentary as you explore the place. Contact City Sightseeing Tours (tel: 01708 866000; www.city-sightseeing.com).

TOP 10 SIGHTSEEING TOURS			
CITY	**PRICE**	**TIMES/FREQUENCY**	**START POINT**
Bath	£9	Every 15 min (peak), hourly (off peak)	Bath Spa train station
Cambridge	£8	Every 15–30 min	Cambridge train station
Cotswold villages	£14.50	Daily 2pm	Rother Street, Stratford-upon-Avon
Edinburgh	£8.50	Every 10–30 min	Waverley Bridge
Glasgow	£8.50	Daily 10–4	George Square
London	£16	Every 15–20 min	Baker Street, Coventry Street, Marble Arch
Oxford	£9	Every 10–20 min	Oxford train station
Stratford-upon-Avon	£8	Every 15–30 min	Pen and Parchment Inn, Bridgefoot
Windsor	£6.50	Every 60 min	Castle Hill
York	£8	Every 10–30 min	Exhibition Square, train station

Ferries

In addition to the main ferry ports such as Dover or Folkestone for overseas arrivals and departures, there are also several dedicated domestic ferry terminals serving the various otherwise inaccessible parts of Britain, including the Scottish Islands and a number of tourist attractions just off the mainland. Vessels range from large vehicle ferries to smaller and faster catamarans and hovercrafts.

Some services are seasonal and also may be badly disrupted by tidal and weather conditions, so always check sailings in advance, especially for longer journeys. Some vessels may be affected more than others, for example hovercraft crossings may be suspended while catamaran services are still running.

BUYING TICKETS

Information about timetables and fares is available direct from the ferry companies. Tickets can be reserved in advance from the ferry operator by phone or online, through travel agents and tourist information offices, and also from train stations as part of a train journey—for example to the Isle of Wight from Portsmouth or Lymington. Advance reservation is advised and may be compulsory at peak holiday times, if you require a specific crossing time or if you have a vehicle. Those on foot can usually just turn up and pay, as there is a wide choice of frequent passenger services. On vehicle ferries, the price will include the vehicle and a number of passengers (usually up to five).

So many factors affect the ticket price—such as the length of stay, size and type of vehicle—that it is best to browse the websites or discuss your needs with the operator before booking.

ON BOARD

Ferries are generally comfortable, with refreshments, toilets and TVs. Foot passengers should turn up at least 10 minutes before departure time. Boarding could involve steep ramps, so take care with buggies. On passenger ferries, buggies and larger items of luggage may be stored out on the deck to leave the inside clear. Otherwise, there are luggage storage areas inside. Staff will be on hand to help. Once on board

A ticket to Ryde: a ferry from the mainland to the Isle of Wight

there should be plenty of seats and you can explore the vessel. Smoking is allowed in designated areas only.

Drive your vehicle on board through the back of larger ferries where you will be directed to a parking space. Passengers can then go up to the decks. A signal sounds when it is time to return to the car.

MAJOR DOMESTIC FERRY ROUTES		
ROUTE	**OPERATOR**	**BOOKINGS**
Aberdeen–Orkney and Shetland	Northlink Ferries, Kirkwall, Orkney KW15 1QX	0845 6000 449; www.northlinkferries.co.uk
Liverpool–Isle of Man	Isle of Man Steam Packet Company Limited, Imperial Buildings, Douglas IM1 2BY	0870 552 3523; www.steam-packet.com
Lymington–Yarmouth, Portsmouth–Ryde and Fishbourne	Wightlink Ferries, Portsmouth PO1 2XB	0870 582 7744; www.wightlink.co.uk
Penzance–St. Mary's, Isles of Scilly	Isles of Scilly Steamship Company, Isles of Scilly Travel Centre, Quay Street, Penzance TR18 4BZ	0845 710 5555; www.islesofscilly-travel.co.uk
Southampton–Cowes	Red Funnel Ferries	0870 444 8898; www.redfunnel.co.uk
Southsea–Ryde	Hovertravel Ltd, Quay Road, Ryde, Isle of Wight PO33 2HB	01983 811000; www.hovertravel.co.uk
Western Isles, Skye, Arran and small islands west of Scotland	Caledonian MacBrayne (CalMac) Ltd, The Ferry Terminal, Gourock PA19 1QP	0870 565 0000; www.calmac.co.uk

Domestic flights

Generally speaking, domestic air travel is a relatively expensive option in Britain but, thanks to often ruthless competition from an increasing number of low-cost airlines, prices are coming down. In addition, new routes are being established all the time. These include Stansted to Blackpool, which offers an inexpensive and convenient service compared to the arduous road or rail options from the south. Note that routes can close without much advance notice, so keep an eye on the airlines' websites.

Advertisements for apparently fantastic offers often appear in newspapers but, even if you act immediately, it is almost impossible to reserve tickets at the advertised prices. But if you are flexible about departure dates and times, some real bargains can be had. Check carefully what the price includes, such as taxes and other charges, credit-card booking fees and so on. Be aware that some advertised fares are one-way only. All domestic flights and those to destinations within the European Union (EU) carry a £10 departure tax (usually included in the price). For flights to other destinations the charge is £20. Also take into consideration the cost and inconvenience of having to get to, and away from, a local airport.

SOME LOW-COST AND DOMESTIC AIRLINES		
AIRLINE	**CONTACT**	**FLY FROM**
Air Wales/Awyr Cymru	0870 777 3131 www.airwales.co.uk	Aberdeen, Cardiff, Glasgow International, Liverpool, Newcastle, Norwich, Plymouth
bmi baby	0870 264 2229 www.bmibaby.com	Aberdeen, Birmingham, Cardiff, Durham Tees Valley, East Midlands, Edinburgh, Glasgow International, Inverness, Jersey, Leeds-Bradford, London Gatwick, London Heathrow, Manchester, Newquay, Norwich, Stornoway
easyJet	0905 560 7777 www.easyjet.com	Aberdeen, Belfast, Bournemouth, Bristol, Doncaster, East Midlands, Edinburgh, Glasgow International, Inverness, Liverpool, London Gatwick, London Luton, London Stansted, Newcastle
Euromanx	0870 787 7879 www.euromanx.com	Bristol, East Midlands, Edinburgh, Glasgow International, Liverpool, London City, London Stansted, Manchester, Ronaldsway (Isle of Man), Southampton
Flybe	0870 567 6676 www.flybe.com	Aberdeen, Birmingham, Bristol, Edinburgh, Exeter, Glasgow International, Leeds-Bradford, Liverpool, London Gatwick, London Luton, Manchester, Newcastle, Norwich, Ronaldsway (Isle of Man), Southampton, Southend
Ryanair	0906 270 5656 www.ryanair.com	Aberdeen, Birmingham, Blackpool, Bournemouth, Bristol, Cardiff, Doncaster, Durham Tees Valley, East Midlands, Edinburgh, Glasgow Prestwick, Leeds-Bradford, Liverpool, London Gatwick, London Luton, London Stansted, Manchester, Newcastle, Newquay
Isles of Scilly Travel Skybus	0845 7105 555 www.islesofscilly-travel.co.uk	Bristol, Land's End, Newquay, Southampton, St. Mary's (Isles of Scilly)
Scot Airways	0870 5050 707 www.scotairways.co.uk	Dundee, Edinburgh, London City, Southampton
Jet2.com	0871 226 1737 www.jet2.com	Bournemouth, Leeds-Bradford, London Gatwick, Manchester, Newcastle

BUYING A TICKET

You can reserve tickets direct from the airlines by phone or online, or through travel agents. If reserving online the tickets will be posted to you. If time is short you can collect them at the airport, but some companies may charge for this.

If you have reserved far enough in advance you may be able to amend or cancel tickets for a charge.

Online travel agents include:
www.cheapflights.co.uk
www.ebookers.com
www.expedia.co.uk
www.lastminute.com
www.opodo.co.uk
www.travelbag.com
www.travelocity.com

ON BOARD

● For security reasons no sharp objects (including scissors and cutlery) are allowed in hand luggage. Lists of prohibited items are displayed at airports.

Regional airports are easy to use

Any items found will be confiscated.
● Domestic flights are relatively short, with few frills, but simple refreshments will be available on longer journeys.
● Smoking is prohibited on board and allowed only in designated areas of airports.

REGIONAL AIRPORTS

Aberdeen Dyce, Aberdeen AB21 7DU, tel: 0870 040 0006; www.baa.com
Birmingham International Birmingham B26 3QJ, tel: 0870 733 5511; www.bhx.co.uk
Blackpool Squires Gate Lane FY4 2QY, tel: 01253 343434
Bournemouth Cavendish Road BH1 1RA, tel: 01202 314545
Bristol International Bristol BS48 3DY, tel: 0870 121 2747; www.bristolairport.co.uk

Cardiff International Vale of Glamorgan CF62 3BD, tel: 01446 711111; www.cial.co.uk
Doncaster Sheffield Robin Hood Doncaster DN9 3RH, tel: 0870 833 2210
Dundee Riverside DD2 1UH, tel: 01382 662200
Durham Tees Valley Darlington DL2 1LU, tel: 01325 332811
Edinburgh Edinburgh EH12 9DN, tel: 0870 040 0007; www.edinburghairport.com
Exeter Exeter EX5 2BD, tel: 01392 367433; www.exeter-airport.co.uk
Glasgow Paisley PA3 2SW, tel: 0870 040 0008; www.glasgowairport.com
Leeds Bradford Leeds LS19 7TU, tel: 0113 250 9696; www.lbia.co.uk
Liverpool Liverpool L24 1YD, tel: 0870 750 8484; www. liverpooljohnlennonairport.com
Manchester Manchester M90 1QX, tel: 0161 489 3000; www.manchesterairport.co.uk
Newcastle Woolsington, Newcastle upon Tyne NE13 8BZ, tel: 0870 122 1488; www.newcastleinternational.co.uk
Newquay St. Mawgan TR8 4HP, tel: 01637 860600; www.newquay-airport.co.uk
Nottingham East Midlands Castle Donington DE74 2SA, tel: 01332 852852; www.nottinghamema.com
Prestwick Aviation House, Prestwick KA9 2PC, tel: 01292 511000; www.gpia.co.uk
Southampton Wide Lane, Southampton SO18 2NL, tel: 0870 040 0009; www.southamptonairport.com

Budget airlines are changing travel habits in Europe

Cycling in Britain

Thanks to organizations such as Sustrans (Sustainable Transport), Britain's network of cycle routes now covers more than 7,000 miles (11,340km). Routes are suitable for a range of journeys and include off-road sections, such as canal towpaths, holiday routes for experienced riders, and urban routes for commuters, school runs or shopping trips.

There are also countless outlets all over the country offering bicycle and equipment rental and practical advice. Local tourist information offices should have details.

ON THE ROAD

In urban areas some parts of the road network have designated cycle lanes, denoted by painted white lines, signposts and/or painted illustrations of a bicycle on the road or footpath. Many stretch for a distance, running along footpaths (some of which have separate sections for cyclists and pedestrians), while others cover just a few paces. With the exception of small children, cycling is not allowed on the pavement and cyclists must obey the general rules of the road, such as traffic lights and one-way streets. Where cycle lanes run along main roads, they may have their own dedicated traffic lights. Bicycles are not allowed on motorways. Cycling among traffic and pedestrians can be dangerous, so care and vigilance is needed at all times.

SAFE CYCLING

● Wear bright clothing and fluorescent clothing at night. Use your lights at night. Helmets are not compulsory, but are advisable. Many Londoners wear masks to protect against pollution.
● Make other road-users aware of your movements. Indicate clearly and in advance.
● Watch out for car doors opening without warning.
● Avoid cycling along the inside of traffic when there is a left turning ahead.
● Always lock your bicycle to a fixed object.

BICYCLES ON PUBLIC TRANSPORT

Although most rail operators will carry bicycles on board, individual company regulations differ, so contact National Rail Enquiries or check with the train company in

advance. Space for bicycles is very limited, so reserve as far ahead as possible, especially at peak times. A reservation charge may apply. Outside peak times there may be space in the guard's (luggage) van if you arrive with a bicycle, but there is no guarantee.

Folding bicycles are usually carried free on most trains and other forms of public transport, but it may be wise to check with the relevant company. In London you can take your bicycle on the surface lines of the Underground network— District, Circle, East London, Hammersmith and City and Metropolitan lines—but not on the deeper lines that have elevators and escalators. A map showing which parts of the network you can use is available from any Underground station.

Some passenger ferries have limited space for bicycles so, again, check in advance. Coaches accept folding bicycles carried in a protective case.

It is advisable to wear a helmet when you're cycling in Britain

USEFUL CONTACTS
National Rail Enquiries
Tel: 0845 748 4950;
www.nationalrail.co.uk
CTC Cotterell House, 69 Meadrow, Godalming GU7 3HS; tel: 0870 873 0060; www.ctc.org.uk. National cycling organization.
A to B Magazine 19 West Park, Castle Cary BA7 7DB; tel: 01963 351649; www.atob.org.uk
Spokes.org.uk Scottish-based cycling organization with loads of information on bicycles north of the border.
Sustrans 2 Cathedral Square, Bristol BS1 5DD (head office); tel: 0845 113 0065; www.sustrans.org.uk
Transport for London
Tel: 020 7222 1234
www.tfl.gov.uk. Publishes a series of 19 free cycling maps covering the whole of the London area.

Taxis

Taxis are a relatively expensive way of getting around, but are useful in certain circumstances, such as airport trips for groups. There are essentially two types of taxi: licensed taxis, such as the traditional black London cab (not confined to the capital), which display a licence on the rear of the vehicle and the private hire operator or minicab.

Like its red buses, London's black cabs are world famous and the design remains distinctive. You can still rely on a London cabby (driver) to know where he's going; drivers must pass exams, called 'The Knowledge', to demonstrate that they know the city well enough to take passengers anywhere in London by the most direct route. Fares in London taxis are set by the regulatory Public Carriage Office; licensed taxis inside and outside London should have meters.

ON THE MOVE

IN LONDON

● London's cabs are metered and fairly expensive, but are a quick and safe way to get about.
● You'll find designated taxi stands outside train stations and large hotels, and at numerous points throughout the city.
● To hail a cab in the street look for an illuminated orange 'TAXI' light on top of the cab and stick out your arm. Tell the driver your destination through the open window, then get in the back seat.
● You can also book through Black Cab London (tel: 0871 871 8710), but you may be charged extra.
● For more information on London taxis and charges, visit **www.tfl.gov.uk**.

OUTSIDE THE CAPITAL

Elsewhere in Britain you will find private taxi firms, including some using traditional black cabs. Ranks are usually found outside stations and at other points around larger towns and cities, such as shopping malls. All private taxis are licensed and regulated and should have meters. Vehicles can range from ordinary saloon (sedan) and estate cars (station wagons) to seven-seaters.
● If you are going a long way or are unsure of the distance, ask for a price quote before you set off.

TIPS

● Taxis become scarce at busy times, especially on Friday and Saturday nights after 10pm, so it may be wise to reserve a ride home in advance if you are going out in the town.
● A tip of 10–15 per cent of the total fare is expected and customary (especially in London), but not compulsory.

The iconic black London cab is also found in some other major cities in Britain

● Unlike black cabs, it is acceptable to sit in the front passenger seat of ordinary taxis.
● Private taxis can also be booked by phone; look in the *Yellow Pages* for local firms.

MINICABS

Minicabs are saloon cars that should be reserved only by telephone or from a minicab company's office. It is not advisable to hail one in the street, and lone women should be wary. Although licensing and regulatory reforms are under way, minicab drivers may be untrained or uninsured, and vehicles may be substandard.
● Avoid minicabs touting at airports and stations as they overcharge and are even more likely to be unlicensed or uninsured. Take licensed cabs from taxi stands or book with a recommended minicab firm in advance.

A taxi stand in Brighton: licensed cabs such as these are approved by local councils and are reliable

VISITORS WITH CHILDREN

The British can be intolerant of children in public places, and this is often most obvious on public transport. However, if you avoid using trains (especially on commuter routes) and the London Underground at peak times, your journey will be much less stressful.

TRAINS
- Call 08457 484950 or visit www.nationalrail.co.uk to check for any possible problems regarding your journey.
- Avoid the rush hour—before 9.30am or between 4.30 and 7pm—as commuter trains can be extremely crowded, and, on the busiest routes to and from London, it is often impossible to get a seat.
- Large stations will have elevators, but these can be unreliable.
- Don't try to push a buggy through the ticket barrier unless it is open. Instead, show your ticket at one of the staffed gates to be let through.
- Newer trains with sliding doors should pose few problems for buggies, but beware of large or high gaps between the platform and the train.
- Many train companies have a family carriage, with extra room for buggies and larger tables. Some companies also offer special travel packs for children, including simple games and crayons. First Great Western (www.firstgreatwestern.co.uk),

runs routes west from London and has good facilities.
- Baby-changing facilities are only likely on trains with toilets for passengers with disabilities.

THE UNDERGROUND
The London Underground is also best avoided during rush hours.
- Most Underground stations do not have elevators. Stairs and escalators are often steep and long so you may need to rely on help from fellow passengers.
- Take particular care with the gap between the platform and the train, and with children near sliding doors.

AIRLINES
- When checking in always explain that you are travelling with small children. You may get an empty seat beside you, or one close to the front of the plane where the movement will be less extreme.
- You may be called first to board the aircraft.
- Children under two usually travel for a nominal fare and are not allocated a separate seat. If a child is sitting on your lap you

will be given a special seat belt that attaches to your own.
- Most airlines provide children's travel entertainment packs, and may have other facilities.

FERRIES
- Motion sickness can affect small children on ferries, so invest in some travel sickness wristbands, which are safe and surprisingly effective.
- A night crossing can be a good family choice if you reserve a cabin in advance. Cabins are generally clean and spacious.

Family train tickets save money

VISITORS WITH A DISABILITY

While the majority of Britain's tourist attractions are geared to visitors with disabilities, public transport still lags behind. Avoid peak times if possible. Guide dogs are welcome on all forms of public transport and staff are generally very helpful. Whichever form of transport you intend to use, it is best to phone in advance if you need special help or services. Shopping malls and main streets in major towns sometimes have motorized buggies on loan (often free) to those with disabilities. There are also a number of free 'land train' vehicles for transport around shopping areas. All London black taxis have wheelchair access, as have an increasing number of modern cabs in larger towns and cities.

The Royal Association for Disability and Rehabilitation (RADAR, tel: 020 7250 3222; www.radar.org.uk) has two publications, 'If only I'd known that a year ago' has transport information and Holidays in

Britain and Ireland—A Guide for Disabled People covers 1,400 places to stay.

TRAINS
- With the exception of the old 'slam-door' types, trains usually

have wheelchair access.
- Arrange for assistance at least 24 hours in advance by contacting the station you are departing from. Information is available from National Rail Enquiries (tel: 0845 748 4950;

minicom: 0845 605 0600; www.nationalrail.co.uk). Useful advice is also available from Tripscope (tel: 0845 758 5641; www.tripscope.org.uk).
• Portable ramps are at most stations, and some trains carry lightweight versions for use at unstaffed stations.
• There are usually accessible toilets on long-distance trains and many regional services.
• Eurostar trains are wheelchair-accessible.

LONDON UNDERGROUND AND DOCKLANDS LIGHT RAILWAY (DLR)
• Each Underground station has a wide access gate, so you can avoid the ticket barrier.
• A map detailing accessibility is available from www.tfl.gov.uk.
• To check that elevators are operating at stations you are visiting call 020 7308 2800 (office hours) or 020 7222 1234 (other times).

• Most DLR stations are accessible by elevator or ramp. Call Customer Services on 020 7363 9700 during office hours.
• There are elevators, escalators and/or ramps on every DLR platform, and tactile edges for those with visual impairments. Each train has a designated wheelchair bay.

BUSES AND COACHES
While a number of urban single-deck buses are accessible for wheelchairs, double-decker buses and coaches are not.
• Manual wheelchairs can be carried on board, but only if folded and if there is room. Powered vehicles or wheelchairs are not permitted on coaches.
• Low-floor accessible buses are being introduced in London.

FERRIES
Improvements have been made to UK ports to cater for those with disabilities, but contact the

port in advance. It may be necessary to reserve a cabin with accessible facilities, particularly on longer crossings.

AIR TRAVEL
Most airlines can help passengers with special requirements. There are designated parking spaces for visitors with disabilities in BAA-run airports. Call 0800 844844 to book one.
• **Heathrow** The Disabled Living Foundation (tel: 020 8745 7495, minicom: 08745 7565), produces a leaflet with advice and a plan of the terminals. All Heathrow Express trains (tel: 0845 600 1515) are wheelchair-accessible.
• **Gatwick** Tel: 0870 000 2468.
• **Stansted** The Stansted Express train is wheelchair-accessible. Tel: 0870 574 7777.
• **Luton** The shuttle bus is wheelchair-accessible and there are elevators at Luton Parkway station (tel: 01582 405 100).

VISITORS WITH PETS

No longer do Britons have to go on foreign holidays without their pets, and no longer do visitors to Britain have to leave their pets at home. The Pet Travel Scheme (PETS) was introduced in February 2000 and now allows residents of 54 qualifying countries to bring their pets into Britain.

ELIGIBLE COUNTRIES
Countries that can participate in the PETS scheme have to meet certain criteria. Only those countries that represent a low risk of introducing rabies and other diseases to Britain are eligible. In Europe 24 countries, including France, Germany, Spain and Italy, are members of PETS. The scheme has been extended to 30 other countries worldwide, including Australia, Canada, Japan and the US.
• For the full list of participating countries visit www.defra.gov.uk.
• The scheme applies only to pet cats and dogs, including guide dogs, but not breeds that are banned in Britain.

APPROVED ROUTES
Visitors coming from long-haul

countries with pets must travel by routes approved by PETS. A number of airlines have agreed routes with PETS. Animals imported by air must travel in a container which has had a seal fixed to it for the whole journey, so that risk of exposure to rabies is reduced.

PROCEDURES
To bring your pet into Britain you must follow a set of procedures.
• Before any other procedures for PETS are carried out, your pet must be fitted with a microchip.
• After the microchip has been fitted your pet must be vaccinated against rabies.
• It must then have a blood test to confirm that it is protected against rabies.

• An official PETS certificate must then be obtained from a government-authorized vet.
• Before departing for Britain your pet must be treated for ticks and worms.

THE JOURNEY
Only travel with a pet if it is fit and healthy enough to withstand the trip. Use a well-ventilated carrying container with which it is familiar. Ensure the animal has enough space, food and water, but give it only a light meal before the journey.

QUARANTINE
Animals that are brought into Britain from countries that don't meet the PETS criteria are quarantined for six months in special holding areas.

This chapter is divided into the seven regions of Britain (▷ 6–7). Places of interest are listed alphabetically in each region. At the front of each regional section that region's key sites are listed. For the location of all the sites in each region turn to the atlas (▷ 423–446).

The Sights

THE WEST COUNTRY

Blessed with Britain's mildest climate, the West Country is a magnet for British holidaymakers. From Stonehenge to the futuristic Eden Project, attractions span 5,000 years of history. Towns and cities in the West Country–Wells and Bath among them–don't so much sprawl as sit tidily in folds in the landscape.

KEY SIGHTS

Swans have lived at Abbotsbury since medieval times

Here comes the sun: sunrise at the Avebury stone circle

The sea has eroded the Bedruthan Steps from arches in the cliffs

ABBOTSBURY

➕ 430 G20 ℹ The Esplanade, Weymouth DT4 7AN, tel 01305 785747 www.abbotsbury-tourism.co.uk

Thatched ironstone cottages line the streets of this village, while beyond a huge 15th-century tithe barn, and the hilltop St. Catherine's Chapel of c1400 are tangible reminders of the Benedictine abbey, founded in 1026, that gave the village its name. Built in the 15th century to store a tenth of all local produce that was harvested, the abbey is now a themed play area. Abbotsbury Swannery (mid-Mar to end Sep daily 10–6; Oct–early Nov daily 10–5, last admission 1 hour before closing), set up by monks in the 14th century, gives unrivalled opportunities to see swans close up. There are feeding sessions daily, 12 and 4. The swans build their nests between March and end April. Hatching is mid-May to end June, and cygnets gain their wings in September and October;
Don't miss West of the village, the Sub Tropical Gardens (Mar–end Oct daily 10–6; rest of year daily 10–4) are awash with pinks, yellows and purples as late spring brings camellias, rhododendrons and perfumed magnolias.

ANTONY

➕ 428 D21 • Torpoint, Plymouth PL11 2QA ☎ 01752 812191 🕐 Apr–end May, Sep–end Oct (also Sun, Jun–end Aug) Tue–Thu 1.30–5.30 (last admission 4.45) 🎫 House and garden £5, child (5–16) £2.50, family £7.50. Woodland garden: adult £4, child (5–16) free. Combined gardens for Antony, formal garden and woodland garden £4.20, child £2.10 🚻 🅿 www.nationaltrust.org.uk

Cornwall's finest Georgian mansion is very much a family house, the seat of the Carews.

Built by Sir William Carew between 1711 and 1721, and replacing a Tudor house, the building is made of silver-grey Pentewan stone, with two colonnaded wings of red brick. Inside it retains its original oak panelling, single four-poster beds, portraits by Sir Joshua Reynolds (1723–92) and a portrait of Charles I (1600–49) at his trial.
    The formal gardens contain the national collection of day lilies and summer border plants, as well as azaleas, rhododendrons and magnolias. The grounds also feature an 18th-century dovecote.

AVEBURY

➕ 430 H18 ℹ Green Street, Avebury SN8 1RF, tel 01672 539425

Set in an area of chalk downlands and now a World Heritage Site, the village of Avebury is enclosed by the largest prehistoric stone circle in the British Isles. Built of local sarsen stones between 2600BC and 2100BC, it consists of two stone circles surrounded by a larger henge (a banked circular enclosure) along which stand 200 huge standing stones. A 15m- (50ft-) wide processional avenue of megaliths once led 1.5 miles (2.5km) beyond West Kennet to the site of the Sanctuary, a temple complex from around 3000BC. Fyfield Down, a National Trust nature reserve east of the village, is littered with natural sarsen stones.
    To the south, and reached by a 15-minute walk, is Silbury Hill, Europe's largest artificial mound (2700BC), which allegedly took around 80 million man hours to construct. Its original purpose remains a mystery, but it is thought to have ritual significance.
    Across the road, a path climbs to West Kennet Long Barrow, a huge stone-chambered tomb built around 3700–3500BC, and in use for over 1,000 years.

Don't miss The Alexander Keiller Museum (Apr–end Oct daily 10–6; rest of year daily 10–4), by Avebury Manor, explains the history of the Avebury landscape.

BATH

See pages 68–71

BEDRUTHAN STEPS

➕ 428 C20 ℹ Red Brick Building, North Quay, Padstow PI 28 8AF, tel 01841 533449; Mar end Oct

According to legend, a giant called Bedruthan used these great coastal rock stacks as stepping stones. They can be seen from the clifftop coast path and a viewpoint near the parking area. The National Trust has built a secure stairway to the beach from the clifftop at Carnewas. It is unsafe to bathe here and there is a risk of being cut off by the tide.

BERKELEY CASTLE

➕ 430 G18 • Berkeley GL13 9BQ ☎ 01453 810332 🕐 Apr–end Sep Tue–Sat 11–4, Sun 2–5; Oct Sun 2–5. Butterfly House closed Oct 🎫 Castle and gardens: adult £7.50, child £4.50, family £21. Gardens only: adult £4, child £2. Butterfly House: adult £2, child £1 🖥 🏛 🚻 🅿 www.berkeley-castle.com

Dominating the village of Berkeley and home of the Berkeleys for almost 850 years, this 12th- and 14th-century castle is a rambling fortress surrounded by walls 3m (14ft) thick and graced by Elizabethan terraced gardens and a vast park. The Great Hall, with its original timber roof, marks where the rebel barons of the West Country met in 1215 before going on to Runnymede to force King John to seal the Magna Carta (▷ 29).
    In the keep are the dungeons, including the cell where Edward II was murdered in 1327 after his deposition.

Bath

Britain's most complete Georgian city, and one of the most elegant, Bath is home of the country's only hot spring, producing up to one million litres (26,000 gallons) of water a day.

The Georgian Theatre Royal opened in 1805

Mineral waters have been available in Bath for centuries

The Royal Crescent is the grandest of Bath's streets

SEEING BATH

It is difficult to imagine a more beautiful city than Bath—great architecture, plenty to see and compact enough to explore on foot—and its World Heritage Site status has ensured its preservation. The city is built from eye-pleasing, honey limestone, and has a striking setting amid seven hills, where the Cotswolds meet the Mendip Hills, and on the banks of the River Avon and the Kennet and Avon Canal. The hills can make walking tiring, but you are more than compensated by the views. With more than 20 museums and historic sites, a huge choice of accommodation and plenty of specialist shops—including a daily antiques market in Bartlett Street—there is definitely something for everyone. In between sightseeing, you can take in vibrant streetlife from any number of cafés in the form of street entertainment. If you're based in London, Bath makes a great day out, as it's only about two hours by fast train from London Paddington.

RATINGS					
Good for kids	●	●	●	○	
Historic interest	●	●	●	●	●
Specialist shopping	●	●	●	●	●
Walkability	●	●	●	○	

TIPS

● Bath is ideal for a weekend break, with a huge choice of accommodation at all prices.
● Go early to the Pump Room and Roman Baths in order to avoid the crowds.
● Parking in the city is a real problem, so either come by public transport or use the park-and-ride service.

HIGHLIGHTS

PUMP ROOM AND ROMAN BATHS

✚ 71 B2 • Stall Street BA1 1LZ ☎ 01225 477785
🕐 Mar–end Jun and Sep–end Oct daily 9–5; Jul–end Aug daily 9–9; rest of year daily 9.30–4.30,
www.romanbaths.co.uk
The high-ceilinged, chandelier-lit Georgian Pump Room (1796) is a great Bath institution, where a chamber trio provides accompaniment to afternoon tea (or you can sample the hot spa water, which may be an acquired taste), within sight of the King's Bath. This room was originally built for a serious purpose: A group of doctors, led by William Oliver (inventor of the Bath Oliver biscuit), felt that invalids should be able to come together to drink Bath's mineral waters. But Richard 'Beau' Nash, the city's Master of Ceremonies, had greater

The Roman Baths (opposite) are the focus of the town. Characters in period costume (left)

BUILDING OF BATH MUSEUM

✚ 71 B1 • Countess of Huntingdon's Chapel, The Vineyards, The Paragon BA1 5NA ☎ 01225 333895 ⊙ Mid-Feb to end Nov Tue–Sun and public holidays 10.30–5

This highly informative museum explains how Bath developed into the place it is.

JANE AUSTEN CENTRE

✚ 71 B1 • 40 Gay Street BA1 2NT ☎ 01225 443000 ⊙ Mar–end Oct daily 10–5.30, Sun 10.30–5.30; rest of year daily 11–4.30

An exhibition charts the life and works of the great novelist (1775–1817) who made two long visits to Bath in the 18th century, and also lived here from 1801 to 1806. The city features in *Persuasion* (published posthumously in 1817) and *Northanger Abbey* (1818).

AMERICAN MUSEUM IN BRITAIN

✚ 71 off C1 • Claverton Manor BA2 7BD ☎ 01225 460503 ⊙ Late Mar–end Oct Tue–Sun 2–5.30. Gardens: late Mar–Oct Tue–Sun 12–5.30

www.americanmuseum.org

This gracious manor house has re-creations of American homes from different states from the 17th to 19th centuries, as well as folk art and exhibits about Native Americans and the Shakers—a Christian sect known for their elegant furniture.

THERMAE BATH SPA

✚ 71 B2 • The Hetling Pump Room, Hot Bath Street BA1 1SJ ☎ 01225 331234 ⊙ Daily (phone for times; due to open 2006)

www.thermaebathspa.com

Occupying two fantastic, former spa buildings, Bath's most contemporary spa experience includes a steam room, massage rooms, gym, rooftop open-air pool and a whirlpool.

ambitions. Realizing that a Pump Room could be useful as a meeting place, he hired musicians to play and fashionable visitors flocked in.

ROMAN BATHS

✚ 71 B2 • Stall Street BA1 1LZ ☎ 01225 477785 ⊙ Mar–end Jun and Sep–end Oct daily 9–5; Jul–end Aug daily 9–9; rest of year daily 9.30–4.30

From the genteel elegance of the Georgian Pump Room you suddenly walk into Roman times in the finest bath-house site in Britain. A self-guiding tour leads past displays of finds from the site down to the waters. The highlight of the visit are the pool and the Roman Bath (the Great Bath). The spring, still bubbling up at a constant 46°C (116°F), was sacred to the goddess Sulis, who was thought to possess curative powers. The Romans made a sanctuary around the spring, dedicated to Sulis Minerva, and both Celts and Romans bathed and made offerings.

The Sun God from the Temple of Sulis Minerva (below)

Wedding dresses are on display in the Museum of Costume

BATH ABBEY

✚ 71 C2 ✉ Abbey Churchyard BA1 1LY ☎ 01225 422462 ⊙ Easter–late Oct Mon–Sat 9–6, Sun 1.15–2.45, 4.30–5.30; rest of year Mon–Sat 9–4.30, Sun 1–2.30, 4.30–5.30

Not in fact an abbey but a church, this building (begun in 1499) represents one of the crowning examples of the Perpendicular style. Legend has it that the shape of the church was dictated to its founder, Bishop Oliver King, in a dream by angels. This story is immortalized on the west front, which shows the carved angels ascending and descending on ladders, and the founder's signature—a carving of olive trees surmounted by crowns. The airy interior is most notable for the size of its windows and the delicate fan vaulting, completed by George Gilbert Scott in the late 19th century. The huge east window depicts 56 scenes from Christ's life, while the floor and walls, crammed with elaborate memorials and Georgian inscriptions, make fascinating reading. The Norman Chapel (also known as the Gethsemane Chapel) has clear traces of the older, Norman chapel on this site.

MUSEUM OF COSTUME AND ASSEMBLY ROOMS

✚ 71 B1 ✉ Bennett Street BA1 2QH ☎ 01225 477789 ⊙ Mar–end Oct daily 10–6; rest of year daily 11–5

This large and prestigious collection displays fashionable dress for men and women dating from the late 16th century to the present. The star attraction is the silver tissue dress dating from the 1660s, although many visitors are interested in the early 19th-century clothes, familiar to many from film adaptations of Jane Austen's novels.

NO. 1 ROYAL CRESCENT

✚ 71 A1 ✉ 1 Royal Crescent BA1 2LR ☎ 01225 428126 ⊙ Mid-Feb to end Oct Tue–Sun 10.30–5; early–late Nov Tue–Sun 10.30–4; Dec to mid-Feb Sat–Sun 10.30–4

This house was designed by John Wood the Younger (1767–74) and offers a chance to see inside one of the town houses in Bath's most celebrated architectural set piece, the Royal Crescent. It has been restored to its appearance of 200 years ago, with pictures, china and furniture of the period and a kitchen with a dog-powered spit used to roast meat in front of the fire. The first-floor

THE SIGHTS

windows are the only ones of the original height—all the others were lengthened in the 19th century. Wood's father (also John) was the architect of The Circus (1754–70), a circular piazza close by.

BACKGROUND

Roman Bath was founded in AD44 as the settlement of *Aquae Sulis*. Bath prospered through the wool trade in medieval times, but its modern importance dates from the 18th century, after its Roman hot springs were rediscovered in 1755. They were made fashionable by the Welsh dandy Richard 'Beau' Nash (1674–1762), who carried out his role as official Master of Ceremonies with panache. He was paramount in attracting London's high society to the baths and springs, as well as to the grand balls and assemblies.

BASICS

✠ 430 G18

🛈 Abbey Chambers, Abbey Church Yard, Bath BA1 1LY, tel 0906 711 2000 (60p a minute); May–end Sep Mon–Sat 9.30–6, Sun 10–4; rest of year Mon–Sat 9.30–5, Sun 10–4

❓ The Bath Pass (available for 1, 4, 7 or 15 days) gives free entry to more than 30 attractions in the Bath and Bristol area; details from the tourist information office, tel: 0870 242 9988 or www.bathpass.com. Also free guided walks and open-top bus tours, plus riverboat trips and punts from Pulteney Bridge.

🚉 Bath Spa, 1 mile (1.5km) from central Bath

www.visitbath.co.uk
An informative website with details on attractions, accommodation, shopping, spa treatments, famous people, a virtual tour and what's on. Links to most of the main sights.

The Royal Crescent's green is used for all kinds of events

Bath Abbey took its present form in the 17th century

The Cheesewring pillar balances precariously on Bodmin Moor

Bowood House's splendid Orangery was designed by Robert Adam, also responsible for the front façade of the house

THE SIGHTS

BODMIN MOOR

⊞ 428 D20 🛈 The Shire Hall, Mount Folly Square, Bodmin PL31 2DQ, tel 01208 76616
www.bodminmoor.co.uk

Best seen from the A30 road west of Launceston (▷ 82), Bodmin Moor is a bleak, wild terrain punctuated by gnarled granite 'tors' (outcrops), and home to rare plants such as bog orchids, as well as birds such as lapwings and snipe. On the moorland fringes, the De Lank and Fowey rivers are important territories for otters.

There are no major settlements, but some of the village churches have fine features, including whimsical carved 16th-century pew ends at Altarnun, and 15th- and 16th-century stained glass at St. Neots.
Don't miss The Cheesewring close by, a strangely shaped rock outcrop near Minions, with a Bronze Age stone circle.

BOURNEMOUTH

⊞ 430 H20 🛈 Westover Road, Bournemouth BN1 2BU, tel 01202 451700 🚊 Bournemouth
www.bournemouth.co.uk

The glory of this large Victorian seaside resort is its 7 miles (11km) of golden sands, offering safe, clean bathing beneath sandstone cliffs. In Lower Gardens is the helium-filled, tethered Bournemouth Eye Balloon (Apr–end Sep daily 7.30am–11pm; rest of year daily 9–dusk) giving a bird's-eye view of the town from 150m (500ft). The Bournemouth Symphony Orchestra, based at the Pavilion Theatre, has an international reputation. The Russell-Cotes Art Gallery and Museum (Tue–Sun 10–5), on the cliffs, has a rich Victorian art collection.
Don't miss Hengistbury Head, good for breezy walks and fine harbour views, just east of town.

BOWOOD HOUSE AND GARDENS

⊞ 430 G18 • Calne SN11 0LZ
☎ 01249 812102 🕓 End Mar–early Nov daily 11–5.30 (grounds 11–6)
💰 Adult £6.50, child (5–15) £4.30, child (2–4) £3.40; season tickets available. Rhododendron Walks: adult £3.70, or £2.70 if combined with house
🖭 🏛 🚻 🅿
www.bowood.org

The family home of the Marquis and Marchioness of Lansdowne since 1754 stands in parkland created by the 18th-century landscape gardener Capability Brown. Built in 1624, the house was finished by the architect Robert Adam (among others) in the 18th century. The main draws of Bowood, however, are the gardens and grounds, featuring terraced rose gardens, Arboretum, Doric Temple, cascade waterfall, Hermit's Cave and woodland walks. For children, there is a playground and the Soft Play Palace.
Don't miss The Rhododendron Walks, a woodland garden ablaze with rhododendrons and azaleas (late Apr–early Jun).

BRADFORD-ON-AVON

⊞ 430 G18 🛈 15 St. Margaret's Street, Bradford-on-Avon BA15 1DE, tel 01225 865797 🚊 Bradford-on-Avon
www.bradfordonavon.co.uk

Almost every route into this hill-side town is down a steep incline lined with mellow Bath-stone weavers' cottages, old inns and flower-decked shops. The tall but tiny Saxon Church of St. Laurence is one of the most complete examples from that time, while The Hall (1610) is a fine example of Jacobean architecture. By the River Avon and the Kennet and Avon Canal, Barton Farm Country Park has a well-preserved 14th-century stone tithe barn with a timbered roof.

BRIXHAM

⊞ 429 E21 🛈 The Old Market House, The Quay, Brixham TQ5 8TB, tel 0906 6801268
www.theenglishriviera.co.uk

Perhaps when you think of Brixham, you think of boats. It is one of the few thriving fishing ports left in the region from where you can sail or take a pleasure cruise to surrounding resorts. It has a working atmosphere in its narrow streets and Victorian cottages rising above the quayside where a full-scale replica of Sir Francis Drake's ship of 1577, Golden Hind, is moored.

There is also a strong tradition of local art here, on show by the harbour at the Strand Art Gallery, with local artists' work on sale.
Don't miss The clifftop walks to the east along Berry Head, which are outstanding.

BROWNSEA ISLAND

⊞ 430 H20 • Poole Harbour BH13 7EE ☎ 01202 707744 🕓 Oct daily 10–4; mid-Mar to mid-Jul and Sep daily 10–5; mid-Jul to end Aug daily 10–6; check time of last boat 💰 Landing fee: adult £4.20, child (5–16) £2, family £10.40; additional ferry charge 🛈 Guided nature tours (tel 01202 709445) 🏛 🚻 🅿 Near Poole Quay
www.nationaltrust.org.uk/brownsea

This tranquil 200ha (500-acre) island is reached by boat from Poole Quay and Sandbanks (on the edge of Bournemouth). Its woodlands, marshland and wild heath are a haven for many forms of wildlife, including wading birds, herons, sand lizards, red squirrels, mink and other animals. The visitor office has an exhibition about the island, and there are marked nature trails.

In 1907 Lord Baden-Powell (1857–1941) took 20 boys to camp here, and in so doing established the Boy Scout movement.

Millennium Square was part of a rejuvenation project for the city

BRISTOL

A strong sense of maritime past pervades the premier city in southwest England, where a huge millennium facelift has created tree-lined avenues and turned Queen Square into a traffic-free haven.

Bristol was a leading port and commercial hub from the 12th century, and from the 15th to 18th centuries it was England's second city after London. Maritime wealth endowed it with imposing churches, notably the late 13th-century St. Mary Redcliffe (Redcliffe Hill) and the eclectic cathedral, with a Norman chapter house.

The former docks (most of the business has moved to Avonmouth) are now busy with places to eat and family attractions, including museums and boat trips. In the Harbourside area are @Bristol (daily 10–5, and until 6 at weekends and on public holiday), covering the Imagarium (a state-of-the art planetarium), Wildwalk (a journey through evolution) and the science and technology museum, Explore. At Great Western Dock is the SS *Great Britain* (Apr–end Oct daily 10–5.30; rest of year daily 10–4.30), the world's first steam-powered ocean liner, built by the English engineer and inventor Isambard Kingdom Brunel (1806–59) and launched in 1843. In the original Temple Meads station built by Brunel, the British Empire and Commonwealth Museum evokes Britain's Empire days, with the story of exploration, trade and conquest, and the legacy on life today.

The Old City, with its Georgian merchants' buildings, is now home to banks and restaurants, while East Side presents a scene of international influence with foods and goods from Asia and the Caribbean; meanwhile the West End around Park Street is the hip area, with funky shops selling the latest fashions and gifts.

The elegant Georgian suburb of Clifton has honey-coloured stone terraces, crescents and squares similar to those found in Bath (▷ 68–71). There are modern malls such as Broadmead and the traditional covered market at St. Nicholas, a market site since 1743.

Clifton Suspension Bridge (in Clifton) is the symbol of the city and probably Brunel's best-known design. It is a delicate engineering miracle spanning the Avon Gorge. Begun in 1836, it was finally opened in 1864, and its 215m (702ft) span was at the time the world's greatest. By the bridge are fine views from a camera obscura tower, best seen on a bright day. Close by is the visitor centre, and there are free daily tours of the bridge.

Clifton Suspension Bridge is 215m (702ft) long and was constructed as a result of a design competition held in 1829

RATINGS

Good for kids	●●●
Historic interest	●●●●
Specialist shopping	●●●
Maritime interest	●●●●

BASICS

✚ 430 G18

ℹ The Annexe, Wildscreen Walk, Harbourside, Bristol BS1 5DB, tel 0906 711 2191 (50p a minute)

🚉 Bristol Temple Meads

www.visitbristol.co.uk

The splendid Great East Window
at Buckfast Abbey

Some believe the Cerne Abbas
Giant to be a fertility symbol

Chesil Beach is an extraordinary
feature of the Dorset coast

BUCKFASTLEIGH

✚ 429 E20 🛈 Leonards Road,
Ivybridge PL21 0SL, tel 01752 897035
www.buckfastleigh.org

This southern gateway town to
Dartmoor is home to the South
Devon Valley Railway (late May–
early Nov, www.southdevon
railway.org for details), a nostalgic
steam line which runs along
a 7-mile (11km) stretch of the
River Dart as far as Totnes
(▷ 88–89).
   The station site is shared by
the Buckfast Butterfly Farm
(Easter–end Oct daily) and
Dartmoor Otter Sanctuary
(Easter–end Oct and Mar daily),
and combined tickets are
available. Watch butterflies from
all over the world fly free and then
learn about their life cycle at this
environmental haven.
   The Otter Sanctuary is a refuge
for this endangered species, with
usually 10 to 12 in residence at
any one time. It focuses on
breeding otters and promoting
public awareness of their
habitats. There is an underwater
viewing area for observing these
normally elusive animals.
   To the north, off the A38 road,
is Buckfast Abbey, whose Abbey
Church is a capacious, austere mix
of Early English and Norman
styles. The abbey is home to a
community of around 40 monks
and there is an audio-visual
presentation, exhibition, tea
rooms and shops selling honey
and Buckfast Tonic Wine.

BUCKLAND ABBEY

✚ 429 D20 • Yelverton PL20 6EY
☎ 01822 853607 🛈 Abbey and
grounds: Easter–end Oct Fri–Wed
10.30–5.30; Nov–end Dec, mid-Feb to
Easter Sat–Sun 2–5 💷 Abbey and
grounds: adult £6, child (5–16) £3,
family £13. Grounds only: adult £3.20,
child £1.60; free Nov–end Mar
🍴 🎁 🎨 🅿
www.nationaltrust.org.uk

Don't come to Buckland Abbey
expecting visions of hooded
figures and Gregorian chants.
This medieval monastery was
converted into an imposing
Elizabethan mansion after the
Dissolution of the Monasteries in
the mid-16th century (▷ 31). It
is best known for its connection
with the buccaneer and explorer
Sir Francis Drake (c1540–96),
who moved into Buckland Abbey
in 1582 and stayed for 13 years.
The house remained the
property of the Drake family until
1794, and it passed into the care
of the National Trust in 1938.
Don't miss The box-hedged
herb garden and massive stone
Great Barn in the grounds.

CERNE ABBAS

✚ 430 G20 🛈 11 Antelope Walk,
Dorchester DT1 1BE, tel 01305 267992
www.cerneabbas.org.uk

Carved into the chalk hillside
northeast of the village of the
same name is the Cerne Abbas
Giant, a 55m (180ft) figure of a
naked man holding a club, and
leaving no doubts as to his virility.
The figure may be associated
with fertility rites and possibly
dates from before the Roman
occupation or could be (according
to a recent theory) a 17th-century
caricature of Oliver Cromwell, but
his origins remain a mix of fact
and speculation. There is a
viewing point by the A352 road.
Cerne Abbas itself derives its
name from a Benedictine abbey
founded here in AD987. Only the
abbey guesthouse and 15th-
century gatehouse remain.

CHEDDAR GORGE

See page 76

CHELTENHAM

✚ 430 G17 🛈 77 The Promenade,
Cheltenham GL50 1PP, tel 01242
522878 🚉 Cheltenham
www.visitcheltenham.com

A good base for touring the
Cotswolds (▷ 276–277), this
Regency town (it received the
royal approval of George III) is
renowned for its handsome
terraces, wrought-iron balconies,
leafy thoroughfares, parks, floral
displays, horse racing, a music
festival in July and a literature
festival in October.
   The town spreads south along
The Promenade, a wide, leafy
street with pavement cafés and
elegant shops.
   The Art Gallery and Museum
(Mon–Sat 10–5.20, closed
public holidays) in Clarence Street
has an excellent section about the
Arts and Crafts movement. Close
by is the Holst Birthplace Museum
(Feb–end Nov Tue–Sat 10–4;
plus some public holidays), which
is dedicated to Gustav Holst
(1874–1934), composer of
The Planets.
Don't miss Pittville Park has
lakes and a showpiece Pump
Room, built in 1825 in the Greek
Revival style. A mineral spring
was discovered here in 1715.
You can still take the salty waters.

CHESIL BEACH

✚ 430 G20 🛈 The Esplanade,
Weymouth DT4 7AN, tel 01305 785747

This huge wall of shingle—18
miles (30km) long, up to 15m
(50ft) high and more than 160m
(525ft) wide—is one of the
south coast's most pronounced
natural features, and is famous
for its colony of terns. Stormy
seas and strong currents continue to pile pebbles on the
bank: from pea-sized stones at
the western end of the bank
gradually increasing to large
cobbles in the east. The beach is
separated from the mainland by
a channel and tidal lagoon called
The Fleet, and joins the mainland
at Abbotsbury (▷ 67).
Swimming at any time is
extremely unsafe.

An aerial view gives an idea of the scale of the Eden Project

EDEN PROJECT

Unique in Britain, this is one of its most visited creations, examining our relationship with the natural world.

Constructed in a disused china clay mine near St. Austell, the Eden Project is a 15ha (37-acre) floral and rainforest gateway into the world of plants. Two gigantic framed structures dubbed 'biomes' house a diverse range of wild and cultivated plants.

Each biome contains areas representing the vegetation of a number of countries: The humid tropics biome has plants and products from Amazonia, West Africa, Malaysia and Oceania; humidity and temperature are controlled to re-create rainforest conditions. A waterfall also cascades from high above the plants. The warm temperate biome focuses on Southern Africa, the Mediterranean and California, and has a magical array of Californian wild flowers. A fascinating video of the construction can be viewed in a small building next door. The grounds outside Eden make up the roofless biome—plants from Britain's own temperate climate, including native Cornish flora.

The story of the development of Eden is short but impressive. Conceived in 1994, it wasn't until May 1997 that the Millennium Commission granted the first £37.5 million. In October 1997, the nursery where Eden's plants are grown and quarantined was purchased and a year later building got under way. It took six months to clear the site of 1.8 million tonnes of soil.

Don't miss The Eden village has animated displays, performance artists, storytelling and workshops throughout the day.

RATINGS	
Good for kids	●●●●○
Scientific interest	●●●●○
Specialist shopping	●●●○○
Time needed	3–4 hours

TIPS
● Come by bus or coach to avoid a long wait to get in.
● If you walk or cycle you get a £3 discount.

BASICS
✚ 428 D21 • Bodelva, St. Austell PL24 2SG
☎ 01726 811911
🕐 Late Mar–end Oct daily 9.30–6 (last admission 4.30); Nov–late Mar daily 10–4.30 (last admission 3)
💷 Adult £12.50, child (5–15) £5, family £30
🚉 St. Austell
🚌 Shuttle from St. Austell every 30–60 min
🍴 💻 🏛 🚻 🅿

www.edenproject.com

The main parts of the project are the eco-friendly biomes that house a wide range of plants

Pale stone buildings characterize Cirencester's Cecily Hill

CIRENCESTER

🔢 430 H18 ℹ️ The Corn Hall, Market Place, Cirencester GL7 2NW, tel 01285 654180
www.cotswold.gov.uk

During the Roman occupation, Cirencester was *Corinium*, England's second most important city after London. Now it is a sedate market town, focusing around its Market Place (markets Mon and Fri), which in turn is dominated by St. John the Baptist Church, one of the grandest Cotswold 'wool churches', built when the wool trade brought great local prosperity during the 15th century.

The town's most attractive street, Cecily Hill, leads into Cirencester Park, laid out geometrically in the 18th century: There is free access for walking. The Corinium Museum (Apr–end Oct daily 10–5; rest of year Tue–Sat 10–5, Sun 2–5) celebrates the city's Roman heritage. Craft workshops take place in the Brewery Arts Centre (Mon–Sat 9.30–5).

CLOVELLY

🔢 428 D19 ℹ️ Clovelly, near Bideford, EX39 5TA, tel 01237 431781 💷 Entrance to village: adult £4.50, child (7–16) £3, family £13.50
www.clovelly.co.uk

Of all Devon's picture-postcard villages, this is one of the most visited. It can be overcrowded in peak season. Visiting Clovelly requires stamina and suitable footwear, as all visitors (and residents) must walk down to it; but a Land Rover service takes you back up to the parking area (Easter–end Oct). Its single cobbled street, known as Up-Along and Down-Along, is lined with colour-washed cottages (some 16th-century), and slopes steeply 120m (400ft) to the tiny harbour.

CHEDDAR GORGE

A dramatic natural spectacle, enjoyed either by a drive along the road, a walk along the top or a tour of the adjoining limestone caves.

🔢 429 F19 ℹ️ The Gorge, Cheddar BS27 3QE (closed in winter), tel 01934 742343
www.cheddarsomerset.co.uk or www.cheddarcaves.co.uk

RATINGS	
Good for kids	●●●●●
Historic interest	●●●
Natural interest	●●●●●

TIPS

● It's best to visit in autumn, when the leaves are turning.
● The gorge is most vertigo-inducing from the lookout tower above—reached by climbing the 274 steps of Jacob's Ladder or by the public footpath from the east, leading from Blackrock Gate.

Cheddar Gorge cuts dramatically beneath towering limestone cliffs, through the Mendip Hills for nearly 2 miles (3km). It is thought to have been formed by meltwater during the various ice ages over the past two million years. The B3135 road winds along the foot of the gorge, with numerous stopping places from where to admire the scene. Cave systems riddle the gorge: The Cheddar Caves (Jul–end Aug daily 10.30–5.30; rest of year daily 10.30–5) have two show caves—Gough's Cave and Cox's Cave—with tinted rock formations, stalagmites and stalactites.

The tourism industry started in the 17th century and has left the village of Cheddar with an abundance of souvenir and cream-tea shops. In centuries past the caves formed the ideal conditions for maturing cheese, and while most cheddar cheese is now manufactured elsewhere (and not just in Britain), you can still see it being made at the Cheddar Cheese Dairy and Craft Village, near the entrance to the gorge.

About 6 miles (9.5km) south are the Wookey Hole Caves (Apr–end Oct daily 10–5; rest of year daily 10–4), where you take a 40-minute guided tour. The first cave dive was made in the Witch's Parlour in 1935, and 25 caverns have since been discovered. Part of the Wookey Hole Caves are the River Axe ravine and the Victorian papermill (handmade paper), a mirror maze and old-fashioned pier amusements.

Natural hues such as subtle pink, green and grey can be identified in the rock at Gough's Cave

THE SIGHTS

Corfe Castle has been a romantic ruin for several centuries

Through the arch from Corsham is the manor of Corsham Court

The grounds of Cotehele are a nature conservation area

CORFE CASTLE

✚ 430 G20 • near Wareham BH20 5EZ
☎ 01929 481294 🕐 Mar, Oct daily 10–5; Apr–end Sep daily 10–6; rest of year daily 10–4 💷 Adult £5, child (5–16) £2.50, family £12.50 🍴 ☐
🔲 🚻 🅿 On edge of village
www.nationaltrust.org.uk

Reduced to a jagged ruin after a long siege during the English Civil War (1642–48) but still dominating the view from miles around, Corfe Castle stands on a steep mound at a breach in the Purbeck Hills. It was built in Norman times and added to by King John. At the time of its demise the castle was the family seat of royalist Sir John Bankes, Attorney General under Charles I. His wife, Lady Bankes, played a key part in the defence of the castle against a Cromwellian siege, and the Roundheads were so impressed by her bravery that she was permitted to take the keys to the castle with her when she was defeated.

Much of the grey stone used to build the village of Corfe was quarried from the castle itself. The village has several good tea rooms, shops, restaurants and pubs.
Don't miss A steam-train ride on the Swanage Steam Railway from Swanage to Corfe (May–end Sep daily, during most days Apr and Oct, and some days rest of year; **www.swanagerailway.co.uk**).

CORSHAM COURT

✚ 430 G18 • Corsham SN13 0BZ
☎ 01249 701610 🕐 Late Mar–end Sep Tue–Sun and public holidays 2–5.30; rest of year Sat–Sun 2–4.30 💷 House and gardens: adult £5, child £2.50. Gardens only: adult £2, child £1
☐ 🔲 🚻 🅿

Set in the small Cotswold town of Corsham is this Elizabethan manor of 1582, altered over the centuries and largely the work

of architects John Nash and Thomas Bellamy.

The current owners, the Methuen family, bought the manor in 1745. The State Rooms and Picture Gallery display works by Reynolds, Rubens and Van Dyck. Landscaped by Capability Brown, the peacock embellished grounds feature formal lawns edged with flowering shrubs and herbaceous borders, avenues of mature trees, a lake and a Gothic bath house.

COTEHELE

✚ 428 D20 • St. Dominick, near Saltash PL12 6TA ☎ 01579 351346; 01579 352739 (recording) 🕐 House: Easter–end Sep Sat–Thu 11–5 Oct Sat–Thu 11–4.30. Gardens: daily 10.30–dusk 💷 Adult £7.40, child (5–16) £3.70, family £18.50. Garden and mill only: adult £4.40, child (5–16) £2.20, family £11 ☐ 🔲 🚻 🅿
www.nationaltrust.org.uk

In a secluded position above the River Tamar, Cotehele is a remarkable Tudor survival. Built between 1485 and 1627 by the Edgcumbe family, it became their second home when they moved to Plymouth Sound in 1533, although relatives continued to

live there. Still unlit by electric light, the house is filled with collections of furnishings, tapestries and armour.

There is much to see in the grounds, with a medieval dovecote, an 18th-century tower and craft workshops. There are also woodland and riverside walks.
Don't miss The restored sailing barge *Shamrock*, at Cotehele Quay, an outstation of the National Maritime Museum in Greenwich (▷ 124).

DARTMOOR NATIONAL PARK

✚ 429 E20 ℹ Tavistock Road, Princetown, Yelverton PL20 6QF, tel 01822 890414
www.dartmoor-npa.gov.uk

The highest land in southern England, filling most of the space between Exeter (▷ 78) and Plymouth (▷ 84), is a granite plateau of rugged, desolate beauty. The pony-grazed, heathery moors are speckled with the remains of prehistoric settlements and punctuated by streams and tors (jagged outcrops), such as the outstanding viewpoints of Hound Tor and Hay Tor. Walkers should be competent navigators, as even the shortest distance can be confusing. There are signs and painted stones as guides, but it's best to buy a map from one of the visitor offices in any main town.

Beneath the tors are cob-and-thatch villages such as Lustleigh and North Bovey. The verdant east side includes the Teign Valley and dramatic Becky Falls.
Don't miss Castle Drogo (Easter–end Oct daily 11–5), near Drewsteignton, architect Sir Edwin Lutyens' 20th-century masterpiece, a blend of Arts and Crafts and medievalism.

Bowerman's Nose rock is typical of the granite outcrops to be found on Dartmoor

A blue plaque tells of Dorchester's connection with Thomas Hardy

Dunster's Yarn Market is a reminder of its wool-trading days

The Tarr Steps cross the River Barle in Exmoor National Park

DARTMOUTH

➕ 429 E21 ℹ️ The Engine House, Mayor's Avenue, Dartmouth TQ6 9YY, tel 01803 834224
www.dartmouth.org.uk

A web of crisscrossing cobbled streets and narrow alleyways gives the ancient town and deep-water port of Dartmouth an unrivalled setting at the mouth of the River Dart. The steep green hills on either side flank a yacht-filled estuary. Enjoy the scene by taking a boat trip or climb to the roof of the small 14th-century fortification of Dartmouth Castle (Apr–end Jun and Sep daily 10–5; Jul–end Aug daily 10–6; rest of year Sat–Sun 10–4), guarding the mouth of the river.

The Paignton and Dartmouth Steam Railway reaches the river from the east side, ending at Kingswear on the opposite bank.

DORCHESTER

➕ 430 G20 ℹ️ 11 Antelope Walk, Dorchester DT1 1BE, tel 01305 267992
🚆 Dorchester
www.westdorset.com

This county town features as Casterbridge in *The Mayor of Casterbridge* (1886) by West Country author Thomas Hardy (1840–1928).

East of town, the National Trust maintains two of his houses: Max Gate (Apr–end Sep Mon, Wed, Sun 2–5), which he designed and lived in from 1885 until his death; and his birth-place, Hardy's Cottage (mid-Mar to end Oct Thu–Mon 11–5), near Higher Bockhampton, an isolated thatched cottage in the forest. His heart is buried nearby in Stinsford churchyard. Hardy's study is re-created in the Dorset County Museum (Jul–end Sep daily 10–5; Mon–Sat 10–5, rest of year) in the town centre; where also on show are items from Maiden Castle, Europe's

largest Iron Age hillfort (south of town), stormed by the Romans during a violent battle in AD43.

DUNSTER

➕ 429 E19 ℹ️ 17 Friday Street, Minehead TA24 5UB, tel 01643 702624
www.dunster-exmoor.co.uk

Outstanding in an area known for the beauty of its villages, Dunster has a broad High Street, lined with cottages and former merchants' houses, which leads from the unusual 17th-century octagonal Yarn Market towards the entrance of Dunster Castle (Sat–Wed 11–5, mid-Mar to end Oct; Sat–Wed 11–4, early Nov).

The castle has been the home of the Luttrell family for 600 years. Between 1868 and 1872 the architect Anthony Salvin attuned the castle for comfortable living, but retained the 17th-century plasterwork and oak staircase. St. George's Church, once both a Benedictine priory and parish church, is the largest in Exmoor and dates mainly from the 15th century.

EDEN PROJECT

See page 75

EXETER

➕ 429 E20 ℹ️ Civic Centre, Dix's Field, Exeter EX1 1RQ, tel 01392 265700
🚆 Exeter St. Davids/Exeter Central
www.exeter.gov.uk

During World War II, Exeter was subject to a massive bombing raid that all but destroyed the historic town. It continues as a regional and shopping hub, although the city's core is a mixture of ancient buildings, such as the Guildhall in the High Street, scattered among bland postwar redevelopments.

The best-preserved streets include Southernhay, Stepcote Hill and the gracious close around the miraculously intact

cathedral, considered the finest specimen of the decorated Gothic style in the country. It has the largest expanse of continuous vaulting in the world, as well as an ornate west façade and 13th-century misericords (carved benches). The old quayside area is lively with places to eat, bars and craft shops, and there are boat tours and walkways.

EXMOOR NATIONAL PARK

➕ 429 E19 ℹ️ Fore Street, Dulverton TA22 9EX, tel 01398 323841
www.exmoor-nationalpark.gov.uk

High moors look out over rolling pastures and wooded river valleys to some of Britain's highest cliffs. The coast path makes the most of the views, but drives along the A39 and along lonely roads over the moor are exhilarating too. Virtually together are the resorts of Lynton, up on the hill, and Lynmouth, down by the sea—the two are joined by a cliff railway; close by are the dramatic Valley of Rocks, with jagged outcrops and feral goats, and Watersmeet, where two rivers join in a wooded valley. Farther east, Selworthy has an array of thatched cottages, while inland Dunkery Beacon commands a colossal view over Exmoor, Devon and South Wales. The area around Malmsmead was immortalized in RD Blackmore's novel *Lorna Doone* (1869), based on a real Exmoor family of outlaws.

FALMOUTH

➕ 428 C21 ℹ️ 28 Killigrew Street, Falmouth TR11 3PN, tel 01326 312300
🚆 Falmouth
www.visitcornwall.com

This port and resort faces the Fal estuary (also known as Carrick Roads), a vast natural harbour filled with boats of all sizes.

Planes hang from everywhere in the Fleet Air Arm Museum

Glastonbury Tor makes a dramatic statement at dusk

The docks at Gloucester are ringed by fine warehouses

Numerous pleasure craft ply the harbour and the River Fal to Truro. Guarding each side of the estuary are two perfect examples of 16th-century military architecture, built during the reign of Henry VIII (1491–1547); St. Mawes Castle (Jul–end Aug daily 10–6; Apr–end Jun and Sep daily 10–5; Oct daily 10–4; rest of year Fri–Mon 10–4), reached by ferry; and the larger Pendennis Castle (Jul–end Aug daily 10–6; Apr–end Jun and Sep daily 10–5; Apr–end Sep closes Sat at 4; Oct–end Mar, daily 10–4), on the town side. In Discovery Quay, the National Maritime Museum Cornwall (daily 10–5) is Cornwall's prime attraction of its kind, chronicling the county's maritime heritage and showing 120 craft from the National Small Boat Collection.

FLEET AIR ARM MUSEUM

⊞ 429 F19 • RNAS Yeovilton, Ilchester BA22 8HT ☎ 01935 840565 ◷ Apr–end Oct daily 10–5.30; Nov–end Mar 10–4.30 (last admission 90 min before closing) 👤 Adult £9.50, child £6, family £28 ▢ 🏧 🚻 🅿
www.fleetairarm.com

Housed in a huge hangar, this major aviation museum tells the story of the men and women of the flying navy. Highlights include the chance to experience life aboard an aircraft carrier, and the interactive Leading Edge exhibition, with dramatic lighting and engine sounds. Or you can become a virtual pilot in the Lockheed Martin Merlin Experience. There is also the opportunity to climb inside a Concorde as the test flight craft is housed here. You'll be surprised at just how small it is.

The Zodiac Clock is a prominent feature of Gloucester Cathedral

Permanent displays include a wide collection of models, photographs, uniforms and equipment.

FOWEY

⊞ 428 D21 🛈 5 South Street, Fowey PL23 1AR, tel 01726 833616
www.fowey.co.uk

Pronounced foy, this particularly appealing Cornish port rises steeply beside its estuarine harbour, with a jumble of narrow streets and crooked alleys peeking between rooftops to the water. The town stages a highly popular Regatta and Carnival week in mid-August, and there is a lively boating scene at the harbourside, with several choices of boat trips. The ferries extend the scope for walks: You can take the ferry to Polruan and walk along the wooded riverbank to Bodinnick, where another ferry brings you back to Fowey. In high season, the town gets very busy so it's best to park at the top and walk down.

GLASTONBURY

⊞ 429 F19 🛈 9 High Street, Glastonbury BA6 9DP, tel 01458 832954
www.glastonburytic.co.uk

Modern Glastonbury retains a sense of the past; people of all faiths and New Age culture adherents congregate here. Many legends surround this town. One claims that King Arthur is buried in Glastonbury Abbey (Apr–end Sep daily 9.30–6; rest of year 10–4.30; opening times extended slightly in some months), which is on the site of a fourth-century monastery. Another legend claims that Joseph of Arimathea came here with the Holy Grail, and that he buried it in the Chalice Well. **Don't miss** Glastonbury Tor offers spectacular views over the counties of Somerset, Wiltshire and Dorset from the 15th-century tower on its summit.

GLOUCESTER

⊞ 430 G17 🛈 28 Southgate Street, Gloucester GL1 2DP, tel 01452 396572 🚉 Gloucester
www.gloucester.gov.uk

The jewel of Gloucester's compact historic heart is the cathedral (daily 7.30–6), housing the tomb of Edward II (1284–1327), magnificent medieval stained glass in its east window, and 14th-century fan vaulting in its cloisters—little wonder it was used for the filming of *Harry Potter and the Philosopher's Stone* (2002).

Cathedral Green is fringed by buildings from the 15th to 18th centuries and the transformed Victorian docks have shops, bars, restaurants and cafés in the preserved warehouses.

Among the city's museums is the National Waterways Museum (daily 10–5; last admission 4), which charts the story of Britain's waterways.
Don't miss The trip along the historic canal within the docks aboard the *Queen Boadicea II*.

LULWORTH COVE

Lulworth Cove is part of an astounding coastline with numerous geological oddities such as a rock arch, fossil forest and strange natural geometry.

RATINGS

Good for kids	●●●●●
Historic interest	●●
Natural beauty	●●●●●
Walkability	●●●●●

TIP

● To explore another part of the Army Ranges, start farther east from Tyneham (an abandoned village used for military exercises), and head out to the clifftops. To check public access times to the Lulworth Army Ranges ☎ 01929 462721 (extension 4819).

BASICS

⊞ 430 G20
🛈 The Esplanade, Weymouth DT4 7AN, tel 01305 785747

www.weymouth.gov.uk

MAKE A DAY OF IT

Abbotsbury (▷ 67)
Corfe Castle (▷ 77)
Dorchester (▷ 78)
Weymouth (▷ 90)

It's a steep climb along the cliff overlooking Lulworth Cove (above) and Durdle Door (above left), a natural sea-eroded arch. You can walk back along the beach

DRAMATIC SCENERY

On the Purbeck Heritage Coast between Swanage and Weymouth, Lulworth Cove is an oval bay with cross-sections of spectacularly folded rock strata. A 1-mile (1.5km) walk west along the well-worn (and steep) track from the parking area leads to the natural limestone arch of Durdle Door, above a long, clean and (mostly) pebbly beach.

Close to the west side of the Cove, the waves foam into Stair Hole, another natural sculpture. Here the earth's forces have lifted, twisted and folded the rock strata over 90 degrees. The cliffs present a risk of falling rocks so take great care when walking beneath them; public notices warn of the dangers of climbing on the rocks.

PLANTS AND WILDLIFE

The wide range of habitats resulting from this geological diversity supports a variety of birdlife: kittiwakes, shags, cormorants and fulmars on the cliffs, along with buzzards, kestrels and occasional peregrines. Lulworth has its own butterfly, the Lulworth Skipper, first discovered in 1832. This small brown-and-black species is seen in July and August and is very rare outside Dorset. Among the variety of vibrant wild flowers found here are five rare species of orchid.

At Easter, most weekends, in August and at certain other times you are allowed into the Lulworth Army Ranges. This coastal strip extends east to Kimmeridge over some of the wildest scenery on the south coast. The presence of the army has saved this landscape from modern intrusions, and the area is a stronghold for plants such as Adonis blue, early spider orchid and wild camomile. Walking is tough going, with steep gradients and dizzying drops. You must keep to the paths at all times as there are unexploded munitions lying around. You can enter from the east side of Lulworth Cove through a gate.

Just below the cliffs are the remains of a fossil forest. Trees from the Jurassic period became submerged in a swamp, allowing algae to grow around them, and sediments trapped by the algae hardened into the round limestone 'burrs' seen today.

Don't miss Boat trips give dramatic views of the coastline; the Heritage Centre (summer daily 10–6; rest of year daily 10–5) has informative videos and displays; the modern Rock Gallery tells the story of Lulworth from 150 million years ago to the present day.

The low hedges at Hidcote divide the different outdoor rooms

Turn back time with a walk along the cloisters at Lacock Abbey

Sunset at the end of the world— Land's End

HIDCOTE MANOR GARDEN

➕ 435 H17 • Hidcote Bartrim, near Chipping Campden GL55 6LR
☎ 01386 438333 ◎ Mid-Mar to end Nov Sat–Wed 10–6 (last admission 5.30, or 4.30 from Oct) 👍 Adult £6.60, child (over 5) £3.30, family £16.10 🍴
🖥 🏛 🚻 🅿
www.nationaltrust.org.uk

Hidcote represents one of the great innovative garden designs, the creation of horticulturist Major Lawrence Johnston between 1907 and 1948. The gardens are made up of a series of structured outdoor 'rooms', each with its own character and separated by walls and hedges of copper and green beech, box, holly, hornbeam and yew. There are outstanding herbaceous borders, old roses and rare or unique plants and trees from all over the world.

The varied styles of the garden rooms peak at different times of year, making Hidcote impressive during any season. It can get overcrowded on public holidays and Sundays.

ISLES OF SCILLY

➕ 428 B20 ℹ Wesleyan Chapel, Well Lane, St. Mary's TR21 0JD, tel 01720 422536
www.simplyscilly.co.uk

Lying 28 miles (45km) off Land's End, this archipelago of 100 isles and islets (only five of which are inhabited) offers an idyllic retreat. Attractions are distinctly low-key: wild flowers, birdwatching, tiny villages, walking, boating, beaches, cycling and snorkelling.

St. Mary's, where the ferry and helicopter arrive from Penzance, has enough of interest to fill a day, with a concentration of prehistoric sites and a coastal path circling the island.

On car-free Tresco, the subtropical gardens of Tresco

Abbey (daily 10–4) are the major attraction.

The other inhabited Scillies are windswept Bryher, St. Agnes and St. Martin's—the latter with some of the best beaches in southwest England.

KINGSTON LACY

🍴 430 G20 • Wimborne BH21 4LA
☎ 01202 883402 (Mon–Fri 9–5); 01202 880413 (recording) ◎ House: Easter–end Oct Wed–Sun 11–5 (last admission 4). Garden and park: Easter–end Oct daily 10.30–6; Nov–late Dec Fri–Sun 10.30–4; Feb to mid-Mar Sat–Sun 10.30–4 👍 Adult £8, child (5–16) £4, family £20. Park and garden only: adult £4, child £2, family £10 🍴
🏛 🚻 🅿
www.nationaltrust.org.uk

For more than 300 years Kingston Lacy was the home of the Bankes family after they were ousted from Corfe Castle (▷ 77) by the Roundheads in the Civil War. The 17th-century house was designed by Sir Roger Pratt and radically altered during the 19th century by Sir Charles Barry. The lavish interior has intricate marble and woodcarving, paintings by Peter Paul Rubens, Anthony van Dyck and Peter Lely, and a Spanish Room with walls of gilded leather.

The park features shady walks, azaleas, camellias, formal lawns, a Victorian fernery and a sunken garden planted with hyacinths, begonias and heliotrope.

LACOCK ABBEY

➕ 430 G18 • Lacock, near Chippenham SN15 2LG ☎ 01249 730227
◎ Apr–end Nov Wed–Mon 1–5.30 (closed Good Fri). Grounds and cloisters: Mar–end Nov daily 11–5.30 (closed Good Fri). Museum: Mar–end Oct daily 11–5.30 (closed Good Fri) 👍 Abbey, grounds, cloisters and museum: adult £7.40, child (5–16) £3.70, family £18.90. Museum, grounds and cloisters: adult £4.60, child £2.30,

family £11.80. Abbey, grounds and cloisters: adult £6, child £3, family £15.30 🍴 🖥 🏛 🚻 🅿
www.nationaltrust.org.uk

Lacock Abbey was founded in 1232 and retains much of its medieval fabric, including the cloisters, sacristy and nuns' chapter house. After the Dissolution of the Monasteries in the mid-16th century, it became a family home, and later acquired an octagonal Tudor tower, 17th-century hall and brewery.

Owned largely by the National Trust and immaculately preserved, the village of Lacock is mostly grey-stone houses and half-timbered thatched cottages dating from medieval times to the 19th century.
Don't miss The Fox Talbot Museum commemorates abbey resident and photographer William Fox Talbot (1800–77), who in 1840 invented the positive/negative process that led to the development of modern photography.

LAND'S END

➕ 428 B21 ℹ Station Road, Penzance TR18 2NF, tel 01376 362207
www.visitcornwall.co.uk

Mainland Britain culminates in spectacular fashion at its southwest tip, with jagged granite cliffs plunging into the Atlantic.

Land's End has been commercialized since Victorian days when Grace Thomas set up her First and Last House and sold refreshments to visitors. Today it has expanded to include restaurants, animal attractions, crafts and gift shops and exhibitions. Once on the cliff path, however, you can soon leave the crowds behind.

One of the most dramatically remote and rugged sections of the Cornish cliffs extends south east to Porthcurno and Treen.

The formal gardens at Lanhydrock House are stunning

The sign announces where you are on the Lizard Peninsula

A giant's head pokes up through the greenery at Heligan

THE SIGHTS

LANHYDROCK HOUSE

✚ 428 D20 • Lanhydrock, near Bodmin PL30 5AD ☎ 01208 73320 ◷ House: Easter–end Sep Tue–Sun 11–5.30; Oct Tue–Sun 10–5. Gardens: daily 10–6. Winter gardens: Nov–end Feb daily dawn–dusk ▧ Adult £7.90, child (5–16) £3.95, family £19.75. Gardens and grounds: adult £4.40, child £2.20 ⅃
▣ ⅃ ℙ
www.nationaltrust.org.uk

Only the gatehouse, entrance porch and north wing remain of the original house, which was built in 1642 but nearly completely destroyed by a fire in 1881. Around 50 display rooms reflect the life of a wealthy Victorian household. This archetypal masters/servants life ranges from the state rooms and the children's nursery wing to the warren of kitchens, larders and sculleries below stairs.

The house is surrounded by exceptional grounds filled with magnolias, rhododendrons and camellias. Adjoining the house are the formal gardens with clipped yews and bronze urns.

LAUNCESTON

✚ 428 D20 ⅈ Market House Arcade, Market Street, Launceston PL15 8EP, tel 01566 772321
www.visitcornwall.co.uk

Once a walled town (one gateway survives), a hub of straw hat-making and the capital of Cornwall, this small town clusters around a hilltop Norman castle (Apr–end Jun and Sep daily 10–5; Jul–end Aug daily 10–6; Oct daily 10–4), where you can climb to the top of the keep. Despite decay over the centuries and a battering in the Civil War (when it was taken four times), an impressive amount survives. Elsewhere in town are pleasant Georgian and earlier façades, some of the finest around Castle Street, where the Lawrence

House Museum (Apr–end Sep Mon–Fri 10.30–4.30; early Oct Mon–Fri 10.30–1.30) records local history.

THE LIZARD

✚ 428 C21 ⅈ 79 Meneage Street, Helston TR13 8RB, tel 01326 565431 www.visitcornwall.com

The Lizard peninsula stretches from Helston in the north to Lizard Point, the most southerly point of the British mainland. This is an area of contrasts, with rugged cliffs and open flat moorland on the west side, and softer verdant landscapes around the Helford River to the east.

Especially attractive are the thatched waterside cottages at Cadgwith and Helford, 10 miles (16km) northeast. Inland, the Goonhilly Earth Station (mid-Mar to late May and Oct daily 10–5; late May–end Sep daily; for other times of year tel: 0800 679593) is the futuristic receiving station for satellite-relayed phone calls and has tours from its visitor centre. **Don't miss** Kynance Cove, a beach beneath cliffs of serpentine rock (so named because it resembles snake skin).

LONGLEAT

✚ 430 G19 • near Warminster BA12 7NW ☎ 01985 844400 ◷ House: mid-Feb to end Sep daily 10–5.30; Oct–end Dec daily 11–3; guided tours only in winter, phone for times. Safari park: mid-Feb to end Oct Mon–Fri 10–4, Sat–Sun and public holidays 10–5. Other attractions: Apr–end Oct daily 11–5.30. Timed tickets (house): guided tours only Oct–Easter 11–3 ▧ House: adult £9, child (4–16) £6. Safari park: adult £10, child £7; additional charges for some attractions. Passport ticket (all attractions and unlimited access): adult £18, child £14 ⅃ ☐ ▣ ⅃ ℙ
www.longleat.co.uk

Britain's first safari park lies beside a sumptuous Elizabethan mansion

(completed 1580), with formal gardens and parkland landscaped by Capability Brown in the 18th century. The drive-through reserve gives an opportunity to encounter hundreds of exotic animals roaming free, including white tigers, lions and gorillas. You can drive your own car or take the safari bus.

Visit the world's longest hedge maze (1.7 miles/2.7km) or take a trip on a safari boat on the huge lake.

Among some of the treasures inside the house are hunting scenes by John Wootton and 17th-century Flemish tapestries.

LOST GARDENS OF HELIGAN

✚ 428 D21 • Pentewan, St. Austell PL26 6EN ☎ 01726 845100 ◷ Mar–end Oct daily 10–6 (last admission 4.30); rest of year daily 10–5, (last admission 3.30) ▧ Adult £7.50, child (5–15) £4, family £20 ⅃ ☐ ▣ ⅃ ℙ
www.heligan.com

The largest garden reclamation project in Europe has revealed a series of magnificent gardens that fell into neglect in the years during and after World War I, as the estate gardeners were enlisted and Heligan became forgotten.

Restoration began in 1990 when the new owners discovered the old garden scheme buried within seemingly impenetrable thicket. The Jungle features giant Australian tree ferns, palms and bamboo; the Productive Gardens have more than 300 varieties of fruits and vegetables, including pineapples grown in specially heated glasshouses; the Pleasure Grounds reveal gardens of many countries, summerhouses and pools, and a crystal grotto; and the Lost Valley is an area of woodlands and wetlands.

LULWORTH COVE

See page 80

The Cobb at Lyme Regis makes a dramatic place for a stroll out to sea—especially when the sea is crashing against the rocks

Milton Abbas's white-painted houses stand in neat rows

LUNDY ISLAND

➕ 428 D19 ℹ️ Lundy Shore Office, The Quay, Bideford EX39 2LY, tel 01271 863636
www.lundyisland.co.uk

Although two hours' journey on the MS *Oldenburg* from either Bideford or Ilfracombe, this remote island in the Bristol Channel is well worth the trip. Measuring about 3 miles (5km) long and about 0.5 mile (1km) across, it has granite cliffs rising to 130m (400ft) and is the haunt of basking sharks, naturalized Asian sika deer, mountain goats and its very own Lundy ponies. The hub of island life is the Marisco Tavern, a very friendly pub that brews its own beer. Accommodation, ranging from a lighthouse to a 13th-century castle, is limited and in great demand, and is run by the Landmark Trust.

LYDFORD GORGE

➕ 429 E20 • The Stables, Lydford, Okehampton EX20 4BH ☎ 01822 820320 🕐 Easter–end Sep daily 10–5.30; Oct 10–4; rest of year, waterfall only, daily 10.30–3 👣 Adult £4.50, child (5–16) £2.20 🅿️ Easter–end Oct 🏧 🚻 🅿️
www.nationaltrust.org.uk

Outside the village of Lydford and on the western edge of Dartmoor, this secretive wooded gorge stretches for 1.5 miles (2.5km). The path leading down to it passes the 30m (90ft) White Lady waterfall on its way through the deep ravine where the river has formed a series of potholes, including the thundering Devil's Cauldron. You'll need stout footwear as the paths are narrow and can be slippery. Lydford itself has a ruined castle, the 16th-century oak-timbered

Castle Inn and the 15th-century Church of St. Petrock.

LYME REGIS

➕ 429 F20 ℹ️ Guildhall Cottage, Church Street, Lyme Regis DT7 3BS, tel 01297 442138
www.lymeregistourism.com

On a coastline renowned for its Jurassic fossils—snail-like ammonites can even be seen embedded in garden walls—is this old port and sedate Regency seaside resort. It has a tangle of narrow streets, with galleries, cafés, craft and antiques shops, set above a gently shelving beach. The favourite place of Jane Austen (1775–1817), she set part of her novel *Persuasion* (1817) here. The snaking breakwater known as The Cobb was where a cloaked Meryl Streep stood in the British movie of *The French Lieutenant's Woman* (1981), based on John Fowles's novel of 1969.

MILTON ABBAS

➕ 430 G20
ℹ️ 1 Greyhound Yard, Blandford Forum DT11 7EB, tel 01258 454770
www.ruraldorset.com

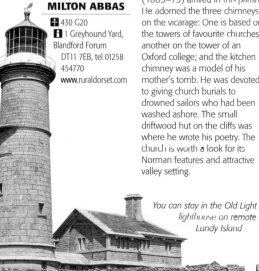

Milton Abbas has a single street with neat thatched white cottages set back from neatly trimmed grass verges. It was created between 1771 and 1790 by the owner of Milton Abbey, Joseph Damer, later Earl of Dorchester. He found that the village of Middleton spoiled the view from his house, so he demolished it, replaced it with an artificial lake and built this new model village for his tenants, out of sight. With the exception of the Abbey Church and Abbot's Hall, the ruined abbey buildings were removed to make way for a Gothic mansion—now housing a public school—set in parkland landscaped by Capability Brown.

MORWENSTOW

➕ 428 D19 ℹ️ The Crescent, Bude EX23 8LE, tel 01288 354240
www.visitcornwall.com

In 1834 the eccentric poet and cleric Reverend Robert Hawker (1803–75) arrived in this parish. He adorned the three chimneys on the vicarage: One is based on the towers of favourite churches; another on the tower of an Oxford college; and the kitchen chimney was a model of his mother's tomb. He was devoted to giving church burials to drowned sailors who had been washed ashore. The small driftwood hut on the cliffs was where he wrote his poetry. The church is worth a look for its Norman features and attractive valley setting.

You can stay in the Old Light lighthouse on remote Lundy Island

Samuel Coleridge hangs outside his cottage in Nether Stowey

One of the prettiest towns in the Cotswolds, the ancient wool town of Painswick is firmly on the tourist route

THE SIGHTS

NETHER STOWEY

🏠 429 F19 🛈 Bridgwater House, King Square, Bridgwater TA6 3AR, tel 01278 436438; Mon–Fri (closed public holidays)
www.somersetbythesea.co.uk

At the heart of this village at the foot of the Quantock Hills is the conservation area of Castle, St. Mary and Lime streets, with architecture dating from medieval times. In Lime Street you will find Coleridge Cottage. Nether Stowey's most famous inhabitant, the poet Samuel Taylor Coleridge (1772–1834), lived here with his family from 1796 until 1800, while he wrote works including *Kubla Khan* (1797) and *The Rime of the Ancient Mariner* (1798). The cottage is owned by the National Trust, which has preserved the great poet's reading room, bedroom and various memorabilia.

PADSTOW

🏠 428 C20 🛈 Red Brick Building, North Quay, Padstow PL28 8AF, tel 01841 533449
www.visitcornwall.com

Overlooking the Camel Estuary, Padstow is the quintessential Cornish fishing port and well known for its seafood restaurants. Life revolves around the harbour (boat trips available), from which a tight maze of narrow streets and alleys leads off. A passenger ferry runs to Rock, where there are walks to Pentire Head, while on the Padstow side you can walk north to Stepper Point for views along the coast. For cyclists, the Camel Trail is a scenic 26-mile (42km) traffic-free route along an old rail track partly following the estuary. Bicycles can be hired locally.

PAINSWICK

🏠 430 G18 🛈 Subscription Rooms, Kendrick Street, Stroud GL5 1AE, tel 01453 760960
www.cotswold.gov.uk

This little Cotswold-stone town slopes to the Painswick Brook, where several former textile mills can be seen. Ninety-nine 200-year-old yews clipped into arches and geometric shapes punctuate the almost surreal churchyard, along with an array of 17th- and 18th-century tombstones in a range of shapes and styles—some hexagonal, others triangular or adorned with scrolls. On the edge of town, Painswick Rococo

Sir Francis Drake was one of Plymouth's most famous and stoic residents—taking on the Spanish in style

Garden (mid-Jan to end Oct) is a careful re-creation of an exuberant 18th-century design using a painting by Thomas Robins in 1748.

PLYMOUTH

🏠 429 D21 🛈 Plymouth Mayflower, 3–5 The Barbican, Plymouth PL1 2LR, tel 01752 266030/306330 🚉 Plymouth
www.visitplymouth.co.uk

The maritime past is writ large over this major naval port. Although badly damaged during World War II, it has managed to retain historic areas. Notable are the Barbican, on the west side of Sutton Harbour (including New Street), Prysten House and the grassy Hoe, where the lighthouse known as Smeaton's Tower looks over Plymouth Sound. Just below is the Plymouth Dome (Apr–end Oct daily 10–5; rest of year Tue–Sat 10–4), where there is an informative and entertaining interpretation of Plymouth's history. It was from Plymouth in 1588 that the navigator Sir Francis Drake (c1540–96) sailed to crush the Spanish Armada, though he did have time to finish his game of bowls first, or so the story goes. In 1620 a more peaceable crew, the Pilgrim Fathers, set off from Plymouth aboard the *Mayflower* for a new life in North America.
Don't miss The Plymouth *Mayflower* Museum (daily 10–4), in Barbican Quay, provides a vivid journey through Plymouth's past; opposite is the National Marine Aquarium (summer daily 10–6; rest of year daily 10–5), Britain's biggest and Europe's deepest aquarium.

POLPERRO

🏠 428 D21 🛈 The Guildhall, Fore Street, East Looe PL13 1AA, tel 01503 262072; Easter–end Oct
www.visitcornwall.com

Jousting tournaments take place at Powderham Castle

Stone circle: Restormel Castle's Norman design was formidable

Salisbury Cathedral's spire stands us a proud monument to the city

Perhaps the most engaging of Cornish fishing villages, Polperro has colour-washed houses set around a small harbour sheltered by two sea walls at the mouth of a steep valley. Craft shops, galleries, pubs and restaurants are in plentiful supply, although this is still a working fishing port. Cars are banned from the narrow streets, and access is on foot—or by horse-drawn carriage—from the parking area above the main village, or you can walk in from Talland Bay, 1 mile (1.5km) east along the scenic coast path.

PORT ISAAC

➕ 428 C20 🛈 Red Brick Building, North Quay, Padstow PL28 8AF, tel 01841 533449
www.visitcornwall.com

A fishing village since medieval times, Port Isaac has clung to its Cornish character despite the steady flow of tourists. Narrow, twisting streets, fish cellars and 'drangs' (geranium-filled alleys) are particular features. The narrowest of all is Squeezebelly Alley. Boat trips are available at the harbour. The fishing fleet still sails at dawn and the day's catch will end up on the menus of many local restaurants, so it's worth visiting one of them.

POWDERHAM CASTLE

➕ 429 E20 • Kenton, Exeter EX6 8JQ
☎ 01626 890243 🛈 45-min guided tours every half hour end Mar–end Oct Sun–Fri 10–5 💷 Adult £7.45, child £4.10, family £19.90 🍴 🛈 🏧 🚻
🅿
www.powderham.co.uk

This archetypal English castle is steeped in history, having belonged to the earls of Devon since 1391. Overlooking the Exe Estuary, it is set in fine natural parkland, grazed by a herd of deer, and also has a heronry and hosts jousting tournaments in the

summer. The house, which was much modified during the 19th and 20th centuries, has a banqueting hall, music room and a chapel once a medieval barn. There's also a resident ghost—reportedly a grey lady haunting the area around the staircase.

RESTORMEL CASTLE

➕ 428 D20 • near Lostwithiel PL22 0BD ☎ 01208 872687 🛈 Easter–end Jun, Sep daily 10–5; Jul–end Aug daily 10–6; Oct daily 10–4 💷 Adult £2.30, child (5–16) £1.20 🍴 Snack kiosk 🏧 🚻 🅿
www.englishheritage.org.uk

Norman castle sites are often reduced to a few grassy humps, but this is an exception, occupying a high mound defended by a deep moat, above the Fowey Valley. The considerable 12th- and 13th-century remains include the gate, keep, kitchens and private rooms, with the walls standing almost at their original height. The castle was a symbol of power and wealth and was once home to Edward the Black Prince (1330–76), heir to the English throne. It was abandoned long before the Civil War, but briefly held a Parliamentarian garrison before falling to the Royalists in 1644.

SALISBURY

➕ 430 H19 🛈 Fish Row, Salisbury SP1 1EJ, tel 01722 334956 🚉 Salisbury
www.visitsalisburyuk.com
www.salisbury.gov.uk

England's tallest spire (123m/404ft) announces Salisbury Cathedral from miles around. Started in 1220 and completed in only 38 years, it is uniformly Early English (the first period of Gothic architecture before it evolved into Decorated and then Perpendicular styles). In the north aisle a dial-less clock dates from 1386 and is probably the

oldest mechanism in working order in the world. The miniature fan-vaulted roof in the grilled Audley Chantry is adorned with ancient roundels (decorative medallions), while the cloisters are the largest of any English cathedral. The library over the East Walk contains one of the four original copies of the Magna Carta—England's first bill of rights, imposed on King John by rebel barons in 1215 (▷ 29).

Outstanding in a city that is already well endowed with fine streets is Cathedral Close—England's largest—whose houses date from the 14th to 18th centuries. Among them is Mompesson House (Apr–end Oct Sat–Wed 12–5), a fine example of Queen Anne-style architecture. Another house contains the Salisbury and South Wiltshire Museum (all year Mon–Sat 10–5; Jul–end Aug Sun 2–5), with archaeology galleries presenting the area's rich prehistoric heritage, including Stonehenge (▷ 87).

Alongside the impressive architecture are huge green swathes of parkland, where you can walk, take a picnic, play tennis and rent a rowing boat on the river, or listen to live music outdoors in summer. The spacious Market Square has a lively market on Tuesday and Saturday.

Don't miss Old Sarum (Apr–end Jun and Sep daily 10–5; Jul–end Aug daily 9–6; Oct daily 10–4; rest of year daily 11–3), about 2 miles (3km) north of the city centre, is the dramatic remains of the settlement that preceded modern Salisbury. It was inhabited from the Iron Age until Norman times. Now deserted, it retains huge Iron Age earthworks, and the scant remains of a Norman palace, castle and cathedral.

ST. IVES

See page 86

A causeway, submerged at high tide, leads to St. Michael's Mount

THE SIGHTS

ST. JUST-IN-ROSELAND

🔢 428 C21 ℹ️ Millennium Rooms, The Square, St. Mawes TR2 5AG, tel 01326 270440
www.visitcornwall.com

This heavily restored church sits tranquilly by the Fal Estuary, but it is the churchyard rather than the building that draws thousands of visitors each year. It slopes down from the lychgate and is a riot of subtropical and flowering shrubs alongside indigenous broad-leafed species. In the early 20th century, the Reverend Humfrey Davis endowed its many paths with granite steps, each carved with words of wisdom—'God is Love', 'O sweet St. Just in Roseland, thy name forever dear'—some from the scriptures or hymns, others that he devised himself.

ST. MICHAEL'S MOUNT

🔢 428 C21 • Marazion, near Penzance TR17 0EF ☎ 01736 710265
🅖 Easter–end Oct daily 10.30–5.30; pre-reserved guided tours only rest of year. Private gardens: Apr–end May daily 🕖 Mon–Fri (except gardens); adult £5.50, child (5–16) £2.75, family £13.75. Ferry: adult £1 each way, child (under 15) £0.50. Private gardens: £3
🍴 💻 🏨 Easter–end Oct 🏨 🅿 At Marazion ❓ Phone ahead in bad weather to check ferry is operating
www.nationaltrust.org.uk

The great granite crag of St. Michael's Mount rises dramatically out of Mounts Bay near Penzance. It mirrors Mont St-Michel in Normandy, as French monks arrived here in the 11th century and established a priory. Over the centuries it was a castle, and then a private house, owned by the St. Aubyn family since 1660. The warren of rooms leads up to the 14th-century church at the highest point, for sweeping views towards Land's End (▷ 81) and the Lizard peninsula (▷ 82).

ST. IVES

St. Ives is renowned for its modern art gallery, and arty fishing port, brimming with character. Other highlights are excellent surfing and bathing beaches.

🔢 428 C21 ℹ️ The Guildhall, Street-an-Pol, St. Ives TR26 2DS, tel 01736 796297 🚇 St. Ives
www.visitcornwall.com

RATINGS				
Good for kids	●	●	●	● ○
Cultural interest	●	●	●	● ●
Historic interest	●	●	●	○
Specialist shopping	●	●	●	

TIP
● The town gets crowded. Use the park-and-ride at Trenwith, by the leisure centre (then a short bus ride or 10-minute walk downhill via steps); or park at Lelant Saltings Station, eight minutes by train.

St. Ives began life as a small fishing community that built its wealth on pilchards. During the 20th century, tourism, surfing and the town's reputation as a centre of art became a magnet for holidaymakers. The hub of the old fishing quarter is Downlong, a maze of tiny stepped streets and alleys with names like Salubrious Place and Teetotal Street.

Mediterranean light qualities and the magnificent coastal scenery have attracted painters and sculptors to St. Ives since the 1880s. They have included the potter Bernard Leach (1887–1979), the painter Ben Nicholson (1894–1982) and his sculptor wife Dame Barbara Hepworth (1903–75). Her studio and house in Barnoon Hill is now the Barbara Hepworth Museum and Sculpture Gallery (Mar–end Oct daily 10–5.30; rest of year Tue–Sun 10–4.30), where everything is much as she left it when she died.

Housed in a stylish, modern building with views out to sea, the Tate St. Ives gallery (Mar–Oct daily 10–5.30; rest of year Tue–Sun 10–4.30) has an international reputation due to the work of the St. Ives School. The curved atrium allows light to flood into the gallery, which has innovative and often controversial exhibitions of modern art to rival its namesakes in London (▷ 129).

The Penwith Gallery (daily 10–1, 2–5) and St. Ives Society of Artists Gallery (Mar–early Nov Mon–Sat 10–5.30) showcase good local art. An arts festival in September offers a varied schedule of music and literature, while shopping tends naturally towards art, clothes (lots of surfing gear) and gift shops.

Don't miss The Penwith peninsula has cliff scenery, old tin mines and prehistoric sites; Iron Age Chysauster Ancient Village (5 miles/ 8km southwest) has the oldest identifiable village street in Britain.

The gallery Tate St. Ives is an airy space for 20th-century works

Geese flock to the Wildfowl and Wetlands Trust at Slimbridge

The mysterious stones are only part of the original complex here

SLIMBRIDGE

➕ 430 G18 • Slimbridge GL2 7BT
☎ 01453 890333 🕐 Apr–end Oct
daily 9.30–5; rest of year daily 9.30–4
🎟 Adult £6.75, child £4, family £17.50
🖥 🏛 🍴 🅿
www.wwt.org.uk

The Wildfowl and Wetlands Trust
—the inspiration of the English
artist and naturalist Sir Peter Scott
(1909–89)—was established
on the saltmarshes at Slimbridge
in 1946.

Now equipped with an
observation tower and state-of-
the art visitor centre, Slimbridge is
the winter home of species such
as white-fronted geese and
Bewick's swans that migrate
every year from Siberia—they pair
for life and some pairs have been
coming here for over 20 years.

The reserve is now home to
the largest and most varied
collection of wildfowl in the
world, including rare and
endangered swans, geese, ducks
and pink flamingos.

SNOWSHILL MANOR

➕ 430 H17 • Snowshill, Broadway
WR12 7JU ☎ 01386 852410 🕐 House
and garden: Easter–end Apr Thu–Sun
12–5, also open Mon public holidays,
Easter–end Oct; May–end Oct Wed–Sun
12–5. Shop and restaurant: 11–5.30
🎟 Adult £7, child (5–16) £3.50, family
£17.80. Garden, shop and restaurant:
adult £4, child £2, family £10
❓ Entrance to manor by timed ticket
only (every 10 min)—pre-reserving
necessary only on public holidays
🍴 🏛 🍴 🅿
www.nationaltrust.org.uk

From the outside, Snowshill
Manor appears to be a traditional
Cotswold Tudor manor house,
set in walled gardens. Within it
reveals the hand of the eccentric
sugar plantation owner and
architect Charles Paget Wade,
who acquired the house in 1919
and gave it to the National Trust

STONEHENGE

**A World Heritage Site that is simply the most familiar
standing stone site in Europe.**

➕ 430 H19 • Stonehenge, SP4 7DE
☎ 01980 624715; 01980 626267
(recording) 🕐 Mid-Mar to end May
daily 9.30 6; Jun–end Aug 9–7; Sep
to mid-Oct 9.30–6; mid- to late Oct
9.30–5; late Oct to mid-Mar 9.30–4.
Closed 24–26 Dec and 1 Jan 🎟 Adult
£5.50, child (5–15) £2.80, family
£13.80 ❓ Admission includes audio
tour 🖥 🏛 🍴 🅿
www.english-heritage.org.uk

RATINGS	
Good for kids	●●●
Historic interest	●●●●
Mystical interest	●●●●●
Time needed	1–2 hours

MAKE A DAY OF IT
Avebury (▷ 67)
Longleat (▷ 82)
Salisbury (▷ 85)

This immensely significant site, Europe's most famous prehistoric
wonder, stands at the core of a ceremonial landscape containing
450 protected ancient monuments of national importance.
Stonehenge retains a powerful atmosphere of mystery and awe
because very little is known about the site. Was it a temple or a
huge astronomical calendar? Why did people build it and how
was this great engineering feat achieved?

What you see are the remains of a sequence of monuments
erected in three phases between around 3050 to around
1600BC. The outer circular bank and ditch are the oldest parts,
probably constructed over 5,000 years ago. About 475 years later
a double circle of 80 bluestones (so called because of their
natural colour) was erected. These stones weighed up to
four tonnes each and were brought more than 200 miles
(320km) from the Preseli Hills in southwest Wales (▷ 289). It is
believed that they were floated on rafts across the Bristol
Channel, then dragged over tracks of logs.

In 1650BC the bluestones were taken down and two rings of
sarsen stones, brought from the nearby Marlborough Downs,
were erected as an outer ring of standing stones, with lintels
across the top of them, and an inner horseshoe of five pairs of
uprights with lintels. Later still, some of the bluestones were lined
up between the two rings of sarsens and in an inner horseshoe.

The largest bluestone—the so-called Altar Stone—was set at the
mid point, where it still lies. The Altar Stone draws the eye
towards the Heelstone, over the peak of which the sun rises on
21 June, the longest day of the year. This occurrence has led
many to believe that the site had a connection with sun worship,
and there are many visitors around this time.

One of the temples created to the wishes of Henry Hoare II on the lake he had dammed from the River Stour

Torquay is a long-established and popular holiday resort

in 1951. His fascination with craftsmanship extended to collecting a vast range of seemingly unrelated objects such as bicycles, clocks, toys, Japanese samurai armour and such curios as a Georgian iron-toothed man trap. His living quarters, in the smaller cottage on the far side of the garden, were equipped in an equally inventive manner.

STOURHEAD

🔲 430 G19 • Stourton, Warminster BA12 6QD ☎ 01747 841152 ⏰ Garden: daily 9–7 (or dusk, last admission 30 min before closing). House: Easter–end Oct Fri–Tue 11–5 (or dusk) (last admission 4 in Oct). Tower: Easter–end Oct daily 12–5 💷 Garden and house: adult £9.90, child (5–16) £4.80, family £23.50. Garden or house: adult £5.80, child £3.20, family £14.20. Garden only (Nov–end Feb): adult £4.30, child £2.10, family £10.50. Tower: adult £2.15, child £1.10, family £5.20 🍴 🛍 ♿ 👥 🅿 www.nationaltrust.org.uk

The estate surrounds a Palladian-style mansion built between 1721 and 1725 by the Scottish architect Colen Campbell (1679–1726). It is crammed with treasures that include the Regency library, paintings by Canaletto (1697–1768) and Sir Joshua Reynolds (1723–92), and furniture designed by Thomas Chippendale (1718–79).

Henry Hoare II, son of a wealthy banker, laid out pleasure gardens between 1741 and 1780, inspired by his tour of Europe. They are a stunning attraction in their own right and feature the Pantheon and Temple of Apollo, a grotto, and a temple to Flora, all set around a central lake.
Don't miss There are beautiful walks on the estate, especially to King Alfred's Tower, a triangular folly made of red brick, from where there are great views.

TINTAGEL CASTLE

🔲 428 D20 • Tintagel PL34 0HE ☎ 01840 770328 ⏰ Easter–late Oct daily 10–6 (until 7 for part Jul and Aug); Oct daily 10–5; rest of year daily 10–4. Closed 24–26 Dec and 1 Jan 💷 Adult £3.90, child (5–15) £2.90 ♿ 👥 www.englishheritage.org.uk

Fact mingles with legend at this spectacularly sited 13th-century clifftop ruin. The site has attracted competing claims for its origins: an Iron-Age enclosure, a Celtic monastery, a Roman signal station and (perhaps spuriously) as the court of King Arthur. Legend has it that Arthur was born here in the late 5th century to Queen Igraine.

Access is up a long, steep flight of steps. Cars must be left at the village of Tintagel next to the castle, where the National Trust maintains a small 14th-century manor house known as the Old Post Office (Apr–end Sep daily 11–5.30; Oct daily 11–4), whose central hall rises the full height of the building.

King Arthur has close associations with Tintagel Castle

TORQUAY

🔲 429 E20 ℹ️ Vaughan Parade, Torquay TQ2 5JG, tel 09066 801268 🚂 Torquay www.theenglishriviera.co.uk

Torquay is the major town of the English Riviera. It is part of an area known as Torbay, which also includes Paignton and Brixham (▷ 72). Its almost balmy climate and safe beaches make it the country's second most visited seaside resort after Blackpool (▷ 164–165).

One feature of the town is its well-kept municipal parks. The Rock Walk, also known as Royal Terrace Gardens, features exotic shrubs and trees, and it is enchantingly lit at night.

Bygones Lifesize Victorian Street (Jul–end Aug Mon–Thu 10–10, Fri–Sun 10–6; Mar–end Jun and Sep–end Oct daily 10–6; Nov–end Feb Mon–Fri 10–4, Sat–Sun 10–5), in St. Marychurch, is a re-creation of a Victorian shopping street.

On the east side of town, Kent's Cavern (Mar–end Jun and Sep–end Oct daily 10–4; Jul–end Aug daily 10–4.30; Oct daily 10–4; Nov–end Feb Mon–Fri 11.30–3.30, Sat–Sun 10–3.30) reveals evidence of Palaeolithic inhabitants.
Don't miss The Model Village (daily from 10; for closing and illumination times tel: 01803 315315), near the cliff railway leading to Babbacombe Beach, is a masterpiece of miniature landscape gardening.

TOTNES

🔲 429 E20 ℹ️ The Town Mill, Coronation Road, Totnes TQ9 5DF, tel 01803 863168 🚂 Totnes www.totnesinformation.co.uk
Totnes has a pervasive sense of the past. On a mound above the River Dart are the Norman remains of Totnes Castle (Apr–end Jun and Sep daily 10–5; Jul–end Aug daily

The palms at balmy Trelissick Garden are superb

10–6; Oct daily 10–4), while in the town's compact centre are 15th-century St. Mary's Church and the 16th-century Guildhall. The Butterwalk hosts a costumed Elizabethan charity market on Tuesday in summer and a general market on Friday and Saturday. In Fore Street, the Elizabethan Museum (Easter–end Oct Mon–Fri 10.30–5) features displays on local history.
Don't miss The chance of the 12-mile (20km) trip along the River Dart to Dartmouth (▷ 78), or the steam-train ride on the South Devon Railway to Buckfastleigh (▷ 74).

TRELISSICK GARDEN

✚ 428 C21 • Feock, Truro TR3 6QL
☎ 01872 862090 ◷ Mid–Feb to end Oct daily 10.30–5.30 (or dusk); rest of year daily 11–4 (late Dec 12–4)
▨ Adult £5, child (5–16) £2.50, family £12.50 🔟 🞑 ⊞ 🏫 🅿
www.nationaltrust.org.uk

Endowed with panoramic views along the Fal Estuary, Trelissick is a garden and extensive woodland park with walks that are accessible all year. At the heart of the estate is the garden, where tender and exotic plants thrive in the sheltered conditions. The magnolias, camellias and rhododendrons produce magnificent spring blossoms, and there are more than 100 species of hydrangea. There is also a walled garden with fig trees and climbers, a shrub garden and the Cornish Apple Orchard.

Try to time your visit to see one of the musical or theatrical events that are occasionally staged here.

TRURO

See page 90

TYNTESFIELD HOUSE

See page 90

The interior of the Gothic cathedral is interrupted by scissor arches

WELLS

England's smallest city has some of its finest ecclesiastical sights.

✚ 429 G19 ℹ Town Hall, Market Place, Wells BA5 2RB, tel 01749 672552
www.somerset.gov.uk/celebratingsomerset

RATINGS	
Good for kids	● ●
Historic interest	● ● ● ●
Religious interest	● ● ●
Walkability	● ● ● ● ●

The limestone city of Wells, beneath the southern slopes of the Mendip Hills, displays the unspoiled perfection of an entire range of ecclesiastical buildings set around a green at the top of the main street. Relatively small crowds make the city a prime base for exploring Somerset's countryside and sights, such as Cheddar Gorge (▷ 76), Exmoor (▷ 78) and Bath (▷ 68–71).

The glories of the cathedral begin with its extraordinarily ornate west front (mid-13th century) decorated with more than 400 separate statues, originally in vivid hues and gold. The severe Early English nave is dominated by two unique curving scissor arches, boldly crossing it and interrupting the view. These were added in the 14th century to strengthen the base of the sinking central tower. Leading off the north transept is a well-worn flight of stone steps to the impressive octagonal chapter house.

Next to the cathedral, the 13th-century Bishop's Palace (Apr–end Oct Mon–Fri and public hols 10.30–6, Sun 12–6, last admission 5) is still the private residence of the Bishop of Bath and Wells and has imposing state rooms. Surrounded by a moat with swans and set in landscaped gardens (which include the ruins of the Great Hall), it is entered by the drawbridge and gatehouse.

Other attractions are comparatively low key, with everything within a few minutes' walk. Close to the cathedral is the marketplace (market Wednesday and Saturday), and the Wells and Mendip Museum (Easter–end Oct daily 10–5.30; rest of year Wed–Mon 11–4), in a Tudor building, records the area's history.
Don't miss The 14th-century Vicar's Close, said to be the oldest complete medieval street in Europe, now accommodates staff of the cathedral and school; the 14th-century Astronomical Clock in the north transept has mounted knights emerging on the hour.

The Westbury White Horse can be seen from a long distance

Forest fire: See blazing autumnal foliage at Westonbirt Arboretum

For traditional seaside entertainment, Weymouth can't be beaten

THE SIGHTS

TRURO

🕂 428 C21 🛈 Boscawen Street, Truro TR1 2NE, tel 01872 274555 🚉 Truro
www.truro.gov.uk

Tin and copper mining made Truro prosperous in the 18th and 19th centuries, and evidence of that heyday survives in Lemon Street, with its Georgian houses of Bath stone, and in the elegantly curved Walsingham Place. Truro's triple-spired cathedral—the first to be erected on a new site since Salisbury Cathedral in 1220—was built between 1880 and 1910 to the design of John Pearson, who showed ingenuity in creating a soaring structure within the cramped site of the former parish church. In River Street, the Royal Cornwall Museum (Mon–Sat 10–5) chronicles the county's history, and displays portraits by the 18th-century Cornish artist John Opie.

TYNTESFIELD HOUSE

🕂 429 G18 • Wraxall, North Somerset BS48 1NT ☎ 0870 458 4500 (information); 0870 241 4500 (bookings) 🕐 Restricted opening times (please call for details) 💷 Please call for details of prices 🖥 🛉
www.nationaltrust.org.uk

For an insider's view of the conservation work that restores and maintains Britain's stately homes, visit Tyntesfield House, near Bristol. The house was built for a wealthy merchant, William Gibbs, in 1864, and remained in the Gibbs family until 2002, when it was acquired by the National Trust. Although the Victorian interiors survive intact, an extensive, costly and fascinating programme of restoration is underway. The house itself is an arresting Gothic Revival masterpiece, with pinnacles, turrets and a

sumptuous chapel that has few peers in Britain. While restoration work continues at Tyntesfield House, opening times are likely to be erratic. Tours are by timed ticket only, and there is limited parking on the site; it's best to use the park-and-ride service from Nailsea.

WELLS

See page 89

WESTBURY WHITE HORSE

🕂 430 G19 🛈 The Library, Edward Street, Westbury BA13 3BD, tel 01373 827158

This huge, awkward-looking depiction of a horse carved on a chalk hillside is the oldest of its kind in Wiltshire. The original Saxon horse—said to have commemorated King Alfred's victory over the Danes at the Battle of Ethandun (Edington) in AD878—was remodelled in 1778 and altered from cart breed to blood breed by a presumptuous Mr. Gee. At the top of the hill is Bratton Castle, a large prehistoric earthwork with a long barrow. Superb views extend far across Wiltshire and Somerset.

WESTONBIRT ARBORETUM

🕂 430 G18 • near Tetbury GL8 8QS ☎ 01666 880220 🕐 Daily 10–8 (or dusk if earlier) 💷 Oct–end Nov: adult £7.50, child (under 18) £1; Mar–end Sep: adult £6.50, child £1; Jan–end Feb: adult £5, child £1 🖥 🍴 🛉 🅿
www.forestry.gov.uk/westonbirt

Worth visiting at any time of year but especially magnificent in autumn, this is among the largest and most diverse collections of trees and shrubs in Europe. The 18,000 trees, set in 240ha (600 acres) of landscaped, wooded grounds crisscrossed with trails (many suitable for visitors in

wheelchairs), were planted from 1829 to the present day and come from all over the world. There is a visitor office with an exhibition and video. Various events are held throughout the year, from concerts to open-air plays in summer to autumn.

WEYMOUTH

🕂 430 G20 • The Esplanade, Weymouth DT4 7AN, tel 01305 785747 🚉 Weymouth
www.weymouth.gov.uk

Once King George III (1738–1820) began visiting this Dorset seaside town in 1789, it soon became a fashionable holiday place. Much of the original character of the town has been retained in its Georgian façades, ironwork balconies and bow windows that characterize the wide Esplanade.

The long arc of golden sand, which offers safe bathing in the sheltered bay, hosts numerous traditional attractions such as Punch and Judy puppet shows. The harbour is a starting point for boat trips and ferries to the Channel Islands, and is overlooked by Brewers Quay, a brewery converted into courtyards and cobbled alleys with attractions and specialist shops. In Barrack Road, Nothe Fort (May–end Sep daily 10.30–5.30; rest of year Sun and public holidays 2.30–5.30) is a huge Victorian fort with coastal views and 70 rooms to explore. **Don't miss** A 15-minute walk (or a train ride from the Esplanade) east along the seafront leads to Lodmoor Country Park (open at all times). These 142ha (350 acres) of parkland include an RSPB (Royal Society for the Protection of Birds) nature reserve and the popular Sea Life aquarium (daily from 10, closing time varies throughout the year).

THE SOUTH EAST AND EAST ANGLIA

Lullingstone Roman Villa, Bignor Roman Villa and Fishbourne Roman Palace suggest that the South East has been Britain's busiest and wealthiest region since the Romans invaded. Stately homes, world-famous university cities and magnificent royal castles constructed since add to the impression of power.

KEY SIGHTS

The 16th-century Moot Hall is Aldeburgh's oldest building

An old-style bus is exhibited at the Amberley Working Museum

The hall at Audley End House prepares visitors for a treat

ALDEBURGH

🕂 432 M17 🛈 152 High Street, Aldeburgh IP15 5AQ, tel 01728 453637 www.suffolkcoastal.gov.uk

Local fishermen still launch their boats here from the shingle beach and sell the day's catch from their huts. The 14th-century Church of St. Peter and St. Paul has a stained-glass window commemorating the composer Benjamin Britten (1913–76), who lived in Aldeburgh from 1947 to 1957. He is buried in the churchyard beside the English tenor Sir Peter Pears (1910–86), his partner and a co-founder of the internationally renowned annual music festival based around Snape Maltings, inland at Snape, each June.

Britten's famous opera, *Peter Grimes,* is based on *The Borough* by the 18th-century Aldeburgh poet George Crabbe (1754–1832) and which was thought to have been set here.

ALFRISTON

🕂 431 L20 🛈 25 Clinton Place, Seaford BN25 1NP, tel 01323 897426 www.sussexcountry.co.uk

Alfriston's high street is a wonderful example of an old Sussex village, with many fine medieval, tile-hung and timber buildings, antiques shops, inns and tea shops. By the church and The Tye (village green) is the first property acquired by the National Trust, the 14th-century thatched Clergy House (Good Fri to mid-Dec Sat–Mon, Wed, Thu; Mar Sat–Sun), purchased in 1896 for £10.

Don't miss Carved on the South Downs, 2 miles (3.5km) north-east of Alfriston, is the Long Man of Wilmington, Europe's largest known representation of the human form. Of unknown date or purpose, the figure stands 70m (235ft) tall.

AMBERLEY WORKING MUSEUM

🕂 431 K19 • Amberley, near Arundel BN18 9LT ☎ 01798 831370 🕓 Mid-Mar to end Mar, May–end Jul, Sep–end Oct Wed–Sun 10–5.30; Apr, Aug daily 10–5.30 🖾 Adult £7.20, child (5–16) £4, family £20 🚇 Amberley ▯ 🏧 🛗 🅿 www.amberleymuseum.co.uk

There's a little bit of everything at this open-air industrial history museum on the site of a former limeworks in the South Downs, covering 150 years of working life in southeast England. On display are a 1920s bus garage, a rural telephone exchange from the 1930s, the Connected Earth exhibition of telecommunications down the ages and the SEEBOARD Electricity Hall, showing a range of domestic appliances from the past. Among the craftspeople at work are a blacksmith and a walking-stick maker.

A narrow-gauge railway and vintage buses travel the length of the museum.

Don't miss Wandering around the thatched village of Amberley.

Geese run free at Arundel's Wildfowl and Wetland Trust

ARUNDEL

🕂 431 K20 🛈 61 High Street, Arundel BN18 1AJ, tel 01903 882268 🚇 Arundel www.sussexbythesea.com

From a distance, Arundel looks rather French, with its castle and spiky Gothic Revival cathedral on a hilltop. The compact, hilly core takes only a few minutes to walk through, but has plenty of brick, flint and timbered architecture to enjoy and antiques shops in which to browse. Arundel Castle (Apr–end Oct Sun–Fri) has been home to the dukes of Norfolk and their ancestors for more than 850 years. Largely rebuilt in Gothic style in the 19th century, it is rich in furnishings and art treasures. Close by is the Roman Catholic Cathedral of Our Lady, completed in 1873. To the north, the River Arun flows through the Wildfowl and Wetland Trust (WWT) Arundel nature reserve (daily), where hundreds of swans, geese and ducks can be observed at close quarters.

ASHDOWN FOREST

🕂 431 K19 🛈 Ashdown Forest Llama Park, Wych Cross, near Forest Row RH18 5JN, tel 01825 712040 www.sussexcountry.co.uk

This former royal hunting ground is the single largest tract of open land in southeast England, and one of the last surviving areas of lowland heath in Europe. The whole area is open to walkers, although the maze of paths can be disorienting. A number of parking areas along the B2026 make good starting points. This was the landscape that inspired the *Winnie the Pooh* stories; the author A. A. Milne (1882–1956) lived nearby, and the sandy tracks, Scots pines and Poohsticks Bridge still closely resemble E. H. Shepherd's (1879–1976) illustrations in the books.

AUDLEY END HOUSE AND GARDENS

🕂 431 L17 • Audley End, Saffron Walden CB11 4JF ☎ 01799 522399 🕓 House: Apr–end Sep Wed–Mon

Beachy Head has a lighthouse to warn ships away from the cliffs

Beaulieu Palace House is a magnificent building

See Venus's head mosaic in the floor at Bignor Roman Villa

12–5 (last admission 4); tours only, Mar and Oct 10–4. Grounds: Apr–end Sep Wed–Sun and public holidays 10–6 (last admission 4); Oct Thu–Mon, 10–5 (last admission 4). Times may vary during summer evening concerts 🚇 Audley End, 1 mile (1.5km) 💷 House and grounds: adult £8.95, child (5–16) £4.50, family £22.40. Grounds only: adult £4.60, child £2.30, family £11.50 🚻 ⚿ 🍴 🅿
www.english-heritage.org.uk

One of England's greatest Jacobean country houses lies just west of Saffron Walden. Built between 1605 and 1614 by Thomas Howard, first Earl of Suffolk, on the scale of a great royal palace, it was reduced in size over the next century, with modifications by architects Sir John Vanbrugh (1664–1726) and Robert Adam (1728–92). James I decided it was 'too large for a king'.

The interior is largely the influence of the third Baron Braybrooke, who inherited the house in 1825 and filled the many rooms (30 are now open to the public) with furnishings and works of art. The gardens and parkland that surround the house were landscaped by Capability Brown (1715–83), with Palladian bridges and temples.
Don't miss The busy medieval market town of Saffron Walden (1 mile/1.5km east), named after the saffron crocuses growing in the surrounding fields, makes a good detour for its timber-framed buildings, turf maze and grand church.

BATEMAN'S

➕ 431 L19 • Burwash, Etchingham TN19 7DS ☎ 01435 882302 🕐 Late Mar–end Oct Sat–Wed, Good Fri 11–5, grounds 5.30 (last admission 4.30) 💷 Adult £5.90, child (5–16) £2.95, family £14.75 ♿ Not good access for wheelchairs 🚻 ⚿ 🍴 🅿
www.nationaltrust.org.uk

The English writer Rudyard Kipling (1865–1936), probably most famous as the author of the two *Jungle Books* (1894–95), made this small Jacobean house his home from 1902 until his death. It remains much as it was when he lived here and is filled with traces of his extraordinary life and work. The magnificent book lined study is where he wrote *Puck of Pook's Hill* (1906) and *Rewards and Fairies* (1910).

The grounds include a mulberry garden, rose garden and a wild garden where a watermill grinds corn into flour most Saturday afternoons.
Don't miss The 1928 Rolls-Royce Phantom, in which Kipling loved to explore the Sussex countryside, is still in the garage.

BEACHY HEAD AND THE SEVEN SISTERS

➕ 431 L20 🛈 Seven Sisters Country Park Visitor Centre, Exceat BN25 4AD (just off A259 between Eastbourne and Seaford), tel 01323 870280
www.sevensisters.org.uk

The high chalk ridge of the South Downs ends at the south coast in spectacular style with a range of dazzling white cliffs at Beachy Head known as the Seven Sisters. Useful starting points are from the visitor office: You can walk out to Cuckmere Haven, the village green at East Dean and Birling Gap, where steps lead to a pebble beach. A path heads along the clifftops, but keep away from the sheer edge, as the cliff can crumble away without warning.

BEAULIEU

➕ 430 H20 • Beaulieu, Brockenhurst SO42 7ZN ☎ 01590 612345 🕐 May–end Sep daily 10–6; rest of year daily 10–5 💷 All sights: adult £15.50, child (5–12) £7.75, youth (13–17) £8.75, family £43 🚻 🍴 ⚿ 🍴 🅿
www.beaulieu.co.uk

Ancestral home of the Montagu family, 16th-century Beaulieu Palace House is best known as the site of the National Motor Museum (or Beaulieu Motor Museum), where 250 vintage vehicles and the Motorsport Gallery celebrate Britain's achievements in the sport.

Beaulieu Palace House contains furniture, paintings, portraits and family memorabilia, and staff in Victorian costume explain domestic life. The estate also includes the remains of a 13th-century Cistercian abbey, housing an exhibition of monastic life.

A high-level monorail transports visitors through the grounds and gardens, or you can explore Beaulieu at ground level by following the Mill Pond Walk.

BIGNOR ROMAN VILLA

➕ 431 J19 • Bignor RH20 1PH ☎ 01798 869259 🕐 Mar–end Apr Tue–Sun, public holidays 10–5; Jun–end Sep daily 10–6; May and Oct daily 10–5 💷 Adult £4.20, child (5–15) £1.80 🚻 ⚿ 🍴 🅿
www.pyrrha.demon.co.uk

Set beneath the South Downs near Bury, Bignor is one of the grandest Roman houses in Britain and one of the largest outside Italy. Occupied between the second and fourth centuries, it was rediscovered in 1811. Within the thatched structures that preserve the villa are spectacular mosaics of the Venus and Cupid Gladiators, the Gorgon Medusa and Zeus's cupbearer, Ganymede. The 25m (80ft) mosaic pavement on the north corridor is the longest on display in Britain. A hole in the floor reveals the hypocaust (underfloor heating system), and the results of other excavations are exhibited in a small museum.

The sheer size and beauty of Blenheim Palace can be appreciated from the landscaped grounds

Those big skies are evident on the Norfolk coast at sunset

THE SIGHTS

BLENHEIM PALACE

⚐ 430 H17 • Woodstock OX20 1PX
☎ 01993 811325 (recording), 01993 811091 ⏲ Palace and gardens: mid-Mar–end Oct daily 10.30–5.30 (last admission 4.45). Park: daily 9–4.45
🎫 House and gardens peak season: adult £13, child £7.50, family £35. Park and gardens: adult £8, child £4, family £20 🍴 ☕ 🏛 👥 🅿
www.blenheimpalace.com

One of the largest private houses in Britain and the ultimate in English baroque was designed by Sir John Vanbrugh (1664–1726) and Nicholas Hawksmoor (1661–1736) and was given by Queen Anne to John Churchill, first Duke of Marlborough (1650–1722), in recognition of his crushing victory over the French at the Battle of Blenheim in 1704. It is still the home of the Churchill family, now occupied by the 11th Duke and his family.

The gilded state rooms overlook lawns and formal gardens laid out by Capability Brown (1715–83). Beautiful Blenheim Lake, spanned by Vanbrugh's Grand Bridge (and it is grand), forms the focal point of the grounds. From the house, look along past the lake to a massive column at the top of which the first duke stands surveying his empire. Also in the grounds are a butterfly house, maze, people-sized games of chess and draughts, and a wooden playground area. A fun miniature railway takes you in brightly painted carriages from the house to the maze and games area.

Don't miss The Churchill Exhibition, a major highlight, is the room where Sir Winston Churchill (1874–1965), Britain's prime minister during World War II, was born on 30 November. He is buried, with his wife, in the village of Bladon nearby.

BODIAM CASTLE

⚐ 432 L19 • Bodiam, near Robertsbridge TN32 5UA ☎ 01580 830436 ⏲ Daily 10–6 (last admission 5), mid-Feb to end Oct; Sat–Sun 10–4 or dusk (last admission 3), rest of year
🎫 Adult £4.40, child (5–16) £2.20, family £11 ☕ 🏛 👥 🅿
www.nationaltrust.org.uk

With its tall drum towers at each corner and walls rising virtually to their original height over a wide, waterlily-filled moat, this substantial ruin recalls a fairytale castle. Bodiam was built by Sir Edward Dalnygrigge in 1385, both as a defence and a comfortable home. There is also a small museum of castle finds with a scale model of Bodiam Castle as it was in 1385.

THE BROADS

⚐ 437 M15 🛈 18 Colegate, Norwich NR3 1BQ, tel 01603 610734
www.broads-authority.gov.uk

Between Norwich and the North Sea coast lie the Broads, a complex of six slow-moving rivers and 41 broads (shallow lakes), providing 122 miles (196km) of navigable waterways. Formed by peat digging in medieval times, this is Britain's largest protected wetland, and the natural habitat of many rare plants and animals. Hiking, angling and birdwatching are all popular activities in the area, but the best way to see the Broads is by boat. The focus of activity is the small town of Wroxham, 8 miles (13km) northeast of Norwich, where boats can be hired.

BROADSTAIRS

⚐ 432 M18 🛈 2 Victoria Parade, Broadstairs CT10 1QL, tel 01843 861232
🚉 Broadstairs
www.broadstairs.gov.uk

With its seven sandy bays, Broadstairs is a bewitching

combination of a sedate, old-fashioned resort and a fishing port with winding streets and ancient fishermen's cottages. Writer Charles Dickens (1812–70) was a regular visitor from 1837. Dickens House Museum (Apr to mid-Oct), on Victoria Parade, was once the home of Mary Pearson Strong, on whom Dickens based the character of Miss Nancy Trotwood for his novel *David Copperfield*. The parlour re-creates the scenes of the book, much as in the original illustrations by H. K. Browne ('Phiz'). The novel was written nearby at Dickens' seafront home, which is now called Bleak House.

THE BURNHAMS

⚐ 437 L15 🛈 Staithe Street, Wells-next-the-Sea NR23 1AN, tel 01328 710885
www.northnorfolk.org/tourism

This scattering of villages with the prefix Burnham lies along the coast of north Norfolk, an area of lonely salt marshes, vast sandy beaches and flint church towers. Burnham Market has a wide village green surrounded by mostly 17th- and 18th-century houses. Burnham Thorpe is famous as the birthplace of Admiral Lord Nelson (1758–1805), the hero of the Battle of Trafalgar. The house was demolished in 1803 and replaced by the present rectory, but All Saints' Church has a marble bust of Nelson. Burnham Overy Staithe is a former port overlooking salt marshes, with a tower windmill beyond.

CAMBRIDGE

See pages 96–97

CANTERBURY

⚐ 432 M19 🛈 12–13 Sun Street, The Buttermarket, Canterbury CT1 2HX, tel 01227 378100 🚉 Canterbury East, Canterbury West
www.canterbury.co.uk

Half-timbered buildings lean over the streets of Canterbury

Much remains of the medieval city that grew up catering to millions of pilgrims who journeyed each year to the shrine of the English saint, Thomas Becket (▷ 29). Becket was murdered in Canterbury Cathedral (where he was Archbishop) in order to please King Henry II, in 1170. The pilgrims' journey was immortalized in *The Canterbury Tales*. The cathedral, approached via the ornate 16th-century Christ Church Gate, dates from around 1070. Its main glory is the 12th- and 13th-century stained glass featuring pilgrim scenes. In the northwest transept a stone marks the spot where Becket died.

Several charitable hospitals founded in medieval times to accommodate pilgrims include Eastbridge Hospital (Mon–Sat; closed Christmas week and Good Fri), 35 High Street. Another example is the Poor Priests' Hospital in Stour Street (daily; closed Sun Oct–May), within which is the Museum of Canterbury (closed Sun Nov–end May, Good Fri and Christmas week), charting 2,000 years of the city's history.

Medieval city walls enclose three sides of Canterbury and its narrow, crooked alleys (notably Mercery Lane) lined with timbered leaning buildings. One of the original 14th-century gates, West Gate (closed Sun, Christmas week and Good Fri), on St. Peter's Street, still survives. The underground Roman Museum (closed Sun during Nov–end May), in Longmarket, houses the remains of a Roman house and re-created interiors.

Don't miss Outside the city are the ruins of St. Augustine's Abbey (daily; Oct–end Mar Wed–Sun), founded in AD597, and burial place of the missionary who brought Christianity to Britain.

Brighton's flamboyant Royal Pavilion was commissioned in 1787

BRIGHTON

Brighton is probably Britain's liveliest seaside resort, raucous but Bohemian, with top arts and clubbing venues and some fanciful Regency architecture.

🚑 431 K20 🛈 Bartholomew Square, Brighton BN1 1JS, tel 0906 7112255 (recording) 01273 292590 🚉 Brighton www.visitbrighton.com

RATINGS	
Good for kids	●●●○
Historic interest	●●●○
Specialist shopping	●●●●●
Walkability	●●●●●

Brighton's reputation for glamour and flamboyance began in the late 18th century when the Prince Regent, later King George IV (1762–1830), first visited and followed his father

TIP
● There is plenty of parking on Madeira Drive, below the esplanade, but otherwise parking in town can be tricky.

in starting a trend for seaside holidays and sea bathing. The Royal Pavilion (daily), the king's astonishing palace (1815–23) in the centre of town, is an oriental extravaganza bristling with Indian-style minarets and onion domes. Its carefully restored interior, famous for its sumptuous decor and elaborate chinoiserie, makes it one of the most extraordinary palaces in Europe. Across the gardens is the former royal stable block, similarly exotic, now housing the Dome concert hall and the Brighton Museum and Art Gallery (closed Mon, except public holidays), with lively exhibits on Brighton's social history, and collections of art nouveau furniture and 20th-century fashion.

CENTRAL HIGHLIGHTS
Brighton had humble beginnings as a fishing village. Behind the elegant sweep of Regency seafront terraces you'll find The Lanes, a warren of narrow streets and alleys with smart antiques, gifts and designer clothing shops, cafés, restaurants and galleries. North Laine, tucked between The Lanes and the station, is crammed with more than 320 shops—selling everything from 1950s kitsch to funky fashions—plus cafés and pubs. And by the train station there's a huge Sunday market with antiques and collectables.

THE SEAFRONT
White stucco buildings create a wonderfully elegant seafront: Lewes Crescent, at the west end, is its grandest moment. Brighton Pier pulsates with seaside amusements. Near the pier are artsy shops, and at weekends during the summer it's a lively area, with street entertainers and beach volleyball. Brighton Sea Life Centre (daily) has an underwater tunnel that allows close viewing of sharks and other marine life.

Cambridge

One of the best university towns in England covers more than 700 years of academic history, and is packed with ancient colleges and other architectural landmarks.

King's College Chapel is famous for its fan-vaulted ceiling

A spectacular sundial, part of popular Queens' College

Fine art lies beyond the entrance to the Fitzwilliam Museum

RATINGS	
Good for kids	● ● ●
Historic interest	● ● ● ● ●
Specialist shopping	● ● ● ●
Walkability	● ● ● ● ●

SEEING CAMBRIDGE

Modern industry may be the first sight of Cambridge as you enter from the flat countryside that surrounds it, so the dense and incongruously beautiful core of this historic city may be a very nice surprise. About half of the university's 30 or so colleges have medieval origins, and are mainly within 10 minutes' walk of each other. You can visit most of them, although some charge an entrance fee, and many are closed while exams are being held.

HIGHLIGHTS

THE COLLEGES

The obvious starting point is King's Parade; climb the tower of the University Church (also known as Great St. Mary's) for a rare high-level view. On one side is the Classical Senate House, where university students receive their degrees, next to Gonville and Caius College (pronounced *keys*—and everyone drops the Gonville part). In the other direction, Market Hill hosts a bustling market (Mon–Sat).

Don't miss King's College Chapel, known throughout Britain for its Chapel Choir, whose annual Christmas Eve carol service attracts crowds who start waiting outside at dawn. It's well worth catching a choral evensong. The chapel was built between 1446 and 1515 under kings Henry VI (1421–71), Henry VII (1457–1509) and Henry VIII (1491–1547). It is perhaps the greatest example of the uniquely English late Gothic Perpendicular style, typified by its wedding-cake fan vaulting that made it the largest single-span vaulted roof of its time. By the altar is Peter Paul Rubens' masterpiece *The Adoration of the Magi*, donated by Major A. E. Allnatt in 1961.

Trinity is the largest college in Cambridge, founded in 1546 by Henry VIII, and its Great Court is the largest of the courtyards at both Cambridge and Oxford universities. One of Trinity's other major features is the Wren Library—designed by Sir Christopher Wren (1632–1723) and completed in 1695—which houses almost 60,000 historic books and manuscripts, including the original manuscript of *Winnie the Pooh* by A. A. Milne (a Trinity student). Trinity's neighbour, and the second-largest college, is St. John's, founded in 1511. Its notable features include the elegant turreted gatehouse, the Bridge of Sighs and the 13th-century School of Pythagoras.

The Corn Exchange is now a place for drinking and relaxing

The best of the rest include: Queens', with its half-timbered Cloister Court and matchstick-like Mathematical Bridge; Emmanuel's garden; Jesus, with cloister-like seclusion and an impressive chapel; and Clare, an elegant Renaissance creation with a stone bridge.

Punting is one (quite difficult) way of getting along The Backs

THE CITY

Among the large stretches of greenery spread around the city are The Backs (the area along the river that gives classic back-door views of Queens', King's, Trinity, Clare and St. John's colleges, and glimpses into their gardens), where you can go punting, Jesus Green and Parker's Piece. Around Jesus Lock are the college boathouses, where you can watch crews rowing on the river, possibly in training for the Oxford v. Cambridge boat race (Mar). Farther away from the city centre, the University Botanic Garden (daily) has mature trees, a scented garden, rockeries and several national collections of species.

Two of Cambridge's best museums are free: The Fitzwilliam Museum (Tue–Sun and some public holiday Mon), in Trumpington Street, has a collection of fine jewellery, porcelain, furniture and glass, paintings by Paul Cézanne, Picasso, Peter Paul Rubens, John Constable and William Blake, watercolours by J. M. W. Turner and prints by Rembrandt. In contrast, intimate little Kettle's Yard (Tue–Sun and public holiday Mon) is a stylish gallery offering a marriage of 18th-century furnishings, antique Oriental rugs and avant-garde art.

FARTHER AFIELD

Out of town, but served by free buses from Cambridge rail station, the Imperial War Museum Duxford (daily) occupies a former military airbase. It has Europe's main collection of military and civil aircraft, plus vehicles, submarines and helicopters. The Normandy Experience re-creates what it was like for an infantryman landing on D-Day, while an innovative building houses the American Air Museum.

Don't miss The Chelsea buns at Fitzbillies' Bakery, 52 Trumpington Street, are famous for being delicious.

BASICS

✚ 436 K17
🏛 The Old Library, Wheeler Street, Cambridge CB2 3QB, tel 0906 586 2526
❓ Walking tours daily, call 01223 457574 for details
🚉 Cambridge

www.visitcambridge.org

TIPS

● Parking is a real problem in the city, so use public transport; or if you come by car, use the park-and-ride service.
● Punting is definitely harder than it looks, and punting traffic jams are a common sight on the River Cam in summer. You can rent a chauffeur at any of the rental places; details from the tourist office.

Chartwell was the beloved home of Churchill for many years

A proud figurehead stands at the prow at Chatham dockyard

There are some delightfully detailed mosaics at Fishbourne

CASTLE RISING

✚ 437 L15 • Castle Rising PE31 6AH
☎ 01553 631330 ◎ Apr–end Oct daily 10–6; rest of year Wed–Sun 10–4
💷 Adult £3.85, child (5–15) £2.20, family £11.50 🚻 ♿ 🅿
www.english-heritage.org.uk

When it was built in the 12th century, Castle Rising was the largest castle in the country. The roof has gone now, but the grand staircase approach survives in good condition and the keep walls stand at their original height. One of its more famous inhabitants was Isabella of France (1292–1358), the queen of England whose son, Edward III (1312–77) locked her up here in 1330 following her part in the murder of his father, her husband Edward II. She is said to still haunt the castle.

CHARTWELL

✚ 431 K19 • Mapleton Road, Westerham TN16 1PS ☎ 01732 868368 (recording), 01732 868381 ◎ Jul–end Aug Tue–Sun and public holidays 11–5 (last admission 4.15); late Mar–end Jun, Sep–end Oct Wed–Sun and public holidays 11–5 (last admission 4.15)
💷 House, garden and studio: adult £8, child (5–16) £4, family £20. Garden and studio: adult £4, child £2, family £10
🍴 🎁 ♿ 🅿
www.nationaltrust.org.uk

This Victorian house was the country home of Britain's prime minister during World War II, Sir Winston Churchill (1874–1965), from 1924 until his death. The rooms look as if he has just stepped outside: there are books, maps, pictures, photographs and personal belongings, including hats, uniforms and Churchill's famous cigars. He and his wife, Lady Clementine Spencer-Churchill, added several features to the grounds, including a small lake and Churchill's studio, where he loved to paint. The studio is still full of his works, some of which display a definite talent. He said he gained great strength from painting and it helped to combat his 'Black Dog' depressions.

Don't miss The playhouse in the garden, created by Churchill for his children, shows the delight he took in his family; Lady Churchill's Rose Garden and the Golden Rose Walk are both a treat for rose lovers.

CHATHAM HISTORIC DOCKYARD

✚ 432 L18 • Dock Road, Chatham ME4 4TZ ☎ 01634 823807 (recording), 01634 823800 ◎ Mid-Feb to end Oct 10–6; Nov, early Feb Sat, Sun 10–4
💷 Adult £10, child (5–16) £6.50, family £26.50 🚆 Chatham, 1 mile (1.5km) 🍴 🚻 🎁 ♿ 🅿
www.chdt.org.uk

Chatham is the world's most complete dockyard to survive from the age of sail and was once England's most important naval dock. It closed in 1984 to become a working museum. In dry dock are three battleships, while the Wooden Walls exhibition re-creates the sights, sounds and smells of the Royal Dockyard from 1758. Inside the working Ropery, traditional techniques are used to make rope to rig the world's greatest sailing ships.

The Museum of the Royal Dockyard celebrates 400 years of the history of Chatham and the Royal Navy.

Don't miss A river cruise on the paddlesteamer *Kingswear Castle* (Jul–end Sep).

CHICHESTER

✚ 431 J20 ℹ 29A South Street, Chichester PO19 1AH, tel 01243 775888 🚆 Chichester
www.chichester.gov.uk

This small, pleasant city still has its original Roman street plan, with two main routes crossing west to east and north to south, enclosed by remains of the city wall (itself partly rebuilt in medieval times). A 16th-century market cross marks the central point. Close by, the cathedral, smaller than most, is early Norman in style, with Early English additions, and has an unusual detached belfry, a tapestry by English artist John Piper (1903–92) and stained glass by the French painter Marc Chagall (1887–1985).

During the 18th century, Chichester was enhanced by such buildings as Pallant House (closed Mon except public holidays), now a museum with an outstanding collection of British modern art.

Just west of the city is Fishbourne Roman Palace (Feb to mid-Dec daily; rest of year Sat–Sun), the largest known Roman residence in Britain, built around AD75. Much of the villa has been excavated and several rooms have been built over the museum to protect the delicate remains from the weather. The palace has the largest collection of in-situ mosaics in Britain and a Roman garden replanted to the original first-century plan.

CHILTERN OPEN AIR MUSEUM

✚ 431 J18 • Newland Park, Gorelands Lane, Chalfont St. Giles HP8 4AB
☎ 01494 872163 (recording), 01494 871117 ◎ Late Mar–end Oct daily 10–5 (last admission 4) 💷 Adult £6.50, child (5–16) £4, family £18.50 🚆 🎁 ♿ 🅿
www.coam.org.uk

More than 30 historic buildings dating from around 1500 to the 1950s have been rescued from demolition and re-erected here on the outskirts of Chalfont St. Giles. There are houses, barns, granaries, an apple store, forge,

An ancient barn still looks steady at Chiltern Open Air Museum

factory, toll house, sports pavilion, an Edwardian cast-iron public toilet and a mission hall, each appropriately furnished. Hands-on activities include brickmaking, straw plaiting and rag rugmaking.

Don't miss High Wycombe Toll House is a three roomed house built in 1826 for the collector of tolls on the London to Oxford road at High Wycombe, 9 miles (14km) east of Chalfont St. Giles.

DOWN HOUSE

🔠 431 K18 • Luxted Road, Downe BR6 7JT ☎ 01689 859119 🕐 Apr–end Sep Wed–Sun, public holidays 10–6; Oct Wed–Sun 10–5; Nov–late Dec and early Feb–end Apr Wed–Sun 10–4. Call to reserve during Aug if arriving by car 💷 Adult £6.60, child (5–16) £3.30, family £16.50 🔲 🔳 🔳 🅿

Charles Darwin (1809–82), one of the most influential scientists of modern times, occupied Down House from 1842 until his death. On the ground floor, the drawing room, dining room, billiard room and study have been furnished and decorated to portray the domestic daily life of his family. In the study are his writing desk and chair, where he wrote the ground-breaking *On the Origin of Species by Means of Natural Selection* (published in 1859), along with some of the 5,000 objects associated with his research. On the first floor is an exhibition covering Darwin's life and work.

ELY

🔠 437 L16 🛈 Oliver Cromwell's House, 29 St. Mary's Street, Ely CB7 4HF, tel 01353 662062 🚊 Ely www.ely.org.uk

Dwarfing the old-fashioned town that huddles on a rise in the flat farmlands of the Fens, Ely Cathedral dates from the 11th

Dover Castle was known as the Key to England under Henry III

DOVER CASTLE

England's oldest fortress, whose history spans the Iron Age to the Cold War.

🔠 432 M19 • Dover CT16 1HU ☎ 01304 201628 (recording), 01304 211067 🕐 Apr–end Sep daily 10–6, Oct 10–5; Nov–end Mar daily 10–4 💷 Including Secret Wartime Tunnels: adult £8.95, child (5–16) £4.50, family £22.40 🚊 Dover Priory, 1.5 miles (2.5km) 🛈 Tours of Secret Wartime Tunnels last about 50 min (last tour 1 hour before closing) for up to 30 people; first-come, first-served. Interactive audio tours (separate tour for battlement walk) in English, French, German and Japanese: £1.50 🔳 🔲 🔳 👫 🅿 Visitors with disabilities may use Palace Green parking area next to keep www.english-heritage.org.uk

RATINGS	
Good for kids	●●●○
Historic interest	●●●●●
Photo stops	●●●●●
Value for money	●●●○

TIP

● Reserve the Secret Wartime Tunnels tour as soon as you arrive, especially in summer.

On clear days you can see the coast of France from this giant fortress, perched on the famous White Cliffs and commanding the shortest sea crossing between England and the Continent. The castle's maze of tunnels, created for defence during the Napoleonic Wars (1800–15), reveal a fascinating secret world from the darkest days of World War II.

No fortress in England can claim a longer history than Dover Castle. Within the ramparts of an Iron Age fort, the Romans built a lighthouse, which still stands, while in the Saxon period the earthworks were re-used for a town. The Church of St. Mary in Castro within the castle walls is one of the most complete Saxon churches in southern England.

The Norman keep, built in the 1180s, houses two exhibitions that highlight the castle's key role when the country was under threat of invasion. The 1216 Siege Experience retraces how a group of rebel barons invited Prince Louis of France to invade England and take the throne from King John. A Castle Fit for a King covers preparations for Henry VIII's visit to Dover in 1539. The castle saw dramatic action during World War II. In 1940 it was from the underground tunnels here that Vice Admiral Ramsay and Prime Minister Sir Winston Churchill masterminded the evacuation from Dunkirk of 388,000 troops in Operation Dynamo. The tour of the Secret Wartime Tunnels re-creates Britain at war through sounds, smells and archive film clips. The lights dim, the drone of bombers can be heard overhead and the sound of people at work fills the Anti-Aircraft Operations Room, the Telephone Exchange and Repeater Station.

Ely Cathedral's imposing West Tower dominates the town

Flowers of every hue welcome you to the gardens of Great Dixter

Hampton Court is crowned with a huge clock and bell tower

THE SIGHTS

century. The east end was rebuilt in Purbeck marble around 1250, while the collapse of the tower in 1322 necessitated the erection of the breathtakingly delicate lantern tower, lodged on eight oak pillars. In the cathedral precinct is the prestigious King's School, founded by Henry VIII. Combined tickets are available for the cathedral, the attached Stained Glass Museum (daily) and Ely Museum (daily), an absorbing local collection in the Old Gaol in Market Street. Also included is Oliver Cromwell's House (daily), the former home in St. Mary's Street of the man who defeated Charles I and became leader of the country as Lord Protector in 1653 (▷ 32). **Don't miss** The riverfront on the Ouse is particularly attractive.

EXBURY GARDENS AND STEAM RAILWAY

➕ 430 H20 • Exbury SO45 1AZ ☎ 023 8089 9422 (recording), 023 8089 1203 🕐 Daily 10–5.30, early Mar–early Nov 💷 Mid-Mar to mid-Jun (depending on flowering season): adult £7, child (3–15) £1.50; train £3. Rest of year: adult £5, child £1; train £2.50 🍴 🚻 👪 🅿
www.exbury.co.uk

One of the world's finest displays of rhododendrons, azaleas and camellias lies within this wonderful 80ha (200-acre) landscaped woodland garden on the east bank of the Beaulieu River. Created by the English collector and taxonomist Lionel de Rothschild (1882–1942) in the 1920s, this is a garden for all seasons. Come in early spring to see magnolias and camellias in bloom and the daffodil meadow a carpet of shimmering gold. Mid-spring brings rhododendrons and vibrant azaleas. The rose garden and herbaceous gardens are at their best in the summer, while autumn features displays

of colour from Japanese maples, deciduous azaleas and flourishing dogwoods.

FELBRIGG HALL

➕ 437 M15 • Felbrigg, near Norwich NR11 8PR ☎ 01263 837444 🕐 House: late Mar–end Oct Sat–Wed 1-5. Garden: late Mar to mid-Jul and Sep–end Oct Sat–Wed 11–5; mid-Jul to end Aug daily 11–5 💷 Adult £6.60, child (5–16 £3.10, family £16.20 🍴 🛍 🚻 🅿
www.nationaltrust.org.uk

In the tranquil countryside of Norfolk is one of the great 17th-century houses of East Anglia. It was begun in the 1620s by a lawyer, Frances Windham, whose grandson William made modifications and filled the rooms with pictures (including many seascapes) he had acquired on a Grand Tour of Italy. Intricate plaster ceilings and a fine library are further high notes of the interior, while outside the walled garden contains a fully functioning dovecote and the National Collection of Colchicums. There is free access to the large estate, where waymarked trails thread their way past venerable trees. **Don't miss:** The nearby 15th-century parish church, standing all alone: it has box pews, memorial brasses and interesting family monuments.

GREAT DIXTER

➕ 432 L19 • Northiam TN31 6PH ☎ 01797 252878 🕐 House and gardens: Apr–end Oct Tue–Sun, plus bank-holiday Mondays, 2-5. Gardens open from 11am Sun, Mon during bank-holiday weekends 💷 House and gardens: adult £7.50, child £3. Gardens only: adult £6, child £2.50 🛍 Garden centre 🚻 🅿
www.greatdixter.co.uk

The highly respected gardening author Christopher Lloyd (1922–2006) created one of

the most experimental, exciting and constantly evolving gardens of our time at Great Dixter. Yew topiary, riotous mixed borders, an exuberant Exotic Garden, carpets of meadow flowers, formal pool and natural ponds contribute to the overall effect. The house, Lloyd's birthplace and home, dates from around 1450, but was restored and enlarged by architect Sir Edwin Lutyens (1869–1944) in 1912. **Don't miss** The Long Border in midsummer.

HAMPTON COURT PALACE

➕ 431 K18 • Hampton Court, East Molesey KT8 9AU ☎ 0870 752 7777 (recording), 020 8781 9500 🕐 Late Mar–late Oct daily 10–6; rest of year daily 10–4.30. Last admission 1 hr before closing. Gardens: 7am–dusk 💷 Adult £12, child (5–16) £7.80, family £35; tickets £1 less if booked online 🚉 Hampton Court 🍴 🛍 🏛 🚻 🅿
www.hrp.org.uk

This magnificent Tudor palace on the banks of the River Thames was begun in 1514 as a country residence for Thomas Wolsey (c1475–1530), Lord Chancellor and cardinal to Henry VIII. Fourteen years later, Wolsey presented it to the king, and for centuries it was home to British monarchs. The palace is a mix of styles—extensive Tudor buildings have late17th-century baroque additions by Sir Christopher Wren. Costumed guides and audio tours lead the way through corridors, grand apartments, lavish bedrooms and vast kitchens that remain much as they were when in use. In summer you can arrive by riverboat from Westminster (tel: 020 7930 2062), Richmond or Kingston-upon-Thames (tel: 020 8546 2434). **Don't miss** The Maze, planted in 1690, and fiendishly frustrating.

The gatehouse at Battle Abbey, near Hastings, was added in 1338

Hever Castle can tell a tale or two about the Boleyn family

Holkham Hall hides a wealth of artworks and rich furnishings

HASTINGS

➕ 432 L20 🛈 Queens Square, Priory Meadow, Hastings TN34 1TL, tel 0800 18106 (recording), 01424 781111 🚉 Hastings **www.visithastings.com**

Forever associated with the Norman invasion, Hastings is a mix of faded seaside resort and attractive fishing port. The old town, a labyrinth of narrow streets, lies east of the centre. The Victorian East Hill Cliff Railway (summer daily 10–5.30; rest of year daily 11–4) climbs to the sandstone cliffs for coastal walks to Fairlight Cove. Across the valley, the Norman ruins of Hastings Castle (daily) crown West Hill. **Don't miss** The site of the 1066 Battle of Hastings, at Battle, where Battle Abbey (daily) marks the spot of the Norman victory (▷ 28).

HATFIELD HOUSE

➕ 431 K18 • Hatfield AL9 5NQ ☎ 01707 287010 🕐 House: Easter Sat–end Sep Sat–Wed 12–4 (guided tours only Mon except public holidays). Park and West Gardens: daily 11–5.30. East Gardens: Mon 11–5.30 💷 House, park and gardens: adult £8, child (5–15) £4, family £22. Park and gardens: adult £4.50, child £3.50. Park only: adult £2, child £1 🚉 Hatfield 🍽 🎁 Garden centre and shop ♿ 🅿 **www.hatfield-house.co.uk**

A sumptuous 1611 Jacobean house, Hatfield was the childhood home of Queen Elizabeth I (▷ 31). It stands on the site of the Royal Palace of Hatfield, of which a wing survives. Inside are magnificent state rooms, furniture, tapestries and paintings. Historic mementoes collected over the years by the Cecils, residents for 400 years, include the national collection of model soldiers. **Don't miss** The Grand Staircase, a superb example of Jacobean craftsmanship.

HEVER CASTLE AND GARDENS

➕ 431 K19 • Hever, near Edenbridge TN8 7NG ☎ 01732 865224 🕐 Castle: Mar–end Oct daily 12–6; Nov 12–5. Gardens only: Mar–end Oct daily 11–6; Nov 11–5. Last admission 1 hour before closing 💷 Castle and gardens: adult £9.20, child (5–14) £5, family £23.40. Gardens only: adult £7.30, child £4.00, family £19.40 🚉 Hever 🍽 🎁 🎒 🎒 🅿 **www.hevercastle.co.uk**

A part doubled-moated 13th-century castle and part Tudor manor house, Hever Castle was the childhood home of Henry VIII's second wife, Anne Boleyn (1501–36). She lived here with her family until she married the king in 1533 (▷ 31).

The castle owes much of its present appearance to lavish early 20th-century renovations by American-born British newspaper magnate William Waldorf Astor (1848–1919), who bought the castle and added mock medieval features and an entire neo-Tudor village behind it for servants and guests. In the gatehouse is an alarming array of instruments of discipline, torture and execution. The Astor family adorned the grounds with formal Tudor, rose and Italian gardens, yew topiary in the form of chessmen, a yew maze and a water maze.

HIGHCLERE CASTLE

➕ 430 H19 • near Newbury RG20 9RN ☎ 01635 253204 (recording), 01635 253210 🕐 Jul–end Aug Mon–Fri 11–4; please call for times for rest of year (last admission 1 hour before closing). Subject to occasional closure; check in advance 💷 Castle and gardens: adult £7.50, child (4–15) £3.60, family £18. Gardens and grounds only: free 🛈 Annual season ticket £25 🍽 🎒 🎒 🎒 🅿 **www.highclerecastle.co.uk**

This great 19th-century house was designed in the 1830s by Sir Charles Barry (1795–1860), one of the architects of the Houses of Parliament in London. The interiors, a heady blend of Gothic, Moorish and rococo influences, are filled with treasures that include items of Tutankhamun's treasure, found in 1922 by the fifth Earl of Carnarvon and Howard Carter when they discovered his tomb. The present (eighth) earl is the Queen's horseracing manager, and the Horseracing Exhibition celebrates Highclere's 100-year association with the sport. Within the grounds are walled gardens and an orangery.

HOLKHAM HALL

➕ 437 L15 • Holkham, near Wells-next-the-Sea NR23 1AB ☎ 01328 710227 🕐 Jun–end Sep Thu–Mon 1–5 (last admission 4.30); Easter and public holidays in May and Aug Sun–Mon 12–5 (last admission 4.30). Park: all year 💷 Hall: adult £6.50, child £3.25. Bygones Museum: adult £5, child £2.50. Hall and Bygones Museum: adult £10, child £5, combined family ticket £25. Park: free 🍽 🎒 🎒 🅿 **www.holkham.co.uk**

Built between 1734 and 1764 by the agriculturalist Thomas Coke (1697–1759), first Earl of Leicester, and home to seven generations of his family, this is regarded as one of the greatest examples of the English Palladian style. Beyond its austere, grey façade lies a treasure house of ancient statues, furnishings and paintings by Peter Paul Rubens, Anthony Van Dyck, Thomas Gainsborough and others. The Bygones Museum (Easter, early May–end Oct Thu–Tue 10–5.30), housed in the stable block, is packed with more than 4,000 domestic and agricultural objects, ranging from Victorian money boxes to vintage cars.

The National Trust has restored the secluded Ightham Mote

The Needles are a distinctive landmark on the Isle of Wight

The celebrated writer Jane Austen wrote three novels in Chawton

HOUGHTON HALL

➕ 437 L15 • Houghton, near King's Lynn PE31 6UE ☎ 01485 528569 🅾 Park, grounds, soldier museum and walled garden: Wed, Thu, Sun and public holidays 11–5.30. House: late Mar–late Sep Wed, Thu, Sun and public holidays 2–5.30 (last admission 4.30) 🎟 Adult £7, child (5–16) £3, family £16. Excluding house: adult £4.50, child £2 🔲 🏛 🚻 🅿
www.houghtonhall.com

Britain's first prime minister, Sir Robert Walpole (1676–1745) had this Palladian mansion built in the 1720s. The work of architects James Gibb, Colen Campbell and others is complemented by the elaborate interior decoration of William Kent. Bedrooms are decorated in the style of ancient Rome, while the magnificent two-storey hall was inspired by the hall in the Queen's House in Greenwich. In the north office wing the Cholmondeley Soldier Museum has about 20,000 models.

IGHTHAM MOTE

➕ 431 L19 • Ightham, Ivy Hatch, Sevenoaks TN15 0NT ☎ 01732 811145 (recording), 01732 810378 🅾 House and gardens: late Mar–end Oct Wed–Fri, Sun–Mon 10–5.30. Estate: dawn–dusk 🎟 Adult £7, child (5–16) £3.50, family £17.50 🍴 🔲 🏛 🚻 🅿
www.nationaltrust.org.uk

Part of the pleasure of visiting this moated manor house is touring through the woods of the Weald of Kent. The half-timbered building dates from 1330 but its main features span many centuries. The Great Hall is the oldest room, while the chapel is Tudor, the drawing room has a Jacobean fireplace and the billiard room is unmistakably Victorian.

In fine weather there is access to the tower for views of the estate that offers secluded walks through woodland and farmland.

ISLE OF WIGHT

➕ 430 H20 🅸 81–83 Union Street, Ryde PO33 2LW, tel 01983 813818 🅿 (to catch ferry) Portsmouth Harbour, Southampton, Lymington Pier 📧 Wightlink ☎ 0870 582 7744, Hovertravel ☎ 01983 811000, Red Funnel Ferries ☎ 0870 444 8898
www.wightlink.co.uk
www.hovertravel.co.uk
www.redfunnel.co.uk
www.islandbreaks.co.uk

A spectacular coastline, a wide range of family attractions and a mild climate make the Isle of Wight a popular holiday destination. You can leave your car on the mainland as the island has excellent public transport.

THE WEST

Scenery varies from the lonely marshes of the north coast to the southern landslipped cliffs around St. Catherine's Point. The best viewpoint of all is Tennyson Down, named after the 19th-century poet who lived nearby; a path leads along the ridge to the cliff end above the chalk pinnacles known as The Needles. At Alum Bay a chairlift descends to the beach for close-up views of multihued sand cliffs. On the north coast, Yarmouth is a characterful port with whitewashed cottages and a castle.

THE EAST

This area includes a string of quiet resorts—Ryde, Sandown, Shanklin and Ventnor, with golden sands, calm waters and esplanades. In Ventnor's balmy climate, subtropical species flourish in the Ventnor Botanic Garden (daily). Southeast of the yachting resort of Cowes (which hosts a famous regatta each August) is Osborne House (daily), Queen Victoria's Italianate seaside retreat, which she had built between 1845 and 1851.

Outside the island's capital, Newport, Carisbrooke Castle (daily) is an impressive Norman ruin, where you can still see the treadwheel that prisoners were forced to walk to draw water from the well; later, donkey power was used instead. **Don't miss** Godshill and Shorwell, two of the island's most striking thatched villages.

JANE AUSTEN'S HOUSE

➕ 431 J19 • Chawton, Alton GU34 1SD ☎ 01420 83262 🅾 Mar–end Nov daily 11–4; rest of year Sat–Sun 11–4 🎟 Adult £4.50, child (8–18) £1 🏛 🚻 🅿 Close by
www.janeaustenmuseum.org.uk

In the middle of the village of Chawton is the red-brick 17th-century house in which novelist Jane Austen (1775–1817) lived with her mother and sister Cassandra during her most prolific writing years, from 1807 to 1817. Here she revised *Sense and Sensibility*, *Pride and Prejudice* and *Northanger Abbey*, and wrote *Mansfield Park*, *Emma* and *Persuasion*. The house, which has been restored to its appearance in the early 1800s, is full of family belongings, including manuscripts, Jane's writing table and even her comb.

KNEBWORTH HOUSE

➕ 431 K17 • Knebworth SG3 6PY ☎ 01438 812661 🅾 Times vary widely and are subject to change during special events—call for details 🎟 All attractions: adult £9, child (4–16) £8.50, family £31. Gardens and park: adult £7, child £7, family £24, season ticket £32 🅿 Knebworth 🔲 🏛 🚻 🅿
www.knebworthhouse.com

The country park has a maze, state-of-the-art adventure playground, deer park, gardens designed by Sir Edwin Lutyens (1869–1944) and a herb garden

The Banqueting Hall at Knebworth House would improve any meal

Leeds Castle, sitting on its pretty islands, was once a residence of Henry VIII but now hosts sports events and conferences

designed by Gertrude Jekyll (1843–1932). Since 1974 it has hosted major open-air rock concerts. The house dates from Tudor times but was embellished in 1843 by Victorian novelist Sir Edward Bulwer Lytton into the high Gothic fantasy seen today.

KNOLE

➕ 431 L19 • Sevenoaks TN15 0RP ☎ 01732 450608 (recording), 01732 462100 🕙 House: late Mar–end Oct Wed–Sun and public holidays 12–4. Garden: late Mar–late Oct Wed 11–4. Park: daily 🅿 House: adult £7.50, child (5–16) £3.75, family £18.75. Garden: adult £2, child £1 🚉 Sevenoaks, 1.5 miles (2.5km) 🍴 🚻 🅿
www.nationaltrust.org.uk

England's largest country house has curious vital statistics: 365 rooms (one for each day of the year), 52 corridors (one for each week) and seven courtyards (one for each day of the week). The original 15th-century house was extended and remodelled by the first Earl of Dorset in 1603 with trademark Jacobean curly gables and tall chimneys. It has been the Sackville family home since 1603 and was the birthplace of author Vita Sackville-West (1892–1962) and the setting of Virginia Woolf's (1882–1941) novel *Orlando* (1928). Its 13 sumptuous state rooms, decorated in the early 17th century, have furniture, tapestries and paintings, and even an early royal toilet.
Don't miss The walk around the free deer park to see these elegant animals.

LAYER MARNEY TOWER

➕ 432 L17 • Layer Marney CO5 9US ☎ 01206 330784 🕙 Apr–early Oct Sun–Thu 12–5 🅿 Adult £3.50, child (3–16) £2, family £10 🚉 Colchester 🍴 🚻 🅿
www.layermarneytower.co.uk

Layer Marney Tower, an astonishing sight in the quiet Essex countryside, is the tallest Tudor gatehouse in the country, built by Henry, first Lord Marney, in the early 16th century. Unfortunately the grand architectural scheme, including a courtyard that would have rivalled Hampton Court Palace (▷ 100), was never completed, and all that stands is one of four sides. Within the grounds are the parish church and a medieval barn where farm animals roam.
Don't miss The wildlife walk passes a large herd of red deer and other livestock.

LEEDS CASTLE

➕ 432 L19 • near Maidstone ME17 1PL ☎ 0870 600 8880 (recording), 01622 765400 🕙 Apr–end Oct daily 11–5; rest of year daily 10.15–3.30 🅿 Adult £13, child (4–15) £9, family £39 🚉 Bearsted 🍴 🛍 🚻 Shop, garden centre 🚻 🅿
www.leeds-castle.com

Set on two islands in the middle of a lake and rising dream-like above its own watery reflection, Leeds Castle was originally a Norman stronghold and was a royal residence from 1278 to 1552, for no fewer than six medieval queens. It was fortified and enlarged by a series of royal incumbents and became a firm favourite of Henry VIII and his first queen, Catherine of Aragon (1485–1536). The landscaped grounds consist of formal gardens, including the English-cottage-style Culpeper Garden and Mediterranean-style Lady Baillie Garden, a maze leading to a secret grotto, a vineyard and an aviary.
Don't miss The unusual Dog Collar Museum (same hours as castle), with a collection dating back more than 400 years.

LULLINGSTONE ROMAN VILLA

➕ 431 L18 • Lullingstone Lane, Eynsford, Dartford DA4 0JA ☎ 01322 863467 🕙 Apr–end Sep daily 10–6; Oct–end Nov, Feb–end Mar daily 10–4; Dec–end Jan Wed–Sun 10–4 🅿 Adult £3.70, child (5–16) £2.80 🚉 Eynsford, 0.75 mile (1km) 🍴 🅿
www.english-heritage.org.uk

Possibly the luxury summer house of an important Roman official, the villa's mostly fourth-century remains include painted walls and fine mosaic floors. In around AD390, Lullingstone's occupiers converted to Christianity and installed a chapel in one of the rooms. This is one of the first surviving Christian chapels in England. The free interactive audio tour paints the picture of the occupants. Combine this with a visit to Lullingstone Castle close by (Sat–Sun and public holidays, May–end Aug), a Tudor and Queen Anne family mansion.

MARWELL ZOOLOGICAL PARK

➕ 430 H19 • Colden Common, near Winchester SO21 1JH ☎ 07626 943163 (recording), 01962 777407 🕙 Late Mar–late Oct daily 10–6; rest of year 10–4 🅿 Adult £12, child (3–14) £8.50, family £39 🚉 Winchester 🍴 🛍 🚻 🅿
www.marwell.org.uk

Marwell is a conservation and breeding centre for endangered species. In the parkland live over 200 species of animal and bird including rhinos, hippos, giraffes, zebras, tigers, jaguars, cheetahs and monkeys. Tropical World, World of Lemurs and Night Life are popular exhibits. Attractions for children include a miniature railway, adventure playground, and an area where animals can be touched.
Don't miss Use the frequent road train for larger distances.

Oxford

Oxford rivals Cambridge as one of the world's foremost university towns, with 39 colleges and Britain's oldest library. It's also a hotbed of interesting buildings and has some pretty riverside walks.

Rowing is a big part of student life in Oxford

Is the Radcliffe Camera Britain's most attractive library?

Tradition says morris dancers must dance on May Day

SEEING OXFORD

Enclosed by the rivers Cherwell and Thames, Oxford is a beautiful city of honey-coloured Cotswold stone. This world-famous seat of learning is a compact historic city and easily explored on foot. The university's colleges stand in cloistered seclusion and can be hard to identify as they are not clearly signed, but between them display a wonderful array of ancient, Classical and modern architecture. Don't miss the back lanes and alleys, particularly Merton Street/Oriel Street, and Queen's Lane/New College Lane (leading beneath the Bridge of Sighs; just off here the Turf Tavern is a popular students' pub). The high street, known as The High, runs from Carfax Tower east to Magdalen Bridge over the River Cherwell, dividing the city into north and south.

HIGHLIGHTS

VIEWS OVER THE CITY

At the beginning of a visit to Oxford, it's a good idea to get your bearings from the rooftops. You can climb the tower of St. Michael's Church in Cornmarket Street, the city's oldest building. Or survey the city from Carfax Tower, a remnant of the 14th-century St. Martin's Church, at the busy crossroads known as Carfax, the city's focal point. Another excellent vantage point is the University Church of St. Mary the Virgin, High Street, dating from 1280. This parish church also serves the university and for a time was the university's reference library and venue for degree ceremonies. Climb the 27m (90ft) tower to the external viewing gallery. It also served as a courtroom for the trials of bishops Latimer, Ridley and Cranmer in 1555–56: They were found guilty of heresy and were burned at the stake in Broad Street: 100m (110yd) away you will find the Martyrs' Memorial commemorating the event.

TIPS

● Visit in term-time for the real student atmosphere.
● Come by public transport or use the park and-ride services from the outer ring roads.
● They may look private, but you can visit many colleges; some have a small admission charge.
● City Sightseeing hop-on, hop-off open-top buses give a useful overview with live commentary.

The University Museum (left) has natural history exhibits such as dinosaur skeletons

PITT-RIVERS MUSEUM AND UNIVERSITY MUSEUM

➕ 107 B1 • Parks Road OX1 3PP
☎ 01865 270927 ◷ Daily 12–4.30

This cavernously old-fashioned museum is an anthropology collection of more than 250,000 objects—among them masks and shrunken heads. Or just admire the Victorian Gothic architecture.

Balliol College and bicycles are quintessentially Oxford

CHRIST CHURCH

➕ 107 B3 • St. Aldates OX1 1DP ☎ 01865 286573 ◷ College: Term time Mon–Sat 10.30–11.45 and 2.30–4.30, Sun 3–4.30; out of term Mon–Sat 9–4.30, Sun 1–4.30. Picture Gallery: Apr–end Sep Mon–Sat 10.30–5, Sun 2–5; Oct–end Mar Mon–Sat 10.30–1, 2–4.30

Founded in 1524, Oxford's largest and most visited college has the biggest quadrangle, and its chapel, Christ Church Cathedral (predating the college), is England's smallest cathedral. Within the Great Hall you will find features from the *Alice in Wonderland* stories written by former don Charles Dodgson, better known as Lewis Carroll (1832–98), while Ante Hall became Hogwarts Hall in the *Harry Potter* movies.

Christ Church Picture Gallery is the only public gallery in any college in either Oxford or Cambridge, and has a collection of 300 paintings, with Italian Old Masters—among them Tintoretto, Leonardo da Vinci, Michelangelo and Carracci—being well represented.

THE RIVERS THAMES AND CHERWELL

➕ 107 B3, C3

These waterways slice through remarkably verdant land close to central Oxford. The tree-lined Cherwell (pronounced *charwell*) is the place for punting and provides almost rural views of Magdalen College

MUSEUM OF OXFORD

➕ 107 B2 • Town Hall Building, St. Aldates OX1 1DZ ☎ 01865 252254 ◷ Tue–Fri 10–4, Sat 10–5, Sun 12–4

This museum gives a succinct survey of the city from prehistoric times to the present, from mammoths to Morris Motors. It has archaeological finds, including a Roman pottery kiln, paintings and furniture from houses in Oxford, and re-created interiors such as a Victorian kitchen and a student's college room.

THE OXFORD STORY

➕ 107 B2 • 6 Broad Street OX1 3AJ ☎ 01865 728822 ◷ Jan–end Jun, Sep–Dec Mon–Sat 10–4.30, Sun 11–4.30; Jul–end Aug daily 9.30–5

For a wackier look at the past, sit at a desk and take a ride through re-created tableaux of great events and famous faces from the past 900 years.

MODERN ART OXFORD

➕ 107 B2 • 30 Pembroke Street OX1 1BP ☎ 01865 722733 ◷ Tue–Sat 10–5, Sun 12–5

This stylish gallery occupies a former brewery and is free of charge. It has changing exhibitions of contemporary art from Britain and beyond, as well as talks, live music and children's activities, plus a café selling very good cakes, and a shop.

(pronounced *mordlin*), one of the richest and most spacious colleges, founded in 1458 and set in its own deer park—walks through here are really stunning. University rowing crews train on the Thames (also known here as the Isis). Stroll through the Oxford Botanic Garden, founded in 1621 and the oldest of its kind in Britain, to Christchurch Meadow and the confluence of the rivers, or rent a punt or rowing boat from Magdalen Bridge or the Cherwell Boathouse in Bardwell Road.

RADCLIFFE SQUARE

➕ 107 C2 • Between Broad Street and High Street ☎ Sheldonian Theatre: 01865 277299. Bodleian Library: 01865 277000 ◷ Sheldonian Theatre: daily 10–12.30, 2–4.30. Bodleian Library: guided tours Mar–end Oct Mon–Fri 10.30, 11.30, 2, 3; Sat 10.30, 11.30

This is an eye-catching architectural group belonging to the university. The Sheldonian Theatre (built between 1664 and 1668) was the first major architectural work by architect Sir Christopher Wren, who was Professor of Astronomy at the time. The interior assumes the shape of a Roman theatre and its grand ceremonial hall is used for university functions and concerts. High above, the cupola is an excellent viewpoint. Close by, the Bodleian Library is one of six copyright libraries in the UK, entitled to receive a copy of every book published in the country. The circular domed Radcliffe Camera of 1737–49, designed by James Gibbs, is a reading room for the library.

ASHMOLEAN MUSEUM

➕ 107 B2 • Beaumont Street ☎ 01865 278000 ◷ Tue–Sat 10–5 and public holidays (Jun–end Aug Thu to 7.30), Sun 12–5 (except Cast Gallery); closed during St. Giles' Fair early Sep

Britain's oldest public museum (opened in 1683), the Ashmolean houses Oxford University's priceless collections from the time of early man to the 20th century. Come here to see material about early cultures in Europe, Egypt and the Near East, and an antiquities department covering everything from the Stone Age to Victorian times.

On a separate site in Beaumont Street, the Cast Gallery has a staggering 100,000 casts (not all on show at one time), which together give a privileged overview of Classical sculpture. The University Museum nearby has fascinating collections on natural history (▷ opposite).

OTHER HISTORIC COLLEGES

Merton College (founded 1264) has peaceful gardens and the 14th-century Mob Quad, Oxford's oldest quadrangle, while New College (founded 1379) is famous for its hall, cloister, chapel and gardens enclosed by the old city wall. Peep into St. John's College, founded 1555, with its arcaded Canterbury Quad, and Queens College (founded 1341) for buildings by Sir Christopher Wren and Nicholas Hawksmoor. Farther out in Parks Road is Keble College (1870), a relative newcomer whose elaborate red-brick buildings are a Victorian *tour de force*.

BACKGROUND

Everywhere in this city of spires and greenery you sense learning has been going on a long time: since 1167 in fact, when a number of English scholars, expelled from the Paris Sorbonne, settled here to found the university. As with its ancient rival, Cambridge (▷ 96–97), students are attached to individual colleges, mostly set around quadrangles (or quads), each with a chapel and dining hall. Most of the central colleges have medieval origins and display a mix of architectural styles, from Renaissance to modern. The colleges originated in the 13th century, when a series of town-versus-gown (townspeople against students) confrontations hastened the establishment of halls of residence. These were succeeded by the first colleges. Since 1974, all but one of them has admitted both men and women—St. Hilda's remains the sole women-only college.

BASICS

🏛 450 J18

ℹ 15–16 Broad Street OX1 3AS, tel 01865 726871

❓ Guided walking tours of the city and colleges from the tourist information centre (first-come, first-served). Punts and rowing boats available from Magdalen Bridge or the Cherwell Boathouse, Bardwell Road.

🚇 Oxford

🚌 From London services run every 10–20 min from Victoria Coach Station via Marble Arch (pay on board), then hourly throughout the night.

www.oxford.gov.uk
A comprehensive official site covering all aspects of the city. Click on 'visiting' for information about the city and its attractions, accommodation and details of guided walks and tours. Click on 'transport' for bus and train information and details of the park-and-ride services.

Below left: Dons wearing mortar boards are a familiar sight in the streets around the colleges

THE SIGHTS

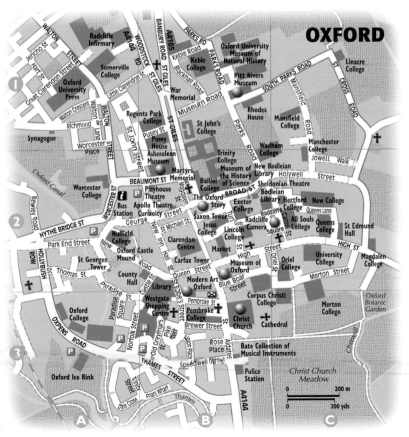

OXFORD

The New Forest's ponies are very much part of the landscape

Norwich Cathedral has the largest cloisters of any English cathedral

The playful and appealing otter is kept safe at the Otter Trust

NEW FOREST

➕ 430 H20 🛈 New Forest Visitor Information Centre, New Street, Lyndhurst SO41 9BH, tel 01590 689000 🚉 Brockenhurst
www.thenewforest.co.uk

Strikingly remote, grazed by free-ranging ponies and cattle, and one of England's largest stretches of open, undeveloped country, the New Forest is excellent for walking, camping and picnicking (▷ 280–283). Established in 1079 as a hunting forest for Norman royalty, it has remained largely intact. At Lyndhurst, the New Forest Museum and Visitor Centre (daily) has an exhibition on the area. Some of the most popular attractions lie in the southeastern corner, including Beaulieu (▷ 93), Exbury Gardens (▷ 100) and Bucklers Hard, a hamlet with a nautical air, and the launching point of several ships from the fleet of Admiral Lord Nelson (1758–1805). **Don't miss** The Bolderwood and Rhinefield ornamental drives—roads planted with giant fir, redwood and cypress trees.

NORWICH

➕ 437 M16 🛈 The Forum, Millennium Plain, Norwich NR2 1TF, tel 01603 727927 🚉 Norwich
www.visitnorwich.co.uk
www.museums.gov.norfolk.uk

Norwich is one of Britain's most complete medieval cities. Outstanding among the jumble of old streets is cobbled Elm Hill, full of antiques, crafts and specialist shops. Northeast in the city is the cathedral, founded in 1096 and with a 15th-century spire rising to 96m (315ft). It has a magnificent stone-vaulted roof with 1,106 carved stone bosses depicting the Bible story.
   Southwest of the cathedral is the busy marketplace, a maze of narrow alleyways with stalls selling just about everything six days a week. Norwich's newest public building is the architecturally acclaimed Forum, home to Origins (daily), an interactive journey through 2,000 years of Norwich and Norfolk's history. The Royal Arcade is where you'll find Colman's Mustard Shop and Museum (Mon–Sat 9.30–5), and can buy tiny tins of Norwich's most famous product. In Bridewell Alley, the Bridewell Museum (Apr–end Oct) chronicles local trades and industries.
   Looking down on the marketplace, 12th-century Norwich Castle (daily) has a fine museum and art gallery, where there is a huge collection of ceramic teapots and works by the early 19th-century Norwich School of landscape painters. **Don't miss** Dragon Hall (Apr–end Oct Mon–Sat; rest of year Mon–Fri), a 15th-century merchants' hall in King Street; The Sainsbury Centre for the Visual Arts (closed Mon), an outstanding art collection in a modern building by architect Norman Foster, at the University of East Anglia, 3 miles (5km) west of Norwich.

ORFORD

➕ 432 M17 🛈 Station Building, Woodbridge IP12 4AJ, tel 01394 382240
www.orford.org.uk

Orford, with its brick-and-timber cottages, was a thriving port when Henry II (1133–89) built Orford Castle (daily) here as a coastal defence in 1165. Its unique polygonal keep survives almost intact with a spiral staircase inside each of the three immense towers.
   Orford is now separated from the sea by 10-mile (17km) Orford Ness (ferries Jul–end Sep Tue–Sat; Apr–end Jun, Oct Sat only), the largest vegetated shingle spit in Europe. It is an important location for breeding and passage birds and has rare shingle flora species.

OTTER TRUST

➕ 437 M16 • Earsham, Bungay NR35 2AF ☎ 01986 893470 🕐 Apr (Good Fri if earlier)–end Sep daily 10.30–6 💷 Adult £6, child (3–15) £3 🍴 🏛 👥 🅿
www.ottertrust.org.uk

Set on the banks of the River Waveney, the Otter Trust maintains the world's largest collection of otters. The animals are kept in near-natural enclosures. There are British otters, which tend to be shy and retiring, and the more playful and extrovert Asian short-clawed otters. The Trust enjoys great success in breeding British otters for release into the wild. For the best views arrive at feeding times (12 and 3pm).
   The reserve also shelters European waterfowl, wallabies and deer.

OXFORD

See pages 104–107

PARHAM HOUSE AND GARDENS

➕ 431 K19 • near Pulborough RH20 4HS ☎ 01903 744888 (recording), 01903 742021 🕐 House: Easter–late Sep Wed, Thu, Sun and public holidays 2–6, plus Tue and Fri, Aug. Gardens: 12–6 💷 House and gardens: adult £6.50, child (5–15) £2.50, family £15.50. Gardens: adult £5, child £1, family £10 🍴 🏛 👥 🅿
www.parhaminsussex.co.uk

Built in 1577, the house contains an impressive variety of furniture and textiles, and an important collection of needlework. The 18th-century Pleasure Grounds include a lake, specimen trees and bulbs, and a maze. Descendants of the original 17th-century deer herd roam the park.

PORTSMOUTH

Home of Britain's naval heritage, with fabulous historic ships and boat tours.

At first sight Portsmouth may not seem a great place for a day out. But it has pockets of huge historic interest, mostly concentrated around the waterfront. It has been a naval base since the 12th century and the hub of one of the most powerful sea-borne fighting forces in history. The city is the home port of the Royal Navy and consequently was heavily bombed during World War II.

A couple of minutes' walk from Portsmouth Harbour station is the Historic Dockyard (daily) with its celebrated warships. Naval officers guide you round Nelson's flagship HMS *Victory* to recall the appalling conditions on board and see the spot where Nelson died in battle in 1805 (▷ 35). Close by is the world's first iron-clad battleship, HMS *Warrior*, launched in 1860. Rescued in 1982 after sinking in 1545, Henry VIII's warship *Mary Rose* features a rich array of finds that provides an unrivalled time capsule of Tudor life. Also in the dockyard, the Royal Naval Museum charts the history of British maritime defence.

TOWN HIGHLIGHTS
Soaring high over the shops and restaurants of the Gunwharf Quays development, the 170m (558ft) Spinnaker Tower (daily) opened in 2005 to give the best viewing platform on the south coast: The glass floor on one level gives a dizzying sense of being on top of things, while from the top level you are exposed to the bracing fresh air. At the end of the High Street lies Old Portsmouth, an area of cobbled streets lined with Tudor and Georgian houses and pubs. These streets were once full of press gangs seeking new naval recruits, whom they forced to join a leaving ship.

OTHER SIGHTS
Over the water at Gosport (reached by ferry), Explosion! Museum of Naval Firepower (Apr–end Oct daily; rest of year Thu, Sat–Sun) displays hardware from the Battle of Trafalgar to the present.

Southsea Castle (daily), on Clarence Esplanade, was built in 1595 to protect Portsmouth against French invasion. Next door, the D-Day Museum and Overlord Embroidery (daily) records the largest invasion force ever gathered: for D-Day (6 June 1944). Its focal embroidery measures 83m (272ft).

Don't miss The 45-minute cruise from the Historic Dockyard to see modern warships; a sail out to Spitbank Fort (Tue–Sun).

RATINGS				
Good for kids	●	●	●	●
Historic interest	●	●	●	●	●
Maritime interest	●	●	●	●	●

BASICS
✚ 430 J20 ⓘ Clarence Esplanade, Southsea PO5 2PB, tel 023 9282 6722
🚇 Portsmouth Harbour

www.visitportsmouth.co.uk

Above: HMS Victory *served for more than 60 years before earning her rest here in dry dock*
Below: Lord Nelson had his last hours on board HMS Victory, *but he is remembered with pride*

Although often besieged, Pevensey Castle was never fully captured

The elegant Drawing Room at Polesden Lacey would have been the perfect setting for Mrs Greville's soirées

THE SIGHTS

PENSHURST PLACE AND GARDENS

➕ 431 L19 • Penshurst, Tonbridge TN11 8DG ☎ 01892 870307 ◉ House: late Mar–end Oct daily 12–4.30. Gardens: late Mar–end Oct daily 10.30–6 💺 House and grounds: adult £7, child (5–16) £5, family £20. Grounds only: £5.50, child £4.50, family £17 🍴 🎁 🚻 🅿️
www.penshurstplace.com

Begun in 1340 for London merchant Sir John de Pulteney, this fortified manor house contains extensive collections of furniture, tapestries, paintings, porcelain and armour acquired by the Sidney family. The lofty chestnut-beamed Baron's Hall, dating from 1341, is among the outstanding original features. For younger visitors there is an adventure playground and a woodland trail.
Don't miss The Tudor walled garden has more than 1 mile (1.5km) of yew hedging dividing it into self-contained rooms.

PETWORTH HOUSE AND PARK

➕ 431 J19 • Petworth GU28 0AE ☎ 01798 342207 ◉ House and Servants' Quarters: late Mar–end Oct Sat–Wed 11–5 (extra rooms shown Mon–Wed, except public holidays). Pleasure Ground: early Mar Sat–Wed 12–4; late Mar–early Nov Sat–Wed 11–6; Nov to mid-Dec Wed–Sat 10–3.30. Park: daily 8–dusk 💺 House, Servants' Quarters and Pleasure Ground: adult £7.50, child (5–16) £4, family £19. Pleasure Ground: adult £2, child £1. Park: free 🅿️ Petworth 🍴 🚻 🎁 🚻 🅿️
www.nationaltrust.org.uk

No other National Trust property can rival Petworth for its art collection. The 300 oil paintings include 20 by Anthony Van Dyck, 20 by J. M. W. Turner and work by Joseph Reynolds and Titian, as well as ancient and neoclassical sculpture. The deer park has been captured on canvas by Turner. The Red Room and the Carved Room of the late 17th-century mansion contain English sculptor Grinling Gibbons' (1648–1721) finest limewood carvings, while the kitchens incorporate Victorian technology.

PEVENSEY CASTLE

➕ 431 L20 • Pevensey BN24 5LE ☎ 01323 762604 ◉ Apr–end Sep daily 10–6; Oct–end Mar Sat–Sun 10–4 💺 Adult £3.70, child (5–16) £1.90 🅿️ Pevensey & Westham ♿ 🍴 🎁 🚻 🅿️
www.english-heritage.org.uk

William the Conqueror (1027–87) landed at Pevensey for his invasion of England in 1066, and occupied the remains of this Roman fort. What survives today is the Roman outer wall and towers, standing almost to their full height, and the partially subsided Norman castle. In World War II the fortifications and gun emplacements were added, together with a blockhouse for anti-tank weapons.

POLESDEN LACEY

➕ 431 K19 • Great Bookham RH5 6BD ☎ 01372 458203 (recording), 01372 452048 ◉ House: mid-Mar to early Nov Wed–Sun, public holidays 11–5. Garden, grounds and walks: daily 11–6 (or dusk) 💺 House, garden, grounds and walks: adult £8, child (5–16) £4, family £20. Garden, grounds and walks: adult £5, child £2.50, family £12.50 🚆 Boxhill & Westhumble, 2 miles (3km) 🍴 🛍 🎁 🚻 🅿️
www.nationaltrust.org.uk

Choose good weather to visit Polesden Lacey, for one of its treasures is the garden and views of the Surrey countryside. In the early 20th century, this Regency house of 1824 was home to society hostess Mrs Ronald Greville, who remodelled it in 1909. King George VI and Queen Elizabeth spent part of their honeymoon here in 1923. The house is much as it was at the time of Mrs Greville's celebrated parties, with the elaborate menus and lists of distinguished guests.

PORTSMOUTH

See page 109

ROLLRIGHT STONES

➕ 430 H17 • near Chipping Norton ◉ Open access 💺 Nominal charge for King's Men 🅿️ In layby (pull-off)
www.english-heritage.org.uk
www.rollrightstones.co.uk

Three groups of stones—The King's Men, The King Stone and The Whispering Knights—together span nearly 2,000 years of the Neolithic and Bronze Ages. The King's Men is a large circle of about 70 stones, while The King Stone is a prominent outlier stone. A little more difficult to find are The Whispering Knights, about 5 minutes' walk east from the main layby (pull-off).

SANDRINGHAM

➕ 437 L15 • The Estate Office, Sandringham PE35 6EN ☎ 01553 772675 ◉ House: Apr–end Sep daily 11–4.45; Oct daily 11–3. Museum: Apr–end Sep daily 11–5; Oct daily 11–4. Gardens: Apr–end Sep daily 10.30–5; Oct daily 10.30–4 💺 House, museum and gardens: adult £7.50, child (5–15) £4.50, family £19.50. Museum and gardens: adult £5, child £3, family £13. Garden tours from £1.50 ❓ Guided garden tours: Fri–Sat 11 and 2 🍴 🎁 🚻 🅿️
www.sandringhamestate.co.uk

Sandringham is the Norfolk country retreat of Queen Elizabeth II. It was built in 1870 for the Prince of Wales (later Edward VII). The main ground-floor rooms are much as they were in Edwardian times, while the old stable, coach houses

Boats are still a major part of the landscape at Sandwich

Mermaid Street in Rye is a delight of jumbled old houses

and power house contain a museum of Royal Family possessions. There is free access to the many paths in the surrounding country park.

SANDWICH

⊞ 432 M19 🔢 The Guildhall, Sandwich CT13 9AH, tel 01304 613565; Apr–end Oct 🚉 Sandwich www.whitecliffscountry.org.uk www.open-sandwich.co.uk

The sea has receded from what was once England's major port, but Sandwich is still one of the best-preserved medieval towns in Britain. The Guildhall Museum (closed Mon and Dec–end Feb) covers the history of Sandwich. Walk beside the River Stour on the earth ramparts to the Old Toll Bridge, from where the Sandwich River Bus takes you to Richborough Roman Fort (Easter–end Sep daily). Dating to the Roman invasion of AD43, the fortified walls and foundations of a triumphal arch remain.

SHEFFIELD PARK GARDEN

⊞ 431 K19 • Sheffield Park TN22 3QX ☎ 01825 790231 🕐 Jan to mid-Feb Sat–Sun 10.30–4; mid-Feb to end Oct Tue–Sun 10.30–6 or dusk; Nov–end Dec Tue–Sun 10.30–4 💷 Adult £5.50, child (5–16) £2.75, family £13.75 🚉 Sheffield Park; Bluebell Railway from Horsted Keynes 🎫 Joint ticket with Bluebell Railway available, call 01825 720800 ▢ 🚼 🍴 🅿 www.nationaltrust.org.uk

This garden was laid out in the 18th century by Capability Brown and expanded in the early 20th century. The garden is best in early summer, when the rhododendrons and azaleas are in bloom, and in autumn when the foliage is a riot of colour. The main features are four large lakes on different levels linked by cascades and waterfalls.

RYE AND WINCHELSEA

Rye and Winchelsea are two captivating historic small-town gems with a wealth of domestic architecture.

⊞ 432 L19 🔢 The Heritage Centre, Strand Quay, Rye TN31 7AY, tel 01797 226696 🚉 Rye, Winchelsea www.rye.org.uk www.rye.co.uk

RATINGS	
Good for kids	●●●○
Historic interest	●●●○
Specialist shopping	●●●●○
Walkability	●●●●○

TIP
● Camber Sands, 5 miles (8km) east of Rye, is better for bathing; a bicycle path from Rye avoids the busy road.

MAKE A DAY OF IT
Bodiam Castle (▷ 94)
Great Dixter (▷ 100)
Hastings (▷ 101)

Just 2 miles (3km) apart, Rye and Winchelsea were two of the five medieval Cinque Ports, part of a confederation that supplied ships to the navy in return for privileges from the king. The sea has since receded, leaving shingle beaches and two small towns seemingly suspended in time.

The larger of the two, Rye, is a huddle of cobbled streets, medieval half-timbered, red-tiled houses and elegant Georgian buildings, with the most photogenic spots along Mermaid Street. The antiques shops and galleries are great for browsing. Parts of the 14th-century defences still remain, such as the Landgate Arch and Ypres Tower, a 13th-century look-out that houses the Rye Castle Museum (Apr–end Oct Thu–Mon; rest of year Sat–Sun).

Facing the church, in West Street, is the early 18th-century Lamb House (Apr–end Oct Wed and Sat pm), home of the American novelist Henry James (1843–1916) from 1898 until his death. It was later occupied by the author E. F. Benson.

Winchelsea, the smallest town in England (population 400), began life at sea level until its destruction in a storm in 1287. It was rebuilt to a grid pattern (the first example of town planning in medieval England) on the clifftop, fortified with walls and gateways against French invaders. Most buildings have 17th- and 18th-century façades but many are much older. Three gates survive of the medieval defences. At the centre, St. Thomas's Church is a fragment of a once larger building, with only the choir and side chapels remaining, but it retains impressive canopied tombs; the 20th-century stained-glass windows tell the town's story. Medieval Court Hall (May–end Sep Tue–Sun and Mon public holidays), restored in the 16th century, houses the local museum.

Don't miss The view from St. Mary's Church tower in Rye.

Windsor and Eton

The adjoining towns of Windsor and Eton together provide the site of Europe's largest castle and one of Britain's most famous public schools.

School's out: Students at Eton College wear distinctive uniforms

TIPS

● Tour companies operate a daily service to Windsor, collecting from many London hotels (details from hotels).
● Windsor Castle's State Apartments and Chapel can close at short notice, so call in advance.

Windsor Old Town is a lovely place to take a break

SEEING WINDSOR AND ETON

Both Windsor and Eton are easily explored on foot and have plenty of attractions to fill a whole day. Less than an hour from London, Windsor's historic grandeur is apparent immediately on arrival. The curving, elevated approach by train from London offers splendid views of the River Thames, Windsor Castle and Eton College, and also crosses Isambard Kingdom Brunel's 1849 wrought-iron bridge.

In addition to the obvious lure of its castle, Windsor has vast open spaces and several other attractions. It is also well stocked with shops, concentrated in a handful of places over a compact area—with everything from main-street names to designer boutiques, antiques, art, gifts and collectables—plus numerous restaurants and cafés, some with outdoor dining.

HIGHLIGHTS

WINDSOR CASTLE

✉ Windsor SL4 1NJ ☎ 020 7321 2233 🕐 Castle: Mar–end Oct daily 9.45–5.15; rest of year daily 9.45–4.15. East end of the north terrace: Aug–end Sep. Semi-state rooms: Oct–end Mar. Subject to closure on certain days (especially in Jun); call first 🎫 Adult: £12, child £7
www.royal.gov.uk

Windsor Castle towers above the town on a chalk cliff overlooking the River Thames. It is the largest inhabited castle in the world and has been one of the principal residences of the sovereigns of England since William the Conqueror (1027–87) built it. Much of the present-day construction, however, dates from the 19th century.

There are several buildings to visit within the castle complex. St. George's Chapel (worshippers only Sun), begun in 1475 by Edward IV and completed in 1509, is a masterpiece of Perpendicular Gothic architecture. Ten monarchs are buried here. In the northwest chapel the monument to Princess Charlotte (who died in 1817 in childbirth) shows her ascending to heaven with an angel carrying her stillborn child. The chapel's fan-vaulted ceiling is particularly beautiful, as are the elaborate 15th-century choir stalls covered in vignettes and surmounted by banners of the 26 Knights of the Garter, whose installation has taken place here since 1348.

The baroque State Apartments, restored following the fire of 1992, are hung with works from the Royal Collection, the world's finest private art collection, with drawings and paintings by Michelangelo, Canaletto, Peter Paul Rubens and many others. Among the prestigious names who decorated the rooms were the Dutch-born English sculptor and woodcarver Grinling Gibbons (1648–1721) and the Italian interior decorator Antonio Verrio (c1640–1707).

Also on display is Queen Mary's Dolls' House, designed by Sir Edwin Lutyens in 1924. The furnishings are at one-twelfth size, and the plumbing and lighting really work.

Also noteworthy is Prince Albert's marble and mosaic memorial chapel designed by Sir George Gilbert Scott (1811–78). A spectacle not to be missed is the pomp of the Changing the Guard, which is dependent on the weather (Jul–end Mar alternate days except Sun 11am; rest of year Mon–Sat 11am).

WINDSOR TOWN

It is worth exploring Windsor's shops and noteworthy buildings. The Guildhall on the High Street was completed in 1707 by Sir Christopher Wren (1632–1723). Its Tuscan columns on the ground floor do not touch the ceiling; apparently, the town council insisted on having them, but Wren left the gap to prove that they were structurally superfluous.

Farther up the High Street you will pass the 19th century parish church of St. John the Baptist. From here you can continue up Park Street to the Long Walk, which skirts Windsor Great Park. This 3 mile (5km) avenue was laid out by Charles I and planted with elms. Within the park is the 14ha (35-acre) woodland Savill Garden (daily), which is worth visiting at any time of the year, but is particularly beautiful in spring when the azaleas and camellias are in bloom.

ETON COLLEGE

✉ Windsor SL4 6DW ☎ 01753 671177 🕐 Apr, Jul–end Aug daily 10.30–4.30; May–end Jun, Sep daily 2–4.30; 1-hour guided tour Apr–end Sep daily 2.15 and 3.15 Across the river from Windsor, over the pedestrian-only Windsor Bridge, is Eton, its appealing main street fronted by Britain's most famous public school. Henry VI (1421–71) founded it in 1440 for 70 King's Scholars or Collegers who lived in the College and were educated free, and for a small number of students who lived in the town of Eton and paid for their education.

Today it is a boarding school for approximately 1,280 boys between the ages of 13 and 18, distinguished by their traditional 19th-century uniform of black tailcoat, waistcoat and pinstriped trousers. Highlights throughout the visiting season include the School Yard, with its statue of Henry VI, the superb Perpendicular-style College Chapel, the Cloisters and the Museum of Eton Life (late Mar–early Oct daily). Famous old Etonians include the Duke of Wellington (1769–1852) and a number of prime ministers—Sir Robert Walpole (1676–1745), William Gladstone (1809–98) and Harold Macmillan (1894–1986).

Don't miss The Household Cavalry Museum, south of Windsor, has uniforms, weapons, vehicles and other exhibits covering centuries of the Royal Horse Guards, the Life Guards and the First Royal Dragoon Guards; a regular shuttle bus runs from the town to Legoland Windsor, the popular family theme park (▷ 232).

The towers of Windsor Castle are visible from miles around, and its interior includes St. George's Chapel, with the banners of the 26 Knights of the Garter

BASICS
✚ 431 J18
ℹ 24 High Street, Windsor SL4 1LH, tel 01753 743900
❓ City Sightseeing Bus tours every 30 min from Windsor Castle or Windsor & Eton Riverside Station: Apr–Oct 10.30–4.30; Nov to mid-Dec Sat–Sun ☎ 01708 866 000 or book online at www.city-sightseeing. com. Also guided walking tours and boat trips
🚉 Windsor & Eton Riverside (from London Waterloo), Windsor & Eton Central (from London Paddington)

www.windsor.gov.uk
Well-designed, comprehensive official site covering everything in and around Windsor, from accommodation to shopping, what's on and transport, including maps and even ideas for short breaks in the area.

The sky's the limit: a flying show at the Shuttleworth Collection

All roads lead to the landscaped gardens at Sissinghurst

The marina in Southampton shelters impressive yachts

SHUTTLEWORTH COLLECTION

➕ 431 K17 • Shuttleworth Aerodrome, Old Warden Park, Biggleswade SG18 9EA ☎ 09068 323310 (recording), 01767 627288 🕒 Apr–end Oct daily 10–5; rest of year daily 10–4 🎫 Adult £7.50, accompanied child up to 16 free; flying display £15 ❓ On flying days flights normally begin at 2pm; sunset flying displays begin at 6.30 on Sat (earlier in Jul and Aug) 🚍 Biggleswade 🍴 🛒 ♿ 🚻 🅿
www.shuttleworth.org

In an all-grass aerodrome, this collection features around 40 aircraft from 1909 to 1955. Many are the last survivors of their type, including a 1909 Bleriot, 1931 Tiger Moth and a 1941 Spitfire, kept in full working order. The exhibition includes vintage cars, motorcycles, bicycles and horse-drawn carriages. Flying displays take place once or twice a month (May–end Oct), when the museum's airworthy exhibits are flown alongside visiting aircraft, and cars from the collection are given a run.

SISSINGHURST CASTLE GARDEN

➕ 432 L19 • Sissinghurst, near Cranbrook TN17 2AB ☎ 01580 710701 (recording), 01580 710700 🕒 Late Mar–end Oct Fri–Tue 11–6.30 🎫 Adult £7.50, child (5–16) £3.50, family £18.50 ❓ Timed entry tickets. Library and Vita Sackville-West's study close at 5.30. Tower and library may be restricted early and late season 🍴 ♿ 🚻 🅿
www.nationaltrust.org.uk

The writer Vita Sackville-West (1892–1962) and her husband, the diplomat and author Sir Harold Nicolson (1886–1968), created this famous Wealden garden in the 1930s around the ruin of a moated Elizabethan mansion. Sissinghurst, a major influence on garden design,

consists of a series of small, enclosed compartments that between them provide an outstanding display of hues through the seasons. The brick front range (c1490) and the four-storey tower (c1565) are all that survive of the house.

SOUTHAMPTON

➕ 430 H19 ℹ 9 Civic Centre Road, Southampton SO14 7FJ, tel 023 8083 3333 🚉 Southampton Central
www.southampton.gov.uk

Between the modern office blocks and shopping streets, fragments of the old town that was largely destroyed during World War II can be found, including a large section of the medieval town wall and its 13 remaining towers. A self-guiding walking tour follows its route—look out for Walk the Southampton Walls signposts and plaques.

The city's museums reveal the diverse history of this major port from medieval prosperity to the golden age of transatlantic travel. The Medieval Merchant's House (Easter–end Sep, Sat–Sun and public holidays) has been restored and furnished to look as it might have done in 1290, while Solent Sky (Mon–Sat 10–5, Sun 12–5) in Albert Road South tells the history of aviation in the Solent area, including the achievements of R. J. Mitchell, designer of the Spitfire.

The Titanic Voices Exhibition in the Maritime Museum (Tue–Sun) in Town Quay has some haunting recordings of the crew and passengers of the ill-fated ship Titanic. On its maiden voyage from Southampton in 1912, this supposedly unsinkable ship went down, with the loss of more than 1,500 lives.

With a plethora of waterfront bars and restaurants, Town Quay and Shamrock Quay are among the city's liveliest spots.

SOUTHWOLD

➕ 437 N16 ℹ 69 High Street, Southwold IP18 6DS, tel 01502 724729 www.visit-southwold.co.uk

The allure of this port-turned-resort is its sedate, old-fashioned character. Groups of brick and colour-washed cottages cluster around greens beneath three landmarks: the lighthouse, Adnam's brewery and the soaring tower of St. Edmund's Church. In the middle of town there are art galleries, antiques shops, tea rooms and pubs, most selling the highly esteemed Adnam's ales. Below the Sailors' Reading Room—a social club for mariners, with a local history display—some 200 brightly painted beach huts dating from the early 1900s line the beach, near the pier.
Don't miss The Amber Shop and Museum, 15 Market Place (Mon–Sat 9–5, Sun 11–4), has examples of amber from all over the world.

STAMFORD

➕ 436 K16 ℹ Stamford Arts Centre, 27 St. Mary's Street, Stamford PE9 2DL, tel 01780 755611
www.southwestlincs.com

With golden limestone buildings and cobbled streets opening onto spacious squares, this most attractive of towns is a popular film location for period-costume dramas. Barn Hill offers the best overall view of the houses and medieval churches. To the south is Burghley House (Apr–end Oct daily, except during Burghley Horse Trials in early Sep), a 240-room Elizabethan mansion built by William Cecil (1520–98), chief minister to Elizabeth I. The house has a world-famous collection of tapestries, porcelain and paintings and is set in a beautiful deer park designed by Capability Brown.

Waddesdon Manor bears more than a passing resemblance to a French Renaissance chateau

Take a trip into the past at the Weald and Downland Museum

STANDEN

✚ 431 K19 • West Hoathly Road, East Grinstead RH19 4NE ☎ 01342 323029 🕐 House: late Mar–end Oct Wed–Sun and public holidays 11–5. Garden: late Mar–end Oct Wed–Sun and public holidays 11–6; Nov to mid-Dec Sat–Sun 11–3 🎫 Adult £6.50, child (5–16) £3.25, family £16. Garden only: adult £3.90, child £1.90. Joint ticket with same-day admission (Wed–Fri) to Nymans Garden: adult £10, child £5 🚉 East Grinstead 🍴 ♿ 🛍 🅿 www.nationaltrust.org.uk

This is a rare opportunity to see inside one of the greatest houses of the 19th-century Arts and Crafts Movement. Standen was built between 1892 and 1894 by Philip Webb as a country home for London solicitor James Beale. The house has been preserved right down to its original electric light fittings; William Morris carpets, textiles and printed wall coverings include many original to the house. The hillside garden looks far over the Sussex Weald countryside.

SUTTON HOO

✚ 432 M17 • Tranmer House, Sutton Hoo, Woodbridge IP12 3DJ ☎ 01394 389714 🕐 Mid-Mar to end Oct daily 11–5; Nov–end Dec Fri–Sun 11–4; Jan to mid-Mar Sat–Sun 11–4 🎫 Adult £5, child (5–16) £2.50, family £12.50. Parking (when exhibition closed—some Sat) £2.50 🚉 Woodbridge 🍴 ♿ 🛍 🅿 www.nationaltrust.org.uk

In 1939, excavation of an Anglo-Saxon royal burial site led to the discovery of the priceless Sutton Hoo treasure. A warrior's helmet, shield, gold ornaments and Byzantine silver were found close to the sea in the remains of a burial of a 27m (90ft) ship. The exhibition here examines the 50-year excavation of the site, and aspects of Anglo-Saxon life such as craftsmanship, and life

and death in seventh-century England. On display are original finds and a full-size reconstruction of King Raedwald's burial chamber. **Don't miss** The burial mounds, a short walk away.

WADDESDON MANOR

✚ 431 J17 • Waddesdon HP18 0JH ☎ 01296 653211 (recording), 01296 653226 🕐 House and cellars: Apr–end Oct Wed–Sun 11–4. Grounds: Apr–end Dec Wed–Sun 10–5; rest of year Sat–Sun 10–5 🎫 House and grounds: adult £11, child (5–16) £8. Bachelors' Wing: £3. Grounds only: adult £4, child £2. National Trust members free ❓ Timed ticket from 10am, first-come, first-served 🍴 ♿ 🛍 🅿 www.waddesdon.org.uk

Definitely a chateau in character, Waddesdon was built in the 1870s by Baron Ferdinand de Rothschild, a member of the 19th-century banking dynasty, for his extravagant house parties. Breathtaking for their opulence, the 45 rooms on view contain 18th-century French furniture and one of the world's finest collections of French decorative arts. The grounds are filled with specimen trees, fountains, grottoes and a rococo revival aviary of exotic birds. **Don't miss** The interesting and well-stocked wine cellars.

WAKEHURST PLACE

✚ 431 K19 • Ardingly, Haywards Heath RH17 6TN ☎ 01444 894066 🕐 Mar–end Oct daily 10–6; Nov–end Feb daily 10–4.30. Mansion and Seed Bank close 1 hour before gardens 🎫 Adult £8, under 17s free 🚉 Haywards Heath 🍴 🛍 🏛 Garden centre, shop 🛍 🅿 www.kew.org www.nationaltrust.org.uk

The country offshoot of the Royal Botanic Gardens at Kew (▷ 126) is a beautiful creation in its own right. A picturesque watercourse

links lakes and ponds, and the gardens surround an Elizabethan mansion with a rural exhibition.

This is one of the country's most varied gardens, with a worldwide collection, an arboretum, and year-round colour. The Millennium Seed Bank, an £80-million international conservation project, safeguards the world's most endangered plant species in massive underground seed vaults. Its aim is to have saved seeds from around 24,000 plants by 2010. **Don't miss** The virtual tour through interactive screens in the Millennium Seed Bank is impressive and fun.

WEALD AND DOWNLAND OPEN AIR MUSEUM

✚ 431 J19 • Singleton, near Chichester PO18 0EU ☎ 01243 811348 🕐 Apr–end Oct daily 10.30–6; Nov–end Dec, mid-Feb to end Mar daily 10.30–4; Jan to mid-Feb Wed, Sat, Sun 10.30–4 🎫 Adult £7.95, child (5–15) £4.25, family £21.95 🚉 Chichester 🛍 🏛 🅿 www.wealddown.co.uk

Set in the South Downs countryside, this is England's leading museum of historic buildings and traditional rural life. More than 40 of the region's old buildings have been rescued from destruction, carefully restored and reconstructed. They vividly evoke the homes, domestic gardens and workplaces of the past 500 years. Among them are medieval houses, a Tudor farmstead, a working 17th-century watermill, Victorian workers' cottages, a Victorian school, carpenters' and plumbers' workshops, and seven period gardens dating from 1430 to 1900.

There are also frequent demonstrations of traditional rural crafts and trades.

THE SIGHTS

Stripes or spots, Whipsnade has plenty of animals to see

Winchester's cathedral stands on prestigious Cathedral Close

The aroma of the roses at Wisley is a big draw with visitors

WHIPSNADE WILD ANIMAL PARK

⊞ 431 K17 • Whipsnade, Dunstable LU6 2LF ☎ 01582 872171 🕐 Mar–end Sep daily 10–6; Oct daily 10–5; Nov–end Dec daily 10–4 (open until 7 Sun and public holidays Apr–end Oct; last admission 1 hour before close). Great Whipsnade Railway: Easter–end Sep from 12 to 1 hr before park closes (check on the day) 💰 Animal Park: adult £14.50, child (3–15) £11, family £46; cars and all occupants £11, parking £3.50. 🍴 🏛 👥 🅿 External car park £2
www.whipsnade.co.uk

Occupying parkland on the Chiltern Hills is one of Europe's largest wildlife conservation centres, home to more than 2,500 creatures, including rare and endangered species. Its herd of seven Asian elephants is the largest breeding group in Britain, and free-roaming animals include wallabies and Chinese water deer.

Daily demonstrations feature free-flying birds, sea-lion performances and penguin feeding. To get around the park, take the free open-top Safari Tour Bus (a good chance to meet giraffes eye to eye), or alternatively take the Great Whipsnade Railway.
Don't miss The Discovery Centre, a must if you want to encounter crocodiles, snakes, tarantulas and piranhas, in their desert, rainforest and other natural settings.

WINCHESTER

⊞ 430 H19 🛈 Guildhall, The Broadway, Winchester SO23 9LJ, tel 01962 840500 🚇 Winchester
www.visitwinchester.co.uk

England's ancient capital and seat of the Anglo-Saxon kings, Winchester has a compact historic central area that you can easily explore on foot; antiquarian

bookshops are a city speciality; a detailed list is available from the tourist information office.

The city came to prominence under Alfred the Great (AD849–99), who made it the capital of his Wessex kingdom in the ninth century. The highlight of the city is its medieval cathedral, dating from 1079 to 1404, in Norman to Perpendicular styles.

Close by are the free City Museum (daily; closed Nov–end Mar Mon) and Winchester College, founded in 1382 and Britain's oldest and one of its most prestigious schools (daily tours). Near Westgate, the Great Hall, built in 1235 (daily), is all that survives of the city's 13th-century Norman castle. You can visit King Arthur's Round Table—a resplendent medieval fake.
Don't miss The Hospital of St. Cross (closed Sun) is a 12th-century almshouse, still home to 25 monks and reached by a tranquil walk across water meadows; by ancient tradition, Wayfarer's Dole (bread and beer) is still given to anyone who asks for it at the porter's lodge.

WINDSOR AND ETON

See pages 112–113

WISLEY, RHS GARDEN

⊞ 431 K19 • Wisley, Woking GU23 6QB ☎ 01483 224234 🕐 Mar–end Oct Mon–Fri 10–6, Sat–Sun and public holidays 9–6; rest of year Mon–Fri 10–4.30, Sat–Sun 9–4.30 💰 Adult £7, child (6–16) £2 🚇 Woking or West Byfleet (then taxi); reduced entry for rail travellers: adult £5.50, child £1.60 ❓ Free to visitors with registered visual impairment and carers of visitors in wheelchairs 🍴 🍽 🏛 Plant sales, shop 👥 🅿
www.rhs.org.uk

The flagship of the Royal Horticultural Society opened as a place of gardening excellence in 1904. Wisley demonstrates British

gardening at its best, offering a blend of landscaped gardens and horticultural tips for keen gardeners. Much of the most important work takes place in trial fields, while elsewhere a series of model gardens serves the needs of a variety of conditions.
Don't miss The plants for sale—the garden centre has around 10,000 of them.

WOBURN ABBEY

⊞ 431 J17 • Woburn MK17 9WA ☎ 01525 290333 🕐 Abbey: Apr–end Sep daily 10–5.30; Nov–end Dec weekends 10–5.30; last admission 1.5 hours before close. Park: Apr–end Sep daily 10–5; rest of year daily 10–4.30 💰 Abbey and Deer Park (when private apartments open): adult £9.50, child (5–15) £5, family from £24. Abbey and Deer Park (when apartments closed): £9.50, child free, family from £19. Abbey Grounds and Deer Park only: car, motorcycle £3 (including passengers), pedestrian/ cyclist £1, visitor from Woburn Safari Park free ❓ Visitors with wheelchairs should call the house in advance for arrangements to be made 🍴 🍽 🏛 👥 🅿
www.woburnabbey.co.uk

Monastic in name only, Woburn is in fact an 18th-century mansion of Palladian composition, on the site of a Cistercian monastery founded in 1145. It has been home to the dukes of Bedford since 1547 and presently is the home of the 15th Duke. On show here is one of the finest private art collections in Britain, with works by Thomas Gainsborough, Joshua Reynolds and other masters.

In the grounds are a deer park and Woburn Safari Park (mid-Mar to end Oct daily; rest of year Sat–Sun), Britain's largest animal safari park, where you sit in your car and drive around while the animals roam free.

LONDON

London has been the world's most influential capital city, with sights, such as Tower Bridge and Big Ben, resonating across every continent. And as the British set out from London for the four corners of the world, so people of hundreds of other nationalities have arrived, making it perhaps the most diverse capital in the world.

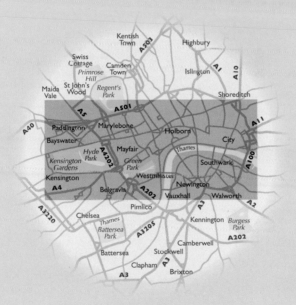

KEY SIGHTS

London

ℹ Britain and London Visitor Centre, 1 Lower Regent Street, London SW1Y 4XT, tel 0870 156 6366 (information on London only, 4p per minute); Mon 9.30–6.30, Tue–Fri 9–6.30, Sat–Sun 10–4 (Jun–end Oct Sat 9–5)
www. visitbritain.com • Information on Britain
www.visitlondon.com • Information on London

HOW TO GET THERE

✈ Airports
London Heathrow, 12 miles (19km) west of central London.
London Gatwick, 30 miles (48km) south of central London.
Also, **Stansted**, **Luton** and **London City** (mainly short-haul destinations).

🚆 Train stations
Mainline stations: Charing Cross, Euston, Fenchurch Street, King's Cross, Liverpool Street, London Bridge, Marylebone, Paddington, St. Pancras, Victoria and Waterloo.

The famous clock tower housing Big Ben

TIPS

• Ride the British Airways London Eye (▷ 120) for unrivalled views of London.
• Go to Harrods (▷ 235). Even if you don't want to buy anything, it's worth visiting this huge, luxurious store.
• Take a boat trip on the Thames for a different perspective of the city.
• Skip lunch and take afternoon tea at Fortnum and Mason (▷ 236).
• Wander off the beaten track; take a street map and explore areas such as Bloomsbury or the City on foot.
• Outside term time, the London School of Economics and Political Science rents student rooms to visitors, providing a basic but inexpensive base in central London.

SEEING LONDON

London is a bustling metropolis with some of the best monuments, museums and galleries in the world. Many of its attractions are some distance apart and you'll need to use its extensive public transport system to reach them. The Underground (Tube) is the quickest way to get around but buses offer views as well as a chance to get to grips with the geography of London. Taxis are everywhere in the centre and are useful for short distances but longer journeys are expensive. Another option is to take one of the open-top bus tours of the main tourist sights of central London, with a commentary in several languages, and the opportunity to get on and get off as many times as you like.

If you set out determined to see everything London has to offer you'll end up frustrated and exhausted. To get the most out of a visit, choose carefully—visit museums, for instance, in which you have a particular interest. It's also worth buying a London Pass as it includes free entry to over 60 attractions and allows you to jump the queue at selected attractions. It costs from £12 per day (with an option to include free travel on public transport) and is available from the Britain and London Visitor Centre (see above), tel: 0870 242 9988 or www.londonpass.com.

BACKGROUND

Although it is very much a 21st-century city, London retains a strong sense of its past. Its roots go back to the first century AD, when the Romans established a garrison at a site on the north bank of the Thames after their invasion of Britain in AD43. Its importance was underlined in the 11th century, when William the Conqueror built the Tower of London. Most of the medieval city was devoured by the Great Fire of 1666, but London soon recovered, and continued to grow in Georgian times, when elegant streets and squares were laid out in Mayfair and fashionable shops opened in Bond Street and Oxford Street.

At the Great Exhibition of 1851 in Hyde Park, London was displayed to the world as the largest city on the planet. By the beginning of the 20th century, London was the capital of the largest empire the world had ever known. After the devastation of the Second World War came the 'swinging London' of the 1960s and the youth culture of coffee bars and boutiques, while skyscrapers and concrete high-rises changed the city skyline forever. The late 1990s heralded a boom that saw London riding high on a wave of prosperity and self-confidence, which looks set to continue, and ensure its reputation as one of the world's most vibrant cities.

DON'T MISS

BRITISH MUSEUM
A vast array of antiquities from around the world (▷ 122–123)
NATURAL HISTORY MUSEUM
Dinosaurs to lichens: millions of specimens from the natural world (▷ 126)
ST. PAUL'S CATHEDRAL
Its iconic dome dominates the London skyline (▷ 127)
SCIENCE MUSEUM
Innovative hands-on museum that brings science to life (▷ 128)
TATE MODERN
Superb modern art in a dynamic setting (▷ 129)
TOWER OF LONDON
Symbolizes nearly 1,000 years of Britain's royal history (▷ 130)

BUCKINGHAM PALACE

Buckingham Palace is a world-famous symbol of monarchy and focus for ceremonial and public occasions as well as one of Queen Elizabeth II's main residences.

The palace so familiar to millions from newsreels and postcards has had centuries of piecemeal architectural changes. Originally plain Buckingham House, it was built in 1702 as the Duke of Buckingham's city mansion. King George III snapped it up as a private residence in 1761 and work began on embellishments and additions. When Queen Victoria and Prince Albert moved into the palace in 1837, a whole new wing was added to accommodate their fast-growing family, closing off the three-sided quadrangle and removing the Marble Arch that provided its grand entrance. The present forecourt, where the Changing the Guard ceremony (▷ 242) takes place, was formed in 1911, as part of the Victoria Memorial scheme.

THE STATE ROOMS

Of the palace's 660 rooms, visitors can see about 20. Enter the palace through the Ambassadors' Court and go through John Nash's dramatic Grand Hall to climb the curving marble of the Grand Staircase, with its gilt-bronze balustrade, to the first-floor State Rooms. Beyond the small Guard Room, hung with Gobelin tapestries, is the Green Drawing Room, an ante-chamber to the Throne Room, where official visitors gather before being presented to the Queen. Some of George IV's fine Sèvres porcelain can be seen here. Ahead is the Throne Room, a theatrical 20m (65ft) space leading up to the chairs of state.

This leads into the 47m (155ft) Picture Gallery, displaying works by Peter Paul Rubens, Rembrandt van Rijn and Anthony van Dyck. The Silk Tapestry Room, with its monumental French pedestal clock, links the Picture Gallery with the East Gallery, leading into the Ball Supper Room and the vast Ballroom, used for investitures and state banquets.

More Gobelin tapestries are displayed in the West Gallery, which leads to the State Dining Room, in white and gold with deep-red walls. Next is the sumptuous Blue Drawing Room, with a dazzling Nash ceiling and huge Corinthian columns. The opulence continues in the Music Room, with its domed ceiling and columns of lapis lazuli.

A blaze of white and gold greets you in the White Drawing Room, where there is more wonderful French furniture, such as a veneered roll-top desk from 1775. The intricately designed Minister's Staircase leads to the ground floor and the Marble Hall, displaying statues of nymphs. Other attractions are the Queen's Gallery, with an important collection of paintings and the nearby Royal Mews.

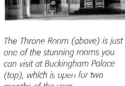

The Throne Room (above) is just one of the stunning rooms you can visit at Buckingham Palace (top), which is open for two months of the year

RATINGS	
Value for money	●●
Good for kids	●●
Historic interest	●●●●

BASICS

✚ 425 E4 • Buckingham Gate SW1A 1AA

☎ General: 020 7766 7324. Credit card booking line: 020 7766 7300

🕐 Late Jul–late Sep (precise dates vary) daily 9.30–6.30 (last admission 4.15); timed ticket system with admission every 15 min

💷 Adult £13.50, child (5–17) £7, family £34

🚇 Victoria, Green Park, Hyde Park Corner

🎧 Self-guiding tours

📖 Official guidebook £4.95 in English, Chinese, French, German, Italian, Japanese, Russian and Spanish

🏧 🚻

www.royal.gov.uk
Informative, accessible site

Rising fortunes: Business is booming at Canary Wharf

The British Library is Britain's biggest 20th-century public building, with eight of its fourteen floors above ground and the rest below

BRITISH AIRWAYS LONDON EYE

✚ 426 H4 • Westminster Bridge Road SE1 7PB ☎ 0870 5000 600 (reservations) 🕐 Jul–end Aug daily 9.30am–10pm; May–end Jun, Sep daily 9.30–9; rest of year daily 9.30–8 💷 Adult £12.50, child (5–15) £6.50 🚇 Waterloo, Westminster, Embankment, Charing Cross 🚢 Riverboat to Waterloo Millennium Pier ℹ Arrive 30 min before the flight 🛍 Souvenir book and guide £5, in English, French, German, Spanish and braille 🍴 In the Flight Zone, County Hall, and outside in Jubilee Gardens 🎫 Jubilee Gardens www.ba-londoneye.com

The world's largest observation wheel offers the best overview of London from 135m (443ft) above the Thames. The capsules have unobstructed views from large windows and the wheel is in constant, very slow motion. Reservations recommended, especially at peak times.

BRITISH LIBRARY

✚ 425 F1 • 96 Euston Road NW1 2DB ☎ 020 7412 7332 🕐 Public areas, exhibitions and bookshop: Mon, Wed–Fri 9.30–6, Tue 9.30–8, Sat 9.30–5, Sun 11–5. Reading rooms open to readers only 💷 Free 🚇 King's Cross, St. Pancras, Euston, Euston Square 🍴 🍷 🎫 www.bl.uk

Britain's national library, once housed in the British Museum (▷ 122–123), got its very own building in 1998. The collection includes every book published in the UK since 1911. There are currently about 150 million items in more than 400 languages. Enter via the information desk and walk round the floor-to-ceiling glass shaft to see some of the beautiful bindings of the King's Library, consisting of 60,000 volumes that once belonged to George III (1738–1820) and that were

donated by his son George IV (1762–1830) in 1823. The outer walls store the British Library's stamp collection—the world's finest.

The John Ritblat Gallery displays more treasures, including various editions of the Magna Carta, the 13th-century charter of rights (▷ 29), and a surviving manuscript in Shakespeare's own hand. The Workshop of Words, Sounds and Images explains how books and newspapers are created, and how sound is recorded. **Don't miss** Leonardo da Vinci's notebook and the earliest printed book, the *Diamond Sutra*.

BRITISH MUSEUM

See pages 122–123

BUCKINGHAM PALACE

See page 119

CANARY WHARF

Museum in Docklands ✚ 427 off M2 • No. 1 Warehouse, West India Quay E14 4AL ☎ 0870 444 3857 🕐 Daily 10–6 💷 Adult £5, child (under 16) free; valid 1 year 🚇 Canary Wharf, West India Quay DLR 🍴 🍷 🎫 www.museumindocklands.org.uk

The Docklands area has suffered many ups and downs over the centuries. By the 15th century, the docks were key to London's growth. And by 1930 there were

100,000 workers employed in the area. The Museum in Docklands, which opened in a 19th-century warehouse in 2003, tells the story of the port, its people and the passing cargoes.

After the massive redundancies of the 1960s and 1970s, the regeneration of Docklands began. The aim was to create a business district, and the area has certainly become busier with each passing decade. Britain's tallest building, Canary Wharf Tower, stands at 244m (800ft) and is the only skyscraper in the world to be clad in stainless steel. Unless you work here, access is not permitted.

Instead of the dockers, there are now 55,000 office workers based in Docklands. You can travel past the skyscrapers on the Docklands Light Railway (DLR) route to Greenwich and beyond—the monorail is raised above the ground.

CHARLES DICKENS MUSEUM

✚ 426 H1 • 48 Doughty Street WC1N 2LX ☎ 020 7405 2127 🕐 Mon–Sat 10–5, Sun 11–5 💷 Adult £5, child (under 16) £3, family £14 🚇 Russell Square, King's Cross, Chancery Lane 🎫 www.dickensmuseum.com

Charles Dickens (1812–70), the prolific novelist and commentator on Victorian society, lived at this Georgian terraced house in

The Dalí Universe collection is displayed in County Hall

A detail of the ornate roof inside the Royal Opera House

Charles Dickens has left an indelible stamp on London

Bloomsbury from 1837 to 1839. It's been dedicated to his life and work, displaying original manuscripts, first editions, letters, personal effects and 19th-century paintings. Perhaps the most interesting room is the study where he completed his first full-length novel, *The Pickwick Papers*, while only in his 20s, and where he later wrote *Oliver Twist* and *Nicholas Nickleby*.

CHELSEA

Chelsea Physic Garden 🔲 425 off E5 •
66 Royal Hospital Road SW3 4HS
☎ 020 7352 5646 ⏰ Early Apr–late Oct Wed 12–5, Sun 2–6 💷 Adult £5, child (5–15) £3.50 🚇 Sloane Square
⬜ ⬜ ⬜
www.chelseaphysicgarden.co.uk

Britain's second-oldest botanical garden (Oxford's is older) was founded in 1673 by the Society of Apothecaries of London to study plants for medical purposes, which is still the case.

The 2ha (5-acre) walled plot has around 5,000 species, rare trees and a rock garden created in 1772 with basaltic lava brought back from Iceland by English botanist Sir Joseph Banks (1743–1820), who accompanied Captain James Cook (1728–79) on his first voyage to the Pacific.

On display are flowering shrubs and rare peonies, as well as culinary herbs, edible flowers, poisonous plants and plants used to make dyes and fibres.

At the behest of Charles II (1630–85), the Royal Hospital Chelsea (Mon–Sat 10–12, 2–4, Sun 2–4; closed Oct–end Apr Sun) was built by Sir Christopher Wren (1632–1723) in the late 17th century as almshouses for veteran soldiers. It still serves that purpose today, and the Chelsea Pensioners, as the residents are known, are a familiar sight (▷ left). Their dress uniform is a scarlet tunic and a tricorn hat.

The hospital has a small museum with uniforms and medals, and the panelled Great Hall. Outside, you can wander in the south grounds, the site of the annual Chelsea Flower Show since 1913 (▷ 242).

COUNTY HALL

🔲 426 I14 • County Hall, Westminster Bridge Road SE1 7PB. **Dalí Universe:**
☎ 020 7620 2720 ⏰ Daily 10–6.30
💷 May–end Sep: adult £9.75, child (8–16) £6.25, child (4–7) £4, family £29. Oct–end Apr: adult £8.50, child (8–16) £5.50, child (4–7) £3.50, family £24. **London Aquarium:** ☎ 020 7967 8010 ⏰ Daily 10–6 💷 Adult £11.75, child (3–14) £8.25, family £36. **Namco Station:** ⏰ Daily 10am–midnight
🚇 Waterloo, Westminster ⬜ ⬜ ♿

www.daliuniverse.com
www.londonaquarium.co.uk
www.namcostation.co.uk

The former headquarters of the Greater London Council house two major attractions.

Laid out in a labyrinth, Dalí Universe is dedicated to surrealist artist Salvador Dalí (1904–89). It features a permanent exhibition of more than 500 works, including the red Mae West Lips sofa. The Dalí collection is complemented by a changing programme of blockbuster art exhibitions; Picasso was a recent subject.

One of Europe's largest aquariums, the London Aquarium occupies three floors and represents a variety of environments. The highlight is the three-level Atlantic and Pacific exhibit, where large sharks and stingrays glide menacingly about. There are brightly patterned fish to

enjoy in the coral reef and Indian Ocean exhibitions, and you can stroke a stingray on the simulated beach.

County Hall is also home to Namco Station, a huge leisure complex.

COVENT GARDEN

🔲 426 H3 • Covent Garden Market WC2E 8RF ☎ 020 7836 9136
⏰ Open access 💷 Free
🚇 Covent Garden 🍴 ⬜ ⬜ ⬜
www.coventgardenmarket.co.uk (market)
www.coventgardenlife.com (general)

Covent Garden became the site of a fruit and vegetable market in the 19th century, but when market traders moved out in 1974 it was turned into the present Piazza, with shops, stalls, eating places and street entertainers (who have to prove their worth by audition), such as the gold-painted man below.

There's still a daily market (10.30–6.30), with a wonderful range of crafts, jewellery, clothing and accessories (Tue–Sun) and antiques (Mon).

To the northwest of the Piazza is the magnificently refurbished Royal Opera House (▷ 237). On the opposite side is the former Flower Market, now London's Transport Museum (Sat–Thu 10–6, Fri 11–6; closed until 2007). The Theatre Museum (Tue–Sun 10–6), on Russell Street, has collections to please any thespian, and nearby are two of the area's famous theatres, the elegant Theatre Royal Drury Lane and the Lyceum (▷ 238), on Wellington Street.

British Museum

Britain's largest museum, covering 33ha (81.5 acres), has more than four million objects on display in around 90 galleries. It is unrivalled for the variety and quality of its treasures, the result of more than 200 years of collecting, excavation and unashamed looting.

The Egyptian Sculpture Gallery (above) displays ancient discoveries, and elsewhere there are jewel-encrusted treasures like this helmet (right). The façade of the British Museum (inset, right) is all neoclassical elegance

RATINGS				
Good for kids	● ●			
Historic interest	● ● ● ● ●			
Specialist shopping	● ● ● ●			

TIPS

● Get your bearings in the Great Court, where you can pick up floor plans and information.
● Don't expect to see everything in a day; focus on what interests you and make for one or two galleries, or on one or two collections.
● Visit in the evening, when the Great Court's restaurants and shops are open. On Thursdays and Fridays the major galleries stay open late.

SEEING THE BRITISH MUSEUM

There are two entrances: one (the main entrance) on Great Russell Street (south) and the other on Montague Place (north). Both lead into the covered Great Court, the hub of the museum and the main information office. The collections are arranged by geography, culture and theme, but the layout and size of the place can be bewildering. Note that collections from the same culture are not necessarily on the same floor.

HIGHLIGHTS

GREAT COURT AND READING ROOM

Sir Robert Smirke's imposing, neoclassical building is entered via the Great Court, added in 2000 and designed by Norman Foster. The curved glass canopy has created a huge, light space and it's worth lingering here to enjoy the sculpture displays.

At the heart of the court is the circular Reading Room, completed in 1857 to the design of Smirke's brother, Sydney. Karl Marx and other intellectuals once beavered away here, and today you can see the domed ceiling and floor-to-ceiling bookcases from a viewing area.

MAIN FLOOR
Rosetta Stone (Room 4)

Though not impressive to look at, the Rosetta Stone was instrumental in solving puzzles of the ancient Egyptian world. The black basalt slab, discovered by Napoleon's army in the Nile Delta in 1799, reproduces the same text in three languages: Greek, Demotic and Egyptian. This offered the first opportunity for modern scholars to crack the code of Egyptian hieroglyphics by comparing them with known scripts.

Elgin Marbles (Room 18)

The question of where they should be—in Greece or in Britain—still causes passionate debate. These frieze reliefs, carved between 447 and 431BC, were taken by Lord Elgin, then British ambassador in Constantinople, from the Parthenon in Athens. Elgin obtained a licence from the Turkish Sultan to remove the stones, which had suffered severe damage in 1687, and, arguing that they would not survive if they remained in Greece, brought them to Britain.

UPPER FLOORS
Portland Vase (Room 70)

This ancient cameo-glass vase was probably made in Rome between AD5 and 25. It eventually reached the hands of the third Duke of Portland in 1786, who lent it to potter Josiah Wedgwood (▷ 34), who copied its cameo design and made it famous.

Sutton Hoo Ship Burial (Room 41)

These treasures are from an Anglo-Saxon royal burial ship that survived intact in Suffolk (▷ 115) and was excavated in 1939. The ship was probably a monument to Raedwald, the last pagan king of East Anglia, who died in about 625. Besides fine gold jewels, the boat contained silver bowls and plates, silver drinking horns, a shield, a sword with jewelled gold hilt and an iron helmet with bronze and silver fittings.

Lewis Chessmen (Room 42)
Carved from the tusks of walruses, these squat figures were discovered on the island of Lewis in the Outer Hebrides of Scotland in 1831 by a crofter. Scandinavian in origin, they depict the figures used on a chess board and are believed to date from the 12th century.

Egyptian Mummies (Rooms 61–66)
Rows of preserved bodies wrapped in bandages and surrounded by their prized possessions and preferred foods have a gruesome fascination. The craftsmanship and elegance of the items are breathtaking.

Lindow Man (Room 37)
Nicknamed 'Pete Marsh' by the archaeologists who found him in a peat bog in Cheshire (▷ 26), Lindow Man is a well-preserved 2,000-year-old corpse. Among several theories is one that he was sacrificed during a Druid ceremony, in which he was beaten to death. There are signs of a blow to his head and a wound to his throat, and mistletoe grains were found in his gut, suggesting that he was fed a hallucinatory meal before being knocked out, strangled and drowned.

LOWER FLOORS
Assyrian Reliefs
Vivid carved figures carrying pots and weapons, taking part in daily activities or military campaigns, were cut into panels for the Assyrian kings' palaces and temples, and have survived from 880–612BC. Like comic strips, they relate their stories from one end of a wall to the other. Some of the most striking friezes come from the great palace of King Sennacherib, who came to the throne of Assyria in 704BC.

BACKGROUND
Wealthy physician Sir Hans Sloane (1660–1753) spent his life collecting assorted coins, books and natural history specimens that, on his death, amounted to 80,000 items. The government bought the collection and put it on display as the British Museum in 1759. As the collection grew, more galleries were added, but space was a major problem and in 1998 the British Library (▷ 120) was moved and the Great Court was given an overhaul.

BASICS

✚ 426 G2 • Great Russell Street WC1B 3DG

☎ 020 7323 8299

🕐 Sat–Wed 10–5.30, Thu–Fri 10–8.30. Great Court: Sun–Wed 9–6, Thu–Sat 9am–11pm. Check times for temporary exhibitions.

💷 Free; charges for some temporary exhibitions

🚇 Holborn, Tottenham Court Road, Russell Square, Goodge Street

🎧 90-min tours of highlights: daily 10.30, 1, 3, adult £8, child (under 11) £5. 'eyeOpener' 50-min introductory tours: daily every half hour 11–3.30, free. Audiotours in several languages, £3.50. Foreign language tours: 020 7323 8181

📖 £5 (English only) and £6 (in several languages)

🍴 Court Restaurant on upper floor of Great Court: Sat–Wed 11–5 (last orders), Thu–Fri 11–9. Reservations, 020 7323 8990

☕ Court Café (Great Court): Sun–Wed 9–5.30, Thu–Sat 10–9. Gallery Café, next to Room 12: daily 10–5

📚 Bookshop, selling art, history and archaeology titles, children's shop and guide shop

www.thebritishmuseum.ac.uk
Good level of practical information and educational links; plenty of background and attractive illustrations.

You can climb on board HMS Belfast *to experience life at sea*

Some of the exhibits at the Imperial War Museum

Kenwood House is famous for its summer open-air concerts

THE SIGHTS

DESIGN MUSEUM

🔲 427 M4 • 28 Shad Thames SE1 2YD
☎ 08708 339955 🕐 Sat–Thu 10–5.45,
Fri 10–9 💷 Adult £6, child (over 12) £4,
under 12s free 🚇 London Bridge,
Tower Hill (or Tower Gateway for DLR)
🚢 St. Katharine's Pier 📷 🏧 ♿
www.designmuseum.org

In 1989 a 1950s warehouse on
Butler's Wharf was converted into
the Design Museum, the first in
the world to be dedicated to
20th- and 21st-century design.
One of London's most inspiring
attractions, it has an evolving
permanent collection of design
classics, while temporary
exhibitions range from
retrospectives of the works of
great designers to thematic shows.

GREENWICH

🔲 431 K18 • Cutty Sark and Old Royal
Naval College, King William Walk SE10
9HT. National Maritime Museum and
Royal Observatory: Greenwich Park SE10
9NF ☎ Cutty Sark: 020 8858 3445. Old
Royal Naval College: 020 8269 4747.
National Maritime Museum and Royal
Observatory: 020 8858 4422 🕐 Cutty
Sark: daily 10–5. Old Royal Naval
College: daily 10–5; grounds: daily 8–6.
National Maritime Museum and Royal
Observatory: early Jul–early Sep daily
10–6; rest of year daily 10–5 💷 Cutty
Sark: adult £4.50, child (5–15) £3.20,
family £12. Old Royal Naval College: free.
National Maritime Museum: free, charge
for special exhibitions 🚇 Cutty Sark DLR
🚉 Greenwich 🚢 Riverboat from
Westminster Millennium Pier (1hr)
🏧 Cutty Sark and National Maritime
Museum 🍴 Regatta Café and Upper
Deck Coffee Bar (both National Maritime
Museum) 🎁
www.cuttysark.org.uk
www.greenwichfoundation.org.uk
(for Old Royal Naval College)
www.nmm.ac.uk

Approach Greenwich by river for
views of some of London's finest
architecture. Historic buildings
and the museums are the big
draw, but it's also worth browsing
the craft stalls at the weekend
market.

The sleek tea clipper *Cutty Sark*,
by Greenwich Pier, was built in
1869 to carry cargo between
Britain and the Orient. Climb on
board to get an idea of the
cramped living conditions
endured by the crew.

The monumental Old Royal
Naval College was created by Sir
Christopher Wren (1632–1723)
in 1664 as a hospital for sailors.
Two areas are open to the public:
the Painted Hall and the chapel.

New galleries have given the
National Maritime Museum more
space to tell the story of Britain's
maritime history, from the failed
16th-century invasion of the
Spanish Armada to the 19th
century. Among the collection of
ships, paintings, navigational
instruments and explorers' relics
is the jacket Nelson was wearing
when he was fatally wounded at
the Battle of Trafalgar in 1805.

The Royal Observatory was
founded by Charles II in 1675 to
tackle the problem of finding
longitude at sea. Take a look
through the telescopes and time-
measuring instruments. The Gate
Clock measures Greenwich
Mean Time, the standard by
which time is set around the
world. Stand astride the
Greenwich Meridian, marked by
a brass strip, and you'll have one
foot in the eastern hemisphere
and the other in the western.

HAMPSTEAD

🔲 431 K18 ☎ Hampstead Heath
Information Centre 020 7482 7073
🕐 Open access 💷 Free
🚇 Hampstead 🚉 Hampstead Heath
www.cityoflondon.gov.uk/openspaces

Hampstead Heath is a
wonderfully diverse public open
space of 320ha (790 acres).
Londoners come here to exercise
and picnic and swim in the three
ponds (Kenwood Pond for
women, Highgate Pond for men
and Hampstead Pond for mixed
bathing). South of the ponds is
Parliament Hill, from the top of
which are extensive views over
central London.

At the northern end of the
heath is Kenwood House
(Apr–end Oct daily 10–5; rest of
year daily 10–4), built in 1616
and remodelled by Robert Adam
in 1764 for the Earl of Mansfield.
It was left to the nation in 1927
by the first Earl of Iveagh, along
with its outstanding collection of
paintings. Here you will find
Rembrandt brooding *Portrait of
the Artist* (c1665) and Vermeer's
The Guitar Player (c1676),
among other important works by
English and Dutch masters.

The English poet John Keats
(1795–1821) came to live in
Hampstead in 1818, fell in love
with his next-door neighbour,
Fanny Brawne, and became
engaged to her in 1819. During
his brief time at what is now
known as Keats House (Tue–Sun
1–5, regular guided tours) in
Keats Grove he wrote some of
his best-loved poems.

Built in 1695, red-brick Fenton
House (Mar Sat–Sun 2–5;
Apr–end Oct Sat–Sun 11–5,
Wed–Fri 2–5) on Windmill Hill,
off Hampstead Grove, is one of
the best of its period still
surviving in London. Period
furnishings are complemented
by a collection of ceramics and
17th-century needlework and the
Benton Fletcher Collection of
17th- and 18th-century
instruments.

Sigmund Freud (1856–1939),
the founder of psychoanalysis,
lived at 20 Maresfield Gardens,
in south Hampstead, from 1938,
after escaping Nazi-occupied
Vienna. The Freud Museum
(Wed–Sun 12–5) is devoted to
his life and work and includes his
famous analysis couch.

The Albert Memorial, Queen Victoria's tribute to her husband. His statue is holding a catalogue for 1851's Great Exhibition

The Inns of Court can offer a secluded, college-like atmosphere

IMPERIAL WAR MUSEUM

✚ 426 J5 • Lambeth Road SE1 6HZ
☎ 020 7416 5320; 020 7416 5000 (recording) 🕐 Daily 10–6 💷 Free (except for some special exhibitions) 🚇 Lambeth North, Elephant and Castle, Southwark, Waterloo 🎧 Audio guides £3.50 📖 £3.50 💻 🚻 ♿
www.iwm.org.uk

An imposing pair of naval guns guards the entrance to this fascinating but sobering museum, and provides a taster of the collection, which covers wars involving Britain or the Commonwealth since 1914. The museum's real emphasis and strengths are in its focus on the effects of war in the 20th century on the lives of soldiers and civilians alike. It leaves you with no doubt as to what war is really like.

Military equipment is on show in the Large Exhibits Gallery, where tanks, artillery, planes and submarines are haphazardly parked, or suspended. Other displays include a re-creation of World War I trench warfare and the World War II Blitz, accompanied by sounds and smells. The Secret War exhibition features one of the remaining German Enigma machines, used to encode messages. The art galleries give an impressive insight into war; the centrepiece is *Gassed* by John Singer Sargent (1856–1925).

The Holocaust Exhibition (not for children under 14) examines the Nazi persecution of Europe's Jewish communities and other groups from 1933 to 1945.

HMS *Belfast* (Mar–end Oct daily 10–6; rest of year daily 10–5) is moored near Tower Bridge. The only surviving armoured warship to be built in the first half of the 20th century, it had an active career during World War II.

INNS OF COURT

Lincoln's Inn ✚ 426 H2 • WC2A 3TL ☎ 020 7405 1393; **Gray's Inn** ✚ 426 H1 • 8 South Square WC1R 5ET ☎ 020 7458 7800; **Inner Temple/Middle Temple** ✚ 426 J2–J5 • King's Bench Walk EC4Y 7HL/Middle Temple Lane EC4Y 9BT ☎ Inner Temple 020 7797 8250; Middle Temple 020 7427 4830 💷 Free 🚇 Chancery Lane (closed Sun), Blackfriars, Holborn, Temple
www.lincolnsinn.org.uk
www.graysinn.org.uk
www.innertemple.org.uk
www.middletemple.org.uk

Four Inns of Court were created in the 14th century to provide accommodation for lawyers and their pupils: Gray's Inn, Lincoln's Inn and two inns at Temple. They are the home of London's legal profession, and every barrister (higher court advocate) must be a member of an Inn.

Lincoln's Inn (Mon–Fri 9–5.30) spans 400 years; 15th-century Old Hall is the setting for the Jarndyce v. Jarndyce case in Dickens' novel *Bleak House*, while gas lamps light the 17th-century houses in New Square.

Blitz bombing destroyed much of Gray's Inn (gardens only Mon–Fri 12–2.30), but the most important buildings have been restored. These include the 17th-century gateway into the gardens, first laid out in 1606 by English philosopher and statesman Sir Francis Bacon (1561–1626).

Two Inns of Court make up the Temple (Inner Temple gardens Mon–Fri 12–3. Middle Temple Hall Sep–Jul Mon–Fri 10–12, 3–4; closed Aug. Middle Temple gardens May–end Jul, Sep Mon–Fri 12–3). The 12th-century Temple Church still stands at the heart of this network of alleys, gardens and courtyards, where the first recorded performance of Shakespeare's *Twelfth Night* took place.

KENSINGTON

Kensington Palace ✚ 424 A4 • Kensington Gardens W8 4PX ☎ 0870 751 5170 🕐 Mar–end Oct daily 10–6; rest of year 10–5 💷 Adult £11, child (5–15) £7.20, family £32 🚇 High Street Kensington, Queensway, Notting Hill Gate 📖 Sound guide included in price; guidebook in English and German £3.95 🍴 Orangery Restaurant 🚻 ♿
www.kensington-palace.org.uk

A royal home for more than 300 years, 17th-century Kensington Palace is probably most famous as the home of Diana, Princess of Wales. The Royal Ceremonial Dress Collection includes some of her dresses.

The Queen's Apartments, including Queen Mary's Bedchamber, and King's Apartments, with ceiling paintings by William Kent (c1685–1748), are of interest for their opulence.

Hyde Park was opened to the public by James I in the 17th century. Members of the Household Cavalry exercise their horses along Rotten Row and at 10.30am and 12pm you can watch them riding to and from the Changing the Guard ceremony at Buckingham Palace (▷ 119).

The city's greenery extends west into Kensington Gardens, the grounds of Kensington Palace. The Serpentine Gallery hosts changing exhibitions of contemporary art (daily 10–6 during exhibitions, free). North of here are two sculptures: *Physical Energy* (1904), by George Frederick Watts (1817–1904), and *Peter Pan* (1912) by Sir George Frampton (1860–1928), commemorating the hero of J. M. Barrie's story. Close by, the Diana, Princess of Wales Memorial Playground opened in 2000. Queen Victoria's beloved husband, Prince Albert, who died of typhoid, is commemorated in the dazzling Albert Memorial.

THE SIGHTS

A river runs through it: Climb Richmond Hill to get panoramic views across London and the snaking River Thames

Follow the story of evolution at the Natural History Museum

THE SIGHTS

MADAME TUSSAUD'S

✚ 425 D1 • Marylebone Road NW1 5LR ☎ 0870 400 3000 (reservations only; fee applies) ◉ Mon–Fri 9.30–5.30, Sat–Sun 9–6 (extended hours peak times). Auditorium shows every 20 min daily 10.30–closing (peak times), Mon–Fri 12.30–closing, Sat–Sun 10.30–closing (off-peak times) (not recommended for under 5s) ◢ Adult £19.99, child (5–16) £15.99, family (must reserve ahead) £68 (includes Auditorium) but prices vary according to time and season, call ahead to check. ◉ Baker Street ✚ Reserve a timed ticket in advance to avoid a long wait ◰ Guidebook £4.50 ◻ ⊞ ⋔ www.madame-tussauds.com

Madame Tussaud's waxworks collection changes all the time—celebrities know they've made it when their waxwork appears here. Have your photograph taken with just about anyone, from James Bond to Beethoven. One of the highlights is the Chamber of Horrors. Next door, the Auditorium—formerly known as the London Planetarium—opened in 1958 and is one of the largest in the world. Its centrepiece is an eight-minute audio-visual star show.

MUSEUM OF LONDON

✚ 427 K2 • London Wall EC2Y 5HN ☎ 0870 444 3852 ◉ Mon–Sat 10–5.50, Sun 12–5.50 ◢ Free ◉ Moorgate, Barbican, St. Paul's, Bank ◰ £4.95, in English only ◻ ⊞ ⋔ www.museumoflondon.org.uk

Laid out in a striking building near the Barbican, the Museum of London is the world's largest urban history museum and Europe's biggest archaeological archive. Most impressive is the Roman London Gallery, which explains the development of *Londinium*. Large models illustrate the city's growth, and a huge array of ordinary items shows how people lived and worked.

NATURAL HISTORY MUSEUM

✚ 424 B5 • Cromwell Road SW7 5BD ☎ 020 7942 5000 ◉ Mon–Sat 10–5.50, Sun 11–5.50. Wildlife Garden: Apr–end Oct daily 12–5 (except during bad weather) ◢ Free. Special exhibitions around £5, child (5–16) £3 ◉ South Kensington ◼ Tours of Darwin Centre (over 10s only), free, reservations required ◰ £3.50, English only ⋔ ◻ ⊞ ⋔ www.nhm.ac.uk

England's most significant collection of dinosaur remains, and over 70 million items (not all on display) from whales to meteorites, are kept at the outstanding Natural History Museum.

The galleries are divided into the Life Galleries and the Earth Galleries, where state-of-the-art displays explain the making of the planet. Dinosaurs (Gallery 21) is one of the most popular galleries: the lighting is low, and there is an animatronic re-creation of a *Tyrannosaurus rex* in action. For a new take on arthropods (Gallery 33) visit Creepy Crawlies to see how many millions of insects, spiders and crustacea inhabit our world.

The Earth Galleries include Visions of Earth, a dramatic, ethereal space highlighting some fantastic geological specimens. Power Within focuses on volcanoes and earthquakes, including a simulation of the earthquake that shook Kobe, in Japan, in 1995. Other galleries focus on Earth's natural treasury of gemstones.

Meet some of the scientists who work on the museum's unique collections in a Darwin Centre Live talk or delve deeper and join a tour of the museum's vast storerooms, where you can see specimens collected by Captain Cook and Charles Darwin.

RICHMOND

✚ 431 K18 ✚ Tourist Information Centre, Old Town Hall, Whittaker Avenue, Richmond, Surrey TW9 1TP, tel 020 8940 9125 ◉ Richmond ◉ Richmond www.visitrichmond.co.uk

Several important attractions make Richmond-upon-Thames an excellent day trip. Ham House (Apr–end Oct Sat–Wed 1–5; closed Thu, Fri), in Ham Street, is one of the most beautiful and well-preserved Stuart houses in Britain, filled with rare furniture, paintings and textiles. Built in 1610, it was the home of the Tollemache family, who were deeply involved in the Civil War and Restoration court politics (▷ 32).

Originally enclosed as a hunting ground by Charles I in 1637, Richmond Park (open access during daylight hours) is the largest open space in London. Herds of graceful deer still graze here. In spring, the Isabella Plantation is a particularly beautiful area of the park.

There's something to see all year round at Kew's Royal Botanic Gardens near Richmond (Apr–end Aug Mon–Fri 9.30–6.30, Sat–Sun 9.30–7.30; Sep–Oct daily 9.30–6; Nov–end Jan daily 9.30–4.15; Feb, Mar daily 9.30–5.30), which were created under George III and developed into one of the world's foremost facilities for horticultural research.

The Temperate House, once the world's largest greenhouse, has an elevated gallery from where to view the plants, including the Chilean wine palm, planted in 1846.

The Princess of Wales Conservatory opened in 1987: Arid desert moves gradually to orchid-filled tropics. British native wild flowers are the theme at Queen Charlotte's Cottage and Gardens.

Heart of gold: looking down the aisle of St. Paul's towards the altar

ST. PAUL'S CATHEDRAL

Britain's only domed cathedral, St. Paul's is second only in size to St. Peter's in Rome.

Sir Christopher Wren's masterpiece is a dramatic combination of vast, airy spaces and elaborate decoration. A wide flight of steps leads up to the west front entrance, flanked by two clock towers.

THE DOME AND GALLERIES

Eight pillars support the huge dome, 111m (364ft) high and weighing about 65,000 tonnes. The acoustics are such that someone standing on the opposite side of the gallery will hear your whispers clearly after several seconds' delay. The frescoes on the dome depict scenes from the life of St. Paul and were painted by Sir James Thornhill between 1716 and 1719. The Golden Gallery runs around the outer dome, a breathtaking 85m (280ft) from the cathedral floor. A hole in the floor gives a dizzying view down.

THE CHANCEL

This part of the cathedral is a riot of 19th-century Byzantine-style gilding. In the north choir aisle is a marble sculpture, *Mother and Child*, by Henry Moore (1898–1986). A marble effigy of poet John Donne (1572–1631) stands in the south choir aisle. This is one of the few effigies that survived the Great Fire of London in 1666, and you can make out scorch marks on its base.

The Duke of Wellington (1769–1852), hero of the Napoleonic Wars and prime minister from 1828 to 1830, lies in a simple Cornish granite casket. Admiral Nelson (1758–1805), who died in action at the Battle of Trafalgar, lies in the middle of the crypt. Nelson's coffin went with him into battle, and after his death he was preserved in it in French brandy for the journey home. At Gibraltar the coffin was put into a lead-lined casket and steeped in distilled wine. Finally his remains were encased in two more coffins before being buried under Cardinal Wolsey's 16th-century sarcophagus.

THE CATHEDRAL'S HISTORY

The first St. Paul's was built in 604, rebuilt 300 years later after a Viking attack and replaced by a Norman cathedral, Old St. Paul's, in 1087. After its destruction in the Great Fire of 1666, Sir Christopher Wren (1632–1723) was commissioned to build a new one. It was finally completed in 1710.

RATINGS	
Good for kids	●●
Historic interest	●●●●●
Value for money	●●●●●

TIP

● There are free organ recitals at 5pm every Sunday, but bring some loose change for the collection at the end.

BASICS

✚ 427 K2 • St. Paul's Churchyard EC4M 8AD

☎ 020 7246 8348

🕐 Mon–Sat 8.30–4.30. Daily for services. Triforium tours (Library, West End Gallery, Trophy Room and Wren's Great Model); advance reservation required, tel: 020 7246 8357 (Mon–Fri 9–2); £12

💷 Cathedral, Crypt and Galleries: adult £8, child (6–16) £3, family £19.50

🚇 St. Paul's, Blackfriars

🚉 Blackfriars

🚌 £4

🎧 Guided tours (in English only) Mon–Sat 11, 11.30, 1.30 and 2. Adult £2.50, under 16s £1. Audio tours (9.45–3): £3.50 in English, French, German, Italian and Spanish

🍴 Refectory restaurant

☕ Crypt Café

🚻 🔧

www.stpauls.co.uk
Virtual tour of the cathedral. Good to look at, but a fairly basic level of background and information.

The next Einstein? Hands-on activities at the Science Museum

The Globe now looks as it did when it first opened in 1599

Somerset House is one of the finest buildings on the Strand

ROYAL ACADEMY OF ARTS

✚ 425 F3 • Burlington House, Piccadilly W1J 0BD ☎ 020 7300 8000 (general), 020 7300 5760 (recording) ⊙ Exhibitions: Sat–Thu 10–6, Fri 10–10. Fine Rooms: Tue–Fri 1–4.30, Sat–Sun 10–6 ⓦ Adult £8–£11, child (12–18) £3, child (9–11) £2, family £25 ◖ Tours of Fine Rooms Tue–Fri 1pm, free ◎ Green Park, Piccadilly Circus ⦿ ▢ ♿ ♈
www.royalacademy.org.uk

Burlington House was built as a Palladian mansion for the Earl of Burlington in around 1720. Since 1768 it has been the Royal Academy of Arts, England's first formal art school. English portrait painter Sir Joshua Reynolds (1723–92) was the first president, and painters John Constable (1776–1837) and J. M. W. Turner (1775–1851) were among the first students. Today the Royal Academy hosts major exhibitions of art from international collections. The Royal Academy Summer Exhibition (Jun to mid-Aug) is a hugely popular show of work by both amateurs and professionals.

ST. PAUL'S CATHEDRAL

See page 127

SCIENCE MUSEUM

✚ 424 B5 • Exhibition Road SW7 2DD ☎ 0870 870 4868 ⊙ Daily 10–6 ⓦ Main museum free (charges for some special exhibitions); IMAX: adult £7.50, child (16 and under) £6; Robots: adult £9, child (16 and under) £7.50, family £22–£29; SimEx Simulator: adult £3.75, child (16 and under) £2.75; Motionride Simulator: adult £2.50, child (16 and under) £1.50 ◎ South Kensington ⦿ £2 ▢ ♿ ♈
www.sciencemuseum.org.uk

Come to the Science Museum for a celebration—and explanation—of humankind's greatest inventions and scientific achievements.

Most people start in the popular Launch Pad, a truly hands-on gallery aimed at children. The ground floor focuses on power and space; main attractions include the full-size replica of the *Apollo 10* command module and the 1829 rail locomotive *Rocket*. The Flight gallery exhibits the Gypsy Moth plane *Jason*, flown from Britain to Australia by aviator Amy Johnson (1903–41) in 1930. Galleries on the upper floors tell the story of the science and art of medicine and the Wellcome Wing brings you up to date with interactive exhibitions about current medical science.

SHAKESPEARE'S GLOBE

✚ 427 K3 • 21 New Globe Walk, Bankside SE1 9DT ☎ 020 7902 1400, 020 7401 9919 (Box office) ⊙ May–end Sep daily 9–4; rest of year daily 10–5. Theatrical performances May–end Sep daily ⓦ Exhibition and theatre tour: adult £9, child (5–15) £6.50, family £25. Theatre performance: adult £13–£29, child (under 16) £11–£27, plus (600) £5 standing only tickets ◎ Blackfriars, Cannon Street, London Bridge, St. Paul's, Southwark ⦿ £5 ⦿ Daily 12–2.30, 5.30–11 ◖ May–Sep daily 10–15 min after end performance; Oct–end Apr daily 10–6 ♿ ♈
www.shakespeares-globe.org

The original Globe was one of Britain's first purpose-built theatres, erected by a company that included Shakespeare in 1599. It was destroyed by fire during a production of *Hamlet* in 1613. A project began in 1969 to create an accurate, functioning reconstruction, using materials, tools and techniques closely matching those of Elizabethan times, but it was 1997 before it was finished.

The theatre is built of unseasoned oak and held together with 6,000 oak pegs. It is crowned with the first thatched roof to be built in the city (understandably) since the Great Fire in 1666. In the middle, an elevated stage and an open-air yard are surrounded on three sides by covered tiers of benches that seat 1,500. Productions are held in the afternoon (May–end Sep only), much as in Shakespeare's day, subject to fine weather.

SIR JOHN SOANE'S MUSEUM

✚ 426 H2 • 13 Lincoln's Inn Fields WC2A 3BP ☎ 020 7405 2107 ⊙ Tue–Sat 10–5; first Tue each month also 6–9pm ⓦ Free; donations box provided ◖ Guided tour Sat 2.30 (tickets sold from 2) £3 ◎ Chancery Lane (closed Sun), Holborn ♿ ♈
www.soane.org

From the moment you knock to be allowed in, it's clear that this is a museum unlike any other. Sir John Soane (1753–1837) was Professor of Architecture at the Royal Academy of Arts and arranged his eccentric and eclectic collection of art and objects for the benefit of his students, filling every inch of space in his house. You'll find yourself wandering among Classical and Renaissance statues and busts, marbles and bronzes, urns, altars, antique gems, odd bits of demolished London buildings, Indian ivory-inlaid furniture, Peruvian ceramics, cork models of Greek temples, Napoleonic medals, thousands of architectural drawings, and a couple of mummified cats. The Picture Room is a highlight: The ingenious use of hinged screens instead of walls allowed Soane to fit more than 100 works into this small room, including William Hogarth's celebrated *A Rake's Progress* (1733). Just enjoy the experience: A floorplan suggests the route Soane himself recommended.

Tate Modern now fills the renovated Bankside building

Tower Bridge is beautiful when illuminated at night, providing an impressive gateway to the city

THE SIGHTS

SOMERSET HOUSE

✚ 426 H3 • Strand WC2R 0RN ☎ 020 7845 4600 🕐 Daily 10–6; extended hours for Courtyard, River Terrace Café and Admiralty Restaurant 🚇 Somerset House: free. Courtauld Institute of Art Gallery, Gilbert Collection, Hermitage Rooms (each): adult £5–£6, child (under 16) free. Courtauld Institute of Art Gallery: free Mon 10–2 🚇 Temple (closed Sun), Covent Garden, Charing Cross, Embankment 🚢 Riverboat to Embankment Pier 🎫 £4.95 🍽 Admiralty Restaurant ☕ River Terrace Café 🏛 🚻
www.somerset-house.org.uk

The rejuvenation of this great riverside landmark has given London a new arts complex in a splendid 18th-century setting.

The Courtauld Institute of Art Gallery houses a stunning assembly of six private collections, featuring Old Masters, Impressionist and post-Impressionist paintings, sculpture and applied arts. A suite of softly top-lit rooms displays works by Paul Cézanne, Vincent Van Gogh, Paul Gauguin and Edouard Manet.

The Gilbert Collection consists of more than 800 superb works of art, donated by Sir Arthur Gilbert (1913–2001). The collection moves from mosiac to pietra dura (hard stone) to 18th-century micromosaic from Rome. Make time to see the lavish silver and gold tableware.

The Hermitage Museum in St. Petersburg lends a regularly changing display of objects to the Hermitage Rooms.

TATE BRITAIN

✚ 426 G5 • Millbank SW1P 4RG ☎ 020 7887 8008 (recording), 020 7887 8000 🕐 Daily 10–5.50 🚇 Free, donations welcome. Charge for special exhibitions 🚇 Pimlico, Vauxhall, Westminster 🚢 From Tate Modern (every 40 min) 🚌 Mon–Fri 11, 12, 1.15, 2, 3; Sat–Sun 12, 2.30, 3. Free.

Audiotours free, English, French, German, Italian, Spanish 🎫 £4.99 🍽 💻 🏛 🚻
www.tate.org.uk/britain/

The Tate Gallery, now Tate Britain, transferred its international collection to Tate Modern (▷ below) in 2000, allowing its British collection from 1500 to the present day (the world's largest) to spread out considerably. Despite this, the gallery still owns far more than it can display, and the paintings on show, presented chronologically, are changed every year. All the great names of British art are represented, from Nicholas Hilliard's 16th-century portrait of Queen Elizabeth I and fashionable 17th-century portraits by Sir Peter Lely and Sir Godfrey Kneller, through the work of major 18th-century figures such as William Hogarth, Joshua Reynolds and Thomas Gainsborough, and progressing into innovative 19th-century paintings by William Blake, John Constable and J. M. W. Turner, who is especially well represented. The Pre-Raphaelites are represented in force, and the collection moves into the 20th century with work by J. S. Lowry, Henry Moore, Barbara Hepworth, Francis Bacon, David Hockney and Lucian Freud. A boat service links the gallery with Tate Modern.

TATE MODERN

✚ 427 K3 • Bankside SE1 9TG ☎ 020 7887 8008 (recording), 020 7887 8000 🕐 Sun–Thu 10–6, Fri–Sat 10–10 🚇 Free, donations welcome. Charge for special exhibitions 🚇 Southwark, Blackfriars, St. Paul's 🚢 From Tate Britain (every 40 min) 🚌 Daily 11, 12, 2, 3 (and 6.30, first Fri of month), free. Audiotours £2, English, French, German, Italian, Spanish 🎫 £4.99, English only 🍽 💻 🏛 🚻
www.tate.org.uk/modern/

Tate Modern, housed in the spectacularly restored Bankside Power Station, is one of the world's leading museums of modern art, and even approaching the gallery is stimulating, especially if you cross the Millennium Bridge, with its wonderful river views, from St. Paul's Cathedral.

Every year there are three additional special loan exhibitions and several shows focusing on a single artist, theme or period. The permanent themed displays always include works by the most influential artists of the 20th century, covering significant artistic periods and movements, with combinations of film media, installations, painting, photography and sculpture. Works by European artists include *The Kiss* by Auguste Rodin. American artists are represented by Richard Hamilton's *The Large Glass* and Andy Warhol's *Marilyn Diptych*, among others.

TOWER BRIDGE

✚ 427 M3 • SE1 2UP ☎ 020 7403 3761 🕐 Apr–end Sep daily 10–6.30; rest of year daily 9.30–6 🚇 Adult £5.50, child (5–15) £3, family £10–£14 🚇 Tower Hill, London Bridge, Tower Gateway DLR 🚢 Riverboat to Tower Millennium Pier 🎫 £2.50 🏛 🚻
www.towerbridge.org.uk

London's best-known bridge links the Tower of London (▷ 130) and the south bank of the River Thames. It opened to the public in 1982. The hydraulically operated bascules are the main draw, designed to allow tall ships to sail through and still lifted more than 900 times a year.

The neo-Gothic towers are an attraction in themselves. Climb to the upper walkways and engine rooms, where an exhibition details the controversies that preceded the eventual construction of the bridge, opened in 1894.

RATINGS

Historic interest	●●●●●
Good for kids	●●●●●
Value for money	●●●●

TIPS

● Crowds can be a problem in the summer. To save waiting, buy tickets in advance by telephoning 0870 756 7070 or online at www.hrp.org.uk.
● There are free daily guided tours by yeoman warders; times are posted every morning at the main entrance.

BASICS

✚ 427 M3 • Tower of London EC3N 4AB ☎ 0870 756 6060 (recording), 0870 756 7070 (tickets) 🕐 Mar–end Oct Tue–Sat 9–6, Sun–Mon 10–6; rest of year Tue–Sat 9–5, Sun–Mon 10–5. Last admission 1 hr before closing. All internal buildings close 30 min after last admission; Tower closes 1 hr after last admission. To watch the Ceremony of the Keys (▷ 242) apply in writing at least 6–8 weeks in advance for free tickets to The Ceremony of the Keys Office, HM Tower of London, London EC3N 4AB 💷 Adult £14.50, child (5–15) £9.50, family £42 🚇 Tower Hill, Tower Gateway DLR 🚢 Tower Millennium Pier 📖 £3.95, English, French, German, Italian, Japanese, Russian, Spanish 🎧 Audioguide, £3, in English, French, German, Italian, Japanese, Russian, Spanish 🍴🛍️🏧🚻

www.hrp.org.uk
Straightforward site with links, historical background and full visitor information.

Crime and punishment: Prisoners rarely left the Tower in one piece

TOWER OF LONDON

Prison, palace, home to the Crown Jewels and symbol of 1,000 years of Britain's royal history.

In previous centuries, prisoners accused of treason would enter the Tower of London by boat through Traitors' Gate–some, such as Henry VIII's second wife, Anne Boleyn, taking their final journey. Today the visitors' entrance is through the Middle Tower and you'll probably get out alive.

THE WHITE TOWER

At the heart of the Tower is its oldest medieval building, the White Tower, thought to date from 1078 and built to serve as a fortress and a royal residence. There's an exhibition about small arms, from the Royal Armouries collection, and spiral stairs lead to the gloriously simple Chapel of St. John the Evangelist. John Flamsteed (1646–1719), Charles II's astronomer, observed the stars from the turrets before moving to new headquarters at Greenwich (▷ 124).

THE CROWN JEWELS

First stop for many visitors is the Jewel House, where displays tell the history of the Coronation Regalia (Crown Jewels) before reaching the treasury, where the jewels are kept. An excellent visual story of the jewels entertains those waiting to view the exhibits, and it is possible to repeat the circuit round the jewels immediately for a second look.

The jewels mainly date from the restoration of the monarchy in 1660 (▷ 32). Among the priceless stones in the collection is the world's biggest cut diamond, the 530-carat First Star of Africa.

TOWER GREEN

The famous prisoners incarcerated and executed here over the years provide the human interest. The Bloody Tower gets its name from the supposed murder of the two princes, Edward and Richard, sons of Edward IV and allegedly the victims of their ambitious uncle, Richard III. The Queen's House, a black-and-white building next to the Bloody Tower, was the scene of Guy Fawkes' interrogation in 1605 (▷ 32) and of a daring escape when the Earl of Nithsdale, imprisoned after the 1715 Jacobite rebellion, made his getaway dressed as a woman. The high-ranking prisoners were kept in the 13th-century Beauchamp Tower. Tower Green was the main focus for suffering and heroics, and was where Anne Boleyn, among others, was beheaded.

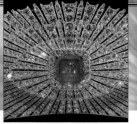

The Cartier tiara at the V&A glitters with expensive jewels

VICTORIA AND ALBERT MUSEUM

🚇 424 C5 • Cromwell Road SW7 2RL
☎ 020 7942 2000 🕐 Mon, Tue, Thu–Sun 10–5.45, Wed, last Fri of month 10–10 💷 Free, except for some special exhibitions and events 🚇 South Kensington 🎟 £3.95 ☕ Free introductory tours daily (1 hr) on the half-hour 10.30–3.30; also 4.30 Wed; meet in the Grand Entrance 🍴 🚻
🏛 🚻
www.vam.ac.uk

In 1852, the aim in creating the V&A (as it is known) was to give everyone access to great art and to provide a source of inspiration for British manufacturers and designers. It retains an exciting freshness and diversity.

Tens of thousands of items are on show, including fashion and textiles, furniture and paintings, jewellery, ceramics, glass, silver and ironwork, and there isn't a hope of seeing more than a small sample on a single visit.

The national collection of photography treats you to more than 300,000 photos, displayed in an elegant gallery that showcases key photographers from all over the world, including William Henry Fox Talbot and Henri Cartier-Bresson.

Tippoo's Tiger (above) is probably the best-known piece in the V & A's Nehru Gallery of Indian Art

TRAFALGAR SQUARE

New Year's Eve, pigeons, Admiral Lord Nelson and two national galleries on London's central square.

Britain and London Visitor Centre
🚇 426 G3 • 1 Lower Regent Street SW1Y 4XT (call in person only)
🕐 Open access 💷 Free 🚇 Charing Cross, Leicester Square

RATINGS	
Good for kids	● ● ●
Historic interest	● ● ● ●
Cultural interest	● ● ● ● ●

One of the world's most famous squares sits at the northern end of Whitehall (▷ 132), commemorating Admiral Lord Nelson's victory against Napoleon and the French at the 1805 Battle of Trafalgar. Nelson towers on his 56m (185ft) column in the middle of the square, guarded by four bronze lions.

Steps lead up to the Corinthian portico of the church of St. Martin-in-the-Fields (Mon–Sat 8–6.30, Sun 8–7), at the northeastern corner of the square. Officially the parish church of Buckingham Palace, St. Martin's has strong royal connections.

The National Gallery's (daily 10–6, Wed to 9pm) collection of Western European art, dating from 1250 to about 1900, is arranged by period. Paintings from 1500 to 1600 are displayed in the West Wing: Don't miss Hans Holbein the Younger's (1497–1543) cryptic *The Ambassadors* (1533). Must-see paintings in the East Wing include *Sunflowers* (1888) in Room 45, which is devoted to Vincent Van Gogh (1853–90). In the North Wing are painters from the Dutch School including Peter Paul Rubens, Rembrandt van Rijn and Jan Vermeer—and Impressionists. One highlight of the Sainsbury Wing, which focuses on the early Renaissance, is Sandro Botticelli's (c1445–1510) *Venus and Mars*.

Tucked away at the back of the National Gallery, the National Portrait Gallery (Sat–Wed 10–5.50, Thu–Fri 10–8.50) is a Who's Who of the key players in British history, science and the arts. Founded in 1856, the collection consists of more than 7,000 paintings, drawings, sculptures and photographs, arranged chronologically over three floors. Dominating the second floor's Tudor Galleries is the magnificent portrait of Elizabeth I (1592) by Marcus Gheeraerts the Younger (1561–1635), a tour de force of political propaganda. Rooms 4–8 are devoted to the Stuarts, while other rooms focus on the 18th century, and include a unique, unfinished sketch (c1810) of Jane Austen by her sister. Victorians fill most of the first-floor rooms. Britain since 1990 occupies the ground floor and includes Bryan Organ's famous 1981 painting of Princess Diana sitting cross-legged, contrasting with the formality of earlier royal portraits.

The National Gallery borders one side of busy Trafalgar Square

The Battle of Britain in stained glass at Westminster Abbey

Members of the Household Cavalry take their duties very seriously at Horse Guards Parade along Whitehall

THE SIGHTS

WALLACE COLLECTION

✚ 425 D2 • Hertford House, Manchester Square W1V 3BN ☎ 020 7563 9500 🕔 Daily 10–5 💷 Free 🚇 Bond Street, Baker Street 🎫 Free guided tours Mon–Fri 1, also Wed, Sat 11.30, Sun 3 📖 £7 🛍 ♿ www.wallacecollection.org

The Hertford family began this world-class collection of art when the fourth Marquess of Hertford, living in Paris during the French Revolution, bought 18th-century paintings, porcelain and furniture to complement his inheritance of fine art. His son, Sir Richard Wallace, added Renaissance ceramics, bronzes, armour and jewellery, and his widow left the enviable collection, including furnishings made for the palaces of Fontainebleau and Versailles, to the nation in 1897.

WESTMINSTER ABBEY

✚ 426 G4 • Parliament Square SW1P 3PA ☎ 020 7654 4900 🕔 Mon–Tue, Thu–Fri 9.30–4.45 (last admission 3.45), Wed 9.30–7, Sat 9.30–2.45 (last admission 1.45). Sun worship only. College Garden: Apr–end Sep Tue–Thu 10–6; rest of year Tue–Thu 10–4 💷 Adult £10, child (11–16) £6, under-11s (2 children per adult) free, family £22 🚇 St. James's Park, Westminster 🎫 90-min tours, £4 per person. Audioguides £3 📖 £3–£8 🛍 ♿ www.westminster-abbey.org

The largest surviving medieval church in London has been the setting for all royal coronations since 1066, and its mausoleum commemorates 3,300 of the nation's most famous historical figures. You enter by the north transept, then turn left to take a one-way, clockwise tour of the church and cloisters. North of the sanctuary is the Lady Chapel, where you can view the white-marble effigy of Elizabeth I, who died in 1603. The main part of the chapel, with its fan-vaulted

ceiling, is an impressive setting for the royal tombs arranged around the altar and aisles.

The south transept, also known as Poets' Corner, is where great poets, authors, artists and actors are honoured with memorials. A few doors down, the Abbey Museum has macabre wax effigies of Queen Elizabeth I, Charles II and Lord Nelson.

WESTMINSTER, PALACE OF

✚ 426 G4 • Parliament Square SW1A 0AA ☎ 020 7219 4272 (House of Commons Information Office), 0870 906 3773 (summer tours tickets) 🕔 Tours during summer recess, Aug, Mon, Tue, Fri, Sat 9.15–4.30, Wed, Thu 1.15–4.30; Sep–early Oct Mon, Fri, Sat 9.15–4.30, Tue–Thu 1.15–4.30; Clock Tower Mon–Fri 10.30, 11.30, 2.30 🚇 Public Gallery (House of Commons) and Visitors Gallery (House of Lords) and Clock Tower free; tours see below 🚇 Westminster 🚢 Westminster Millennium Pier 🎫 Tour during summer recess: adult £7, child (4–16) £5, family £22 📖 Free 🛍 ♿ 🚻 www.parliament.uk

Despite their appearance, the Houses of Parliament, which form the main part of the Palace of Westminster, are 19th-century buildings. The original medieval palace was virtually destroyed by fire in 1834 and the competition to design a replacement in Elizabethan style was won by architect Charles Barry (1795–1860) and his assistant, Augustus Pugin (1812–52). The famous clock tower housing Big Ben (the hour bell), was completed in 1858.

The Jewel Tower (Apr–end Oct daily 10–5; rest of year daily 10–4) was used to store Edward III's treasures. An exhibition in the tower explains the history of Parliament.

For a guided tour of the Houses of Parliament, UK

residents should contact their Member of Parliament. Visitors from overseas are not admitted during session but may enter during the summer recess on a pre-reserved tour. Anyone is able to attend debates in both the House of Commons and the House of Lords (join the queue outside St. Stephen's Entrance and expect to wait one to two hours during the afternoon). To arrange a tour of the Clock Tower (Mon–Fri 10.30, 11.30 and 2.30; free), UK residents should contact their Member of Parliament (overseas visitors are not admitted).

WHITEHALL

✚ 426 G4 ℹ Britain and London Visitor Centre, 1 Lower Regent Street SW1Y 4XT (call in person only) 🕔 Open access 💷 Free 🚇 Charing Cross, Westminster

Whitehall is the broad avenue connecting Trafalgar Square (▷ 131) with Parliament Square. Heading south, the navy was run from the first building on the right, the Admiralty, when the British fleet was considered the most powerful in the world.

Next is Horse Guards Parade, where two members of the Household Cavalry mount guard on horseback daily between 10am and 4pm. Beyond Horse Guards is the gated entrance to Downing Street, where the prime minister and chancellor have their official residences.

At the heart of Whitehall is the Cenotaph, designed by Sir Edwin Lutyens in 1920 to commemorate the victims of World War I.

The Churchill Museum and Cabinet War Rooms (daily 9.30–6), reached by turning right on to King Charles Street, were the secret underground rooms where Sir Winston Churchill oversaw his World War II plans.

WALES

Today the Welsh capital, Cardiff, is a resurgent, politically independent city. But the number of castles watching over Wales testifies to the battles that have been fought for this mountainous country. In addition to castles, visitors will find one of the most popular gardens in Britain, at Bodnant, and the unusual holiday village of Portmeirion.

KEY SIGHTS

The view of Aberdulais Falls from above is the best part of the visit

Striped deckchairs line the seafront at Aberystwyth

Beaumaris Castle, Anglesey: unfinished but still mighty

ABERDULAIS FALLS

🏠 429 E18 • Aberdulais, near Neath SA10 8EU ☎ 01639 636674 🕐 Mar Fri–Sun 11–4; Apr–end Oct Mon–Fri 10–5; rest of year Sat–Sun and public holidays 11–6, Fri–Sun 11–4 💷 Adult £3.20, child (5–16) £1.60, family £8 🍴 Sat–Sun and public holidays, in summer 🏪 🚻 🅿
www.nationaltrust.org.uk

The water thunders into a natural amphitheatre of rock in a wooded setting, and has powered industry for over 400 years. The copper-smelting works founded in 1584 later gave way to flour and grist mills, then tinplate works from 1830 to 1890, and today a hydroelectric plant is installed here. Displays (including letters and engravings) in the information section and turbine house trace the long history of this complicated industrial site.

ABERYSTWYTH

🏠 433 E16 ℹ Lisburne House, Terrace Road, Aberystwyth SY23 2AG, tel 01970 612125 🚉 Aberystwyth
www.aboutaber.co.uk

Aberystwyth is a lively university town with a strong culture of the Welsh language: Welsh and Celtic manuscripts are displayed in the National Library of Wales on Penglais Hill (Reading Rooms Mon–Fri 9.30–6, Sat 9.30–5; National Screen and Sound Archives Mon–Fri 10–5, Gregynog Exhibition Gallery Mon–Sat 10–5). Bay-windowed Victorian and Edwardian hotels and guesthouses line the waterfront, which ends at Constitution Hill, where the electric cliff railway (opened 1896) climbs for fine views of Cardigan Bay. On top is the world's largest camera obscura.
    From town, steam trains on the Vale of Rheidol Railway (May–end Oct) wind their way through a wooded valley to Devil's Bridge.

ANGLESEY

🏠 433 D14 ℹ Station Site, Llanfair PG LL61 5UJ, tel 01248 713177 🚉 Llanfair PG, Holyhead and intermediate stations
www.anglesey-online.co.uk

Wales' largest island can seem surprisingly flat in comparison to the rugged heights of nearby Snowdonia (▷ 145). Its shores are of the most interest to visitors. On the east and southwest coasts are large sandy beaches backed by dunes, while the north coast is more complicated, with a succession of smaller coves. Puffins, razorbills, fulmars and guillemots nesting on South Stack cliffs, off the northern shore, can be watched from the RSPB South Stack Cliff Site visitor office.

HISTORIC SIGHTS
The island is linked to the Welsh mainland in spectacular style by Thomas Telford's (1757–1834) seven-arched Menai Suspension Bridge (1826), spanning the Menai Strait. The island's fertile interior is rich in prehistoric sites, including the Bronze Age burial mound at Bryncelli Ddu (east of Llandaniel Fab), with its stone entrance still intact.
    The coastal town and yachting resort of Beaumaris, on the south-east shore, is the island's main focus for visitors. It is dominated by Beaumaris Castle, dating from 1295 (Mar–end Sep daily 9.30–6.30; rest of year Mon–Sat 9.30–4, Sun 11–4), the last of Edward I's (1239–1307) iron ring of fortresses, a chain of castles built to subdue the Welsh (▷ 29). Although unfinished, the castle is regarded as a perfect example of medieval military architecture, with symmetrical concentric walls designed by James of St. George. The 1614 Courthouse (Easter–end Sep daily 10.30–5) is still in use, while Beaumaris Gaol shows how nasty a Victorian prison could be.

HIKING
For coastal walks, head to the breezy summit of Holyhead (216m/710ft), the highest point in Anglesey, capped by an Iron Age fort. Although it's on the separate Holy Island, it is still part of Anglesey. Or stroll along the dunes from Newborough Warren, in the southeast of the island, to the peninsula and lighthouse of Llanddwyn Island.
Don't miss Britain's longest station name is Llanfairpwllgwyngyllgogerychwyrndrobwllllantysilio-gogogoch, a name invented in the 19th century in a bid to attract more trade. It translates as 'St. Mary's Church in the hollow of white hazel near a rapid whirlpool and the Church of St. Tysilio near the red cave'. Not surprisingly, it's shortened to Llanfair PG.

BLAENAVON WORLD HERITAGE SITE

🏠 429 F18 • Blaenavon Iron Works, North Street, Torfaen NP4 9RQ ☎ 01495 792615 🕐 Ironworks: Apr–end Oct daily 9.30–4.30. Big Pit: mid-Feb to end Nov daily 9.30–5 💷 Big Pit: free. Ironworks: adult £2, child (5–16) £1.50, family £5.50 🍴 🏪 🚻 🅿
www.cadw.wales.gov.uk (Ironworks)
www.nmgw.ac.uk (Big Pit)
www.world-heritage-blaenavon.org.uk

Two major sites recall the town's former role as a mainstay of coal and iron production. The Big Pit National Mining Museum gives free underground tours through a coal mine (closed in 1980), with a ride in a miners' cage lift, and with former miners as guides. You can visit the colliery buildings, pithead baths and smithy on the surface, while underground are the coal faces, levels, air doors and pit-pony stables.
    Blaenavon Ironworks, dating from 1788, is the best-preserved 18th-century ironworks in Europe, and a row of workers' cottages still stands.

People come to Bodnant House to visit the verdant gardens

Caernarfon Castle is run by Cadw, the Welsh heritage trust, and been restored to its original majesty

BODELWYDDAN CASTLE

434 E14 • Bodelwyddan, near St. Asaph LL18 5YA ☎ 01745 584060 🕙 Nov–end Mar Sat–Sun 10.30–4, Thu 9.30–6; Sep–end Oct, Apr to mid-Jul Sat–Thu 10.30–5; mid Jul to early Sep daily 10.30–5 🚶 Adult £4.50, child (5–16) £2, family £12. Gardens only: adult £2, child £1, family £4 🏛 👪 P
www.bodelwyddan-castle.co.uk

This 19th-century mock castle, complete with turrets and battlements, is now the Welsh headquarters of the National Portrait Gallery, and houses a large collection of Victorian portraits, including Victorian portraiture photographs.

There is plenty of interest here for all ages, with World War I practice trenches, an adventure playground, parkland, walled gardens and a woodland walk.

BODNANT GARDEN

434 E14 • Tal-y-Cafn, Colwyn Bay LL28 5RE ☎ 01492 650460 🕙 Mid-Mar to end Nov daily 10–5 🚶 Adult £5.50, child (5–16) £2.75 🛒 🏛 Shop and garden centre 👪 P
www.bodnantgarden.co.uk

Situated above the River Conwy, with views across the valley to Snowdonia (▷ 145), Bodnant is one of the most visited of all British gardens.

By turns formal and informal, it was first planted in 1875 by the Aberconway family, whose descendants still run the shop and plant centre. There are Italianate terraces, a huge lily pond and a deep wooded valley known as The Dell. Spring brings shows of daffodils, camellias, magnolias and cherry blossom, while early summer has rich displays of rhododendrons, azaleas and laburnum. Late summer bursts into bloom with roses, clematis and waterlilies.

BRECON BEACONS NATIONAL PARK

429 F20 🛈 Old Cattle Market Car Park, Brecon LD3 8ER, tel 01874 623156
www.breconbeacons.org

While lacking the drama of the very highest peaks of Snowdonia National Park (▷ 145), these highlands of South Wales have exhilarating walks and views, particularly on the precipitous sandstone ridge that rises to Pen y Fan (886m/2,907ft).

The eastern flanks comprise the Black Mountains, a series of ridges and lonely valleys; here a road edges past the ruins of 13th-century Llanthony Priory and over the Gospel Pass to drop steeply to the second-hand bookshop mecca and charming market town of Hay-on-Wye. The Georgian town of Brecon and its surroundings mark the central ground of the national park and make a good base for visits. To the west is Black Mountain (confusing, since there are Black Mountains to the east), a bleak moorland expanse dominated by the craggy ridge of Carmarthen Fan. In the south the Waterfall Country is a tremendous series of waterfalls along the gorges of the Hepste, Melte and Nedd. **Don't miss** Sgwd yr Eira, a magnificent waterfall in the Waterfall Country, where you can squeeze your way along a ledge behind the curtain of the fall.

CAERLEON ROMAN FORTRESS AND BATHS

429 F18 🛈 High Street, Caerleon, Gwent NP6 1AE, tel 01633 423134 🕙 Apr–end Oct daily 9.30–5; rest of year Mon–Sat 9.30–5, Sun 11–4 🚶 Baths: adult £2.50, child (5–16) £2, family £7 🏛 👪 P
www.cadw.wales.gov.uk

One of three Roman legionary bases in Britain founded in AD75, Caerleon retains a well-preserved

rectangular fortress, with a 6,000-seat amphitheatre and excavated remains of the barracks. Amid the modern town and preserved under cover are the baths, which included an open-air pool, heated changing rooms and an exercise hall. Excavated items are on display at Caerleon Legionary Museum (Mon–Sat 1–5, Sun 2–5). **Don't miss** Demonstrations of a Roman legionary's life take place in the museum's Capricorn Centre, with a reconstructed barrack room, food preparation and replica armour to try on.

CAERNARFON

433 D14 🛈 Castle Ditch, Castle Street, Caernarfon LL55 1SE, tel 01286 672232
www.caernarfon.com

This market town is dwarfed by the magnificent harbourside Caernarfon Castle (Jun–end Sep daily 9.30–6; Apr, May, Oct daily 9.30–5; Nov–end Mar Mon–Sat 9.30–4, Sun 11–4), built in 1283 by Edward I (1239–1307) to consolidate his conquest of Wales (▷ 29). Edward I's son, the future Edward II (1284–1327), was born here. In 1969 the castle was the setting for Prince Charles's investiture as Prince of Wales. Substantial lengths of the medieval town wall snake through the town.

On a hill above the town lie the foundations of the Roman settlement fort of Segontium (founded AD77) with a museum displaying finds from this far-flung outpost of the Roman Empire. On Caernarfon Airparc, where the RAF Mountain Rescue Service was formed in 1943, is Caernarfon Airworld Museum (daily 9–5.30), an indoor interactive museum with historic and modern aircraft, trial flights and pleasure flights.

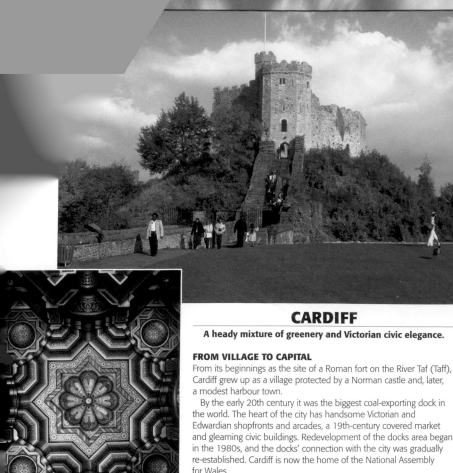

CARDIFF

A heady mixture of greenery and Victorian civic elegance.

FROM VILLAGE TO CAPITAL

From its beginnings as the site of a Roman fort on the River Taf (Taff), Cardiff grew up as a village protected by a Norman castle and, later, a modest harbour town.

By the early 20th century it was the biggest coal-exporting dock in the world. The heart of the city has handsome Victorian and Edwardian shopfronts and arcades, a 19th-century covered market and gleaming civic buildings. Redevelopment of the docks area began in the 1980s, and the docks' connection with the city was gradually re-established. Cardiff is now the home of the National Assembly for Wales.

THE CASTLE AND CIVIC CENTRE

The focus of the city is Cardiff Castle (daily 9.30–6), a Norman fortress dating from Roman times. In the 19th century it was transformed into a flamboyant, neo-Gothic extravaganza by the third Marquess of Bute and his designer William Burges (1827–81).

Northeast of the castle, the white Portland-stone buildings of the Civic Centre, built in the 19th and 20th centuries, are laid out on broad avenues. In front is the elaborate City Hall and the National Museum and Gallery (Tue–Sun 10–5), with an Evolution of Wales exhibition and the largest collection of Impressionist and post-Impressionist paintings outside France.

Don't miss Cardiff Castle's marble and cedarwood décor in the Arab Room, and the fireplace with castle frieze in the Banqueting Hall.

ON THE WATERFRONT

Cardiff's docks have become vibrant Cardiff Bay, fringed with restaurants, bars and shops. Among the attractions are Techniquest (Mon–Fri 9.30–4.30, Sat–Sun 10.30–5), a science discovery complex and planetarium; arts and crafts exhibitions in a restored warehouse; Butetown History and Arts Centre (Tue–Fri 10–5, Sat–Sun 11–4.30), tracing the area's history; and the Pierhead Building (Mon–Fri 9.30–4.30), with a display about the National Assembly for Wales.

The white-wood Norwegian Church (daily 10–4) is a cultural centre with events and exhibitions, built for Scandinavian sailors who brought timber beams for the South Wales coal mines. Goleulong Lightship 2000 (Mon–Sat 10–5, Sun 2–5) has a light tower, engine room, chapel and cabins to explore. The new Millennium Centre hosts opera, ballet and musicals in a dramatic modern building opened in 2004.

Admire the Islamic ceiling in the Arab Room (above) at Cardiff Castle, which stands on a defensive site above the city

RATINGS	
Good for kids	●●
Historic interest	●●●
Specialist shopping	●●●
Walkability	●●

BASICS
✛ 429 F18
🛈 St. David's House, 16 Wood Street, Cardiff CF10 1ES, tel 0870 909 2005
🚆 Cardiff Central

www.visitcardiff.info

Herbert Tower is the focus of Caerphilly Castle

One of the fantastic painted ceilings at Gothic Castell Coch

The sheer cliffs fall away from Carreg Cennen Castle

CAERPHILLY CASTLE

⊞ 429 F18 • Castle Street, Caerphilly CF83 1JD ☎ 02920 883143 ⏰ Jun–late Sep daily 9.30–6; Apr–end May, Oct daily 9.30–5; rest of year Mon–Sat 9.30–4, Sun 11–4 (closed 24 Dec–1 Jan) 💷 Adult £3, child (5–16) £2.50, family £8.50 🚊 Caerphilly 📷 🚻 🅿 www.cadw.wales.gov.uk

The largest medieval fortress in Wales, and one of the largest in Britain, Caerphilly Castle has a somewhat incongruous setting beside a modern industrial town. Its design was complex, with concentric outer walls—walls within walls—further defended by a water-filled moat and artificial lakes and islands. One of the towers has been permanently leaning to one side since the 17th century, when Parliamentarians tried to blow it up during the Civil War (▷ 32). The walls stand once again at their original height following restoration in the 19th and 20th centuries. There is an exhibition of working replica siege engines, which are periodically demonstrated (call in advance to find out times).

CALDICOT CASTLE

⊞ 429 F18 • Church Road, Caldicot NP26 4HU ☎ 01291 420241 ⏰ Mar–end Oct daily 11–5; Nov–Feb Sat–Sun 11–4 💷 Adult £3.50, child (5–18) £2, family £10; additional charges for special events/activities 📷 🚻 🅿 www.caldicotcastle.co.uk

Set in a country park, Caldicot is a restored 13th-century castle on a Norman motte, built by Humphrey de Bohun, Earl of Hereford. Its elaborate defences included portcullises, heavy gates and murder holes.

Although the castle was restored by the antiquary J. R. Cobb from 1855, much of the original stonework is still intact. ther surviving architectural ails include latrine turrets, a hooded fireplace and window-seats.

Don't miss Taking a look at the sculpted heads and ornate windows on the twin turrets of the main gatehouse.

CARREG CENNEN CASTLE

⊞ 429 E17 • Trapp, near Llandeilo SA19 6UA ☎ 01558 822291 ⏰ Apr–end Oct daily 9.30–6.30; rest of year daily 9.30–dusk 💷 Adult £3, child (5–16) £2.50, family £8.50 📷 🚻 🅿 www.cadw.wales.gov.uk

Carreg Cennen perches on an inland cliff on the western side of the Brecon Beacons National Park (▷ 135). Built in about 1300, it was originally an Anglo-Norman stronghold, designed to repel Welsh advances. Even in its ruinous state, its massive towers are still very impressive, while on the south side a sheer 90m (295ft) drop forms a natural defence. Despite this, the Welsh rebel Owain Glyndwr (c1350–1416) took the castle in the 15th century (▷ 30), and the Yorkists later destroyed it during the Wars of the Roses (1455–85) to prevent its use as a Lancastrian base.

Don't miss The passageway cut into the cliff leading to a natural cave beneath the fortifications.

CASTELL COCH

⊞ 429 F18 • Castle Road, Tongwynlais, near Cardiff CF15 7JQ ☎ 029 2081 0101 ⏰ Apr–end May, Oct daily 9.30–5; Jun–end Sep daily 9.30–6; rest of year Mon–Sat 9.30–4, Sun 11–4. Usually closed for six weeks in Jan–Feb for conservation work 💷 Adult £3, child (5–16) £2.50, family £8.50 🚻 🅿 www.cadw.wales.gov.uk

On the edge of Cardiff is this unfinished Victorian Gothic fantasy, designed in 1875 by William Burges (who also designed Cardiff Castle, ▷ opposite) for John Patrick Crichton Stuart, third Marquess of Bute (1713–92), as a hunting lodge. Burges created a fairytale place with sharp conical roofs and outrageously lavish interiors with painted ceilings and walls, sculpted and gilded figures, and elaborate furnishings.

Don't miss The clever details in the wall decoration of the drawing room—such as the painted ribbons that seem to support the family portraits, and the frog holding a bottle of cough mixture for the frog in its throat.

CELTICA

⊞ 433 E16 • Y Plas, Aberystwyth Road, Machynlleth SY20 8ER ☎ 01654 702702 ⏰ Daily 10–6 (last admission to main exhibition 4.20) 💷 Adult £5, child (5–16) £4, family £16 🚊 Machynlleth ❓ Discounted rail/admission ticket available 📷 🚻 🅿 www.celticawales.com

Welsh and Celtic history is vividly brought to the fore in this unusual museum housed in Y Plas, a Victorian mansion set in grounds which include a Celtic maze. Headsets guide visitors through a series of themed rooms, where life-size electronic figures tell their own tales. An interpretive centre uses murals and replicas to explore history, while the Historium is devoted to temporary exhibitions.

A coat of arms from Castell Coch

A wind turbine at the Centre for Alternative Technology

The huge Dan-yr-Ogof cave was discovered in 1912

A Victorian dam: Craig Coch Reservoir in the Elan Valley

THE SIGHTS

CENTRE FOR ALTERNATIVE TECHNOLOGY

➕ 434 E16 • near Machynlleth SY20 9AZ ☎ 01654 705950 🕐 Easter–end Oct daily 10–5.30; Nov–Easter daily 10–dusk; extended opening hours during school summer holidays; closed Christmas and two weeks in Jan 🏛 Easter–end Oct: adult £8, child (5–18) £5.50, family from £24. 10% discount if you arrive by bus or bike 🖥 🏧 🏃 🅿
www.cat.org.uk

Within a disused slate quarry on a remote hillside in mid-Wales, a community of half a dozen self-sufficient families has been established to showcase how 'green' energy and alternative technology can be used in various aspects of everyday life. It has been arranged foremost with visitors in mind: A water-powered cliff railway (summer only) carries you up to the site from the parking area. From there you can wander among solar-powered buildings, pumps and turbines, organic gardens and farm animals.

CHIRK CASTLE

➕ 434 F15 • Chirk, near Wrexham LL14 5AF ☎ 01691 777701 🕐 Apr–end Sep Wed–Sun 12–5 (gardens 11–6); Oct Wed–Sun 12–4 (gardens 11–5); also public holidays (last admission 1 hr before closing) 🏛 Adult £6.40, child (5–16) £3.20, family £15.80. Garden only: adult £4, child £2, family £10 🚂 Chirk 🍴 🏧 🏃 🅿
www.chirk.com
www.nationaltrust.org.uk

On a rise in the hills of the northern Welsh borderlands, 14th-century Chirk Castle is one of the few erected by Edward I (1239–1307) to survive intact, with its squat towers and forbidding exterior walls. Inside, however, much has changed: The Myddelton family, resident since 1595, added elegant state

rooms with Adam-style furniture, tapestries and portraits, a 17th-century Long Gallery, and decorations in a medieval idiom by the 19th-century designer Augustus Pugin (1812–52).

The grounds are planted with roses and yews in the formal gardens.

DAN-YR-OGOF NATIONAL SHOWCAVES

➕ 429 E17 • National Showcaves Centre for Wales, Dan-yr-Ogof, near Abercrave, Upper Swansea Valley SA9 1GJ ☎ 01639 730801, 01639 730284 (winter helpline) 🕐 Apr–end Oct daily from 10. First admission to caves 10.30; last admission varies (usually about 3). Also open school holidays at Christmas and Feb half-term 🏛 Adult £9.50, child (4–16) £6 🖥 🏧 🏃 🅿
www.dan-yr-ogof-showcaves.co.uk

The focus of this complex of attractions in the Brecon Beacons National Park (▷ 135) was discovered by local farmers Jeff and Tommy Morgan in 1912. Their voices are used to guide visitors through the caves, which include the Bone Cave, where 42 Bronze Age skeletons were found, and the Dome of St. Paul's in the Cathedral Cave, where waterfalls feed into an underground lake. Elsewhere are a Dinosaur Park, Barney Owl's Adventure Playground (undercover in a converted barn), a replica Iron Age farm, a Shire Horse Centre and Victorian Farm.

Separate charges give entrance to a dry skiing slope and trekking facility.

DOLAUCOTHI GOLD MINES

➕ 433 E17 • Pumsaint, Llanwrda SA19 8RR ☎ 01558 825146 (recording), 01558 650177 🕐 Mar–end Oct daily 10–5 (last underground tour 4.30) 🏛 Site only (includes gold-panning): adult £3.20, child (5–16) £1.60, family

£8. Underground tour: adult £3.80, child £1.90, family £9.50 🖥 🏧 🏃 🅿
www.nationaltrust.org.uk

Britain's only known Roman gold mine may date back as early as the Bronze Age. It was also in use from Victorian times until the 1930s.

A long guided tour (children under 5 are not admitted) leads through the most recent site and explores the Roman/Victorian caves and passages. Visitors are kitted out with helmets and lamps for the underground sections, and are encouraged to pan for gold in the mine yard. **Don't miss** Roman axe marks can still be seen in the rock at the entrance to the mining passage.

ELAN VALLEY

➕ 434 E16 ℹ Elan Valley Visitor Centre, Rhayader LD6 5HP, tel 01597 810880 (Rangers' Office), 01597 810898 (Visitor Centre) 🕐 Visitor Centre: mid-Mar to end Oct daily 10–5.30
www.elanvalley.org.uk

Created between 1893 and 1952 to provide water for Birmingham, this Welsh version of the Lake District (▷ 172) has dams and reservoirs within the bleak Cambrian Mountains. Initially the scheme caused controversy as it involved flooding existing communities, yet the lakes are now attractions in themselves.

The earlier dams are built in an elaborate Victorian style, and the area is rich in wildlife, including the rare red kite (identified by its large wingspan and forked tail). Some of the birds fly over to Gigrin Farm (not open to the public) near Rhayader.

The Elan Valley Visitor Centre has an exhibition, café and details of walks. The Elan Valley has 12 Sites of Special Scientific Interest (SSSIs) including meadow, ancient woodland and upland mire.

CONWY

The best-preserved medieval town in Wales memorably evokes the era of English rule. It also makes an excellent base for exploring Snowdonia and the coast.

THE FORTIFICATIONS

Conwy was built by Edward I after his conquest of the area in 1283 (▷ 29). His military architect, James of St. George, created a walled and fortified town based on those in Switzerland and France. By the 18th century Conwy had settled into its role as a trading post and river-ferry port on the route to Holyhead and Ireland.

The town's most striking feature is the virtually intact 1,280m (4,200ft) town wall that extends from the castle and contours above the streets. Three double-towered gateways and 21 towers punctuate the wall; a walk along it gives wonderful views over the town rooftops, the surrounding countryside and the River Conwy.

Also built by Edward I, the formidable castle (Apr–end May daily 9.30–5; Jun–end Sep daily 9.30–6; Oct daily 9.30–5; Nov–end Mar Mon–Sat 9.30–4, Sun 11–4) has eight massive round towers guarding the estuary. Inside, only one stone arch remains of the eight that were constructed in the 1340s to support the roof of the great hall.

DOMESTIC ARCHITECTURE

One of Conwy's greatest treasures is Plas Mawr (Apr–end May Tue–Sun 9.30–5; Jun–end Aug 9.30–6; Sep 9.30–5; Oct 9.30–4), the Elizabethan town house completed in 1585 for Robert Wynn. Designed to spread upwards rather than outwards, the house was partly influenced by European architecture—such as the canalside houses of Bruges in Belgium. In 1993 the Welsh heritage body Cadw embarked on a meticulous restoration project that resulted in a re-creation of Wynn's great hall, kitchen, bedrooms and banqueting room, many decorated in elaborate and many-hued plasterwork.

On the corner of Castle Street, Aberconwy House (Apr–end Oct Wed–Mon 11–5), with its stone steps and overhanging upper storey, represents the sole surviving merchant's building of medieval Conwy. It contains period furniture, and a video traces its history, which included a spell as a Temperance Hotel. On the quayside, reached through the Lower Gate, is the Smallest House (Apr–end Jun, Sep–end Oct daily 10–6; Jul–end Aug daily 10–9), a very narrow one-up, one-down dwelling.

Don't miss The row of 12 privies on the town wall (between Mill Gate and Tower 18), some with grooves for the wooden seats, projecting outwards (probably over the old course of the Gyffin stream).

Thomas Telford's 1826 suspension bridge leading to Conwy's castle is closed to traffic. In the town you can visit the Smallest House (inset)

BASICS

434 E14

Conwy Castle Visitor Centre, Conwy LL32 8LD, tel 01492 592248

Conwy

www.conwy.gov.uk

MAKE A DAY OF IT

Bodnant Garden (▷ 135)
Caernarfon (▷ 135)
Llanberis (▷ 141)
Llandudno (▷ 141)
Snowdonia National Park (▷ 145)

Erddig has been restored to how it looked in 1922

Rhossili Beach on the Gower Peninsula can rival anywhere in the world for golden sand, and it is often deserted

ERDDIG

⊞ 434 F15 • near Wrexham LL13 0YT
☎ 01978 315151 (recording), 01978 355314 ⏱ House: late Mar–end Sep Sat–Wed, Good Fri 12–5; Oct Sat–Wed 12–4; last admission 1 hr before closing. Tapestry Room and small Chinese Room: Wed and Sat. Garden: late Mar–end Jun, Sep Sat–Wed, Good Fri 11–6; Jul–end Aug Sat–Wed 10–6; Oct Sat–Wed 11–5; Nov–end Dec Sat–Sun 11–4 💷 Adult £7.40, child (5–16) £3.70, family £18.40. Garden and outbuildings only: adult £3.80, child £1.90, family £9.20 🍴 ⛪ 👫 🅿
www.nationaltrust.org

For 240 years this 17th-century red-brick mansion was occupied by the Yorke family, but it then fell into near dereliction and was rescued by the National Trust in the 1970s. It is chiefly of interest not for its architecture but for the unusually close bond between its owners and their staff. You enter not through the front door but through the servants' quarters. The house is set in formal gardens overlooking a canal lined with lime trees.
Don't miss The portraits of servants, dating from the 1790s and 1830s, along with verses about them.

GOWER PENINSULA

⊞ 428 D18 ℹ Gower Heritage Centre, Parkmill, Gower, Swansea SA23 2EM, tel 01792 371206
www.explore-gower.co.uk

The Gower Peninsula is something of a scenic microcosm on the doorstep of industrial Swansea (▷ 146) and the old-fashioned seaside resort of Mumbles. Its wide sandy beaches attract crowds at weekends in summer, and footpaths skirt virtually the entire length of its dramatically varied coastline, along the cliff-bounded heights of the southern shores and the lower-lying marshes on the north side.

CLIFF AND BAY VIEWS

For an overview, head up the moorland ridge of Cefn Bryn, near the sweeping sands of Three Cliffs Bay. At the western tip of Gower, Rhossili Down provides a walk at two levels—along its crest and along the beach far below, where shipwrecks are revealed at low tide. From there you can walk past Worms Head, a long finger of rock accessible via a causeway and across a natural arch (Devil's Bridge) for two hours before and after low tide. The coast turns a corner to enter Mewslade Bay with startlingly jagged cliffs. At Oxwich Bay there are nature trails through dunes and woods. On the north coast the village of Llanrhidian overlooks salt marshes and tidal sandbanks, where cockles are harvested.

Make sure you leave time to see Gower's castles. Oxwich and Pennard are eerie ruins on the south coast, while to the north Weobley Castle (Apr–end Oct daily 9.30–6; rest of year daily 9.30–5) is a more substantial survival, a fortified manor house dating mainly from the 13th and 14th centuries.

GREENWOOD FOREST PARK

⊞ 433 E14 • Greenwood Forest Park (Gelli Gyffwrdd), Y Felinheli LL56 4QN ☎ 01248 671493, 01248 670076 (info-line) ⏱ Jul–end Aug, Easter daily 10.30–6; Mar–end Apr, May–end Jun 10–5.30; Sep–end Oct 11–5 💷 Varies according to season and number of activities. Adults £4.95–£7.50, child (under 16) £3.95–£6.50, family £15.65–£24.95 🍴 ⛪ 👫 🅿
www.greenwoodforestpark.co.uk

Children of all ages can let off plenty of steam in this imaginative forest park in the foothills of Snowdonia (▷ 145). There are boisterous activities such as a sled run down a 70m (220ft) slide, a jungle boat ride and mini tractors.

Elsewhere are longbow archery, traditional craft displays, ducks, peacocks, rabbits, an arboretum and gardens, a sculpture trail and a rainforest boardwalk.

HARLECH CASTLE

⊞ 433 E15 • Castle Square, Harlech LL46 2YH ☎ 01766 780552 ⏱ Mar–end May, Oct daily 9.30–5; Jun–Sep 9.30–6; Nov–Mar Mon–Sat 9.30–4, Sun 11–4 💷 Adult £3, child (5–16) £2, family £8.50 🚂 Harlech ⛪ 👫 🅿
www.cadw.wales.gov.uk

The walls and six drum towers of this 13th-century castle stand virtually at their original height. Built as one of Edward I's iron ring of fortresses designed to subdue the Welsh, it is defended by a massive gatehouse and commands views of the sea, the Snowdonia mountains and the Lleyn Peninsula. Fortified steps (open in summer only) lead to the foot of the castle.

The song *Men of Harlech* was inspired by a long siege against the castle when it was held by the Lancastrians during the Wars of the Roses.

LAUGHARNE

⊞ 428 D17 ℹ Visitor Centre, 113 Lammas Street, Carmarthen SA31 3QA, tel 01267 231557
www.dylanthomasboathouse.com

Pronounced *larn*, this quiet town on the Taf Estuary grew up around 12th- to 16th-century Laugharne Castle (Apr–end Sep daily 10–5), now an imposing ruin.

The Welsh poet Dylan Thomas (1914–53) settled here in 1949, and Dylan Thomas' Boathouse (daily 10–5.30) and writing shed, where he lived and worked in his final, tragic and alcohol-blighted years, make a poignant visit. Creating the right atmosphere is the paper-strewn desk (with discarded papers on the floor)

The Mountain Railway steams up Snowdon from Llanberis

Llandrindod Wells's streets are lined with Victorian façades

Ruined Criccieth Castle's towers dominate Lleyn's skyline

where Thomas wrote his best-known work, *Under Milk Wood* (1954), basing the town of Llareggub on Laugharne. He and his long-suffering wife Caitlin are buried in St. Martin's churchyard.

LLANBERIS

✚ 433 E14 ⓘ Visitor Office, 41b High Street, Llanberis LL55 4EU (closed winter), tel 01286 870765 www.llanberis.org

Llanberis is a busy mountain resort spread out at the foot of Snowdon, the highest mountain in Wales. From here steam trains on the rack-and-pinion Snowdon Mountain Railway (mid-Mar to end Nov daily, weather permitting) grind their way to the summit, from where you can walk back via a number of strongly contrasting routes. At a lower level, the Llanberis Lake Railway (for timetable, www.lake-railway.co.uk) steams its way along Llyn Padarn. Electric Mountain (Jun–end Aug daily 9.30–5.30; Apr–end May, Sep–end Oct 10.30–4.30; Oct–end Nov, Feb–end Mar Wed–Sun 10.30–4.30) offers a tour of one of Europe's largest pumped storage stations, hidden deep inside a mountain.

In Padarn Country Park, the Welsh Slate Museum (Easter–end Oct daily 10–5; rest of year Sun–Fri 10–5) paints a vivid picture of the lives of workers in the slate quarries that functioned here from 1861 to 1969.

LLANDRINDOD WELLS

✚ 434 F16 ⓘ Old Town Hall, Memorial Garden, Llandrindod Wells LD1 5DL, tel 01597 822600 🚉 Llandrindod Wells www.llandrindod.co.uk

Period shopfronts, frilly wrought-iron canopies, and broad avenues lined with villas and hotels assert Llandrindod as one of the best-preserved Victorian spa towns in Britain. Within Rock Park you can

sample the rusty-tasting waters that gush from a fountain, or visit the restored Pump Room, while the lake is a popular strolling area. Among many period buildings is the Automobile Palace, an early motor showroom (1909) housing the National Cycle Exhibition (Mar–end Oct daily 10–4), a collection of more than 250 historic bicycles from Victorian examples to more comfortable-looking modern versions.

Try to visit in late August, when the whole town dresses in period costume during Llandrindod's Victorian Week.

LLANDUDNO

✚ 434 E14 ⓘ Visitor Centre, 1–2 Chapel Street, Llandudno LL30 2SY, tel 01492 876413 🚉 Llandudno www.llandudno-tourism.co.uk

A well-preserved example of Victorian seaside architecture, Llandudno has an elegant seafront, with hotels and guesthouses overlooking a pebble beach and iron-railed pier. Venture by cable-car or steep tramway to Great Ormes Head for fine views over Conwy Bay and the Snowdonia mountains. The Great Orme Mines (Feb–end Oct daily 10–5) were dug for copper by Bronze Age settlers around 4,000 years ago and claim to be the oldest metal mines in the world open to the public; excavations can sometimes be seen in progress.

LLANGOLLEN

See page 143

LLEYN PENINSULA

✚ 433 D15 ⓘ Min y Don, Station Square, Pwllheli LL53 5HG, tel 01758 613000 🚉 Pwllheli www.gwynedd.gov.uk

This tranquil arm of land jutting out between Tremadog and Caernarfon bays forms part of

an unspoiled, rugged coastline and a rural, hilly interior. At the base of the peninsula is Porthmadog, a small town linked to Snowdonia by two steam railways—the Welsh Highland Railway (timetable, www.whr.co.uk) and the Ffestiniog Railway (timetable, www.festrail.co.uk).

Two other popular places on the southern coast are Criccieth, with a castle on a headland overlooking the beach, and Pwllheli. Elsewhere, the peninsula is all about wildlife, tranquillity, and ancient and sacred sites. Tre'r Ceiri is an Iron Age settlement memorably set beside the coastal mountain of Yr Eifl; Bardsey Island, off the tip of the Lleyn Peninsula, was the site of a 5th-century Celtic monastery. **Don't miss** Plas-yn-Rhiw on the south coast (Mar–end May Thu–Mon 12–5; Jun–end Sep Wed–Mon 12–5; Oct Sat–Sun 12–4) is a 16th-century manor house with ornamental gardens overlooking the bay known as Hell's Mouth.

MONTGOMERY

✚ 434 F16 ⓘ Vicarage Garden, Church Street, Welshpool SY21 7DD, tel 01938 552043 www.montgomery-powys.co.uk

While none of the border towns of mid-Wales are of great size, Montgomery is scarcely more than a village, yet with imposing Georgian buildings recalling its once greater status as a county town. The finest buildings are in Broad Street, and include the 1748 Town Hall. Overlooking the town are the sparse ruins of the 13th-century castle, well worth climbing for its views A 16th-century former inn, The Old Bell (Apr–end Sep Wed–Fri, Sun 1.30–5, Sat 10.30–5) houses local history displays about the town and the Cambrian Railway.

The Great Glasshouse is the National Botanic Garden of Wales's most exciting feature, housing plants from all over the world

Children can take the wheel at Oakwood Park

NATIONAL BOTANIC GARDEN OF WALES

✚ 429 E17 • Middleton Hall, Llanarthne SA32 8HG ☎ 01558 668768 🕐 Nov–end Mar daily 10–4.30; rest of year daily 10–6; last admission 1 hr before closing 💷 Adult £7, child (5–15) £2, family £16 🍴 🍽
🚻 🎁 🅿
www.gardenofwales.org.uk

When it opened in 2000 this was Britain's first new national botanic garden in nearly 200 years. Essentially a teaching and research facility, the garden is laid out with visitors in mind, with plants along a broadwalk linking a Japanese garden, a double-walled garden and a marsh lining the lake and pond. The gardens occupy the estate of a Georgian mansion that has long since vanished, from which time Paxton's Tower, a two-storey triangular eyecatcher, survives. **Don't miss** The Great Glasshouse, a striking glass dome designed by Norman Foster, housing plants of Mediterranean ecosystems.

The mallard is one of the species you can see at the National Wetlands Centre

NATIONAL WETLANDS CENTRE WALES

✚ 429 E18 • Llanelli Centre, Penclacwydd, Llwynhendy, Llanelli SA14 9SH ☎ 01554 741087 🕐 Summer daily 9.30–5 (grounds 9.30–6); winter daily 9.30–4.30 (grounds 9.30–5) 💷 Adult £5.50, child £3.50 (4–16), family £14.50 🍽 🚻 🎁 🅿
www.wwt.org.uk

One of nine centres in Britain to be run by the Wildfowl and Wetlands Trust (WWT), this reserve lies on the east side of Carmarthen Bay. Hundreds of ducks, geese, swans and flamingoes enjoy life here—some are tame enough to be fed by hand. There are observatory hides for birdwatchers, as well as a Millennium Discovery Centre, Millennium Wetlands play area with Water Vole City tunnels and Swans Maze. **Don't miss** Spotting the little egret, a resident species of bird whose numbers shot up from just two in 1995 to several hundred now.

NATIONAL WOOL MUSEUM

✚ 433 D17 • Dre-Fach Felindre, Llandysul SA44 5UP ☎ 01559 370929 🕐 Apr–end Sep daily 10–5; rest of year Tue–Fri 10–5 💷 Free 🍽 🚻 🎁 🅿
www.nmgw.ac.uk

This museum doubles as a working woollen mill, producing modern goods that are offered for sale. Yarns are produced on 19th-century machinery and woven on both hand and power looms. You can also watch demonstrations of traditional hand-carding, spinning and weaving. The museum traces the history of Dre-Fach Felindre and its heyday as the 'Huddersfield of Wales' (referring to the major textile-producing town in northern England), when 40 mills were based here.

OAKWOOD PARK

✚ 428 D17 • Canaston Bridge, Narberth, Pembrokeshire SA67 8DE ☎ 08712 206211 🕐 Easter–end Jul daily 10–5; Aug 10–10; Sep–end Oct 10–5 💷 Adult £13.75, child (3–9) £12.75. After 5.30 (Aug) £9.50 🍴 🍽
🚻 🎁 🅿
www.oakwood-leisure.com

One of Pembrokeshire's biggest family attractions, Oakwood Park has rides such as the wooden rollercoaster Megafobia, the 46m (150ft) high skycoaster, Vertigo, and the UK's only shoot-and-drop tower, The Bounce, which shoots riders into the air at high speed—and watches them drop. KidzWorld is aimed at younger children, while Techniquest is an indoor science discovery centre. **Don't miss** Fireworks displays in late-opening sessions (Aug).

PEMBROKE CASTLE

✚ 428 C18 • Pembroke SA71 4LA ☎ 01646 681510 🕐 Apr–end Sep daily 9.30–6; Mar, Oct 10–5; Nov–Feb 10–4 💷 Adult £3, child (over 5) £2, family £8 ❓ Guided tours (Jun–end Aug daily) £1 extra 🚇 Pembroke 🍽 🚻 🎁 🅿
www.pembrokecastle.co.uk

Surrounded by water on three sides, this massive Norman fortress remained invincible until the 17th-century Civil War (▷ 32), when the Parliamentarians took it. During the Wars of the Roses, Lady Margaret Beaufort came here and gave birth to the future king, Henry VII (1457–1509), the first Tudor king of England. Life-size figures in the great hall of the gatehouse represent Earl William de Valence and family at a medieval banquet. Other displays trace the story of Henry VII and describe the horrors of punishment in the castle dungeon. **Don't miss** Wogan Cavern, a huge limestone cave originally used as a boat store.

LLANGOLLEN

A romantic, green vale beneath limestone crags and home of the world-famous musical Eisteddfod.

LLANGOLLEN TOWN

The Vale of Llangollen has attracted tourists since the late 18th century. A good starting point is the market town of Llangollen, host since 1947 of the annual International Eisteddfod in July, when performers from all over the world compete in dance, song and instrumental music (below). The venue is the impressive Royal International Pavilion. Indoor attractions here include the Motor Museum and Canal Exhibition (Mar–end Oct Tue–Sun 10–5), with cars and cycles dating from 1912 and a display about the building of the canals, and the Llangollen Museum (daily 10–6), recording the social and industrial history of this fascinating corner of Wales.

On a hill above town is the half-timbered house, Plas Newydd (House: Apr–end Oct Sat–Wed 12–5; Gardens: Apr–end Oct Sat–Wed 12–5.30). This was the home of the Ladies of Llangollen—Lady Eleanor Butler and Miss Sarah Ponsonby—who fled their families in 18th-century Ireland in order to live together, and who welcomed a stream of celebrated visitors to their much-extended cottage between 1780 and 1829. The house is furnished as it was in their day and an exhibition in one room tells the ladies' remarkable story.

THE GREAT OUTDOORS

The canal wharf is the starting point for horse-drawn barge trips through the vale, including a dizzy stretch across Thomas Telford's monumental Pontcysyllte Aqueduct, 38m (126ft) above the River Dee, and reaching the river at the sweeping weir of Horseshoe Falls. Steam trains on the Llangollen Railway (Jun–end Oct daily, Christmas and school holidays) lead through 13km (8 miles) of scenery, stopping at Berwyn, above the river gorge and a 15-minute walk from Horseshoe Falls.

Wide views of the vale beyond Llangollen can be enjoyed from the ruins of 13th-century Castell Dinas Brân (Crow City Castle), perched on a hill above town. In a tranquil position 3.5km (2 miles) north of Llangollen are the remains of 13th-century Valle Crucis Abbey (Apr–end Sep daily 10–5), including the elaborately carved west front with distinctive rose window. The valley was named after Eliseg's Pillar, a ninth-century Christian cross that still stands near the abbey ruins.

About 11 miles (18km) west of Llangollen is 17th-century Rug Chapel (Mar–end Sep Wed–Sun 10–5). In contrast to its plain exterior, its interior is a riot of decoration, with carved wooden angels, a painted ceiling, gallery and a mural depicting a prone skeleton.

Take a barge trip high up across the Pontcysyllte Aqueduct or see carvings like the one above at Plas Newydd in Llangollen

RATINGS			
Good for kids	● ●		
Historic interest	● ● ● ●		
Outdoor fun	● ● ● ●		
Walkability	● ● ●		

BASICS
✚ 434 F15
ℹ Town Hall, Castle Street LL20 5PD, tel 01978 860828

www.llangollen.org.uk

Carregwastad Point on the Pembrokeshire Coast, Britain's only sea-based national park, is reached by the long and twisting coastal path

Italianate architecture characterizes Portmeirion

THE SIGHTS

PEMBROKESHIRE COAST NATIONAL PARK

🗺 433 C17 ℹ National Park Visitor Centre, The Grove, St. David's SA62 4NW, tel 01437 720392
www.visitpembrokeshire.com
www.pembrokeshirecoast.org.uk

The Pembrokeshire Coast Path, a 186-mile (300km) National Trail, weaves around an intricate seaboard, giving excellent views. The scenery divides between the more rugged north and the level cliffs in the south.

Near St. David's (▷ 145), Whitesands Bay is a long beach, with St. David's Head a short walk north looking across towards Ireland. Strumble Head, at the tip of a remote section of cliffs, has some of the best views to the south from the Iron Age hillfort site of Garn Fawr. Fishguard is a harbour town with ferries to Rosslare in Ireland. Inland, the Preseli Hills are dotted with prehistoric sites, including Bronze Age stone circles and Neolithic burial chambers; it was from here that the bluestones of Stonehenge originated (▷ 87). On the hillfort site of Castell Henllys (Apr–end Oct daily 10–5) is a reconstructed Iron Age village.

One of many outstanding coastal viewpoints is Wooltack Point near Marloes, which overlooks Skomer and Skokholm islands (▷ opposite).Bosherston Lily Ponds lie close to the beach of Broad Haven; the coast path going west passes the rock pillars of Elegug Stacks and the natural arch known as the Green Bridge of Wales. Many tidal creeks drain into the harbour of Milford Haven; overlooking one inlet is Carew Castle (Apr–end Oct daily 10–5), the ruined shell of a medieval fortress-turned-Elizabethan-mansion
Don't miss The ancient, primitive hermitage chapels of St. Non, St. Justinian (both near St. David's)

and St. Govan (near Bosherston), are each sheltered remotely in the cliffs.

PENRHYN CASTLE

🗺 433 E14 • Llandygai, Bangor LL57 4HN ☎ 01248 353084; 01248 371337 infoline 🕐 Mar–end Jun and Sep–end Oct Wed–Mon 12–5; Jul–end Aug Wed–Mon 11–5. Garden: Mar–end Jun and Sep–end Oct Wed–Sat 11–5; Jul–Aug Wed–Mon 10–5 💷 Adult £7, child (5–16) £3.50, family £17.50. Gardens and stable block exhibitions only: adult £5, child £2.50 🍴 🎁 🚻 🅿
www.nationaltrust.org.uk

This stately mock-castle overlooking the Menai Strait and Anglesey follows the 19th-century fashion for neo-Norman architecture. Ostentatious in the extreme, it was built by Thomas Hopper between 1820 and 1840 and has more than 300 rooms.

The Pennant family flaunted their wealth here (gained from Jamaican sugar, slavery and Welsh slate) with a slate bed weighing 1 tonne, which was made for Queen Victoria, stained-glass windows in the great hall, and a grand staircase with ornate lamp-holders, carved masks and encrusted pillars.

You can tour the grounds in a staff-driven buggy (reservation necessary). Look out for a walled garden and exotic tree and shrub collection.

PISTYLL RHAEADR

🗺 434 F15 ℹ Vicarage Gardens, Church Street, Welshpool SY21 7DD, tel 01938 552043
www.pistyllrhaeadr.co.uk

At the end of a long, sparsely populated valley is this dramatic waterfall (the name means 'waterfall spout'), the tallest in Wales. A narrow ribbon of water drops into a wooded rock basin from a height of

73m (240ft), broken in mid-flight by a man-made rock arch placed there to enhance the whole effect.

During a tour of Wales in the 19th century, the English writer and traveller George Henry Borrow (1803–81) recorded the fall as 'an immense skein of silk agitated and disturbed by tempestuous blasts'. Visitors can walk to the top or watch the spectacle from the picnic area at ground level.

PORTMEIRION

🗺 433 E15 • Portmeirion LL48 6ET ☎ 01766 770000 🕐 Daily 9.30–5.30 💷 Adult £6, child (over 5) £3, family £14.40 🚂 Boston Lodge 0.6 mile (1km) on Ffestiniog Railway 🍴 🛍 🎁 🚻 🅿
www.portmeirion-village.com

The Italian Riviera comes to the shores of Snowdonia in this surreal 20th-century creation, by architect Sir Clough Williams-Ellis, occupying a headland overlooking the Dwyryd estuary. His aim was to show that a beautiful location could be developed without its being spoiled. The result is a storybook version of a Mediterranean village in which parts of other buildings from elsewhere in Britain have been ingeniously recycled.

Portmeirion has a piazza at its heart and buildings that include a belvedere, campanile, pantheon and triumphal arch, overlooked by pastel-hued cottages decorated with carvings and paintings. A Victorian mansion, Castell Deudraeth, houses a restaurant and rooms; cottages are let as self-catering accommodation. Distinctive Portmeirion pottery is sold at the village shop.

POWIS CASTLE

🗺 434 F16 • Welshpool SY21 8RF ☎ 01938 551944 (recording), 01938 551929 🕐 Castle: Apr–end Sep Thu–Mon 1–5; Sep–end Oct 1–4.

Take a tour of the Rhondda Heritage Park by bus

Snowdon in reflective mood in Llynnow Mymbyr

The lantern ceiling is a major feature of St. David's Cathedral

Garden: 11–6 (5.30 when castle opens till 4), Nov–end Dec Fri–Sun 11–4
🅱 Adult £8.80, child (5–16) £4.40, family £22. Garden only: adult £6.20, child £3.10, family £15.20
🅱 Welshpool 2 miles (3km) via footpath 🍴 🚌 ♿ 🅿
www.nationaltrust.org.uk

The border fortress with red sandstone walls appears as a forbidding bulk, but conceals an elegant stately home, influenced by 600 years of architecture. The Herbert family, who acquired it in 1584, added an Elizabethan long gallery and 17th-century state bedroom. Yet the grounds steal the show: During the 18th century the architect William Winde laid out the terraced gardens, planted with huge clipped yew hedges. There are statues, an aviary and an orangery, with views across the Severn Valley. Edward Clive, son of Clive of India, was made Earl of Powis in 1804 and restored the castle. You can visit the Clive Museum.

RHONDDA HERITAGE PARK

➕ 429 E18 • Trehafod, Rhondda Cynon Taff CF37 2NP ☎ 01443 682036
🅾 Daily 10–6 (last tour 4.30); Oct–Easter Tue–Sun 🅱 Adult £5.60, child (5–16) £4.30, family £16.50. Energy Zone: adult free, child £2
🅱 Trehafod 🍴 🍽 🚌
♿ 🅿
www.rhonddaheritagepark.com

Based at the former Lewis Merthyr Colliery, this heritage park evokes the sounds, smells and sights of what life was like in a coal mine until the large-scale closures of South Wales' mines in the 1970s and 1980s.

The underground tour, led by ex-miners, vividly re-creates working conditions on a shift—there is even a simulated explosion. The multimedia exhibition Black Gold uses the lives of a real miner and his predecessors to illustrate the Rhondda's coal industry from the 1850s, and there are displays about the mining valley communities.

For children of all ages there is the Energy Zone play area (Easter–end Oct).

ST. DAVID'S

➕ 433 C17 🅸 Pembrokeshire Coast National Park Visitor Centre, The Grove SA62 4NW, tel 01437 720392
www.stdavids.co.uk

Its cathedral raises St. David's to the status of a city, yet it is scarcely more than a village in character and size.

Tucked away in a dip next to the substantial ruins of the Bishop's Palace (daily 9.30–6), St. David's Cathedral dates from the 12th century but is on the site of a sixth-century monastery founded by David, patron saint of Wales. David was thought to have been born at a point marked by Non's Well, close by on a grassy headland on the coast.
Don't miss The 16th-century wooden ceiling of the cathedral nave and brightly decorated tower lantern ceiling.

SKOMER AND SKOKHOLM

➕ 428 C18 🅸 Tourist information, 19 Old Bridge, Haverfordwest SA61 2EZ, tel 01437 763110
www.wildlifetrust.org.uk/wt.sww/

These two island reserves off the western tip of the Pembrokeshire mainland are (together with more remote Grassholm Island) among Europe's foremost breeding sites for sea birds. Porpoises and dolphins are regular visitors.

Skokholm has the first bird observatory built in Britain, founded here in the 17th century. Colonies of guillemots, razorbills and storm petrels live here, along with about 160 grey seal pups, born each year around the beaches and caves of the island. Skomer is also where 160,000 pairs of Manx shearwaters live. Ferries leave from Martinshaven (Apr–end Sep).

It is also possible to stay on Skokholm (call tourist office).

SNOWDONIA NATIONAL PARK

➕ 433 E15 🅸 Snowdonia National Park Authority, Penrhyndeudraeth LL48 6LF, tel 01766 770274
www.eryri-npa.gov.uk

Covering a large chunk of north-west Wales, Snowdonia takes its name from Snowdon (1,085m/3,560ft), the highest mountain in England and Wales (known as Yr Wyddfa in Welsh). This area of wild peaks and lakes draws great numbers of walkers and climbers, particularly to the area around Snowdon. Glyder Fawr, Carnedd Dafydd and Moel Siabod are among other shapely peaks, while there are easier walks in the forests around the village of Betws-y-Coed and along the Aberglaslyn Pass near the village of Beddgelert.

Built of sturdy stone around a spacious square, Dolgellau, near looming Cader Idris (889m/2,915ft), is the only town inside the national park. Others lying close to the boundary include the historic castle towns of Conwy (▷ 139) and Caernarfon (▷ 135), the Victorian seaside resort of Llandudno (▷ 141) and Blaenau Ffestiniog, in its industrial setting amid mountains of slate scraps and where slate caverns may be visited.
Don't miss The steam railways winding around the lake shores and through majestic mountain scenery, especially the Snowdon Mountain Railway from Llanberis (▷ 141) to the summit.

Boats moored in Tenby's attractive harbour

Watch traditional weaving at Trefriw Woollen Mills

The Welsh Wildlife Centre has nature activities for children

SWANSEA

🚻 429 E18 ℹ Plymouth Street, Swansea SA1 3QG, tel 01792 468321; Mon–Sat 9.30–5.30, Sun 10–4

This industrial city on the south coast boasts two fine museums, virtually adjacent in the regenerated dockland district. The National Waterfront Museum (daily 10–5, admission free) opened in time for the 200th anniversary of Nelson's victory at Trafalgar in 1805. The theme is mostly industrial history—Nelson's fleet was kitted out with copper hulls and cannonballs from the city's giant metal manufacturers, and a focal point among the modern interactive displays is a tin-plate rolling mill. The nearby Swansea Museum (Tue–Sun, 10–5, free) tells the city's own story, with floating exhibits as well as graphic accounts of the Blitz in World War II (▷ 39), the Mumbles lifeboat and Cape Horn coal trade.

Don't miss The interactive shops where you can compare modern goods with those of a 19th-century co-operative in North Wales or a pawnbroker's in Tredegar.

TENBY

🚻 428 D18 ℹ The Croft, Tenby SA70 8AP, tel 01834 842404 🚉 Tenby www.virtualtenby.co.uk

Sections of its 13th-century wall, notably the fine Five Arches gateway, still stand around this cheerful harbour town and resort whose beaches make it a popular choice of families. Georgian houses crowd around the harbour, where a 19th-century fort can be seen on St. Catherine's Island (reached on foot at low tide). The Tudor Merchant's House (Mar–end Oct Sun–Fri 11–5) is a restored building dating from the late 15th century.

Don't miss The boat trip (Apr–end Oct, weather dependent) to Caldey Island, home since 1929 to a Cistercian community that has restored the medieval monastery. The monks make perfumes, cream, craft items and honey and sell them in the monastery shop.

TREDEGAR HOUSE

🚻 429 F18 • Newport NP10 8YW ☎ 01633 815880 ◷ Easter–end Sep Wed–Sun 11.30–4 🎟 Adult £5.40, child under 15 free 🍴 🛍 ♿ 🚻 🅿

Regarded as the finest Restoration (dating from the 1660s) house in Wales, Tredegar was the seat for 500 years of the Morgan family, and they had it built in red brick around two sides of a courtyard. One wing survives from the original 15th-century building, while interior highlights include the Brown Room, completely furnished in 17th-century oak with elaborate and grotesque carvings, and the King's Room, furnished as it was in the 1930s and 1940s, when it was occupied by Evan Morgan, the last member of the family to live here.

Don't miss A look at the unusual window sundial, with two painted flies that signify time flying.

TREFRIW WOOLLEN MILLS

🚻 434 E14 • Trefriw LL27 0NQ ☎ 01492 640462 ◷ Mon–Fri 9.30–5.30, Sat 10–5. Weaving and upper floors: Mon–Fri 10–5 🎟 Free 🛍 ♿ 🚻 🅿 www.trefriw-woollen-mills.co.uk

The busy clatter of machinery makes it clear that this is very much a working mill, owned by the same family for more than 140 years. Traditional tapestry-style, double-weave products are made on machinery dating from the 1950s and 1960s. Visitors can see the weaving process and

the hydroelectric turbines that replaced the waterwheels in the 1930s and 1940s.

Rugs, bedspreads and clothing are on sale in the shop.

WELSH WILDLIFE CENTRE

🚻 433 D17 • Cilgerran, near Cardigan SA43 2TB ☎ 01239 621600 ◷ Apr–end Sep daily 10–5. Reserve open daily, all year 10.30–5 🎟 Included in car-parking charges: £3 per car 🛍 ♿ 🚻 🅿

The nature reserve here covers woods, meadows, reedbeds and marshes along the River Teifi—as well as a former slate quarry and former railway bed. The diversity of habitats gives rise to an abundance of wildlife, including otters and one of the largest British colonies of Cetti's warbler. The limestone plantlife features rare species such as dotted sedge. For birdwatching make for the treetop hide; for children there's a wildlife adventure playground.

YNYSLAS

🚻 433 E16 ℹ Ynyslas Information Centre, c/o Countryside Council for Wales, Plas Gogerddan, Aberystwyth SY23 3EE, tel 01970 871640; Apr–end Sep daily 9.30–4.30 🎟 Free 🚻 🅿 www.ccw.gov.uk

Seven species of orchid grow in the dunes on this fine section of coast north of Aberystwyth (▷ 134). The reserve juts out into the watery expanses of the Dovey estuary, looking across to Aberdovey and the southern border of Snowdonia National Park (▷ 145).

It is fascinating to watch how the dunes are constantly changing as they shift in the wind. The visitor complex explains how they are formed, describes the wildlife and conducts walks in the reserve.

WYE VALLEY

The River Wye builds up to a glorious finale as it meanders through the steep-sided wooded Wye Valley, at its best in autumn when the leaves turn russet red.

The Wye Valley was once busy with charcoal burning which supplied local ironworks. During the latter years of the 18th century the valley became popular with Romantic poets in their quest for a deeper appreciation of nature.

MONMOUTH

This small market town of Georgian and older buildings stands where the Monnow flows into the River Wye. The Monnow itself is spanned by a uniquely designed 13th-century fortified bridge. The arcaded Shire Hall dominates the marketplace, Agincourt Square, while Monmouth Castle was the birthplace of Henry V (1387–1422). East of town rises The Kymin, a hill with fine views and two Georgian follies—the Naval Temple and the Round House (the latter a banqueting hall)—both owned by the National Trust.

William Wordsworth's poem *Composed a Few Miles above Tintern Abbey* was inspired by the majestic ruins of Tintern Abbey (Apr–end May and Oct daily 9.30–5; Jun–end Sep daily 9.30–6; Nov–end Mar Mon–Sat 9.30–4, Sun 11–4). Although turned into a roofless shell during the Dissolution of the Monasteries under Henry VIII (▷ 31), parts of the 12th- to 13th-century Cistercian abbey stand at their original height, notably the abbey church, where elaborate window tracery survives. The Cistercians tended to choose beautiful settings for the sites of their abbeys, and this is no exception, with views along the gorge. Farther south and on the west side of the gorge, the Wynd Cliff gives expansive views over the area.

CHEPSTOW

Guarding a vital crossing point into Wales and at the foot of the hilly town of Chepstow, the impressive fortress of Chepstow Castle (Apr–end May and Oct daily 9.30–5; Jun–end Sep daily 9.30–6; Nov–end Mar Mon–Sat 9.30–4, Sun 11–4) was built in 1067 as the Norman invaders pushed westwards (▷ 28). The stone keep is original, but the towers, walls, gatehouses and barbicans were added later. It was adapted for musketry and cannon after the Civil War (▷ 32).

Don't miss Symonds Yat (northeast of Monmouth), a rock viewpoint overlooking a huge loop of the river. A hand-operated chain ferry and a suspension bridge are useful aids to exploring the gorge on foot.

The view from Symonds Yat takes in the River Wye, which snakes past Tintern Abbey (inset)

RATINGS

Good for kids	●●
Historic interest	●●
Photo stops	●●●●●
Outdoor fun	●●●●

BASICS

➕ 429 G18

🏢 Shire Hall, Agincourt Square, Monmouth NP25 3DY, tel 01600 713899

🚉 Chepstow

www.monmouth.org.uk

TIP

● The best of the walks through the gorge are along the waymarked Offa's Dyke Path and (lower level) Wye Valley Walk.

Henry V is captured in stained glass at Monmouth

THE MIDLANDS

The birthplaces of Shakespeare and the Industrial Revolution; outstanding medieval castles and manor houses; and the home of the family of Diana, Princess of Wales: all are excellent reasons for touring the Midlands. The region is often overlooked by British holidaymakers

KEY SIGHTS

The ride of your life: Alton Towers' Nemesis rollercoaster

Nightlife and narrowboats: Birmingham's restored Gas Street Basin, the heart of the city's canal system, attracts revellers and boaters

ALTHORP

➕ 435 J16 • Althorp, near Northampton NN7 4HQ ☎ 01604 770107 🕐 Jul–end Sep daily 11–4 🎫 Adult £12, child (5–17) £10, family £29.50. Extra fee for visiting upstairs. Discounts for online or telephone reservations 🍴 ♿ 🛍 🅿
www.althorp.com

Following her death in a car crash in Paris, Diana, Princess of Wales (1961–97), was buried on a private island in a lake within the grounds of her family home. As home of the Spencers since 1508, Althorp has become something of a shrine to her, and a six-room exhibition celebrates her life. The mansion, modified in the 18th century in Classical style, sits among trees and pastures, and some private apartments are open to the public.

ALTON TOWERS

➕ 435 H15 • near Alton ST10 4DB ☎ 0870 520 4060 🕐 Daily 9.30–5 or later according to season; rides 10am to about 1 hr before closing 🎫 Premium season: adult £29, child (4–11) £21, family £78. Special internet tariffs available 🛍 🍴 ♿ 🛍 🅿
www.altontowers.com

As theme parks go, Alton Towers rates as one of Europe's biggest, with plenty of new attractions added each year. There are knuckle-whitening rollercoaster rides such as the unmissable Nemesis, AIR, Ice Show, the Haunted House Strikes Back, Rita—Queen of Speed, and features for younger children such as Adventureland and Old MacDonald's Farmyard. There are also extensive landscaped gardens. Reservations are available for major rides, and is recommended at busy times. **Don't miss** Visiting near Halloween when some of the rides take place in the dark.

AVONCROFT MUSEUM OF HISTORIC BUILDINGS

➕ 435 G16 • Stoke Heath, Bromsgrove B60 4JR ☎ 01527 831363 🕐 Mar Tue–Thu and Sat–Sun 10.30–4; Apr–end Jun and Sep–Oct Tue–Fri 10–4.30, Sat–Sun 10–5; Jul–end Aug daily 10.30–5; Nov Sat–Sun 10.30–4 🎫 Adult £5.20, child (5–16) £2.60, family £14 🛍 🍴 ♿ 🅿
www.avoncroft.org.uk

More than 20 historic buildings spanning 600 years of history have been rescued and reconstructed on a large open site in the Worcestershire countryside. They range from the venerable to the humble, from 15th- and 16th-century timber-framed buildings to a 1940s prefab of a kind erected hastily across Britain to house those who had lost their homes during bomb raids. The National Telephone Kiosk Collection pays homage to the very British (but now largely superseded) red phone box, while other exhibits include a cock-fighting pit and a working windmill.

BELVOIR CASTLE

➕ 436 J15 • near Grantham NG32 1PD ☎ 01476 870262 🕐 Easter–end Sep Tue–Thu, Sat, Sun, bank-holiday Mondays 11–5; Mar, Oct Sat (grounds only), Sun 11–5. Castle closed during special events 🎫 Castle and grounds: adult £10, child (5–16) £5, family £26. Gardens: adult £5, child free 🍴 🛍
♿ 🍴 🛍
www.belvoircastle.com

Pronounced beaver, the castle is a startling Regency-Gothic edifice in pinkish stone, with a jumble of towers and turrets. It has been home to the dukes of Rutland since 1508, although the present structure, the third on the site, dates from the early 19th century. It contains some opulent interiors, notably the Picture Gallery, including works by Thomas Gainsborough, Nicolas Poussin, Bartolomé Murillo and Hans Holbein. Beneath the castle terrace are the Rose and Statue Gardens; farther away are the lush Duchess's Spring Gardens, restored to their former glory and with plants fed by natural springs close to a summer house.

BIRMINGHAM

➕ 435 H16 ℹ The Rotunda, 150 New Street, Birmingham B2 4PA, tel 0121 202 5099
www.birmingham.org.uk

Britain's second city is at the heart of the industrial Midlands. While lacking the townscape of Britain's major historic cities, Birmingham does have notable pockets of interest. Since the 1980s there has been a marked improvement in the city's image, and around its remarkably intricate canal network, new walkways, shops and public areas have been created. Gas Street Basin, where narrowboats are often moored, makes a good starting point for waterside walks along the canal's towpaths.

Birmingham's obvious central point is around Victoria Square and Centenary Square, by the Grecian former Town Hall. Close by is the eclectic Birmingham Museum and Art Gallery (Mon–Thu and Sat 10–5, Fri 10.30–5, Sun 12.30–5) with one of the world's largest collections of Pre-Raphaelite paintings (free). A stylish contemporary art gallery with changing exhibitions and free admission is the Ikon Gallery in Brindleyplace (Tue–Sun and public holidays 11–6).

A canalside stroll leads north from the centre to the Jewellery Quarter, which retains much Victorian character and is still the focal point for jewellery-making; there are great numbers of specialist workshops operating

Live crafts are on view at the Black Country Living Museum

Eat as much chocolate as you can at Cadbury World

Charlecote Park has had at least two famous guests

on a small scale. The Museum of the Jewellery Quarter in Vyse Street (Apr–end Oct Tue–Sun and public holidays 11.30–4) occupies the extraordinarily antiquated workshops of Smith and Pepper, in operation from 1899 to 1981 for the manufacture of bangles. In that time, virtually nothing changed, and when the factory closed down it was left untouched until it became a museum (entrance free).

Birmingham noticeably lacks green space and trees, and so the Birmingham Botanical Gardens (Apr–end Sep Mon–Sat 9–7, Sun 10–7; Oct–end Mar closes 5 or dusk if earlier) in Westbourne Road, Edgbaston, can be a welcome contrast. This is the foremost plant collection in the Midlands, with four glasshouses, themed gardens and aviaries. A visit to Cadbury World (▷ below) is a must for anyone who wants some free chocolate.
Don't miss Millais' *The Blind Girl* (1846) and English historical painter Ford Madox Brown's *Last of England* in the Birmingham Museum and Art Gallery.

BLACK COUNTRY LIVING MUSEUM

🔢 435 G16 • Tipton Road, Dudley DY1 4SQ ☎ 0121 557 9643 ◉ Mar–end Oct daily 10–5; Nov–end Feb Wed–Sun 10–4; call for Christmas opening 💷 Adult £9.95, child (5–17) £5.75, family £28 ⬛ 🏛 🍴 🅿
www.bclm.co.uk

The industrial area of the West Midlands known as the Black Country has changed immeasurably over the past 50 years, and this brilliant evocation turns the clock back to the early years of the 20th century. All kinds of buildings from around the area have been moved here and rebuilt to create a canalside village, with shops, school, a mill,

boat dock, brass foundry and back-to-back houses. You can take a canal trip into limestone caverns, watch a silent film in the 1920s Limelight Cinema, have a beer in the Bottle and Glass Inn, or have fun at the old-fashioned fairground. There's always lots happening in the way of glass-cutting, metalworking, sweet-making and other crafts. Visitors can try out a lesson in the old-fashioned school, where strict discipline is observed. The coal mine gives a glimpse of the miners' working day.
Don't miss The tramcar ride.

BUXTON

🔢 435 H14 🛈 The Crescent, Buxton SK17 6BQ, tel 01298 25106
www.visitbuxton.co.uk

Buxton makes an excellent base for exploring the Peak District National Park (▷ 296–297). This former spa town has a distinctly genteel air, with the old pump room (now an art gallery), well-manicured Pavilion Gardens, its own Opera House, the grand, domed former Devonshire Royal Hospital and the grandiose Palace Hotel. Close to St. Ann's Well, which dispenses pure water, is the Crescent, built in the 1780s and Buxton's architectural glory. On the southern edge of town, Poole's Cavern (Mar–end Oct daily 10–5) is a spectacular show cave with the longest horizontal view of any cave in Britain.
Don't miss The 1854 thermal baths are now the modern Cavendish Arcade, crammed with shops, but they still feature the original plunge baths.

CADBURY WORLD

🔢 435 H16 • Linden Road, Bournville, Birmingham B30 2LD ☎ 0121 451 4180 (recording), 0121 451 4159 (tickets) ◉ Reservation essential, times vary. 20 Jan–end Dec usually daily (closed some

days in Feb, Nov and Dec) 💷 Adult £10.50, child (5–16) £7.90, family £32 🍴 ⬛ 🏛 🍴 🅿
www.cadburyworld.co.uk

Chocoholics should beat a path to this extremely popular attraction next door to the Cadbury factory. The history section tells the story of chocolate and there are interactive exhibits, a ride through the chocolate world, free samples, and a shop from which only the most self-restrained will walk away empty-handed. You can also taste melted chocolate straight from the production line.

CALKE ABBEY

🔢 435 H15 • Ticknall, near Derby DE73 1LE ☎ 01332 863822 ◉ House: late Mar–end Oct Sat–Wed 1–5.30. Garden and church: late Mar–end Oct Sat–Wed 11–5.30. Park: most days until 9 or dusk 💷 House and garden: adult £6.30, child (5–16) £3.10, family £15.70. Garden only: adult £3.80, child £1.90, family £9.50 🍴 🏛 🍴 🅿
www.nationaltrust.org.uk

Despite its name, Calke Abbey is a baroque country mansion mostly built between 1701 and 1703. Little changed over the years, and, occupied by the reclusive Harpur Crewe family up to 1924, it steadily decayed. The National Trust took it over and opened it to the public in 1989, deliberately leaving some of the rooms in their unrestored state. It makes a poignant visit—with the family wealth long gone, the atmosphere is of lost grandeur. The park, designated as a National Nature Reserve and managed for its nature conservation value, has 19th-century glasshouses, an ice house, walled flower garden and an orangery.
Don't miss Visiting the brewhouse tunnel that the servants took to get to the house cellars.

The Eastgate Clock in Chester can be seen from all over town

Church Stretton, nestling at the foot of Long Mynd, was once a fashionable resort and makes a good base for walking

CHARLECOTE PARK

435 H17 • Wellesbourne CV35 9ER
☎ 01789 470277 House: mid-Mar to end Sep Fri–Tue 12–5; Oct Fri–Tue 12–4.30. Grounds: mid-Mar to end Oct Fri–Tue 10–5.30; Nov to mid-Dec Sat–Sun 11–4 (also shop and restaurant) Adult £6.60, child (5–16) £3.30, family £16 www.nationaltrust.org.uk

History is writ large on this grand country house in the Warwickshire countryside. It has been the home of the Lucy family and their forbears, the Montforts, for 900 years, although the present rose-pink brick structure dates from 1551. Guests have included Elizabeth I (1533– 1603), who slept here for two nights in 1572, and the young William Shakespeare (1564– 1616), who is alleged to have been caught poaching on the estate. Herds of fallow deer, red deer and Jacob sheep roam the park; estate buildings open to visitors include the brewhouse, gatehouse, coach house and tack room. The grounds were landscaped by Capability Brown. **Don't miss** The Victorian kitchen, which gives an idea of what life was like below stairs.

CHATSWORTH HOUSE

See page 152

CHESTER

434 F14 Town Hall, Northgate Street CH1 2HJ, tel 01244 402111 www.chestertourism.com

A Roman city called Deva, then a medieval port and cathedral city, and, after the River Dee silted up, a place where prosperous Georgian merchants settled: Chester has many layers of history. It has the most complete medieval city walls in Britain. You can walk along or beside them to get an overview of the city. One of the original city gateways is

Eastgate, surmounted by a highly ornate clock dating from 1897; just to the south, the wall passes the partly excavated site of the largest Roman amphitheatre in the country, and close by the Roman Garden has re-erected Roman columns.

The best Roman remains are in the Grosvenor Museum (Mon–Sat 10.30–5, Sun 2–5), with Roman tombstones and other displays on the city's history. The Dewa Roman Experience (Mon–Sat 9–5, Sun 10–5), beneath the site of the original Roman fort, admirably evokes Roman Chester with a re-created street complete with the sounds, sights and smells of Roman life, as well as archaeological excavations and artefacts.

WITHIN THE WALLS

Central Chester is a crossing of two main streets (both largely traffic free): along these run the Rows, two tiers of arcaded shopping streets, one above the other. The scheme dates from medieval times and is unique in Britain. The black-and-white buildings at The Cross are 19th-century Tudor replications, but Chester has many original examples of half-timbered

architecture. To the north is Chester Cathedral (daily 9–5), part of the most complete medieval monastic complex in Britain. Although heavily restored, it has retained stunning engraved 13th-century choir stalls and carvings such as the one below.

You can see Europe's largest bat enclosure, called the Twilight Zone, at Chester Zoo (daily from 10; closing hours vary with season; for times call 01244 380280). **Don't miss** Walking the city walls, especially on the east side, and taking a boat trip on the River Dee.

CHURCH STRETTON AND LONG MYND

434 F16 Church Street, Church Stretton SY6 6DQ, tel 01694 723133 www.southshropshire.org.uk

Some of the highest and least spoiled uplands in central England, Long Mynd has bracken- and bilberry-covered hillsides. There are a few steep roads leading over the top, or you can walk into deep valleys such as Ashes Hollow and the Carding Mill Valley.

At the foot of the hills, Church Stretton makes a useful base for the area's activities, which include horseback riding, golf and gliding. East of the town, Caer Caradoc is perhaps the area's finest viewpoint, and is capped by the ramparts of an Iron Age hillfort. For more information about the area, visit the Secret Hills Discovery Centre (Apr–end Sep daily 10–5; Oct–Mar daily 10–4.30) near Craven Arms. **Don't miss** Stokesay Castle (Mar–end May and Sep–end Oct Thu–Mon 10–5; Jun–end Aug daily 10–6; rest of year Fri–Sun 10–4), one of England's best-preserved fortified medieval manor houses.

CHATSWORTH HOUSE

England's answer to the Palace of Versailles, Chatsworth is a country house on the grandest scale, with furniture and art to impress, and plenty for children in the grounds.

The restoration of medieval Haddon Hall began in 2000

➕ 435 H14 • Chatsworth, Bakewell DE45 1PP ☎ 01246 565300 ⓘ Park: all year. House, garden, farmyard and adventure playground: late Mar to mid-Dec daily. House: daily 11–5.30. Garden 11–6 (Jun–end Aug opens at 10.30). Farmyard and adventure playground: daily 10.30–5.30 ♿ Park: free. House and garden: adult £9.50, child (5–16) £3.50, family £22.50. Garden only: adult £5.75, child £2.50, family £14. Farmyard and adventure playground: adult or child (over 3) £4.25, family pass (all attractions) £38 📷 House £3.50, gardens £3.50, park £1, children's guide £1 🍴 🛍 🏛 🎁 🅿 £1.50
www.chatsworth.org

RATINGS			
Good for kids	●	●	●
Historic interest	●	●	● ●
Specialist shopping	●	●	●

THE HOUSE

This palatial home of the Duke and Duchess of Devonshire is set in the Peak District. The original house dates from 1551, but most of what you see was built between 1686 and 1707. The Painted Hall is magnificently baroque, with marble floors, a painted ceiling and a spectacular staircase. Among the 30 rooms on show are the State Bedroom, where George II (1683–1760) died. The present queen's grandparents, George V (1865–1936) and Queen Mary, slept in this room when they visited Chatsworth in 1933. Great works of art are spread throughout the house, and among the highlights are works by Antonio Canova, Rembrandt van Rijn, Paolo Veronese and Tintoretto. The library contains around 17,000 books.

THE GROUNDS AND ESTATE

The 18th-century landscaper Capability Brown laid out the park, and in the 19th century Joseph Paxton (1803–65) was head gardener before he went on to design the Crystal Palace in London for the Great Exhibition of 1851.

There is plenty to explore on the estate, including a cottage garden, a kitchen garden, an excellent farm shop, a maze, 5 miles (8km) of paths leading past rare trees and shrubs, ponds, artful fountains and outdoor sculptures. Perhaps the most memorable feature outside is the 200m (660ft) water cascade. It was designed in 1696, with every step of the stone slope built slightly differently to vary the sound that the water makes. Children are encouraged to splash and paddle in the water, which is shallow and safe. Elsewhere are a play area for younger children and a woodland adventure playground among the trees. A daily milking demonstration takes place at 3.30.

Don't miss The trompe l'oeil violin on a door of the Music Room.

CLUMBER PARK

➕ 435 J14 • The Estate Office, Clumber Park, Worksop S80 3AZ ☎ 01909 476592 ⓘ Daily dawn–dusk; Apr–end Sep only some facilities ♿ Pedestrians, cyclists and those arriving by public transport free 🍴 🛍 🏛 🎁 Shop and plant sales 🅿 Car/motorcycle £4, caravan/minibus £5.20
www.nationaltrust.org.uk

One of the largest country parks in Europe, Clumber is the 1,500ha (3,700-acre) estate of a country house that was demolished in 1938. However, several features remain, including an estate village and Gothic Revival chapel. Encompassing forest, parkland, heathland and a huge serpentine lake, the park is large enough for a half day's walking, or you can follow one of several bicycle trails (bicycle rental Apr–end Oct, including tandems and child carriers).

The walled organic kitchen garden features a palm house, conservatory, vines, fig trees and herbaceous borders. There is a lively variety of special events most weekends from Easter to the end of September.

COVENTRY CATHEDRAL

➕ 435 H16 • 4 Priory Row, Coventry CV1 5ES ☎ 024 7622 7264 ⓘ Daily 9–5 ♿ Suggested donation £3 🛍 🏛 🎁 🅿
www.coventrycathedral.org

On 14 November 1940 a bomb destroyed the medieval cathedral at Coventry. Its ruins now stand alongside the new cathedral, designed by the Scottish architect Sir Basil Spence (1907–76) and consecrated in 1962. Widely regarded as a masterpiece of modern architecture, Spence's edifice shows that contemporary style can still produce a feeling of spirituality. It has a great sense of internal space, height, peace and

THE SIGHTS

The Old House in Hereford is a perfect example of half-timbering

Special weekend events at Kenilworth Castle feature living history displays, medieval entertainment and plays by Shakespeare

light, and is further distinguished by a parade of modern works of art. Most notable are the tapestry *Christ in Glory* by Graham Sutherland (1903–80), bronzes by Sir Jacob Epstein (1880–1959) and the Great Baptistry Window by John Piper (1903–92).

Don't miss The West Screen, a wall of glass engraved with saints and angels.

HADDON HALL

🚹 435 H14 • Bakewell DE45 1LA ☎ 01629 812855 🕐 Apr–end Sep daily 10.30–5.15; Oct Thu–Sun 10.30–4.45 💷 Adult £7.25, child (5–16) £3.75, family £19 🚫 No wheelchair access to house 🍴 🚻 👬 🅿 www.haddonhall.co.uk

One of the finest examples of an English medieval manor house, Haddon Hall has been in the family of the present owner, Lord Edward Manners, for over 800 years. It was modified between the 12th and 16th centuries, but has changed little since, although restoration of the house began in 2000. Intricately carved panelling adorns the Long Gallery, and the chapel has 15th-century wall paintings. Outside, the castellations and towers are for picturesque effect rather than defence. The garden terraces above the River Wye feature clipped yews and roses.

HARDWICK HALL

🚹 435 H14 • Doe Lea, near Chesterfield S44 5QJ ☎ 01246 850430 🕐 Hall: Apr–end Oct Wed–Thu, Sat–Sun (also public holidays) 12.30–4.30. Garden: Apr–end Oct Wed–Mon 11–5.30. Park: daily 8–6 or dusk 💷 Adult £7.20, child (5–16) £3.60, family £18. Garden only: adult £3.90, child £1.95, family £9.75 🍴 🚻 👬 🅿 www.nationaltrust.org.uk

Built for the intriguing Bess of Hardwick, properly known as

Elizabeth, Countess of Shrewsbury (1527–1608) in the 1590s, this outstanding late 16th-century house strongly evokes life in the Elizabethan period. Much of the original furniture and tapestries remain, and there is needlework by Mary, Queen of Scots (1542–87), who was held prisoner here for 15 years (▷ 31). The orchard and herb garden lie within the original walled courtyards, while beyond spreads a park grazed by rare breeds of cattle and sheep.

Don't miss The portrait of Mary, Queen of Scots, in the Long Gallery or the 16th-century tapestries.

HEREFORD

🚹 434 G17 🚹 1 King Street, Hereford HR4 9BW, tel 01432 268430 www.visitherefordshire.co.uk

Hereford looks its best in the area towards the River Wye, with a striking Georgian streetscape in Castle Street, and tree-shaded walks in Castle Green and along the river.

Dominating the skyline since the 12th century, Hereford Cathedral (daily 7.30–5.30) is built of golden sandstone and was modified during late medieval times. To the north, the half-timbered Old House (Tue–Sat 10–5), built in 1621, is one of the city's finest town houses. The Hereford Cider Museum (Apr–end Oct Tue–Sat and public holidays 10–5; rest of year Tue–Sat and public holidays 12–4) in Pomona Place looks at the world of cider-making.

Don't miss The chained library in the cathedral and the Mappa Mundi, a unique world map of 1290, also in the cathedral.

IRONBRIDGE GORGE MUSEUMS

See page 154

See page 154

JODRELL BANK SCIENCE CENTRE AND ARBORETUM

🚹 434 G14 • near Macclesfield SK11 9DL ☎ 01477 571339 🕐 Apr–end Oct daily 10.30–5.30; rest of year daily 10.30–3.30 (call for Christmas and New Year times) 💷 Adult £1.50, child (4–16) £1. Planetarium/3D Show £1 (children under 4 free) 🚻 👬 🅿 www.jb.man.ac.uk

Find out about gravity, space travel, radio waves and the movement of the planets at the Science Centre. The main focus is the Lovell Telescope, in operation since 1957 and one of the largest fully steerable radio telescopes in the world. You can zoom in with a remote camera to see what the telescope is receiving through radio waves.

Also on site is the second largest planetarium in Britain after London, and many child-friendly exhibits. Outside, the arboretum has national collections of rowan and apple tree species, and a birdwatching hide.

KENILWORTH CASTLE

🚹 435 H16 • Castle Mews, Kenilworth CV8 1NE ☎ 01926 852078 🕐 Jun–end Aug daily 10–6; Mar–end May, Sep–end Oct 10–5; Nov–end Feb 10–4, closed 24–26 Dec and 1 Jan 💷 Adult £4.95, child (5–16) £2.50, family £12.40 🚻 👬 🅿 www.english-heritage.org.uk

No other English castle ruin even approaches 12th-century Kenilworth for sheer size. It has huge sandstone walls, a Great Hall and a mighty Norman keep. Robert Dudley (c1532–00), the Earl of Leicester, transformed it into a Tudor palace, and Elizabeth I (▷ 30–31), with whom he was having an affair, visited him here in 1575. Sir Walter Scott (1771–1832) stayed close by, while writing his novel *Kenilworth* (1821).

THE SIGHTS

The Feathers Hotel is one of Ludlow's most famous buildings

LICHFIELD

✚ 435 H15 ℹ Donegal House, Bore Street WS13 6NE, tel 01543 308209
www.visitlichfield.com

The glory of Lichfield is its cathedral (daily 7.40–5.30), with its trio of dark sandstone spires soaring over half-timbered houses and the former 17th-century Bishop's Palace in the cathedral close. The west front is adorned with 113 statues, including 24 English kings, while inside its many treasures include an eighth-century illuminated manuscript known as the *St. Chad's Gospels* (on display daily, Easter–end Oct). Lichfield's most famous son was the man of letters Samuel Johnson (1709–84); the house where he was born in Breadmarket Street is now The Samuel Johnson Birthplace Museum (Apr–end Sep daily 10.30–4.30; rest of year 12–4.30).

Try and time your visit to see one of the many musical events at the cathedral.

LINCOLN

✚ 436 J14 ℹ 9 Castle Hill, Lincoln LN1 3AA, tel 01522 873213
www.visitlincolnshire.com

Lincoln is visible for miles around in the low-lying landscape, with its castle and majestic twin-towered cathedral prominent on a high hill. From the modern pedestrianized shopping streets at the foot of the hill, a walk up appropriately named Steep Hill leads into Minster Yard and Lincoln Cathedral (summer daily 7.15am–8pm; winter Mon–Sat 7.15–6, Sun 7.15–5), mostly of the 13th and 14th centuries and in the top league of England's ecclesiastical architecture. Highlights include the elaborate west façade, stained-glass rose windows

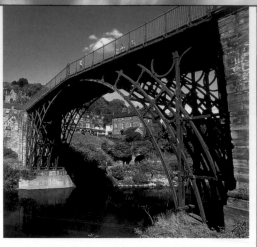

IRONBRIDGE GORGE MUSEUMS

Several outstanding museums stand in the true birthplace of the Industrial Revolution.

✚ 434 G16 • Coach Road, Coalbrookdale TF8 7DQ ☎ 01952 432166, 0800 590258 🕐 Nov–end Mar daily 10–5; some small sites closed (call for details). Pipeworks daily 1–5
🎟 Passport to all sites: adult £12.95, child (5–16) £8.25, family £40 🍴 🛍
🏛 👬 🅿
www.ironbridge.org.uk

RATINGS				
Good for kids	●	●	●	●
Historic interest	●	●	●	● ●
Walkability	●	●	●	●

The Iron Bridge of 1779 did more than just span the modest River Severn: It was the first structure of its kind to be built of iron, and has come to symbolize the start of the Industrial Revolution. It was in this valley in 1709 that the ironmaster and engineer Abraham Darby I (1678–1717) pioneered the smelting of iron ore with coke rather than charcoal, making the mass-production of metal feasible.

The Gorge is dotted with nine sites that all belong to the museum. The largest is Blists Hill Victorian Town, reconstructed on the site of an 18th-century industrial estate, with working factories, shops and workers' cottages staffed by costumed actors and craftspeople (below). Coalport China Museum occupies what was the Coalport China Works. Close by is the entrance to the Tar Tunnel, where you go underground to see what was a natural source of bitumen when Ironbridge was functioning. Across the river stands the Jackfield Tile Museum, within a huge Victorian tile factory that is again making decorative tiles for sale.

South of Jackfield Bridge the Broseley Pipeworks, which used to manufacture clay tobacco pipes, has been left as it was when it closed in 1957 after 350 years of production. Beyond the Iron Bridge (which has an exhibition in its tollhouse) the Museum of the Gorge gives an overview of the development of the gorge as a whole, including a scale model of the area as it was in 1796. North of here the Coalbrookdale Museum of Iron contains the original blast furnace built by Abraham Darby I, while the Darby Houses were homes to the ironmasters. Enginuity is a hands-on attraction aimed at children that invites them to try such engineering tasks as stoking a furnace. The Hay Inclined Plane at Blists Hill is an astonishing engineering feat linking two canals by means of a steep tramway.

Don't miss Seeing glassmakers and potters display their skills at the Coalport China Museum.

The Malvern Hills are full of hiking trails, all of which are surprisingly easy, with huge views all the way

The story of silk production is told at Macclesfield Silk Museum

and 14th-century carved choir stalls. Close by are the Bishop's Palace (Apr–end Jun and Sep–end Oct daily 10–5; Jul–end Aug daily 10–6; rest of year Thu–Mon 10–4), and Lincoln Castle (Apr–end Sep Mon–Sat 9.30–5.30, Sun 11–5.30; rest of year Mon–Sat 9.30–4, Sun 11–4), dating from Norman times and retaining gateways, towers and a 19th-century prisoners' chapel.

Museum attractions include the free Usher Gallery (Tue–Sat 10–5, Sun 1–5) in Lindum Road, with fine and decorative arts and memorabilia of the locally born poet Alfred, Lord Tennyson (1809–92), and the Museum of Lincolnshire Life (May–end Sep daily 10–5; rest of year Mon–Sat 10–5), Burton Road.

LITTLE MORETON HALL

🞣 434 G15 • Congleton CW12 4SD
☎ 01260 272018 ◉ Mar–end Oct Wed–Sun 11.30–5; Nov to mid-Dec Sat–Sun 11.30–4 🎫 Adult £5.25, child (5–16) £2.50, family £12.50 🍴 🎟
🏛 🅿
www.nationaltrust.org.uk

Little Moreton Hall is the perfect example of a moated timber-framed manor house. The black-and-white timbering is quite eyecatching. The Long Gallery was the final phase of building, completed 140 years after the Great Hall was begun in the 1440s. Although a visit will probably not last long, this building is a treat for those interested in English architecture. Check in advance for special Living History weekends.

LUDLOW

🞣 434 G16 ℹ Castle Street, Ludlow SY8 1AS, tel 01584 875053
www.ludlow.org.uk

Georgian brickwork and earlier half-timbering grace the streets of this hilltop town, with Broad Street a particularly harmonious example of townscape. Ludlow Castle (Jan Sat–Sun 10–4; Feb–end Mar, Oct–end Dec daily 10–4; Apr–end Jul, Sep daily 10–5; Aug daily 10–7), a border fortress begun in the late 11th century, was enlarged in the 14th century into a palace for the powerful Roger Mortimer. Near the ancient Butter Cross, the Church of St. Laurence assumes a practically cathedral-like grandeur, and has a fine set of 15th-century carved misericords (benches in the choir). The town has emerged as a regional foodie capital, with an excellent range of restaurants. The annual Ludlow Festival (▷ 253), has drama and music performed in the castle grounds.

LYME PARK

🞣 435 G14 • Disley, Stockport SK12 2NX ☎ 01663 766492 (recording), 01663 762023 ◉ House: Apr–end Oct Fri–Tue 1–5, holiday Mon 11–5 (timed ticket only). Park: Apr–end Oct daily 8am–8.30pm; rest of year daily 8–6. Garden: Apr–end Oct daily 11–5; Mar and Nov to mid-Dec Sat–Sun 12–3 🎫 House: adult £4.50, child (5–16) £2.30. House and garden: adult £6.20, child £3.10, family £15. Park: £4 per car, refundable on purchase of house and garden ticket. Garden only: adult £3, child £1.50 🍴 🎟 🏛 🅿
www.nationaltrust.org.uk

One of the finest examples of English Palladian architecture, the grey-stone Hall was begun in the 16th century and remodelled in 1725 by the Venetian architect Giacomo Leoni, giving the house Classical proportions and baroque ceilings. Some of the Elizabethan interiors survive, and contrast strongly with later rooms. In the Saloon, the great woodcarver, Grinling Gibbons (1648–1721), added virtuoso carving.

The large grounds have strongly contrasting views, with urban Manchester (▷ 174) on one side and the rural Peak District (▷ 156) on the other. There is ample scope for walks in the huge deer park, which contains woodland, ornamental gardens and an 18th-century hunting lodge known as The Cage. The scene in the 1995 BBC television adaptation of *Pride and Prejudice* where Darcy emerges from a lake was filmed here.

MACCLESFIELD SILK MUSEUM AND PARADISE MILL

🞣 435 G14 • Park Lane, Macclesfield SK11 6TJ ☎ Heritage Centre 01625 613210; Paradise Mill 01625 612045 ◉ Silk Museum: Mon–Sat 11–5, holiday Mon 12–4. Paradise Mill: guided tours Mon–Sat 1.15, 2.15, 3.15. Heritage Centre: Mon–Sat 10–5, Sun 12–4; closed Good Fri 🎫 One site: adult £3.10, others £2.10. Two sites: adult £4.15, others £3.15. Three sites: adult £6.20, others £5.20 🍴 🎟 🏛 🅿
www.silk-macclesfield.org

Three related attractions tell the story of silk production in the town of Macclesfield. The Silk Museum in Park Lane has exhibits about all aspects of the industry, including the workers' lives, the operation of looms, and manufactured silk. The Heritage Centre on Roe Street, close by, has a collection of silk costumes and displays related to the development of the silk industry in the town, housed within a former Sunday School. You can also explore a re-creation of a Victorian school room. A short walk away is Paradise Mill, a 19th-century silk-producing mill in operation until 1981. Inside, little has been changed, with handlooms that were installed in 1912 still in working order.

Nottingham still celebrates the legendary outlaw, Robin Hood

Peaceful walks are an attraction at Dovedale in the Peak District

Shrewsbury's Old Market Hall still has its coat of arms

THE SIGHTS

MALVERN HILLS

434 G17 21 Church Street, Malvern WR14 2AA, tel 01684 892289 www.malvernhills.gov.uk

Malvern water has been noted for its purity since the 18th century. Malvern Wells still has a spa atmosphere in its ornate Victorian buildings, although Great Malvern, to the north, is older; its magnificent priory church has some stunning 15th-century stained glass.

The long narrow ridge of the Malvern Hills rises suddenly away from the town. From a distance they look like a jagged mountain range, but close up the Malverns are much less daunting. Several marked walks reveal far-ranging views of the Cotswolds (▷ 276–277) and the border with Wales.
Don't miss Herefordshire Beacon is an Iron Age hillfort on the Malvern Hills.

MR STRAW'S HOUSE

435 J14 • 7 Blyth Grove, Worksop S81 0JG 01909 482380 Late Mar–end Oct Tue–Sat 11–4.30 Adult £4.60, child (5–16) £2.30, family £11.50. Admission by pre-reserved timed ticket only Private road; parking only for those with timed tickets www.nationaltrust.org.uk

From the exterior, this appears to be a perfectly ordinary Edwardian house. Yet its owner, a tradesman by the name of Mr Straw, changed virtually nothing in more than 60 years of living here from 1923. After his death it was opened to the public by the National Trust in the mid-1990s. Mr Straw's letters, photographs, clothing, furniture, wallpaper and other household items have been preserved intact, creating a fascinating time capsule. There is a lovely traditional suburban garden.

NOTTINGHAM

435 J15 1–4 Smithy Row, Nottingham NG1 2BY, tel 0115 915 5330 www.visitnottingham.com

Although not the most attractive of cities, Nottingham has a real buzz, with a vibrant mix of bars, pubs and clubs.

The Castle Museum and Art Gallery (daily 10–5) includes the Story of Nottingham gallery and has underground tours through passages cut below the city (in which Ye Olde Trip to Jerusalem pub is built). For more underground tours, visit the City of Caves (daily 10–5) beneath the Broadmarsh Shopping Centre, dug out over the centuries. The Galleries of Justice (Apr–end Oct Tue–Sun and public holidays 10–5; rest of year Tue–Fri 10–4, Sat–Sun 10–5), in Shire Hall, vividly re-enact a trial in a Victorian court and the grim hardship of life in a prison cell.

PEAK DISTRICT NATIONAL PARK

435 H14 Old Market Hall, Bridge Street, Bakewell DE45 1DS, tel 01629 813227 www.peakdistrict.org

Ringed by industrial cities such as Manchester and Sheffield, the Peak District provides an exhilarating sense of freedom and space.

The Peak District is really two landscapes: The Dark Peak is an area of bleak, open gritstone moors with dramatic rocky edges, such as Stanage Edge, while the White Peak is formed of classic limestone country with stone-walled pastures cut by deep dales (valleys), such as Dovedale, Lathkill Dale and Monsal Dale.

Of the many villages worth a look in the area are Tissington, with wide grassy borders and a

Jacobean hall, and Eyam, where you can follow the moving story of a village that, finding itself ravaged by plague in 1665, deliberately isolated itself from the outside world. The canalside village of Cromford had the world's first water-powered mill in 1771, now a museum.

The ruins of Peveril Castle (May–end Aug daily 10–6; Apr and Sep–end Oct daily 10–5; Nov–end Mar Wed–Sun 10–4) overlook Castleton at the heart of the Peak's cave district, with several caverns open to the public. The Blue John Cavern at Castleton (summer daily 9.30–5.30; rest of year 9.30–dusk), with its vast stalactite- and stalagmite-covered interior, also includes the Blue John Mine that extracts Blue John stone, one of the rarest and most beautiful forms of fluorspar. Also worth visiting in the Peak District are Buxton (▷ 150), Chatsworth House (▷ 152), Haddon Hall (▷ 153), and Lyme Park (▷ 155). For a walk and tour, ▷ 296–299.

QUARRY BANK MILL AND STYAL COUNTRY PARK

434 G14 • Quarry Bank Road, Styal SK9 4LA 01625 527468 Estate: daily, dawn–dusk. Mill: Apr–end Sep daily 10.30–5.30; rest of year Tue–Sun 10.30–5. Apprentice House and garden: Tue–Fri 2–4.30, Sat–Sun and holidays 11–5 Mill and Apprentice House: adult £8, child (5–16) £4.70, family £18. Mill only: adult £5.50, child £3.70, family £15

www.quarrybankmill.org.uk

On the wooded fringes of Manchester, the River Bollin runs through Styal Country Park, a rewarding area for walks marred only by the noise of aircraft from Manchester Airport, which is just a short distance away.

Wedgwood pottery: one of Stoke-on-Trent's claims to fame

Learning is fun at Snibston Discovery Park

Southwell's imposing minster is visible from miles around

The main focus of the park is Quarry Bank Mill, a water-powered cotton mill built in 1784, and restored by the National Trust. The looms clatter away, and exhibits evoke the working life of the mill. You can also see spinning and weaving demonstrations.
Don't miss The Apprentice House shows how a mill apprentice would have lived 160 years ago; reserve as soon as you arrive as places are limited.

SHREWSBURY

🗺 434 F15 🛈 The Music Hall, The Square, Shrewsbury SY1 1LH, tel 01743 281200
www.shrewsburytourism.co.uk

Black-and-white Tudor houses and Georgian red brick distinguish the old town of Shrewsbury, on a peninsula tightly enclosed by a great loop of the River Severn, guarded on its landward side by Shrewsbury Castle (Mon–Sat 10–5, Sun 10–4), which contains the Shropshire Regimental Museum. Examples of half-timbered buildings include Owen's Mansion and Ireland's Mansion, close to the arcaded Old Market Hall of 1596, while the narrow alley of the Bear Steps leads past a timber-framed hall now housing an art gallery.
About 6 miles (9.5km) south-east of Shrewsbury, Wroxeter Roman City (daily) had a population of 6,000 in Roman times, but was later abandoned. It has the remains of a second-century municipal baths and a museum.

SHUGBOROUGH ESTATE

🗺 435 G15 • Milford, near Stafford ST17 0XB ☎ 01889 881388 🕐 Late Mar–end Oct daily 11–5 🎟 Whole site: adult £8, child (5–16) £5, family £20. National Trust members: house free; all sites £5 🍴 🛒 ♿ 🚻 🅿
www.shugborough.org.uk

The ancestral home of the earls of Lichfield is a crisply classical 17th- and 18th-century mansion. During the 1740s, rococo plasterwork was added to the sumptuous state rooms. In addition to period furniture, paintings, ceramics and silver, there are photographs by the late Patrick, Earl of Lichfield (1939–2005), a cousin of the Queen and a celebrated photographer. You can visit the servants' quarters, kitchen, brewhouse and coach house, plus a Victorian schoolroom and puppet shop. The park has some unusual classical monuments, as well as Park Farm, with an agricultural museum and rare farm breeds.

SNIBSTON DISCOVERY PARK

🗺 435 H15 • Ashby Road, Coalville LE67 3LN ☎ 01530 278444 🕐 Daily 10–5; closed usually 2nd week in Jan 🎟 Adult £5.50, child (5–15) £3.50, family £15 🛒 ♿ 🚻 🅿
www.leics.gov.uk/museums

Snibston is a well-designed museum where learning and fun go hand in hand—though not to the detriment of the seriousness of subjects such as conditions down a 19th-century coal mine, where men, women and children worked in sometimes appalling situations. Using former industrial buildings and the Coalville mine buildings, the park mixes indoor and outdoor educational activities, including outdoor science and water playgrounds.

SOUTHWELL

🗺 436 J15 🛈 The Gilstrap Centre, Castlegate, Newark NG24 1BG, tel 01636 655765
www.southwellminster.org.uk
www.nationaltrust.org.uk

The minster (Apr–end Sep daily 8–7; rest of year daily 8–dusk) is the architectural highlight of this small Nottinghamshire town (pronounced suthall). Dating from Norman times, the chapter house (begun 1292) has superbly delicate carving, celebrating the foliage of Sherwood Forest in stone. In Upton Road, The Workhouse (Apr–end Jul and Sep, Oct Thu–Mon 12–5; Aug daily 11–5), the best-preserved building of its kind in Britain, evokes the grim life of the destitute. Opened in 1824 to shelter and feed the sick and poor, the workhouse is typical of the many that once dotted the country.

STOKE-ON-TRENT

🗺 434 G15 🛈 Bagnall Street, Hanley, Stoke-on-Trent ST1 3AD, tel 01782 236000
www.visitstoke.co.uk

Potteries are known to have existed since at least 1300 in the Six Towns (Burslem, Fenton, Hanley, Longton, Stoke and Tunstall) that make up the Stoke-on-Trent conurbation. Some of the most desirable ceramics in the world have come from this region. Twelve of the potteries have factory tours, and two of these are large-scale attractions with visitor centres—Wedgwood (Mon–Fri 9–5, Sat–Sun 10–5; closed 24 Dec–2 Jan) and Spode (Mon–Sat 9–5, Sun 10–4); the Spode factory dates from the 18th century, and tours run on weekdays. These and many other potteries have factory shops with big discounts.
For an overview of the history of Staffordshire pottery, visit the free Potteries Museum and Art Gallery (Mar–end Oct Mon–Sat 10–5, Sun 2–5; rest of year Mon–Sat 10–4, Sun 1–4) in Hanley. The Gladstone Pottery Museum (daily 10–5), in Longton, occupies the area's last working Victorian pottery factory.

Stratford-upon-Avon

Home of Britain's greatest playwright and the Royal Shakespeare Company, Stratford has become a very popular stop on the tourist route, but is still the top destination for literary pilgrims. A wealth of Tudor architecture and plenty of other attractions awaits.

The Royal Shakespeare Theatre (above) was built after the original burned down in 1926 Anne Hathaway's Cottage is where Shakespeare wooed his wife-to-be (right inset). The Garrick Inn (right) was named after impresario David Garrick

RATINGS

Good for kids	● ● ●
Historic interest	● ● ●
Literary interest	● ● ● ● ●

BASICS

✚ 435 H17

🛈 Bridgefoot, Stratford-upon-Avon CV37 6GW, tel 0870 160 7930

❓ Avon Boating runs short river cruises in Victorian and Edwardian craft from near the theatres; www.avon-boating.co.uk

🚃 Stratford-upon-Avon

www.shakespeare-country.co.uk

TIPS

● Hop-on hop-off tours, run by City Sightseeing are a useful way to get to Anne Hathaway's Cottage and Mary Arden's House.
● Combined tickets are sold for the Shakespeare houses: New Place, Nash's House, Hall's Croft, Anne Hathaway's Cottage and Mary Arden's House.

SEEING STRATFORD

Even without the Shakespeare (▷ 30–31) connection, Stratford is a very appealing town on the River Avon, with many historical buildings. One of the most photogenic spots is Church Street. Many of the buildings have Georgian frontages, but the 15th-century almshouses are timber-framed, and the King Edward VI School is thought to be where Shakespeare was educated. The Guildhall Chapel dates from the 13th century and is still a place of worship.

HIGHLIGHTS

SHAKESPEARE'S BIRTHPLACE

Henley Street CV37 6QW ☎ 01789 204016 🕐 Apr–end May and Sep–end Oct Mon–Sat 10–5, Sun 10.30–5; Jun–end Aug Mon–Sat 9–5, Sun 9.30–5; Nov–end Mar Mon–Sat 10–4, Sun 10.30–4

The site most visitors head for first is this building in the middle of town. Whether this marks the Bard's true birthplace is open to question, but it has become his shrine. Since his birth in 1564, this half-timbered Tudor house has changed, but the interior has been refurbished to give a good impression of the young Shakespeare's life.

ROYAL SHAKESPEARE COMPANY

The Royal Shakespeare Company (RSC) maintains Stratford's theatrical traditions, with events at its three theatres—the Royal Shakespeare Theatre, the Swan and the Other Place. The Royal Shakespeare, on Waterside, is a 1930s building and the main venue for Shakespeare's plays (including *Hamlet*, whose hero is pictured below), while the Swan occupies the shell of the first Memorial Theatre, erected in 1879, destroyed in a fire in 1926 and then rebuilt. There are backstage tours (usually Mon–Fri and Sun, except matinee days; call 01789 403405 or visit www.rsc.org.uk for details), while the Royal Shakespeare Company Collection (daily) is an exhibition of costumes.

To rub shoulders with thespians, visit the 16th-century Dirty Duck near the Memorial Theatre, which is the watering hole of RSC actors.

ANNE HATHAWAY'S COTTAGE

Cottage Lane, Shottery CV37 9HH ☎ 01789 204016 🕐 Apr–end May and Sep–end Oct Mon–Sat 10–5, Sun 10.30–5; Jun–end Aug Mon–Sat 9–5, Sun 9.30–5; Nov–end Mar Mon–Sat 10–4, Sun 10.30–4

Shakespeare's wife lived in this pretty thatched cottage. You can walk along the country lane from Hall's Croft to avoid the traffic. The house stayed in the Hathaway family until the 19th century, and much of the family furniture remains.

MARY ARDEN'S HOUSE AND THE SHAKESPEARE COUNTRYSIDE MUSEUM

Station Road, Wilmcote CV37 9UN ☎ 01789 204016 🕐 Apr–end May and Sep–end Oct Mon–Sat 10–5, Sun 10.30–5; Jun–end Aug Mon–Sat 9.30–5, Sun 10–5; Nov–end Mar Mon–Sat 10–4, Sun 10.30–4

The childhood home of Shakespeare's mother is 3 miles (5km) north of town. Walk along the towpath of the Stratford-upon-Avon Canal or take the train one stop beyond Stratford. The Shakespeare Countryside Museum surrounds the cottage and has displays about life and work here, and Glebe Farm, a working blacksmith's and falconer's.

HOLY TRINITY CHURCH

Old Town CV37 6BG ☎ 01789 415563 ⊙ Mar–end Oct Mon–Sat 8.30–5, Sun 2–5 (until 6, May–end Sep); rest of year Mon–Sat 9–4, Sun 2–5
Out of town by the river is the 13th-century church where Shakespeare was baptized in 1564 and buried in 1616, as shown by the baptismal entry and burial notice in the parish register here. His gravestone is in front of the altar.

HALL'S CROFT

Old Town CV37 6BG ☎ 01789 204016 ⊙ Nov–end Mar daily 11–4; Apr–end May and Sep–end Oct daily 11–5; Jun–end Aug Mon–Sat 9.30–5, Sun 10–5
This half-timbered house is named after the respected physician Dr. John Hall, who married Shakespeare's daughter, Susanna in 1607. It contains period furnishings, and a small display has been made of medicine in Shakespeare's day.

HARVARD HOUSE

High Street CV37 6HP ☎ 01789 204016 ⊙ Apr–end May Fri–Sun and public holidays 12–5; Jun–early Sep Wed–Sun and public holidays 12–5
Now containing the Neish Collection of Pewter, this house was the home of Katherine Rogers, mother of clergyman John Harvard (1607–38), who emigrated to Massachusetts shortly before his death. His generous bequests to the newly founded US college at Cambridge led to its being named after him.

BACKGROUND

Before the birth of the world's greatest playwright, to John and Mary Shakespeare, Stratford was a busy but unexceptional market town, where merchants built imposing half-timbered houses.

MORE TO SEE

NEW PLACE

Chapel Street CV37 6EP ☎ 01789 204016 ⊙ Jul–end Aug Mon–Sat 9.30–5, Sun 10–5; Apr–end May and Sep–end Oct daily 11–5; Nov–end Mar daily 11–4
The house where Shakespeare died in 1616 no longer exists, but its site in Chapel Street is marked by a garden next to Nash's House (daily), itself owned by the first husband of his granddaughter Elizabeth and now containing displays on the town's history.

TEDDY BEAR MUSEUM

Greenhill Street CV37 6 LF ☎ 01789 293160 ⊙ Mar–end Dec daily 9.30–5.30; Jan–end Feb daily 10–4
This lovingly assembled collection of ancient and modern teddies (some owned by famous people) includes several rarities.

BUTTERFLY FARM

Swan's Nest Lane CV37 7LS ☎ 01789 299288 ⊙ summer daily 10–6; rest of year daily 10–dusk
On the opposite bank from the RSC theatres, this claims to be Europe's largest live butterfly and insect exhibit, where eye-catching exotic creatures inhabit a re-created tropical landscape of pools and waterfalls.

THE MIDLANDS STRATFORD-UPON-AVON 159

Tatton Park was built between 1780 and 1813

STONELEIGH ABBEY

🔲 435 H16 • Stoneleigh, near Kenilworth CV8 2LF ☎ 01926 858535 🕐 House: Good Fri–end Oct Tue–Thu, Sun and public holidays 11–4. Grounds: 10–5 🖭 Grounds only, £2 per person. Guided tours of West Wing and Stables: adult £6, first child (5–12) free, additional child £2.50 ❓ Abbey: 90-min guided tours only at 11am, 1pm and 3pm; reservations not essential, but advisable to arrive slightly early 🖳 🖺 🏠 🅿 www.stoneleighabbey.org

Like many other abbeys that aren't really abbeys, Stoneleigh is a country house occupying a medieval monastic site. On the guided tour around this Georgian building visitors are taken to the room where Queen Victoria (1819–1901) slept, the dining room where she and her husband, Prince Albert (1819–61) dined in 1858, and the bath that was made specially for her visit. It is also recorded that novelist Jane Austen (1775–1817) paid a visit to the house in 1806.

STRATFORD-UPON-AVON

See pages 158–159

SUDBURY HALL AND NATIONAL TRUST MUSEUM OF CHILDHOOD

🔲 435 H15 • Sudbury, Ashbourne DE6 5HT ☎ 01283 585305 🕐 Apr–end Oct Wed–Sun 1–5; early Dec Sat–Sun 11–4 🖭 Hall and Museum (including gardens): adult £9, child (5–16) £4.50, family £20. Hall or museum: adult £5.50, child £3.50, family £12.50 🖳 🖺 🏠 🅿 www.nationaltrust.org.uk

Considered one of the finest houses of its period in England, Sudbury Hall dates from the late 17th century. Its greatest qualities are the interiors, with carving by Grinling Gibbons (1648–1721),

WARWICK CASTLE

A castle almost too perfect-looking to be real, enlivened by jousting tournaments and lifelike waxworks.

🔲 435 H16 • Warwick CV34 4QU ☎ 0870 442 2000 🕐 Apr–end Sep daily 10–6; rest of year daily 10–5 🖭 Summer: adult £16.95, child (4–16) £9.95, family £45 ❓ Audiotour £2.95 📖 £3.95 🖈 Warwick 🅿 www.warwick-castle.co.uk

RATINGS	
Good for kids	●●●
Historic interest	●●●●
Value for money	●●

MAKE A DAY OF IT
Coventry Cathedral (▷ 152)
Hidcote Manor Garden (▷ 81)
Kenilworth Castle (▷ 153)
Stratford-upon-Avon (▷ 158–159)

Architecturally, Warwick is one of the finest examples of a medieval castle in England, with its exteriors dating back to the 14th and 15th centuries. To appreciate it from the outside, walk around the walls and through the gardens, landscaped by Capability Brown in the 1750s, with the subsequent addition of a Victorian Rose Garden and Peacock Garden. The castle is owned by the Tussaud's Group (who run Madame Tussaud's in London, ▷ 126) and is run as a modern tourist attraction.

The interior was thoroughly upgraded in the 17th to 19th centuries, and the private apartments are furnished as they would have been in 1898. The Royal Weekend Party uses waxwork figures to replicate aristocratic life of that time, one guest being the young Winston Churchill (1874–1965). The Kingmaker is an exhibition devoted to the castle's most significant and influential owner, Richard Neville, Earl of Warwick (1428–71). You can see Neville preparing for his final battle in 1471. Also look for the arms and armour exhibition and the eerie Dungeon and Torture Chamber.

WARWICK

Many visitors to the castle unfortunately miss the town of Warwick itself, which was given a handsome makeover after a disastrous fire in 1694. As a result, it has some of the finest 18th-century streetscapes in England, notably in the High Street and Northgate Street. Predating the fire are two medieval gateways, the old houses in Castle Lane, the 15th-century Beauchamp tomb in the Church of St. Mary and (near the West Gate) Leycester Hospital (closed Mon). The last of these is a wonderfully complete group of half-timbered buildings (mostly 16th-century). Visitors can look into the chapel, courtyard and great hall.

Don't miss Weekend events such as re-enacted battles (above), jousting and falconry displays (May to end Sep).

He looks friendly enough at the West Midlands Safari Park

The best approach to Worcester Cathedral is via the river path

The tourist information office is housed in Worcester's Guildhall

painted ceilings and murals of mythological subjects by Louis Laguerre, and a spectacular staircase carved by Edward Pierce. The Gallery—one of the longest in England—has an opulent decorative plasterwork ceiling.

In the 19th-century service wing, the National Trust Museum of Childhood looks into the world of the child, past and present, with collections of antique toys and dolls. Younger visitors also get the opportunity to play the role of chimneysweep and climb inside a chimney.

TATTON PARK

➕ 434 G14 • near Knutsford WA16 6QN ☎ 01625 534435 (recording), 01625 534400 ⏰ Park: Apr–end Sep daily 10–7; rest of year Tue–Sun 11–4. Gardens: Apr–end Sep Tue–Sun 10–6; rest of year Tue–Sun 11–3. Mansion: Apr–end Sep Tue–Sun 1–5. Farm: Apr–end Sep Tue–Sun 12–5; rest of year Sat–Sun 11–3. Old Hall: Apr–end Sep Sat–Sun 12–4 (guided tours only). Last admission 1 hr before closing 💷 Mansion, Gardens, Tudor Old Hall and Farm (per attraction): adult £3, child (4–15) £2, family £8; car entry to park £4 ☕ 🍴 Shop and garden centre 👶 🅿 www.tattonpark.org.uk

The Classical Georgian mansion and 405ha (1,000-acre) park at Tatton stage a lively variety of events throughout the year, including flower shows, antiques fairs, vintage car shows, drama and concerts with fireworks. The house has furniture that was specially made by furniture makers Waring and Gillow of Lancaster, and paintings by Canaletto (1697–1768). The Tudor Old Hall was its precursor.

The grounds have plenty to entice, with a Japanese garden, rose garden, fern house, maze and rare-breeds farm, as well as woodland walks and several bicycle trails.

WALL ROMAN SITE (LETOCETUM)

➕ 435 H16 • Watling Street, Wall WS15 0AW ☎ 01543 480768 ⏰ Jun–end Aug daily 10–6; Apr–end May and Sep–end Oct daily 10–5 💷 Adult £2.90, child (5–16) £1.50 www.english-heritage.org.uk

As with most Roman remains in Britain, there is little above foundation level to be seen here. Yet the museum and audiotour help to bring the place back to life.

Known to the Romans as Lectocetum, Wall was established as a military base in around AD50 at the junction of two routes—Watling Street and the Ryknield Way—and grew into a busy town, providing overnight accommodation for travelling Roman officials and imperial messengers. The bathhouse is one of the most complete Roman relics of its kind in Britain, and there are also remains of a mansio, where travellers could rest and change their horses.

WEST MIDLANDS SAFARI PARK AND LEISURE PARK

➕ 434 G16 • Spring Grove, Bewdley DY12 1LF ☎ 01299 402114 ⏰ Mid-Mar to end Oct daily from 10 (closing time varies, the earliest is 4) 💷 All visitors over 4 years £7.99, under 4s free 🍴 ☕ 🛍 👶 🅿 www.wmsp.co.uk

The 4-mile (6.5km) drive through this hugely popular safari park takes about an hour and gives visitors a close encounter with lions, giraffes, zebras and more, as well as with some endangered species such as white rhinoceroses and Bengal tigers. You may also get the chance to feed antelopes. Throughout the day there are live shows that might feature a reptile encounter, feeding the hippos or a sea-lion show.

The leisure park area has traditional rather than ultra-scary rides and is suitable for all the family.

Don't miss Pets' Corner for younger children, where they can touch and feed the animals, and giraffe rides for older children.

WORCESTER

➕ 434 G17 ℹ The Guildhall, High Street, Worcester WR1 2EY, tel 01905 726311 www.visitworcester.com

The city of Worcester is a mix of the sublime and the mundane: amid some insensitive 20th-century development and fine streets of Georgian mansions and timber-framed buildings is the cathedral (daily 7.30–6), with a superb crypt, cloister and monuments, including that of King John (1167–1216) and the 14th-century Beauchamp tomb. The Royal Worcester Porcelain Works (visitor office: Mon–Sat 9–5.30, Sun 11–5, closed Easter Sun; tours Mon–Fri, reservations advised) dates from 1751 and offers a factory tour and a museum, where examples of this delicate china through the ages is on display in period settings.

During the Battle of Worcester in 1651, Charles II (1630–85) made his headquarters near the cathedral at the 11th-century Commandery (Mon–Sat 10–5, Sun 1.30–5), which now houses the Civil War Visitor Centre, focusing on the trial of Charles I and Cromwell's campaign (▷ 32–33).

Another famous person associated with this area is the British composer Edward Elgar (1857–1934), whose statue stands near the cathedral. He was born outside the city at Lower Broadheath, at what is now the Elgar Birthplace Museum (daily 11–5; closed 23 Dec–31 Jan).

THE NORTH

The inhabitants of the north of England have a pride in their region that is unmatched elsewhere. It's a justifiable pride, because two of the most charming national parks in Britain, the Lake District and the Yorkshire Dales, are here, while the abundant historical sights are balanced by exciting cities.

KEY SIGHTS

Alnwick Castle is watched over by statues on its towers

ALNWICK CASTLE AND GARDEN

➕ 439 H9 • Alnwick NE66 1NQ
☎ 01665 511100 ⏰ Castle: Apr–end Oct daily 11–5. Garden: Apr, May, Oct 10–6; Jun–end Sep 10–7; Nov–end Jan 10–4; Feb–end Mar 10–5 💷 Castle and grounds: adult £12, child (5–15) £2.95. Castle: adult £7.95, child £2.95. Garden: adult £6, child under 16 free with paying adult 🚻 🏧 🍴 🅿
www.alnwickcastle.com

Younger visitors can have fun spotting the features that were filmed here for the Harry Potter movies. Alnwick Castle is the quintessential medieval English fortress, with towers and battlements set in parkland by the River Aln. The castle was founded in 1095, and by 1147 it had the appearance that it essentially has today. The Percy family, later the dukes of Northumberland, have owned it since 1309. The interiors are a surprise, remodelled in the 19th century in sumptuous neo-Renaissance style, with much gilding and carving.

BAMBURGH CASTLE

➕ 443 H9 • Bamburgh NE69 7DF
☎ 01668 214515 ⏰ Mid-Mar to end Oct daily 11–5 💷 Adult £5.50, child (5–15) £2.50 ♿ Difficult wheelchair access 🚻 🏧 🍴 🅿
www.bamburghcastle.com

Sitting on an outcrop of rock overlooking the North Sea, Bamburgh has huge walls and turrets, and a massive square keep. Despite its apparent strength, it was the first castle ever to be taken by artillery—by King Edward IV's army in 1464. Its shattered remains were restored in the 18th and 19th centuries. The interiors were remodelled in the 19th century, but are still impressive—especially the King's Hall—while the armoury and dungeon are exciting for children.

High and mighty: Durham is dominated by its cathedral

DURHAM

Durham is a World Heritage Site with a magnificent cathedral and captivating views.

➕ 439 H11 🛈 Millennium Place DH1 1WA, tel 0191 384 3720 🚉 Durham
www.virtualdurham.co.uk

RATINGS	
Good for kids	●●
Historic interest	●●●●●
Specialist shopping	●●●
Religious interest	●●●●●

MAKE A DAY OF IT

Beamish, The North of England Open Air Museum (▷ 164)
Hadrian's Wall (▷ 168)
Newcastle upon Tyne (▷ 175)

The heart of the university city of Durham is compact, historic and largely traffic-free. High on the cliff above the River Wear is the mighty three-towered cathedral (Oct–end Apr Mon–Sat 9.30–6.15, Sun 12.30–5; May–end Sep Mon–Sat 9.30–8, Sun 12.30–8). It was built mostly over 40 years from 1093 and both rounded Norman and pointed Gothic arches can be seen. Huge cylindrical pillars are carved with geometric designs, while at the east end lies the body of St. Cuthbert, one of the region's major saints. The Bishop's throne is the most elevated in Britain—fittingly, for the prince-bishops of Durham were a law unto themselves, and even the king needed permission to enter their lands. The cloisters and precincts represent the most complete survival of a medieval monastery in England; off the cloister, the Treasury (Mon–Sat 10–4.30, Sun 2–4.30) has relics of St. Cuthbert.

On the opposite end of the hilltop is the Norman castle (Jul–end Sep daily; rest of year Mon, Wed, Sat, Sun afternoons), whose great circular keep contains the Gallery and Chapel, and the medieval Great Hall. There is also a series of 18th-century state rooms. Since 1832 it has been part of Durham University. In an attractive cobbled street, the Durham Heritage Centre (Jun–end Sep daily 11–4.30; Apr–end May, Oct Sat–Sun 2–4.30) in St. Mary le Bow Church in North Bailey tells the city's story.

Don't miss The Galilee Chapel, at the cathedral's west end, is decorated with carved zigzags, giving a jazzy setting for the tomb of the Venerable Bede (c673–735), Britain's first historian.

THE SIGHTS

The Royal Border Railway Bridge, spanning the River Tweed, was built in the style of an aqueduct in the 1840s by Robert Stephenson

Blackpool's The Big One will have you screaming in your seat

THE SIGHTS

BEAMISH, THE NORTH OF ENGLAND OPEN AIR MUSEUM

🔲 439 H11 • Beamish DH9 0RG
☎ 0191 370 4000 🕐 Apr–end Oct daily 10–5. Town and tramway: Nov–end Mar Tue–Thu, Sat–Sun 10–4
💷 Apr–end Oct: adult £12, child (5–16) £7; rest of year: £4 for all 🚌 Bus 720 from Durham, 709 from Newcastle upon Tyne ♿ Difficult wheelchair access 🔲 🏛 🍴 🅿
www.beamish.org.uk

A painstaking reconstruction of a northern town from a bygone era, full of buildings transported from other places, Beamish is filled with details of past times. Its aim is to tell the story of the people of northeast England between 1825 and 1913. Costumed staff welcome visitors to shops stocked with period goods, and to the pub and newspaper office. You can take part in a lesson in the village school, ride on an electric tram, visit the dentist's surgery, catch a replica 1825 steam train and visit a factory. The schoolroom teaches how hard schooldays were, and the chapel shows how religion dominated many lives.

BEMPTON CLIFFS

🔲 440 K12 • Bempton Cliffs Nature Reserve, 11 Cliff Lane, Bempton, Bridlington YO15 1JD ☎ 01262 851179
🕐 Visitor office: Mar–end Nov daily 10–5; Feb and Dec Sat–Sun 9.30–4
🚆 Bempton, 1 mile (1.5km) 💷 Free
🔲 🏛 🍴 🅿 £3.50
www.rspb.org.uk

One of the major bird sites on the east coast, these sheer 120m (400ft) chalk cliffs are home to more than 200,000 breeding seabirds. There are five safe viewing points (two accessible to wheelchairs) and a visitor office, run by the Royal Society for the Protection of Birds (RSPB). Bird species (depending on the season) include puffins, guillemots, razorbills, kittiwakes, fulmars and migrating birds. It is one of the country's most important breeding sites for Britain's largest seabird, the gannet, with several thousand nests. Also look out for seals and porpoises. A footpath follows the coast to the east round the spectacularly indented cliffs of Flamborough Head.

BERWICK-UPON-TWEED

🔲 443 H9 ℹ 106 Marygate TD15 1BN, tel 01289 330733 🚉 Berwick-upon-Tweed
www.berwickonline.org.uk

Positioned near the Scottish border, Berwick was for long under threat of invasion and is guarded by Britain's only complete set of 16th-century ramparts, which you can walk around in their entirety. Here, three great bridges span the River Tweed— the Royal Border Railway Bridge, the Royal Tweed Bridge and the Berwick Bridge.

Berwick itself reveals its quirky side within the walls, a place full of unexpected levels and grey stone houses. Prominent in the town, Berwick Guildhall (guided tours Easter–end Sep Mon–Fri 10.30am and 2pm) houses the Cell Block Museum in the Town Gaol. Berwick Barracks (daily), the earliest surviving in Britain, date from the early 18th century and contain The King's Own Scottish Borderers Regimental Museum and the Berwick Museum and Art Gallery, including Chinese ceramics, medieval carvings and Impressionist paintings.
Don't miss The Breakyneck Steps, beside the White Wall of the castle, plunge from the heights to the riverbank.

BEVERLEY

🔲 440 K13 ℹ 34 Butcher Row HU17 0AB, tel 01482 867430 🚉 Beverley
www.eastriding.gov.uk

Surprisingly little known, Beverley is one of the best-looking old market towns in the north of England.

The main attraction is its architecture. It has streets lined with mostly 18th- and 19th-century houses, two marketplaces and the North Bar of 1409, a rare early brick gateway. Beverley Minster dates mostly from the 13th century. It is a large, long building with twin towers and an interior full of light and elaborate carving. The Percy Tomb in Beverley Minster is a masterpiece of the mid-14th-century Decorated style, with a very elaborate stone canopy, carved with fruit, flowers, figures and angels.

Though smaller, St. Mary's Church, at the other end of the town, is equally impressive. It was mostly rebuilt in the 15th century, and its painted roof, dating from around 1445, depicts 40 English kings. The carving of a rabbit in St. Michael's Chapel—with a pilgrim's staff and pouch— is reputedly the inspiration for the White Rabbit in Lewis Carroll's Alice's Adventures in Wonderland (1865). Also take a look at the Minstrels in St. Mary's Church, small carvings of five players at the top of a nave pillar.
Don't miss Enjoying a beer at the White Horse, a fascinating old-fashioned gaslit pub.

BLACKPOOL

🔲 439 F13 ℹ 1 Clifton Street FY1 1LY, tel 01253 478222 🚉 Blackpool
www.blackpooltourism.com

What Blackpool does, it does extremely well: donkey rides, amusement arcades and big rides. During the 19th century, local factory workers traditionally came here for their annual week's holiday to enjoy the famous promenade, the long sandy beach and its theatres. Blackpool Tower (daily; closed

Bradford's National Museum of Photography, Film and Television

Owned by the National Trust, Brimham Rocks can be explored via a network of maintained footpaths

Mon–Fri in winter, except Feb half-term), a scale copy of Paris's Eiffel Tower, dates from this time and you can still visit the Grand Theatre. Blackpool Pleasure Beach (Apr–end Oct daily; Nov–end Dec and Mar Sat–Sun) is the main draw. The original Big Dipper was opened here in 1923 and is still going strong, rivalled today by one of Europe's biggest rollercoasters, The Big One. **Don't miss** The best time to visit is in the autumn, when you can see the famous Blackpool Illuminations, huge moving tableaux of fairytales and brilliantly lit trams.

BLACKWELL, THE ARTS AND CRAFTS HOUSE

➕ 439 F12 • Bowness-on-Windermere LA23 3JR ☎ 015394 46139 🕐 Apr–end Oct daily 10.30–5; rest of year daily 10–4 🚶 Adult £5, child (under 16) £2.75, family £13 ▣ ▦ ♿ 🅿
www.blackwell.org.uk

One of the most important examples of an Arts and Crafts house in Britain, Blackwell was designed by the English architect Mackay Hugh Baillie Scott (1865–1945), and completed in 1900 for Edward Holt, heir to a Manchester brewing company. After a restoration project costing £3.25 million, the Lakeland house was opened to the public in 2001. Baillie Scott was influenced by William Morris (1834–96) and author John Ruskin (1819–1900), and the Arts and Crafts' rural motifs are evident everywhere: stained-glass windows, and tiles and friezes of wild flowers, berries and animals. Overall, however, the interior is strikingly modern, even minimalist. The house hosts art exhibitions throughout the year. **Don't miss** Brantwood (daily 11–5), John Ruskin's home in Coniston.

BRADFORD

➕ 439 H13 🏛 City Hall, Centenary Square BD1 1HY, tel 01274 753678 🚆 Bradford Interchange, Saltaire
www.visitbradford.com

Bradford played a major role in the wool trade during the Industrial Revolution. European merchant settlers brought wealth and prestige and with it the city became the wool capital of the world. Legacies of this past include fine, gritstone buildings and early Victorian architecture. The City Hall, with its Italianate clock tower, and the neo-Gothic Wool Exchange are two fine examples.

The main attraction is the National Museum of Photography, Film and Television (Tue–Sun and public holidays), housed in a curved, glass-walled building. Inside are five floors of interactive displays on all forms of visual media, including an IMAX cinema. There's something here for all the family—exhibits on the earliest days of television, methods of advertising and news gathering, and plenty of buttons to press and games to play.

Learn more about the city's past in the Bradford Industrial Museum (Tue–Sat, Sun pm and public holidays), housed in the former Moorside Mills northeast of the city itself. There are working textile machines, workers' cottages and shire horses like those that once pulled the city's trams and buses.

Now a World Heritage Site, Saltaire, 4 miles (7km) north of central Bradford, is a remarkable Victorian factory village. It was built in the 1850s by the philanthropic wool baron Sir Titus Salt to house his workers in decent conditions around his colossal Italianate woollen mill. A school, hospital, two churches, Sunday school, washhouse and shops were all part of Salt's design. Today, Salt's

Mill has shops, businesses and the 1853 Gallery (daily 10–6, free), the world's largest permanent collection of paintings by the local artist David Hockney (born 1937). Walk along the back streets of Saltaire to see how the more fortunate 19th-century mill workers lived. **Don't miss** The excellent Animation display in the National Museum of Photography, Film and Television.

BRIMHAM ROCKS

➕ 439 H12 • Brimham Rocks, Summerbridge, Harrogate HG3 4DW ☎ 01423 780688 🕐 Daily 8–dusk 🚶 Free 🚌 Bus 24 Harrogate/Pateley Bridge with a 2-mile (3km) walk from Summerbridge ▣ ▦ ♿ 🅿 Car £3 (up to 4 hr), £4 (over 4 hr)
www.brimhamrocks.co.uk

Aspiring rock climbers beat a path to this vast series of strange rock formations scattered across nearly 400ha (1,000 acres) of elevated moorland on the edge of the Yorkshire Dales (▷ 314–315). The weird sculptural effects of wind, ice and rain have produced a series of gritstone towers and pinnacles, some appearing to balance precariously on the flimsiest foundations. Look for the Dancing Bear, David's Writing Desk and the Idol.

CAMELOT THEME PARK

➕ 434 G13 • Charnock Richard, Chorley PR7 5LP ☎ 08702 204820 🕐 Apr–end Sep daily 10–5; Oct–end Mar Sat–Sun 🚶 Adult £16, child £16, child under 1m (3ft) free, family £55 ▣ ▦ ♿ 🅿
www.camelotthemepark.co.uk

Camelot is a medieval fantasy theme park. Attractions include jousting tournaments, big rides such as a looping rollercoaster and a go-carting circuit, plus carousels, a farm and gardens.

Castle Howard is an imposing baroque country house

CASTLE HOWARD

➕ 440 J12 • Castle Howard, near Malton YO60 7DA ☎ 01653 648333
🕐 House: Mar–end Nov daily 11–4. Garden: daily 10–dusk all year
💷 House and garden: adult £9.50, child (4–16) £6.50. Garden: adult £6.50, child £4.40, family—one child free
🚌 Bus 840 from York train station mid-Apr to end Sep 🍴 ☕ 🏛 🎁
🅿
www.castlehoward.co.uk

A ruler-straight road leads through the great estate of this palatial baroque house, the first building to be designed by the playwright and architect Sir John Vanbrugh (1664–1726), in 1699, with the assistance of the vastly more experienced Nicholas Hawksmoor (1661–1736).

The domed hall and wide façades are familiar to millions of Britons through the fondly remembered 1981 television adaptation of Evelyn Waugh's *Brideshead Revisited*, and for many people Castle Howard has come to epitomize a nostalgia for England before World War II. It is still the home of the Howard family.

The dome and many rooms were destroyed in a disastrous fire in 1940, but the damage was repaired and the house's restoration continues. You can take a tour through rooms decorated with Howard family heirlooms, and paintings by Peter Paul Rubens, Canaletto and Hans Holbein. There are exhibitions dedicated to the filming of *Brideshead Revisited*, the building of the house, and the role of women at the house over the centuries.

The gardens feature the formal Italianate Temple of the Four Winds, the great Pyramid and the huge Mausoleum. There is also an adventure playground, farm shop, plant nursery and holiday park.

The abbey's cellarium is part of this unique World Heritage Site

FOUNTAINS ABBEY AND STUDLEY ROYAL WATER GARDEN

Heart-stopping vistas greet visitors to Britain's most complete monastic ruins, with a medieval deer park and elegant 18th-century water gardens.

➕ 439 H12 • Ripon HG4 3DY
☎ 01765 608888 🕐 Abbey, Hall and Water Garden: Mar–end Oct daily 10–5; Nov–end Feb 10–4. Deer Park: daily dawn–dusk 💷 Adults £5.50, child (5–16) £3, family £15
🚉 Harrogate 🍴 🏛
www.fountainsabbey.org.uk

RATINGS	
Panoramic landscapes	●●●●●
Historic interest	●●●●
Good for kids	●●
Walkability	●●●●●

MAKE A DAY OF IT
Brimham Rocks (▷ 165)
Harrogate (▷ 170)
Ripon (▷ 177)
Wharfedale, Swaledale and Wensleydale (▷ 184)

Fountains Abbey was established in 1132 by 13 monks looking for a simple life, and this damp, rocky, desolate ravine fitted the bill perfectly, with a supply of stone and timber for building, shelter from the rough northern weather and an abundance of spring water. The abbey became extremely wealthy, but Henry VIII closed it down during his dissolution of the country's monasteries in 1539 (▷ 31). Yet it has survived as Britain's largest abbey ruin and you can still see the church tower, dating from around 1500, soaring above the Norman nave. Wander too among the remains of the monastic quarters and into the vaulted interior of the cellarium (storehouse).

The later owners beautified the estate and it was sold to Sir Stephen Proctor, who commissioned the building of Fountains Hall (1598–1604), partly from stone taken from the abbey.

In the 18th century the neighbouring estate of Studley Royal fell into the hands of local MP John Aislabie, who began to landscape the grounds, a project begun in 1720 and completed after his death in 1746 by his son, William. The result is a remarkable creation, a water garden of geometric pools, follies and a landscape of rocky outcrops. In 1768 William acquired Fountains Abbey and Fountains Hall. He extended the gardens to include the sweeping lawn as an approach to the abbey and added Anne Boleyn's Seat, a viewpoint above the valley with a framed view of the ruins.

Close by are the Banqueting House, the Temple of Piety, the Temple of Fame, the Gothic Tower and the fishing lodges that overlook the lake at the garden's eastern end.

Don't miss Taking the path that rises steeply from the Water Gardens via the Serpentine Tunnel to Anne Boleyn's Seat; the Seven Bridges Walk goes through re-created wilderness.

Take an X-ray of yourself at the Catalyst Museum

Art and science meet at inventor William Armstrong's Cragside

Gannets on the Farne Islands share their home with other birds

THE SIGHTS

Don't miss The informative costumed characters, among them Vanbrugh, the fifth Earl of Carlisle and the Housekeeper from 1850.

CATALYST MUSEUM

434 G14 • Mersey Road, Widnes WA8 0DF ☎ 0151 420 1121 ◐ Tue–Fri and public holidays 10–5; Sat–Sun 11–5. Also most Mon 10–5 during school holidays Adult £4.95, child (5–16) £3.50, family £14.95 Runcorn (far side of Runcorn–Widnes Bridge)
www.catalyst.org.uk

The chemical industry is the focus of this family-oriented attraction in a former soap factory. It makes an unusual day out, with plenty of hands-on exhibits, including puzzles, touch-screen computers and a giant bubble machine. Archive footage and lifelike reconstructions delve into the chemical industry through the ages, from the production of medicines and soaps to toys, photography and clothing. An all-glass lift whisks you to the Observatory Gallery for views of the River Mersey.

CRAGSIDE

439 H10 • Cragside, Rothbury, Morpeth NE65 7PX ☎ 01669 620150 ◐ House: mid-Mar to end Sep normally Tue–Sun 1–5.30, but closed until 2007. Estate and garden: mid-Mar to end Oct Tue–Sun 10.30–7; Nov–end Dec 11–4 House, gardens and estate: adult £8.50, child £4, family £20. Gardens and estate: adult £5.70 (£2.80 in winter), child £2.60 (£1.30 in winter), family £14 (£7 in winter)
www.nationaltrust.org.uk

This spectacular 19th-century house was built for the industrialist and inventor William Armstrong (1810–1900) and was the first house in the world to be lit entirely by electric light—powered by a hydroelectric plant that he installed. The house has Arts and Crafts furniture and interiors, and immediately conveys the lifestyle of a rich 19th-century businessman. The huge grounds include a deep wooded valley—a vivid display when the rhododendrons and azaleas are in bloom—and one of Europe's largest rock gardens. There is also a devious maze, and the grounds are one of the red squirrel's last strongholds. Displays recall Armstrong and his inventions, which include the breech-loading gun.

DUNSTANBURGH CASTLE

443 H9 • near Alnwick NE66 2RD ☎ 01665 576231 ◐ Apr–end Sep daily 10–6; Oct 10–4, Nov–end Mar Thu–Mon 10–4 Adult £2.50, child (under 16) £1.30 Craster (via Alnwick) from Newcastle upon Tyne
www.english-heritage.org.uk

You will have to walk to see Dunstanburgh Castle, as the ruin stands on an outcrop of rock on a lonely stretch of coast, 1 mile (1.6km) from the road. A particularly memorable approach is from the fishing village of Craster, from where the walk is about twice as far along the coast path. The site was fortified during the Iron Age, although the present structure was begun in 1314 by Thomas, Earl of Lancaster. Built to protect a small harbour, it was originally surrounded on three sides by the sea (and by a moat on its fourth).

DURHAM

See page 163

FARNE ISLANDS

443 H9 • c/o The Sheiling, 8 St Aidan's, Seahouses NE68 7SR ☎ 01665 721099/720651 ◐ Landing permitted on Inner Farne and Staple Island: Apr and Aug–end Sep daily 10.30–6. May–end Jul (breeding season) Staple Island 10.30–1.30, Inner Farne 1.30–5 (Excluding boat): May–end Jul: adult £5, child (5–16) £2.50. Apr, Aug–end Sep: adult £4, child (5–16) £2 From Seahouses harbour (2½ hr) Wheelchairs have access to Inner Farne only, preferably at high tide Inner Farne
www.nationaltrust.org.uk

The National Trust specifically advise wearing a hat when visiting this archipelago of 28 islands (15 at high tide) during the breeding season, to protect visitors from dive-bombing terns. The Farne Islands are one of Britain's foremost seabird breeding grounds. On the boat trip from Seahouses harbour you may spot seals bobbing in the water before you land on Inner Farne and Staple Island, which support huge populations of puffins, razorbills, eiders, kittiwakes, cormorants and oystercatchers. Other islands can be viewed from the boat.

HADRIAN'S WALL

See page 168

HALIFAX

439 H13 Piece Hall, Halifax HX1 1RE, tel 01422 368725 Halifax
www.calderdale.gov.uk

In the heart of the Pennine Hills, Halifax became a powerhouse of the textile industry during the Industrial Revolution. The focus of its pre-industrial heritage is Piece Hall, built as a woollen market in 1779, with 350 small rooms set on a series of colonnaded tiers around a vast open space. Today, the hall has small gift shops, cafés, a market and open-air concerts. The main tourist attraction is Eureka! The Museum for Children (daily), aimed at 3- to 12-year-olds, where children can learn about themselves and the world.

Hadrian's Wall at Housesteads: A National Trail follows the line of the wall. Visit the Mithraic Temple at Carrawburgh (inset)

HADRIAN'S WALL

Walk along the longest and most spectacular Roman remains in Britain.

Northumberland preserves the best remains of this once 76-mile (120km) monument, built between AD122 and 128 on the orders of the Roman emperor Hadrian (AD76–138). He had it built to control trade over the border rather than to keep out the barbarians to the north. The B6318 road, which runs parallel to it for part of the way, follows the line of the Roman military way that served the regular forts and observation turrets along the wall. A deep defensive rampart—the vallum—was dug later on the south side of the wall.

HIGHLIGHTS

In many places the wall has long since disappeared, but there are well-preserved sections between Chollerford in the east and Haltwhistle in the west. At Housesteads Roman Fort (Apr–end Sep daily 10–6; Oct–end Mar daily 10–4) the latrines have seating for 12 soldiers and a water channel for sponges (used in place of toilet paper). Close to here is Vindolanda Fort (Apr–end Sep daily 10–6; Feb–end Mar, Oct–end Nov 10–5; Dec–end Jan 10–4), with reconstructions of part of the wall and buildings, and a museum displaying local excavations.

Chesters Roman Fort (Apr–end Sep daily 10–6; rest of year daily 10–4) was a cavalry fort with the remains of the bathhouse (look for the niches where clothes were placed), headquarters and barracks. Corbridge Roman Site (Apr–end Sep daily 10–6; Oct 10–4; Nov–end Mar Sat–Sun 10–4) is a former Roman garrison town and was the supply base for the Roman invasion of Scotland in AD80, with some well-preserved granaries.

For an idea of Roman-style bathing, visit the reconstructed bathhouse at Hadrian's outpost, Segedunum Roman Fort (Apr–end Aug daily 9.30–5; Sep–end Oct 10–5; Nov–end Mar 10–3.30) at Wallsend. A 35m (115ft) tower gives a superb view of the remains of the fort itself. At South Shields, Arbeia Roman Fort (Apr–end Oct Mon–Sat 10–5.30; rest of year Mon–Sat 10–3.30) has a reconstructed gatehouse and re-created scenes of camp life. At the west end of the wall, the finest monument is Birdoswald Fort (Mar–end Nov daily 10–5.30).

Don't miss The Mithraic Temple at Carrawburgh has the remains of a place of worship for the soldiers, dedicated to the god Mithras.

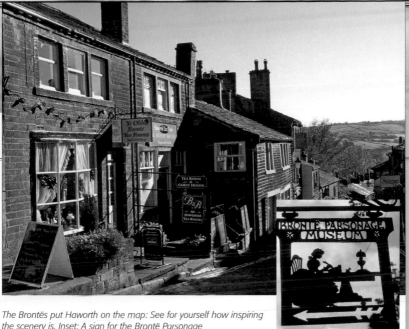

The Brontës put Haworth on the map: See for yourself how inspiring the scenery is. Inset: A sign for the Brontë Parsonage

HAWORTH

Haworth is the hub of the countryside associated with the literary Brontë family.

When Haworth was home to the Brontë family in the 19th century, it was still a textile-manufacturing village. The steep, cobbled streets are surrounded by wild moorland, and the look of the village has changed little since the Brontës lived here, despite the gift shops and tea rooms.

THE PARSONAGE

Haworth became home to the Brontës in 1820 when Patrick Brontë (1777–1861) was appointed its rector. It was while living at the Parsonage here that the three sisters—Charlotte (1816–55), Emily (1818–48) and Anne (1820–49)—wrote their most famous novels, respectively *Jane Eyre* (1847), *Wuthering Heights* (1847) and *The Tenant of Wildfell Hall* (1848). You can follow well-trodden paths past the Brontë Falls to the ruins of Top Withins farmhouse, reputedly the model for nature-loving Emily's *Wuthering Heights*.

The Parsonage sits at the top of Main Street, overlooking the church. Built in 1778, it has been restored to how it would have looked in the Brontës' day. Mementoes include the children's handwritten miniature books, the sofa on which Emily died and Charlotte's wedding bonnet.

The great tragedy of the family is that they all died at a young age. The girls' brother, Branwell, a drunk and opium addict, died of tuberculosis in 1848 at the age of 31. Emily also succumbed to the disease and died three months later, at the age of 30. Anne faded away, dying in Scarborough in 1849, having journeyed there to see if the sea air would cure her. Charlotte died on 31 March 1855 at the age of 39 in the early stages of pregnancy. Two other sisters, Maria and Elizabeth, died in childhood.

Don't miss The tiny statue of Charlotte in the cabinet to your left as you enter her room, together with the description of her by her biographer, friend and fellow novelist Mrs Elizabeth Gaskell (1810–65).

OTHER SIGHTS

Inside the Parish Church of St. Michael and All Angels, where Patrick Brontë was vicar for 41 years, are memorials to the family. Visit the Brontë Weaving Shed (Mon–Sat 10–5.30, Sun 11–5), on North Street, where you can see traditional 19th-century commemorative Brontë Tweed being made.

RATINGS

Good for kids	● ● ●
Historic interest	● ● ● ●
Literary interest	● ● ● ● ●
Walkability	● ● ● ● ●

BASICS

➕ 439 H13

ℹ️ 2–4 West Lane, Haworth BD22 8EF, tel 01535 642329

🚉 Keighley and Worth Valley Railway (01535 645214), connecting with mainline services at Keighley

🗓️

www.visithaworth.com

TIP

● Steam trains from Keighley run by the Keighley and Worth Valley Railway are a good way to get to the village.

MAKE A DAY OF IT

Bradford: National Museum of Photography Film and Television (▷ 165)
Halifax: Piece Hall or Eureka! The Museum for Children (▷ 167)
Hebden Bridge (▷ 170)
Skipton: Castle (▷ 178)

Bookish visitors can browse in the library at Harewood House

Victorian style in Harrogate: The spa town is being smartened up

Barges motor along the Rochdale Canal, at Hebden Bridge

THE SIGHTS

HAREWOOD HOUSE AND BIRD GARDEN

✚ 440 H13 • Harewood, near Leeds LS17 9LQ ☎ 0113 218 1010 ⓒ Grounds and Bird Garden: daily 10–4.30 (or 1 hr before dusk). House: daily 11–4. Terrace Gallery: daily 11–4. Old Kitchen: daily 12–4. Adventure Playground: Mar–end Nov daily 10–6 🅿 All sites: adult £11 (Mon–Fri), £13 (Sat–Sun), child (5–16) £6.50 (Mon–Fri), £8 (Sat–Sun), family £35 (Mon–Fri), £40 (Sat–Sun). Grounds and Bird Garden: adult £8.25/£10.25, child £5.50/£7, family £29.50/£32.50 🚌 Bus 36 from Harrogate or Leeds 🍴 ▫ 🏛 🎫 🅿 www.harewood.org

This showpiece country house was designed for the Lascelles family (the earls of Harewood) by John Carr in 1759. Much of the furniture is by Thomas Chippendale (1718–79) from nearby Otley. There's plenty to enjoy outside, with an adventure playground, a rose garden, lakeside walks, a Spiral Meadow in the kitchen garden and a Bird Garden with over 100 species of bird.
Don't miss Thomas Chippendale's lavishly carved and gilded State Bed.

HARROGATE

✚ 440 H13 🛈 Royal Baths Assembly Rooms, Crescent Road HG1 2RR, tel 01423 537300 🚉 Harrogate www.harrogate.gov.uk

Its spa days may have declined, but Harrogate still exudes style, with Victorian buildings and hotels ranged around the expansive 80ha (200-acre) green known as The Stray. You can stroll through the lushly planted Valley Gardens and go boating on the lake. Or why not sample the waters from Europe's strongest sulphur well at the Royal Pump Room Museum (Apr–end Oct Mon–Sat 10–5, Sun 2–5; rest of year Mon–Sat

10–4) in Crown Place, or look into the former Promenade Room that now houses the Mercer Art Gallery (Tue–Sun and public holidays)? The 1897 Royal Baths in Crescent Road still have the original Turkish baths, decorated appropriately in Moorish style with plush tiles, in addition to saunas and solariums.

Harrogate is a leading events venue and the annual Antiques Fair attracts dealers from around the world. Harlow Carr Botanical Garden (Mar–end Oct daily 9.30–6; Nov–end Feb 9.30–4) is one of the show gardens of the north.
Don't miss Having afternoon tea at Betty's Tearoom on Parliament Street, a Harrogate institution.

HAWKSHEAD

✚ 439 F12 🛈 Main Car Park, Hawkshead LA22 0NT, tel 015394 36525 www.hawkshead-village.com

With its whitewashed houses, narrow streets and cobbled alleyways, Hawkshead has hardly changed since the days when William Wordsworth (1770–1850) attended school here. The traffic-free central area has allowed it to keep its dignity. For centuries Hawkshead was a thriving market town at the heart of the local woollen industry, but it dwindled into insignificance in the 19th century. Wordsworth carved his name on his desk at Hawkshead Grammar School, now a museum (Easter–end Oct Mon–Sat 10–12 and 1.30–5, Sun 1–5), and as a boy attended Hawkshead church. The Beatrix Potter Gallery (Apr–end Oct Sat–Wed 10.30–4.30) has illustrations by the famous children's author Beatrix Potter (1866–1943), who lived at Near Sawrey.

HAWORTH

See page 169

HEBDEN BRIDGE

✚ 439 G13 🛈 Hebden Bridge Visitor and Canal Centre, New Road, Hebden Bridge HX7 8AD, tel 01422 843831 🚉 Hebden Bridge www.calderdale.gov.uk

This spectacular little Pennine town is set in the steep-sided valley of Calderdale, with double-decker houses—one house at the top entered from one street, another underneath entered from a street below—clinging tenaciously to the hillsides. Heptonstall, above Hebden Bridge, became the local focus for hand-weaving in the pre-Industrial age, but was overtaken by the large mills in Hebden Bridge during the 19th century.
Don't miss Walking from Hebden Bridge to Heptonstall via the packhorse bridge and the steep cobbled lane known as The Buttress.

HEXHAM

✚ 439 G10 🛈 Wentworth Car Park, Hexham NE46 1QE, tel 01434 652220 🚉 Hexham www.hadrianswallcountry.org

Hexham, a market town on the River Tyne, is dominated by its abbey church. Begun by St. Wilfrid in about AD675, it contains the crypt built by the saint, but otherwise dates mostly from 1180 to 1250. Look out for the Roman standard-bearer's tombstone, the ancient crypt and the Frith Stool (a Saxon seat in the chancel). Moot Hall, near the marketplace, is a miniature castle pierced by a gateway, erected in the late 14th century as the entrance to barracks for the local garrison; it now houses an art gallery and library. Hexham makes a good base for exploring the most impressive parts of Hadrian's Wall (▷ 168).

The Lady Isabella waterwheel, Isle of Man, is the largest in Europe

With calm waters and small islands, Derwentwater, near Keswick, is one of the Lake District's most attractive lakes

HOLKER HALL

🔲 439 F12 • Cark-in-Cartmel, near Grange-over-Sands LA11 7PL
☎ 015395 58328 🕐 Apr–end Oct Sun–Fri 10.30–5. Lakeland Motor Museum: Apr–end Oct Sun–Fri 10.30–4.45. Gardens: Apr–end Oct Sun–Fri 10–6 💷 All sights: adult £9.25, child (6–16) £5.50
🍴 💻 🏛 🎪 🅿
www.holker-hall.co.uk

The hall itself dates from the 17th century, but much of what you see today is from the 1870s, when architects Paley and Austin added a new wing, an imposing cantilevered staircase and well-disguised modern comforts such as fake books to hide the light switches. The grounds overlook Morecambe Bay, and have woodland trails as well as formal gardens. The Lakeland Motor Museum has more than 100 vehicles on display, including the Campbell Bluebird exhibition dedicated to the father-and-son team of Sir Malcolm (1885–1949) and Donald Campbell (1921–67), who between them set a series of water-speed records on nearby Coniston Water from the 1930s to the 1960s.

HULL

🔲 436 K13 🛈 1 Paragon Street, HU1 3NA, tel 01482 223559 🚉 Hull
www.hullcc.gov.uk/visithull

The large port of Kingston upon Hull (or Hull, as it is commonly known) is only patchily inviting at first look. World War II bombing devastated large areas of the city. However, much investment has gone into rejuvenating the waterfront, including a waterside walkway and marina, and the old town. The best areas are the narrow cobbled High Street, with old warehouses, Victorian shopping arcades, a lively covered market and the streets around the vast Holy Trinity Church.

There is also still considerable activity along the quaysides as trawlers land their catches.

The Deep (daily 10–6, last entry 5) is billed as 'the world's only submarium'. It puts the marine world into chronological context, from the Big Bang onwards, and has all kinds of marine life and push-button gadgets. Hull's other museums (Mon–Sat 10–5, Sun 1.30–4.30) are all free and include the lively trio of Wilberforce House, the home of slavery abolitionist William Wilberforce (1759–1833); Streetlife, a transport museum popular with children; and the more sober Hull and East Riding Museum, with re-creations of an Iron Age village and a well-displayed Roman section. The charmingly old-fashioned Hull Maritime Museum (Mon–Sat 10–5, Sun 1.30–4.30), in Queen Victoria Square, has details on the city's history of whaling, fishing and shipping, and nearby is the equally absorbing Ferens Art Gallery (Mon–Sat 10–5, Sun 1.30–4.30).
Don't miss Two impressive modern structures are the Tidal Surge Barrier (1980), at the entrance to the River Hull from the Humber, and the mighty Humber Bridge (1981).

ISLE OF MAN

🔲 438 D12 🛈 Department of Tourism and Leisure, Sea Terminal Buildings, Douglas IM1 2RG, tel 01624 686801
🛳 Isle of Man Steam Packet Company
☎ 01624 661661, www.steam-packet.com (Heysham, Liverpool–Douglas)
www.gov.im

Best known perhaps for the annual motorcycle races—the Isle of Man Tourist Trophy (TT), held on various courses for almost a century—the Isle of Man is a curious fragment of the British Isles. Measuring 33 miles by 13 miles (53km by 21km) and in the

Irish Sea off the northwest of England, the island is a Crown dependency, not part of the UK, and has lenient taxation and the world's oldest continuous parliament (the Tynwald). But the landscape has much more to interest the visitor: sandy beaches, dramatic moors and mountains, and a generous smattering of Celtic crosses, standing stones and ancient burial grounds.

The capital, Douglas, has a Victorian waterfront, horse-drawn trams and the Manx Museum (Mon–Sat 10–5), but Peel, on the west coast, makes a more characterful base. Train enthusiasts should take a trip on the island's narrow-gauge railway.
Don't miss Peel Castle and Castle Rushen in Castletown are both impressive.

KENDAL

🔲 439 G12 🛈 Town Hall, Highgate LA9 4QL, tel 01539 725758 🚉 Kendal
www.kendaltown.org

For 600 years up to the 19th century, this town of grey stone on the eastern threshold of the Lake District (▷ 172) also flourished as a milling town. Today, although the manufacturing industries have dwindled, Kendal still possesses many former weavers' yards as well as numerous ginnels (alleyways), most just off Highgate and Stricklandgate.

The town's best-known former residents are Henry VIII's sixth wife Catherine Parr (1512–48), born in the now-ruined hilltop castle, and portraitist George Romney (1734–1802). Some of Romney's works are displayed in Abbot Hall Gallery (Mon–Sat), along with paintings by J. M. W. Turner and John Constable.
Don't miss The Museum of Lakeland Life (Mon–Sat) recalls local life from the 17th to 19th centuries.

The Lake District has a vast array of tranquil, beautiful lakes to visit

KESWICK

439 F11 Moot Hall, Market Place CA12 5JE, tel 017687 72645
www.keswick.org

Keswick's position on Derwentwater is the key to its appeal as the major centre in the northern Lake District. Walkers venture from here all year round to the summit of Skiddaw, into the crag-lined valley of Borrowdale or along the gentle paths by the lake. The Keswick Launch (Apr–end Nov daily 10–6; rest of year Sat–Sun 10–6) connects points around the lake.
Don't miss Castlerigg Stone Circle, 38 chunks of volcanic stone.

LAKE DISTRICT NATIONAL PARK

439 F12 National Park Authority, Murley Moss, Oxenholme Road, Kendal LA9 7RL, tel 01539 724555
www.lake-district.gov.uk

This is an extraordinarily diverse area of mountains and lakes tucked into England's northwest corner. There's a wide choice of walking routes, from the high summits of Scafell Pike and Helvellyn to strolls through tranquil valleys and along lake shores. Or you can see it on a cruise: Options include the Victorian steam yacht *Gondola* for a trip on Coniston Water, or a lake steamer on Ullswater.

There's also a range of indoor attractions for rainy days, including visits to the houses of the area's most famous residents. Among them are Hill Top (Mar–end Oct Mon–Wed, Sat–Sun 10.30–4.30 (some Thu in Aug)), home of Beatrix Potter (1866–1943), and Rydal Mount (Mar–end Oct daily 9.30–5; closed Tue, rest of year), home of William Wordsworth (1770–1850). He and his sister Dorothy lived at Dove Cottage in Grasmere (daily 9.30–5.30).

The Corn Exchange, built in 1863, is now a stylish market for jewellery, clothing, music and other collectable items

LEEDS

One of the fastest-growing cities in England, Leeds displays true northern grit alongside a cultural renaissance.

439 H13 Gateway Yorkshire, The Arcade City Station LS1 1PL, tel 0113 242 5242 Leeds City Leeds/Bradford Airport
www.leeds.gov.uk

RATINGS				
Historic interest	●	●	●	
Shopping	●	●	●	●
Good for kids	●	●	●	
Walkability	●	●	●	

Industry and commerce are synonymous with this city, whose architecture tells of great expansion in the 19th century. The Classical Town Hall is one of Britain's grandest, and the Victorian glass-roofed arcades and elliptical Corn Exchange are period gems as well as bustling shopping venues. Nightlife, music and theatre are other major draws.

In central Leeds, the City Art Gallery (Mon–Sat 10–5 (Wed 10–8), Sun 1–5), on the Headrow, has an impressive range of 19th- and 20th-century paintings and sculptures. Next door is the Henry Moore Institute (daily 10–5.30 (Wed 10–9)) with major exhibits from 1850 to the present by Henry Moore, Barbara Hepworth, Andy Goldsworthy and others. Telling the story of medical treatment through the ages, the Thackray Medical Museum (daily 10–5), on Beckett Street, is of mainstream appeal, with interactive displays exploring Victorian slum life.

After many years of ignoring the River Aire and the Leeds–Liverpool Canal planners have developed along the banks of both, with a dynamic waterfront culture of pavement cafés and specialist shops. Here, the Royal Armouries Museum (daily 10–5) houses the national collection of arms and armour.

Outstanding among the more outlying attractions is Leeds Industrial Museum (Tue–Sat 10–5, Sun 1–5), within Armley Mills, once the largest woollen mill in the world. The museum now tells the story of the growth of Leeds as one of the world's great industrial cities. Temple Newsam (Apr–end Oct Tue–Sun 10.30–5; Nov–end Mar Tue–Sun 10.30–4), east of the city, is a large 16th-century house with rich collections of fine art, as well as Europe's largest working rare breeds farm.
Don't miss The elephant armour and Henry VIII's tournament armour in the Royal Armouries Museum.

Horned helmet at the Royal Armouries Museum

LIVERPOOL

One Mersey waterfront, two cathedrals, four Beatles and several superb museums put Liverpool in a class of its own.

Its days as one of the great ports of the British Empire have long gone, but the grandeur of its architecture echoes the boom years—Liverpool has more landmark buildings than any English city outside London and is to be European Capital of Culture 2008.

ARCHITECTURAL HIGHLIGHTS

Walk from Lime Street Station, past neoclassical St. George's Hall (1854), along Dale Street and Water Street to the waterfront. Here is the Royal Liver Building (1911 by W. Aubrey Thomas), a main landmark, with the famous sculptural Liver Birds perched high on the 10-storey tower.

Red-brick Albert Dock (1846) was imaginatively restored in 1988 into gift shops, cafés and major museums. Fans can visit the Beatles Story (daily 10–6), dedicated to the world-famous group. There's a mock-up of The Cavern club, the white piano on which John Lennon (1940–80) composed *Imagine* (1971), and other memorabilia.

At either end of Hope Street are the two cathedrals. The vast, sandstone Anglican Liverpool Cathedral was started in 1904 but inaugurated in 1978, to Giles Gilbert Scott's design; its tower can be seen from north Wales. The concrete Metropolitan Cathedral (Roman Catholic) was built in 1967 and is sometimes affectionately known as the Mersey Funnel. It was designed by Frederick Gibberd, and is brilliantly lit by blue stained-glass windows.

MUSEUMS AND GALLERIES

The Walker Art Gallery (daily 10–5), on William Brown Street, houses one of the UK's best provincial art collections, including works by local artist George Stubbs (1724–1806), noted for his paintings of horses. The impressive Maritime Museum (daily 10–5), in Albert Dock, gives an insight into the city's maritime past. Next door, Tate Liverpool (Tue–Sun 10–5.50) houses an excellent collection of modern art. Just beyond Albert Dock is the Museum of Liverpool Life (daily 10–5), where you can learn more about what makes this city tick—from the character of the residents to music and sport.

THE BEATLES CONNECTION

From Albert Dock, the Magical Mystery Tourbus goes to Strawberry Fields, Penny Lane and The Cavern, locations closely associated with the Beatles. Other tours take in the childhood homes of John Lennon and Sir Paul McCartney where the group often rehearsed.

RATINGS

Good for kids	● ● ●
Historic interest	● ● ● ●
Musical interest	● ● ● ● ●
Walkability	● ● ●

BASICS

✛ 434 F14

🛈 Atlantic Pavilion, Albert Dock L3 4EA, tel 051 237 3925

❓ Magical Mystery Tourbus from Albert Dock, daily 2.10pm (also 11.40 in summer), tel 0871 222 1967

🚉 Liverpool Lime Street
www.visitliverpool.com
www.liverpool08.com

TIPS

● Save on what could be a very expensive day out by visiting these free attractions: Walker Art Gallery, Merseyside Maritime Museum, HM Customs and Excise National Museum, Museum of Liverpool Life and Tate Liverpool.
● Ride the ferry across the Mersey (Pier Head) for the best introduction to the city.

The Royal Liver Building is the principal landmark for Liverpool, which is to be European Capital of Culture in 2008

The Beatles (inset) are forever linked with the city

Lindisfarne Castle has stood on Holy Island for nearly 500 years

LINDISFARNE (HOLY ISLAND)

➕ 443 H9 • Holy Island, Northumberland TD15 2SH
☎ 01289 389244
www.lindisfarne.org.uk

Joined at low tide by a causeway to the mainland, Holy Island (known as Lindisfarne before 1082) retains the sense of isolation that drew monks and hermits here from early medieval times onwards. You need to take note of the signs for safe crossing times. The most famous monk was St. Cuthbert (died AD687), bishop of the monastery. The museum beside the ruins of 12th-century Lindisfarne Priory (Apr–end Sep daily 9.30–5; Oct daily 9.30–4; Nov–end Jan 10–2; Feb–end Mar 10–4) recounts the life of the early monks. Lindisfarne Castle (Apr–end Oct Tue–Sun 12–4.30 or 10.30–3 depending on tides, but check tides) was built in the 1540s and restored in 1903 by the architect Sir Edwin Lutyens; its interior is a combination of the 16th century, comfortable Edwardian furnishings and Lutyens' quirks.
Don't miss Trying Lindisfarne mead, a honey alcoholic drink made at St. Aidan's Winery. And take a look at the copy of the Lindisfarne Gospels (an illuminated seventh-century manuscript now kept in the British Library) in St. Mary's Church.

LIVERPOOL

See page 173

MARTIN MERE

➕ 434 F13 • The Wildfowl and Wetlands Trust, Burscough L40 0TA
☎ 01704 895181 ⏰ Mar–end Oct daily 9.30–5.30; rest of year daily 9.30–5
💷 Adult £5.95, child (4–15) £3.75, family £15.50 🖥 🍴 👥 🅿
www.wwt.org.uk

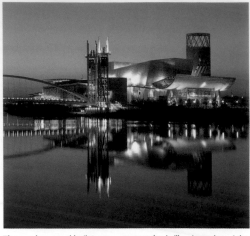

The modern, steel-built Lowry arts complex is illuminated at night

MANCHESTER

From theatres, clubs and café society to wealthy football clubs, Manchester has survived industrial meltdown to become one of the most vibrant cities in Britain.

➕ 434 G14 ℹ Town Hall Extension, Lloyd Street M60 2LA, tel 0161 234 3157 🚉 Manchester Piccadilly
www.manchester.gov.uk

RATINGS			
Historic interest	● ● ●		
Cultural interest	● ● ●		
Shopping	● ● ● ●		

Manchester grew from a small town in the late 18th century to become one of the most important cities of the Industrial Revolution. It made its money from cotton, earning it the nickname Cottonopolis. Waves of decline and rebuilding followed, culminating in Manchester's successful hosting of the 2002 Commonwealth Games, which has created entire new areas.

THE HIGHLIGHTS
Great buildings, such as the neo-Gothic Town Hall (tours Sat and Wed 2pm), and the Royal Exchange (the former Cotton Exchange), speak of the wealth of the late 18th century, and you are free to wander around these buildings. The top attraction is Urbis (Tue– Sun 10–6), housed in a shimmering glass building near the cathedral. Inside, state-of-the-art interactive displays and exhibits lead you through a journey exploring life in different cities of the world.

Recently restored and given a striking new stone and glass extension to the original, stone-built, porticoed Victorian building, the Manchester Art Gallery (Tue–Sun 10–5) can finally show off its artistic wealth, which includes a great collection of modern pieces as well as its noted Pre-Raphaelite paintings. The first floor is home to the Manchester Gallery, with works by L. S. Lowry (1887–1976) and others. In the Castlefield district, the Museum of Science and Industry in Manchester (daily 10–5) is an excellent free visit, with Robert Stephenson's 1830 locomotive *Planet*.

SALFORD QUAYS
Salford Quays houses two major free tourist attractions. Within a gleaming steel-built structure, The Lowry (galleries: Sun–Fri 11–5, Sat 10–6) encompasses theatres and galleries, including an exhibition of Lowry paintings, with some of his earlier, iconic images of matchstick men in the streets of industrial Manchester. Across a footbridge is the Imperial War Museum North (Nov–end Feb daily 10–5; Mar–end Oct 10–6), an ingenious building made of three shards of fractured steel to represent the world's conflicts on land, sea and air.

Splendid Newby Hall was designed by Robert Adam

One of several Wildfowl and Wetlands Trust (WWT) sites in the UK, Martin Mere is a wetland habitat for birds, with swans, ducks and geese from every corner of the world. Winter is a particularly good time to visit, when thousands of pink footed geese, and whooper and Bewick's swans can be seen under floodlight in the evening.

A resident of Martin Mere

NEWBY HALL AND GARDENS

➕ 440 H12 • Newby Hall, Ripon HG4 5AE ☎ 01423 322583 🌐 Jul, Aug daily 12–5 (gardens 11–5.30); Apr–end Jun, Sep Tue–Sun and public holidays, same times 🎫 House and garden: adult £8.20, child (4–16) £5.70. Garden: adult £6.90, child £5. Miniature railway: all £1.50 🍴 🛒 ♿ 🏛 👶 🅿
www.newbyhall.com

A treasure house of art and furniture, this 17th-century building has antique sculptures and Gobelin tapestries brought back from the Grand Tour of Europe in the 1760s by William Weddell, the owner. He commissioned the architect Robert Adam to extend the house, adding a sculpture gallery. Much of the furniture was designed by Adam and made by Thomas Chippendale. The gardens, developed in the 20th century, have superb borders. There is also an adventure playground, miniature railway and sculpture exhibition.

The 1928 Tyne Bridge is the symbol of the city, and was built by Dorman Long, who also created the Sydney Harbour Bridge

NEWCASTLE UPON TYNE

The locals of this resurgent city compensate for the biting North Sea winds with a natural warmth and exuberance.

➕ 439 H10 ℹ 132 Grainger Street NE1 5AF, tel 0191 277 8000 (also at central train station and city library) www.newcastle.gov.uk

RATINGS		
Historic interest	● ● ●
Good for kids	● ●
Shopping	● ● ●

AROUND THE TYNE

The River Tyne provides some of Newcastle's key landmarks. The semicircular Tyne Bridge has as its companions the High Level Bridge (1849), with two decks (the upper for trains and the lower for motorized traffic), the hydraulically operated Swing Bridge (1876) and the innovative Gateshead Millennium Bridge (2000), with its unique blinking-eye mechanism that makes it pivot to allow ships to pass. The bridges join Newcastle to Gateshead, where a major attraction is the huge Baltic Centre for Contemporary Art (gallery: Fri–Wed 10–6, Thu 10–8, free). Occupying a former flour mill, this lively arts complex includes The Sage, an ultra-modern theatre and arts venue, and has a rooftop restaurant.

Newcastle dates back to Roman times, and the 'new castle'—of which the impressive keep and chapel survive—was begun in 1080. On the riverfront is 16th-century Bessie Surtees' House (Mon–Fri 10–4), built of timber and originally home to rich merchants. Early legacies of the boom years as a coal port include elegant Victorian architecture by John Dobson in Grey Street; climb the 164 steps of Grey's Monument for an overview. Around here is the main shopping area, with the indoor Grainger Market (Mon, Wed 9–5, Thu–Sat 9–5.30) offering all kinds of goods.

MUSEUMS AND GALLERIES

The city is particularly known for its lively nightlife, but has enough cultural highlights (many free) to justify a visit. The Laing Art Gallery (Mon–Sat 10–5, Sun 2–5) focuses on 19th-century art. The Hancock Museum (Mon–Sat 10–5, Sun 2–5) on Barras Bridge is the region's leading natural history museum. Two of Newcastle's liveliest attractions are the Centre for Life (Mon–Sat 10–6, Sun 11–6), delving into evolution, the workings of the brain and emotions, and the Discovery Museum (Mon–Sat 10–5, Sun 2–5), with interactive science, featuring shipbuilding, mirrors, magnets and a Science Maze.
Don't miss An early morning visit to the Sunday Quayside Market along the River Tyne.

The North Yorkshire Moors Railway follows a scenic route

Northumberland National Park features unspoilt countryside

Nostell Priory is an early 18th-century Palladian-style mansion

NORTH YORK MOORS NATIONAL PARK

✚ 440 J12 ℹ North York Moors National Park, The Old Vicarage, Bondgate, Helmsley, York YO62 5BP, tel 01439 770657
www.northyorkmoors-npa.gov.uk
www.moors.uk.net

Though not the highest nor the most dramatically rugged of Britain's national parks, this is a highly distinctive corner of England. Medieval stone crosses, placed as waymarkers, punctuate the bare waste of the moors, which feature the country's largest continuous tract of heather—a really spectacular purple carpet in late summer. There's an exhilarating sense of solitude up here among the skylarks and grouse.

Below are a series of lush, green dales (valleys) such as Esk Dale and Rosedale, each with trademark attractive villages such as Hutton-le-Hole and Coxwold that sport red-tiled roofs, yellowstone walls and spacious village greens (come out of season if you want to avoid the crowds). Make a visit to Ryedale Folk Museum in Hutton-le-Hole to see reconstructed local buildings. The quiet market town of Helmsley, on the park's southern edge, makes a useful base for exploring the area, and has the jagged ruins of a 13th-century castle (Apr–end Sep daily 10–6; rest of year Thu–Mon 10–4) to explore.

Coastal attractions include formidable sandstone cliffs and impossibly squashed-together fishing villages such as Robin Hood's Bay, with a famously steep main street and a smuggling history to rival any other, and Staithes, which has maintained some of its traditional qualities.

You can get a good idea of the landscape by driving or cycling along the many quiet roads, or from the steam and diesel trains on the North Yorkshire Moors

Railway (▷ 309). But the best views of all are from the long-distance footpath, the Cleveland Way, as it snakes along the escarpments, taking in the huge inland cliff of Sutton Bank, the mini-summit of Roseberry Topping and the entire coastal stretch from Saltburn-by-the-Sea to Filey.

Early Christians left some impressive monuments, including the monastic remains of 14th-century Mount Grace Priory (Apr–end Oct daily 10–6; rest of year Thu–Mon 10–4), 11 miles (18km) north of Thirsk, where a silent order of monks once lived, 12th-century Byland Abbey (Apr–end Oct Thu–Mon 10–5; open Wed in Aug) near Coxwold, and Rievaulx Abbey (▷ 177).

Don't miss A trip on the North Yorkshire Moors Railway, which runs from Pickering to Grosmont through the heart of the moors.

NORTHUMBERLAND NATIONAL PARK

✚ 439 G10 ℹ Eastburn, South Park, Hexham NE46 1BS, tel 01434 605555
www.nnpa.org.uk

This quietest and least-frequented of Britain's national parks covers an area known as the Cheviot Hills—uplands spanning the Scottish border, grazed by wild sheep—as well as Hadrian's Wall farther south (▷ 168). Roads into the Cheviots tend to be dead ends, but the drive into Coquet Dale via Alwinton gives a good idea of the sheer emptiness of the landscape. If you want to explore further, Windy Gyle is an excellent walkers' summit, with expansive views into Scotland. West of the park boundary lie the huge plantations of Kielder Forest; this manmade landscape is not to everyone's taste, but offers forest walks, rowing boats on the reservoir of Kielder Water and outstanding cycling.

North of Redesdale, much of the land is used for military training, and parts are closed to the public, while others are accessible only on designated footpaths when the warning flags are not flying. Details are available from tourist information offices.

NOSTELL PRIORY

✚ 435 H13 • Doncaster Road, Nostell, near Wakefield WF4 1QE ☎ 01924 863892 ⏰ House: Apr–end Oct Wed-Sun 1–5. Grounds: Mar daily 11–5; end Mar–end Nov 11–6; Dec 11–4.30 💰 House and grounds: adult £6, child (5–16) £3, family £15. Grounds only: adult £3.50, child £1.50 🚌 Arriva 485, 496/8 Wakefield–Doncaster; Yorkshire Traction 244/5 Barnsley–Pontefract 🚉 Fitzwilliam 1.5 miles (2km) 🍴 🏪 🎫 🅿
www.nationaltrust.org.uk

This mansion takes its name from the priory dedicated to St. Oswald, founded on the site in the 12th century. The interior is the main draw, with plasterwork by Robert Adam (1728–92) and James Paine and furniture by Thomas Chippendale(1718–79). There are paintings by Flemish artist Pieter Breughel the Younger (c1564–1638) and an 18th-century dolls' house, complete with original fittings and scaled-down Chippendale furniture. There are plans to restore the surviving 18th-century garden features. Enjoy the scented rose garden and the lakeside walk to the Menagerie Garden.

PORT SUNLIGHT

✚ 434 F14 ℹ Heritage Centre, 95 Greendale Road, Port Sunlight, Wirral CH62 4XE, tel 0151 644 6466 🚉 Port Sunlight
www.portsunlightvillage.com

In the industrial Wirral peninsula is this visionary garden village utopia, built in 1888 by the

These residences in Port Sunlight are now highly desirable

Rievaulx Abbey: Ruined but still emotive and graceful

Ripon Cathedral has an imposing west front

enlightened Sunlight Soap magnate William Hesketh Lever to house his factory workers—and now an extremely desirable place to live. No two groups of cottages are quite the same, although black-and-white Tudor and bricky Queen Anne and Elizabethan styles predominate. The Village Trail is a self guiding walking tour available from the Heritage Centre (daily 10–4).

At its heart is the Lady Lever Art Gallery (daily 10–5), built for the education of the workers, which has paintings by Edward Burne-Jones, Dante Gabriel Rossetti, J. M. W. Turner, John Constable and Joshua Reynolds, as well as Wedgwood ceramics.

RHEGED

439 F11 • Redhills, Penrith CA11 0DQ 01768 868000 Daily 10–5.30 National Mountaineering Exhibition: adult £5.95, child (5–16) £4, family £17. Any two attractions: adult £9.95, child £6.75, family £27.95. All attractions: adult £20.55, child £14.05, family £58.75 Penrith station, then bus X4 or X5
www.rheged.com

Rheged was the name of an ancient Celtic kingdom that dominated northwest England and southern Scotland in the sixth century AD. Today it is Cumbria's largest visitor complex, and Europe's largest grass-covered building. The central attraction is *Rheged—the Movie* (daily, various times), a film that plays on a giant IMAX screen and charts 2,000 years of the area's history.

Another reason to visit is the Helly Hansen National Mountaineering Exhibition (daily 10–5.30), a permanent display of equipment, objects and personal items from some of Britain's most famous climbers and expeditions, including the successful 1953 Everest expedition and Mallory and Irvine's earlier fatal attempt to reach the summit of Mount Everest.

RICHMOND

439 H12 Friary Gardens, Victoria Road, Richmond DL10 4AJ, tel 01748 850252
www.richmond.org.uk

Richmond is one of the most tempting historical towns in the Yorkshire Dales. Off cobbled Trinity Church Square, one of England's largest marketplaces, is a steep knot of unspoiled streets such as Frenchgate and Newbiggin Broad, mainly with refined Georgian buildings, and two surviving medieval gateways.

Perched on a precipitous bank above the fast-flowing River Swale, Richmond Castle (Apr–end Oct daily 10–6; rest of year daily 10–4) dates from 1071; within it, Scollard's Hall (1080) may be Britain's earliest surviving domestic building. Still very much in use, the Georgian Theatre Royal (Mon–Sat 10–4) has the oldest unaltered interior (1788) in Britain. The museum displays original playbills and painted scenery made in 1836. **Don't miss** Taking one of the walks around the outside of the castle and down to Richmond Falls on the River Swale.

RIEVAULX ABBEY

440 J12 • Rievaulx Abbey, Rievaulx YO62 5LB 01439 798228 Mar–end Sep daily 10–6; Oct–end Mar Thu–Mon 10–4 Adult £4, child (under 16) £2. Audiotour free
www.english-heritage.org.uk

Rievaulx (pronounced *reevo*) was the first Cistercian monastery to be founded in England, in 1132, and by 1200 there were more than 140 monks and 500 lay brothers leading an austere life of prayer, fasting and work in this remote corner of Rye Dale.

Much of what you see today dates from the 13th century, supremely graceful in spite of the damage following Henry VIII's dissolution of the monasteries in 1539 (▷ 31). Particularly majestic are the soaring arches of the now roofless monastic church. **Don't miss** Rievaulx Terrace and Temples (Mar–end Sep daily 10.30–6; Oct 10.30–5) are an 18th-century landscape feature overlooking the abbey ruins.

RIPON

440 H12 Minster Road, Ripon HG4 1QT, tel 01765 604625 (Mar–end Sep Mon–Sat)
www.ripon.org

One of England's smallest cities, with a population of around 15,000, Ripon is known as the Cathedral City of the Dales. Overlooking the spacious market-place and the knot of narrow streets is the cathedral (daily 8–5.30). Its chief glories include the choir stalls, with late 15th-century carved misericords, and the Saxon crypt—a remnant of the seventh-century monastery.

Ripon's museums pursue the law-and-order theme, for Ripon was once within the jurisdiction of the archbishops of York, who maintained their own law. The Police and Prison Museum (Apr–end Oct daily 11–4; rest of year daily 1–4) in St. Marygate has a cranking machine, turned by prisoners simply to give them something to do, while the Workhouse Museum (Apr–end Oct daily 11–4; rest of year daily 1–4), in the former workhouse in Allhallowgate, illustrates how the old and poor were treated during the 19th century. **Don't miss** The Hornblower, who blows the large horn by the obelisk in Market Square at 9pm every evening, to tell the citizens that the watch has been set.

Fewer fishing boats set out from Scarborough today

Skipton's 14th-century castle was crucial in the Wars of the Roses

Townend has beautifully carved oak furniture

THE SIGHTS

SCARBOROUGH

⊞ 440 K12 ⓘ Unit 3, Pavilion House, Valley Bridge Road, Scarborough YO11 1UZ, tel 01723 373333
www.scarborough.gov.uk
www.discoveryorkshirecoast.com

A headland occupied by the ruins of 12th-century Scarborough Castle (Apr–end Sep daily 10–6; rest of year Thu–Mon 10–4) divides the two curving sandy bays of Scarborough, just outside the southeast corner of the North York Moors National Park (▷ 176). The town became a spa in the 17th century and has a valid claim as Britain's first seaside resort. The oldest part of town huddles beside the fishing harbour in South Bay. Most of Scarborough developed after the railway arrived in 1845. One of the great symbols of Scarborough is the Grand Hotel of 1863, once one of the largest in the world, with its bulbous domes and elaborate balconies.

In The Crescent, the literary Sitwell family lived at what is now Wood End Museum (Jun–end Sep Tue–Sun 10–5; rest of year Wed, Sat–Sun 11–4) for 60 years from 1870, and the house has displays about them as well as a Victorian conservatory and fossil collection. It also houses the Museum of Natural History. Tickets for this also cover the Art Gallery (Jun–end Sep Tue–Sun 10–5; rest of year Thu–Sat 11–4), which has changing exhibitions and views of the town by the 19th-century artist Atkinson Grimshaw, who lived here for may years and specialized in twilight scenes. Also included is the Rotunda Museum (Jun–end Sep daily 10–5; rest of year Tue, Sat–Sun 11–4), whose impressive domed interior contains original glazed showcases dating back to 1829. The Sea Life Centre and Marine Sanctuary (Nov–end Feb daily 10–4; Mar–end Apr 10–5; May–end Oct 10–6) in North Bay is one of the town's main family attractions, with rockpool habitats and a variety of marine life.

Don't miss Enjoying a concert by the Spa Orchestra, either in the Spa Grand Hall or outdoors in the special band area; alternatively there are re-enacted sea battles using model ships on the lake in Peasholm Park during summer. The grave of author Anne Brontë (1820–49) is in the churchyard near the parish church.

SIZERGH CASTLE

⊞ 439 F12 • Sizergh, near Kendal LA8 8AE ☎ 015395 60951 🕐 Mon–Thu, Sun 1.30–5.30, Apr–end Oct (garden 12.30–5.30) 💷 Adults £5.80, child (5–16) £2.90, family £14.80 🍴 ♿ 👫 🅿
www.nationaltrust.org.uk

The home of the Strickland family for over 760 years, this ivy-clad medieval castle/manor house has been much extended. At its core is a 14th-century pele (small, square, defensive) tower; the rest is mostly Elizabethan. Inside, there is an exceptional series of oak-panelled rooms set off by intricately carved mantelpieces and early oak furniture. Each room is hung with portraits of the family and of royalty with whom they have had some connection.

The grounds feature two lakes, a rock garden and a wild garden with local limestone flora.

SKIPTON

⊞ 439 G13 ⓘ 35 Coach Street BD23 1LQ, tel 01756 792809 🚉 Skipton
www.skiptononline.co.uk

The Gateway to the Dales is at its liveliest on market days— Monday, Wednesday, Friday and especially Saturday. The broad, tree-lined main street is full of shops and old pubs, with ginnels (cobbled alleys) running off on either side. Retaining turrets and battlements, Skipton Castle (Mar–end Sep Mon–Sat 10–6, Sun 12–6; rest of year Mon–Sat 10–4, Sun 12–4) dates from Norman times. It played a significant role in the Wars of the Roses (1455–85) and endured a three-year Parliamentarian siege during the Civil War (▷ 32), after which it had to be partly rebuilt.

TOWNEND

⊞ 439 F12 • Troutbeck, Windermere LA23 1LB ☎ 015394 32628 🕐 Wed–Sun 1–5 💷 Adult £3.40, child (5–16) £1.70, family £8.50 ❓ Not suitable for wheelchairs or pushchairs 🍴 💷 ♿ 👫 🅿
www.nationaltrust.org.uk

Come here to see how Lakeland farmhouses used to look. Townend has no electricity, and epitomizes the remoteness of the Lake District in centuries past. It remained the property of the farming Browne family for over 300 years until it was taken over by the National Trust in 1943, though you can still meet the current Mr Browne at the house (most Thursdays). The mainly 17th-century house has the Browne's handcarved furniture and domestic implements, and has a downhouse for washing, cooking, pickling and brewing, and a firehouse with living quarters.

UPPER TEESDALE

⊞ 439 G11 ⓘ Woodleigh, Flatts Road, Barnard Castle DL12 8AA, tel 01833 690909 💷 High Force: adult £1, child £0.50 🅿 B2677 car park £1.50
www.teesdale.gov.uk

Spring gentians and orchids are among the rare post-Ice Age vegetation in this tundra-like part of the northern Pennine Hills.

WHITBY AND THE NORTH YORK MOORS COAST

Whitby is a popular seaside resort set among dramatically positioned fishing villages—an ideal walking base.

Trencherfield Mill is part of the Wigan Pier Experience

➕ 440 J13 🏠 Langhourne Road YO21 1YN, tel 01947 602674
🚆 Whitby
www.discoveryorkshirecoast.com

MAKE A DAY OF IT

North York Moors National Park (▷ 176)
Scarborough (▷ 178)

Whitby is a blend of fishing port and Victorian seaside resort, set along the slopes of the deep valley of the River Esk. Prominent among the boats that pack the harbour are the traditional flat-bottomed fishing cobles. The 13th-century ruins of Whitby Abbey (Apr–end Sep daily 10–6; Oct daily 10–5; Thu–Mon 10–4 rest of year) are reached by 199 steps. The visitor complex gives a vivid audio-visual guide from the days of the abbey's seventh-century founder, St. Hilda, to its shelling by German warships in World War I. The abbey, steps and graveyard of St. Mary's Church feature in Irish writer Bram Stoker's classic novel *Dracula* (1897).

A statue of the great explorer Captain James Cook (1728–79) looks over the town from the West Cliff. He was born close by in Marton and his ships were built at Whitby; the house where he lodged in Grape Lane while an apprentice is now the Captain Cook Memorial Museum (Mar daily 11–3; Apr–end Oct daily 9.45–5), telling the story of his life and voyages of discovery.

Whitby's other strength is as a base for visiting the North York Moors and coast (▷ 176, 306–307). Three extraordinary fishing villages are located near the town. Staithes has escaped prettification and is set along a narrow, steep-sided creek, often bearing the brunt of storms and floods. A 20-minute clifftop walk leads to the village from Runswick Bay, smaller and neater, tightly packed beneath the cliff. Farther south, Robin Hood's Bay was rife with smuggling in the 18th century. It hugs a steep slope, and is densely packed with red pantiled roofs, tiny alleys and crooked lanes. From here there are breezy walks south along the highest cliffs on England's east coast. **Don't miss** Whitby Museum (Tue–Sun 9.30–4.30, some Mon in school holidays) is in Pannett Park and has an idiosyncratic collection of fossils, natural history, Whitby jet and seafaring memorabilia. The Dracula Experience (Apr–end Oct daily 10–5; rest of year Sat–Sun 10.30–5 (later in summer)) provides a blood-curdling encounter with Whitby's fictional past.

Fish and ships: Whitby's working harbour adds to the town's charm

The main settlement is Barnard Castle, named after the substantial ruins of its 11th-century castle (Apr–end Sep daily 10–6; rest of year Thu–Mon 10–4), used as a stronghold of the Balliol family. On the edge of town, the Bowes Museum (daily 11–5) of fine arts occupies an unexpectedly grand building, built in 1869 in the style of a French château. However, the real drama of the valley lies to the west. High Force, a spectacular 21m (70ft) waterfall, is part of the Raby Castle estate and is at its most raging after a heavy rainfall. Take the 10-minute walk down through woodland from the B6277. **Don't miss** Cauldron Snout waterfall, near the vast reservoir of Cow Green, is spectacular as it tumbles down the hillside.

THE WIGAN PIER EXPERIENCE

➕ 434 G14 • Wigan Pier, Trencherfield Mill, Wigan WN3 4EF ☎ 01942 323666
🕙 Mon–Thu 10–5, Sat–Sun 11–5
🚆 Wigan 💷 Adult £5.25, child (over 5) £4.25, family £14.75 🍴 ☕ 📷
♿ 🅿
www.wlct.org

Along the redeveloped Leeds and Liverpool Canal, Wigan Pier is an archive of an industrial town. The Way We Were exhibition offers a taste of what life was like in Wigan in 1900 through re-creations that include a Victorian classroom, a coal mine and a variety theatre. All the sites are interactive, with actors dressed in period costume helping to create the full experience: Slouch in the classroom and you'll be told to sit up straight. The sprawling site was originally overhauled in the mid-1980s and is now undergoing another ambitious regeneration programme. It's worth checking beforehand to see what the latest developments are.

THE SIGHTS

York

A wonderfully complete medieval city, crammed with historic treasures and outstanding museums, York is also home to Gothic York Minster, one of Britain's finest cathedrals. The city is fun to explore on foot, with plenty of entertainment out on the streets.

SEEING YORK

This strikingly beautiful city straddling the River Ouse is one of Britain's premier sights. Despite its distance from London, it is easily accessible by train, and is served by several major roads. York has a multitude of museums and buildings spanning a range of historic periods. Much of the city's compact heart is pedestrianized, so it's a great place to explore on foot, taking in its wealth of shops and vibrant street performers. York is an easy and pleasant city for walking, and a circuit of the city wall is an excellent way to get your bearings. Among the most evocative streets are The Shambles, originally a street of butchers' shops and retaining overhanging, jettied, timber-framed buildings, and Stonegate, where shop signs and frontages span several centuries. Also look for York's distinguished clutch of medieval churches (some no longer used for services). Arguably the finest is Holy Trinity (Goodramgate) with its inward-facing box pews and late 15th-century stained glass.

HIGHLIGHTS

YORK MINSTER

✚ 183 B1 • Deangate YO1 7HH ☎ 01904 557216 🕑 Mon–Sat 9–30–5 (for tourists), Sun 12–5.30 💷 Adult £5, child (under 16) free. Combined ticket (includes undercroft, treasury and crypt): adult £7, child free. Tower: adult £3, child £1
www.yorkminster.org

Dating from 1220–1472, this is Europe's largest Gothic cathedral north of the Alps, with two towers, richly traceried windows and a massive west front. Its medieval stained glass represents a quarter of all the stained glass of the period in England. Look particularly for the Five Sisters within a quintet of lancet windows, and for the depictions of Genesis and Revelation in the superb east window of c1250—the world's largest area of medieval stained glass within a single window. The stone choir screen is carved with images of English monarchs from William I (1028–87) to Henry VI (1421–71), while around the nave and choir are painted stone shields dating from the time when Edward II (1284–1327) held a parliament in York.

There are separate admission charges for certain other parts of the Minster—the treasury, featuring the 11th-century Horn of Ulf, and the crypt, containing part of the 11th-century church that preceded the Minster. Also below ground level, the foundations (or undercroft) reveal an absorbing cross-section of history, from the remains of a Roman fort to the drastic building works carried out in the 1960s to support the collapsing central tower (whose foundations turned out to be completely inadequate). The octagonal Chapter House has lively carvings of flowers and fruits and is unusual in that it lacks a central structural pillar. The long climb up the central tower is rewarded by a panoramic view over the city (extra admission charge).

Reconstructed streets in the Castle Museum bring York's history alive

TIPS

● The York Pass (www.yorkpass.com) gives free entry to more than 30 attractions in and around the city, plus numerous special offers for shopping and dining (adult: one day £19, two days £25, three days £32).
● The city wall (3 miles/5km) is worth walking, but you may prefer to skip the southern part, which looks over relatively modern suburbs.
● A boat trip on the River Ouse is a great alternative way of seeing York and its surroundings, and also offers a glimpse of the Archbishop of York's palace at Bishopthorpe.

York Minster (left and inset) is the city's crowning glory

TREASURER'S HOUSE

✚ 183 B1 • Minster Yard YO1 7JL
☎ 01904 624247 🕐 Apr–end Oct
Sat–Thu 11–4.30

This house beside the Minster was mostly rebuilt in the 17th century—long after the post of Treasurer to the Minster was abolished (in 1547)—after which it passed into private hands. The National Trust has filled it with French furniture and English glass and ceramics.

Displays in the Jorvik Viking Centre illustrate the city's history

THE MERCHANT ADVENTURERS' HALL

✚ 183 C2 • Fossgate YO1 9XD
☎ 01904 654818 🕐 Apr–end Sep
Mon–Thu 9–5, Fri–Sat 9–3.30, Sun 12–4; rest of year Mon–Sat 9–3.30

York's largest (27m by 12m/ 89ft by 40ft) and most impressive medieval half-timbered building is still in use. It has a complex roof with vast crossbeams.

CLIFFORD'S TOWER

✚ 183 B3 • Tower Street YO1 1SA
☎ 01904 646940 🕐 Mar–end Sep
daily 10–6; Oct 10–5; Nov–end Feb 10–4

The four-lobed stone keep of the castle dates from 1245, and replaced a wooden tower built by William I in 1068.

FAIRFAX HOUSE

✚ 183 B2 • Castlegate YO1 9RN
☎ 01904 655543 🕐 Mon–Thu and
Sat 11–5, Sun 1.30–5, Fri guided tours, 11 and 2

Witness wealthy living during the 18th century at this exceptional Georgian town house, which was saved from the brink of collapse in 1984. It contains select items from centuries past, notably a collection of splendid 17th- and 18th-century English clocks.

CITY WALL

You get an immense sense of historic continuity in York, which is enclosed by its virtually complete wall, pierced by bars (gateways). The section between Bootham Bar (on the site of the Roman gateway) and Monk Bar gives some of the choicest views of the old city. Monk Bar, the best-preserved gateway, houses the Richard III Museum (Mar–end Oct daily 9–5; rest of year daily 9.30–4), presenting the story of the monarch (1452–85) portrayed (possibly unfairly) as a murderer by Shakespeare and others, and giving you a chance to reach your own verdict. The heads of criminals and enemies were placed on spikes on Micklegate Bar during the Wars of the Roses (1455–85), and there's a small social history display inside (Feb–end Oct daily 9–5; rest of year Sat–Sun 9–5).

THE SHAMBLES

✚ 183 C2

A short walk south from York Minster leads through some of the city's most memorable streets, where jettied half-timbered buildings overhang the narrow thoroughfare, the walls lean at alarming angles and the buildings on either side almost touch each other at roof level. This was originally a row of butchers' stalls (hence the hooks and rails, from which the meat was hung, still visible above some windows). It has since been smartened up into one of the city's most famous sights and costumed characters such as town criers (below) entertain sightseers. Stonegate has an array of old shop fronts and has such curios as a red devil figurine above a former printer's shop. Farther east, near Aldwark, is the half-timbered Merchant Taylors' Hall (all year Tue 10–4), with a 14th-century roof beyond a 17th- and 18th-century façade, and the jettied Black Swan Inn, whose beamed rooms and inglenook fireplace make it an interesting lunch spot.

YORK CASTLE MUSEUM

✚ 183 C3 • The Eye of York YO1 1RY 🕐 Daily 9.30–5

Housed in the former Debtors' Prison of 1705 and Female Prison of 1780, this museum alone justifies a visit to York. Displays include full-size reconstructions of Victorian and Edwardian shopping streets, collections of costumes and uniforms, and the very cell in which notorious highwayman Dick Turpin (1706–39) spent his last days before facing death on the gallows.

JORVIK VIKING CENTRE

✚ 183 B2 • Coppergate YO1 9WT ☎ 01904 543403
🕐 Apr–Oct daily 10–5; daily 10–4, rest of year

Another of York's must-sees is the fruition of an excavation that uncovered the Viking settlement of Jorvik. The centre presents a unique journey back to 10th-century York, with sights, sounds and smells of life based on archaeological evidence. It ends with a display of finds from the site and a hologram of the Viking helmet found here—the original is in the Yorkshire Museum in Museum Gardens.

NATIONAL RAILWAY MUSEUM

✚ 183 A2 • Leeman Road YO26 4XJ ☎ 01904 621261
🕐 Daily 10–6

Across Lendal Bridge in the west of the city, the National Railway Museum is the definitive national collection of railwayana, and it's free. Over 100 restored locomotives are on display here, including the record-breaking steam locomotive *Mallard*, which reached a heady 126mph (202kph) and is the world's fastest steam engine, a full-size working replica of the *Rocket*, originally built by railway pioneer George Stephenson (1781–1848), the sumptuous royal saloon carriage (car) built for Queen Victoria (1019–1901), and a modern Japanese bullet train. Other displays include railway posters, paintings and photographs. Rail buffs may also like to visit York Model Railway (Mon–Sat 9–6, Sun 10–5), in York Station.

MUSEUM GARDENS

➕ 183 B2

This is a pearl of a picnic place, where you can spread out on the lawn and survey the scene. There are ruins of 13th-century St. Mary's Abbey, the 13th-century remains of St. Leonard's Hospital (including a chapel and vaulted undercroft), a Roman tower known as the Multangular Tower and a large chunk of Roman wall standing at its original height. Also in the gardens is the Yorkshire Museum (daily 10–5), whose exhibits include Roman sculptures and mosaics, Anglo-Saxon finds such as the Ormside Bowl and much-embellished Gilling Sword, Viking weaponry and medieval treasures.

Don't miss The Middleham Jewel in the Yorkshire Museum, a gold pendant adorned with a superb sapphire—one of the finest examples yet found of medieval Gothic jewellery (▷ 316).

BACKGROUND

York was founded by the Roman army in AD71 as the town of Eboracum. The Roman fortress and the roads that led to it form the basis of the city's outline today, and a few remains are visible above ground, such as the walls of the fortress in the foundations of York Minster. After the Romans left, Viking settlers took over, and the town became Jorvik. They established the city's gateways and named the streets, many of them on the Roman lines. In the Middle Ages, York flourished as a trading city, and the walls that were started in Roman times were rebuilt.

BASICS

➕ 440 J13

ℹ George Hudson Street YO1 6WR, tel 01904 554455

🚉 York

www.visityork.org
Comprehensive and clearly laid out guide to visitor attractions and accommodation in the city. A to Z of themes, plus itineraries, shopping and eating.

York's defensive walls have Roman foundations

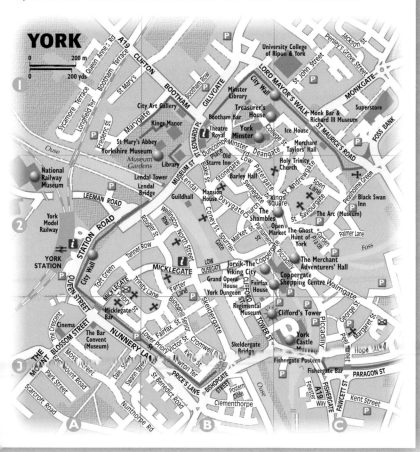

Wharfedale, in the Yorkshire Dales National Park, is a wide valley with fertile fields outlined by stone walls

There are modern figures in the Yorkshire Sculpture Park

THE SIGHTS

WINDERMERE

⊞ 439 F12 🛈 Victoria Street, Windermere LA23 1AD, tel 015394 46499 🚉 Windermere
www.lake-district.gov.uk

The Lake District resorts of Windermere town and Bowness merge together on the east shore of Windermere, England's longest lake (10.5 miles.17km).

For most visitors, the lake, whose wooded shores are dotted with houses, is the major attraction: Steamers ply its length from near Ambleside at the north end to Lakeside at the southern extremity. Just north of Bowness, the Windermere Steamboat Museum (mid-Mar to early Nov daily 10–5) has restored historic craft and offers boat trips. Farther north on the A591, the Brockhole Visitor Centre (Easter–end Oct daily 10–5) supplies information on the area, plus guided walks and children's activities.

YORKSHIRE DALES NATIONAL PARK

⊞ 439 G12 🛈 Yorkshire Dales National Park Authority, Colvend, Hebden Road, Grassington BD23 5LB, tel 01756 752748
www.yorkshiredales.org.uk

The Yorkshire Dales comprise some of the most enticing terrain of the Pennine Hills, the backbone of northern England. Below the bleak gritstone moors run a series of limestone valleys (dales), each with its own subtle character. The villages, built of stone and often ranged around greens, are very much part of the landscape, and many grew up around the now-vanished lead mining industry in the boom years of the 18th and 19th centuries.

WHARFEDALE, SWALEDALE AND WENSLEYDALE

Corridor-like Wharfedale begins at Bolton Abbey, with its ruined 12th-century priory beside the still-functioning priory church, then continues past the mini-gorge of The Strid and the bustling village of Grassington and the overhang of Kilnsey Crag.

Farther north, the scenery is more mellow and expansive in Wensleydale, a valley renowned for waterfalls, crumbly Wensleydale cheese and the forbidding castle ruins of Middleham and Bolton Castle.

Swaledale is a remote and secretive place studded with stone barns and relics of lead-mining, and with the fast-flowing River Swale linking Reeth, with its charming sloping green, and the market town of Richmond (▷ 177).

THE WESTERN DALES

To the west are the Yorkshire Dales' most spectacular limestone landscapes, including the Three Peaks (the three highest hills—Whernside, Ingleborough and Pen-y-Ghent). North of Malham is Malham Cove, a limestone cliff beneath a deep-fissured limestone pavement. To the east, Gordale Scar was formed when a cavern collapsed, leaving a gorge shadowed by huge, formidable crags.

At the northwestern extremity of the national park, the Howgill Fells are a great contrast, formed by high, rounded hills of slate. There are stern, knee-stiffening hikes over them, but the walk up the relatively modest summit of Winder from the town of Sedbergh provides a good taster.

YORKSHIRE SCULPTURE PARK

⊞ 435 H13 • West Bretton, Wakefield WF4 4LG ☎ 01924 832631
🕐 Summer daily 10–6; winter daily 10–5 💷 Free ◻ ⊞ 👫 🅿 £3 per day
www.ysp.co.uk

You don't need to be an aficionado of sculpture to enjoy a visit here. The sculpture park was set up in 1977 and was a pioneer in placing sculpture outdoors. A trail takes you on a tour of the highlights, and there are plenty of places for picnicking.

There are permanent and changing exhibits in this expansive parkland, with works by some of the leading figures of the last 100 years, including Dame Barbara Hepworth (1903–75), Dame Elisabeth Frink (1930–93) and Sir Anthony Caro (born 1924), plus gallery space for smaller exhibits.

Don't miss The sculptures by Yorkshire maestro Henry Moore (1898–1986), in the adjacent country park.

Bronze sculptures by Henry Moore in Bretton Country Park

SCOTLAND

Scotland's turbulent history is reflected in its magical castles and a forceful national identity. But there's much more to the region than whisky, kilts and tales of Highland rebellions. On the spellbinding islands of the Orkneys, the Shetlands and Skye, visitors will find evidence of prehistoric cultures.

KEY SIGHTS

Swords and knives instead of wallpaper at Abbotsford House

Aberdeen's Maritime Museum has some interesting displays, including complicated ships' models and a miniature oil rig

THE SIGHTS

ABBOTSFORD

✚ 443 G9 • Melrose TD6 9BQ
☎ 01896 752043 🕐 Jun–end Sep Mon–Sat 9.30–5, Sun 9.30–5; mid-Mar to end May and Oct Mon–Sat 9.30–5, Sun 2–5 💺 Adult £5, child £2, under 8s free 🚻 🏛 🏃
www.scottsabbotsford.co.uk

This delightful, overblown, turreted grey mansion is a must for an insight into the eclectic mind of the writer Sir Walter Scott (1771–1832), best known for epic romantic poems such as *The Lady of the Lake* (1810) and novels including *Ivanhoe* (1819).

Abbotsford was the home he built for himself in 1812 on the banks of the River Tweed, 2 miles (3km) west of Melrose, and it is filled with historical curiosities, some of which—like the condemned criminals' door from the old Tolbooth in Edinburgh—are built into the fabric of the house. Take a look at the great man's library, the gracious dining room, whose windows look down to the river, and the bristling armoury, its walls covered with guns, knives and other weapons. The overall effect is one of mock, almost theatrical, antiquity—a distillation of the ambience of his novels.
Don't miss Scott's collection of belongings of the famous, including Rob Roy's purse and James IV's hunting bottle.

ABERDEEN

✚ 443 G6 ⓘ 23 Union Street AB11 5BP, tel 01224 288828 🚉 Aberdeen www.agtb.org

Scotland's third city was once its biggest seaside resort, thanks to the miles of golden sands which stretch north from the mouth of the River Don. Today Aberdeen has a businesslike air and is better known as the oil capital of Europe. Its foundations as a royal burgh date back to the early 12th

century, and it grew into a major port for access to the Continent, trading in wool, fish and scholars from its two universities. In fact, the harbour is still the heart of the city. In the late 18th century, the town expanded, and many of Aberdeen's finest granite buildings in the New Town date from the 19th century. Architect Archibald Simpson (1790–1847) is associated with many, including the Union Buildings and Assembly Rooms Music Hall on Union Street.

Provost Ross's House, on Shiprow (1593), houses the lively Aberdeen Maritime Museum (Mon–Sat 10–5, Sun 12–3), with an 8.5m (30ft) scale model of an oil rig. The Aberdeen Art Gallery on Schoolhill has an outstanding collection of 18th- to 20th-century paintings (Mon–Sat 10–5, Sun 2–5).

ARRAN, ISLE OF

✚ 441 C9 ⓘ The Pier, Brodick KA27 8AU, tel 01770 302140 ⛴ Ferry from Ardrossan to Brodick or Kintyre to Lochranza (summer)

Often described as Scotland in miniature, this scenic island between the Ayrshire coast and the Kintyre Peninsula has been a popular holiday resort for generations of Clydesiders. The mountain of Goat Fell (874m/2,867ft) dominates the skyline to the north, and there is plenty of opportunity for outdoor activities, including walking, golf and pony-trekking around the island. The red sandstone Brodick Castle (Castle: Apr–end Oct daily 11–4.30. Country park: all year daily 9.30–dusk) is the single biggest attraction.

BLAIR CASTLE

✚ 442 E6 • Blair Atholl, Pitlochry PH18 5TL ☎ 01796 481207 🕐 Mar–end Oct daily 9.30–4.30 (last admission); Nov–end Mar Tue and Sat 9.30–12.30

💺 House and grounds: adult £6, child £4.30, under 5s free, family £17.50. Grounds only: adult £2.20, child £1.10, family £5.15 🚉 Blair Atholl Village 🚻 🏛 🏃
www.blair-castle.co.uk

This white-turreted mansion north of Pitlochry seems the archetypal Scottish castle. It's been the ancestral home of the Murrays and Stewarts, dukes and earls of Atholl, for more than 700 years, and has its own private army, the Atholl Highlanders, thanks to a favour granted in 1845 by Queen Victoria, who had visited in 1842.

The Highlanders are the only remaining private army in Europe —visitors in May can see them parade under inspection of the Duke of Atholl.

The medieval castle occupied a strategic position on the main route to Inverness and was seized by Cromwell's army in 1652 (▷ 32). In more peaceful times, it was recast as a Georgian mansion by the second duke, and with the advent of the railway in 1863, a Victorian-style remodelling took place, leaving the pretty building you see today. There's lots to see inside, including an original copy of the *National Covenant* and the small tartan-clad room where Bonnie Prince Charlie slept in 1745.
Don't miss The extensive mature gardens. Diana's Grove is a fine planting of tall trees, dating from 1737 and the recently restored, walled Hercules Garden is of a similar vintage.

BRAEMAR AND DEESIDE

✚ 442 F6 ⓘ The Mews, Mar Road, Braemar AB35 5YL, tel 01339 741600 www.braemarscotland.co.uk

In 1852, when Queen Victoria and Prince Albert picked an estate between Ballater and Braemar on which to build their

Caerlaverock Castle dates from the 13th century

holiday home, the entire Dee Valley acquired a cachet which it has never quite lost. Members of the royal family, including the present queen, still spend their summer holidays at Balmoral Castle (exhibition Apr–end Jul daily 10–5), enjoying country sports in the hills and forests.

To the east of the Cairngorms, the Dee valley offers good walking country. West of the busy small town of Braemar, a narrow road leads upstream to the Linn of Dee, where the river plunges down between polished rocks into foaming pools. This is part of the 29,402ha (72,598-acre) Mar Lodge Estate, managed by the National Trust for Scotland (NTS), with signposted walks. The road ends near the earl of Mar's Punchbowl, another beauty spot, where, it is said, the earl brewed punch in a natural bowl in the rocks before the Jacobite uprising of 1715.

From Braemar, the A93 follows the course of the river as it flows east for 60 miles (96km) to the coast at Aberdeen. Ballater is a pleasing little granite-built town, once the terminus of a railway branch line. This is celebrated at the Old Royal Station, now an information centre and tea room (Jun–end Sep daily 9–6; Oct–end May 10–5) which recalls the days when famous guests would alight here on their way to Balmoral. Royal provisions still come from the town, as can be seen by the coats of arms everywhere, from the bakery to the outdoor clothing shops.

East lies Glen Tanar, with birch woods at the Muir of Dinnet, and good walking over the Grampian Hills to the Glens of Angus.

Don't miss The footbridge at Bridge of Feugh, south of Banchory, from where you can watch salmon leaping the Falls of Feugh.

Pines along the shore of Loch Garten

THE CAIRNGORMS

The highest massif in Britain, with alpine plants and rare wildlife is a winter playground for climbers and skiers.

🞣 442 F6 🛈 Cairngorms National Park Authority, 14 The Square, Grantown-on-Spey PH26 3HG, tel 01479 873535
Aviemore 🞣 445 E5 🛈 Grampian Road PH22 1PP, tel 01479 810363
🚉 Aviemore

RATINGS				
Good for kids	●	●	●	
Outdoor pursuits	●	●	●	●
Photo stops	●	●	●	●

The Cairngorm mountains lie between Speyside (▷ 206) and Braemar (▷ opposite), dominated by the four peaks of Ben Macdhui (1,309m/4,295ft), Braeriach (1,295m/4,249ft), Cairn Toul (1,293m/4,242ft) and Cairn Gorm (1,245m/4,085ft). Between them runs the ancient north–south pass of Lairig Ghru, and around the northwest edge are the settlements of Speyside and the skiing resort of Aviemore. The remoteness of the Cairngorms has left them the haunt of golden eagles, ptarmigan, capercaillie and other species that thrive in the deserted corries amid unusual alpine plants. The area was designated Scotland's second national park in 2003.

The once-sleepy station of Aviemore was developed in the 1960s as a ski centre, and while some of the most brutal specimens of architecture from this period have been demolished, it has little to recommend it unless you are part of the ski scene. The Rothiemurchus Estate, 1.5 miles (2.5km) to the south (daily 9–5.30), offers a variety of outdoor pursuits in a beautiful setting of mountains, lochs and Caledonian pine forest. This is the remains of the Old Wood of Caledon that once covered much of the country, harbouring wolves and bears.

Aviemore is linked by the Strathspey Steam Railway (tel: 01479 810725) to Boat of Garten. The Royal Society for the Protection of Birds (RSPB) has a visitor complex here—a camera watches the ospreys nesting on nearby Loch Garten (right). A funicular railway in the Cairngorm ski area east of Aviemore takes visitors up Cairn Gorm to the highest shop and restaurant in Britain (May to mid-Jun and Sep–end Nov daily 10–5.15; sunset dining Jun–end Aug Fri–Sat).
Don't miss The ancient landscapes of Rothiemurchus and watching the ospreys on Loch Garten.

Callander's visitor complex tells the story of local hero Rob Roy

Crarae Garden: a corner of the Himalayas beside Loch Fyne

Cawdor Castle had a starring role in Shakespeare's *Macbeth*

THE SIGHTS

CAERLAVEROCK CASTLE

✚ 438 F10 • Glencaple, Dumfries DG1 4HD ☎ 01387 770244 ◷ Apr–end Sep daily 9.30–6.30; Oct–end Mar Mon–Sat 9.30–4.30, Sun 2–4.30 🖐 Adult £4, child (5–15) £1.60 ▫ 🏛 ♿

www.historic-scotland.gov.uk

The remains of three huge round towers mark out the corners of this ruined, triangular castle, once the home of the Maxwell family. It is set close to the Solway shore, about 8 miles (13km) southeast of Dumfries. Two sides were protected by an arm of the sea, while the third had a moat, earthworks and a mighty gatehouse. The castle saw lots of action before extensive rebuilding during the 15th century. In the 1630s it was remodelled for more comfortable living.

CALLANDER

✚ 442 E8 ℹ Ancaster Square FK17 8ED, tel 0870 720 0628 www.lochlomond-trossachs.org

Callander is a bustling little town, the eastern gateway to the Trossachs (▷ 203). The architecture of its long main street reflects the town's heyday in the late 19th century as a spa, and today it is lined with interesting shops. In the square, the former church is occupied by the tourist information office with, upstairs, the audio-visual Rob Roy Story (Mar–end May, Oct daily 10–5; Jun–end Sep 10–6; Nov–Feb 11–4). Rob Roy MacGregor (1671–1734) was a folk hero and outlaw who took refuge in the Trossach glens.

CAWDOR CASTLE

✚ 445 E5 • Nairn IV12 5RD ☎ 01667 404401 ◷ Daily 10–5.30, Jun to mid-Oct 🖐 Adult £6.80, child (5–16) £4, family £19.50. Gardens only £3.50 🍴 🏛

www.cawdorcastle.com

The name of Cawdor has echoes of Shakespeare's *Macbeth*, and this marvellous castle does not disappoint. It stands inland, between Inverness (▷ 197) and Nairn, with a central tower dating to 1454, a drawbridge and proud turrets. It is the home of Angelika, Dowager Countess of Cawdor, and the presentation of family portraits and treasures is refreshingly light-hearted. The influence of the owner and her late husband is most clearly seen in the gardens, which are symbolically themed.

CRARAE GARDEN

✚ 441 C8 • Inveraray PA32 8YA ☎ 01546 886614 ◷ Daily 9.30–dusk. Visitor centre Apr–end Sep daily 10–5 🖐 Adult £5, child £4, family £14 ▫ 🏛

www.nts.org.uk

This hillside garden lies on the shores of Loch Fyne, between Inveraray and Lochgilphead. It was the creation of Lady Grace Campbell and continued by her son, Sir George Campbell, who began the transformation of a narrow Highland glen into a Himalayan gorge in 1925. Today it is cared for by the National Trust for Scotland (NTS), and has more than 400 species of rhododendron and azalea. This is primarily a woodland garden, with paths winding through eucalyptus and other trees.

Don't miss The Neolithic chambered cairn (c2500BC).

CRATHES CASTLE

✚ 443 G6 • Banchory AB31 5QJ ☎ 01330 844525 ◷ Gardens: all year daily 9–dusk. Castle and visitor centre: Apr–end Sep daily 10–5.30; Oct daily 10–4.30 🖐 Castle or gardens: adult £8, child (5–16) £5. Combined ticket: adult £10, child £7, family £25 📷 £3.50 🍴 🏛

www.nts.org.uk

In 1323, Robert the Bruce gave a parcel of land east of Banchory to Alexander Burnard (Burnett) of Leys. In 1553 a castle was begun on the site and it is now a great example of a baronial-style tower house, famous for its Jacobean ceilings, boldly painted with figures, designs and mottoes.

While the interior of the castle presents the comfortable setting of mellow furnishings, oak-carved panels and family portraits you might expect, it is the 1.5ha (3.75-acre) walled garden glimpsed from the windows that steals the show. Massive hedges of Irish yew topiary dominate the upper garden. The deep herbaceous borders of the lower garden are breathtaking.

CULLODEN

✚ 445 E5 • Culloden Moor, Inverness IV2 5EU ☎ 01463 790607 ◷ Site: daily, all year. Visitor centre: Nov–end Dec, Feb–end Mar daily 11–4; Mar–end May, Sep–end Oct 9–5.30; Jun–end Aug 9–6 🖐 Adult £5, child (5–18) £1, under 5 free, family £13 📷 🍴 🏛 ❓ Audio-visual tour in French, Gaelic, German, Italian and Japanese

www.nts.org.uk

The Jacobite defeat at the Battle of Culloden, fought on 16 April 1746, was the dismal outcome of a civil war that had split families and hastened the end of the clan system in Scotland.

Prince Charles Edward Stuart (1720–88), nicknamed Bonnie Prince Charlie, was brought up in European exile, the heir to the throne of Scotland, which the Catholic Stuarts still claimed through James, the Old Pretender.

Encouraged by the French, Charles landed at Glenfinnan (▷ 196) in 1745 and raised a mixed bag of Highland fighters. Initially the Prince's army was successful, and reached Derby in central England before running

Visit the battlefield at Culloden to see the many memorials

Culross Palace was the main house of Culross in 1597

Take an underwater safari at Deep Sea World

out of steam. The Highlanders then retreated north, but by the spring of 1746 the Hanoverian forces were closing in.

When the two armies met at Culloden, a tactical blunder placed the Prince's Highlanders within range of the government artillery, and the Jacobites were blown away in under an hour. Today memorial stones and flags show where individual clans fell on the battlefield.

It's a good idea to watch the audio-visual exhibition in the visitor complex before exploring the battlefield.

CULROSS

442 E8 🔢 1 High Street, Dunfermline KY12 7DL, tel 01383 720999

Your first impression of this little town may be one of familiarity: Culross (pronounced *cure-oss*) looks like the paintings of very old Scottish burghs, with its winding, cobbled streets and crow-stepped gables. It had an early involvement in coal-mining and salt-panning, mostly through George Bruce, the town's 16th-century entrepreneur. As the local coal ran out, Culross became a backwater. Many of the 17th- and 18th-century houses were never replaced, so, paradoxically, it was Culross's poverty that created the picturesque groupings admired today.

In the 1930s the National Trust for Scotland started buying up properties approaching dereliction. Decades later, many of the houses are fully restored and inhabited. Exceptional buildings, such as the ochre Culross Palace (Bruce's mansion of 1597) and the Town House (1626, where suspected witches were locked in the attic), are open to the public (Easter–end Sep daily 12–5). Other buildings in the town are closed.

CULZEAN CASTLE AND COUNTRY PARK

438 D9 🔢 Maybole KA19 8LE
☎ 01655 884455 ⏰ Castle: Apr–end Oct daily 10.30–5.30. Country park: daily 9.30–dusk, all year 💷 Castle and country park: adult £12, child (5–16) £8, family £30. Park only: adult £8, child £5, family £20 🍴 🛍️ 🎫 🏛️
www.nts.org.uk

Culzean (pronounced *cullane*) is the National Trust for Scotland's most popular property, thanks in part to the surrounding country park—228 lush green hectares (563 acres) of wild gardens and leafy woodland filled with trails.

The golden stone castle, set right at the edge of the cliffs, is handsome rather than beautiful. It is reached via a bridge, and rises high above the terraced garden. Inside, it is like an 18th-century show home, the masterpiece of Scottish architect Robert Adam (1728–92), who worked on it from 1777 to 1792. Highlights include the graceful oval staircase and the Circular Saloon. The top floor was granted to US General Eisenhower in 1945, for his lifetime, as thanks from the people of Scotland for American help during World War II. You can stay in the Eisenhower apartment.

DEEP SEA WORLD

442 F8 • Battery Park, North Queensferry KY11 1JR ☎ 01383 411880 ⏰ Apr–end Oct daily 10–6; rest of year Mon–Fri 10–5, Sat–Sun 10–6 💷 Adult £8.55, child (3–15) £6.30, family £28.70 🚉 North Queensferry 🚌 Free shuttle from Edinburgh daily Jul–Aug, weekend rest of year 🍴 🎫 🏛️
www.deepseaworld.com

This mega-aquarium lies just off the north side of the Forth road bridge, and is an underwater wonder-world.

The complex has the world's longest underwater walkway (112m/360ft), where a perspex tunnel allows visitors to share the sharks' domain without getting wet. Beware—it's quite easy to lose excited small children on the conveyor belt. Explore the tanks full of piranhas, sharks, stingrays and deadly poisonous frogs, and get your hands wet in the rock pool area with safer creatures such as starfish. There is also a seal sanctuary. If you're over 16, don't miss the chance to join a shark dive—reservation is essential.

DOUNE CASTLE

442 E8 • Castle Road, Doune FK16 6EA ☎ 01786 841742 ⏰ Apr–end Sep daily 9.30–6.30; rest of year Sat–Wed 9.30–4.30 💷 Adult £3, child (5–15) £1.20 🎫
www.historic-scotland.gov.uk

The village of Doune lies 8 miles (13km) northwest of Stirling, and it would be easy to pass through and miss the castle completely. Look out for the signs, however, that lead you down a narrow road to this substantial grey ruin, hidden in the trees on a curve of the River Teith.

Built by the powerful Regent of Scotland, Robert Stewart, Duke of Albany, in the late 14th century, the castle is comparatively simple in construction, with a main block of buildings set around a courtyard, and contained by a great curtain wall.

It is an admirable example of medieval concerns for security, with gates to secure the courtyard, further gates to defend the buildings should the courtyard be taken in battle, and separate stairs to the lord's hall and the retainers' hall to ensure that each could be defended in its own right. Even the Duke's bedroom has its own emergency exit.

THE SIGHTS

THE ROYAL MILE

Edinburgh
•

**A castle, a palace, an impressively long main thoroughfare and
a world-famous skyline create the home city of Scotland's ruling élite.
Edinburgh is drenched in history.**

SEEING EDINBURGH

The Scottish capital is divided into two distinct halves by the
the Water of Leith. The Old Town to the south has historic
routes such as Grassmarket and Canongate and a medieval
network of alleys. More breathing space can be found in the
striking Georgian streets of the New Town to the north.

HIGHLIGHTS

EDINBURGH CASTLE

⊞ 192 B2 • Castle Hill EH1 2NG ☎ 0131 225 9846 ◉ Apr–end Oct daily
9.30–6; rest of year daily 9.30–5 💷 Adult £9.80, child (under 16) £3.50
🎧 Guided tours 🍴 ♿
www.historic-scotland.gov.uk

Edinburgh Castle towers over the city from its volcanic rock. Bronze Age
people settled on the top around 850BC, and by the Middle Ages it was a
fortified site and royal residence. The views from the ramp at the entrance
are great. The Half Moon Battery is the defensive wall and walkway on the
east side, built after the Lang (long) Siege of 1567–73. Since 1861 a field
gun has boomed out here Monday to Saturday at precisely 1pm to
enable mariners to fix the time accurately. The Crown Room displays the
ancient regalia of Scotland—crown, sceptre and sword—locked away after
the parliamentary union with England in 1707 (▷ 33) and unearthed by
Sir Walter Scott in 1818. The Stone of Destiny is also here, on which
Scottish kings were crowned. Originally at Scone Palace, it was stolen by
Edward I and remained in London until recovered from Westminster
Abbey in 1996. The Scotch Whisky Heritage Centre (Oct–end Apr daily
10–6; rest of year daily 9.30–6.30) is below the castle.

PALACE OF HOLYROODHOUSE

⊞ 193 E1 • EH8 8DX ☎ 0131 556 5100 ◉ Apr–end Oct daily 9.30–6; rest of year
daily 9.30–4.30 💷 Adult £8.50, child (under 17) £4.50, under 5 free, family £27.50
🎧 Guided tours only Nov–end Mar 🍴 ♿
www.royal.gov.uk

Filled with works of art from the Royal Collection, this towered palace
sits at the foot of the Royal Mile and is the Queen's official residence
in Scotland, which means it may be closed at short notice. The palace
started in the 15th century as a guesthouse for Holyrood Abbey, and
its name is said to come from the Holy Rood, a fragment of Christ's
cross belonging to David I (c1080–1153). Bonnie Prince Charlie
(1720–88) held court here in 1745, followed by George IV on his
triumphant visit to the city in 1822. The state rooms, designed for
Charles II and hung with Brussels tapestries, are particularly good.

MUSEUM OF SCOTLAND

⊞ 192 C3 • Chambers Street EH1 1JF ☎ 0131 247 4422 ◉ Tue 10–8, Mon,
Wed–Sat 10–5, Sun 12–5 💷 Free 🎧 Free tours daily 🍴 🛈 ♿
www.nms.ac.uk

This entertaining museum showcases the Scottish collections from
the Royal Museum next door. It is a superb, well-explained collection
that covers the shaping of Scotland through geology and glaciation,
what is known of the lives of the earliest settlers in Scotland and the
founding of Scottish identity.

*New Year's Eve is spectacular in
Edinburgh (above)
Musicians play at the Edinburgh
Festival in August every year
(left)*

RATINGS				
Good for kids	●	●	●	●
Historic interest	●	●	●	●
Specialist shopping	●	●	●	●
Walkability	●	●	●	●

BASICS

⊞ 443 F8
🛈 3 Princes Street (above Mall)
EH2 2QP, tel 0131 473 3800; Apr, Oct
Mon–Sat 9–6, Sun 10–6; May–Jun,
Sep Mon–Sat 9–7, Sun 10–7; Jul–Aug
Mon–Sat 9–8, Sun 10–8; Nov–Mar
Mon–Sat 9–5, Sun 10–5
🚉 Edinburgh Waverley

www.edinburgh.org
Listed information is brief and general
so use the search facilities for
accommodation, food and drink,
events and leisure ideas.

TIPS

● A free bus service links the
four national galleries.
● The exact fare is required
for Lothian Buses and First
Edinburgh, but journeys
shouldn't cost much more
than £1 (£2 on night buses).

ARTHUR'S SEAT

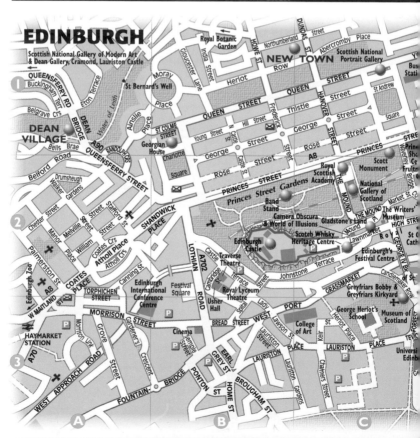

🗺 193 off E2

Arthur's Seat is the 251m (823ft) high remains of a 325-million-year-old volcano. There is access to Holyrood's hills and lochs.

ROYAL BOTANIC GARDEN

🗺 192 off B1 • 20A Inverleith Row EH3 5LR ☎ 0131 552 7171 🕐 Mar and Oct daily 10–6; Apr–end Sep daily 10–7; Nov–end Feb daily 10–4 🎫 Free

The garden has 15,500 species in 28ha (70 acres) of landscaped grounds and 10 greenhouses.

CANONGATE KIRK

🗺 193 E2 • Canongate EH8 8BR ☎ 0131 556 3515 🕐 Jun–end Oct Mon–Sat 10.30–4, Sun 10–12.30 🎫 Free 🚻

Canongate Kirk was built in 1688 after James VI of Scotland converted the abbey church at Holyrood to a chapel.

OUR DYNAMIC EARTH

🗺 193 E2 • Holyrood Road EH8 8AS ☎ 0131 550 7800 🕐 Jul–end Aug daily

NATIONAL GALLERY OF SCOTLAND

🗺 192 C2 • The Mound EH2 2EL ☎ 0131 624 6200 🕐 Fri–Wed 10–5, Thu 10–7 🎫 Free 🚌 Free bus runs between all four national galleries 🚻 www.natgalscot.ac.uk

Designed by New Town architect William Playfair (1789–1857), the National Gallery of Scotland has a collection of 20,000 paintings, sculptures and drawings. The main focus are paintings by Europe's great masters but Scottish artists are displayed in their own section downstairs. Favourites include Sir Henry Raeburn's over-the-top tartan-clad chieftan, *Colonel Alastair Mcdonnell of Glengarry* (1812), and the land- and seascapes of William McTaggart (1835–1910).

NEW TOWN

🗺 192 B1

The New Town covers 1sq mile (2.5sq km) to the north of Princes Street, and is characterized by broad streets of grand, terraced houses with large windows and ornamental door arches. The Georgian House (Mar, Nov daily 11–3; Apr–end Jun, Sep, Oct 10–5; Jul, Aug 10–7), on Charlotte Square's north side, is a meticulous re-creation of an 18th-century home, down to the Wedgwood dinner service on the dining table.

ROYAL MILE

🗺 192 C2

The Royal Mile is the name of the long street that links Holyrood Palace with Edinburgh Castle. About 60 narrow closes lead off on either side. Lady Stair's Close, near St. Giles Cathedral, is the best known and leads through to the Writers' Museum (Mon–Sat 10–5, Sun 2–5 during Edinburgh Festival). Drop into the Museum of Edinburgh (Aug only

Mon–Sat 10–5, Sun 12–5) to get a feeling of the interiors of these old houses. The 1490 John Knox House (Jul–end Aug Mon–Sat 10–5.30, Sun 12–5.30), on the corner of Royal Mile, is where John Knox (c1505–72), the founder of the Church of Scotland, preached. The house shows how the medieval High Street looked.

NATIONAL GALLERY OF MODERN ART AND DEAN GALLERY

🔢 192 off A1 ✉ 74 Belford Road EH4 3DR ☎ 0131 624 6200 🕐 Daily 10–5
💷 Free, may be a charge for temporary exhibitions 🔲

A sweeping, living sculpture of grassy terraces and ponds is the first thing you see as you arrive here. Among the works in the permanent collection are those by Pablo Picasso, Georges Braque, Henri Matisse and Barbara Hepworth. The work of the early 20th-century group of painters known as the Scottish Colourists is striking. Stroll across the road to the Dean Gallery. This collection majors on Dada and the Surrealists, and the Scottish sculptor Eduardo Paolozzi (1924–2005).

BACKGROUND

The name Edinburgh derives from the city's original name Dunedin and the 12th-century term burgh, denoting a town with certain rights, such as trading or taxation. Edinburgh was a royal burgh, and by the time Robert the Bruce (▷ 28) granted a new charter to the city in 1329, it was on the road to becoming the capital of Scotland. The 16th and 17th centuries saw religious and political turmoil, but the city survived. Unlike Glasgow (▷ 198–200), Edinburgh's people didn't get their hands dirty during the Industrial Revolution, preferring to develop services such as banking. In the 1990s, political power was devolved from London to the Scottish capital.

Greyfriars Bobby, a famous city landmark (top); Holyroodhouse (middle); the Camera Obscura on the Royal Mile (bottom)

10–5; Nov–end Mar Wed–Sun 10–6
💷 Adult £8.95, child £5.45
This science park tells the story of the Earth in slick, easy chunks of virtual-reality science.

GREYFRIARS BOBBY

🔢 192 C2 • George IV Bridge
This bronze statue is of a Skye terrier, Bobby, the devoted companion of a farmer who regularly dined in Greyfriars Place.

SCOTTISH NATIONAL PORTRAIT GALLERY

🔢 192 C1 • 1 Queen Street EH2 1JD
☎ 0131 624 6200 🕐 Fri–Wed 10–5, Thu 10–7 💷 Free 🔲 ♿
Scottish worthies and the national photography collection are represented in this gallery.

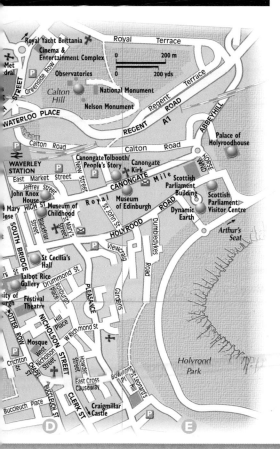

Scott's ship Discovery is a major attraction in Dundee

The Dutch connection: a gable on a cottage in Crail, East Neuk

Romantic Eilean Donan Castle is exceptionally photogenic

THE SIGHTS

DUNDEE

➕ 443 F7 ℹ️ 21 Castle Street DD1 3AA, tel 01382 527527
www.dundeecity.gov.uk

Dundee sprawls along the northern shore of the Firth of Tay, but speed past inland on the ring road and you'll miss a treat, for Dundee's waterfront has undergone a transformation. The focus is Discovery Point and a famous heroine of polar exploration, the three-masted Royal Research Ship Discovery, which was built here in 1901. The story of her planning and construction is told in the museum alongside (Easter–end Oct Mon–Sat 10–6, Sun 11–6; rest of year Mon–Sat 10–5, Sun 11–5), with models and sailors' belongings that bring the city's ship-building history to life. Discovery's maiden voyage, under the command of a young Robert Falcon Scott (1868–1912), was to Antarctica, where in 1902 she became frozen in the pack ice. She was to remain there for two long winters, while scientific research was undertaken and Scott made an unsuccessful attempt to reach the South Pole. It's a fascinating story, making the tour of the ship's cramped quarters even more interesting.

On the other side of the rail station, Sensation Dundee is a tribute to modern research (Apr–end Oct daily 10–6; rest of year daily 10–5). It's a lively hands-on science centre dedicated to the five senses.

Dundee's second major attraction is an excellent industrial museum in the middle of the city, called the Verdant Works (Easter–end Oct Mon–Sat 10–6, Sun 11–6; rest of year Wed–Sat 10.30–4.30, Sun 11–4.30). It's a good idea to watch the short film first. Save money by buying a joint entrance ticket for Verdant Works and Discovery.

Don't miss The poky corner on board Discovery where the ship's doctor Edward Wilson (1872–1912) painted watercolours of the trip.

DUNKELD AND HERMITAGE

➕ 442 F7 ℹ️ The Cross, Dunkeld PH8 0AN, tel 01350 727688 🚉 Dunkeld and Birnam

With the exception of the diminutive 13th-century cathedral, the original settlement of Dunkeld was destroyed by the Jacobites after their victory at Killiecrankie in 1689. It was rebuilt, with terraced houses packed tightly into just two main streets, Cathedral Street and High Street, with a tidy little square, the Cross. By the partly restored cathedral stands the Parent Larch, a tree imported from Austria in 1738 and the parent of many of the trees in the nearby forests, planted between 1738 and 1830 by the dukes of Atholl.

A pleasant walk beside the River Braan leads past the tallest Douglas fir in Britain (64.3m/ 211ft) to the Hermitage, an 18th-century folly. To the east, the Loch of the Lowes is in the care of the Scottish Wildlife Trust and is famous for breeding ospreys (Apr–end Sep daily).

EAST NEUK

➕ 443 G8 ℹ️ Museum and Heritage Centre, 62–64 Marketgate, Crail KY10 3TL, tel 01333 450869 (seasonal) ℹ️ Tourist Information Office, Harbourhead, Anstruther KY10 3AB, tel 01333 311073 (seasonal) ❓ Fife Coastal Path links the villages

Neuk is the Scottish word for a corner, and East Neuk is the name given to eastern Fife, where old fishing villages face south to Edinburgh and the Lothians. These old towns have narrow streets that quickly get congested in summer, so be prepared to explore on foot.

Crail is the farthest east of the string, with a charter dating to 1178 and a photogenic 16th-century harbour. Former trading links with the Netherlands show up in the architecture, characterized by pantile roofs and high, stepped gables. The square-towered tolbooth even has a Dutch bell, cast in 1520.

Next in line to the west is Anstruther, a larger resort town and former herring port. The Scottish Fisheries Museum (Apr–end Sep Mon–Sat 10–5.30, Sun 11–5; rest of year Mon–Sat 10.30–4.30, Sun 12–4.30) is housed in historic waterfront buildings around a courtyard, and illustrates the past and present life of Scottish fishermen and their families. The town also has a history of smuggling, which took place mainly on the Dreel burn (stream) and at the 16th-century Smuggler's Inn.

Continue west to Pittenweem, the main fisheries port for the East Neuk. The town began in the seventh century, when St. Fillan based himself in a cave here (in Cove Wynd) while converting the local Picts to Christianity. Artists seem to be attracted to the town and there are several small art galleries to explore.

The tiny houses of the next village, St. Monans, crowd around its harbour, where ship-building as well as fishing brought prosperity in the 19th century. The splendid, squat Auld Kirk (old church), standing alone at the western end, was built in 1362.

Elie is the farthest west of the East Neuk villages, and its golden sands made it a popular holiday resort during the late 19th century. A causeway leads to a rocky islet with views out to sea and a busy watersports complex.

Charles I is immortalized in the walls of Falkland Palace

Neptune's Staircase on the Caledonian Canal allows boats to pass from one level to another—see the walk on pages 326–327

Don't miss The stone windmill on the coast between Pittenweem and St. Monans, once used to evaporate seawater for the valuable salt industry.

EDINBURGH

See pages 190–193

EILEAN DONAN CASTLE

444 C5 • Dornie, by Kyle of Lochalsh IV40 8DX ☎ 01599 555202 Apr–end Oct daily 10–5.30; Mar–Easter, Nov daily 10–3.30 Adult £4.75, child £3.75, family £9.75 www.eileandonancastle.com

Probably the most photographed castle in Scotland, Eilean Donan is perched on a rock near the northern shore of Loch Duich, joined to the mainland by a bridge. There has been a fortification on the site since the 13th century, and a MacRae stronghold was destroyed here by government troops in 1719. The Eilean Donan you see today, complete with stone walls up to 4.3m (14ft) thick, is the result of rebuilding between 1912 and 1932. It is said that its creator, Lieutenant Colonel John MacRae-Gilstrap, saw an image of how it might look in a dream. It has starred in films such as *The World Is Not Enough*.

FALKIRK WHEEL

442 E8 • Lime Road, Tamfourhill, Falkirk FK1 4RS ☎ 08700 500208 Apr–end Oct daily 9–6; Nov–end Mar daily 9.30–5 Free. Boat ride: adult £8, child (5–16) £4.25, under 5s free, family £21.50 Falkirk Grahamston Advance reservation essential for boat trips www.thefalkirkwheel.co.uk

Is it engineering or art? That's one of the questions that comes up at first sight of this unique 35m (115ft) structure. It opened in 2002 to link the canals that run across the middle of Scotland,

replacing 11 locks, which had been dismantled in 1933. The wheel is a cross between a lock and a lift, a state-of-the-art method of raising and lowering boats between two different levels of the Forth and Clyde ship canal and the Union Canal. Watch from the glass-sided visitor centre as the great structure rotates, and take a 40-minute boat ride up onto the higher canal, through a tunnel, and back down on the wheel.

FALKLAND PALACE

443 F8 • Falkland, Cupar KY15 7BU ☎ 01337 857397 Mar–end Oct Mon–Sat 10–6, Sun 1–5.30 Adult £10, child £7, family £25 www.nts.org.uk

Stuart monarchs used this handsome Renaissance-fronted fortress in the heart of Fife as a hunting lodge and retreat. The twin towers of the palace gatehouse dominate the little town of Falkland, with its clusters of 17th-century red-roofed houses. The palace itself dates to the 15th century. Mary, Queen of Scots (1542–87) spent part of her childhood here, but when the future Charles II (1630–85) fled to exile in 1651, it fell into ruin. In 1887 its fortunes changed when John Patrick Crichton Stuart, the third Marquess of Bute, started rebuilding and restoring it. A series of rooms reflect the different periods of occupation, including the Chapel Royal and the King's Room, with a magnificent bed and tapestries.

FORT WILLIAM

442 D6 • Cameron Square PH33 6AJ, tel 01397 703781 Fort William

Fort William's location on a road and rail junction at the head of Loch Linnhe and the foot of the Great Glen makes it a convenient touring base for the northwest of

Scotland. The town's heyday as a military outpost is long gone—the fort, which withstood Jacobite attacks in 1715 and 1745, was demolished in 1864 for a rail station. The town grew after this period, and is unappealing in itself, but its position makes it popular with walkers and climbers.

Fort William's biggest attraction lies to the east: the rounded bulk of Ben Nevis (1,343m/4,406ft), Britain's highest mountain. Conditions at the top can be extremely cold even on warmer days below, and visitors should take all necessary precautions before attempting to climb it. On the first Saturday in September you may be overtaken by runners—entrants in the annual Ben Nevis Race, established in 1937. The record currently stands at 1 hour 25 minutes.

FYVIE CASTLE

446 G5 • near Turriff AB53 8JS ☎ 01651 891266 Jul–end Aug daily 11–5; Apr–end Jun, Sep Sat–Wed 12–5. Grounds: all year daily 9.30–dusk Adult £8, child (5–16) £5, under 5s free, family £20 www.nts.org.uk

The magnificent Fyvie Castle, set in a landscaped park in the valley of the River Ythan, has a 46m (150ft) frontage, dominated by a large gatehouse. It is said that five of Scotland's great families—the Prestons, Meldrums, Setons, Gordons and Leiths—each built a tower as they owned the castle in turn. The oldest part dates from the 13th century and incorporates the architectural highlight: a spiral staircase of broad stone steps known as a wheelstair, a 17th-century addition by Alexander Seton. Opulent interiors were created in the early 20th century, making a rich backdrop to the weapons collections and the portraits.

Princess Margaret (1930–2002) was born at Glamis Castle

Nungate Bridge in Haddington crosses the River Tyne and leads in to Church Street and Scotland's largest parish church

GLAMIS CASTLE

➕ 443 F7 • by Forfar DD8 1RJ
☎ 01307 840393 🕐 Mar–end Oct daily 10–6; Nov–end Dec 12–4 💷 Adult £7, child (5–16) £3.80, under 5s free, family £20 🍴 🎫
www.glamis-castle.co.uk

A grand, turreted building 5 miles (8km) west of Forfar, Glamis (pronounced *glahms*) Castle has been the seat of the earls of Strathmore and Kinghorne since 1372. It's essentially a medieval tower house that was extended and remodelled to palace proportions. Explore the castle on a guided tour and then roam the stunning park.

Glamis was the childhood home of Queen Elizabeth, the Queen Mother (1900–2002), and there is a special exhibition on her life in the Old Coach House. In the village of Glamis, the Angus Folk Museum (Jul–end Aug daily 11–5, Sun 1–5; Easter–end Jun, Sep Fri–Tue 12–5, Sun 1–5), in a row of 18th-century cottages, gives an idea of life at the other end of the social scale.

Don't miss Duncan's Hall at the castle, the setting of William Shakespeare's *Macbeth*.

GLASGOW

See pages 198–200

GLEN AFFRIC

➕ 445 D5 ℹ Castle Wynd, Inverness IV2 3BJ, tel 01463 234353

This peaceful valley, 30 miles (48km) southwest of Inverness and running parallel with the Great Glen, is one of the best-loved beauty spots in the Highlands. Its scenery combines forest and moorland, river and loch with mighty mountains such as Carn Eighe (1,182m/3,878ft). A narrow road leads up from Cannich to where you can park at the River Affric, passing the

Dog Falls and a picnic area at Loch Beinn a Mheadhoin on the way up. Crested tits and crossbills may be seen all year in the woods, while golden eagles and capercaillie are rarer sightings.

GLEN COE

➕ 442 D7 ℹ Ballachulish PA39 4JR, tel 01855 811296 (seasonal)

Whether your first approach to Glen Coe is from the wide, watery wasteland of Rannoch Moor, or up from Loch Leven, you cannot fail to be impressed by the majesty of this long, steep-sided valley. On a clear day you can see the tops of the Aonach Eagach ridge to the north (966m/3,169ft) and the peaks of the Three Sisters to the south, leading down from Bidean nam Bian (1,148m/3,766ft). At the top, eastern end, the glen is guarded by the massive bulk of Buachaille Etive Mor, the Great Shepherd of Etive (1,019m/3,343ft).

This is prime mountaineering country, and not for the unfit or unwary. In winter it becomes its own snow-filled world, offering an extra challenge to climbers. There is a ski station with a chairlift at the eastern end, on the flanks of Meall a'Bhùiridh (1,108m/3,635ft). Learn more about the glen's remarkable geology at the Inverrigan Visitor Centre (Mar–Easter daily 10–4; Easter–end Aug daily 9.30–5.30; Sep–end Oct daily 10–5; Nov–end Feb Fri–Mon 10–4).

Memories last long in the Highlands, and there is still a frisson between the Macdonalds and Campbells that dates back to a February night in 1692. At a time when clan leaders were required to swear allegiance to the monarchs, William and Mary, Alastair Macdonald of Glencoe postponed the task. When he missed the deadline, Campbell of Glenlyon was sent to make an

example of him. Campbell's men were billeted here for two weeks before turning on their hosts in an act of cold-blooded slaughter that left 38 dead. The betrayal has never been forgotten.

GLENFINNAN

➕ 441 C6 ℹ Cameron Square, Fort William PH33 6AJ, tel 01397 703781 🚉 Glenfinnan

On 19 August 1745, Prince Charles Edward Stuart (Bonnie Prince Charlie) raised his standard here at the top of Loch Shiel, a rallying cry to supporters of his father's claim to the throne of Scotland. It was the start of the Stuarts' final campaign, which would end in disaster at Culloden (▷ 188). The occasion is recalled by a pillar monument topped by the statue of a kilted soldier, built here in 1815, which provides a focus for the magnificent view down the loch. The National Trust for Scotland has an informative visitor office near by (Apr–end Jun, Sep–end Oct daily 10–5; Jul–end Aug daily 9.30–5.30; Nov Sat–Sun 10–4).

HADDINGTON

➕ 443 G8 ℹ Quality Street, North Berwick EH39 4HJ, tel 01620 892197 (seasonal)

This handsome market town is set in prime agricultural country on the River Tyne, 18 miles (29km) east of Edinburgh. It was granted the status of a royal burgh in the 12th century, and later became the county town for East Lothian. Protestant reformer John Knox was born here around 1513. The original medieval town was laid out to a triangular streetplan that can still be traced along High Street, Market Street and Hardgate. Painted in bright, warm hues, the 18th-century Georgian buildings of the High Street make an attractive façade.

The pepperpot towers of
Inveraray Castle are unmistakable

The Kessock Bridge, spanning the Moray Firth north of Inverness, is
a good place to spot dolphins frolicking in the waters

THE SIGHTS

HIGHLAND FOLK MUSEUM

✚ 442 E6 • Duke Street, Kingussie
PH21 1JG ☎ 01540 661307
🕐 Kingussie: mid-Apr to end Aug
Mon–Sat 9–5; Oct Mon–Fri 9.30–4.
Newtonmore: mid-Apr to end Aug daily
10.30 5.30; Sep daily 11–4.30; Oct
Mon–Fri 11–4.30 💷 Kingussie: adult
£2.50, child (5–16) £1.50. Newtonmore:
adult £5, child £3. 🚇 Kingussie
🚌 Newtonmore 🏧
www.highlandfolk.com

Two sites in Kingussie and
Newtonmore, 2.5 miles (4km)
apart and signposted from the
A9, make up the Highland Folk
Museum. Together they offer an
unsanitized picture of rural life in
the Highlands over the centuries,
through reconstructed buildings,
a working croft and collections of
everyday objects. Kingussie has
a large collection of farming
implements and machinery, and
a reconstructed blackhouse,
a traditional stone cottage,
from Lewis (▷ 203–204).
Newtonmore has a reconstructed
18th-century village, including a
tailor's workshop, a church and a
school. Staff in traditional
costume demonstrate farming
skills and crafts.

INNER HEBRIDES

See page 202

INVERARAY

✚ 442 D8 🚻 Front Street PA32 8UY,
tel 01499 302063

Spread out along a bay near the
head of Loch Fyne, Inveraray was
for centuries the capital of Argyll.
The ruling family, the Campbell
dukes of Argyll, had a castle nearby,
and when the untidy village
threatened the view, the third
duke moved the lot to its present
purpose-built site. This creates a
harmony in the buildings. They
include the parish church, which
causes the main street to flow

around it. The tall brown-stone
tower belongs to All Saints'
Episcopalian Church, famous for
its peal of 10 bells and for
panoramic views from the top
(mid-May to end Sep daily 10–1,
2–5). The town's courthouse
and jail of 1820 now house an
entertaining exhibition about
prison life (Apr–end Oct daily
9.30–6; rest of year daily 10–5).

To the north, Inveraray Castle
is an 18th-century mansion
(Apr–end May, Oct Mon–Thu, Sat
10–1, 2–5.45, Sun 1–5.45;
Jun–end Sep Mon–Sat 10–5.45,
Sun 1–5.45).
Don't miss A visit to the Loch
Fyne Oyster Bar for fresh and
smoked seafood, at the head of
Loch Fyne.

INVEREWE GARDENS

✚ 444 C4 • Poolewe, Achnasheen IV22
2LG ☎ 01445 781200 🕐 Garden:
Apr–end Oct daily 9.30–9; rest of year
9.30–4. Visitor centre: Apr–end Sep
daily 9.30–5; Oct daily 9.30–4 💷 Adult
£8, child (5–16) £5.25, family £16
🚤 Private jetty in the garden allows
access by private or cruise boat. 🎧 Free
guided tours Apr–end Sep Mon–Fri
1.30pm 🍴 🏧
www.nts.org.uk

In 1862 Osgood Mackenzie
(1842–1922) inherited the
Inverewe estate from the Laird
of Gairloch, his stepfather, and
on this barren, wind-blown
promontory started to plant
sheltering belts of trees.
Inverewe benefits from the
warmth of the Gulf Stream, and
although the garden is on a
latitude more northerly than
Moscow, it rarely suffers from
extreme frosts. Masses of soil
and fertilizing seaweed had to
be imported, and this seemed to
be an unpromising start to what
has become Scotland's best-
known woodland garden. In fact,
Mackenzie had to wait 20 years
before the trees were sufficiently

established for him to begin
serious planting.

The planting is varied and exotic,
with something flowering at most
times of the year.

Inverewe is surrounded by
some of the most beautiful
scenery in the Highlands; make
the most of a visit to this remote
spot and explore the area.

INVERNESS

✚ 445 E5 🚻 Castle Wynd IV2 3BJ,
tel 01463 234353 🚇 Inverness
✈ Inverness

The administrative capital of the
Highland region, Inverness is a
service town for the surrounding
area, filled in summer with
visitors planning highland
expeditions.

Inverness's lack of antiquities
is due, the locals will tell you, to
the Highlanders' habit of burning
the town down at regular intervals
after Oliver Cromwell (1599–
1658) built a fort here in 1652.
The architecture is mostly 19th
century, including the red
sandstone castle with its
monument to Flora MacDonald,
who helped Bonnie Prince
Charlie to escape in 1746 after
his defeat at nearby Culloden
Moor (▷ 188).

A 60-mile (100km) slash
across the country from Inverness
to Fort William, the Great Glen
follows a geological fault. It is
lined with roads and a series of
lochs, of which the longest and
best known is Loch Ness. Narrow
and up to 230m (750ft) deep in
places, some believe Loch Ness
harbours a monster (known as
Nessie). The first recorded
sighting was in the seventh
century, and you can find out
about more recent searches at
Drumnadrochit's Loch Ness 2000
Visitor Centre (Nov–Easter daily
10–3.30; Easter–end May
9.30–5; Jun, Sep 4–6; Jul–end
Aug 9–8; Oct 9.30–5.30).

SCOTLAND G–I 197

Glasgow

Known as a gritty but friendly city, Glasgow has some handsome architectural treasures, along with regenerated cultural pursuits. Make sure you look up—much of the finest architecture is above street level.

Rodin's The Thinker *at the Burrell Collection*

BASICS

🔸 442 E8

🔸 Greater Glasgow and Clyde Valley Tourist Board, 11 George Square, Glasgow G2 1DY, tel 0141 204 4400; Mon–Sat 9–8, Sun 10–6

🔸 Glasgow Central and Queen Street

🔸 Glasgow Underground (or Clockwork Orange) links different parts of the city, tel 0141 333 3708

www.seeglasgow.com

SEEING GLASGOW

Once Scotland's industrial powerhouse, Glasgow has rediscovered its artistic side in recent years. It was European City of Culture in 1990, then City of Architecture and Design in 1999—a long way from its roots in ironworks and ship-building. The industrial decline of the 1960s and 1970s caused big problems, but, in typical style, the city picked itself up and is now, arguably, a more exciting place than its east coast rival, Edinburgh (▷ 190–193).

HIGHLIGHTS

BURRELL COLLECTION

Pollok Country Park, 2060 Pollokshaws Road G43 1AT ☎ 0141 287 2550 🔘 Mon–Thu, Sat 10–5, Fri and Sun 11–5 🔸 Free; charge for some special exhibitions 🔸 Pollokshaws West 🔸 Free guided tours 🔲 🔲 🔲
This priceless collection of 9,000 pieces of art from around the world was given to Glasgow in 1944 by Sir William Burrell (1861–1958). You'll find August Rodin's *The Thinker* in the Courtyard. Intriguing old stone doorways lead into different parts of the museum. In the Ancient Greece and Rome section, look for fragments of delicate Roman mosaics. Don't overlook the Islamic Art section at the farthest end of the museum, dripping with Oriental carpets. The corridor between the café and the entrance is aglow with medieval glass, suspended along the windows that form the outer skin of the building.

GALLERY OF MODERN ART (GoMA)

Royal Exchange Square, Queen Street G1 3AZ ☎ 0141 229 1996 🔘 Mon–Wed, Sat 10–5, Thu 10–8, Fri and Sun 11–5 🔸 Free 🔸 Queen Street, Glasgow Central 🔸 Tours most weekends 🔲 🔲 🔲
GoMA, in a former tobacco baron's mansion, is set on four floors linked by a glass lift. Among the ever-changing display, look out for Peter Howson's painting *Patriots* (1991), with three loutish men and their snarling bulldogs, as well as huge striped canvases by pop artist Bridget Riley (born 1931) and works by Andy Warhol (1927–87) and David Hockney (born 1937).

GLASGOW SCIENCE CENTRE

50 Pacific Quay G51 1EA ☎ 0141 420 5000 🔘 Daily 10–6; late opening IMAX cinema Thu–Sat 🔸 Science Centre: adult £6.95, child (3–16) £4.95; combination tickets available 🔸 Cessnock 🔸 Exhibition Centre 🔲 🔲 🔲
The main attraction at the Science Centre is the Science Mall, with four floors of 500 interactive exhibits. Highlights include distorting mirrors, seeing how an artificial arm picks up signals from your body, and a walk-on piano for those under seven. The other main elements on the site are the 24m (80ft) screen in the IMAX theatre, and the dizzying 122m (400ft) viewing tower designed to turn 360 degrees in the wind.

GLASGOW NECROPOLIS

🔸 11 George Square G2 1DY, tel 0141 204 4400 🔘 Daily 10–6 🔸 Free
This is Glasgow's 'city of the dead', stuffed with ostentatious monuments to the wealthy 19th-century industrialists who developed

ST. MUNGO MUSEUM OF RELIGIOUS LIFE AND ART

2 Castle Street G4 0RH ☎ 0141 553 2557 ◷ Mon–Thu, Sat 10–5, Fri and Sun 11–5 🎟 Free 🚇 High Street 🍴 ♿

www.glasgowmuseums.com
Enter this modern museum near the medieval cathedral through a Zen gravel garden. It is set out over three floors, with an art collection, religious items and a section about religion in Glasgow.

The Gallery of Modern Art (above) is one of the most interesting contemporary art galleries in Britain. Right: Victorian George Square and City Chambers. Left: the Scottish Football Museum

the city. Their competitive spirit showed even after death, with extraordinary monuments commissioned from the finest architects of the day. There's a great view of the crowded Necropolis skyline from the third floor of the St. Mungo Museum (▷ above).

HUNTERIAN MUSEUM AND ART GALLERY

University of Glasgow, 82 Hillhead Street G1 8QQ ☎ 0141 330 5431/4221 ◷ Mon–Sat 9.30–5 🎟 Free 🚇 Hillhead 🚆 Glasgow Queen Street ▢ ♿ 🚻 www.hunterian.gla.ac.uk
William Hunter (1718–83) was a Glasgow-trained physician who left his scientific collections—including anatomical specimens used in teaching—to his old university. The collection was opened for show in 1807, making this the oldest public museum in Scotland. The magnificent art collection, in a separate building on campus, originates from Hunter's own purchases of 17th-century Flemish, Dutch and Italian masters. There's also a coin collection and displays of geology and archaeology, including Roman finds from Scotland.

THE MACKINTOSH TRAIL

🏛 11 George Square G2 1DY, tel 0141 204 4400
Charles Rennie Mackintosh (1868–1928) was born in Glasgow, and at the age of 16 was apprenticed to a firm of architects. He was an outstanding student, praised for the originality of his architecture, a distinctive fusion of the flowing lines of art nouveau with the simplicity of the Arts and Crafts Movement. He left his mark on Glasgow, with principal points of interest forming the Rennie Mackintosh Trail.

The Glasgow School of Art (tours Apr–end Sep daily 10.30, 11, 11.30, 1, 1.30, 2, 2.30, Oct–end Mar Mon–Sat 11, 2) was founded in 1845. Mackintosh won the competition to design the new building at 167 Renfrew Street in 1896. It is known as his masterpiece and still looks fresh and modern over 100 years later.

The Willow Tearooms, opened in 1903, are a short walk away above a jewellery shop at 217 Sauchiehall Street and offer a restored Mackintosh interior upstairs in the Salon de Luxe.

THE TENEMENT HOUSE

145 Buccleuch Street, Garnethill G3 6QN ☎ 0141 333 0183 ◷ Mar–end Oct daily 2–5 🎟 Adult £5, child (5–16) £4 🚇 Cowcaddens 🚆 Charing Cross www.nts.org.uk
In the 19th and early 20th centuries, most Glaswegians lived in tenement houses, sharing communal facilities. They could be overcrowded, with families sharing one room. This example was the home of Agnes Toward from 1911. Agnes never threw anything away and when she died in 1975, her house became a unique time capsule of social history.

TALL SHIP AT GLASGOW HARBOUR

100 Stobcross Road G3 8QQ ☎ 0141 222 2513 ◷ Mar–end Oct daily 10–5; rest of year daily 10–4 🎟 Adult £4.95, child (5–16) £2.50 🚇 Partick 🚆 Finnieston/ Exhibition Centre ▢ ♿ www.thetallship.com
The best view of this fine steel-hulled sailing ship is from the windows of the Science Centre opposite. The SV Glenlee, built on the Clyde in 1896, is one of five Clyde-built ships left afloat.

A Mackintosh detail from the House for an Art Lover

The grand entrance hall of the City Chambers, opened by Queen Victoria in 1888 (right); the Botanic Gardens (below left); the futuristic Glasgow Science Centre (below right)

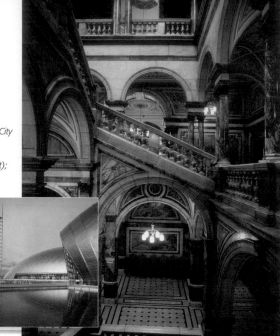

PEOPLE'S PALACE

Glasgow Green G40 1AT ☎ 0141 271 2951 ◉ Mon–Thu, Sat 10–5, Fri and Sun 11–5 🎫 Free 🚇 High Street, Argyle Street, Bellgrove ◻ ⊞ www.glasgowmuseums.com
Set on Glasgow Green, this museum captures the character of the city.

CLYDEBUILT

Braehead Shopping Centre, Kings Inch Road G51 4BN ☎ 0141 886 1013 ◉ Mon–Sat 10–5.30, Sun 11–5.30 🎫 Adult £4.25, child (5–16) £2.50, family £10 🚇 Gilmour Street 🚢 Waterbus
www.scottishmaritimemuseum.org
Runs through Clydeside's golden age of ship-building in the 19th and 20th centuries.

SCOTTISH FOOTBALL MUSEUM

Hampden Park G42 9BA ☎ 0141 616 6139 ◉ Mon–Sat 10–5, Sun 11–5 🎫 Adult £8, child (5–16) £4, family £20 🚇 Bridge Street ◻ ⊞
www.scottishfootballmuseum.org.uk
Hampden Park is Scotland's national football stadium.

BOTANIC GARDENS

730 Great Western Road G12 0UE ☎ 0141 334 2422 ◉ Daily 7–dusk; glasshouses: Apr–end Oct daily 10–4.45; rest of year daily 10–4.15 🎫 Free 🚇 Partick
The highlight is the Kibble Palace, a huge domed glasshouse.

The House for an Art Lover (Apr–end Sep Mon–Wed 10–4, Thu–Sun 10–1; Oct–end Mar Sat–Sun 10–1) is a fantasy, designed in 1901 without the imposed limitations of budget or client, by Mackintosh and his wife, Margaret MacDonald (1864–1933). In 1996 artists and craftspeople made the dream a reality at 10 Dumbreck Road in leafy Bellahouston Park.

At the university's Hunterian Gallery, Mackintosh House is the exquisite re-creation of the interior of the home which the Mackintoshs made together, with original furniture, as it appeared in 1906. You can clearly see the influence of Japanese style.

At Queen's Cross, 870 Garscube Road, northwest of the city, St. Matthew's Free Church is Mackintosh's only complete church, designed in 1897. It follows a simple Gothic Revival style, the attention to detail extending to the carvings of birds and foliage on the oak pulpit. The church was restored and is now home to the Charles Rennie Mackintosh Society (Mar–end Oct Mon–Fri 10–5, Sun 2–5).

Hidden down Mitchell Lane, between Buchanan and Union streets, the Lighthouse is Glasgow's museum of architecture and design. Completed in 1985, the building was the first public commission by Mackintosh. It later became the headquarters of the *Glasgow Herald* newspaper. As well as a permanent Mackintosh display, there are extensive temporary exhibitions. There's a breathtaking panorama from the top of the Lighthouse (Mon, Wed–Sat 10–5, Tue 11–5, Sun 12–5).

BACKGROUND

Trade and religion have shaped Glasgow. St. Kentigern (518–603) is said to have built Glasgow's first church, where the cathedral now stands. The settlement became a royal burgh in 1611 and the Protestant Revolution later that century allowed commerce to flourish. As a port on the west coast, Glasgow was perfectly located for trade with the English colonies in America, importing tobacco, cotton and rum. The Industrial Revolution helped Glasgow become the workshop of the Western world. Money flowed in as ships built on the Clyde flowed out; the opulent City Chambers (Mon–Fri 9–5) on George Square suggest how wealthy the city was. The city is now adapting to post-industrial life, with an emphasis today on culture and entertainment.

Kelso Abbey was once the largest of the Border abbeys

The Mull of Kintyre is a windswept, isolated spot with exhilarating views across to Ireland

JEDBURGH

⊞ 439 G9 ⓘ Murray's Green TD8 6BE, tel 0870 608 0404 (seasonal) www.jedburgh-online.org.uk

Jedburgh lies on the old main road into Scotland, and has witnessed many conflicts—in fact, so frequently was the town's castle attacked, rebuilt and attacked again that it was finally demolished in 1409. The broken tower and red sandstone walls of the ruined abbey (Apr–end Sep daily 9.30–6.30; rest of year 9.30–4.30) still dominate the town.

This was one of the great medieval Border abbeys (along with Kelso, ▷ right, Dryburgh, and Melrose, ▷ 204), and the shepherding skills of the monks were the basis on which the town's weaving industry and wealth grew. Mary, Queen of Scots reputedly stayed in a house in the town in 1566, leaving it briefly to visit her wounded lover, the Earl of Bothwell (c1535–78).
Don't miss Mary, Queen of Scots' death mask, at Mary, Queen of Scots' House (Mar–end Nov Mon–Sat 10–4, Sun 11–4.30), taken from her severed head.

JOHN O'GROATS

⊞ 446 F2 ⓘ County Road, John o'Groats KW1 4YR, tel 01955 611373 (seasonal) www.visitjohnogroats.com

In popular imagination, John o'Groats is the most northerly settlement on the British mainland, 873 miles (1,405km) from Land's End in Cornwall (▷ 81), although the inhabitants of tiny Scarfskerry, a few miles to the northwest, have been known to take exception to the claim. It is named after a Dutchman, Jan de Groot, who lived here in 1509; today there are souvenir

shops and cafés. Queen Elizabeth the Queen Mother (1900–2002) restored the nearby Castle of Mey as a holiday home (May–end Jul, mid-Aug to end Sep Sat–Thu 10.30–4).
Don't miss The true most northerly point in Britain: the exposed headland of Dunnet Head, between John o'Groats and Thurso.

KELSO

⊞ 443 G9 ⓘ Town House, The Square TD5 7HF, tel 0870 608 0404 www.kelso-online.co.uk

Kelso is one of the most elegant of the Border towns. A poignant fragment is all that remains of Kelso Abbey, destroyed by the English in 1545. Nearby is the handsome five-arched bridge over the River Tweed built by John Rennie in 1803. From the parapet there is a fine view across to Floors Castle (Apr–end Oct daily 10–4.30), the largest inhabited house in Scotland, a monument to the wealth and privilege of the dukes of Roxburghe. Fine art, tapestries and French furniture are all on view.

An 18th-century mansion northwest of Kelso, Mellerstain House (Easter and May–end Oct Sun–Mon, Wed–Fri 12.30–5; also Oct Sat 12.30–5) is famous for its architecture and elegant interiors, and is still the family home of the Earl of Haddington. The delicate plasterwork is reminiscent of the decoration of Wedgwood pottery.

KILLIN

⊞ 442 E7 ⓘ Breadalbane Folklore Centre, Falls of Dochart, Main Street FK21 8XE, tel 01567 820254 www.killin.info

The little flower-filled village of Killin lies at the western end

of Loch Tay, in the ancient district of Breadalbane, and is a popular touring, walking and fishing area. It has its own attractions, notably the Falls of Dochart, which run through the middle. The hills are full of colourful legends, brought to life at the Breadalbane Folklore Centre in St. Fillan's Mill (Jul–end Aug daily 9.30–6.30; Jun and Sep daily 10–6; Mar–end May and Oct daily 10–5). If you can't tell your fairies from your kelpies, this is the place to get educated.

KINTYRE

⊞ 441 C9 ⓘ Harbour Street, Tarbert PA29 6UD, tel 01880 820429 ⓘ Mackinnon House, The Pier, Campbeltown PA28 6EF, tel 01586 552056 ✕ Campbeltown 🚢 Ferry: Lochranza on Arran to Claonaig (summer) and Tarbert (winter) www.campbeltownferry.com

In 1098, Norse king Magnus Barelegs hauled his ship over the narrow neck of land at Tarbert to claim the beautiful Kintyre peninsula. Despite swift, modern access it still has the feeling of a world apart. The eastern road, via the holiday village of Carradale, is slower, allowing time to enjoy the views to Arran (▷ 186).

The Mull of Kintyre was made famous by occasional resident Sir Paul McCartney in his hugely successful song (the former Beatle owns a home and a recording studio in the area). It is the southernmost tip of this peninsula, looking across to Northern Ireland, only 12 miles (20km) away. Tarbert, at the top, is an appealing little port, while Campbeltown, at the southern end, remains an important focus for the local farming community, and the home of the Springbank distillery. Try to visit the golden sands in Machrihanish Bay—they are often deserted.

THE SIGHTS

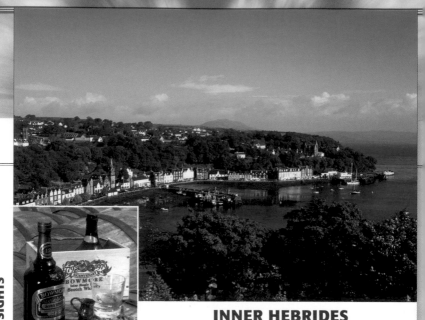

RATINGS

Historic interest	● ● ○
Outdoor activities	● ● ● ○
Photo stops	● ● ● ○
Wildlife interest	● ● ● ○

BASICS

➕ 441 • The main islands are identified by a red dot

ℹ️ The Pier, Craignure, Isle of Mull PA65 6AY, tel 01680 812377

ℹ️ Bowmore, Islay PA43 7JP, tel 01496 810254

ℹ️ Harbour Street, Tarbert PA29 6UD, tel 01880 820429

🚢 Mull: ferry from Oban, Kilchoan and Lochaline. Coll, Tiree, Colonsay: ferry from Oban. Islay and Jura: ferry from Tarbert. Gigha: ferry from Tayinloan on the Kintyre peninsula. All Caledonian MacBrayne, tel 01475 650100 (recording), 0870 565 0000 (reservations), www.calmac.co.uk

❓ Islay has a whisky trail leaflet, detailing the opening times for the Laphroaig, Lagavulin and Bowmore distilleries

TIPS

● Ferry services to the islands are infrequent and may change according to weather conditions; plan your visit carefully.
● Reserve ahead; accommodation on the smaller islands is limited.

Visit sheltered Tobermory Harbour on Mull and (inset) the Bowmore Distillery on Islay

INNER HEBRIDES

Explore the various communities of Scotland's Western Isles.

The Inner Hebrides islands hug the western shores of Scotland, and include Mull, Iona, Coll, Tiree, Colonsay, Islay, Jura and Gigha.

MULL

Mull is the largest island, covering 350sq miles (900sq km), with high mountains in the south and the rugged inlets of Loch Scridain and Loch na Keal in the west. The main settlement is Tobermory, with its attractive waterfront. The remoteness of the western coast, its sculpted appearance created by lava flow 50 million years ago, makes it an ideal habitat for golden eagles, buzzards and peregrines. To see birds of prey up close, visit Wings Over Mull, a conservation complex at Craignure (Apr–end Oct daily 10.30–5.30). A short ride away on a narrow-gauge railway (Apr–end Oct daily 10–5.30), Torosay Castle is a stately home built in 1858 (house: Apr–end Oct daily 10.30–5; gardens: summer daily 9–7).

IONA AND STAFFA

Fionnphort on Mull is the main access point for Iona, a magical island and the cradle of Christianity in Scotland since the sixth century. Make straight for the abbey (May–end Sep Mon–Fri 10–4.30, Sat–Sun 1–4.30; Oct–end Apr Sun, Tue, Thu 1–4), but spare time for the remains of the 13th-century priory, built for Augustinian nuns. Excursions take in the island of Staffa, with its hexagonal basalt columns and Fingal's Cave.

THE OTHERS

To the west of Mull, the low-lying islands of Coll, Tiree, Colonsay and Oronsay are known for sandy beaches and rare birds. By comparison, Islay is positively cosmopolitan, a working island with seven distilleries, the Museum of Islay Life at Port Charlotte (Apr–end Oct Mon–Sat 10–5, Sun 2–5), and an annual festival of music and whisky, the Feis Ile (late May/early Jun). With its three high conical mountains, Jura is easily recognized. Standing stones and cairns date habitation here back to 7000BC. Gigha is famous for the gardens of Achamore House (daily, all year). Canna, Rum, Eigg and Muck make up the Small Isles group south of Skye and are reached from Mallaig. Each has its own identity, but they share a reputation for unusual birdlife. Rum is the biggest, with the mountains of Askival (812m/2,658ft) and Sgùrr nan Gillean (764m/ 2,503ft), and Muck is the smallest, occupied by just one farm.

Wool has been dyed and woven on Harris since the 1840s

LOCH LOMOND AND THE TROSSACHS NATIONAL PARK

Between them, Loch Lomond and the Trossachs offer magnificent scenery of wild woods, Britain's largest freshwater lake and forest-covered hills.

442 D8 🛈 National Park Gateway Centre, Loch Lomond Shores, Ben Lomond Way, Balloch G83 3QL, tel 0845 345 4978 🚌 Balloch, Tarbet and Ardlui on west side of Loch Lomond www.lochlomond-trossachs.org

RATINGS				
Outdoor pursuits	●	●	●	●
Good for kids		●	●	●
Photo stops	●	●	●	●
Walkability	●	●	●	

The romantic beauty of the Highland landscape, epitomized by this accessible and scenic area, was first discovered in the late 18th century. It was novelist and poet Sir Walter Scott who did much to bring it to the popular eye, with his poem *The Lady of the Lake* (1810), set in identifiable locations across the Trossachs, ending at Loch Katrine. Today, Scotland's first designated national park (opened in 2002) stretches from the western shores of Loch Long across to Callander (▷ 188), and from Killin (▷ 201) in the north to Balloch in the south.

This is great hiking country, with waymarked trails and an attractive stretch of the West Highland Way long-distance footpath running along the eastern shore of Loch Lomond. Stretching for 24 miles (38.6km), the loch is a watersports' playground, with 38 pretty islands scattered throughout. Ben Lomond, on the eastern shore, is a popular Munro hill climb (974m/3,192ft). Luss, off the A82, is the best village to explore. The Loch Lomond Shores Visitor Centre explains the geology and history of the region (Easter–end Jun daily 9.30–6; Jul–end Aug 9.30–6.30; 10–5 rest of year).

The Trossachs is the area to the east of Loch Lomond, including the wooded hills of the Queen Elizabeth Forest Park, and the peaks of Ben Venue (729m/2,391ft) and Ben Ledi (879m/2,874ft). Some of the best scenery is between Aberfoyle and Loch Katrine, with easy walking and a steamboat ride among the islands.
Don't miss Visiting the dramatic pass to the high point of Rest and Be Thankful, on the A83 west of Arrochar.

Loch Ard is a typical calm Trossachs lake

KIRKCUDBRIGHT

438 E11 🛈 Harbour Square DG6 4HY, tel 01557 330494

This pretty harbour town lies southwest of Castle Douglas and has retained much character. The street plan is medieval, the castle ruin 16th-century, and its popularity with painters dates from 1901, when artist E. A. Hornel (1864–1933) settled here. Broughton House, where he lived and worked, is now a gallery and museum. It is said that local residents approached Hornel and his friends for their advice on colour schemes whenever their house fronts needed repainting—hence the harmonious shades seen in the High Street.

More paintings by Kirkcudbright artists can be seen in the Tolbooth Art Centre (Jun–end Sep Mon–Sat 11–5, Sun 2–5).

LEWIS AND HARRIS

444 B3 🛈 26 Cromwell Street, Stornoway, Isle of Lewis H51 2DD, tel 01851 703088 🛈 Pier Road, Tarbert, Isle of Harris HS3 3DJ, tel 01859 502011 ⛴ Ferry from Uig on Skye to Tarbert, from Otternish on North Uist to An T-ob (Leverburgh) and from Ullapool to Stornoway ✈ Flights from Glasgow and Edinburgh to Stornoway ❓ No public transport on Sundays

Lewis and Harris are joined by a narrow neck of land, but retain strong individual identities. They share a strong Gaelic culture and a traditional observance of the Sabbath—so plan ahead if you're here on a Sunday.

Lewis has large undulating peat moors scattered with lochs. Steornabhagh (Stornoway) is the administrative focus and a busy fishing port. Good roads lead through the crofting communities that hug the shore and to the mountainous southwest corner, where the white sands of Uig and Reef compete with green islands to steal the view.

The ruins of Melrose Abbey are haunting when illuminated

Planes of all kinds are at North Berwick's Museum of Flight

The ornate Italian chapel on Orkney, crafted by prisoners of war

THE SIGHTS

Harris is the most beautiful of the Outer Hebrides, with high mountains and deep-cut bays. The subtle browns, greens and smoky greys of the landscape are reflected in the island's most famous export, Harris tweed, a high-quality, hand-woven cloth.

The island has many prehistoric monuments and monoliths, including the remarkable avenue and circle of 13 stones at Calanais (Callanish), dating to around 3000BC (Visitor Centre: Apr–end Sep Mon–Sat 10–6; rest of year Wed–Sat 10–4). Just up the coast, Dun Carloway Broch is an excellent example of a circular Iron Age dwelling. Set back from the beach at Bosta is a reconstructed Iron Age house that can be compared with the evocative 19th-century Black House at Arnol (Apr–end Sep Mon–Sat 9.30–6.30; Oct–end Mar 9.30–4.30).

MELROSE

⊞ 443 G9 🛈 Abbey House TD6 9LG, tel 0870 608 0404
www.scot-borders.co.uk

The Romans built a massive fort here, by a bridge over the River Tweed, and called it Trimontium after the three peaks of the Eildon Hills. There's little left to see now, but the Three Hills Roman Heritage Centre in this compact Borders town sets it all in context (Mar–end Oct daily 10.30–4.30).

The more visible history of Melrose dates from 1136, when David I (c1085–1153) founded the pink sandstone abbey (Apr–end Sep daily 9.30–6.30; rest of year Mon–Sat 9.30–4.30, Sun 2–4.30). Repairs in the 19th century were at the instigation of novelist Sir Walter Scott; the ruins are majestic, and the stone carving outstanding—look up to see saints, dragons, flowers and a pig playing the bagpipes.

Don't miss The burial place of Robert the Bruce's heart in the abbey, marked by an engraved inscription.

NEW LANARK WORLD HERITAGE SITE

⊞ 442 E9 • New Lanark Mills, Lanark ML11 9DB ☎ 01555 661345 🛈 Visitor Centre: Jun–end Aug daily 10.30–5, 11–5 rest of year 🎫 Adult £5.95, child (5–16) £3.95, family from £16.95 🅿 ♿ 🍴
www.newlanark.org

Robert Owen (1771–1858) purchased the cotton mills here in 1799 and established a utopian society—a model community with improved conditions for the workers and their families. There was a school, day nursery, institute for adult education and a village store run by a cooperative. The site slowly declined, but in 1973 the New Lanark Conservation Trust started to restore it, with the results seen today.

Don't miss The walk to the three waterfalls upstream.

NORTH BERWICK

⊞ 443 G8 🛈 1 Quality Street EH39 4HJ, tel 01620 892197

North Berwick is a small resort east of Edinburgh, on the shores of the Firth of Forth, with several attractions, making it an interesting day trip from Edinburgh.

East, towards Tantallon Castle, the Museum of Flight (Mar–end Oct daily 10–5; Oct–end Mar Sat–Sun 10–4) is Scotland's national collection of historic aircraft, with more than 50, from a Glasgow-built flying machine that inspired the Wright brothers to an Avro Vulcan bomber.

Twenty days of blasting from King James V's cannons in 1528 could not destroy Tantallon Castle (Mar–end Sep daily 9.30–6.30; Oct–end Mar Sat–Wed 9.30–4.30). Set high on a promontory, and protected by the sea on three sides and on the fourth by a wall 15m (50ft) high and 3.7m (12ft) thick, it was almost impregnable. From the 14th century the fortress was the stronghold of the Red Douglases, earls of Angus. It was the sixth earl, Archibald Douglas, who incurred the king's wrath, having kept him a virtual prisoner in Edinburgh.

A modern building at the harbour, the Scottish Seabird Centre (Apr–end Oct daily 10–6; Nov–end Jan Mon–Fri 10–5; Feb, Mar Sat–Sun 10–5.30) is the key to the birdlife of the Firth of Forth, and in particular the famous gannet colony that inhabits the Bass Rock.

ORKNEY ISLANDS

⊞ 446 F2 🛈 6 Broad Street, Kirkwall KW15 1NX, tel 01856 872856 ⛴ Ferry: from Aberdeen (7 hr) or Scrabster, by Thurso (1 hr 40 min) ✈ Kirkwall
www.visitorkney.com

This low-lying group of more than 90 islands and skerries lies 20 miles (32km) off the northern coast of Scotland. Orkney joined Scotland in the 13th century as part of a dowry when Margaret of Denmark married the Scottish king James III (1452–88).

Today these islands ring with Norse-sounding placenames, although Picts and Celts pre-dated the Vikings by at least 4,000 years, leaving extraordinary signs of their presence at Maes Howe and Skara Brae.

Hoy is the second-largest of the Orkney islands. Its best-known feature is the columnar stack of red sandstone, known as the Old Man of Hoy. Standing at 137m (450ft), it's a challenge for climbers.

The heather-covered hills of Cuilags and Ward Hill offer excellent walking country, with

The ruined Earls Tower looks out over Perth and Perthshire

Highland Games are very popular festivals throughout Scotland, with marching bands and special sports, seen here at Pitlochry

views over Scapa Flow. This sheltered natural harbour was home to the Royal Navy during both world wars, and was the site of the scuttling of the German fleet after the end of World War I. Learn more at the fascinating Scapa Flow Visitor Centre and Museum at Lyness (May–end Sep Mon–Sat 9–4.30, Sun times depend on ferry timetable; rest of year Mon–Fri 9–4.30). A group of Italian prisoners of war confined on the islands during World War II created the Italian Chapel (daily, dawn–dusk) in two Nissen huts.

The buildings of Kirkwall's narrow, paved streets date from the 16th to the 18th centuries. Dominating everything is the red sandstone bulk of St. Magnus Cathedral on Broad Street, begun by Earl Rognvald in 1137 and completed in the 15th century (Apr–end Sep Mon–Sat 9–6, Sun 1–6; rest of year Mon–Sat 9–1, 2–5).

A 7m (23ft) grassy mound in a field to the south of Loch of Harray, on the road from Stromness to Finstown, Maes Howe (Apr–end Sep daily 9.30–6.30; Oct–end Mar 9.30–4.30) looks unpromising at first sight. Under the turf, however, lies a chambered grave dating from around 2800BC that is a treasure of World Heritage status. You have to bend double to walk through the 14.5m (47ft) entrance passage before you emerge into the beautifully formed inner chamber. While the contents are long gone, the structure itself has survived undamaged, barring some runic graffiti left by passing Vikings. Don't miss the nearby Ring of Brodgar, a magnificent stone circle.

A visit to Skara Brae (Apr–end Sep daily 9.30–6.30; rest of year Mon–Sat 9.30–4.30, Sun 2–4.30) is essential. Northwest

of Kirkwall, it is the site of a village inhabited between 3100 and 2500BC. The sands subsequently encroached and covered the houses, which lay undiscovered until a storm in 1850 revealed stone structures. Excavations showed six similar houses linked by passageways. As you walk around the site, you look down into the houses from above, through what would have been roofs of skin and turf. Slabs of stone created hearths, cupboards in the walls, bed surrounds, clay-lined troughs in the floor, and even a dresser, suggesting a delightfully unexpected degree of sophistication.

Orkney's second town, Stromness, boomed in the early 19th century. The winding main street is paved and cobbled; follow it all the way to its southern end, to the maritime displays in the Stromness Museum on Alfred Street (Apr–end Sep daily 10–5; Oct to mid-Feb, mid-Mar to end Apr Mon–Sat 11–3.30).

PERTH

🔲 442 F7 🚹 Lower City Mills, West Mill Street PH1 5QP, tel 01738 450600 (seasonal) 🚉 Perth

The Roman settlement of Perth was founded along the banks of the River Tay in the first century AD. Today it is a lively city, with great shops and bohemian cafés. The Perth Mart, in the old cattle market, is the venue for the pedigree bull sales, the biggest of their kind in Europe, held in October and February.

Balhousie Castle, along the edge of the North Inch park, has the Black Watch Regimental Museum (Mon–Sat 10–4.30, May–end Sep; rest of year 10–3.30).

Open-top bus tours depart from the rail station to Scone Palace (daily 9.30–5.30, Apr–end

Oct). In the grounds of this lived-in stately home is Moot Hall, the earliest crowning place of Scottish kings and first home of the Stone of Destiny (▷ 191).

PITLOCHRY

🔲 442 E7 🚹 22 Atholl Road PH16 5DB, tel 01796 472215 🚉 Pitlochry

Pitlochry, a bustling town beside the River Tummel, has one long main street. At the geographical heart of Scotland, it's been a popular holiday resort since the 19th century, and has two distilleries: Bell's Blair Atholl (Easter–end Sep Mon–Sat 9.30–5, Sun 12–5; Oct–Easter tours at 11, 1 and 3 only) and the tiny Edradour (Mar–end Oct Mon–Sat 9.30–6, Sun 11.30–5; Nov–end Dec Mon–Sat 9.30–5, Sun 11.30–5; Jan–end Feb Mon–Sat 10–4, Sun 12–4). A footbridge leads to the Festival Theatre and Plant Collectors Garden (Easter–end Oct Mon–Sat 10–5, Sun 11–5). There's a view from the bridge to the salmon ladder, installed as part of the hydroelectric dam system along the river.

ROSSLYN CHAPEL

🔲 443 F8 • Roslin EH25 9PU ☎ 0131 440 2159 🕐 Mon–Sat 9.30–6, Sun 12–4.45 💷 Adult £6, under 18s free ♿ 🚻
www.rosslynchapel.org.uk

In a tiny mining village 6 miles (10km) south of Edinburgh, this is the most mysterious building in Scotland: It was made famous by Dan Brown's The Da Vinci Code. A church was founded here in 1446. It was to be a large cruciform structure, but only the choir was ever built, along with parts of the east transept walls. It is linked with the Knights Templar and believed by some to be the hiding place of the Holy Grail.

Grantown-on-Spey is a good place for fly-fishing for salmon

SCOTTISH CRANNOG CENTRE

🏠 442 E7 • Kenmore, South Loch Tay, near Aberfeldy PH15 2HY ☎ 01887 830583 🕐 Mid-Mar to end Oct daily 10–5.30; Nov daily 10–4 💰 Adult £4.75, child (5–16) £3, family £14 🏠
www.crannog.co.uk

Crannogs were circular, communal dwellings built on stilts above the surface of a loch, and 2,000 years ago central Scotland was apparently littered with hundreds of them. One has been reconstructed near Kenmore at the eastern end of Loch Tay, its design based on ongoing underwater excavations on the opposite side of the loch at Fearnan. Informative tours show some of the remarkable discoveries from the site, and take you across the uneven pier into the hut itself, where you can learn how archaeologists have gleaned clues to the way of life of the original crannog dwellers. Back on land, there are demonstrations of ancient skills such as fire-making. Reserving ahead is essential in mid-summer.

SPEYSIDE

🏠 446 F5 ℹ️ 17 High Street, Elgin IV30 1EG, tel 01343 542666 ℹ️ High Street, Grantown-on-Spey PH26 3EH, tel 01479 872773 (seasonal)
www.maltwhiskytrail.com

The River Spey flows from the Cairngorms (▷ 187) near Aviemore and winds northeast through gentle hills and woodland to pour into the sea between Lossiemouth and Buckie. On the way, it flows under a magnificent iron bridge at Craigellachie designed by engineer Thomas Telford (1757–1834), lends its name to the historic Strathspey Railway and the town of Grantown-on-Spey, and picks up a long-distance trail,

SHETLAND ISLANDS

Shetland has an unusually cosmopolitan air, thanks to its northern trade routes, and a culture that is more Viking than Scottish.

🏠 446 G3 ℹ️ Market Cross, Lerwick ZE1 0LU, tel 01595 693434 🚢 Ferry to Lerwick from Kirkwall (8 hr) or Aberdeen (14 hr) ✈️ Sumburgh
www.visitshetland.com

RATINGS	
Coastal attractions	●●●●●
Good for kids	●●●
Historic interest	●●●●●
Specialist shopping	●●●

Shetland, a grouping of more than 100 islands, is the most northerly part of Britain, lying as close to Bergen in Norway as to Aberdeen.

The capital is the harbour town of Lerwick, due to Dutch herring fishermen who used its sheltered harbour in the 17th century. In the shops, traditional knitwear is the thing to buy; if you can't see what you want, dextrous workers will make you a bespoke garment. The Shetland Museum in a splendid new building on Hays Dock is a terrific introduction to the islands (due to open late 2006; daily).

Complex layers of history were uncovered at Jarlshof Prehistoric and Norse Settlement (Apr–end Sep daily 9.30–6.30), near Sumburgh, when a storm dislodged the covering turf. The obvious survivor is the shell of the 17th-century Laird's House, which overlies a broch (a prehistoric circular stone tower). Around it are the remains of a Viking farm with a communal longhouse. Further layers have revealed a settlement from the second century BC, and a 14th-century medieval farm, creating an intriguing record of life here.

The double-skinned circular tower of Mousa Broch dates from 100BC to AD300, and is the best-preserved example of its kind in Scotland. Access in summer is via a small passenger boat from Leebitton, in Sandwick (boat trips on *Solan IV* mid-Apr to mid-Sep weather permitting. Reservations essential, tel: 01950 431367 or 07901 872339).

A tiny grass-covered island off the southwest coast, St. Ninian's Isle is a green jewel. It is joined to the land by a curved tombolo of silvery shell sand, which permits access except during the highest tides of the year, and is a lovely area for walks. St. Ninian was the first Christian missionary to reach Shetland, and the ruins of a 12th-century church still stand. In 1958 a hoard of intricately worked Pictish silver was discovered, buried under the nave. The treasure is now in the Museum of Scotland in Edinburgh (▷ 191), but replicas can be seen in the Shetland Museum in Lerwick.

Much of Unst's fame rests on its status as the most northerly of the Shetland isles. The nature reserve at Hermaness is home in summer to 100,000 screaming seabirds which nest on and around the cliffs. There's a regular ferry service from Yell to Unst.

Vikings were here: See remains of old settlements at Jarlshof

Take the bridge over Swilken Burn at St. Andrews Old Golf Course

The distinctive peak of Sgurr nan Gillean

the Speyside Way. Speyside is a name associated with the area between Elgin, Keith and Grantown, and more particularly with the production of some of Scotland's famous single malt whiskies. Eight distilleries, mostly founded in the early 19th century, are linked by the signposted Malt Whisky Trail: Glen Grant, Glen Moray, Cardhu, Strathisla, Glenlivet, Benromach, Dallas Dhu and Glenfiddich. Each offers guided tours and whisky tastings, but opening times and admissions vary so check ahead (the tourist office has a leaflet with all the information).

ST. ANDREWS

✚ 443 G7 ⓘ 70 Market Street KY16 9NU, tel 01334 472021

This attractive, breezy city has a sandy bay and a narrow harbour, and Scotland's oldest university, founded in 1413 and where Prince William was a student. It is also the home of the Royal and Ancient Golf Club, founded in 1754 and still the ruling authority on the game. Check out its history at the British Golf Museum on Bruce Embankment (Apr to mid-Oct daily 9.30–5.30; rest of year Thu–Mon 10–4).

Near the gaunt ruins of the cathedral stand the remains of the 12th-century St. Rule's Tower. Climb the spiral stairs of the 33m (108ft) tower for views that reveal the medieval grid of the city streets. The two main roads are North Street, leading to St. Andrews Links (golf course), and South Street, with the city gateway of 1589, the West Port.

North along the shore lie the spectacular ruins of the castle, rebuilt in 1390, where a battle and siege took place in 1546 (Apr–end Sep daily 9.30–6.30; rest of year daily 9.30–4.30). **Don't miss** The bottle-shaped dungeon in the castle.

SKYE

The amazing island of Skye is part of Scotland's soul

✚ 444 B5 ⓘ Bayfield House, Bayfield Road, Portree IV51 9EL, tel 01478 612137 ⛴ Ferry: Mallaig to Armadale (40 min, summer), Glenelg to Kylerhea (15 min, summer), Skye Bridge at Kyle of Lochalsh

RATINGS					
Coastal attractions	●	●	●	●	●
Good for kids	●	●	●		
Outdoor pursuits	●	●	●	●	
Photo stops	●	●	●	●	●

Skye is the largest and best known of the Inner Hebrides, its name woven into the story of Bonnie Prince Charlie's flight after the Battle of Culloden (▷ 188–189) in the 18th century, and the loss of a way of island life and emigration to the New World in the 19th century. Every view of the island is dominated by the Cuillin (pronounced *coolin*), jagged mountains that reach their highest peak in the south with Sgurr Alasdair (1,009m/3,310ft). These are the Black Cuillin, distinct from the scree-covered granite of the lower Red Cuillin, but all are challenges for climbers. In the north of the island, ancient lava flows have produced sheer cliffs, with crags and pinnacles such as the Old Man of Storr, created where softer rocks buckled under the weight of the lava. The unusual formations of the Quiraing on the Trotternish peninsula can be examined more closely if you walk with care.

The harbour town of Portree is the focus of island life, and its Aros Experience offers the best introduction to Skye's natural history (daily 9–6).

The Skye bridge sets one massive concrete foot firmly on the little 2.4ha (6-acre) island of Eilean Ban, a nature reserve run by a charitable trust for the local community. Access is via the Bright Water Visitor Centre on the pier at Kyleakin (May–end Oct Mon–Sat 10–4), which has information on local wildlife and history.

The western side of Skye is wilder, with the long fingers of Waternish and Duinish stretching to the Outer Hebrides. Dunvegan is the family seat of the MacLeods, and claims to be Scotland's oldest inhabited castle, occupied since the 13th century (mid-Mar to end Oct daily 10–5; rest of year daily 11–4). Among its treasures is the Fairy Flag, a now tattered scrap of cloth, with apparently potent powers to rescue the clan at times of peril.

Broadford is the main place in the south, with access to the magnificently scenic road to Elgol. If you haven't already seen otters in the coastal waters, take a look at them at the Kylerhea Otter Haven (daily dawn–dusk).

Fine restaurants and Scottish islands don't always go together, but Skye offers some excellent dining (▷ 367). At Carbost, the Talisker Distillery produces a fragrant, peaty single malt whisky (Nov–end Mar Mon–Fri 2–4.30; Apr–end Oct Mon–Sat 9.30–4.30).

Monuments to the great warriors at Stirling Castle

Threave Garden has stunning herbaceous borders

Traquair House has retained many of its original features

THE SIGHTS

STIRLING

442 E8 Royal Burgh of Stirling Visitor Centre, The Esplanade FK8 1EH, tel 01786 479901 Stirling www.stirling.co.uk

Stirling Castle's position high on a rocky outcrop has given it a prominent role in Scottish history. The castle, where Mary, Queen of Scots spent her childhood, served as a royal palace (Apr–end Sep daily 9.30–6; rest of year daily 9.30–5). Mary was crowned in the Chapel Royal in 1543. The town was of particular importance in the Wars of Independence fought against England. Notable Scottish victories include Stirling Bridge (1297), fought at the Old Bridge, when William Wallace (c1270–1305) cleverly split the opposing army, and Bannockburn (1314), when Robert the Bruce (1274–1329) took charge. Both men are commemorated as local heroes, Wallace with the National Wallace Monument on the hill of Abbey Craig (Nov–end Feb daily 10.30–4; Mar–end May and Oct daily 10–5; Jun daily 10–6; Jul–end Aug daily 9.30–6; Sep daily 9.30–5), and Bruce with a heritage centre on the field of Bannockburn, below the castle (Apr–end Oct daily 10–5.30; Feb–end Mar, Nov–end Dec daily 10.30–4).

THREAVE GARDEN AND ESTATE

438 E10 • Castle Douglas DG7 1RX 01556 502575 Garden and estate: daily, all year. Visitor centre and countryside centre: Mar–end Oct daily 9.30–5.30; Feb and Nov–end Dec daily 10–4. House: Mar–end Oct Wed–Fri and Sun, 11–3.30 (guided tours only, admission by timed ticket) Garden: adult £10, child (5–16) £8, family £20
www.nts.org.uk

Threave is an investment in the future. The National Trust for

Scotland has created a teaching garden, where horticulturalists come to learn and try out new ideas. It offers a mixture of established splendours such as a vast walled garden alongside less formal, more experimental areas. The garden was created during the Victorian era and Threave House dates from 1872.

TORRIDON

445 C5 Auchtercairn, Gairloch IV21 2DN, tel 01455 712130 (seasonal)

A spectacular wilderness of massive, bare mountains, Torridon, Scotland's first national nature reserve, lies on the northwest coast. The 1,000m (3,282ft) bulk of Beinn Eighe looms above the lonely pass between Shieldaig and Kinlochewe, shedding white quartzite scree like snow. To the west, Liathach (1,055m/3,460ft) is the tallest peak in the range, closely followed by Beinn Alligin (985m/ 3,232ft). The mountains are for serious walkers only, but there's a more accessible path along the north shore of Loch Torridon to Red Point. The National Trust for Scotland has a visitor centre by Torridon village (Easter–end Sep daily 10–6).

TRAQUAIR

443 F9 • Innerleithen EH44 6PW 01896 830323 Jun–end Aug daily 10.30–5; mid-Apr to end May and Sep daily 12–5; Oct daily 11–4 House and grounds: adult £5.80, child (5–14) £3.25, family £16.80
www.traquair.co.uk

An air of romance and secrecy surrounds Traquair, a beautiful old castle buried in the trees about 6 miles (10km) southeast of Peebles. It started out as a royal hunting lodge for King James III (1452–88), and at one point the River Tweed ran so

close that he could fish from his windows. In the 17th century, however, the river was re-routed by Sir William Stuart. The castle has been in the continuous ownership of the Maxwell Stuarts since 1491.

Traquair's sense of mystery comes from its connections with the doomed Stuart cause to take over the Scottish throne. Mary, Queen of Scots called by here in 1566, and the famous Bear Gates have not been opened since 1745, when Bonnie Prince Charlie last rode through. The fifth earl of the Maxwell Stuarts was incarcerated for helping him and promised that the gates would not be opened until a Stuart was on the throne.

The Traquair Brewery was successfully revived in 1965. Taste the results in the shop.

ULLAPOOL

445 D4 Argyle Street, Ullapool IV26 2UR, tel 01854 612135 Badentarbat to Summer Isles cruises, summer; ferry to Lewis www.ullapool.com

An 18th-century planned town, Ullapool may no longer be the hub of the North Atlantic fishing industry, but it is a good touring base. The road north leads into a sparsely populated country of peatbog and loch, heather moorland and bare, rocky mountains. This is the 11,000ha (27,000-acre) national nature reserve of Inverpolly, and the prominent lumps of rock are mountains of weathered, red Torridonian sandstone, of which the most accessible is Stac Pollaidh (612m/2,008ft). The area is rich in wildlife and there are sandy beaches at Achnahaird, Garvie, Reiff and Badentarbat. **Don't miss** Remote Achiltibuie, north of Ullapool. Reached via a winding, single-track road, it has views to the Summer Isles.

This chapter gives information on things to do in Britain other than sightseeing. Britain's best shops, arts venues, nightlife, activities and events are listed region by region.

What to Do

SHOPPING

With, by a considerable margin, the largest amount of retail space of any European country and a population of dedicated shoppers, Britain can meet most retail requirements. Beyond the cheap and cheerful mementoes–models of London buses, Union Jack T-shirts and the like–souvenir-hunting is a rewarding experience, with many distinctively British products on offer.

BRITISH SPECIALITIES

Tweed and tartan, both woven woollen cloths, are two famously Scottish textiles. Both have made a fashionable comeback on catwalks in recent years and are excellent purchases. The most highly regarded tweed is Harris tweed, which is handwoven by islanders on the Outer

Old Scottish families may have several clan tartans…

Hebrides. The Harris Tweed Authority (tel: 01851 702269, www.harristweed.com) preserves its authenticity. Tartan, or plaid, is actually a relatively recent invention, having first appeared at the start of the 18th century. By the end of the 18th century tartan became established as a means of identifying Scotland's clans and districts. There are many tartan patterns today; some are authentic, others are modern designs.

Clothes are another good purchase, if expensive. Men's tailors line Savile Row in London, where Prince Charles goes to have his suits made. Home-grown women's fashion

designers range from stalwarts Jasper Conran and Katharine Hamnett to new labels such as Clements Ribeiro, and Antoni and Alison. Less dressy clothing from Britain includes hardwearing Fair Isle woollen sweaters from the Shetland Islands, Barbour and Burberry jackets, and even Wellington boots from Hunter. Although functional rather than fashionable, prices can be high for these items; a Barbour jacket costs well over £100.

Since the late-18th century the potteries of Stoke-on-Trent have produced some of Britain's finest bone chinaware. Names at the heart of the industry include Wedgwood, founded by Josiah Wedgwood (1730–95), Josiah Spode (who founded the Spode factory in 1776) and Royal Doulton, which earned a royal warrant in 1901. Details of all the factory shops, which offer keen prices, and the visitor attraction Ceramica are available from Stoke-on-Trent's Tourist Information Centre; tel: 01782 236000, www.visitstoke.co.uk.

Also in the Midlands, Nottingham is renowned for lace, and the highlight of the city is the central Lace Market.

Britain is a great destination for book-lovers. Second-hand shops are found in most towns, but Hay-on-Wye has the highest concentration. The large chains–Waterstones, Borders and Ottakars, and the more academic Blackwell's–carry enormous ranges and can usually order titles within days.

Music (particularly CDs) is less of a bargain, with prices

comparing unfavourably to those in North America. However, again, it's hard to fault the sheer choice on offer. The big chains–HMV and Virgin–cover every genre and also sell videos, DVDs and books. Specialist shops, such as the record shops of Manchester's Northern Quarter, provide vinyl records

… these are just two of the countless designs

to DJs and keen collectors, who also congregrate at record fairs. Bootleg recordings, such as those sometimes sold at Camden Market, London, may disappoint.

DEPARTMENT STORES

Clothes, perfumes, jewellery, home furnishings and electrical goods are all typically found in department stores. And some of the best in the world are found in Britain. London boasts the greatest number, among them Harrods and Harvey Nichols in Knightsbridge, Selfridges and Liberty in the West End, and several branches of John Lewis. But most cities will have

at least one good department store—look out for branches of the John Lewis Partnership and House of Fraser—and shoppers no longer have to schlep to London to shop at the most fashionable. Harvey Nichols has opened shops in Leeds, Birmingham, Manchester and Edinburgh, while Selfridges now has branches in Birmingham and Manchester. Many stores allow you to shop over the internet.

MARKETS
Market squares were often the focal point of towns, and many towns still have a market once or twice a week. Expect to find fruit and vegetables, butcher's

Berwick Street in Soho has one of London's top markets

and fishmonger's stalls and household items. Prices are often lower than in shops, but haggling is not usual.

SHOPPING MALLS AND FACTORY OUTLETS
Britain has not escaped the shopping mall. These tend to have little to offer the visitor other than the convenience of finding the usual main street shops and brands under one roof, and lots of parking spaces. But factory outlets such as McArthurGlen and Bicester Village, which usually sell designer clothing at discounted prices, do attract bargain-hunters, including shoppers from other countries.

TAX-FREE SHOPPING
If the goods you buy are going to be exported to a non-EU country, you are exempt from Value Added Tax (VAT; currently 17.5 per cent), where it is applied. This can be a considerable saving (but you have to spend a minimum amount, which varies from shop to shop) and it is usually reclaimed at the airport on departure rather than deducted in the shop. Most major department stores participate and will have details of their tax-free shopping policies and help with your claim. For more information: tel: 020 8222 0101; www.globalrefund.com.

SALES
Twice a year, shops slash their prices in order to sell the previous season's remaining stock. The January sales see the best bargains, starting immediately after Christmas and continuing into February. Determined bargain-hunters camp out overnight in the streets in order to be first in

FARMERS' MARKETS
Evidence of Britain's renewed interest in good food can be found in many town squares and city streets at weekends. Farmers' markets differ from the usual local markets (often held mid-week) by selling produce direct from farmers. Prices are keen, and the produce, from homegrown fresh meat and vegetables to home-made breads and preserves, is good quality. For dates and locations contact: London Farmers' Markets (tel: 020 7704 9659; www.lfm.org.uk); National Association of Farmers' Markets (tel: 08454 588420; www.farmersmarkets.net); Scottish Association of Farmers' Markets (tel: 01478 640276; www.scottishfarmersmarkets.co.uk).

line when the sales open at Harrods (▷ 235) or Selfridges (▷ 235). Summer sales begin in June or July and last until the end of August.

HOURS
Core opening hours are from 9am to 5pm (with no break for lunch). In towns and cities, however, most shops stay open to at least 5.30pm or 6pm, and late opening, until 8pm, 9pm or 10pm, is common in busy areas, while supermarkets are likely to remain open into the night. Many shops will open for at least a few hours on Sundays.

Properly made pork pies are a traditional snack

SHOPPERS' RIGHTS
In Britain the Office of Fair Trading (www.oft.gov.uk) safeguards the rights of shoppers and encourages a fair and competitive market. Your statutory rights ensure that the goods you purchase are of 'satisfactory quality', 'fit for their purpose' and described accurately. You may be entitled to a refund if the goods don't meet these criteria; you must keep the receipt as proof of purchase.

THE LISTINGS
In our listings prices are subject to change. We have given the closest train station, if it is within 4 miles (6km) of the site.

With so many shops in Britain, it can be a time-consuming business finding one that sells exactly what you are looking for. This chart tells you what to expect in the most essential stores on Britain's main shopping streets. Call the head office to find your nearest branch. Many will sell goods online.

WHAT TO DO

NAME	Women's clothing and/or shoes	Men's clothing and/or shoes	Children's clothing and items	Pharmacy and toiletries	Jewellery and accessories	Souvenirs and gifts	Books, music and magazines	Sports and outdoor kit	Food and drink	Household and electrical goods	HEAD OFFICE
BHS	✔	✔	✔		✔	✔				✔	020 7262 3288
Blacks	✔	✔						✔			0800 056 0127
The Body Shop				✔	✔	✔					01903 731500
Boots		✔	✔	✔	✔	✔			✔	✔	0845 070 8090
Borders							✔				020 7379 7313
Clarks	✔	✔	✔								01458 443131
Crabtree & Evelyn				✔		✔			✔		01235 864824
Debenhams	✔	✔	✔	✔	✔	✔	✔	✔		✔	0844 561 6161
Dixons										✔	0870 333 1222
Dolcis	✔	✔	✔								01582 723131
Edinburgh Woollen Mills	✔	✔	✔		✔	✔					01387 380611
Evans	✔										0870 606 9666
Goldsmiths					✔	✔					0116 232 2000
H&M	✔	✔	✔								020 7323 2211
Habitat										✔	0870 411 5501
Harvey Nichols	✔	✔	✔	✔	✔			✔	✔	✔	0870 873 3833
HMV							✔				020 7432 2000
Holland & Barrett				✔					✔		02476 244400
House of Fraser	✔	✔	✔	✔	✔	✔		✔		✔	020 7963 2000
Jessops										✔	0116 232 6000
Jigsaw	✔										020 8392 5678
JJB	✔	✔	✔					✔			01942 210120
John Lewis	✔	✔	✔	✔	✔	✔	✔	✔		✔	0845 604 9049
Laura Ashley	✔		✔		✔					✔	0871 983 5999
Liberty	✔	✔	✔	✔	✔	✔				✔	020 7734 1234
Marks & Spencer	✔	✔	✔	✔	✔	✔			✔	✔	0845 302 1234
Monsoon	✔		✔		✔						020 7313 3000
Mothercare			✔	✔							0845 330 4030
Next	✔	✔	✔		✔					✔	0845 600 7000
Paperchase						✔					020 7467 6200
Past Times				✔	✔	✔			✔		0870 120 1939
Russell & Bromley	✔	✔	✔		✔						020 8460 1122
Selfridges	✔	✔	✔	✔	✔				✔	✔	08708 377 377
Thorntons						✔			✔		0800 454537
Topshop	✔		✔		✔						020 7636 8040
Virgin Megastores							✔				020 7299 0444
Wallis	✔										0845 121 4520
Waterstone's							✔				020 8742 3800
WH Smith							✔				0870 444 6444
Whittard of Chelsea						✔			✔		0800 015 4394
Woolworths	✔	✔	✔	✔	✔	✔	✔	✔	✔	✔	0845 608 1100

The Body Shop chain was started in 1976 by Anita Roddick with a few handmade products using natural ingredients and as little packaging as possible

NUMBER OF SHOPS	DESCRIPTION	SHOP WEBSITE
140	Mid-range clothing store with some household goods and lighting	www.bhs.co.uk
60	For outdoor equipment, clothing and camping gear	www.blacks.co.uk
1,700	Pioneering retailer of cosmetic products using natural, sustainable resources	www.thebodyshop.com
1,400	Chemists and opticians plus cosmetics, children's clothing and food	www.boots.com
20	Retailer of books, CDs and very wide range of magazines and papers	www.borders.co.uk
500	Retailer of shoes for men, women and children	www.clarks.co.uk
40	For luxurious toiletries and fragrances made from herb and flower essences	www.crabtree-evelyn.co.uk
125	Dependable department store retailing fashion brands and homeware	www.debenhams.com
380	Electrical goods from TVs and refrigerators to cameras and computers	www.dixons.co.uk
65	Retailer of shoes for men, women and children	www.alexon.co.uk
250	Fine woollen sweaters, accessories and other clothing	www.ewm.co.uk
300	Fashion retailer for the larger woman	www.evans.ltd.uk
160	Jewellery, clocks and watches	www.goldsmiths.co.uk
75	Bargain clothing store for women and children	www.hm.com
40	Design-led furniture and household goods for modern homes	www.habitat.net
5	High-end, trend-setting department stores for followers of fashion	www.harveynichols.com
165	Sells CDs in all genres of music and DVDs, videos and books	www.hmv.co.uk
500	Health foods, vitamin supplements and alternative remedies	www.hollandandbarrett.co.uk
50	Classy department store retailing fashion brands and homeware	www.houseoffraser.co.uk
240	Sells all kinds of photographic equipment and accessories, including digital	www.jessops.com
40	Smart clothes for young women	www.jigsaw-online.co.uk
450	Sportswear and shoes for men, women and children	www.jjb.co.uk
25	Reliable department store retailing fashion brands and homeware	www.johnlewis.co.uk
205	Upscale selection of famously floral women's clothing and home furnishings	www.lauraashley.com
3	Classy department store retailing fashion brands and homeware	www.liberty.co.uk
355	The mainstay of the middle classes, selling food, clothing and homeware	www.marksandspencer.com
400	Women and children's clothing, specializing in sleek party dresses	www.monsoon.co.uk
245	Baby and toddler clothes, toys and equipment	www.mothercare.com
295	Smart, practical clothing for men, women and children	www.next.co.uk
20	All sorts of things made from paper plus trendy stationery	www.paperchase.co.uk
80	Specializing in reproduction period home and giftware	www.past-times.com
35	High-quality, fashionable shoes, boots and bags	www.russellandbromley.co.uk
5	Smart, youthful department store retailing fashion brands and homeware	www.selfridges.co.uk
410	Sells own-brand chocolates and toffees	www.thorntons.co.uk
280	Economical clothing store with finger on fashion's pulse	www.topshop.co.uk
150	Sells CDs in all genres of music and DVDs, videos and books	www.virginmega.co.uk
252	Ladies' fashions	www.wallis-fashion.co.uk
200	Britain's biggest chain of bookstores with superb coverage in larger branches	www.waterstones.co.uk
550	Large shops sell countless magazines, stationery, even books and CDs	www.whsmith.co.uk
100	A mecca for tea and coffee drinkers, with many blends available	www.whittard.co.uk
810	Stores majoring on good-value clothing for children, music and homeware	www.woolworths.co.uk

ENTERTAINMENT

As cinema has grown in popularity, so intimate, bijou venues have made way for huge but somewhat soulless multiplexes showing the latest blockbusters. So-called 'high-brow' culture—theatre, opera, ballet—is steadily becoming less élitist and more affordable. However, good seats are not cheap and popular performances are booked up quickly, but mid-week performances are often good value.

Smoking is banned in venues such as cinemas and theatres (except in designated areas), but alcohol is sometimes served in independent cinemas, and theatres have bars and cafés or restaurants. At the theatre order your interval drinks in advance and avoid the mad scramble for the bars.

CINEMA

Every year the British film industry produces a minor hit or two and grabs a couple of Oscars, but never really challenges Hollywood. British cinemas are much the same:

It's easy to catch a world-famous show such as Riverdance

dominated by multiplexes but interspersed with interesting, independent picture houses such as the Cornerhouse in Manchester, the Watershed in Bristol and the Phoenix Picture House in Oxford. Usually tickets can be reserved in advance and collected on the door (a good idea with popular films), or you can just turn up and pay, but be prepared to wait.

CLASSICAL MUSIC, OPERA AND DANCE

Larger venues across London that can cater for the scale of classical music and dance performances—Barbican Hall, the South Bank Centre and the Royal Opera House—are

also home to national companies. Birmingham and Bournemouth also have excellent orchestras. Both the BBC National Orchestra of Wales (tel: 0800 052 1812; www.bbc.co.uk/wales/now) and Welsh National Opera (tel: 029 2063 5000; www.wno.org.uk) are based in Cardiff, while Glasgow is home to Scottish Opera (tel: 0141 248 4567; www.scottishopera.org.uk) and Scottish Ballet (tel: 0141 331 2931; www.scottishballet.co.uk). Multipurpose spaces, such as the Lowry in Manchester, host a range of performances. Tickets are available from:
• Bournemouth Symphony Orchestra–tel: 01202 670611; www.bsolive.com
• City of Birmingham Symphony Orchestra–www.cbso.co.uk
• English National Ballet–www.ballet.org.uk
• English National Opera–www.eno.org
• London Symphony Orchestra– tel: 020 7638 8891; www.lso.co.uk

CONTEMPORARY LIVE MUSIC AND COMEDY

Britain's rock and pop heritage has bequeathed a number of historic venues. Regardless, it's still easy to find a band raising the roof somewhere on a Saturday night. Larger venues, from Carling Academy Brixton in London to Glasgow's Barrowlands, host big-name bands, while smaller venues (including the back rooms of

pubs) book up-and-coming acts. Characterless stadiums such as Wembley Arena are the preserve of household names and pop acts. Harder to find are jazz, blues and world music clubs—Ronnie Scott's in

A huge range of music is on offer

London is probably the best-known venue.

Comedy clubs have become increasingly evident in cities; chains such as Jongleurs provide live acts most nights.

THEATRE

Britons are very keen theatre-goers, and theatres have an unparalleled supply of British drama to draw on—from William Shakespeare to adopted Irishman Oscar Wilde (1854–1900), and contemporary playwrights such as Harold Pinter (born 1930). Theatre-going is not the formal, dressy occasion it once was, but most of the audience make an effort to look smart.

Unsurprisingly, London has the greatest range of venues, with contemporary productions at the Donmar Warehouse, musicals in the West End and authentically staged Shakespearean plays at Shakespeare's Globe. Regional hotspots include the West Yorkshire Playhouse in Leeds, the Theatre Royal in Plymouth and Manchester's Royal Exchange. Bristol's Old Vic repertory group is highly rated, while the cliff-top Minack Theatre in Cornwall is a stunning venue.

The epicentre of Shakespearean drama is Stratford-upon-Avon, but an outdoor performance of *A Midsummer Night's Dream* by a local group on a summer evening somewhere is just as enjoyable.

One traditional festive genre is pantomime. A bawdy blend of fairytales, topicality, cross-dressing (a feature of Shakespeare's plays) and audience participation, it's an acquired taste, but popular with families at Christmas.

TICKETS

The easiest ways to buy tickets are from the venue's box office, direct from the performance company or through a ticket agency for larger events—a debit or credit card is useful, but an extra charge may be added. Agencies accredited by the Society of Ticket Agents and Retailers ensure that booking fees and terms and conditions are clearly identified. Major agencies include:

- First Call—tel: 0870 840 1111; www.firstcalltickets.com
- Keith Prowse— tel: 0870 842 2248; www.keithprowse.com/uk
- Ticketmaster— tel: 0870 150 0541; www.ticketmaster.co.uk

Note that the cheaper the ticket, the poorer your view will be. A £5 seat may be stuck at the back or behind a pillar, but spending more (up to £75 for theatre tickets) buys a better view.

Bright lights, big city: For nightclubs like Brighton's Ocean Rooms (above), head for Britain's cities

Going out: Clubbers in London

NIGHTLIFE

Time's up for the customary eleventh-hour downing of drinks as Britain relaxes its licensing laws and embraces European-style nightlife. In the past pubs were obliged to stop serving at 11pm—a time when citizens on the Continent would be getting ready for a night on the town—and bars and clubs had trouble securing licences to serve drinks after 2am. But today pubs can stay open all day and night (local council permitting). Despite this, many still keep to traditional hours, and may close between the lunchtime and evening sessions.

Britain's biggest cities, especially London, offer thrilling nightlife that compares with anything in Paris, New York or Sydney. Whether it's cutting-edge dance clubs or quieter bar-clubs for 30-something customers, it's not difficult to find somewhere in London, Brighton, Bristol, Birmingham, Cardiff, Leeds, Nottingham, Manchester, Glasgow or Edinburgh.

Elsewhere, the story can be less encouraging. University towns and cities, such as Oxford, Cambridge and York, often have an excellent choice of evening entertainment, but Friday and Saturday nights can also be exciting in many of the nondescript provincial towns.

- The legal age for buying and drinking alcohol is 18. Children are often allowed in certain areas of pubs up until around 9pm, but

children under 14 are not usually allowed in the bar area. Note, however, that children are by no means welcome in all pubs.

● Bars and clubs are generally for over-18s only, but some nights may be designated over-21s or over-25s.

PUBS

Pubs today differ from their predecessors in several respects. Unlike the male-dominated bastions of the past, most now encourage female customers and families. Pubs that are part of a chain, often with generic names such as The Slug and Lettuce, are especially welcoming. Some pubs

Most pubs offer a wide range of beers

provide non-smoking areas or even ban smoking completely. From summer 2007, smoking will be banned in all pubs, bars and clubs in England (▷ 407). Most pubs serve (sometimes very good) food plus coffee and tea. Free houses (independent pubs) offer the most interesting experience: As they are not tied to a large brewing group, they can stock local beers from small, specialist brewers. In the countryside, pubs are usually the only option for a night out.

BARS

The relaxation of its licensing laws is reflected in Britain's changing drinking habits. In

some areas bars are taking over from pubs and nightclubs as the focal points for socializing. During the day they resemble cafés, serving food and coffee, while at night they often become small nightclubs, complete with DJ and dance floor. Outdoor, European-style drinking is more widespread (weather permitting).

CLUBS

Most towns and cities will have at least one nightclub, but choose carefully. The options might be bewildering in some cities but small towns may have just one dingy venue, playing uninspiring chart music. Britain's cosmopolitan communities ensure that most musical preferences are represented: jazz, funk, soul, dub, rock, world, and even country and western.

But dance music's many strands dominate the club scene, and regions develop their own particular sounds: garage in London; techno in Birmingham; drum and bass in Bristol; big beat in Brighton; and house music in Liverpool and Manchester. A few superclubs survive, such as Fabric and the Ministry of Sound in London, but smaller, intimate clubs cultivate a more loyal clientele. Dress codes vary, so check before you set out. Most places accept smart-casual: no T-shirts, jeans or trainers. And beware that door staff can be decidedly fickle.

LISTINGS

Local listings magazines such as London's *Time Out* (www. timeout.com) are available from newsstands and tourist information offices. The London *Evening Standard*'s free weekly magazine *Metro Life* is another excellent source of information, as is the paper's website, www.thisislondon.co.uk. On Saturday *The Guardian* newspaper includes *The Guide*, a pocket-size weekly

listing of arts, entertainment and nightlife.

GAY AND LESBIAN SCENE

With openly gay politicians, policemen and pop stars, British society seems to have finally put its hang-ups about homosexuality behind it. A gay and lesbian scene that has existed discreetly for hundreds of years has never been so visible, with pubs, bars and clubs for every taste and a calendar of summer festivals and events.

London (particularly Old Compton Street in Soho), Brighton and Manchester have the most noticeable gay communities, although most

Manchester has one of Britain's liveliest gay and lesbian scenes

major cities will have gay venues if not districts. Outside these places, however, be wary of open displays of affection.

Regular gay publications include *Gay Times* (www. gaytimes.co.uk) and *Attitude*; *Diva* (www.divamag.co.uk) is for lesbians. They contain features and listings information and are available from most newsstands. Free papers *Pink Paper* (www.pinkpaper.com), *Boyz* (www.boyz.co.uk) and *QX* (www.qxmagazine.com) can be picked up in most venues.

Your best starting point is the London Lesbian and Gay Switchboard (tel: 020 7837 7324; www.llgs.org.uk).

SPORTS AND ACTIVITIES

It doesn't take long to realize that the British are mad about sport. After all, they invented and refined many of the world's main sports, including football (soccer), rugby, cricket, golf and boxing. The sports pages of national newspapers (particularly at the weekend), carry results of the major matches and preview forthcoming fixtures. The sport section of the BBC's website (www.bbc.co.uk) also has details of fixtures. Even small towns and villages will compete in local cricket and football leagues at weekends.

Whether it's on foot, on horseback, by bicycle or in a kayak, glider, balloon or boat, there is no better way of seeing the country than getting out in the fresh air; and Britons follow a huge range of organized pursuits.

ANGLING
Coarse and fly-fishing require a licence, which you can buy at post offices. Local tackle shops are good sources of information and equipment. Fly-fishing can be more expensive but tuition

Cricket: Ask a spectator for a brief explanation of the rules

is readily organized. Fishing boats from ports may also offer trips to visitors.

BALLOONING
Hot-air ballooning is a popular way of viewing the countryside. There are many operators in England, especially in rural areas and close to Bristol, where a major balloon festival is held in August. Tourist information centres list operators.

BEACHES
Britain is not short of coastline and has some spectacular beaches—if you know where to look. Europe's Blue Flag organization (www.blueflag.org) awards flags to beaches that

meet its strict standards of safety and cleanliness. There were 113 Blue Flag beaches in the UK in 2005, with high concentrations in Wales (such as St. David's) and in Devon (such as Woolacombe). But many fine beaches don't make the grade; the Marine Conservation Society's free *Good Beach Guide* (www.goodbeachguide.co.uk) recommends good beaches.

CLIMBING
The British Mountaineering Council (BMC) represents climbers, hillwalkers and mountaineers. It provides weather reports and has databases of clubs and locations.
● BMC–tel: 0870 010 4878; www.thebmc.co.uk

CRICKET
The Marylebone Cricket Club (MCC), based at London's Lord's cricket ground (www.lords.org), administers the 42 Laws of cricket.

Domestic fixtures are played between the 18 top English and Welsh county sides, over three or four days, while international Test cricket is a series of five-day matches between national teams. Test matches can sell out quickly, especially for fixtures against Australia. County games, although less passionate, are more accessible. The England Cricket Board (www.ecb.co.uk) lists fixtures and contact details for county clubs.

CYCLING
Most towns have cycle shops and rental facilities. Cities vary in cycle-friendliness: York has an exemplary network of cycle paths; cycling in London can be frightening. Cyclists are not

Those keen on a flutter will enjoy a day at the races

allowed on main 'A' roads and motorways (designated 'M'), and some of the smaller 'B' roads may have fast traffic, but country lanes are safe and scenic. Sustrans publishes *Cycling in the UK* (£14.95) and detailed maps. For details about travelling with a bicycle, ▷ 61.

FOOTBALL (SOCCER)
Football tops the table as the most popular spectator sport in England and Scotland, with most towns and cities fielding a team. England's Premier League of 20 teams—including Manchester United, Liverpool, Arsenal and Chelsea—has a worldwide audience and

largely avoids the financial problems afflicting some of Europe's other leagues.

The national season runs from August to the end of May, culminating in the FA Cup Final. Domestic leagues are governed by the Football Association (www.thefa.com) or the Scottish Football Association (www.scottishfa.co.uk). The FA lists fixtures, as do newspapers. Most matches take place on Saturday, but there are also Sunday and midweek games.

GOLF

The town of St. Andrews in Scotland is famous for being the 'home of golf'. Golf was

Scotland boasts more than 500 golf courses

first played on the Old Course in around 1400, and the sport remains accessible and inexpensive in Scotland. Visitor regulations at England's private clubs tend to be more complex; some require a letter of introduction or handicap certificate. Public courses are open to anyone.
● The Golfclub Great Britain– tel: 020 8390 3113; www.golfclubgb.co.uk

HERITAGE RAILWAYS

Steam engines run on about 30 restored, privately operated rail lines, and make an enjoyable, nostalgic experience. Information on heritage steam railways in the UK and

Ireland—including details of trains, operating days and events—is available from the Heritage Railway Association (www.heritagerailways.com). Five of the best steam train trips are: The Watercress Line in Hampshire (tel: 01962 733810; www.watercressline. co.uk); Keighley and Worth Valley Railway in Yorkshire's Brontë Country (tel: 01535 645214; www.kwvr.co.uk); Severn Valley Railway in the West Midlands (tel: 01299 403816; www.svr.co.uk); North Yorkshire Moors Railway (tel: 01751 472508; www. northyorkshiremoorsrailway. com); and Talyllyn Railway in North Wales (tel: 01654 710472; www.talyllyn.co.uk).

HORSE RACING

The British love a flutter (a small wager), and the country's bookies (betting shops) do good business on major races such as the Aintree Grand National. The flat-racing season runs from late March to early November, and National Hunt (over jumps) between August and late June. There are numerous racecourses around the country but book in advance for major meetings.

HORSEBACK RIDING

Horseback riders visiting Britain can look forward to an extensive choice of riding centres and some beautiful locations. Riders share bridleways and rights of ways with mountain bikers. The British Horse Society (www.bhs.org.uk) has a directory of riding holiday firms.

MOTOR RACING

Britain has a long history of motor racing, and is home to several Formula One teams, such as Williams and McLaren. The British Grand Prix takes place at Silverstone in Northamptonshire (tel: 08704 588290; www.silverstone-circuit.co.uk).

MOUNTAIN BIKING

Mountain biking is well established in Britain, and a series of purpose-built trails has been developed. Those in Wales managed by Mountain Biking Wales (www.mbwales.com) offer some of the best cycling in the world. Outside these hubs mountain bikers are permitted on bridleways (including long-distance paths), rights of way, but not footpaths.

RIVER SPORTS

Kayaks and canoes can be rented along several rivers and at lakes in Britain: Rivers in Wales and the Lake District are particularly good spots. Expect sedate conditions. Most rivers

Sailing on Errwood Reservoir in the Peak District

are privately owned and may be closed at certain times of the year.
● Punting—where the punter uses a long pole to propel a flat-bottomed boat—is a speciality of Oxford and Cambridge.
● British Canoe Union—tel: 0115 982 1100; www.bcu.org.uk

RUGBY

Britain's second winter sport is played between September and the end of May. In Wales rugby union—with 15 players per side—is the national sport, while the north of England is the base for rugby league, the 13-a-side variant.

Ticket and fixture information:
- Rugby Football Union, Twickenham, London: www.rfu.com
- Scottish Rugby Union, Murrayfield, Edinburgh: www.sru.org.uk
- Welsh Rugby Union, Millennium Stadium, Cardiff: www.wru.co.uk

SAILING
Many people sail yachts and dinghies at weekends. Local sailing clubs, marinas and specialist agencies offer yacht charter (with or without a skipper) and dinghy rental.
- Royal Yacht Association–tel: 0845 3450 400; www.rya.org.uk

SCUBA DIVING
The British Sub-Aqua Club (BSAC) has more than 1,600 branches nationwide. Since visibility and currents change during the year local advice is essential. Dives on the coast's plentiful wrecks should be attempted only with guidance.
- BSAC–tel: 0151 350 6200; www.bsac.com

SNOWSPORTS
Each winter, snowfall in the Cairngorms draws some optimistic skiers to Aviemore in Scotland, the country's most developed ski resort.

SURFING AND WINDSURFING
The Pembrokeshire coast and the beaches of Cornwall, Devon and Dorset are some of the best surf spots in Britain. Wetsuits are essential, but all equipment can be rented from surfing bases. Windsurfers have more choice, with excellent coastal stretches and inland reservoirs. Contact the British Surfing Association (BSA) for information and weather reports. The Royal Yachting Association (see Sailing) represents windsurfers.
- BSA–tel: 01637 876474; www.britsurf.co.uk

TENNIS
The annual Grand Slam tennis tournament at Wimbledon causes queues along the streets of the London suburb. Most tickets are sold in advance; a few are reserved for sale on the day, but turn up very early. Many players warm up for Wimbledon at the Stella Artois tournament at Queen's Club in West Kensington, London.
- Lawn Tennis Association: www.lta.org.uk

WALKING
Britain's vast web of footpaths is rigorously maintained. Upland areas rarely top 900m (3,000ft), but weather conditions can deteriorate rapidly. Take a compass, some food and water and a waterproof jacket; and tell someone where you are going.
- Ramblers' Association–tel: 020 7339 8500; www.ramblers.org.uk

HEALTH AND BEAUTY

A revival of spa culture has swept the country in recent years, and professionally run spas are now found across Britain.

The original spa towns of Harrogate and Bath, which have had spas since the Romans visited, have renovated their historic facilities. They are open to the public (Bath's spa is due to open in 2006) for complementary therapies or just relaxing by the pools. There are 10 other spa towns in Britain, including Cheltenham, Malvern and Llandrindod Wells, although they don't yet have comparable projects. It is also rare for a smart hotel not to offer some beauty treatments–many have full spas with pools and massages.
- Spa Business Association– tel: 01225 758214; www. spabusinessassociation.co.uk

FOR CHILDREN

You don't have to go far to find somewhere to amuse children for a day. The range of options is enormous, from first-class zoos and other wildlife attractions to heritage steam railways, and from child-oriented museums to fun-packed water parks.

The premier theme parks include large, very popular places such as Alton Towers (▷ 149) and Legoland Windsor (▷ 232). Family tickets are always available, but costs can accumulate. The old dictum that 'children should be seen and not heard' no longer applies and most attractions offer reduced-price tickets, children's menus and other facilities. Look out for special offers (such as two-for-one tickets) during school holidays that may be advertised in newspapers or tourist offices.

FESTIVALS AND EVENTS

If you want to catch a special event, major or minor, you'll be spoiled for choice. Sporting, cultural, religious or traditional, every month is packed with dates for the diary. A select number of them form 'The Season'—an eclectic variety of fashionable occasions that are notable social gatherings rather than just events. These include the opera festivals held at Glyndebourne and Garsington, and the Royal Academy Summer Exhibition. As the socialite's handbook *Debrett's* notes, knowing what to wear and where to sit is as much of a minefield as acquiring the right tickets. In the past The Season was an opportunity for the upper classes and upwardly mobile to meet, quaff champagne and catch up on the progress of old school chums. Increasingly today it is an excuse for the business classes to meet, quaff champagne and catch up on the progress of old clients.

ARTS AND CULTURE

There are more than 100 major arts and cultural festivals a year, all listed by the British Arts Festivals Association. In Wales the most important annual festival is the Royal National Eisteddfod, a celebration of Welsh song, theatre and language in August. In the same month Scotland's showpiece, the Edinburgh Festival, takes place. Perhaps the best, and certainly the largest, example of British multiculturalism is the Notting Hill Carnival in London around the public holiday at the end of August. There are music festivals for every taste, from the rock and alternative vibes of Glastonbury (June) to the rarefied opera festivals of Glyndebourne and Garsington, for which tickets are almost impossible to acquire. Other 'Season' arts events are more accessible: the Royal Academy's Summer Exhibition and the Last Night of the Proms at the Royal Albert Hall (both in London) for lovers of pomp and ceremony, and the Hay-on-Wye Literary Festival.

- British Arts Festivals Association– tel: 020 7247 4667; www.artsfestivals.co.uk

SPORT

April is a busy month for sporting occasions. The Flora London Marathon—probably the biggest mass-participation sports event in the country

with almost 50,000 runners— is preceded by the world's top steeplechase, the Grand National at Aintree. The annual Varsity Boat Race—a 150-year-old race between coxed rowing eights from the universities of Oxford and Cambridge—is curiously compelling, and thousands of spectators crowd the banks of the Thames between Putney Bridge and Mortlake for this free event. The 149th race in 2003 saw Oxford win by the closest ever margin: just 30.5cm (12in).

There's less stuffiness at the FA Cup Final that marks the end of the English and Welsh domestic footballing season in May, but just as much flag-waving as at the Proms. Tickets, however, are practically impossible to get. For a grandstand view and little of the hassle, reserve your place in front of a large-screen TV at any number of pubs and bars, but choose your venue carefully, as some are extremely partisan while others may be more 'neutral'. North of the border the Scottish equivalent is equally anticipated.

The end of the football season heralds the start of the 'summer' cricket matches. However, with the first games in mid-April, the weather is usually still decidedly chilly, so it's a good idea to wrap up warm and bring an umbrella. Sporting events of The Season include the two-week

Wimbledon Tennis Championship, with ample television coverage; Cowes Week, a yachting jamboree on the Isle of Wight; and Glorious Goodwood, a race meeting at Britain's most scenic race-course, in West Sussex.

TRADITIONAL EVENTS

Summer brings village fetes and agricultural shows to rural areas, while in London the Queen's (official) birthday is celebrated with the Trooping the Colour pageant in June. But the most uniquely British event takes place in the autumn: Guy Fawkes (or Bonfire) Night. Having failed to blow up the Houses of Parliament in the Gunpowder Plot of 1605, Guy Fawkes was hung, drawn and quartered. Effigies of Guy Fawkes are often burned on bonfires across England on 5 November (or the weekend nearest that day) and fireworks mark the event.

In the depths of winter (25 January) the Scots celebrate their national poet Robert Burns (1759–96), while in Wales the main festival is St. David's Day, on 1 March.

- Local tourist offices have detailed events calendars or check in advance at www.visitbritain.com
- www.whatsonwhen.com allows you to search for events by category.

WHAT TO DO

THE WEST COUNTRY

Beyond its beaches, the southwest of England has much to offer. Bristol is the main metropolitan centre, while Bath and Bournemouth also provide good opportunities for shopping and entertainment. Outdoor activities are a major draw, especially sailing, surfing, diving and fishing—unsurprising, perhaps, with so much beautiful coastline.

KEY TO SYMBOLS	
⊞	Shopping
☺	Entertainment
☮	Nightlife
☾	Sports
✪	Activities
♡	Health and Beauty
✿	For Children

SHOPPING

Many local specialities are edible or drinkable: fudge, clotted cream, Cornish pasties and cider (scrumpy is the non-sparkling variety). They may not be the sort of items that travel well, but are definitely worth trying. Popular with painters since the 1880s, St. Ives is still a base for many artists, who offer their work for sale. But Bath has the region's most rewarding and diverse selection of shops.

PERFORMANCE AND NIGHTLIFE

Bournemouth has a highly regarded professional symphony orchestra, while Bristol enjoys an above-average number of jazz gigs. The best theatrical productions are often staged at Bristol's Old Vic, Bath's Theatre Royal and the Minack Theatre, a stunning open-air venue on a clifftop at Porthcurno, near Penzance, in Cornwall.

Although the West Country lacks the metropolitan diversity of other parts of England, it has a strong array of clubbing venues. Bournemouth's huge nightclubs pull in the crowds, while Bristol's distinct musical identity—influenced by the city's Afro-Caribbean communities—has spawned artists such as Massive Attack and Tricky. It also has many fashionable bars. For listings in Bristol and Bath check out the fortnightly *Venue* magazine, available from tourist offices.

SPORTS, ACTIVITIES AND FESTIVALS

Watersports are the big draw in the southwest. Devon and Cornwall have a number of prime surf spots, with Newquay, on Cornwall's north coast, hosting international surfing competitions at Fistral Beach. The waters of Cornwall and the Isles of Scilly are good for snorkelling and scuba diving, but currents can be treacherous in places. Sailing is popular around Falmouth, Poole and Salcombe. Fishing has provided a living for many towns and villages, which now offer fishing trips for visitors. Fossil hunters head to the cliffs and coves of Dorset (especially near Lyme Regis), as do cavers and climbers. And there are several multi-activity centres in the region. Walkers can tackle sections of Britain's longest national trail, the South West Coast Path. For spectators, local cricket and rugby teams enjoy a higher profile than the region's football teams. The events calendar includes fairs, music events such as the Glastonbury Festival and quirky traditions, including the dramatic Burning Barrels festival in Ottery St. Mary.

BABBACOMBE DOWNS

🎭 BABBACOMBE THEATRE
Cary Point, Babbacombe Downs, Torquay TQ1 3LU
Tel: 01803 328385
www.babbacombe-theatre.com
This is a place to visit for old-fashioned seaside variety shows and comedy, as well as drama productions.
🎫 Box office: mid-Feb to end Dec Fri–Mon 10–5, Tue–Thu 10–9 (5 when no performance) 🎟 Adult £13, child (under 16) £7 📦 🚇 Torquay

BARNSTAPLE

⭐ THE TARKA TRAIL
The Stone Barn, Fremington Quay, Barnstaple EX31 2NH
Tel: 01271 372586
www.biketrail.co.uk
Try the 180-mile (290km) Tarka Trail, through the area described in author Henry Williamson's 1927 book *Tarka the Otter*. Bicycles can be hired from three Biketrail shops along the route. You need National Cycle Network Map No.27. See Sustrans, ▷ 61.
🎟 Bicycle rental from £6.50 per half day (£9.50 per day) 📦 Fremington Quay Heritage Centre 🚇 Barnstaple

BATH

🏛 CAROLINE NEVILL MINIATURES
22A Broad Street, Bath BA1 5LN
Tel: 01225 443091
A leading supplier of dolls' houses and miniature furniture. The range includes Tudor, Regency and Victorian styles, as well as more contemporary designs. The tiny contents, including furniture, books, paintings and silver-ware, are exquisitely crafted.
🎫 Mon–Sat 10.30–5 🚇 Bath Spa

🏛 GEORGE BAYNTUN
Manvers Street, Bath BA1 1JW
Tel: 01225 466000
www.georgebayntun.com
A bookshop engaged in buying, selling, binding and restoring old and rare books since 1829. Specializes in English literature, particularly classics and modern first

editions, plus antique prints (including views of Bath). The shop has retained much of its 19th-century character.
🎫 Mon–Fri 9–1, 2–5.30, Sat 9.30–1 🚇 Bath Spa

🏛 THE GLASS HOUSE
1–2 Orange Grove, Bath BA1 1LP
Tel: 01225 311183
www.realshoppinguk.com
Decorative glass in many forms, including jewellery and stained glass. Also on sale are Bath Aqua Glass, a hand-blown and attractively tinted glass (inspired by Roman and Georgian glass), Bristol Blue Glass, made since the 1780s, and lesser-known

Beautiful decorative art at the Glass House in Bath

Exmoor Cranberry Glass from Porlock Weir in Somerset.
🎫 Mon–Sat 9.30–6, Sun 12–6 🚇 Bath Spa

🏛 GUILDHALL MARKET
High Street, Bath BA2 4AW
Tel: 01225 477945
A traditional market experience in an 18th-century building—a market has existed on this site since its Royal Charter of 1284. The huge range of items includes antique and modern jewellery, rugs, food, electrical supplies, tools and old-fashioned sweets (candy).
🎫 Mon–Sat (also Sun in Dec) 9–5 (times for individual traders vary)
📦 🚇 Bath Spa

🎭 THEATRE ROYAL BATH
Sawclose, Bath BA1 1ET
Tel: 01225 448844
www.theatreroyal.org.uk
Opened in 1805, and steeped in history, with drama, opera, ballet; plus fringe productions and jazz in the Ustinov Studio.
🎫 Box office: Mon–Sat 10–8, Sun and public holidays 12–8
🎟 £10–£30, 40 standby tickets costing £5 available from 12 on day of performance
🍴 🚻 🚇 Bath Spa

🍷 WOODS
9–13 Alfred Street, Bath BA1 2QX
Tel: 01225 314812
Stylish bar in a Georgian building. Popular with visiting actors and a glitzy crowd.
🎫 Closed Sun evening
🚇 Bath Spa

♨ THERMAE BATH SPA
Hetling Pump Room, Hot Bath Street, Bath BA1 1SJ
Tel: reservations: 01225 331234
www.thermaebathspa.com
Due to open some time in 2006, this spa draws on natural thermal springs. Bathers can enjoy an open-air roof-top pool, steam rooms, massage and treatments.
🎫 Daily 9am–10pm (last entry 8pm)
🎟 Two hours £19, 4 hours £29, all day £45 (not including treatments) 🍴 📦
🏛 🚇 Bath Spa

BISHOPS LYDEARD

♨ CEDAR FALLS
Bishops Lydeard, Taunton TA4 3HR
Tel: 01823 433233
www.cedar-falls.co.uk
Health farm offering short breaks, treatments and alternative therapies plus a golf course, tennis courts and outdoor pool.
🎫 Call for details 🎟 Full day from £79; individual treatments from £9.50 🍴 🚻

BOURNEMOUTH

🎭 BOURNEMOUTH INTERNATIONAL CENTRE (BIC)
Exeter Road, Bournemouth BH2 5BH
Tel: 01202 456400; box office: 08701 113000
www.bic.co.uk
Arts and leisure complex hosting theatre, music and even wrestling. Concerts by the Bournemouth Symphony Orchestra.
🕐 Box office: daily 10–5.30 (or until 30 min after performance starts). By phone: Mon–Sat 9.30–9, Sun 9.30–5 (9 if there is a show) 🎫 Various 🍴 🎧 🚉 Bournemouth

🎭 THE OPERA HOUSE
570 Christchurch Road, Boscombe, Bournemouth BH1 4BH
Tel: 01202 399922, information: 08708 301414
www.operahouse.co.uk
The club that gave the south coast's clubbers an alternative to Brighton, where guest and resident DJs play house and trance.
🕐 Thu–Sat 9pm–3am 🎫 £3–£10 🚉 Bournemouth

BRISTOL

🌿 ARNE HERBS
Limeburn Nurseries, Limeburn Hill, Chew Magna, Bristol BS40 8QW
Tel: 01275 333399
www.arneherbs.co.uk
Herbs, both rare and household but all pesticide-free, are sold at Anthony Lyman-Dixon's nurseries.
🕐 Daily 10–4

🛍 BROADMEAD
Broadmead Shopping Centre, Bristol BS1 3DX
Tel: 0117 925 7053
www.bristolbroadmead.co.uk
One of the region's leading shopping districts. Department stores, major chains and specialist shops, some concentrated in the Mall Galleries Shopping Centre. There is also a range of markets.
🕐 Mon–Sat 9–6 (8 Thu), Sun 11–5; individual stores may differ 🍴 🎧 🚉 Bristol Temple Meads

🛍 ST. NICHOLAS MARKET
Corn Exchange, Bristol BS1 1JQ
Tel: 0117 922 4017
The antithesis of Bristol's modern shopping areas, this 18th-century open-air and covered market has been the traditional focal point for shopping in the city since 1743. Antiques, organic fruit and vegetables, and exotic delicacies. Great for olives and local honey, second-hand books and trendy clothing (modern fashion and retro).
🕐 Mon–Sat 9.30–5 (also Sun 11–4, Dec) 🍴 🎧 🚉 Bristol Temple Meads

Broadmead in Bristol: a magnet for shopaholics

🎭 BRISTOL OLD VIC
King Street, Bristol BS1 4ED
Tel: 0117 987 7877
www.bristol-old-vic.co.uk
This is Britain's oldest working theatre, as well as one of Britain's top companies. Also houses the New Vic Studio.
🕐 Box office: Mon–Sat 10–8 (Wed 10.30–8) 🎫 Adult £5–£22, child (under 19) £5–£19 🍴 🎧 🚉 Bristol Temple Meads

🎵 COLSTON HALL
Colston Street, Bristol BS1 5AR
Tel: 0117 922 3682; bookings: 0117 922 3686
www.bristol-city.gov.uk/colstonhall
Concert hall presenting major artists in pop music, classical

music and opera, and stand-up comedy. Reservations advised.
🕐 Mon–Sat 10–8.30 (Sun from 5pm if performance) 🎫 Various 🎧 🎵 🚉 Bristol Temple Meads

🎬 IMAX THEATRE@BRISTOL
Anchor Road, Harbourside, Bristol BS1 5DB
Tel: 0845 3451235
www.at-bristol.org.uk/imax
3D movies shown every 75 minutes on the IMAX screen.
🕐 Mon–Fri 11.15–4.30, Sat–Sun 12.30–6 🎫 Adult £6.50–£7.50, child (3–15) £4.50–£5.50, family £19–£22 🍴 🚉 Bristol Temple Meads

🎵 THE OLD DUKE
45 King Street, Bristol BS1 4ER
Tel: 0117 927 7137
Said to be the oldest-established jazz venue in the country. Live music every night, including trad, blues and jazz funk. Three-day jazz festival over August public holiday.
🕐 Daily 11–11 🚉 Bristol Temple Meads

🏏 GLOUCESTERSHIRE COUNTY CRICKET CLUB
County Ground, Nevil Road, Bishopston, Bristol BS7 9EJ
Tel: 0117 910 8000; box office 0117 910 8010
www.glosccc.co.uk
There's an Edwardian pavilion at this tree-fringed cricket club.
🕐 Box office: Apr–end Sep Mon–Fri 9.30–4 🎫 Adult £12–£15, child (5–15) £6 £7 🍴 🎧 🚉 Bristol Temple Meads (2 miles/3km)

BURTON BRADSTOCK

🪂 FLYING FRENZY
1 Mill Terrace, Burton Bradstock, Bridport DT6 9PW
Tel: 01308 897909
www.flyingfrenzy.com
Paragliding over Dorset, with taster days that guarantee solo flying, and four-day courses.
🕐 All year (subject to weather). Advisable to reserve at least one month in advance 🎫 Taster day £110 (second person flies half price). Includes equipment 🎧

CHEDDAR GORGE

🌐 CHEDDAR GORGE CHEESE COMPANY

The Cliffs, Cheddar Gorge BS27 3QA
Tel: 01934 742810
www.cheddargorgecheeseco.co.uk
This is more than a shop selling cheese; watch many varieties of Cheddar cheese being made and taste them.
🕐 Mid-Jul to end Aug daily 10–6; Apr to mid-Jul and Sep–end Oct daily 10–5; rest of year daily 10–4.30 💷 Adults £1.75, children free 🍴

CHELTENHAM

🌐 THE COURTYARD

Montpellier Street, Cheltenham GL50 1SR
Tel: 01242 519707
www.visitcheltenham.gov.uk
Escape the chain stores on two levels of chic boutiques and specialist shops around a sunken piazza and elevated walkway.
🕐 Generally Mon–Sat 9–5.30 💻 🍴
🚉 Cheltenham Spa

🎭 EVERYMAN THEATRE

Regent Street, Cheltenham GL50 1HQ
Tel: 01242 572573
An attractive and decorative venue staging drama, musicals, opera and ballet. Also runs a large educational department with numerous workshops.
🕐 Box office: Mon–Sat 9.30–8.30 (6 in Aug), Sun from 2 hours before a performance 💷 £10–£25 🍴 💻
🚉 Cheltenham

🎠 CHELTENHAM RACECOURSE

Prestbury Park, Cheltenham GL50 4SH
Tel: 01242 537642 (24 hours)
www.cheltenham.co.uk
Home of National Hunt racing. The annual highlight is March's The Festival and the Cheltenham Gold Cup race. Reserve tickets in advance.
🕐 16 meetings Oct–end May; call for dates. Advance reservations required for special events
💷 £6–£30 🍴 💻 🚉 Cheltenham Spa

CIRENCESTER

⭐ COTSWOLD WATER PARK

Keynes Country Park, Spratsgate Lane, Shorncote, Cirencester GL7 6DF
Tel: 01285 861459
www.waterpark.org
Britain's largest lakeland park with 133 lakes for watersports. Equipment can be rented.
🕐 Open access 💷 Free admission to park, but individual charges for activities
💻 🚉

EAST PORTLEMOUTH

⭐ SALCOMBE DINGHY SAILING

3 Cross Lane Cottages, East Portlemouth, Salcombe TQ8 8PB
Tel: 01548 842786
www.salcombedinghysailing.co.uk

Where better to sample cheddar than Cheddar Gorge?

Sail in the sheltered estuary, with tuition available. Choose from a 90-minute, half-day or full-day sail. Boat rental.
🕐 Daily 10–5.15; reserve in advance
💷 Individual tuition: £42 single session, £75 half day, £110 full day; rental from £45

EXETER

🎭 EXETER PHOENIX

Bradninch Place, Gandy Street, Exeter EX4 3LS
Tel: 01392 667080
www.exeterphoenix.org.uk
An impressive cultural centre offering exhibitions, art-house films, music gigs and workshops.

🕐 Box office: Mon–Sat 10–8
💷 £4.50–£16 💻 🚉
🚉 Exeter Central

🎭 NORTHCOTT THEATRE

Stocker Road, Exeter EX4 4QB
Tel: 01392 493493
www.northcott-theatre.co.uk
Unusual because it has its own in-house professional theatre company, it also stages touring shows, opera and ballet.
🕐 Box office: Mon–Sat 10–8 (6 on non-performance days) 💷 £11–£16
💻 🚉 🚉 Exeter Central

🍷 COOLINGS WINE BAR

11 Gandy Street, Exeter EX4 3LS
Tel: 01392 434184
Situated on medieval Gandy Street, this is a popular place to enjoy a drink.
🕐 Daily 10am–11pm 🚉 Exeter Central

FALMOUTH

🌐 DUCHY OF CORNWALL OYSTER FARM

Port Navas, Falmouth TR11 5RJ
Tel: 01326 340210
Native and Pacific oysters are supplied to top restaurants from these beds in the Percuil and Helford rivers. The oysters together with mussels and smoked salmon are also sold on site—bring your own bread, lemon and white wine.
🕐 Mon–Fri 8–4, Sat 8–12
🚉 Penmere (4 miles/6.5km)

🎭 FALMOUTH ARTS CENTRE

Church Street, Falmouth TR11 3EG
Tel: 01326 212300
www.falmoutharts.org
A 200-seat theatre and cinema, and four exhibition galleries with a wide-ranging remit: lunchtime recitals, talks, music, dance and drama.
🕐 Box office: Mon–Sat 10–2 (and for 30 min before evening performance)
💷 Various 💻 🚉 Falmouth

GLOUCESTER

🌐 GLOUCESTER ANTIQUE CENTRE

1 Severn Road, Gloucester GL1 2LE
Tel: 01452 529716
Britain's largest provincial antiques market in a converted

Victorian warehouse in the revamped historic dockland area of the city, and with 140 dealers represented.

🕐 Mon–Sat 10–5, Sun 1–5 🎫 Free (50p weekends) 🚗 🚂 Gloucester

⊕ HOUSE OF THE TAILOR OF GLOUCESTER

9 College Court, Gloucester GL1 2NI
Tel: 01452 422856
www.beatrixpottersociety.org.uk

A tiny shop and the location of *The Tailor of Gloucester*, which Beatrix Potter sketched while visiting the city. Books, toys and ornaments, plus merchandise from other children's classics such as *Winnie the Pooh*. Small museum.

🕐 Apr–end Oct Mon–Sat 10–5, rest of year Mon–Sat 10–4 🎫 Shop: free. Museum: adult £1, children free
🚂 Gloucester

🏉 GLOUCESTER RFC

Kingsholm Road, Gloucester GL1 3AX
Tel: 08718 718781; tickets: 08717 211865
www.gloucesterrugbyclub.com

Home to a leading rugby union club, Gloucester's Kingsholm is a notoriously raucous ground.

🕐 Sep–end May 🎫 Adults £18–£32, child (under 16) £9–£11 🚗
🚂 Gloucester

GREAT TORRINGTON

⊕ DARTINGTON CRYSTAL

Great Torrington EX38 7AN
Tel: 01805 626242
www.dartington.co.uk

Known worldwide for its fine crystal. Visitors centre, factory tours, factory seconds shop, plus bargains from other brands such as Denby and Portmeirion pottery and knitwear from the Edinburgh Woollen Mill.

🕐 Mon–Fri 9–5 (shop from 9.30), Sat 10–5, Sun 10–4. Tours: Mon–Fri only. 🎫 Shop: free. Tour: adult £5, child (under 16) free. Visitors centre: adult £2, child (under 16) free 🍴

HAYLE

✪ SHORE SURF SCHOOL

46 Mount Pleasant, St. Ives Bay, Hayle TR27 4LE
Tel: 01736 755556
www.shoresurf.com

A safe introduction to surfing at beaches in the St. Ives Bay area. Lessons for all abilities and age groups (over-8s).

🕐 Daily 10.15–12.45, 2.15–4.45
🎫 Half-day £20, full day £35. Equipment included

HELSTON

⊕ THE LIZARD PASTY SHOP

Beacon Terrace, The Lizard, Helston TR12 7PB
Tel: 01326 290889
www.connections.co.uk/lizardpastyshop

Children will love the House of the Tailor of Gloucester

Ann Muller's small shop sells arguably some of Cornwall's finest pasties. They are hand-made with local ingredients and make a good snack on a trip to the Lizard.

🕐 Mon–Sat 9.30–2.30

✪ THE FLAMBARDS EXPERIENCE

Clodgey Lane, Helston TR13 0QA
Tel: 01326 573404;
recorded information: 08456 018684 (24 hours)
www.flambards.co.uk

Several all-weather attractions: a re-created Victorian village, a life-size street during the World War II Blitz, a Science Centre and rides.

🕐 Late Mar to mid-Apr and Jun–late Jul daily 10–5; mid-Apr to end May and Sep–end Oct daily 10.30–5; late Jul–end Aug daily 10–5.30; rest of year Tue–Thu and Sat–Sun 11–4 🎫 Adult £4.95–£11.50, child (5–14) £3.95–£9.25, family £29.55–£56.40. Return within a month: £5.50 (£2.25, Nov–Easter) 🍴
🚗 🏛

LAUNCESTON

ⓨ JAMAICA INN

Bolventor, near Launceston PL15 7TS
Tel: 01566 86250
www.jamaicainn.co.uk

A coaching inn immortalized by Daphne du Maurier, who stayed here in 1930. The setting, legends and atmosphere of Bodmin Moor inspired her novel *Jamaica Inn* (1936). The Smugglers Museum features smuggling memorabilia and contains The Daphne du Maurier room.

🕐 Daily 11–11. Museum: Easter–end Oct daily 10–5; Nov–Dec and Feb–Easter daily 11–4 🎫 Museum: adult £3.50, child (4–16), family £8.95

LISKEARD

⊕ TRAGO MILLS

Two Waters Foot, Liskeard PL14 6HY
Tel: 01579 348877
www.trago.co.uk

A regional institution, selling thousands of cut-price items from DIY goods to Oriental carpets, all displayed in warehouses. Lower end of the market. Also in Falmouth and Newton Abbott.

🕐 Mon–Sat 9–5.30, Sun 10–4 (viewing from 9.30). Extra 30 min shopping before closing 🚗 🚂 Liskeard

LOSTWITHIEL

⊕ HAYE FARM CIDER

Haye Farm, St. Veep, Lerryn, Lostwithiel PL22 0PB
Tel: 01208 872250

Haye Farm's orchards have been producing traditional Cornish cider since 1200.

🕐 Daily 8–late

WHAT TO DO

NEWQUAY

✪ NATIONAL SURFING CENTRE
Fistral Beach, Newquay TR7 1HW
Tel: 01637 850737
www.nationalsurfingcentre.co.uk
The British Surfing Association holds major surfing championships at their facility on Fistral Beach. Tuition for all levels for ages eight upwards, from half-days to one-week courses.
🕐 Easter–end Oct daily 10.30–1 and 2.30–5; advance reservation recommended 💷 From half a day: £25. Price includes equipment
🚉 Newquay

NEWTON ABBOT

✪ SHILSTONE ROCKS RIDING AND TREKKING CENTRE
Widecombe-in-the-Moor, Newton Abbot TQ13 7TF
Tel: 01364 621281
www.dartmoorstables.com
Half- and full-day escorted rides or treks over Dartmoor on well-trained horses. Hard hats provided.
🕐 Treks at 10 and 2 💷 £25 for 1 hour

PAIGNTON

✪ QUAYWEST WATERPARK
Goodrington Sands, Paignton TQ4 6LN
Tel: 01803 555550
www.quaywest.co.uk
Eight flumes and slides—including the Devil Drop, a 20m (66ft) free fall. Inner tubes, mats supplied.
🕐 Late May–early Sep daily 10–6
💷 All-day ticket: adult £8.95, child (under 13 years) £7.95, child (under 3ft 6in/1.06m) £3.50, family £31 🍴 ▢
🚉 Paignton

PENQUIT

✪ SOUTH WEST COAST PATH
The South West Coast Path Association, Windlestraw, Penquit, Ermington PL21 0LU
Tel: 01752 896237
www.swcp.org.uk
At 630 miles (1,020km), Britain's longest national trail curls round Devon, Cornwall and most of Dorset and Somerset. Highlights are the Iron Coast from Hartland Point in Devon to Bude; the Granite Coast at Land's End; and the stretch around Devon's South Hams. Maps available from local tourist information offices.

PENRYN

⊕ CORNISH CUISINE
The Smokehouse, Islington Wharf, Penryn TR10 8AT
Tel: 01326 376244
www.smokedsalmon-ltd.com
An appetizing selection of smoked Cornish produce: local organic cheeses, hand-lined mackerel and game.
🕐 Mon–Fri 9–4.30
🚉 Penryn

Newquay is a major surfing centre

⊕ MENALLACK CORNISH FARMHOUSE CHEESES
Menallack Farm, Treverva, Penryn TR10 9BP
Tel: 01326 340333
A must for cheese aficionados, Menallack uses unpasteurized milk from local animals to handmake 19 specialist cheeses. All 49 varieties of Cornish cheese are sold in the shop.
🕐 Mon–Fri 9–5, Sat 9–12.30
🚉 Penry

PLYMOUTH

⊕ BARBICAN GLASSWORKS
The Old Fishmarket, The Barbican, Plymouth PL1 2LT
Tel: 01752 224777
www.dartington.co.uk
A former Victorian fish market refurbished as a shop and glassblowing studio. Many top names in glass and pottery, including Dartington Crystal, Wedgwood China and Waterford Crystal. Also candles, woodcarvings, nautical gifts, jewellery and speciality foods.
🚉 Plymouth

▽ MOUNT BATTEN BAR
Lawrence Road, Plymouth PL9 9SJ
Tel: 01752 405500
Take a water taxi from the Mayflower steps to reach this lively bar in the heart of the Mount Batten area. There is a formal restaurant and live bands play most weekends.
🕐 Sun–Wed 12–11, Thu–Sat 11–11
🚉 Plymouth

PORTHCURNO

🎭 THE MINACK THEATRE
Porthcurno, near Penzance TR19 6JU
Tel: 01736 810694; box office: 01736 810181
www.minack.com
Open-air theatre cut into the Cornish cliffs with the Atlantic as a backdrop. Plays, musicals and opera in the 17-week summer season.
🕐 Box office: (pre-season) Easter to mid-May Mon–Fri 9.30–5.30; mid-May to mid-Sep (season) Mon–Fri 9.30–8, Sat– 9.30–5.30. Visitor centre: Apr–end Sep daily 9.30–5.30; rest of year 10–4
💷 Visitor centre: £3, child (12–15) £1.20. Performances: adult £6–£7.50, child (under 16) £3–£4 ▢
🚉 Penzance (10 miles/16km)

ST. IVES

▽ ISOBAR
Street-An-Pol, St. Ives TR26 2DS
Tel: 01736 799199
www.theisobar.com
St. Ives' hippest bar.
🕐 Club: July–end Aug Mon–Sat; rest of year Wed–Sat 💷 Club: free before 9.30pm or 10.30pm, £5 or £6 after
🚉 St. Ives

SALISBURY

🌐 CHARTER MARKET
Market Square, Salisbury
Tel: 01722 434652
www.salisbury.gov.uk
A centuries-old outdoor market with a huge range of reasonably priced fresh farm produce.
🕐 Tue and Sat (except third Tue in Oct) 8–4 🅿 🚉 Salisbury

🎭 SALISBURY PLAYHOUSE
Malthouse Lane, Salisbury SP2 7RA
Tel: 01722 320333
www.salisburyplayhouse.com
Stages Shakespeare, modern drama and annual pantomime.
🕐 Box office: Mon–Sat 10–8 (or 6 if no performance) 💷 £5–£17.50 🅿 ♿
🚉 Salisbury

SALTASH

⛳ ST. MELLION GOLF COURSE
St. Mellion, Saltash PL12 6SD
Tel: 01579 352002
www.st-mellion.co.uk
The West Country's top golf venue.
🕐 All year, open to non-members 💷 Nicklaus Course £57 per round; Old Course £39 per round 🍴 🅿
🚉 Bere Alston (3 miles/5km)

STREET

🌐 CLARKS VILLAGE
Farm Road, Street BA16 0BB
Tel: 01458 840064
www.clarksvillage.co.uk
Over 90 outlets, including Marks & Spencer, Royal Worcester, Dartington Crystal and many shoe shops, with up to 60 per cent discounts.
🕐 Jun–end Aug Mon–Sat 9–7 (8 Thu), Sun 10–5pm; Apr–end May and Sep–end Oct Mon–Sat 9–6 (8 Thu), Sun 10–5pm; rest of year Mon–Sat 9–5.30 (8 Thu), Sun 10–5pm 🍴 🅿

TRURO

🎭 HALL FOR CORNWALL
Back Quay, Truro TR1 2LL
Tel: 01872 262466
www.hallforcornwall.co.uk
First-rate arts centre, hosting ballet, theatre, bands and operas.
🕐 Box office: Mon–Sat 9–6 (later on performance night) 💷 £5–£30 🍴
🚉 Truro

FESTIVALS AND EVENTS

FEBRUARY/MARCH

BATH LITERATURE FESTIVAL
2 Church Street, Abbey Green, Bath BA1 1NL
Tel: 01225 463362
www.bathlitfest.org.uk
Readings and presentations by leading authors in some of the most historic buildings in Bath.
🕐 1 week, late February–early March
🚉 Bath Spa

MAY

BATH INTERNATIONAL MUSIC FESTIVAL
2 Church Street, Abbey Green, Bath BA1 1NL Tel: 01225 463362
www.bathmusicfest.org.uk
Classical music, jazz, contemporary music and world music in various locations in Bath.
🕐 Late May–early June, two weeks
🚉 Bath Spa

JUNE

ROYAL BATH AND WEST SHOW
Royal Bath and West Showground, Shepton Mallet BA4 6QN
Tel: 01749 822200
www.bathandwest.co.uk
Get a taste of rural life at the region's best agricultural show, which includes rare breeds of British farm animals.
🕐 Four days early June

GLASTONBURY FESTIVAL
Pilton, 6 miles (9km) east of Glastonbury
Tel: 0115 912 9129
www.glastonburyfestivals.co.uk
The largest open-air music and performing arts festival in the world. Also theatre, circus, cabaret and children's activities. Tickets sell out in days.
🕐 Late June
🚉 Glastonbury (6 miles/9km)

ROYAL CORNWALL SHOW
Royal Cornwall Showground, Wadebridge PL27 7JE
Tel: 01208 812183
www.royalcornwall.co.uk

This three-day annual country show (first held in 1793) includes an agricultural display, Cornish food and drink, a flower show and a steam fair with traction engines and a traditional fairground.
🕐 Mid-June three days 💷 Adults £5.20–£11.50, child £2.60–£5.70

JULY

CHELTENHAM INTERNATIONAL FESTIVAL OF MUSIC
Various locations
Tel: 01242 227979
www.cheltenhamfestivals.co.uk
Among the top British classical music events, with a reputation for a contemporary bias. The Fringe Festival runs alongside, with jazz, dance, theatre, children's events, street entertainers and fireworks.
🚉 Cheltenham
🕐 Early July, two weeks

AUGUST

BRISTOL INTERNATIONAL BALLOON FIESTA
Ashton Court Estate, Long Ashton, Bristol BS41 9JN
Tel: 0117 953 5884
www.bristolfiesta.co.uk
With 120 hot-air balloons, half a million visitors, and a glow-in-the-dark night flight finale, this is a spectacular, family-friendly annual summer event.
🕐 Thursday–Sunday, mid-August
🚉 Bristol Temple Meads

NOVEMBER

BURNING BARRELS
Ottery St. Mary
Tel: 01404 813964
www.tarbarrels.co.uk
On Guy Fawkes Night the residents of Ottery St. Mary shoulder flaming, tar-soaked barrels and run through the village in a 17th-century tradition. The streets get crowded and chaotic, so this event may not be suitable for children.
🕐 5 November

WHAT TO DO

THE SOUTH EAST AND EAST ANGLIA

WHAT TO DO

What should you expect from the most urbanized region of Britain? Good, varied shopping opportunities, cosmopolitan university cities and a surprising amount of outdoor space is the short answer. The fact is that London dominates much of the south east, with many of the counties adjoining Greater London suffering from dormitory-town syndrome; inhabitants commute daily into London to work. This means that many people in the south east also seek their entertainment in the capital, at the expense of their local nightlife and culture. But if they want to get away from it all most only have to drive a short distance to the coast for beaches, boating and resorts.

KEY TO SYMBOLS

- 🌐 Shopping
- 🎭 Entertainment
- 🍷 Nightlife
- 🏃 Sports
- ✪ Activities
- ♡ Health and Beauty
- ✪ For Children

SHOPPING

Brighton has an eclectic selection of boutiques in The Lanes and the North Laine, while university cities Oxford and Cambridge offer rich pickings. Escape the chain stores in Oxford by walking to Little Clarendon Street in the north of the city. Out-of-town malls include several specializing in discounted designer wear, such as at Bicester. Antiques hunters should investigate Rye and Lewes on the south coast. Canterbury, Norwich and Winchester are far enough from London to be interesting.

PERFORMANCE AND NIGHTLIFE

Despite their proximity to London, there are some notable theatres, cinemas and performance venues in the south east, including Chichester Festival Theatre, Oxford's Phoenix Picturehouse and the Guildhalls of Southampton and Portsmouth. Generally, the region's provincial nightlife doesn't match that of London. There are two exceptions. Brighton is home to the largest gay community in Europe and a sizeable student population, boosting the social scene. Revenge is the city's biggest gay club. And Oxford, home of guitar bands Radiohead and Supergrass (who have a share in the Zodiac venue), has several stylish bars. Or do what most people do: avoid the smaller towns at weekends and catch a train to London.

SPORTS, ACTIVITIES AND FESTIVALS

Suburbanites escape to the South Downs, the Norfolk Broads and the New Forest at weekends. The South Downs, a chalk ridge from Winchester to Brighton, offers superb walking, mountain biking and, at the Brighton end, paragliding. Continue down to the south coast and the Isle of Wight for world-class sailing and windsurfing. Suffolk and Norfolk have some fine walks along the North Norfolk Coast Path, and boating on the Norfolk and Suffolk Broads is equally enjoyable. Unsurprisingly the affluent south east has some spas for destressing after work, and for children there are several excellent theme parks (Thorpe Park and Legoland Windsor) on the periphery of London.

ALDEBURGH

🎵 SNAPE MALTINGS CONCERT HALL
Snape, Saxmundham, Aldeburgh
IP17 1SR
Tel: 01728 687100; box office: 01728
687110
www.snapemaltings.co.uk
Home to the International
Aldeburgh Festival, plus other
events and performances.
🕐 Box office: Mon–Fri 9.30–1, 2–4.30
🎫 Various 🍴 🅿 🚉
🚉 Saxmundham (5.5km/3.5 miles)

ASCOT

🏇 ASCOT RACECOURSE
Ascot SL5 7JX
Tel: 01344 876876
www.ascot.co.uk
Britain's most glamorous
racecourse hosts June's Royal
Ascot week, noted for visitors'
fashions.
🕐 Flat racing May–end Oct; National
Hunt Nov–end Apr 🎫 Adult £6–£49
🍴 🚉 Ascot

ASHFORD

🛍️ MCARTHURGLEN DESIGNER OUTLET ASHFORD
Kimberley Way, Ashford TN24 0SD
Tel: 01233 895900
www.mcarthurglen.com/ashford
Outlet with 70 top name
and designer stores offering
discounts of up to 50 per cent.
🕐 Mon–Wed and Fri 10–6, Thu 10–8,
Sat 9–7, Sun 11–5 🚉 Ashford
International 🚌 Shuttle bus from train
station every 15 min 🍴 🅿

BRIGHTON

🛍️ BRIGHTON FLEA MARKET
31a Upper St. James's Street, Kemp
Town, Brighton BN2 1JN
Tel: 01273 624006
This indoor market has more
than 60 stalls selling antiques,
furniture and collectables.
🕐 Mon–Fri 10–5, Sat 10–4.30, Sun
10.30–4.30 🚉 Brighton

🛍️ RIN-TIN-TIN
34 North Road, Brighton BN1 1YB
Tel: 01273 672424
Buy original 20th-century
nostalgia—old advertising,
packaging, labels, posters,
magazines, glamour and
household items.
🕐 Mon–Sat 11–5.30 🚉 Brighton

🎭 BRIGHTON DOME
29 New Road, Brighton BN1 1UG
Tel: 01273 709709
www.brighton-dome.org.uk
Major complex with three
venues hosting music, dance
and comedy.
🕐 Box office: Mon–Sat 10–6
🎫 Various 🅿 🅿 🚉 Brighton

Comedy, cabaret and more at Brighton's Komedia

🎭 KOMEDIA
44–47 Gardner Street, Brighton
BN1 1UN
Tel: 01273 647101; box office: 01273
647100
www.komedia.co.uk/brighton
Theatre and renowned late
cabaret bar showcasing
comedy, music, cabaret and
international theatre.
🕐 Mon 5–10pm when evening show,
Tue–Sat 12–10 (5 when no evening
performance), Sun 1–10 (when
children's show) otherwise 6–10pm
🎫 Various 🅿 🅿 🚉 Brighton

🌙 REVENGE
32–34 Old Steine, Brighton BN1 1TR
Tel: 01273 606064
www.revenge.co.uk
Brighton's biggest gay nightclub,
with cabaret and dance music.
🕐 Mon–Thu 10.30pm–2am, Fri
10pm–3am, Sat 10pm–4am, Sun
10pm–2am 🎫 £1.50–£8.50
🚉 Brighton

🌙 THE SQUID AND STARFISH
77–78 Middle Street, Brighton BN1 1AL
Tel: 01273 727114
Stylish, unpretentious and
reasonably priced pre-club bar.
🕐 Mon–Sat 4–11, Sun 4–10.30
🚉 Brighton

⭐ SALTDEAN LIDO
Saltdean Park Road, Brighton BN2 8SP
Tel: 01273 888308
Classic open-air swimming
pool built in 1937 in
Hollywood modernist style;
worth seeing for the
architecture alone.
🕐 Late May–end Sep daily 10–6
(weather permitting) 🎫 Adult £4, child
(3–16) £3 🅿

CALSHOT

⭐ CALSHOT ACTIVITIES CENTRE
Calshot Spit, Calshot, Fawley,
Southampton SO45 1BR
Tel: 023 8089 2077
www.calshot.com
One of the largest outdoor
adventure centres in Britain,
with dinghy sailing, windsurfing,
kitesurfing, powerboating,
canoeing, jet skiing, climbing,
skiing, snowboarding, track
cycling and archery.
🕐 All year 🎫 Prices vary 🅿

CAMBRIDGE

🛍️ ALL SAINTS GARDEN ART AND CRAFT MARKET
Trinity Street, Cambridge CB2 1TB
Tel: 01223 457446
www.cambridge-art-craft.co.uk
Outdoor market in the heart
of the city, with all kinds of arts
and crafts.
🕐 Sat 10–5; also Fri Jun–end Aug and
Wed–Sat in Dec 🅿 Food stalls
🚉 Cambridge

CAMBRIDGE ARTS PICTURE HOUSE
38–39 St. Andrew's Street, Cambridge CB2 3AR
Tel: 01223 504444 (box office)
www.picturehouses.co.uk
Cherished Cambridge cinema with three screens showing current and classic films.
Daily Adult £4.20–£6.20, child (3–14) £4.20 Cambridge

CAMBRIDGE ARTS THEATRE
6 St. Edward's Passage, Cambridge CB2 3PJ
Tel: 01223 578933; box office: 01223 503333
www.cambridgeartstheatre.com
Small theatre with repertory and touring productions.
Box office: Mon–Sat 10–8, Sun (performance days only) one hour before curtain up
Various Cambridge

CAMBRIDGE CORN EXCHANGE
Wheeler Street, Cambridge CB2 3QB
Tel: 01223 457555; box office: 01223 357851
www.cornex.co.uk
The city's prime concert venue is also used for festivals and shows.
Box office: Mon–Sat 10–9, Sun 6–9
Various Cambridge

THE EAGLE
Benet Street, Cambridge CB2 3QN
Tel: 01223 505020
Landmark old Cambridge pub—a coaching inn since the 16th century—usually packed with students.
Mon–Sat 11–11, Sun 12–10.30
Cambridge

CHERTSEY

THORPE PARK
Staines Road, Chertsey KT16 8PN
Tel: 0870 444 4466
www.thorpepark.co.uk
One of Britain's best theme parks, with thrilling rides, including the world's first 10-looping rollercoaster.
Mid-Mar to end Oct daily times vary.
Adult £25–£28, child (4–11) £17–£20, family £77–£97
Staines, shuttle to Park half hourly

CHICHESTER

CHICHESTER FESTIVAL THEATRE
Oaklands Park, Chichester PO19 6AP
Tel: 01243 784437; box office: 01243 781312
www.cft.org.uk
This is one of Britain's flagship theatres, with an illustrious reputation. It opened in 1962 with Sir Laurence Olivier as its first director. The smaller, more intimate Minerva theatre was built in 1989.
Box office: Mon–Sat 10–8 (6 when no performance), Sun from 2 hours before performance Various
Chichester

Lakeside shopping centre is one of Europe's largest

CLACTON-ON-SEA

CLACTON FACTORY SHOPPING VILLAGE
Stephenson Road West, Clacton-on-Sea CO15 4TL
Tel: 01255 479595
www.clactonvillage.co.uk
'Seaside village' factory outlet with 48 stores selling designer and high street brands at savings of up to 60 per cent, including fashion, confectionery, jewellery and homewares.
Mon–Sat 10–6, Sun 11–5
Clacton

GRAYS

LAKESIDE SHOPPING CENTRE
West Thurrock Way, Grays RM20 2ZP
Tel: 01708 869933
www.lakeside.uk.com
More than 320 shops, a multiplex cinema, and a sports lake with diving school.
Mon–Fri 10–10 (10–7 public holidays), Sat 9–7.30, Sun 11–5 (some larger stores open at 10.30 for viewing). Closed 25 Dec. Individual stores vary
Chafford Hundred (linked by a bridge)

GUILDFORD

YVONNE ARNAUD THEATRE
Millbrook, Guildford GU1 3UX
Tel: 01483 440000
www.yvonne-arnaud.co.uk
One of the country's leading regional theatres.
Box office: Mon–Sat 10–8 (6 non-performance days)
Adult £13–£24.50, child (under 16) from £7
Guildford

HEACHAM

NORFOLK LAVENDER
Caley Mill, Heacham PE31 7JE
Tel: 01485 570384
www.norfolk-lavender.co.uk
England's premier lavender farm. Contains the National Collection of Lavenders with over 100 different lavenders to see and smell.
Apr–end Oct daily 10–5; rest of year daily 10–4. Guided tours: Easter–end Sep 11, 12, 2, 3 (also 4, Jun–end Aug)
Free. Tours: adult £2.25, child £1.25
King's Lynn (12 miles/19km)

LURGASHALL

LURGASHALL WINERY
Dial Green, Lurgashall, near Petworth GU28 9HA
Tel: 01428 707292
www.lurgashall.co.uk
This 17th-century farm maintains old English country practices by producing a range of fruit wines, fruit liqueurs and meads.
Mon–Sat 9–5, Sun 11–5
Haslemere (6 miles/10km)

MIDHURST

⊕ COWDRAY PARK POLO CLUB
Cowdray Park Estate, Midhurst
GU29 0AQ
Tel: 01730 813257
www.cowdraypolo.co.uk
The home of British polo in beautiful surroundings in the Cowdray Park Estate. The main event is the Gold Cup in July; bring a picnic and enjoy an arena-side view of the action.
🕐 Matches: late Apr–early Oct Sat–Sun, public holiday Mon and some weekdays 🎫 From £10 per car (including driver and passenger; children under 12 free) 🍴 🛒 🚇

MILTON KEYNES

⊕ XSCAPE
602 Marlborough Gate, Milton Keynes
MK9 3XS
Tel: 08712 225670
www.xscape.co.uk
The largest indoor real-snow slope in Britain.
🕐 Daily 9am–11pm 🎫 Adult £16 (child £13) per hour off peak, adult £20 (child £17) per hour peak times 🛒 🚇 Milton Keynes

NEWBURY

⊕ THE WATERMILL THEATRE
Bagnor, near Newbury RG20 8AE
Tel: 01635 45834; box office:
01635 46044
www.watermill.org.uk
Intimate theatre (seating 216 people) within a converted riverside mill, with a superb reputation.
🕐 Box office: Mon–Sat 10–7 (6 non-performance days and last Sat of run) 🎫 From £10 🍴 🚇 Newbury

NORWICH

⊕ THE ASSEMBLY HOUSE
Theatre Street, Norwich NR2 1RQ
Tel: 01603 626402
www.assemblyhousenorwich.co.uk
In a building dating from the 13th century are two concert halls and three galleries with weekly exhibitions.
🕐 Box office: Mon–Fri 8.30–4.30, Sat 10–4 🎫 Various 🍴 🚇 Norwich

⊕ BROADS AUTHORITY
18 Colegate, Norwich NR3 1BQ
Tel: 01603 610734
www.broads-authority.gov.uk
The wetlands of the Norfolk and Suffolk Broads offer gentle sailing. Yachts and motor cruisers are rented from boatyards. Or book through an agency. Blakes (tel: 08702 202498) or Hoseasons (tel: 01502 500505).

OXFORD

⊕ ALICE'S SHOP
83 St. Aldate's, Oxford OX1 1RA
Tel: 01865 723793
www.sheepshop.com
This is the original Old Sheep Shop (from Lewis Carroll's

The Phoenix Picturehouse is an Oxford institution

Through the Looking-Glass), from where the real-life Alice Liddell used to buy her sweets (candy). It stocks a wide range of Alice-themed gifts.
🕐 Daily 11–5 🛒 🚇 Oxford

⊕ BLACKWELL'S
48–51 Broad Street, Oxford OX1 3BQ
Tel: 01865 792792
www.blackwell.co.uk
Blackwell's Oxford empire spans seven shops, including this renowned academic bookshop, the Art and Poster Shop at No 27 and the Music Shop at Nos 23–25.
🕐 Mon–Sat 9–6 (Tue from 9.30), Sun 11–5 🚇 Oxford

⊕ THE COVERED MARKET
The High, Oxford
www.oxfordcity.co.uk/shops/market
Oxford's covered market has been developing since 1773. Today it houses a wide variety of shops, from clothing and footwear to gift shops and jewellers', via butchers' and delicatessens.
🕐 Mon–Sat 8.30–5.30 🚇 Oxford

⊕ THE UNIVERSITY OF OXFORD SHOP
106 High Street, Oxford OX1 4BW
Tel: 01865 247414
www.oushop.com
This shop sells official University of Oxford items.
🕐 Mon–Sat 9–5.30 (also Jun Sun and public holidays 11–4; Jul–end Aug Sun 11–5) 🚇 Oxford

⊕ PHOENIX PICTUREHOUSE
57 Walton Street, Oxford OX2 6AE
Tel: Box office: 01865 512526; recorded information: 01865 554909 (24 hours)
www.picturehouses.co.uk
Opened in 1913, now showing independent and classic films.
🕐 Daily 🎫 Adults: £5.50–£6.50, child (3–14) £4 🛒 🚇 🚇 Oxford

⊕ FREUD
119 Walton Street, Jericho, Oxford OX2 6AH
Tel: 01865 311171
Housed in a converted church, this bar is popular for a late drink.
🕐 Mon–Sat 11am–2am, Sun 12–10.30 🚇 Oxford

⊕ THE RIDGEWAY NATIONAL TRAIL
The National Trails Office, Holton, Oxford OX33 1QQ
Tel: 01865 810224
www.nationaltrail.co.uk/ridgeway
The Ridgeway, which follows a chalk ridge used by prehistoric man, is perhaps Britain's oldest road. It's 85 miles (136km) long and stretches from Overton Hill near Avebury to Ivinghoe Beacon in the Chilterns. There are many places to stop off at along the way.

PORTSMOUTH

🌐 GUNWHARF QUAYS
Gunwharf Quays, Portsmouth PO1 3TZ
Tel: 023 9283 6700
www.gunwharf-quays.com
More than 85 designer outlet stores with up to 70 per cent discounts. Gunwharf Quays is the focus of the redeveloped Portsmouth Harbour.
🕐 Mon–Wed 10–6, Thu–Fri 10–8, Sat 9–8, Sun 11–5; public holidays 10–6 🍴 🛒 🚻
🚉 Portsmouth Harbour

🎭 PORTSMOUTH GUILDHALL
Guildhall Square, Portsmouth PO1 2AB
Tel: 02392 834146; box office: 023 9282 4355
www.portsmouthguildhall.co.uk
Concert hall of 2,000-plus capacity staging rock gigs and classical music events.
🕐 Box office: Mon–Sat 10–6.30 (later on performance days), Sun from 1 hour before performance 🎟 Various 🛒 🚻 🚉 Portsmouth & Southsea

SOUTHAMPTON

🎭 SOUTHAMPTON GUILDHALL
Civic Centre, Southampton SO14 7LP
Tel: 023 8063 2601
www.southampton-guildhall.com
Southern England's largest multipurpose entertainment venue, with rock and pop, classical orchestras and comedy.
🕐 Box office: Mon–Sat 9.30–5
🎟 Various 🛒 🚻 🚉 Southampton Central

⚾ HAMPSHIRE CRICKET CLUB
The Rose Bowl, Botley Road, West End, Southampton SO30 3XH
Tel: 023 8047 2002; ticket office: 08702 430291
www.hampshirecricket.com
Hampshire's headquarters has excellent facilities for spectators.
🕐 Season: Apr–end Sep. Ticket office: Mon–Fri 9–5 🎟 Adult £25–£45, child £15+ 🍴 🛒 🚻 🚉 Southampton Parkway and Southampton Hedge End

TRING

💆 CHAMPNEYS TRING
Wigginton, Tring HP23 6HY
Tel: 01442 291000; reservations: 08703 300300
www.champneys.co.uk
Based in a private mansion in landscaped parkland, this is one of the world's leading 'destination spas', with over 100 treatments. Over-16s only.
🕐 All year 🎟 Day package: 'Relax Day' £89.95 (£99.95 Sat–Sun) 🍴 🛒
🚉 Berkhamsted

VENTNOR

✴ BLACKGANG CHINE
Blackgang, Chale, Ventnor PO38 2HN
Tel: 01983 730052
www.blackgangchine.com

Walk through gently rolling countryside on the Ridgeway

Imaginative themed areas plus play areas set on the wooded slopes of Blackgang Chine on the Isle of Wight. Under 14s must be with an adult.
🕐 Daily 10–5 (later, floodlit evenings in high season, call for details)
🎟 Person (4–60yr) £8.50, family £31. Free return visit within seven days 🛒

WALTON-ON-THE-HILL

✴ WALTON HEATH GOLF CLUB
Deans Lane, Tadworth KT20 7TP
Tel: 01737 812380
www.whgc.co.uk
Walton Heath has hosted the Ryder Cup and the European Open. Visitors must contact the club in advance and have

a handicap certificate or letter of introduction. Limited play at weekends.
🎟 £90–£100 per round 🍴 🛒
🚉 Tadworth

WINCHESTER

🌐 CADOGAN AND JAMES
30–31 The Square, Winchester SO23 9EX
Tel: 01962 877399
Ladies' and gentlemen's outfitters in a square near the cathedral. Quality, unusual town- and countrywear from around the British Isles, including waistcoats, an extensive range of cashmere, plus gifts and accessories.
🕐 Mon–Sat 9.30–5.30 (Sun 11–5 in Dec) 🚉 Winchester

WINDSOR

✴ LEGOLAND WINDSOR
Winkfield Road, Windsor SL4 4AY
Tel: 08705 040404
www.legoland.co.uk
The ever-popular Lego brick is the theme of this family venue in Windsor Great Park with more than 50 interactive rides, live shows, building workshop and other attractions.
🕐 Mar–end Nov daily 10–5, 6 or 7. Closed Dec–end Feb 🎟 1-day: adult £26, child (3–15) £22; 2-day: adult £47, child (3–15) £43 🍴 🛒 🚉 Windsor & Eton Riverside, Windsor & Eton Central 🚌 Shuttle from both stations; tickets including admission, rail travel and shuttle from most major stations in Britain

WYCOMBE

✴ WYCOMBE SUMMIT SKI AND SNOWBOARD CENTRE
Abbey Barn Lane, High Wycombe HP10 9QQ
Tel: 01494 474711
www.wycombesummit.com
England's premier ski and snowboard centre with the longest ski slope in England (300m/985ft). Skiing, snowboarding and ski bobbing. Lessons available. Bar and restaurant.
🕐 Daily 10–10 🎟 One hour. Sat–Sun: adult £15, child (3–16) £12.50; Mon–Fri: adult £13, child (3–16) £11.50 🍴 🛒
🌐 🚉 High Wycombe

FESTIVALS AND EVENTS

MAY

NORFOLK AND NORWICH FESTIVAL
Norwich and Norfolk, various venues
Tel: 01603 614921
www.n-joy.org.uk
Eleven days of classical music, opera, jazz, blues and cabaret.
🔘 Early May 🎭 Various 🚆 Norwich

BRIGHTON FESTIVAL
Brighton, various venues
Tel: 01273 700747
www.brighton-festival.org.uk
International performers from the world of theatre, dance, music and literature.
🔘 Early to late May 🎭 Various
🚆 Brighton

ISLE OF WIGHT WALKING FESTIVAL
Isle of Wight, various locations
Tel: 01983 813800
www.isleofwightwalkingfestival.co.uk
Two weeks of events and walks at Britain's largest walking festival.
🔘 Mid-June

MAY DAY
Magdalen Bridge, Oxford
Tel. 01865 726871
www.visitoxford.org
All-night parties culminate at Magdalen Bridge, where Magdalen College choir sing in the dawn from the chapel tower to hushed crowds.
🔘 30 April to 1 May 🚆 Oxford

JUNE

ALDEBURGH FESTIVAL OF MUSIC AND ART
Snape Maltings, Snape
Tel: 01728 687110
www.aldeburgh.co.uk
Internationally renowned music and arts festival.
🔘 Early to late June
🎭 various
🚆 Saxmundham 3.5 miles (5.5km)

BROADSTAIRS DICKENS FESTIVAL
Broadstairs
Tel: 01843 861827
www.broadstairs.gov.uk/dickensfestival
Week-long celebration of Dickens, including a parade, play, cricket match, Victorian music hall, ball, readings, talks, walks and bathing.
🔘 Mid-June 🎭 Free and various
🚆 Broadstairs

CHICHESTER FESTIVITIES
Chichester, various venues
Tel: 01243 785718
www.chifest.org.uk
An 18-day celebration of music, film, theatre, art and literature.
🔘 Late June to mid-July 🎭 Various
🚆 Chichester

JULY

GOODWOOD FESTIVAL OF SPEED
Goodwood Estate, Goodwood
Tel: 01243 755055
www.goodwood.co.uk
A high-powered gathering of prestigious motor sport cars and bikes.
🔘 Last weekend in June 🎭 Various
🚆 Chichester

WOMAD FESTIVAL
Rivermead, Reading, Berkshire
Tel: 0118 939 0930
www.womad.org
This annual celebration of world music is friendly and fun.
🔘 Late July–early August
🎭 Friday–Sunday 🎭 Friday £35, Saturday £55, Sunday £45, weekend £99.99 🚆 Reading

FARNBOROUGH INTERNATIONAL AIRSHOW
Farnborough, Hampshire
Tel: 020 7227 1043; tickets: 08709 063059
www.farnborough.com
An internationally important biennial airshow.
🔘 Mid-July 1 week 🎭 Adult £10–£22 (in advance), £13–£27 (on day), child (under 16) free 🚆 Farnborough

AUGUST

COWES WEEK
Cowes, Isle of Wight
Tel: 01983 295744
www.cowesweek.co.uk
Yachties and socialites flock to this renowned annual sailing get-together.
🔘 From last Saturday of July or first Saturday of August

ARUNDEL FESTIVAL
Arundel, various venues
Tel: 01903 883474
www.arundelfestival.co.uk
Ten-day arts festival—drama, concerts and family entertainment—in Arundel Park, Castle and other venues.
🔘 Last week August 🎭 Various
🚆 Arundel

SEPTEMBER

RYE FESTIVAL
Rye, various venues
Tel: 01797 224442
www.ryefestival.co.uk
A two-week celebration of music, theatre and literature.
🔘 First two weeks September
🎭 Various 🚆 Rye

NOVEMBER

LEWES BONFIRE NIGHT
Lewes
Tel: 01273 483448
www.lewes.gov.uk
Largest Guy Fawkes night fireworks event in Britain, with fancy dress parades and marching bands.
🔘 5 November (except Sunday)
🚆 Lewes

DECEMBER

THE FESTIVAL OF NINE LESSONS AND CAROLS
King's College Chapel, Cambridge
Tel: 01223 331212
www.kings.cam.ac.uk/chapel
Carol service broadcast on Radio 4.
No advance tickets, start queuing at dawn to get in.
🔘 24 December 3pm 🎭 Free
🚆 Cambridge

WHAT TO DO

LONDON

Ask a Londoner about their city and after grumbling about the traffic, the grime and the house prices, they'll admit that they wouldn't live anywhere else, at least until they reach their 40s. Why? London is a city of youngsters, with most residents aged from 16 to 44. So, the nightlife is never stale and the cultural options are superlative, with august institutions balanced by modern productions. And, as a visit to one of the city's many markets will prove, it's a place where you can buy almost anything.

KEY TO SYMBOLS	
🌐	Shopping
🎭	Entertainment
🍸	Nightlife
🏃	Sports
⭐	Activities
♡	Health and Beauty
✹	For Children

SHOPPING

The city offers shoppers a vast range, from smart department stores and speciality shops to market stalls. The central intersection of Regent Street and Oxford Street can be unpleasantly crowded; there are more interesting shops in areas around King's Road in Chelsea, Neal Street in Covent Garden and towards the east of London. Smart shopping districts include Kensington and Knightsbridge.

PERFORMANCE AND NIGHTLIFE

There is a huge variety of performing arts and entertainment. It's worth looking beyond central London and scanning the pages of the listings guide *Time Out*. Classical music fans should start at the South Bank Centre, which has a full schedule of dance and concerts. The Royal Opera House has a flashy new setting but still has a reputation for high prices and stuffiness. For opera sung in English, try the Coliseum (▷ 237), home of English National Opera.

For a selection of folk, world music, blues, rock 'n' roll and salsa stray out of the centre and into areas such as Camden, Kentish Town or Islington, all of which have lively pub-and-club scenes.

Much of the West End's 'theatreland' now seems to concentrate on long-running musicals. The National Theatre stages classic and experimental work on the South Bank.

Clubbers will find that the more interesting nightlife options lie outside the West End, especially to the east in Shoreditch, Hoxton and Clerkenwell. After a period when superclubs ruled, there's now a genuine variety of venues for every taste and budget.

Those seeking more moderate volume, a little more space and a greater age range might prefer to head for clubs hosting salsa or world music sessions.

SPORTS, ACTIVITIES AND FESTIVALS

London is the setting for several iconic sporting venues: Lord's Cricket Ground (▷ 240), Wimbledon's All England Lawn Tennis Club (▷ 241) and rugby's Twickenham Stadium (▷ 241). London's greatest offering for the active of all ages is its parks, greens and commons: Hampstead Heath, Hyde Park, Battersea Park, Wimbledon Common or Clapham Common.

SHOPPING

ART AND ANTIQUES

GUINEVERE
574–580 King's Road SW6 2DY
Tel: 020 7736 2917
www.guinevere.co.uk
The original antiques emporium on the King's Road, and probably the best. The eclectic selection of fine antiques ranges as much in price as in age and origin.
Mon–Fri 9.30–6, Sat 10–5.30
Fulham Broadway

AUCTION HOUSES

CHRISTIE'S
85 Old Brompton Road SW7 3LD
Tel: 020 7930 6074
www.christies.com
James Christie conducted his first sale in 1766, and went on to hold the greatest auctions of his time. Christie's salerooms are now world famous, auctioning major artworks. Most auctions are free and public; some require a ticket, which should be reserved in advance.
Variable South Kensington

BOOKS

WATERSTONE'S
203–206 Piccadilly W1J 1LE
Tel: 020 7851 2400
www.waterstones.co.uk
Flagship branch of the major chain store. The Piccadilly outlet is Europe's biggest bookshop, with specialist floors focusing on fiction, academic titles, children's books and other subjects. There's a bar on the fifth floor.
Mon–Sat 10–10, Sun 12–6
Piccadilly Circus

CHILDREN

HAMLEYS
188–196 Regent Street W1B 5BT
Tel: 08703 332450
www.hamleys.co.uk
The 'World's Finest Toyshop' and certainly one of the biggest. Five large floors full of toys. Staff demonstrate the latest gadgets. Great fun for all ages.
Mon–Fri 10–8, Sat 9.30–8, Sun 12–6
Oxford Circus

YOUNG ENGLAND
47 Elizabeth Street SW1W 9PP
Tel: 020 7259 9003
www.youngengland.com
Traditional children's clothing including pinafore dresses, kilts, romper suits, baby bootees and velvet-trimmed woollen coats are on offer here. This is the place to come for a high-quality, classic look. Elizabeth Street is a Pimlico jewel—while you're here look out for other outstanding shops such as Philip Treacy hats, Chatsworth Farm Shop and Jeroboam for delicious food.
Mon–Fri 10–5.30, Sat 10–3
Sloane Square, Victoria

Liberty stocks an amazing range of fabrics and much more

DEPARTMENT STORES

HARRODS
87–135 Brompton Road SW1 7XL
Tel: 020 7730 1234
www.harrods.com
Harrods' vast, terracotta building belies its origins as a small grocer's shop in 1849. There are 330-plus departments. The ground-floor food halls are a highlight.
Mon–Sat 10–7 Knightsbridge

HARVEY NICHOLS
67 Brompton Road SW1X 7RJ
Tel: 020 7235 5000 (recorded information)
www.harveynichols.com
This chic department store has marvellous window displays

and an ultra-trendy beauty bar. There are six floors of clothing and housewares, a food market on the fifth floor, and a Stylish café, restaurant and sushi bar.
Mon–Fri 10–8, Sat 10–7, Sun 12–6
Knightsbridge

LIBERTY
210–220 Regent Street W1B 5AH
Tel: 020 7734 1234
www.liberty.co.uk
The mock-Tudor building was actually built in the 1920s. The interior contains a varied stock ranging from ornaments and rugs that seem to have been gathered on some explorer's travels to up-to-date fashion designer apparel.
Mon–Thu 10–8, Sat 10–7, Sun 12–6
Oxford Circus

LILLYWHITE'S
24–36 Lower Regent Street SW1Y 4QF
Tel: 08703 339600
A department store dedicated entirely to sport, Lillywhite's can kit you out for most mainstream sporting activities.
Mon–Sat 10–9, Sun 12–6
Piccadilly Circus

SELFRIDGES
400 Oxford Street W1A 1AB
Tel: 08708 377377
www.selfridges.com
A Victorian façade hides this popular store, now a modern emporium filled with designer clothes, accessories and a huge beauty hall. There is also an eclectically stocked food hall and 18 places to eat and drink.
Mon–Sat 10–8, Sun 12–6
Marble Arch, Bond Street

FASHION

AGENT PROVOCATEUR
16 Pont Street SW1X 9EN
Tel: 020 7235 0229
www.agentprovocateur.com
Seductive underwear sold in a boudoir-style shop by the son and daughter-in-law of Vivienne Westwood, famous for her punk designs in the 1970s.
Mon–Sat 11–7 Knightsbridge, Sloane Square

WHAT TO DO

ANDERSON & SHEPPARD
30 Savile Row W1S 3PT
Tel: 020 7734 1420
Considered to be the best tailor's shop on 'The Row', Anderson's was established in 1906. Expect to pay £2,000 for a classic English gentleman's suit at this traditional shop.
🚇 Mon–Fri 8.30–5 🚇 Piccadilly Circus, Oxford Circus

MULBERRY COMPANY
41–42 New Bond Street W1S 2RY
Tel: 020 7491 3900
www.mulberry.com
Ready-to-wear fashions for men and women, plus accessories, bags, luggage and smaller items, all in top-quality leather.
🚇 Mon–Sat 10–6, Thu 10–7
🚇 Bond Street

FOOD AND DRINK
FORTNUM AND MASON
181 Piccadilly W1A 1ER
Tel: 020 7734 8040
www.fortnumandmason.co.uk
Founded in 1707 as a grocery, this famous store is wood-panelled and lit with chandeliers. The ground-floor food hall is fantastic.
🚇 Mon–Sat 10–6.30, Sun (Food Hall, Lower Ground Floor and Patio Restaurant only) 12–6
🚇 Green Park, Piccadilly Circus

ROCOCO
321 King's Road SW3 5EP
Tel: 020 7352 5857
www.rococochocolates.com
Mouth-watering chocolates, mostly handmade on the premises. Choose from hundreds of varieties including pralines, marzipans and violet creams.
🚇 Mon–Sat 10–6.30, Sun 12–5
🚇 South Kensington, Sloane Square

HOME FURNISHINGS
THE CONRAN SHOP
Michelin House, 81 Fulham Road SW3 6RD
Tel: 020 7589 7401
www.conran.com
Designer Terence Conran's glorious emporium is filled with super-stylish household

items. This is a 'must see' shop for fans of modern interiors—stocking classics, such as Eames chairs—and prices are not as high as you might imagine.
🚇 Mon, Tue, Fri 10–6, Wed, Thu 10–7, Sat 10–6.30, Sun 12–6 🚇 South Kensington

MARKETS
BERWICK STREET
Old-fashioned fruit and vegetable market tucked away in Soho, also selling cheese, bread, herbs and spices. Loud stallholders, media and fashion folk plus a few shady characters from the nearby red-light area set a unique scene.
🚇 Mon–Sat 8–6 🚇 Piccadilly Circus

Fortnum and Mason offers luxurious food shopping

BRICK LANE
Buzzing multi-ethnic East End street market, selling a variety of items such as clothes and food, but specializing in Asian goods. Get here early for the best stuff.
🚇 Sun 🚇 Liverpool Street, Aldgate East

COVENT GARDEN
▷ 121

PETTICOAT LANE
Middlesex Street and Wentworth Street
London's most famous market was originally named after the garments sold by French immigrants in the 1700s. It now has a Cockney feel and sells

cheap clothing. Around 1,000 stalls; busiest on Sunday.
🚇 Mon 8–2, Tue–Fri 8–4, Sun 9–2
🚇 Liverpool Street, Aldgate

PORTOBELLO ROAD
Famous market with hundreds of stalls selling antiques, vintage clothing, and *objets d'art*. Not cheap and there is a lot of junk, but fun to catch the 'Notting Hill' vibe. Runs from Pembridge Road (Notting Hill Gate Underground) north up to Westbourne Park Road (Ladbroke Grove Undergound).
🚇 Mon–Wed, Sat 8–7, Thu 8–1, Fri 8–6 🚇 Notting Hill Gate, Ladbroke Grove

MUSIC
VIRGIN MEGASTORE
1 Piccadilly Circus W1J 0TR
Tel: 020 7439 2500
www.virginmegastore.co.uk
This megastore sells everything from chart hits to specialist stock, as well as computer games.
🚇 Mon–Sat 9am–midnight, Sun 12–6
🚇 Piccadilly Circus

TOILETRIES
JO MALONE
150 Sloane Street SW1X 9BX
Tel: 020 7730 2100
www.jomalone.co.uk
A wonderful shop selling face creams, scented candles and perfumery, now owned by Estée Lauder.
🚇 Mon, Tue, Sat 9.30–6, Wed–Fri 9.30–7, Sun 12–5 🚇 Sloane Square

🎭 ENTERTAINMENT
CINEMAS
CURZON MAYFAIR
38 Curzon Street, Mayfair W1Y 7TY
Tel: 020 7495 0500
www.curzon.net
This well-known art-house cinema first opened in 1934.
🚇 Green Park

ELECTRIC CINEMA
191 Portobello Road W11 2ED
Tel: 020 7908 9696
www.the-electric.co.uk
Originally opened in 1910, the Electric later turned to

WHAT TO DO

repertory cinema—classics and independent films—and now has a brasserie.

🚇 Ladbroke Grove, Notting Hill Gate

IMAX CINEMA
1 Charlie Chaplin Walk, South Bank SE1 8XR
Tel: 08707 872525
www.bfi.org.uk/imax
A 480-seat cinema housed in a space-age balloon, with the biggest film screen in Britain. Visually overwhelming but limited number of films.

🚇 Embankment, Waterloo

ODEON LEICESTER SQUARE
22–24 Leicester Square WC2H 7LQ
Tel: 08705 050007
www.odeon.co.uk
Famous West End showpiece in the heart of London's 'movieland' used for many film premières.

🚇 Leicester Square, Piccadilly Circus

PRINCE CHARLES
7 Leicester Place WC2H 7BP
Tel: information: 09012 727007 (25p per min); reservations: 020 7439 3654
www.princecharlescinema.com
Central independent cinema offering seats at lower than usual West End prices. Foreign-language films shown with English subtitles.

🚇 Leicester Square, Piccadilly Circus

CLASSICAL MUSIC, DANCE, OPERA

BUSH HALL
310 Uxbridge Road, Shepherd's Bush W12 7LJ
Tel: 020 8222 6955
www.bushhallmusic.co.uk
Formerly a ballroom, Bush Hall reopened in 2000 as a small concert hall staging classical concerts, recitals, jazz and rock concerts.

🎫 £5–£35 🚇 Shepherd's Bush

LONDON COLISEUM
St Martin's Lane WC2N 4ES
Tel: 020 7632 8300
www.eno.org
Home to English National Opera (who always sing in English) with regular visits

from Welsh National Opera, Opera North and the Royal Festival Ballet. ENO is known for some innovative productions.

🎫 £5–£70 🚇 Charing Cross, Leicester Square

ROYAL ACADEMY OF MUSIC
Marylebone Road NW1 5HT
Tel: 020 7873 7373
www.ram.ac.uk
Free lunchtime recitals at one of London's four music colleges. Reasonably priced evening chamber and orchestral performances.

🎫 £5–£15 🚇 Regent's Park

Film stars walk the red carpet at Odeon Leicester Square

ROYAL ALBERT HALL
Kensington Gore SW7 2AP
Tel: 020 7589 3203 (info), 020 7589 8212 (reservations)
www.royalalberthall.com
Renowned venue for major concerts and the Proms; cheap tickets are sold on a first-come, first-served basis.

🎫 £3–£50 🚇 South Kensington

ROYAL OPERA HOUSE
Bow Street WC2E 9DD
Tel: 020 7304 4000
www.royaloperahouse.org
Principal venue for world-class classical music, opera and ballet. Home to the Royal Ballet.

🎫 £3–£180 🚇 Covent Garden

SADLER'S WELLS THEATRE
Rosebery Avenue EC1R 4TN
Tel: 020 7863 8000
www.sadlerswells.com
Europe's finest dance venue, offering classical ballet, modern dance and opera.

🎫 £10–£40 🚇 Angel

SOUTH BANK CENTRE
South Bank Centre SE1 8XX
Tel: 020 7960 4242
www.sbc.org.uk
Arts complex comprising the Royal Festival Hall (closed until 2007 for refurbishment) for large-scale classical music performances, the mid-sized Queen Elizabeth Hall for small orchestral concerts and the Purcell Room for chamber music, accompanied singers and solo musicians.

🎫 £6–£65 🚇 Embankment, Waterloo

WIGMORE HALL
36 Wigmore Street W1U 2BP
Tel: 020 7935 2141
www.wigmore-hall.org.uk
London's favourite intimate concert and recital venue, with acoustics of legendary perfection. The architectural elegance, all marble and plaster with cupola, matches the peerless quality of the great classic performances.

🎫 £10–£35 🚇 Bond Street

CONTEMPORARY LIVE MUSIC
CARLING ACADEMY BRIXTON
211 Stockwell Road, Brixton SW9 9SL
Tel: 08707 712000
www.brixton-academy.co.uk
Large auditorium where you can catch touring rock/pop acts.

🎫 £15–£30 🚇 Brixton

CARLING APOLLO HAMMERSMITH
Queen Caroline Street W6 9QH
Tel: 08706 063400
www.carlinglive.com
Large mainstream rock and pop venue on a busy roundabout in the heart of Hammersmith. Good sound and sightlines.

🎫 £10–£40 🚇 Hammersmith

DUKE OF YORK'S THEATRE
St. Martin's Lane WC2N 4BG
Tel: 08700 606623
www.theambassadors.com/dukeofyorks
Hosts acclaimed drama tested elsewhere, whether by Sir Peter Hall's company in Bath, on the Edinburgh Fringe or at the Royal Court Theatre.
£7.50–£40 Leicester Square

JAZZ CAFÉ
5 Parkway, Camden Town NW1 7PG
Tel: 08701 500044
www.meanfiddler.com
Live jazz, soul, world music, hip-hop, R&B—it's all here.
£10–£20 Camden Town

PIZZA EXPRESS JAZZ CLUB
10 Dean Street W1D 3RW
Tel: Jazz Club 020 7439 8722, restaurant 020 7437 9595
www.pizzaexpress.co.uk/jazzsoho.htm
All kinds of modern and contemporary jazz performed in the basement area under the main Pizza Express restaurant in Soho (reserve ahead).
£15–£20 Tottenham Court Road

RONNIE SCOTT'S
47 Frith Street W1D 4HT
Tel: 020 7439 0747
www.ronniescotts.co.uk
Britain's top jazz venue and one of the world's most famous jazz clubs, where the best players perform.
£15–£25; more for special gigs
 Tottenham Court Road

SHEPHERD'S BUSH EMPIRE
Shepherd's Bush Green W12 8TT
Tel: 08707 712000
www.shepherds-bush-empire.co.uk
Friendly mid-sized venue with good acoustics, a balcony and bar.
£10–£30 Shepherd's Bush

THEATRES
ALDWYCH THEATRE
Aldwych WC2B 4DF
Tel: 08704 000805
www.aldwychtheatre.com
Completed in 1905, during a building boom after the demolition of London's old 'theatreland'. Stages drama, dance and musicals.
£15–£39.50 Covent Garden

ALMEIDA THEATRE
Almeida Street, Islington N1 1TA
Tel: 020 7359 4404
www.almeida.co.uk
Housed in a building dating from 1837. Renowned for premiering exciting new plays.
£7–£30 Angel

LONDON PALLADIUM
Argyll Street W1V 1AD
Tel: 08708 901108
www.rutheatres.co.uk
A colossal 2,300-seat theatre built in 1910.
£15–£40 Oxford Circus

Top-flight performances are on offer at the National Theatre

LYCEUM THEATRE
Wellington Street WC2E 7DA
Tel: 08702 439000
On a site once occupied by David Garrick's 1771 concert and exhibition hall.
£17.50–£40 Charing Cross

LYRIC THEATRE
Shaftesbury Avenue W1V 7HA
Tel: 08708 901107
www.rutheatre.com
A friendly theatre, the oldest on Shaftesbury Avenue.
£7–£12 Piccadilly Circus

OLD VIC
The Cut, Waterloo Road SE1 8NB
Tel: 08700 606628
www.oldvictheatre.com

Historic building (1818) where Britain's National Theatre began before transferring to the South Bank in the 1970s. Most theatre greats of the 20th century have appeared here.
£10–£40 Waterloo, Southwark

NATIONAL THEATRE
South Bank SE1 9PX
Tel: 020 7452 3000
www.nationaltheatre.org.uk
Base of the National Theatre Company. Three auditoriums: the Cottesloe, with no fixed seats or staging; the Lyttleton; and the Olivier, named after Sir Laurence Olivier, the NT's first director.
£10–£34 Waterloo

THEATRE ROYAL HAYMARKET
Haymarket SW1Y 4HT
Tel: 08709 013356
www.trh.co.uk
As famed for its beautiful 18th-century pillared façade and the mirrors and gilding in the Grand Saloon bar as for its productions.
£25–£55 Piccadilly Circus

NIGHTLIFE
BARS
THE BUG BAR
The Crypt, St. Matthew's Church, Brixton SW2 1JF
Tel: 020 7738 3366
www.bugbar.co.uk
Beneath an old church on a traffic island in central Brixton. A relaxed vibe, original décor and reasonably priced drinks. Very popular so arrive early. Cool DJs, live band on Wednesdays; lounge bar and restaurant.
 Wed 7pm–2am; Thu, Sun 8pm–2am; Fri, Sat 8pm–3am
£3–£6; free before 9pm Brixton

HOME BAR
100–106 Leonard Street EC2A 4RH
Tel: 020 7684 8618
A large basement where you can chill out on tatty furniture, sip drinks without interruption and enjoy laid-back grooves and upbeat tunes (retro, hip-hop). The crowd is relaxed and the ambience friendly.

WHAT TO DO

Mon–Fri 5pm–midnight,
Sat 6pm–midnight 🖐 Free
🚇 Old Street

MARKET PLACE
11 Market Place W1W 8AH
Tel: 020 7079 2020
www.market-place.com
Set on two floors, Market Place is a classic London DJ bar with panelled walls and very good food. Downstairs is larger, with room to dance and alcove tables.
Mon–Wed noon–midnight, Thu–Sat noon–1am, Sun noon–10.30pm 🖐 Free–£7 🚇 Oxford Circus

MASH
19–21 Great Portland Street W1W 8QB
Tel: 020 7637 5555
Popular retro bar where beers are brewed on the premises. Good pizzas, bar food and serious dining too. DJs four nights a week.
Mon–Sat noon–2am 🖐 Free
🚇 Oxford Circus

SAND
156 Clapham Park Road SW4 7DE
Tel: 020 7622 3022
www.sandbarrestaurant.co.uk
This keeps south Clapham in the loop as far as cool goes. A relaxed place, with recesses for drinking and chatting.
Mon–Sat 5pm–2am, Sun 5pm–1am
🖐 £5 🚇 Clapham Common

ZOO BAR
13–17 Bear Street WC2H 7AS
Tel: 020 7839 4188
www.zoobar.co.uk
Central London bar popular with Londoners after work and buzzing with a party atmosphere. Features a comprehensive cocktail list with a happy hour until 7pm.
Mon–Fri noon–2.30am, Sat noon–3am 🖐 Free 🚇 Leicester Square

CLUBS

333
333 Old Street EC1V 9LE
Tel: 020 7739 5949
www.333mother.com
Excellent club with a music policy that embraces breaks and beats, soul, funk, reggae, drum 'n' bass and hip-hop. Sunday gay nights.
Bar: Mon–Wed, Fri 8pm–3am, Thu 8pm–4am, Sat 8pm–1am. Club: Fri–Sat 10pm–5am 🖐 £5–£10
🚇 Old Street

BAR RUMBA
36 Shaftesbury Avenue WC1D 7ER
Tel: 020 7287 6933
www.barrumba.co.uk
Established basement club with great dancing and regular theme nights including a jazz-funk Monday event and salsa every Tuesday. Music also includes drum and bass, house and hip-hop.

Clubbers partying hard at Brixton's Fridge

Mon, Thu–Fri 8pm–3am, Tue 6pm–3am, Sat 9pm–3am, Sun 8pm–1.30am 🖐 £3–£12; free before 9pm 🚇 Piccadilly Circus

THE END
18A West Central Street WC1A 1JJ
Tel: 020 7419 9199
www.endclub.com
Knowledgeably hosted for dance music aficionados, with house music and drum and bass nights. Excellent sound quality, minimalist décor, centrally located.
Mon, Wed 10pm–3am, Thu 10pm–4am, Fri 10pm–5am, Sat 10pm–7am, Sun tel for details
🖐 £4–£15
🚇 Tottenham Court Road, Holborn

FABRIC
77A Charterhouse Street EC1M 3HN
Tel: 020 7336 8898
www.fabric-london.com
Fabulously cool Fabric is one of London's superclubs and a cutting-edge venue, playing eclectic dance music for an easy-going 20-something crowd. Next to Spitalfields market in Farringdon
Fri 9.30pm–5am, Sat 10pm–7am
🖐 £12–£18 🚇 Farringdon

FRIDGE
Townhall Parade, Brixton Hill, Brixton SW2 1RJ
Tel: 020 7326 5100
www.fridge.co.uk
Hard-partying hedonists dance all night to techno and trance at Brixton's biggest venue. Dance music at weekends and live nights during the week.
Mon–Thu times vary, Fri–Sat 10pm–6am 🖐 £5–£20 🚇 Brixton

HEAVEN
The Arches, Villiers Street WC2N 6NG
Tel: 020 7930 2020
www.heaven-london.com
London's most famous gay club. Popcorn on Monday, playing commercial and funky house; Wednesday is pop, funk and R'n'B; Friday and Saturday nights are explosive, with commercial house.
Mon 10pm–3.30am, Wed 10.30pm–3am, Fri 10pm–4am, Sat 10pm–6am 🖐 £2–£12
🚇 Embankment, Charing Cross

MINISTRY OF SOUND
103 Gaunt Street SE1 6DP
Tel: 08700 602666
www.ministryofsound.com
Perhaps London's most famous club, the Ministry is a huge place where you can experience every aspect of house music. Never mind the unfriendly bouncers, long queues and high admission prices and party past dawn.
Fri 10pm–5am, Sat 11pm–7am
🖐 £12–£15 🚇 Elephant and Castle

NOTTING HILL ARTS CLUB

21 Notting Hill Gate W11 3JQ
Tel: 020 7460 5226
www.nottinghillartsclub.com
Set in a basement, with projector images on the whitewashed walls and fabrics. Reasonably priced drinks include great Cuban rum and beer. Frequent live bands.
🕐 Mon–Wed 6pm–1am, Thu–Fri 6pm–2am, Sat 4pm–2am, Sun 4pm–1am. Last entry 1 hour before closing 💷 £5–£8 🚇 Notting Hill Gate

THE SCALA

275 Pentonville Road N1 9NL
Tel: 020 7833 2022
www.scala-london.co.uk
Former cinema turned clubbing venue with three floors and several bars. Hosts hip-hop and breakbeat nights. Friday is Popstarz, a gay indie night attracting many straight clubbers.
🕐 Fri 10pm–5am, Sat 10pm–6am 💷 £8–£15 🚇 King's Cross

TURNMILLS

63b Clerkenwell Road EC1M 5PT
Tel: 020 7250 3409
www.turnmills.co.uk
Highly regarded club playing house music in a maze-like layout. Friday and Saturday are theme nights and there's a gay evening once a month on a Saturday.
🕐 Fri 10.30pm–7.30am, Sat 10pm–late 💷 £10–£15 🚇 Farringdon

COMEDY CLUBS

CHUCKLE CLUB

Three Tuns Bar, London School of Economics, Houghton Street WC2A 2AE
Tel: 020 7476 1672
www.chuckleclub.com
Students' union bar offering cheap drinks and an established comedy club which pulls in some of the best comics in the business.
🕐 Sat 7.45pm–11pm 💷 £8–£10 🚇 Holborn

COMEDY STORE

1a Oxendon Street SW1Y 4EE
Tel: 08700 602340
www.thecomedystore.co.uk
The best in stand-up comedy with improvisation ('improv') from the Comedy Store Players and big British TV and radio names.
🕐 Tue–Thu, Sun 8pm–10.15pm, Fri–Sat 8pm–10.15pm, midnight–2.15am; over 18s only 💷 £12–£15 🚇 Piccadilly Circus, Leicester Square

JONGLEURS COMEDY CLUB, BATTERSEA

Bar Risa, 49 Lavender Gardens SW11 1DJ
Tel: 08707 870707
www.jongleurs.com

Spend a leisurely afternoon on Hyde Park's Serpentine

Part of a countrywide chain of comedy clubs with consistently high-quality stand-up performers. This was the first, opened in 1983. Originally a 1920s ballroom, it now has bar, grill and late-night venue.
🕐 Thu–Sat from 8.30pm 💷 £9–£15 🚇 Clapham Junction

🏃 SPORTS AND ⭐ ACTIVITIES

BIRD WATCHING

LONDON WETLAND CENTRE

Queen Elizabeth's Walk, Barnes SW13 9WT
Tel: 020 8409 4400
www.wwt.org.uk
Excellent hides and over 130 species of birds annually on a 42ha (105-acre) site. Special events include walks, talks, craft demonstrations and workshops.
🕐 Late Mar–late Oct daily 9.30–6; rest of year daily 9.30–5 💷 Adult £6.75, child (4–16) £4, family £17.50 🚇 Hammersmith 🚆 Barnes

BOATING

HYDE PARK

The Ranger's Lodge, The Old Police House, Hyde Park W2 2UH
Tel: 020 7298 2100
www.royalparks.gov.uk
The Serpentine, a 11ha (27-acre) lake, has facilities for rowing, canoeing and paddle boats.
🚇 Hyde Park Corner, Marble Arch, Knightsbridge

REGENT'S PARK LAKE

Storeyard (Inner Circle), Regent's Park NW1 4NR
Tel: 020 7486 7905
www.royalparks.gov.uk
Boating facilities on the park's lake, which also has islands, a heronry and waterfowl.
🚇 Baker Street, Marylebone, Regent's Park, Great Portland Street, Camden Town

CRICKET

LORD'S

St. John's Wood Road NW8 8QN
Tel: MCC info: 020 7289 1611; tickets: 020 7432 1000
www.lords.org.uk
Historic home of cricket, hosting internationals, one-day games, cup finals and semi-finals.
🚇 St. John's Wood

FOOTBALL

ARSENAL

Arsenal Stadium, Avenell Road, Highbury N5 1BU
Tel: 020 7704 4000
www.arsenal.com
Famous north London club, usually near the top of the Premiership. Relocating to new Emirates Stadium nearby at Ashburton Grove at the start of 2006–07 season.
🚇 Arsenal

CHELSEA
Stamford Bridge, Fulham Road,
Chelsea SW6 1HS
Tel: 08703 001212
www.chelseafc.co.uk
Wealthy team, owned by a
Russian billionaire, that has
played since 1905, winning the
League championship 50 years
later and again 50 years later
in 2005.
🚇 Fulham Broadway

TOTTENHAM HOTSPUR
White Hart Lane, Bill Nicholson Way,
High Road, Tottenham N17 0AP
Tel: 08704 205000
www.spurs.co.uk
Universally known as Spurs,
Tottenham has played at its
White Hart Lane stadium since
renting it from brewers in
1899.
🚇 White Hart Lane

GOLF
RICHMOND PARK GOLF COURSE
Roehampton Gate, Priory Lane,
Richmond SW15 5JR
Tel: 020 8876 1795
www.richmondparkgolfclub.co.uk
Richmond Park Golf Course is
set in parkland bisected by the
River Wissey. Facilities include
a driving range and putting
green.
💷 Weekday £6–£19, weekend £6–£22
🚇 Richmond

GREYHOUND RACING
WALTHAMSTOW STADIUM
300 Chingford Road, Chingford E4 8SJ
Tel: 020 8498 3300
www.wsgreyhound.co.uk
An evening 'at the dogs' is a
fun and inexpensive night out.
Races on Tuesday, Thursday
and Saturday evenings.
🚇 Walthamstow Central then bus 97,
215, 357

ROLLER BLADING
A free two-hour Friday Night
Skate (www.thefns.com) starts
at 8pm from the Duke of
Wellington Arch, in Hyde Park.
You must be good at braking
and turning at speed and
fast enough to keep up

with the marshals. Skaters
are advised to wear body
armour, a helmet and reflective
clothing. The Rollerstroll
(www.rollerstroll.com) is a less
taxing skate in the summer.
Meet at 2pm on Serpentine
Road, Hyde Park.
Slick Willies, 12 Gloucester Road
(tel: 020 7225 0004) rent out skates.
💷 Rental £10 a day 🚇 High Street
Kensington

RUGBY
TWICKENHAM STADIUM
Rugby House, 21 Rugby Road,
Twickenham TW1 1DZ
Tel: 020 8892 2000; tours: 020 8892
8877
www.rfu.com

*London has a number of top
football clubs*

Rugby union's major venue also
has a Museum of Rugby, and
there are tours of the stadium.
🕐 Museum: Tue–Sat 10–5, Sun 11–5.
Closed post-match Sun. Matchdays: no
tours and museum open for match
ticket holders only 💷 Tours/museum:
adult £8, child £5 🚉 Twickenham

SWIMMING
SERPENTINE LIDO
Hyde Park W1J 7NT
Tel: 020 7706 3422
www.serpentinelido.com
Hyde Park's Lido has been in
existence for more than 100
years. You can swim in the
Serpentine or sunbathe in a
deckchair. Also a small pool for
children.

🕐 Early Jun to mid-Sep daily 10–6
💷 Adult £3.50, child (3–15) 80p,
family £8 🚇 Hyde Park Corner

TENNIS
ALL ENGLAND LAWN TENNIS AND CROQUET CLUB
PO Box 98, Church Road, Wimbledon
SW19 5AE
Tel: 020 8944 1066
www.wimbledon.org
Private club founded in 1868.
Centre and No. 1 courts used
only for the Championships;
others used all year by club
members and LTA-sponsored
players.
🚇 Southfields 🚉 Wimbledon

QUEEN'S CLUB
Palliser Road, West Kensington W14 9EQ
Tel: 020 7385 3421
www.queensclub.co.uk
International tennis stars warm
up for Wimbledon in the Stella
Artois tournament, held here
in June.
🚇 Barons Court

♥ HEALTH AND BEAUTY
GEO. F. TRUMPER
20 Jermyn Street SW1Y 6HP
Tel: 020 7734 1370
www.trumpers.com
One of London's first barber
shops (it opened in 1875) still
offers wet shaves, haircuts and
colognes.
🕐 Mon–Fri 9–5.30, Sat 9–5;
reservation essential 💷 Wet shave £30
🚇 Green Park, Piccadilly Circus

PORCHESTER SPA
Porchester Centre, Queensway W2 5HS
Tel: 020 7792 3980
Good-value spa in west
London. Three Turkish hot
rooms, two Russian steam
rooms, a cold plunge pool,
a whirlpool bath and an art
deco swimming pool, all for
less than £20.
🕐 Daily 10–10. Women only: Tue,
Thu–Fri, Sun (10–4). Men only: Mon,
Wed, Sat. Mixed couples: Sun 4–10
💷 Adult £19.45. Mixed couples ticket:
£27.50 🚇 Bayswater

TRIYOGA

6 Erskine Road NW3 3AJ
Tel: 020 7483 3344
www.triyoga.co.uk
Europe's top spot for yoga,
packed with celebrity clients.
Also offers treatments such as
massage, shiatsu and
acupuncture.
🕐 Mon–Fri 6.30am–9pm, Sat 8–8,
Sun 9–7.30 💷 Classes from £12
🚇 Chalk Farm

❋ FOR CHILDREN

BETHNAL GREEN MUSEUM OF CHILDHOOD

Cambridge Heath Road E2 9PA
Tel: 020 8980 2415
www.museumofchildhood.org.uk
Children can play with some
of the 6,000 exhibits in this
collection.
🕐 Sat–Thu 10–5.50 💷 Free
🚇 Bethnal Green

LONDON ZOO

Regent's Park NW1 4RY
Tel: 020 7722 3333
www.londonzoo.co.uk
London Zoo opened in 1828
and is now an internationally
important conservation centre.
Check the events schedule for
feeding times, when the
modernist Penguin Pool
becomes crowded.
🕐 Early Mar–late Oct daily 10–5.30;
rest of year daily 10–4 💷 Adult £14,
child (3–15) £10.75, family £45
🚇 Camden Town

MADAME TUSSAUD'S
▷ 126

NAMCO STATION

County Hall, Riverside Building,
South Bank SE1 7PB
Tel: 020 7967 1066
www.namcostation.co.uk
Three levels of entertainment
with bowling, video games and
rides.
🕐 Daily 10am–midnight 💷 Free
🚇 Waterloo, Westminster

NATURAL HISTORY MUSEUM
▷ 126

SCIENCE MUSEUM
▷ 128

APRIL

FLORA LONDON MARATHON

From Greenwich SE10 to The Mall SW1
Tel: 020 7002 0200
www.london-marathon.co.uk
Some 35,000 runners start the
world's biggest road race.
Apply from August to late
October for the following April.
🕐 Third Sunday in April 💷 Free
🚇 Start: North Greenwich
Finish: Green Park, St. James's Park

MAY

CHELSEA FLOWER SHOW

Royal Hospital, Royal Hospital Road
SW3 4SL
Tel: 020 7649 1885
www.rhs.org.uk
Premier flower show held in
the grounds of Chelsea Royal
Hospital usually attended by
the Queen.
🕐 Late May 🚇 Sloane Square

JUNE

TROOPING THE COLOUR

Horse Guards Parade, Whitehall
SW1A 2AX
Tel: 020 7414 2479
On the Queen's official birthday
the 'colour' (flag) of one of the
Household Cavalry's seven
regiments is 'trooped' in her
presence at this ceremony.
🕐 Third Saturday of June 💷 Free
🚇 Westminster, Charing Cross

WIMBLEDON LAWN TENNIS CHAMPIONSHIPS

The All England Lawn Tennis and
Croquet Club, Church Road,
Wimbledon SW19 5AE
Tel: 020 8944 1066
www.wimbledon.org
International tennis
championships held over two
weeks.
🕐 Last week June, first week July
💷 £4–£83 🚇 Southfields
🚉 Wimbledon

AUGUST

NOTTING HILL CARNIVAL

Notting Hill W10/W11
Tel: 020 7730 3010
Join a million people at one of

CEREMONY OF THE KEYS

Tower of London EC3N 4AB
Tel: 0870 756 7070
www.hrp.org.uk
Every evening at 9.50pm the
ceremony of locking up the
Tower of London begins.
Assemble at the West Gate
at 9.15pm. Apply in writing
for free tickets to The
Ceremony of the Keys Office,
HM Tower of London,
London EC3N 4AB (▷ 130)
at least 6 weeks in advance.
🕐 Nightly 💷 Free 🚇 Tower Hill

CHANGING THE GUARD

Buckingham Palace SW1A 1AA,
Horse Guards SW1A 2AX
Tel: 020 7930 4832
www.royal.gov.uk
Footguards in full dress
uniform of red tunics and
bearskin hats change shifts
in the Guard Mounting
ceremony.
🕐 Buckingham Palace: Early April–
end July daily 11.30; rest of year
alternate days. Horse Guards Arch:
Monday–Saturday 11am, Sunday
10am
🚇 Buckingham Palace: St. James's
Park; Horse Guards: Charing Cross

Europe's biggest street parties.
Fabulous costumes, steel
drums and sound systems.
🕐 Sunday, Monday; August Bank
Holiday weekend
💷 Free 🚇 Ladbroke Grove

OCTOBER/NOVEMBER

STATE OPENING OF PARLIAMENT

House of Lords, Parliament Square
SW1A 0PW
Tel: 020 7219 4272
www.parliament.uk
See the Queen arrive in a
State coach attended by the
Household Cavalry to reopen
Parliament following its
summer recess.
🕐 Date varies, phone to confirm
🚇 Westminster

WHAT TO DO

WALES

Cardiff aside, a visit to Wales will be about experiencing the great outdoors. For such a compact country, Wales crams in a lot: the highest mountains outside Scotland, a breathtaking coastline and a multitude of activities. Despite this, the Welsh capital, Cardiff, can hold its own against any British city, with Britain's most innovative sports stadium, a national orchestra and Wales' most exciting nightlife.

KEY TO SYMBOLS	
⊕	Shopping
🎭	Entertainment
▼	Nightlife
⚕	Sports
✪	Activities
♡	Health and Beauty
❀	For Children

SHOPPING

Although chain stores dominate the Welsh capital, several elegant arcades boost Cardiff's shopping options. Second-hand bookshops abound in Hay-on-Wye, while shops selling outdoor gear can be found in towns in the national parks: Llanberis, Betws-y-Coed and Brecon. Gifts to consider include jewellery made from Welsh gold, and love spoons—traditionally carved from a single piece of wood and intricately designed.

NIGHTLIFE AND PERFORMANCE

Cardiff, home of Welsh National Opera, the BBC National Orchestra of Wales and the BBC National Chorus of Wales, is the place to head for if you want to hear classical music. But even in more isolated areas of Wales there is a strong tradition of music and theatre. Productions are staged in English and Welsh; perhaps the best-known English-language theatre company is Theatr Clwyd, which is based in Mold and performs at the Anthony Hopkins Theatre. For details visit www.theatre-wales.co.uk.

There's also a rich vein of Welsh rock music; established names range from chart-toppers Manic Street Preachers to the Super Furry Animals. Venues in Cardiff especially are likely to have gigs by the latest bands, but don't expect too much of nightlife outside Swansea and Cardiff. *Buzz* magazine (www. buzzmag.co.uk) lists events.

SPORTS, ACTIVITIES AND FESTIVALS

Rugby union, not soccer, is the national sport of Wales, and small towns field premier sides (for fixtures see the Welsh Rugby Union's website: www.wru.co.uk).

Among its wealth of outdoor activities, seven mountain biking centres (www.mbwales.com) maintain trails that have been acclaimed by the International Mountain Biking Association. Standards of watersports are also high, with canoeing and kayaking on the rivers Usk, Dee, Wye, Teifi and Llugy. Great surfing is found on the Pembrokeshire coast. The Wales Tourist Board (www.adventure.visitwales.com) is very informative. Activity centres for under-18s should be accredited by the Adventure Activities Licensing Authority (www.aala.org).

The annual national and international eisteddfods are major music festivals.

ABERGAVENNY

🍴 SKIRRID INN
Llanfihangel Crucorney, Abergavenny NP7 8DH
Tel: 01873 890258
Celebrated for its food, this pub is said to be the oldest in Wales, dating back to the 12th century.
🕐 Mon–Fri 12–2.30 or 3, 6–11; Sat 12–11; Sun 12–12.30, 7–10.30

ABERYSTWYTH

🌐 SIOP Y PETHE
17 Rhodfa'r Gogledd, Aberystwyth SY23 2JH
Tel: 01970 617120
An established stockist of Welsh-language books, CDs and other items, including publications of prize-winning eisteddfod literature.
🕐 Mon–Sat 9–5 (sometimes later)
🚉 Aberystwyth

🎭 ABERYSTWYTH ARTS CENTRE
The University of Wales, Penglais Campus, Aberystwyth SY23 3DE
Tel: 01970 623232
www.aberystwythartscentre.co.uk
Theatre, concert hall, cinema, galleries and shops on the university campus.
🕐 Box office: Mon–Sat 10–8, Sun 1.30–5.30 🍴 Various 🍴 🛍 🅿
🚉 Aberystwyth

BETWS-Y-COED

🍴 BRYN TYRCH HOTEL
Capel Curig, Betws-y-Coed LL24 0EL
Tel: 01690 720223
Traditional pub with beamed bar. Specializes in vegetarian and wholefood meals and has some accommodation. Within sight of Snowdon, and popular with walkers.
🕐 Daily 7am–11pm

BRECON

🌟 MOUNTAIN AND WATER
Brecon LL3
Tel: 01873 831825
www.mountainandwater.co.uk
The Wye Valley is an accessible and highly rated destination for paddle sports, running through 150 miles (240km) of striking scenery. Mountain and

Water rents canoes and runs rafting trips.
🚣 Canoes from £25 per day

CAPEL CURIG

🌟 PLAS Y BRENIN
Plas y Brenin National Mountain Centre, Capel Curig LL24 0ET
Tel: 01690 720214
www.pyb.co.uk
Rock climbing and mountaineering sessions, canoeing, dry-slope skiing. No children under 8 or unaccompanied children under 10. Same-day booking possible.
🕐 All year 🚣 Sample prices: climbing £175–£425, mountaineering/hill-walking £150–£375, kayaking and canoeing £155–£360 🍴

Cardiff's New Theatre offers a wide range of performances

CARDIFF

🌐 CASTLE WELSH CRAFTS
1 Castle Street, Cardiff CF1 2BS
Tel: 029 2034 3038
Opposite the entrance to Cardiff Castle, this giftshop has good-quality traditional products such as carved love spoons, Celtic-design jewellery, slate carvings and lamps. There are also excellent handmade Welsh-language cards, artwork by Welsh artists and tapestries.
🕐 Mon–Sat 9–5.30 (also some Sun)
🚉 Cardiff Central

🎭 CHAPTER ARTS CENTRE
Market Road, Canton, Cardiff CF5 1QE
Tel: 029 2030 4400
www.chapter.org

Theatre, dance, film, art exhibitions and workshops, with performances in English and in Welsh.
🕐 Daily 10am–11pm. Chapter gallery and shop: Tue–Sun 11–8, during exhibitions
🍴 Various 🛍 🚉 Cardiff Central

🎭 COAL EXCHANGE
Mount Stuart Square, Cardiff CF10 6EB
Tel: 029 2049 4917
www.coalexchange.co.uk
The ornate 1880s exchange building in the inner harbour of Cardiff Bay is a stylish live music venue.
🕐 Box office open daily 9–5
🚉 Cardiff Bay (trains from Cardiff Queen Street)

🎭 NEW THEATRE
Park Place, Cardiff CF10 3LN
Tel: 029 2087 8889
www.newtheatrecardiff.co.uk
A traditional theatre—home of Welsh National Opera—with plays, gigs and dance.
🕐 Box office: Mon–Sat 10–8 🍴 🛍
🅿 🚉 Cardiff Queen Street

🎭 SHERMAN THEATRE
Senghennydd Road, Cathays, Cardiff CF24
Tel: 029 2064 6900
www.shermantheatre.co.uk
A mixture of conventional and radical productions, including those by the Sherman Theatre Company.
🕐 Box office: Mon–Sat 10–8 (10–5.30 if no performance) 🛍
🚉 Cardiff Queen Street

🎭 ST. DAVID'S HALL
The Hayes, Cardiff CF10 1SH
Tel: 029 2087 8444
www.stdavidshallcardiff.co.uk
Wales' national concert hall, home of the BBC National Orchestra of Wales and a venue for the biennial Cardiff Singer of the World. Pop, rock and classical music, comedy, children's shows and dance.
🕐 Box office: Mon–Sat 10–8 (or 6 if no performance) 🍴 Various 🍴 🛍 🅿
🚉 Cardiff Central

BAR ICE
4 Churchill Way, Cardiff CF10 2DW
Tel: 029 2023 7177
Pub and nightclub, with an ice-themed interior. Commercial pop music from the 1980s onwards attracts a young, studenty crowd.
⏰ Mon 11–11, Tue 10am–midnight, Wed–Sat 10am–2am, Sun 11–11
🚉 Cardiff Queen Street

CLWB IFOR BACH
11 Womanby Street, Cardiff CF10 1BR
Tel: 029 2023 2199
www.clwb.net
Three floors with different styles—bar and dance floor on ground level; alternative music at the top.
⏰ Mon–Sat 9pm–2am 💷 £3–£10
🚉 Cardiff Central

LIQUID
St. Mary's Street, Cardiff CF10 1FA
Tel: 029 2064 5464
www.liquid-online.com
This branded city-centre super-club is all lava lamps and light shows. Music is from the dance mainstream with some R&B.
⏰ Thu 9.30pm–3am, Fri 9.30pm–2.30am, Sat 9.30pm–3am
💷 Usually free before 10, then various

GLAMORGAN CRICKET CLUB
Sophia Gardens, Cardiff CF1 9XR
Tel: 029 2034 3478
www.glamorgancricket.com
Welsh cricket's only first-class team hold their own with the English counties.
⏰ Apr–end Sep 💷 £8–£15

MILLENNIUM STADIUM
St. Mary's Street, Cardiff CF10 1GE
Tel: 0870 013 8600; ticket hotline 0870 5582582
www.millenniumstadium.com
State-of-the-art sports stadium with retractable roof, hosting major sports and music events.
⏰ Tours (non-match days): Mon–Sat 10–5, Sun 10–4 💷 Tours: adult £5, child £2.50, family £15 🍴 💻
🚉 Cardiff Central

CEREDIGION

LLWYNHELYG FARM SHOP
Sarnau, Llandysul, Ceredigion SA44 6QU
Tel: 01239 811079
Farm shop with strong emphasis on Welsh produce, including 60 types of cheese.
⏰ Mon–Sat 8.30–6.30, Sun 9.30–1.30

CHEPSTOW

CHEPSTOW RACECOURSE
Chepstow NP16 6BE
Tel: 01291 622260
www.chepstow-racecourse.co.uk
Jumps and flats course hosting Coral Welsh National.
⏰ Over 30 meetings a year—some evenings 💷 Members' enclosure £17, public enclosure £12 (under 16s free with paying adult) 🍴 💻 🚉 Chepstow

Cardiff's Millennium Stadium is one of the UK's top venues

CORWEN

WHITE LION HOTEL (Y LLEW GWYN)
Cerrigydrudion, Corwen LL21 9SW
Tel: 01490 420202
Traditional inn by a village square, with garden, real ales and home-made food; 12 rooms. Live Welsh music Friday.
⏰ Mon–Thu 12–11, Fri–Sat 12–12, Sun 12–10.30

DALE

WEST WALES WINDSURF AND SAILING CENTRE
Dale, near Haverfordwest SA62 3RB
Tel: 01646 636642
www.surfdale.co.uk
Sailing and watersports centre for all levels of experience in windsurfing, sailing, surfing and kayaking. No children under 8. Advance reservation necessary.
⏰ All year 💷 Rental rates from £5 per hour for surfboards, dinghies and gear

DOLGELLAU

COED Y BRENIN FOREST
Coed Y Brenin, Dolgellau
Tel: 01341 440728
www.mbwales.com
www.forestry.gov.uk
One of the world's best mountain-biking locations, Coed Y Brenin has many waymarked trails. Bicycle rental available.
🍴 💻 🅿

HARLECH

ROYAL ST. DAVID'S GOLF CLUB
Harlech LL46 2UB
Tel: 01766 780857; secretary 01766 780361
www.royalstdavids.co.uk
Scenic 18-hole course by dunes between Harlech Castle and the sea. Not suitable for beginners or those with high handicaps. Players must hold current handicap certificate. There is also a dress code. Confirm starting time in advance.
⏰ Daily except during events
💷 Mon–Fri £42 per round, £52 per day; Sat–Sun £52 per round, £60 per day
🍴 🚉 Harlech

KNIGHTON

OFFA'S DYKE PATH
Offa's Dyke Centre, West Street, Knighton LD7 1EN
Tel: 01547 528753
www.offasdyke.demon.co.uk
A National Trail, the 177-mile (287km) Offa's Dyke Path follows the England–Wales border from Sedbury Cliffs to Prestatyn, skirting the eighth-century defence built by Mercia's King Offa (died AD796). Hay-on-Wye, Knighton and Llangollen make good bases.
⏰ Centre: Easter–end Nov daily 9–5.30; rest of year Mon–Sat 10–4
🍴 💻 🅿

LLANBERIS

⊕ V12 OUTDOOR

High Street, Llanberis LL55 4EN
Tel: 01286 871534
www.v12outdoor.com
Equipment and clothing for
walkers and climbers.
🕐 Mon–Fri 9.30–5.30, Sat 9–6, Sun 9–5

LLANDUDNO

🎭 NORTH WALES THEATRE

The Promenade, Llandudno LL30 1BB
Tel: 01492 872000
www.nwtheatre.co.uk
A modern waterfront theatre
with the largest stage in Wales,
for drama, concerts and
shows.
🕐 Box office: Mon–Sat 9.30–8.30, Sun
12–4 or 2–8 depending on show
🍴 Various 🖥 🎟 🚇 Llandudno

LLANIDLOES

⊕ THE GREAT OAK BOOKSHOP

35 Great Oak Street, Llanidloes, SY18 6BW
Tel: 01686 412959
A rambling building full of new
and second-hand books, plus
cards and stationery.
🕐 Mon–Fri 9.30–5.30, Sat 9.30–4.30

LLANWRTYD WELLS

⭐ LLANWRTYD WELLS

Llanwrtyd Wells, Powys
Tel: 01591 610666 (visitor information)
There's plenty of easy-going
mountain biking around
Britain's smallest town:
low-level routes on minor
roads, green lanes and hilly
tracks. Bicycle rental available.
🍴 🖥 🅿

MOLD

🎭 CLWYD THEATR CYMRU

County Civic Centre, Mold CH7 1YA
Tel: 0845 330 3565 (box office)
www.clwyd-theatr-cymru.co.uk
Home of the Theatr Clwyd
company, staging modern
and classical drama, plus
visiting companies and
artists.
🕐 Box office: Mon–Sat 10–8
🍴 🖥 🎟 With view of Clwyd hills

NEWPORT

🎵 TJ'S

16–18 Clarence Place, Newport NP19 0AE
Tel: 01633 216608
Dubbed the 'British Seattle',
the rock music in this bar
justifies its reputation.
🕐 Thu, Fri–Sat 9–2am; Bar 11am–8.
Gigs various nights 🚇 Newport

PORTMEIRION

⊕ THE SHIP SHOP

Portmeirion LL48 6ET
Tel: 01766 770000
www.portmeirion.com
Ceramics produced at
Portmeirion Potteries in
Stoke-on-Trent.
🕐 Daily 9.30–5.30
🚇 Boston Lodge on Ffestiniog Railway

*Beautiful ceramics at
Portmeirion's Ship Shop*

ST. DAVID'S

⭐ TWR-Y-FELIN CENTRE

1 High Street, St. David's, Dyfed
SA62 6SA
Tel: 01437 721611
www.tyf.com
Coasteering was invented here
and involves a mix of climbing,
jumping and swimming around
sheltered stretches of coastline.
It's suitable for non-swimmers.
Equipment provided.
🕐 Courses all year 🚌 Variable

SWANSEA

⊕ LOVESPOON GALLERY

492 Mumbles Road, Mumbles,
Swansea SA3 4BX
Tel: 01792 360132
www.lovespoons.co.uk
Devoted to love spoons carved
by Welsh craftspeople.
🕐 Mon–Sat 10–5.30 🚇 Swansea

⊕ SWANSEA MARKET

Oxford Street, Swansea
Tel: 01792 654296
Wales' largest covered market.
Fresh produce from the Gower
peninsula includes cockles and
laverbread.
🕐 Mon–Sat 9–5.30 🚇 Swansea

🎭 SWANSEA GRAND THEATRE

Singleton Street, Swansea SA1 3QJ
Tel: 01792 475242; box office 01792
475715
www.swansea.grand.co.uk
Traditional theatre in the heart
of the city with opera, dance,
drama, musicals, children's
shows, comedy and jazz.
🕐 Box office: Mon–Sat 9.30–8 🍴
🖥 Footlights café-bar 🚇 Swansea

🎵 ESCAPE

Northampton Lane, Swansea SA1 4EH
Tel: 01792 470000
www.escapegroup.com
Mainstream super-club with
bars and music over several
levels. Varied selection of
dance music.
🕐 Fri 9pm–3am, Sat 10pm–4am
🎫 £7–£12 🚇 Swansea

Y FELINHELI

⭐ GREENWOOD FOREST PARK (GELLI GYFFWRDD)

Greenwood Forest Park, Y Felinheli
LL56 4QN
Tel: 01248 671493/670076 (info line)
www.greenwoodforestpark.co.uk
Children can let off steam in
this forest park in Snowdonia.
Activities include a sled run,
family rollercoaster, mini
tractors, a toddlers' village and
boat rides. Don't miss the
animals and open air theatre
in August.
🕐 Easter, July, Aug daily 10.30–6;
Mar–end Jun 10–5.30; Sep, Oct 11–5
🎫 Adult £4.95–£7.50, child (under 16)
£3.95–£6.50, family £15.65–£24.95 🖥
🖼 🍴 🅿

APRIL

INTERNATIONAL FESTIVAL OF MUSICAL THEATRE
Cardiff
Tel: 029 2090 1111
www.cardiffmusicals.com
Varied events to celebrate the musical, with composers, performers, lyricists and producers contributing to over 250 performances in venues around the city.
🚉 Cardiff Central
🕐 Late March–end April

APRIL–SEPTEMBER

HARBOUR AND BAY FESTIVAL
Cardiff Bay, Cardiff
Tel: 029 2087 3690
Celtic food and drink fair, plus musical events and maritime walkabouts.
🕐 Apr–end Sep 🚉 Cardiff Bay

MAY–JUNE

HAY FESTIVAL
Hay-on-Wye
Tel: 01497 821217
www.hayfestival.co.uk
Internationally renowned annual literary festival, held over 10 days.
🕐 Late May to early June

URDD NATIONAL EISTEDDFOD
Different venue every year
Tel: 01970 613100
www.urdd.org
The biggest youth festival in Europe, with over 460 competitions in music, the arts, literature and performance. A total of 96 local and 17 regional eisteddfods (pictured on page 243) are held throughout Wales to choose 15,000 winners for this culminating week. There are stands and exhibitions on eisteddfod field.
🕐 Late May to early June

JUNE

CARDIFF SINGER OF THE WORLD
St. David's Hall, The Hayes, Cardiff CF10 1SH
Tel: 029 2087 8444
www.stdavidshallcardiff.co.uk
New Theatre, Park Place, Cardiff CF11 1FH
Tel: 029 2087 8889
www.bbc.co.uk/wales
www.newtheatrecardiff.co.uk
Biennial international competition for singers of opera (in St. David's) and songs (New Theatre), attracting worldwide TV audiences.
🕐 Late June, odd-numbered years (2007, 2009)

JULY

INTERNATIONAL MUSICAL EISTEDDFOD
Llangollen
Tel: 01978 862001
www.international-eisteddfod.co.uk
Week-long international festival and competition of singers and dancers, first held in 1947 as post-war bid to unite nations.
🕐 Early July

CARDIFF FESTIVAL
Tel: 029 2087 2087
www.cardiff-festival.com
Live outdoor music, international street entertainment, pre-Edinburgh comedy and carnival parade at various venues.
🕐 Mid-July to early August
🚉 Cardiff Central

ROYAL WELSH SHOW
Llanelwedd, near Builth Wells
Tel: 01982 553683
www.rwas.co.uk
Major agricultural event, with livestock, machinery and equipment, stands, displays and other events over four days.
🕐 Late July 🚉 Builth Road

AUGUST

NATIONAL EISTEDDFOD OF WALES
Different venue each year, alternating between south and north Wales
Tel: 029 2076 3777
www.eisteddfod.org.uk
Wales' most important cultural gathering, with competitions in literature, art, drama and music.
🕐 First week in August

BRECON JAZZ FESTIVAL
Brecon
Tel: 01874 611622
Three-day international jazz festival.
🕐 Early August

VICTORIAN FESTIVAL
Llandrindod Wells
Tel: 01597 823441
www.victorianfestival.co.uk
About 300 events, including street theatre, walks, talks, exhibitions, drama and music, with Victorian themes.
🕐 Mid- to late August, one week
🚉 Llandrindod

OCTOBER–NOVEMBER

THE DYLAN THOMAS CELEBRATION
Dylan Thomas Centre, Somerset Place, Swansea SA1 1RR
Tel: 01792 463980
www.dylanthomasfestival.com
An annual literary festival is held around the dates of Dylan Thomas's birth and death, with guest speakers, performances and films celebrating the writer's work and life.
🕐 27 October to 9 November
🚉 Swansea

NOVEMBER

CARDIFF SCREEN FESTIVAL
Various locations
Tel: 029 2033 3300
www.sgrin.co.uk
The highlight of the festival is the showcase featuring work by Welsh filmmakers, but there are also special screenings at cinemas around Wales.

WHAT TO DO

THE MIDLANDS

The Midlands—or the Heart of England, as the regional tourist board prefers—includes a revitalized Birmingham (the second-largest city in Britain), the country's first national park (the Peak District) and Stratford-upon-Avon, birthplace of the playwright who gave the world *Romeo and Juliet*, *Hamlet* and *King Lear*. There's little surprise, then, that the region has plenty to offer visitors prepared to venture beyond London.

KEY TO SYMBOLS	
⊞	Shopping
♬	Entertainment
▽	Nightlife
👤	Sports
✪	Activities
♡	Health and Beauty
✷	For Children

SHOPPING

As the cradle of the Industrial Revolution, this area produced goods that were sent all over Britain and the world. Many towns and cities are traditionally tied to particular industries, and fine china from Stoke-on-Trent, jewellery from Birmingham and lace from Nottingham make good purchases.

PERFORMANCE AND NIGHTLIFE

Culturally, Stratford-upon-Avon grabs the limelight with the Royal Shakespeare Company's cluster of theatres. The Swan is mainly used for productions by Shakespeare's contemporaries, while The Other Place stages modern drama. Popular productions sell out weeks in advance, although some seats are reserved for sale on the day and there's a small possibility of a few last-minute returns. Stratford aside, don't overlook Birmingham's world-class symphony orchestra and ballet company.

Nightlife in the region concentrates on Nottingham and Birmingham, energized by these cities' large student populations. Both have up-and-coming districts, such as Birmingham's Gas Street Basin and Broad Street, buzzing with bars and clubs of varying degrees of trendiness and rowdiness. Birmingham's free listings magazine is called *What's On* (available from tourist offices).

SPORTS, ACTIVITIES AND FESTIVALS

Another result of the Industrial Revolution is the Midlands' impressive canal network, which is gradually being cleaned up. Boating holidays can be taken on many stretches. Look for the 1875 Anderton Boat Lift near Northwich in Cheshire and the Foxton locks in Leicestershire, both great feats of engineering.

The Peak District to the north of the Midlands offers the greatest range of outdoor activities. The national park primarily attracts climbers and hill walkers, but there are also large cave systems to explore and easy bicycle rides along old railway tracks. Other rural retreats are the Shropshire Hills around Church Stretton and the Malvern Hills for walkers, Cannock Chase, and country estates such as Clumber Park, near Worksop. There are many successful football, rugby and cricket teams to interest sports fans.

Festival highlights include the Buxton Festival in July and Ludlow Marches Food and Drink Festival in September.

Trips on popular loops, such as the Stourport Ring through Worcester, Kinver and Birmingham, and the Avon Ring, which passes Stratford-upon-Avon, can be booked through an agency such as Premier Choice (www.uk-waterways.com).

WHAT TO DO

BAKEWELL

✪ PEAK DISTRICT NATIONAL PARK AUTHORITY
Aldern House, Baslow Road,
Bakewell DE45 1EA
Tel: 01629 816200
www.peakdistrict.org
The Peak District is the main draw for walkers in the Midlands, with more than 1,600 miles (2,600km) of public footpaths across moors and limestone gorges. National park rangers take guided walks throughout the year.

The superlative crags and caverns of the Peak District attract many climbers and cavers. Whether you're going up or down, reserve a tour with a qualified instructor from one of the area's outdoor activities operators who provide equipment. The National Park Authority can supply names of operators.

The Peak District is also popular with cyclists, who can try everything from off-road riding to the disused and flat railway route, the Tissington Trail. You can pre-reserve bicycles for rental from one of the National Park Authority's five bicycle rental shops.

BIRMINGHAM

⊕ THE BULLRING
Birmingham B5 4BU
Tel: 0121 632 1500
www.bullring.co.uk
Shoppers are spoiled for choice in Birmingham. The rebuilt Bullring shopping area joins Brindley Place and the Gas Street Basin, all retail nirvanas.
⊙ Mon–Fri 9.30–8, Sat 9–8, Sun 11–5
🍴 ⬛ 🚆 Birmingham New Street, Birmingham Moor Street

⊕ ST. MARTIN'S MARKET
Edgbaston Street, Birmingham B5 4RD
Tel: 0121 303 0300
www.birmingham.gov.uk
This market includes around 350 stalls selling a very wide variety of crafts, including jewellery and pottery, plus fabrics, household items, new

and designer clothes, and second-hand clothes.
⊙ Tue, Fri–Sat 9–5.30 🍴 ⬛
🚆 Birmingham New Street

🎭 BIRMINGHAM HIPPODROME THEATRE
Hurst Street, Birmingham B5 4TB
Tel: 08707 301234
www.hippodrometheatre.co.uk
Home of the Birmingham Royal Ballet, which performs three times a year. Touring shows include Welsh National Opera, West End shows, musicals and comedy.
⊙ Box office: Mon–Sat, 10–8.30
💷 £11–£28 🍴 ⬛ 🚻
🚆 Birmingham Moor Street

Traditional English crafts at Jinney Ring Craft Centre

🎭 BIRMINGHAM REPERTORY THEATRE
Broad Street, Centenary Square,
Birmingham B1 2EP
Tel: 0121 245 2000; box office 0121 236 4455
www.birmingham-rep.co.uk
In existence since 1913, with two theatres—Main House (seating 900) and Studio Theatre (140).
⊙ Box office: Mon–Sat 10–8 (6 when no performance), Sun when a performance (check times) 🍴 🚻
🚆 Birmingham New Street, Birmingham Moor Street, Birmingham Snow Hill

▽ JAMES BRINDLEY
Brindley Place, 12 Bridge Sreet,
Birmingham B1 2JR
Tel: 0121 644 5971
Best visited during the weekend, when you can enjoy a stylish jazz brunch. During the week it attracts a business-suited crowd.
⊙ Mon–Sat 12–11, Sun 12–10.30
🚆 Birmingham Five Ways

▽ THE MEDICINE BAR
The Custard Factory, 1 Gibb Street,
Digbeth, Birmingham B9 4AA
Tel: 0121 693 6333
www.custardfactory.com
Stylish bar serving up organically or locally produced food all day and, they say, 'music and art for sisters and brothers' by night in what was once an old custard factory.
⊙ Thu–Sat 9pm–3.30am 💷 £10
🚆 Bordesley

⚫ WARWICKSHIRE COUNTY CRICKET CLUB
The County Ground, Edgbaston,
Birmingham B5 7QU
Tel: 08700 621902; ticket office: 08700 621902
www.thebears.co.uk
www.edgbaston.com
The second Test ground in the Midlands also boasts Edgbaston Cricket Museum, with 100 years of cricketing memorabilia.
⊙ Apr–end Sep 💷 Adult £10 per day, £30 per match, child (under 16) £5 per day, £15 per match 🍴 ⬛ 🚻
🚆 Birmingham Five Ways

BROMSGROVE

⊕ JINNEY RING CRAFT CENTRE
Hanbury, near Bromsgrove B60 4BU
Tel: 01527 821272
www.jinneyringcraft.co.uk
Rural craft centre with artists and craftspeople in converted farm buildings. Includes pottery, jewellery, candles, art, stained glass, garden design, violins, fabrics and picture framing.
⊙ Tue–Sat (and public holidays) 10.30–5, Sun 11–5 💷 Free 🍴

BUXTON

🎭 BUXTON OPERA HOUSE
Water Street, Buxton SK17 6XN
Tel: 01298 72050; box office: 08451 272190
www.buxton-opera.co.uk
Not just opera but rock, jazz and classical music, contemporary and classical theatre, stand-up comedy and pantomime. Home to the annual summer opera festival.
🕐 Box office: Mon–Sat 10–8 (6 when no performance), Sun from 4 on performance days 💷 Various 💷
🚉 Buxton

CASTLE DONINGTON

🏁 DONINGTON PARK
Castle Donington, near Derby DE74 2RP
Tel: 01332 810048; tickets: 0870 4000699; Museum: 01332 811027
www.donington-park.co.uk
www.doningtoncollection.com
Grand Prix track for cars and motorcycles, and home of the British Motorcycle Grand Prix. Also on site, the Donington Grand Prix Collection.
🕐 Races most weekends, Mar–end Nov. Museum: daily 10–5 (later on race days) 💷 Adult from £10, child (under 15) free. Museum: adults £7, child (6–16) £2.50, family £14 🍴 🚗

CHESTER

🏛 CHESHIRE WORKSHOPS
Burwardsley, near Chester CH3 9PF
Tel: 01829 770401
Large, modern collection of buildings in a rural setting outside Chester where you can see candles being made and a candle-dipping ferris wheel. Also glassmaking demonstrations and workshops for children.
🕐 Daily 10–5 💷 Free 🍴

🏛 CHESTER MARKET
Princess Street, Chester
Tel: 01244 402340
www.chester.gov.uk
Covered market in a modern building in the heart of Chester, on a market site dating from the 14th century. Some 100 stalls.
🕐 Mon–Sat 8–5.30 🚗 🚉 Chester

🍺 OLD HARKERS ARMS
1 Russell Street, Chester CH3 5AL
Tel: 01244 344525
This spacious and lively pub is in a converted Victorian canalside warehouse outside central Chester.
🕐 Daily 11.30–11 🚉 Chester

🏇 CHESTER RACES
The Racecourse, Chester CH1 2LY
Tel: 01244 304600
www.chester-races.co.uk
Small racecourse, known as the Rodee, within sight of the city walls. The country's oldest, dating from the 16th century.
🕐 12 flat-racing fixtures, May–end Sep 💷 £5–£35, reserve festival days in advance 🍴 🚗 🚉 🚉 Chester

Catch a concert at Buxton Opera House

DROITWICH

💧 DROITWICH SPA BRINE BATHS COMPLEX
St. Andrews Road, Droitwich WR9 8DN
Tel: 01905 794894
www.brinebath.com
The water at this natural brine spa is pumped from an underground lake 61m (200ft) below the town and used for its therapeutic properties. Rehabilitation, physiotherapy, hydrotherapy, massage and beauty therapy services are available. There is also a sauna and fitness centre.
🕐 Mon–Fri 11.30–8.30, Sat 10–5, Sun 9.30–4 💷 Adult £7.75 (couples £14), child (10–16) £4.25 🍴 🚗 🚉
🚉 Droitwich Spa

FLASH

🐴 NORTHFIELD FARM RIDING AND TREKKING CENTRE
Flash, near Buxton SK17 0SW
Tel: 01298 22543
www.northfieldfarm.co.uk
Pony-trekking in the Peak District from 40 minutes to two days. Riders of all ages and standards, and riders with disabilities, welcomed.
🕐 Normally starting 10.30 or 2 💷 40 min £12, 1 hour £15, 2 hours £25, one day £48, two days from £110 🚉 Macclesfield (9 miles/14km)

GREAT MALVERN

🏊 MALVERN SPLASH LEISURE COMPLEX
Priory Road, Great Malvern WR14 3DS
Tel: 01684 893423
www.malvernhills.gov.uk
Swimming pool with fitness suite, wave machine and flume, dance studio, sunbeds and sauna. Children's activities with crazy inflatables.
🕐 Daily 7am–10pm 💷 Swim: adult £2.70–£3, child £2–£2.45, family £8–£9.15 🚗 🚉 Great Malvern

HEREFORD

🎭 THE COURTYARD
Edgar Street, Hereford HR4 9JR
Tel: 01432 359252; box office: 08701 122330
www.courtyard.org.uk
Performance venue covering music, film, theatre, comedy, dance and the visual arts.
🕐 Box office: Mon–Sat 10–8
💷 £5–£20 🍴 🚗 🚉 Hereford

IRONBRIDGE

🏛 JONATHAN HARRIS STUDIO GLASS
Coalport China Museum, Coalport, Ironbridge TF1 6TH
Tel: 01952 246381
www.jhstudioglass.com
Handcarved cameo glassware, plus bowls, vases, perfume bottles and paperweights, with glassmaking demonstrations.
🕐 Daily 10–4. Glass made usually Tue–Fri only 💷 Free 🚗 🚉 Telford (5 miles/8km), then shuttle bus (Sat–Sun and public holidays) to Ironbridge Gorge Museums

LEEK

⭐ PEAK DISTRICT HANG GLIDING CENTRE

York House, Ladderedge, Leek ST13 7AQ
Tel: 07000 426445 (best time: 8am–9am or 7pm–8pm)
www.peakhanggliding.co.uk
The oldest British Hang Gliding and Paragliding Association-approved school in Britain; learn to fly in four to seven days.
🕐 Courses usually 4–7 days 💷 £475

LEOMINSTER

🏛 THE MOUSETRAP

3 School Lane, Leominster HR6 8AA
Tel: 01568 615512
www.mousetrapcheese.co.uk
Small, central shop run by cheesemakers Karen and Mark Hindle, selling farmhouse and Continental cheeses. Also biscuits, pickles, chutneys, local beers, ciders and cider brandy. Other branches in Hereford and Ludlow.
🕐 Mon–Sat 9–5 🚇 Leominster

MAMBLE

🏛 MAMBLE CRAFT CENTRE

Church Lane, Mamble, near Bewdley DY14
Tel: 01299 832834
www.mamblecraftcentre.co.uk
Items made by a group of craftspeople—including artists, woodcarvers and textile designers—at work within a converted barn in a rural setting.
🕐 Tue–Sun (also Oct–end Dec Mon and Mon public holidays) 10.30–5
💷 Free 🅿

MELTON MOWBRAY

🏛 YE OLD PORK PIE SHOPPE

Dickinson and Morris, 10 Nottingham Street, Melton Mowbray LE13 1NW
Tel: 01664 482068
www.porkpie.co.uk
Dickinson and Morris have been baking pork pies since 1851 and are the last remaining producers of authentic Melton Mowbray pork pies in Melton Mowbray.
🕐 Mon–Sat 8–5 🚇 Melton Mowbray

🎡 TWINLAKES PARK

Melton Spinney Road, Melton Mowbray LE14 4SB
Tel: 01664 567777
www.twinlakespark.co.uk
Large-scale outdoor and indoor play areas for all ages set in 32ha (80 acres) of Leicestershire Wolds countryside.
🕐 Daily 10–5. Closed 24–26 Dec
💷 Ages 3–60 £7.50, child (under 3) free, family £28, mid-Mar to early Nov; ages 3–60 £4.75, child (under 3) free, rest of year 🍴 🚻 🅿 🚇 Melton Mowbray

NOTTINGHAM

🏛 THE LACE CENTRE

Severns Building, Castle Road, Nottingham NG1 6AA
Tel: 0115 941 3539

Beautiful glassware at Jonathan Harris in Ironbridge

One of several shops in a city famed for lace, but undoubtedly the most unusual, in a 14th-century timbered house. Has displays of lacemaking and also the chance for visitors to try pillow lacemaking.
🕐 Apr–end Oct Mon–Sat 10–5, Sun 11–4; Nov–end Mar Mon–Sat 10–4, Sun 11–4. Lacemaking: Apr–end Oct Thu 2–4 💷 Free 🚇 Nottingham

⛸ NOTTINGHAM ARENA

National Ice Centre, Lower Parliament Street, Nottingham NG1 1LA
Tel: 0115 853 3000; tickets: 08701 210123 (24 hours)
www.nottingham-arena.com
Large modern ice rink and 10,000-seater concert venue,

used for Holiday on Ice shows as well as concerts.
🕐 All year 💷 £10–£50 🚻 🍴 🚇 Nottingham

🎭 NOTTINGHAM ROYAL CENTRE

Theatre Square, Nottingham NG1 5ND
Tel: 0115 989 5500; box office: 0115 989 5555
www.royalcentre-nottingham.co.uk
Houses both the Theatre Royal, Nottingham's top venue for plays, musicals, comedy, opera and classical concerts, and the Royal Concert Hall, a venue that attracts major names of classical and pop music.
🕐 Box office: Mon–Sat 8.30–8.30
💷 Various 🍴 🚻 🅿 🚇 Nottingham

🎬 BROADWAY CINEMA

14–18 Broad Street, Nottingham NG1 3AL
Tel: 0115 952 6600; box office: 0115 952 6611
www.broadway.org.uk
Classy cinema and the best in the East Midlands, screening mainstream titles, as well as an impressive selection of art-house films.
🕐 Box office: Mon–Fri 9–8.45, Sat–Sun, one hour before the first film–8.45pm 💷 Adult £5.50, children (under 12) £2 🚻 See next entry
🚇 Nottingham

🍷 BROADWAY CINEMA BAR

Broadway Cinema, 14 Broad Street, Nottingham NG1 3AL
Tel: 0115 952 1551
Relaxed, movie-mad clientele congregates at the bar of this revered independent cinema for a good selection of beers. Non-smoking café bar upstairs.
🕐 Mon–Fri 9am–11pm, Sat 11–11, Sun 12–10.30 🚇 Nottingham

🍷 MEDIA

The Elite Building, Queen Street, Nottingham NG1 2BC
Tel: 0115 910 1101
www.medianightclub.com
This club's fantastic interior justifies its position as the hottest nightspot in Nottingham, attracting top DJs.
🕐 Daily 9pm–2.30am 💷 From £3
🚇 Nottingham

🎵 ROCK CITY
8 Talbot Street, Nottingham NG1 5GG
Tel: 0115 941 2544
www.rock-city.co.uk
One of the biggest and best rock clubs in the country, with amps turned up to 11.
🕐 Tue 9.30pm–2am, Thu–Fri 9pm–2am, Sat 8.30pm–2.30am
💷 £2.50–£5 🚉 Nottingham

🎵 YE OLDE TRIP TO JERUSALEM
1 Brewhouse Yard, Castle Road, Nottingham NG1 6AD
Tel: 0115 947 3171
www.triptojerusalem.com
Dates back to the 12th century and claims to be the oldest inn in England, where Crusaders would meet on their way to the Holy Land.
🕐 Mon–Sat 11–11, Sun 12–10.30
🚉 Nottingham

🏏 NOTTINGHAMSHIRE COUNTY CRICKET CLUB
Trent Bridge, Nottingham NG2 6AG
Tel: 0115 982 3000; tickets: 0870 168 8888
www.nottsccc.co.uk
One of two Test (international) cricket grounds in the Midlands.
🕐 Apr–end Sep 💷 Adult £10–£55, child (under 16) £5–£15, family £30–£35 🚉 Nottingham

❄ NATIONAL ICE CENTRE
Lower Parliament Street, Nottingham NG1 1LA
Tel: 0115 853 3000
www.national-ice-centre.com
Huge modern ice rink.
🕐 Mon, Wed, Fri 1.30–4, 7.30–10; Tue 10–12; Thu 10–12, 7.30–10, Sat 10–12, 2.30–5, 7.30–10; Sun 10–12, 2.30–5 💷 All ages £3.50 plus £1.50 skate hire (£5.50 including skate hire, Fri evening and Sat–Sun) 📷 🚉 🚉 Nottingham

RAGDALE

💧 RAGDALE HALL HEALTH HYDRO
Ragdale, near Melton Mowbray LE14 3PB
Tel: 01664 434 831
www.ragdalehall.co.uk
A luxurious spa with three swimming pools, two exercise

studios and 400 staff administering beauty treatments.
🕐 All year 💷 Day spa package from £105 🍴 📷 🚉 Melton Mowbray

SHREWSBURY

🛍 THE PARADE SHOPPING CENTRE
St. Mary's Place, Shrewsbury SY1 1DY
Tel: 01743 343178
www.paradeshops.co.uk
A concentration of 30 shops and a coffee house in central Shrewsbury, contained in a Grade II listed (landmark) building with a grand Classical entrance with columns and a pediment. Crafts and specialist shops offering picture framing,

One of many specialist shops in Shrewsbury's Parade

dolls' houses, hobby horses and clocks etc.
🕐 Mon–Sat 9.30–5 📷 🚉 Shrewsbury

STOKE-ON-TRENT

🛍 EDWARDS' CHINA
2–10 Market Lane, Hanley, Stoke-on-Trent ST1 1LA
Tel: 01782 260345
www.edwardschina.co.uk
One of the best shops in Stoke for examples of work by all the major local china manufacturers, as well as top-quality crystal.
🕐 Mon–Sat 9–5.10 📷 🚉 Stoke-on-Trent

STRATFORD-UPON-AVON

🎭 ROYAL SHAKESPEARE THEATRE, SWAN THEATRE AND THE OTHER PLACE
Waterside, Stratford-upon-Avon CV37 6BB
Tel: 01789 403404; box office: 08706 091110
www.rsc.org.uk
Home of the Royal Shakespeare Company (RSC), presenting Shakespeare's plays and other works in the playwright's home town. You can take a guided tour behind the scenes including the RSC Collection, featuring costumes and props from previous productions.
🕐 All year 💷 From £5 🍴 📷 🚉 Stratford-upon-Avon

🎭 STRATFORD PICTUREHOUSE
Windsor Street, Stratford-upon-Avon CV37 6NL
Tel: 01789 415500; information: 01789 415511 (24 hours)
www.picturehouses.co.uk
Modern two-screen cinema showing the latest blockbuster and art-house releases. Works by local artists on display in the roof-top terrace bar.
🕐 All year 💷 Adults: £5.50–£6, child £4–£4.50 📷 🚉 🚉 Stratford-upon-Avon

SILVERSTONE

🏁 SILVERSTONE CIRCUIT
Silverstone NN12 8TN
Tel: 08704 588200; tickets: 08704 588290
www.silverstone-circuit.co.uk
The home of British motor racing, with over 40 motor racing events a year. Also tuition in driving a racing car yourself.
🕐 All year 💷 Various 🍴 📷 🚉

TAMWORTH

❄ THE SNOWDOME
Leisure Island, River Drive, Tamworth B79 7ND
Tel: 08705 000011
www.snowdome.co.uk
Indoor slope for skiers and snowboarders of all abilities.
🕐 Daily 9am–1am 💷 Adult £22, child (under 17) £16 per hour 📷 🚉 🚉 Tamworth

DRAYTON MANOR THEME PARK

Near Tamworth B78 3TW
Tel: 08708 725252 (recorded information); tickets: 08702 406950
www.draytonmanor.co.uk
More than 100 innovative rides, including Fifth Element and Shockwave, plus a zoo.
🕐 Mid-Mar to late Oct daily 10.30–5, (closed some days in Sep and Oct)
💷 Over 12s £17 (£19 weekends, public and school holidays); 4–11s £13 (£15 weekends, public and school holidays); family (tel: 08702 406950) 🍴 🅿

TOWCESTER

CATANGAR LLAMAS

18 High Street, Weston, Towcester NN12 8PU
Tel: 01295 768676
www.llamatrekking.co.uk
Llama trekking along bridleways and country lanes.
🕐 All year, reservation essential
💷 Adult from £35, child (8–12) free if accompanied by adult for each child

WORCESTER

SWAN THEATRE

The Moors, Worcester WR1 3EF
Box office: Huntingdon Arts, Huntingdon Hall, Crowngate, Worcester WR1 3LD
Tel: 01905 611427
www.huntingdonarts.com
Varied and eclectic mix of drama, music, comedy, pantomime and poetry.
🕐 Box office: Mon–Sat 10–5pm
💷 £7–£20 🅿 🚇 Worcester Foregate Street

PERDISWELL PARK GOLF CLUB

Bilford Road, Worcester WR3 8DX
Tel: 01905 754668
Pay and play on this 18-hole, par-68 course in parkland.
🕐 All year 💷 Mon–Fri £10.15, Sat–Sun £13.85 🍴 🅿

WORCESTER RACECOURSE

Pitchcroft, Worcester WR1 3EJ
Tel: 08702 202772
www.worcester-racecourse.co.uk
Racecourse in a picturesque setting by the river. Seventeen race meetings.
🕐 Apr–end Oct 💷 £6–£16 🍴 🅿
🅿 🚇 Worcester Forgate (10-min walk)

FESTIVALS AND EVENTS

APRIL

SHAKESPEARE'S BIRTHDAY CELEBRATIONS

Various locations, Stratford-upon-Avon
Tel: 01789 204016
www.shakespeare.org.uk
Shakespeare was not born on 23 April, but that was the date of his baptism and therefore the date on which his birthday is celebrated annually with a weekend of events.
🕐 Nearest weekend to 23 April, parade Saturday starts at 10.55am
💷 Free 🚇 Stratford-upon-Avon

MAY

CASTLETON ANCIENT GARLAND CEREMONY

Castleton, Derbyshire
Tel: 01433 621192
An endearing annual summer ceremony with a parade to the market square, with participants bearing garlands and stopping for refreshment at every pub on the way.
🕐 Last Saturday in May, parade 5.30pm–8.30pm 💷 Free

JUNE

THE THREE COUNTIES SHOW

Malvern Showground, Malvern
Tel: 01684 584900
www.threecounties.co.uk
Find out about rural England at this agricultural show of produce and crafts from Herefordshire, Gloucestershire and Worcestershire.
🕐 Friday–Sunday, mid-June
💷 Adults £12, child (5–15) £6, family £28 🚇 Great Malvern

LUDLOW FESTIVAL

Castle Square, Ludlow SY8 1AY
Tel: 01584 872150
www.ludlowfestival.co.uk
Open-air theatre in the grounds of Ludlow Castle, with music, opera, dance, comedy, street performers, culminating in a firework finale.
🕐 Two weeks, late June–early July
💷 Various 🚇 Ludlow

JULY

BUXTON FESTIVAL

Various locations in Buxton
Tel: 01298 70395
www.buxtonfestival.co.uk
An established opera festival in the town's lovely Opera House and other venues.
🕐 Two weeks, mid-July 💷 Various
🚇 Buxton

AUGUST

THREE CHOIRS FESTIVAL

Hereford, Gloucester, Worcester
Tel: 01905 640663
www.3choirs.org
Europe's oldest choral festival, held in rotation in each of the cathedrals of Hereford, Gloucester and Worcester. 2007's festival will be held in Gloucester and 2008's in Worcester.
🕐 Early August 💷 Free–various
🚇 Hereford, Gloucester or Worcester

SEPTEMBER

LUDLOW MARCHES FOOD AND DRINK FESTIVAL

The Buttercross, Ludlow SY8 1AW
Tel: 01584 873957
www.foodfestival.co.uk
Britain's premier food and drink festival featuring local produce and related events.
🕐 Friday–Sunday, early September
💷 Free 🚇 Ludlow

ARTSFEST

Various venues, Birmingham
Tel: 0121 685 2605
www.artsfest.org.uk
Over 300 performances throughout the city make this Britain's largest free arts festival.
🕐 Friday–Sunday, early Sep 💷 Free
🚇 Birmingham New Street

OCTOBER

CHESTER LITERATURE FESTIVAL

8 Abbey Square, Chester CH1 2HU
Tel: 01244 319985
www.chesterfestivals.co.uk
Literary events, readings and workshops around Chester.
🕐 Most of Oct 💷 Various 🚇 Chester

THE MIDLANDS N–W/FESTIVALS AND EVENTS 253

THE NORTH

The North of England has two of Britain's most beautiful national parks, sophisticated shopping and a hedonistic attitude to nightlife in Leeds, Manchester, Newcastle and Sheffield. Liverpool is set to be European Capital of Culture in 2008.

KEY TO SYMBOLS	
⊕	Shopping
🎭	Entertainment
▽	Nightlife
⚽	Sports
✪	Activities
♡	Health and Beauty
✪	For Children

SHOPPING

Leeds' occasional label as the 'London of the North' is not without some justification, as the first Harvey Nichols store outside London, in Leeds' Victoria Quarter, was a hit with fashion-conscious locals. On the other side of the Pennines, Manchester replied with a new Selfridges store in 2002, followed by its own Harvey Nichols (in the Millennium Quarter) in 2003. Options elsewhere range from cavernous shopping malls such as Gateshead's Metro Centre to small speciality shops such as Davill's of Ripon. Typical souvenirs for those with a sweet tooth include Harrogate toffee (sold in blue and silver tins) and Blackpool Rock.

PERFORMANCE AND NIGHTLIFE

Pop music remains a force to be reckoned with in the northwest. There's been a steady stream of great bands from Manchester over the years, including Joy Division and the Stone Roses. And Liverpool's reputation for idiosyncratic but ground-breaking groups is upheld by young bands like The Coral. Both cities have a range of venues, from the small to the stadium-sized. There are 150 clubs to choose from in Manchester and the gentrification of several other northern cities has brought safe and enticing districts full of stylish café-bars, such as The Calls in Leeds and Castlefield in Manchester. Nightlife in Newcastle remains brasher, but less self-conscious.

On a less raucous note, both Manchester and Liverpool have highly regarded orchestras: the Hallé and the Royal Liverpool Philharmonic.

SPORTS, ACTIVITIES AND FESTIVALS

Some of the biggest clubs in English football are in this region: Manchester United, Liverpool and Newcastle United. However, it's practically impossible to get tickets for their league matches. A better idea is to try less fashionable teams, such as Everton (in Liverpool) and Manchester City. Rugby league—the fast-paced, 13-a-side variant—has its foundations in the North.

Walkers and riders can explore the Lake District, the Yorkshire Dales and the North York Moors, all offering well-established routes through spectacular scenery. The Lakes and the Dales can get congested on summer weekends—the austere, heather-clad North York Moors are a less-crowded alternative.

The region's great variety of festivals ranges from maritime events in Liverpool to York's popular Viking celebrations, and the thrilling Isle of Man TT motorcycle races.

ALNWICK

⊕ BARTER BOOKS

Alnwick Station, Alnwick NE66 2NP
Tel: 01665 604888
www.barterbooks.co.uk
Huge, eccentric second-hand
bookshop in grandiose former
train station. Books are
displayed in the former waiting
rooms and platform area, and
a model railway runs along
shelves. Substantial local
interest section, plus rare and
antiquarian books.
🕙 Apr–end Sep daily 9–7, rest of year
Fri–Wed 9–5, Thu 9–7 🖸

BEVERLEY

🍷 THE WHITE HORSE

22 Hengate, Beverley HU17 8BL
Tel: 01482 861973
Traditional 16th-century pub
also known as Nellie's.
🕙 Mon–Sat 11–11, Sun 12–10.30pm
🚆 Beverley

BRADFORD

🎭 ALHAMBRA THEATRE

Morley Street, Bradford BD7 1AJ
Tel: 01274 432000
www.bradfordtheatres.co.uk
This traditional theatre hosts
visiting ballet, opera, classical
and modern drama
companies.
🕙 Box office: Mon–Sat, from 10am
💷 From £7 🚆 🚌 Bradford
Interchange

CONISTON

🚣 CONISTON BOATING CENTRE

Lake Road, Coniston
Tel: 015394 41366
Dinghies, motor boats and
canoes for hire on Coniston
Water.
🕙 Daily 10–4.30 💷 From £8 per hour
rowing boat, £15 per 2 hours canoe

FALSTONE

🚣 KIELDER WATER

Kielder Water, Falstone NE48 1BT
Tel: 01434 240398
www.kielder.org
Europe's largest man-made
lake offers a variety of game
fishing. Boat rental available.
No unaccompanied children
under 14.

🎣 Game fishing: mid-Mar to end Oct
🎫 Day ticket (from bank): adult
£16.50. Including boat: £22.50 🚆 🖸
🚆 🍴 At Leaplish

HARROGATE

☕ BETTY'S CAFÉ AND TEA ROOMS

1 Parliament Street, Harrogate HG1 2QU
Tel: 01423 502746
www.bettysandtaylors.co.uk
High-class baker's and
pâtisserie (opened 1919), with
a quintessentially English tea
room attached. Specialities
include Yorkshire curd tarts
and Fat Rascals. Shops in Ilkley,
Northallerton and York too.
🕙 Daily 9–9, closed 1 Jan and
25–26 Dec 🖸 🚆 Harrogate

Mouth-watering delicacies at Betty's in Harrogate

🍷 MONTEY'S

3 Corn Exchange Buildings, The Ginnel,
Harrogate HG1 2RB
Tel: 01423 526652
Friendly café and bar serving
food. Live music most evenings.
🕙 Wed–Sat 5.30pm–11, Sun
7pm–10.30pm 🚆 Harrogate

🌊 THE HYDRO

Jennyfield Drive, Harrogate HG1 2RP
Tel: 01423 556767
www.harrogate.gov.uk
Modern swimming pool and
fitness complex, offering beauty
therapies, massage and crèche.
🕙 Daily 7.30am–9.30pm
💷 Swimming: adult £3.30, child £2.
Under-8s must be accompanied 🖸
🚆 Harrogate

🌊 THE TURKISH BATHS AND HEALTH SPA

Royal Baths, Parliament Street,
Harrogate HG1 2WH
Tel: 01423 556746
www.harrogate.gov.uk/turkishbaths
The newly renovated baths first
opened in 1897. The Moorish
interiors are reason enough to
visit, but keenly priced spa
treatments are tempting.
Admission includes use of the
steam room, plunge pool and
frigidarium (relaxation room).
🕙 Sun–Fri 9.30–7.30, Sat 9.30–4.30
💷 Admission £10.50; massage: from
£18; reflexology: from £27
🚆 Harrogate

KENDAL

LAKE DISTRICT NATIONAL PARK AUTHORITY

Murley Moss, Oxenholme Road,
Kendal LA9 7RL
Tel: 01539 724555
www.lake-district.gov.uk
A magnet for lovers of the
outdoors, 'the Lakes' have
attracted poets, artists and
writers as well as countless
hikers and day trippers. A
network of narrow valleys
(dales) radiates out from a
central core of mountains
including England's highest,
Scafell Pike 978m (3210ft).
Well-maintained paths give a
fantastic range of walks from
easy strolls to challenging
long-distance hikes.

KIRBY MISPERTON

🎢 FLAMINGOLAND THEME PARK AND ZOO

Kirby Misperton, near Malton YO17 6UX
Tel: 0870 752 8000
www.flamingoland.co.uk
White-knuckle experiences,
rides for small children and a
zoo with over 1,000 animals.
🕙 Mar–end Oct Mon–Fri 10–5;
Sat–Sun 10–6 (times vary later in year
according to daylight) 💷 Adult £17.50,
child (4–11) £16.50, family £64 🍴 🖸
🚌 🚆 Malton 5 miles (8km)

KNARESBOROUGH

⭐ BLUE SKY BALLOONS
Moor Lane, Arkendale, Knaresborough HG5 0RQ
Tel: 01423 340140
www.blueskyballoons.co.uk
Hot-air balloon rides over the Yorkshire countryside.
🕐 Daily evenings, Apr–end Sep
💷 Balloon ride: £165 per person
🚇 Knaresborough

LEEDS

🏬 HARVEY NICHOLS
107–111 Briggate, Leeds LS1 6AZ
Tel: 0113 2048888
www.harveynichols.co.uk
Leeds' branch of the London department store is just as chic as the original. Expensive designer clothes are a speciality, and the beauty salon and fourth-floor restaurant are extremely popular.
🕐 Mon–Wed 10–6, Thu–Fri 10–7, Sat 9–7, Sun 11–5 🚇 Leeds

🏬 VICTORIA QUARTER
Briggate, Leeds LS1 6AZ
Tel: 0113 2455333
www.vqleeds.com
Classy, covered shopping area built in 1898, with a stained-glass roof. A wide range of top-quality goods from the first Harvey Nichols store outside London and designer shops such as Vivienne Westwood and Gieves & Hawkes.
🕐 Mon–Sat 10–5, Sun 11–5. Times vary; some shops closed Sun 🚇 Leeds

🎭 CITY VARIETIES
Swan Street, Leeds LS1 6LW
Tel: 0113 2430808
Typical 19th-century music hall. Actors Lillie Langtry (1853–1929) and Charlie Chaplin (1889–1977) appeared here.
🕐 Box office: Mon–Sat 10 to curtain up
💷 Various 🚇 Leeds

🎭 GRAND THEATRE AND OPERA HOUSE
46 New Briggate, Leeds LS1 6NZ
Tel: 0113 2226222
www.leeds.gov.uk/grandtheatre
Grand Victorian theatre—base of Opera North—staging opera, ballet, classical and modern drama, musicals, shows and gigs.
🕐 Box office: Mon–Sat 10–9, Sun 11.30–7 💷 £3–£47 🚇 Leeds

🎭 WEST YORKSHIRE PLAYHOUSE
Playhouse Square, Leeds LS2 7UP
Tel: 0113 2137700
www.wyp.org.uk
Modern theatre hosting a regular season of classical and modern plays.
🕐 Box office: Mon–Sat 9–8
💷 From £5 🍴 🚇 Leeds

🍸 MAJESTYK
City Square, Leeds LS1 4DS
Tel: 0113 2424333
www.majestyk.co.uk

Harvey Nichols brings some London glamour to Leeds

Large, lively central Leeds nightclub in a former cinema. Expect chart tunes, garage, soul and house.
🕐 10pm–2 or 4am 💷 £2–£6 🚇 Leeds

🍸 MOJO
18 Merrion Street, Leeds LS1 6PQ
Tel: 0113 2446387
Intimate, modern bar in central Leeds, serving superb cocktails to rock and indie music.
🕐 Sun–Thu 5pm–1am; Fri–Sat 5pm–2am 🚇 Leeds

🏏 YORKSHIRE CRICKET CLUB
Headingly Cricket Ground, St. Michael's Lane, Leeds LS6 3BU
Tel: 0113 2787394
www.yorkshireccc.com

International ground with fine facilities for spectators.
🕐 Reservations: Mon–Fri 9–5
💷 County match (3–4 days): adult £12, child £6. One-day match: adult £15, child £10 🚇 Headingley or Burley Park

LIVERPOOL

🏬 ALBERT DOCK
Albert Dock, Liverpool L3 4AF
www.albertdock.com
Touristy, with some quirky gift and homeware stalls, but visit for souvenirs.
🕐 Generally Mon–Sat 9–6, Sun 11–5
🍴 🚇 Liverpool Lime Street

🏬 CAVERN WALKS
Matthew Street, Liverpool L2 6RE
Tel: 0151 2369082
wwww.cavernshopping.com
Named for the famous club where The Beatles made their name, offers designer fashion, jewellery and gift shops on two floors. Cricket has chic, stylish fashions that ooze quality and style.
🕐 Mon–Sat 9–5.30 🍴
🚇 Liverpool Lime Street

🏬 JEFFS
80 Bold Street, Liverpool L1 4HR
Tel: 0151 7070880
Affectionately known as the 'Harrods of Liverpool', this place specializes in women's wear, fashions and accessories. Take a break in the Victorian tea room.
🕐 Mon–Sat 9.30–5.30
🚇 Liverpool Central

🏬 PROBE RECORDS
9 Slater Street, Liverpool L1 4BW
Tel 0151 7088815
Legendary record shop and part of Liverpool's music scene for decades, selling vinyl and CDs covering rock, indie, electronic and more. Essential for collectors.
🕐 Mon–Sat 10–6 🚇 Liverpool Central

🎭 EVERYMAN THEATRE
5–9 Hope Street, Liverpool L1 9EL
Tel: 0151 7094776
A wide range of productions—from Shakespeare to modern

WHAT TO DO

playwrights—as well as concerts, exhibitions and dance.

Daily Various
Liverpool Lime Street

PHILHARMONIC HALL

Hope Street, Liverpool L19 BP
Tel: 0151 7093789
www.liverpoolphil.com
Art deco building, home to the Royal Liverpool Philharmonic; also hosts jazz, pop and world music.

Daily; box office: Mon–Sat 10–5, Sun 12–5 £3.50–£35
Liverpool Central

BELUGA BAR

40 Wood Street, Liverpool L1 4AQ
Tel: 0151 708 8896
Don't let this bar's basement location put you off, as it's a fine place to hang out, and the seasonal menu is good value.

Mon–Thu 9am–11pm, Fri–Sun 9am–12am Liverpool Central

RAWHIDE COMEDY CLUB

Royal Court Theatre, 1 Roe Street, Liverpool L1 1HL
Tel: 0870 787 1240
www.rawhidecomedy.com
At Liverpool's leading comedy club, Baby Blue, comedians from the national circuit vie with local wits.

Thu–Sat 7.45pm £5 Thu, £12 Fri, £13.50 Sat Liverpool Lime Street

AINTREE RACECOURSE

Ormskirk Road, Aintree, Liverpool L9 5AS
Tel: 0151 5232600
www.aintree.co.uk
Home to the Grand National, the world's most famous steeplechase (▷ 259 Festivals and Events).

MANCHESTER

CRAFT AND DESIGN CENTRE

17 Oak Street, Manchester M4 5JD
Tel: 0161 8324274
Buy funky jewellery, candles, furniture and the like from the artists' workshops here.

Mon–Sat 10–5.30, Sun in Dec
Manchester Piccadilly

SELFRIDGES

Exchange Square, Manchester M3 1BD
Tel: 0870 8377377
www.selfridges.co.uk
This branch of the fabulous London store aims to be funkier and focused on fashion.

Mon–Fri 10–8, Sat 9–8, Sun 11–5
 Manchester Piccadilly

THE TRIANGLE

Exchange Square, Manchester M4 3TR
Tel: 0161 8348961
The former Corn Exchange has been redeveloped into a complex housing mainstream chains and independent shops.

Mon–Sat 10–7, Sun 11–5
Manchester Victoria

Liverpool's Albert Dock has been redeveloped for shoppers

BRIDGEWATER HALL

Lower Mosley Street, Manchester M2 3WS
Tel: 0161 9079000
www.bridgewater-hall.co.uk
Home of the Hallé and BBC Philharmonic orchestras, this is one of Europe's finest venues for classical music.

Box office: Mon–Sat 10–8, Sun 12–6 (8 on concert nights) Various
 Manchester Piccadilly

ROYAL EXCHANGE THEATRE

St. Ann's Square, Manchester M2 7DH
Tel: 0161 8339833
www.royalexchange.co.uk
The city's best-known theatre with a superb setting in the Royal Exchange and 'in-the-round' aspect.

Daily £3.75–£25.50
 Manchester Piccadilly

THE LOWRY

Salford Quays, Salford, Manchester M50 3AZ
Tel: 0870 787 5780
www.thelowry.com
Two theatres offering a range of music, opera, comedy and drama.

Daily From £5
Salford Central

46 CANAL STREET

46 Canal Street, Manchester M1 3LZ
Tel: 0161 2363766
This bar at the heart of the city's gay scene fills up in the summer, but can be a bit empty at other times—such is the choice in the Gay Village.

Sun–Fri 12–12, Sat 12–1am
From £6 Manchester Piccadilly

CRUZ 101

101 Princess Street, Manchester M1 6DD
Tel: 0161 9500101
www.cruz101.com
A popular Gay Village destination, Cruz 101 is one of Manchester's best gay clubs, with a range of entertainment from club nights to live acts.

Mon, Wed–Sat 10.30pm–3am
Manchester Piccadilly

MANCHESTER ROADHOUSE

8–10 Newton Street, Manchester M1 2AN
Tel: 0161 2379789
www.theroadhouselive.co.uk
Excellent venue to catch young Mancunian bands searching for fame. Also hosts club nights.

Mon–Thu 8pm–2am, Fri–Sun 9pm–3am £3–£7
Manchester Piccadilly

SOUTH

4a South King Street, Manchester M2 6DQ
Tel: 0161 8317756
A small, civilized place attracting a discerning mid-20s crowd to a mix of house and funk.

Fri–Sat 10pm–2.30am Salford

🟡 THE COMEDY STORE
Deansgate Locks, Whitworth Street, Manchester
Tel: 08705 932932
www.thecomedystore.co.uk
Live stand-up performances at the only Comedy Store outside London.
🕐 Performances Wed–Sun 💷 £6–£15
🍴 🅿 🚇 Manchester Deansgate

🟡 TRIBAL SESSIONS AND REDLIGHT AT SANKEYS SOAP
Jersey Street, Manchester M4 6JG
Tel: 0161 6619668
Trendy and popular club nights.
🕐 Fri 10pm–3am, Sat 10.30pm–4am
💷 Fri £8–£12, Sat £10–£12.
Programme may differ during student vacations 🚇 Manchester Piccadilly

🔴 MANCHESTER UNITED FOOTBALL CLUB
Sir Matt Busby Way, Old Trafford, Manchester M16 0RA
Tel: 0161 868 8000; 0870 442 1994
www.manutd.co.uk
Match tickets may be virtually impossible to obtain, but a visit to Old Trafford's Theatre of Dreams museum—covering the history of the club from 1878 to the present day—is the next best thing.
🕐 Daily 9.30–5 💷 Stadium tour and museum: adult £9, child £6, family £25; museum only: adult £5.50, child £3.75, family £15

NEWCASTLE UPON TYNE
🌐 GRAINGER MARKET
Grainger Street, Newcastle upon Tyne
NE1 5QN
Tel: 0191 2115540
www.newcastle.gov.uk
This traditional, early 19th-century indoor market contains the oldest surviving branch of Marks & Spencer, opened in 1895. The market consists of the Grainger Arcade and the impressive vegetable market, with its curved glass roof. There are over 100 stores.
🕐 Mon and Wed 9–5, Tue, Thu–Sat 9–5.30 🍴 🚇 Newcastle

🎬 TYNESIDE CINEMA
10 Pilgrim Street, Newcastle upon Tyne
NE1 6QG
Tel: 0191 2328289
www.tynecine.org
Art-house and foreign-language films.
🕐 Box office: Mon–Sat 10–8.30, Sun from 15 min before first lunchtime screening 💷 From £5 🖥 🅿
🚇 Newcastle

🟡 JAZZ CAFÉ
23–25 Pink Lane, Newcastle upon Tyne
NE1 5DW
Tel: 0191 2326505
Live jazz, latin dance and a cultured crowd make this one of Newcastle's coolest nightspots.
🕐 Tue–Sat 8pm–3am 🚇 Newcastle

The respected Stephen Joseph Theatre in Scarborough

🟡 KLUB IKON
49 Newbride Street, Newcastle upon Tyne
Tel: 0191 2612526
www.ikonnewcastle.co.uk
One of Newcastle's biggest clubs.
🕐 Mon–Sat 9pm–2am (times may vary) 💷 From £3 🚇 Newcastle

OTTERBURN
🔴 REDESDALE RIDING CENTRE
Soppitt Farm, Otterburn NE19 1AF
Tel: 01830 520276
www.redesdaleriding.co.uk
Horseback riding in the Northumberland moorlands. No children under 5.
🕐 All year; times vary
💷 £30 for 2 hours

RICHMOND
🎬 THE GEORGIAN THEATRE ROYAL
Victoria Road, Richmond DL10 4DW
Tel: 01748 825252
www.georgiantheatreroyal.co.uk
The only functioning 18th-century theatre surviving in Britain stages drama, music, comedy, opera and recitals.
🕐 Box office: Mon–Sat 10–5, 7pm on performance days 💷 From £5 🍴 🅿

RIPON
🌐 DAVILLS OF RIPON
24 Westgate, Ripon HG4 2BQ
Tel: 01765 603544
A tiny shop near Market Square, selling bread, cakes and superb handmade chocolates.
🕐 Mon–Tue and Thu–Sat 8.30–5, Wed 8.30–2

ROTHERHAM
🔵 MAGNA SCIENCE ADVENTURE CENTRE
Sheffield Road, Templeborough, Rotherham S60 1DX
Tel: 01709 720002
www.visitmagna.co.uk
Discover science at this awesome, disused steelworks which has been turned into an educational adventure centre. Its four pavilions—Earth, Air, Fire and Water—are aimed at children, with plenty of hands-on activities.
🕐 Daily 10–5 💷 Adult £9, child (5–15) £7, family £28 🍴 🖥 🌐
🚇 Meadowhall

SCARBOROUGH
🎬 STEPHEN JOSEPH THEATRE
Westborough, Scarborough YO11 1JW
Tel: 01723 370541
www.sjt.uk.com
Theatre hosting both repertory and touring productions plus premières of dramas by English playwright and director Sir Alan Ayckbourn (born 1939), the company's artistic director since 1971.
🕐 Box office: Mon–Sat 10–8
💷 From £10.50 🖥 🅿
🚇 Scarborough

WHAT TO DO

STOCKTON-ON-TEES

⭐ TEES WHITE WATER CENTRE

Tees Barrage, Stockton-on-Tees TS18 2QW
Tel: 01642 678000
www.4seasons.co.uk
Purpose-built whitewater canoe course beside the River Tees, with rapids and slalom course.
🕐 Daily 8–8, in summer; 8–6, in winter
💷 Whitewater rafting: £110–£140 group of 6. Day ticket £8 🚻
🚉 Thornaby

YARM

⚫ CLUB M

Tall Trees Hotel, Yarm TS15 9PE
Tel: 01642 387200
www.clubm.co.uk
One of the North's biggest clubs. Plays a wide variety of dance music, including a monthly retro night.
🕐 Fri 9pm–2.30am, Sat 8.30pm–3am. Fri over-20s only 💷 £8–£12 🚉 Yarm

YORK

🏛 BARBARA CATTLE

45 Stonegate, York YO1 8AW
Tel: 01904 623862
www.hl-brown.co.uk
A treasure house in York's historic centre, with fine silver and jewellery, especially 18th- and 19th-century English silverware and rare York silver.
🕐 Mon–Sat 9–5.30 🚉 York

🏛 ROBERT THOMPSON'S CRAFTSMEN LTD

Mouseman Visitor Centre, Kilburn, York YO61 4AH
Tel: 01347 869100
www.robertthompsons.co.uk
Run by the grandsons of founder Robert Thompson (1876–1955), the woodcarver whose work is seen in many of Yorkshire's churches and great houses. Oak furniture and smaller items are finished with Thompson's celebrated trademark mouse.
🕐 Mon–Thu 8–5, Fri 8–3.45, Sat 10–12; closed Christmas and New Year. Visitor Centre: Easter–end Sep daily 10–5; Oct Tue–Sun 10–5; Nov, Dec Wed–Sun 11–4 🍴 🚉 Thirsk (7 miles/11km)

FESTIVALS AND EVENTS

FEBRUARY

VIKING FESTIVAL

York, various locations
Tel: 01904 643211
Longship races and battle re-enactments draw around 10,000 people to York for this jovial salute to its 200-year Viking occupation.

APRIL

GRAND NATIONAL

Ormskirk Road, Aintree, Liverpool
Tel: 0151 5232600
www.aintree.co.uk
This horse race is broadcast live and has many a betting novice laying a wager. Tickets can be bought on the gate or in advance.
🕐 First Saturday in April 💷 From £7

MAY–JUNE

ISLE OF MAN TT RACES

Douglas, Isle of Man
Tel: 01624 644644
Perhaps the most famous (and notorious) motorcycle races in the world take place over two weeks on this mountainous island.
🕐 May to June

JUNE

MERSEY RIVER FESTIVAL

Albert Dock, Liverpool
Tel: 0151 7095111 (tourist office)
Tall ships, sea shanties and the Royal Marines are all part of Europe's biggest free maritime gala, held annually.

ALNWICK MEDIEVAL FAIR

Alnwick
Tel: 01665 605004
The Middle Ages come to Alnwick for one week a year in this thorough re-creation of a medieval fair, complete with costumed revellers, crafts, courts and a ducking stool.
🕐 June to July

JULY

YORK EARLY MUSIC FESTIVAL

York, various locations
Tel: 01904 632220
www.yorkearlymusic.org
Held over three weeks, this is Britain's leading early music festival, with singers and musicians performing in York's historic buildings.

AUGUST

INTERNATIONAL BEATLE WEEK

Atlantic Pavilion, Albert Dock, Liverpool
Tel: 0151 239 9091
www.visitliverpool.com
The biggest annual celebration of The Beatles' music in the world takes place over five days at venues in their home city.
🕐 Late August

GAY FEST

Manchester, various locations
Tel: 0161 2343157
One of the largest Gay Pride events in Europe, Manchester's Gay Fest brings its community on to the streets for a flamboyant parade.

SEPTEMBER

GREAT NORTH RUN

Newcastle, Gateshead
Tel: 0191 4020016
www.ukactivity.com
A half-marathon that sees thousands of runners on the streets of Newcastle and Gateshead.

HARROGATE ANTIQUES FAIR

Harrogate International Centre, Harrogate
Tel: 01823 323363
www.harrogateantiquefair.com
Prestigious antiques fair held over four days.
🕐 Late September to early October

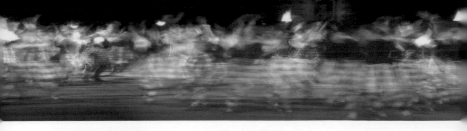

SCOTLAND

WHAT TO DO

Cross England's border into Scotland and it's not just the accent that changes. There's theatre, music, literature and art with a distinctly Scottish feel, as well as the world-famous Edinburgh Festival. Outdoors, some homegrown sports, such as golf, have caught on more readily than others, such as shinty. And beyond the golf courses are the Highlands, some of the most dramatic landscapes in Britain.

KEY TO SYMBOLS	
⊕	Shopping
ⓐ	Entertainment
ⓥ	Nightlife
ⓚ	Sports
✪	Activities
♡	Health and Beauty
✾	For Children

SHOPPING

There may be a generous allocation of uninspiring tartan-fixated souvenir shops in Scotland, but they are balanced by genuinely interesting shopping destinations. Visit Glasgow's Princes Square to see a well-designed shopping complex; Jenners in Edinburgh is a department store that is also a cut above the rest. Whisky, woollens (including cashmere) and, yes, tartan products such as kilts, make respectable souvenirs.

PERFORMANCE AND NIGHTLIFE

Glasgow gives Edinburgh a run for its money in the entertainment stakes. Its contemporary music scene has flourished in venues such as King Tut's Wah Wah Hut. And Glasgow's Royal Concert Hall matches the standard of performances at Edinburgh's prestigious Usher Hall. Dundee's West End is a notable cultural quarter. The fortnightly magazine *The List* covers Glasgow and Edinburgh.

SPORTS, ACTIVITIES AND FESTIVALS

Golf is the national game of Scotland with more than 500 courses to choose from. A useful website is www.scottishgolf.com. Tourist information offices sell golf passes offering discounted rounds at local courses. With its abundance of rivers, lochs and 4,000 miles (6,400km) of coastline, you can enjoy coarse, sea or game fishing in Scotland. For coarse and game fishing you need a permit, available from the tourism offices or tackle shops. The brown trout season is from 15 March to 6 October. You can go salmon and sea trout fishing from 15 January to 30 November. For more information, visit the Salmon and Trout Association's website (www.salmon-trout.org).

Tourist information offices stock maps for walkers, climbers, cyclists and campers. Access to the Scottish countryside is usually open to all walkers but there are some restrictions during the shooting season. In the Highlands there are special phone numbers giving recorded information on access restrictions. Serious hill walkers tick off the list of Munros, a set of 284 peaks over 914.4m (3,000ft) high. Pack insect repellent to ward off summer's armies of midges.

For information on the Edinburgh Festival, Royal Highland Show and other events, ▷ 266.

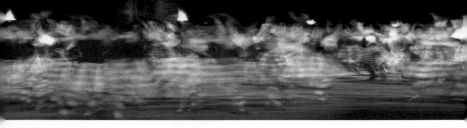

ABERDEEN

🌐 ESSLEMONT & MACINTOSH

26–38 Union Street, Aberdeen AB10 1GD
Tel: 01224 647331

This large independent department store has been a fixture of Aberdeen's 'Granite Mile' since 1873. On a site split between two buildings, discover emporia of clothes, cosmetics, perfume, china, gifts and things for the home.

🕐 Mon, Wed, Fri–Sat 9–5.30, Tue 9.30–5.30, Thu 9 7.30, Sun 12–4 🚻 🚇 Aberdeen

🎵 MUSIC HALL

Union Street, Aberdeen AB10 1QS
Tel: 01224 641122 (box office)
www.musichallaberdeen.com

Big classical concerts are held here, including performances by the Royal Scottish National Orchestra. Also jazz.

🕐 All year 🚻 🚇 Aberdeen

🎵 LEMON TREE

5 West North Street, Aberdeen AB24 5AT
Tel: 01224 642230
www.lemontree.org

The best music venue in Aberdeen, with classical, traditional Irish, funk, blues and rock concerts. Also hosts theatre, dance and comedy. Close to the top of Union Street.

🕐 All year 🚻 Food Thu–Sun 12–3; live jazz Fri and Sun 🚇 Aberdeen

🎬 THE BELMONT

49 Belmont Street, Aberdeen AB10 1JS
Tel: 01224 343536
www.picturehouses.co.uk

This popular art-house cinema also screens classic films and holds French and Italian film festivals.

🕐 Daily 🎫 From £3.70 🚻 🚇 Aberdeen

🍺 OLD BLACKFRIAR'S

52 Castle Street, Aberdeen AB11 5BB
Tel: 01224 581922

Cosy pub dating back to the time of Mary, Queen of Scots.

🕐 Mon–Sat 11am–midnight and Sun 12.30–11.30 🚇 Aberdeen

ABERFELDY

🌟 HIGHLAND ADVENTURE SAFARIS

The Highland Safari Lodge, Dull, Aberfeldy PH15 2JQ
Tel: 01887 820071
www.highlandadventuresafaris.co.uk

Explore the Highlands on a Land Rover tour. Local wildlife includes grouse, deer and golden eagles.

🕐 All year 🎫 2 hour 30 min tour: adult £32.50, child (under 12) £12.50, (13–18) £17.50 🚻 🚇

AVIEMORE

🌟 ROTHIEMURCHUS ESTATE

Near Aviemore PH22 1QH
Tel 01479 812345
www.rothiemurchus.net

Dundee Rep is one of Scotland's leading theatres

The Rothiemurchus Estate south of Aviemore has forests, rivers, lochs and mountains to explore and is home to rare species such as the capercaillie. The activity centre offers guided walks, fishing, shooting and off-road driving.

🕐 Daily 9–5.30 🎫 Variable 🚇 Aviemore

DUMFRIES

🎭 THEATRE ROYAL

Shakespeare Street, Dumfries DG1 2JH
Tel: 01387 254209
www.theatreroyaldumfries.co.uk

The Theatre Royal is Scotland's oldest working theatre, offering plays and pantomimes performed by the resident amateur Guild of Players and touring productions of music and drama.

🕐 All year 🎫 From £6 🚻 🚇 Dumfries

🍺 THE GLOBE INN

56 High Street, Dumfries DG1 2JA
Tel: 01387 252335

This 400-year-old pub was Robert Burns's local. You'll find it down an alley near the foot of the High Street.

🕐 Mon–Wed 10am–11pm, Thu–Sun 10am–midnight 🚇 Dumfries

DUNDEE

🎭 DUNDEE REP

Tay Square, Dundee DD1 1PB
Tel: 01382 223530
www.dundeerep.co.uk

Scotland's leading repertory theatre is in Dundee's West End, the up-and-coming cultural quarter. Also hosts touring productions and shows by the contemporary Scottish Dance Theatre.

🕐 All year. Box office: 10am–8pm 🚻 🚇 Dundee

🍺 SOCIAL

10 South Tay Street, Dundee DD1 1PA
Tel: 01382 202070

The glass-walled side of this trendy bar overlooks Tay Square. Cool, contemporary decoration inside, with different events each night, including live music from R&B to reggae.

🕐 Mon–Sat 11am–midnight, Sun 12–12 🚇 Dundee

EASDALE

🌟 SEA.FARI

Easdale Harbour, Seil Island, near Oban
Tel: 01852 300003
www.seafari.co.uk

Enjoy an exhilarating trip on a rigid inflatable boat to see wildlife such as seals, seabirds, dolphins and the occasional minke whale.

🕐 Trips run all year, weather permitting, but mainly Easter–end Oct 🎫 2 hours from adult £26, child £19.50, family £82.50

WHAT TO DO

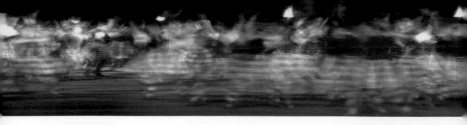

EDINBURGH

🌐 JENNERS
48 Princes Street, Edinburgh EH2 2YJ
Tel: 0131 225 2442
www.jenners.com
Grander than its newest rival Harvey Nichols, Jenners is an Edinburgh institution, founded in 1838. It sells everything from high-quality clothes and shoes to toys, glassware, groceries and perfume. Slightly more expensive than Princes Street's other department stores.
🕐 Mon, Wed, Fri, Sat 9–6, Tue 9.30–6, Thu 9–8, Sun 11–5
🚉 Edinburgh Waverley

🌐 OCEAN TERMINAL CENTRE
Ocean Drive, Leith, Edinburgh EH6 6JJ
Tel: 0131 555 8888
www.oceanterminal.com
Designed by Jasper Conran and opened in 2001, Ocean Terminal is a vast shopping and cinema complex overlooking the Firth of Forth and the royal yacht *Britannia*.
🕐 Mon–Fri 10–8, Sat 10–7, Sun 11–6
🍴 Zinc Bar & Grill (tel: 0131 553 8070)

🌐 ROYAL MILE WHISKIES
379 High Street, Royal Mile, Edinburgh EH1 1PW
Tel: 0131 225 3383
www.royalmilewhiskies.com
This specialist whisky shop opposite St. Giles Cathedral stocks a vast range of malt whiskies, some of which are 100 years old. It's the best place to buy rare whiskies if you want them shipped home.
🕐 Mon–Sat 10–6, Sun 12.30–6
🚉 Edinburgh Waverley

🌐 TARTAN WEAVING MILL AND EXHIBITION
555 Castle Hill, The Royal Mile, Edinburgh EH1 2ND
Tel: 0131 226 4162
www.tartanweavingmill.co.uk
You can hear the weaving looms in the basement everywhere in this massive tartan shop at the top of the Royal Mile. On the way down you can have your photo taken in full Highland rig, consult the 'Clans and Tartans Bureau' for information about your own clan history, then have a go at weaving yourself.
🕐 Daily 9–5.30 🎟 Free 🛒
🚉 Edinburgh Waverley

🎬 DOMINION
18 Newbattle Terrace, Morningside, Edinburgh EH10 4RT
Tel: 0131 447 4771 (box office)
www.dominioncinema.com
This family-run cinema screens independent and mainstream movies, and has traditional leather Pullman seats. Bag a sofa and free wine or beer with the Gold Class service.
🕐 Daily 🚉 Edinburgh Haymarket

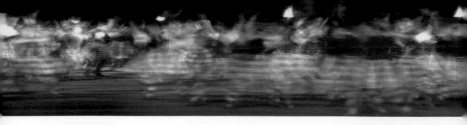

Jenners in Edinburgh is the world's oldest department store

🎭 EDINBURGH FESTIVAL THEATRE
13–29 Nicolson Street, Edinburgh EH8 9FT
Tel: 0131 529 6000
www.eft.co.uk
Prestigious concert venue hosts touring productions of dance, theatre, musicals and comedy, plus ballet and Scottish Opera productions.
🕐 All year. Box office: Mon–Sat 11–8, Sun 11–4 🎟 From £8 🛒 🛒
🚉 Edinburgh Waverley

🎭 EDINBURGH PLAYHOUSE
18–22 Greenside Place, Edinburgh EH1 3AA
Tel: 0870 606 3424
www.getlive.co.uk (theatre information)
The best venue for touring productions of big-budget musicals and dance. A five-minute walk from the east end of Princes Street.
🕐 All year 🎟 From £12 🛒
🚉 Edinburgh Waverley

🎭 QUEEN'S HALL
Clerk Street, Edinburgh EH8 9JG
Tel: 0131 668 2019
www.queenshalledinburgh.co.uk
A more intimate venue than the Usher Hall, this is a hot spot for jazz, blues and soul, as well as classical music and comedy, attracting names such as Courtney Pine and Ruby Turner.
🕐 All year 🎟 From £10 🛒
🚉 Edinburgh Waverley

🎭 USHER HALL
Lothian Road, Edinburgh EH1 2EA
Tel: 0131 228 1155
www.usherhall.co.uk
Edinburgh's most prestigious concert hall attracts excellent orchestras. A distinctive circular building towards the West End, its high dome can be seen from many parts of the city.
🕐 All year 🎟 From £10 🛒
🚉 Edinburgh Haymarket

🍷 BELUGA
30a Chambers Street, Edinburgh EH1
Tel: 0131 624 4546
The Beluga bar-nightclub is the place to see and be seen: a laid-back venue to lunch in by day, and home of the beautiful people by night. A huge waterfall dominates the opulent interior.
🕐 Daily 11am–1am 🎟 Free entry
🚉 Edinburgh Waverley

🍷 BLUE MOON
1 Barony Street, New Town, Edinburgh EH1
Tel: 0131 556 2788
Everybody is welcome at this gay bar, noted for serving the best food in the area all day. The staff are a good source of local knowledge on the best club nights (both gay and straight).
🕐 Mon–Fri 11–11, Sat–Sun 10am–11.30pm 🚉 Edinburgh Waverley

WHAT TO DO

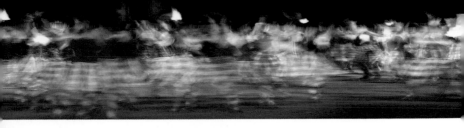

🍷 JOLLY JUDGE
7a James Court, Old Town, Edinburgh EH1 2PB
Tel: 0131 225 2669
Seek out this 17th-century pub for its malt whiskies. At the top of the Royal Mile go down East Entry into James Court.
🕐 Mon and Thu–Sat 12–12, Tue–Wed 12–11, Sun 12.30–11

🍷 STAND COMEDY CLUB
5 York Place, Edinburgh EH1 3EB
Tel: 0131 558 7272
www.thestand.co.uk
Enjoy live comedy from new and well-known comedians at this dark and intimate basement bar. Weekend shows often sell out, so reserving in advance is recommended.
🕐 Mon–Sat 7.30pm–1am, Sun 12.30–midnight 🎫 Free–£9
🚆 Edinburgh Waverley

🏉 MURRAYFIELD STADIUM
Off Roseburn Terrace, Murrayfield, Edinburgh EH12 5PJ
Tel: 0131 346 5000
www.sru.org.uk
Rugby is Edinburgh's most popular sport so reserving in advance for matches is essential. Behind-the-scenes tours are also available.
🕐 Call for match information. Stadium tours Mon–Fri 11 and 2.30
🎫 Vary. Tour: adult £5, child (5–18) £3, family £12 🚆 Edinburgh Haymarket

💧 EDINBURGH FLOATARIUM
29 North West Circus Place, Edinburgh EH3 6TP
Tel: 0131 225 3350
Enjoy floating in a float tank, reflexology, massages and facials. The aromatherapy massage is particularly recommended.
🕐 Mon–Fri 9–8, Sat 9–6, Sun 9.30–4
🎫 1-hour float £25; 1-hour aromatherapy massage £32 🏛
🚆 Edinburgh Waverley

ELGIN

🏛 JOHNSTON'S OF ELGIN CASHMERE VISITOR CENTRE
Newmill, Elgin IV30 4AF
Tel: 01343 554099
www.johnstonscashmere.com

Take a tour of the only Scottish mill still to turn cashmere into clothes: it has been spun, dyed and woven here for over 200 years. The shop sells high-quality cashmere clothes in glorious shades. Tax-free shopping for visitors from outside the EU. Signposted from central Elgin.
🕐 Mon–Sat 9–5.30; also Jun–Oct Sun 11–4.30 🚆 Elgin

FORT WILLIAM

🏛 HEBRIDEAN JEWELLERY
95 High Street, Fort William PH33 6DG
Tel: 01397 702033
www.hebridean-jewellery.co.uk
The distinctive jewellery in this small shop is adorned with

You'll find beautifully made cashmere in Elgin

Celtic designs and handmade in the Hebrides. Other branches are found in South Uist, and Stornoway on the Isle of Lewis. Tax-free shopping for customers from outside the EU.
🕐 Mon–Sat 9–5.30 🚆 Fort William

⭐ NEVIS RANGE
Torlundy, Fort William PH33 6SW
Tel: 01397 705855
www.nevisrange.co.uk
Ski and snowboarding resort north of Fort William, with the highest skiing in Scotland, from easy to difficult.
🕐 Daily; closed early Dec
🎫 Gondola: adult £8, child £4.90; ski rental: £15.50 daily; snowboard rental £17.50 daily 🍽 🏛

🚂 JACOBITE STEAM TRAIN
Fort William Railway Station, Fort William
Tel: 01463 239026
www.steamtrain.info
The steam train that had a cameo role as the Hogwarts Express in the Harry Potter films follows the scenic Road to the Isles via Glenfinnan (where scenes were shot at the great viaduct).
🕐 Mid-Jun to early Oct Mon–Fri 10.20am 🎫 Day return: adult £26, child £15 🏛 🚆

GLASGOW

🏛 GEOFFREY (TAILOR) KILTMAKERS & WEAVERS
309 Sauchiehall Street, Glasgow G2 3HW
Tel: 0141 331 2388
www.geoffreykilts.co.uk
One of Scotland's top kiltmakers and Highland dress specialists, brimming with every kind of kilt, tartan and accessory. Made-to-measure outfits can be sent to you abroad.
🕐 Mon–Wed and Fri–Sat 9–5.30, Thu 9–7, Sun 11–5 🚆 Glasgow Charing Cross

🏛 PRINCES SQUARE
48 Buchanan Street, Glasgow G1 3JX
Tel: 0141 204 1685
www.princessquare.co.uk
An art deco style doorway on Buchanan Street announces this smart indoor shopping complex. Good shops sell clothes, shoes and gifts, including Jo Malone perfumes.
🕐 Mon–Wed and Fri 9.30–6, Thu 9.30–8, Sat 9–6, Sun 12–5 🏛 🍽 🏛
🚆 Glasgow Argyle Street

🏛 TISO GLASGOW OUTDOOR EXPERIENCE
Couper Street, off Kyle Street, Glasgow G4 0DL
Tel: 0141 550 5450
www.tiso.com
A great selection of outdoor equipment, clothing and books. The interactive features—a 15m (50ft) rock pinnacle, waterfall and 7m (23ft) ice wall—enable you to try out the gear.
🕐 Mon–Tue, Fri–Sat 9–6, Wed 9.30–6, Thu 9–7, Sun 11–5
🚆 Glasgow Queen Street

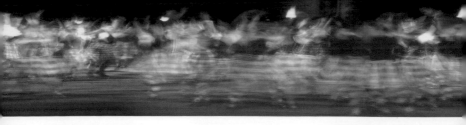

BARROWLANDS
244 Gallowgate, Glasgow G4 0TS
Tel: 0141 552 4601; 0870 903 3444
www.glasgow-barrowland.com
Big-name pop and rock acts play at this engaging venue. Tickets from Ticket Scotland (tel: 0141 204 5151).
All year From £9
St. Enoch
Glasgow Central, Queen Street

CENTRE FOR CONTEMPORARY ARTS (CCA)
350 Sauchiehall Street, Glasgow G2 3JD
Tel: 0141 3524900 (cinema tickets)
www.cca-glasgow.com
Various contemporary art forms, including music, visual art and alternative cinema are catered for at this cutting-edge venue. Films include classics, foreign films and work by leading directors.
Daily Cowcaddens

GLASGOW ROYAL CONCERT HALL
2 Sauchiehall Street, Glasgow G2 3NY
Tel: 0141 353 8000
www.grch.com
Glasgow's most prestigious venue and home of the Royal Scottish National Orchestra, this concert hall has a varied schedule of classical, pop and rock music and holds the Celtic Connections winter festival of concerts and ceilidhs.
All year £5–£30 Buchanan Street Glasgow Queen Street

KING TUT'S WAH WAH HUT
272a St. Vincent Street, Glasgow G2 5RL
Tel: 0141 221 5279/08770 169 0100 (Ticketmaster)
www.kingtuts.co.uk
The heart of the Glasgow music scene. It's an unpretentious, relaxed venue playing cutting-edge indie, pop and rock. Tickets from Ticketmaster.
All year From £4.50
Glasgow Central, Queen Street

THEATRE ROYAL
282 Hope Street, Glasgow G2 3QA
Tel: 0141 240 1133
www.theatreroyalglasgow.com
The best in opera, ballet, dance and theatre at the home of Scottish Opera and Scottish Ballet.
All year From £4
Cowcaddens, Buchanan Street
Queen Street

ARCHES
253 Argyle Street, Glasgow G2 8DL
Tel: 0870 240 7528
www.thearches.co.uk
The nightclub in the Arches complex, with its industrial-style interior, is Glasgow's biggest. The music varies and

Comfortable shopping in Glasgow's Princes Square

can include hip-hop, house, soul or big name DJs.
Club nights Fri–Sun, until late
From £5 St. Enoch
Glasgow Central

SCOTIA BAR
112–114 Stockwell Street, Glasgow G1 4LW
Tel: 0141 552 8681
This traditional pub is Glasgow's oldest, established in 1792. Live folk music on most evenings and poetry readings on Sundays.
Mon–Sat 11am–midnight, Sun 12–12 St. Enoch
Glasgow Central

JEDBURGH

CHRISTOPHER RAINBOW
8 Timpendean Cottages, Jedburgh TD8 6SS
Tel: 01835 830326
Bicycles can be rented here, or delivered. Ideal for the peaceful Four Abbeys Cycleway through Melrose, Dryburgh and Kelso along the Tweed and Teviot rivers.
All year Bicycle rental from £18 a day

KINGUSSIE

HIGHLAND WILDLIFE PARK
Kincraig, Kingussie PH21 1NL
Tel: 01540 651270
www.highlandwildlifepark.org
The reserve–with children's trail, activities and play area–has a viewpoint where you can watch red deer, Highland cattle and bison. A raised walkway takes you over the wolf enclosure.
Apr–end May and Sep–end Oct daily 10–6; Jun–end Aug 10–7; rest of year 10–4 Adult £8.50, child £6.50
Kingussie 4 miles (6.5km)

KIRKCUDBRIGHT

JO GALLANT
Ironstones, 70 High Street, Kirkcudbright DG6
Tel: 01557 331130
www.jogallant.co.uk
Sumptuous textiles are displayed in this stone-fronted building near the Tolbooth Art Centre. The price of the embroidered wall-hangings, cushions and scarves may be high, but so is the quality.
Mon–Sat 10–5 (call first if travelling specially)

LEWIS

OISEVAL GALLERY
Brue, Isle of Lewis HS2 0QW
Tel: 01851 840240
www.oiseval.co.uk
Enjoy beautiful photographs of Hebridean landscapes by James Smith, displayed in a small gallery in the photographer's house. Mail-order service available.
Mon–Sat 10.30–5.30

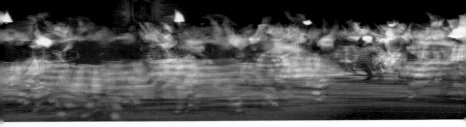

LOCH KEN

✪ GALLOWAY SAILING CENTRE

Castle Douglas, Loch Ken Marina
DG7 3NQ
Tel: 01644 420626
www.lochken.co.uk
Activities on beautiful Loch Ken include sailing, windsurfing, kayaking, canoeing, quad biking and gorge scrambling.
🕐 Apr–end Oct 💷 Lessons from £20. Call for rental rates 🖥️

MELROSE

🏛️ ABBEY MILL

Annay Road, Melrose TD6 9LG
Tel: 01896 822138
This large store selling knitwear, clothes, toys and Scottish food occupies a corn mill, which dates back to the Middle Ages, just outside town, beyond Melrose Abbey.
🕐 Daily 9–5.30, may vary in winter
🖥️

PENICUIK

🏛️ EDINBURGH CRYSTAL VISITOR CENTRE

Eastfield, Penicuik EH26 8HB
Tel: 01968 675128
www.edinburgh-crystal.com
See the famous Edinburgh crystal being made in the factory and choose from beautiful decanters, vases and whisky glasses in the shop. You can talk with the master craftspeople as they work, and see how glass has been made through the ages.
🕐 Mon–Sat 10–5, Sun 11–5 🖥️

✪ PENTLAND HILLS ICELANDICS

Windy Gowl Farm, Carlops, Penicuik EH26
Tel: 01968 661095
www.phicelandics.co.uk
Enjoy short rides or all-day treks in the Pentland Hills on Icelandic ponies from a Trekking and Riding Society of Scotland-approved centre. Tough shoes and warm clothing essential. Minimum age 8 years.
🕐 Fri–Wed, all year, rides at 10 and 2.30 💷 £30 for two hours

PERTH

🏛️ CAITHNESS GLASS VISITOR CENTRE

Inveralmond, Perth PH1 3TZ
Tel: 01738 637373
www.caithnessglass.co.uk
Vases, whisky tumblers, decanters and paperweights are sold at discount prices in the factory shop. Glassmaking can be watched on weekdays year-round and weekends in July and August. The shop offers overseas posting.
🕐 Mid-Jun to early Sep Mon–Sat 9–6; Oct–end May Mon–Sat 9–5, also Sun 10–5, Mar–end Nov, and 12–5 Dec–end Feb 💷 Free 🍴 🏛️ 🚉 Perth 2.5 miles (4km)

Stylish souvenirs at Caithness Glass in Perth

☯ FAMOUS BEIN INN

Glenfarg, Perth PH2 9PY
Tel: 01577 830216
www.beininn.com
The Bein Inn, 5 miles (8km) south of Perth, was built as a resting place for travellers on the route from Edinburgh to the Highlands. It is famous for its small stage, attracting folk, country and rock musicians. There are ten gigs monthly.
🕐 Daily to 11.30pm

PITLOCHRY

🏛️ HERITAGE JEWELLERS

104 Atholl Road, Pitlochry PH16 5BL
Tel: 01796 474333
www.heritage-jewellers.co.uk
This small, exclusive shop sells gold and silver jewellery, cultured pearls, Celtic jewellery made in Orkney and Scottish gold.
🕐 Mon–Sat 10–5, Sun 12–4 🚉 Pitlochry

✪ FREESPIRITS

Riverside Inn, Grandtully, Pitlochry PH9 0PL
Tel: 0845 644 4755
www.freespirits-online.co.uk
This outdoor activities company majors in adrenaline sports around the River Tay, River Tummel and Perthshire. Activities are suitable for age 8 and over.
🕐 All year 💷 Rafting from £30; canyoning £30 🖥️ 🚉 Pitlochry

ST. ANDREWS

🏛️ DAVID BROWN GALLERY

9 Albany Place, St. Andrews KY16 9HH
Tel: 01334 477840
The gallery is worth a visit if you love antiques—but if you love antiques and golf, it's a must. Unassuming on the outside, but an Aladdin's cave within, crammed full of silverware, prints and vintage golfing books.
🕐 Mon–Sat 9–5.30

🏛️ LUCCI

68 Market Street, St. Andrews KY16 9NU
Tel: 01334 477796
One of the better gift shops in town, specializing in interior design and furnishings. Next to the tourist information office.
🕐 Mon–Sat 9.30–7, Sun 12–5 🚉 Leuchars

☯ CENTRAL BAR

79 Market Street, St. Andrews KY16 9NU
Tel: 01334 470290
A St. Andrews institution in the heart of the town, popular with students and locals. Food served until 9pm. On the corner of College Street and Market Street.
🕐 Mon–Thu noon–midnight, Fri–Sat noon–1am 🚉 Leuchars

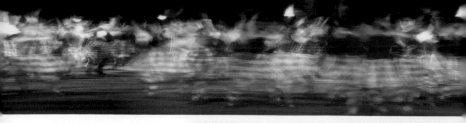

ST. ANDREWS LINKS
Pilmour House, St. Andrews KY16 9SF
Tel: 01334 466666
www.standrews.org.uk
The largest golf complex in Europe consists of six public golf courses, including the Old Course, the New Course and the Jubilee Course. Advance reservation essential–the waiting list is anything from weeks to years. Check the website for the complex rules and requirements.
All year Strathtyrum Course £22; Old Course £115 Leuchars

STOBO

STOBO SPA
Stobo Castle, Stobo EH45 8NY
Tel: 01721 725300
www.stobocastle.co.uk
Treat yourself at this luxurious, £5 million spa in a 19th-century castle south of Edinburgh. Lunch and dinner are included. Reserve in advance. Not suitable for children.
All year Day visit from £160

TAIN

GLENMORANGIE DISTILLERY
Tain IV19 1PZ
Tel: 01862 892477
www.glenmorangie.com
Take a tour of the 'Glen of Tranquillity' distillery and see how this famous whisky is made before having a taste of the real thing. Advance reservation recommended. Just north of the village, overlooking the Dornoch Firth.
Mon–Fri 9–5; also Jun–end Aug Sat 10–4 and Sun 12–4 Adult £2.50

ULLAPOOL

HIGHLAND STONEWARE
Mill Street, Ullapool IV26 2UN
Tel: 01854 612980
www.highlandstoneware.com
See this distinctive pottery being made and hand-painted by craftspeople at the Ullapool factory. You can commission your own designs.
Easter–end Oct Mon–Fri 9–6, and Sat 9–5

FESTIVALS AND EVENTS

JANUARY

CELTIC CONNECTIONS
Glasgow
Tel: 0141 287 5511
www.celticconnections.com
Scotland's biggest folk festival attracts musicians from all over the world for concerts and ceilidhs over two weeks across the city.
Mid-January

UP HELLY AA
Lerwick, Shetland
Tel: 01595 693434
www.shetlandtourism.com
Viking celebrations in Lerwick, with torchlight processions, a ceremonial ship burning and partying.
Last Tuesday in January

APRIL

SPIRIT OF SPEYSIDE WHISKY FESTIVAL
Speyside
Tel: 01343 542666
www.spiritofspeyside.com
Four days of whisky-flavoured fun all over Speyside, from vintage tastings on trains to tours of unusual distilleries. Book ahead.
Late April–early May

JUNE

ROYAL HIGHLAND SHOW
Ingliston, near Edinburgh
Tel: 0131 335 6200
www.royalhighlandshow.org
Scotland's biggest agricultural show: livestock judging, show jumping and country activities.
Late June

JULY

GLASGOW JAZZ FESTIVAL
Glasgow, various venues
Tel: 0141 552 3552
www.jazzfest.co.uk
Five days of the best in international jazz. Sample the Fringe, too.
Early July

AUGUST

INTERNATIONAL ARTS FESTIVAL
Edinburgh, various venues
Tel: 0131 473 2099
www.eif.co.uk
The three-week event is the world's largest arts festival, offering opera, dance, music and theatre.

EDINBURGH FRINGE FESTIVAL
Edinburgh, various venues
Tel: 0131 226 5257
www.edfringe.com
The ever-expanding Fringe hosts hundreds of productions of varying quality in any venues with available space.
Mid to end August

COWAL HIGHLAND GATHERING
Dunoon
Tel: 01369 703206
www.cowalgathering.com
The biggest Highland games in Scotland fields 3,500 competitors. Highland dancing, piping and athletics events over three days.
Late August

SEPTEMBER

BRAEMAR GATHERING
Braemar
Tel: 01339 755377
www.braemargathering.org
Gatherings of competitive pipers, dancers and athletes have occurred here for about 900 years, and the Queen is a regular visitor.
Early September

DECEMBER

HOGMANAY
Princes Street, Edinburgh
Tel: 0131 473 3800
www.edinburghshogmanay.org
Celebrate the New Year with live music and fireworks at Scotland's biggest party. Free entry but obtain a pass in advance–see website.
31 December

This chapter describes 14 drives and 16 walks that explore Britain's national parks and areas of outstanding natural beauty, from the Cotswolds to the Scottish Highlands. The locations of the walks and drives are marked on the map on page 268. All the walks follow well-trodden, waymarked paths. Each walk also has a starting point on each of the drives: This is marked by a red star on the relevant drive.

Out and About

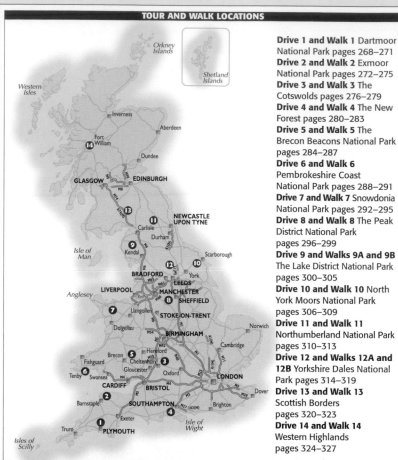

TOUR AND WALK LOCATIONS

1. DRIVE

DARTMOOR NATIONAL PARK

Winding, narrow roads traverse valleys where ponies, cattle and sheep roam free. Dartmoor (▷ 77) is a diverse area of wilderness, with rugged hills and moorland carpeted with colourful heather, tempered by wooded river valleys and ancient villages.

THE DRIVE

Distance: 65 miles (105km)
Allow: 3–4 hours, plus time for wandering
Start/end: Tavistock, map ref 429 D20
Tourist information office: The High Moorland Visitor Centre, Tavistock Road, Princetown PL20 6QF, tel: 01822 890414
OS Landranger maps: 191, 202

Leave Tavistock ❶ on the B3357 that heads eastwards to the moors and climbs on to Dartmoor. You shortly see Vixen Tor away to the right; this is the largest of Dartmoor's many tors—outcrops of weathered granite. Soon after you come to the crossroads at Two Bridges. Turn left and shortly left again to follow the B3212 to continue northeast (signposted Moretonhampstead).

On the way you pass through Postbridge ❷, where the largest and best-preserved of Dartmoor's clapper bridges–planks or stone slabs laid across stones–crosses the East Dart River. The bridge has been used by tin miners and farmers since medieval times.

The next right turning (towards Widecombe in the Moor) is a diversion to Grimspound, a celebrated 3,000-year-old Bronze Age settlement. To reach it follow the lane for 1 mile

(1.5km) and park at the steps on the left by a bend in the road. Grimspound consists of the faint, circular outlines of 24 huts, which probably had roofs of timber and turf. Farther along the B3212 is the Miniature Pony Centre (mid-Mar to end Oct daily 10.30–4.30). Continue on the B3212 to Moretonhampstead ❸.

A series of fires in the 19th century destroyed many of Moretonhampstead's older buildings, but a fine row of 17th-century almshouses survives in Cross Street. The architect Sir Edwin Lutyens' early 20th-century Arts and

OUT AND ABOUT

Crafts masterpiece Castle Drogo is just to the north.

At Moretonhampstead turn right on the A382 (signposted Bovey Tracey). Turn right on to the B3387 for Haytor Vale and the descent to Widecombe in the Moor.

Widecombe in the Moor is a candidate for the most popular Dartmoor village, set neatly in a hollow among granite ridges. The roof of the surprisingly grand late 14th-century church has a whimsical set of bosses featuring a pelican, a scapegoat and three interlocking rabbits forming the special sign of the tin miners—who paid for the majestic church tower.

From Widecombe follow tiny winding lanes to Dunstone ❹ and to Ponsworthy. The road climbs to Dartmeet ❺, where the East and West Dart rivers converge near another old clapper bridge.

The area around Dartmeet is lush and green, and only a few minutes' strolling is needed to escape the bustle of what is a very popular place.

From Dartmeet continue on the B3357 back to Two Bridges, but this time head southwest to Princetown ❻.

At 427m (1,400ft) above sea level, Princetown is England's highest village. It is also among the bleakest, inhabited mostly by staff of the high-security Dartmoor Prison, a grey edifice built originally for prisoners of the Napoleonic Wars (1800–15). The village is also home to the High Moorland Visitor Centre. South

of the village, a dead-end road to Whiteworks reaches perhaps the loneliest settlement in Dartmoor, a row of cottages looking out over empty moor.

From Princetown continue west on the B3212, from which you can divert to Burrator Reservoir. Carry on along the B3212 to Yelverton and the A386, which returns you to Tavistock.

Don't miss Postbridge's ancient clapper bridge

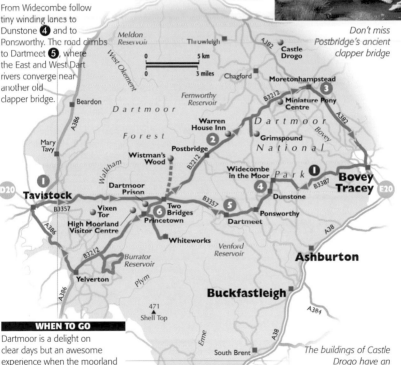

The buildings of Castle Drogo have an unusually modern feel

WHEN TO GO
Dartmoor is a delight on clear days but an awesome experience when the moorland mists roll in.

WHERE TO EAT
Warren House Inn, in a high position with excellent views over the moor (1 mile/1.6km) east of Postbridge on the B3212 (tel: 01822 880209), serves sandwiches, hot meals and cream teas. Badger's Holt at Dartmeet (tel: 01364 631213) is a picturesque restaurant and gift shop in a delightful setting.

PLACES TO VISIT
Castle Drogo
✉ Moretonhampstead, EX6 6PB
☎ 01647 433306
🕐 Late Mar to early Nov Wed–Mon
🎟 Adult £6.50, child £3.20, family £16.20. Gardens only: adult £4, child £2

High Moorland Visitor Centre
✉ Princetown, PL20 6QF
☎ 01822 890414
🕐 Daily 10–5

HAYTOR

Haytor is one of the most prominent of all Dartmoor's many tors. A magnificent viewpoint in itself, it is also surrounded by disused quarries, where the trackbeds of long-vanished tramways make useful routes for walkers.

THE WALK

Length: 4 miles (6.5km) or 5 miles (8km) including Saddle Tor
Allow: 2.5–3 hours
Start/end: Parking area at Haytor map ref 429 E20
OS Landranger map: 191
OS Explorer map: OL28

Leave the parking area ❶ and cross the road to take the wide grassy path up to the rocky summit of Haytor. You can also climb to the top of the tor by a flight of steps carved into the rock. Walk around the left side of the rock mass of Haytor ❷.

The view ahead is over western Dartmoor, one of the most accessible sections of the open moor. Slightly to the left, Hound Tor is particularly prominent, with Greator Rocks to its right. Straight ahead is Haytor Down, and beyond is the wooded valley of the River Bovey. To the northeast (right) are the remains of Haytor Quarry.

Continue around the rock mass and take the first path to the right of the quarry. Walk towards the perimeter fence of the quarry and join a track on the right. The

A carpet of wild flowers on the way up Haytor. Walkers will find that the views from the top are worth the climb

route skirts the right-hand edge of the quarry ❸. Beyond the quarry, bear left to follow the granite tramway. You pass the entrance to the quarry, and then the tramway bears right over a stone embankment to reach a T-junction. Turn left and continue to follow the tramway, bearing to the left. You will eventually see Smallacombe Rocks ❹ on the right. Take any of the paths that lead off to the right across the open moor towards these rocks.

Smallacombe Rocks gives an extensive view of the surrounding moor. You can extend the walk northeast from here, via a demanding route heading down the valley to the east and up to the summit of Hound Tor. Beneath this tor are the excavated remains of a medieval village, where you can see the layout of several houses, complete with fireplaces.

Turn around to face Haytor, and locate a quarry behind Holwell

Tor farther down the slope and to the right. Take the path leading from Smallacombe Rocks to the point just to the left of this quarry. This leads back to the tramway. Turn right along the tramway, walking past a ruined building and the quarry itself ❺. Continue around the back of the quarry and cross over the remains of a bridge (the path is narrow and not particularly well defined, so you will need to clamber over a few rocks). After crossing the bridge, bear left up to the top of Holwell Tor.

❻ From Holwell Tor walk directly across the moor on a narrow and ill-defined path that heads to Low Man, a cliff to the right of Haytor. At Haytor, retrace your steps to the parking area.

❼ From the top of Holwell Tor you can extend the walk by continuing southwards across the moor to Saddle Tor, where you turn left across the low and wide ridge leading back to Haytor. This extension gives far-ranging views.

OUT AND ABOUT

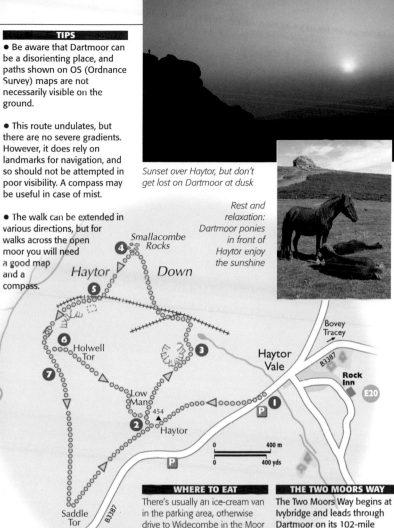

TIPS

● Be aware that Dartmoor can be a disorienting place, and paths shown on OS (Ordnance Survey) maps are not necessarily visible on the ground.

● This route undulates, but there are no severe gradients. However, it does rely on landmarks for navigation, and so should not be attempted in poor visibility. A compass may be useful in case of mist.

● The walk can be extended in various directions, but for walks across the open moor you will need a good map and a compass.

Sunset over Haytor, but don't get lost on Dartmoor at dusk

Rest and relaxation: Dartmoor ponies in front of Haytor enjoy the sunshine

OUT AND ABOUT

WHERE TO EAT

There's usually an ice-cream van in the parking area, otherwise drive to Widecombe in the Moor (about 2 miles/3.5km off the route) for cafés and a pub.

THE TWO MOORS WAY

The Two Moors Way begins at Ivybridge and leads through Dartmoor on its 102-mile (164km) journey across the county of Devon to end at Lynmouth, in Exmoor National Park. It passes to the west of this walk, through Widecombe in the Moor and over Hameldown Tor, passing the Bronze Age site of Grimspound. Farther north it enters the wooded landscape of the Teign Valley and climbs past Castle Drogo (▷ 269). A particularly popular circular walk with a series of wonderful views joins this one at Fingle Bridge in the Teign valley. It then heads along the river via the Fisherman's Path, climbing up to the back entrance to Castle Drogo and returning at high level along the Hunter's Path—a total of 4 miles (6.5km).

Early Bronze Age ruins at Grimspound

EXMOOR NATIONAL PARK

Starting from the pleasant resort of Lynton, this tour of Exmoor (▷ 78) follows the scenic A39 coast road before heading inland to the heart of Somerset.

THE DRIVE

Distance: 65 miles (105km)

Allow: 3 hours plus stops

Start/end: Town Hall, Lee Road, Lynton EX35 6BT, tel: 01598 752225 map ref 429 E19

OS Landranger maps: 180, 181

www.visit-exmoor.info

Leave Lynton town hall and follow signs for the Valley of Rocks ❶, to the west of town.

This moorland valley strongly appealed to the 18th- and 19th-century Romantic poets—William Wordsworth (1770–1850), Samuel Taylor Coleridge (1772–1834) and Robert Southey (1774–1843). It runs closely parallel to the sea and has fantastic rock formations jutting out of its slopes. The finest view is from Castle Rock, which drops 120m (400ft) to the sea but can be climbed easily from its landward side. There is a picnic area left of the entrance to the valley.

From the valley entrance the road passes the Lee Valley estate and continues past the Lee Abbey Christian Community. It then climbs steeply. At the next fork bear right (signposted Woody Bay). Pass the Woody Bay Hotel then, at a T-junction, turn right and just past a telephone box fork right downhill, signed Hunter's Inn.

Make a detour to visit Trentishoe ❷, where the tiny church has an unusual musicians' gallery, a kind that was often removed during the 19th century. Note the notch cut out of the railings to allow the movement of the double bass player's bow. Hunter's Inn is a starting point for walks along the wooded Heddon Valley to the sea at Heddon's Mouth, where there are remains of a small port, including the ruins of a lime kiln; fertilizer was shipped to Wales from here.

Bear left towards Killington, and turn right on the A39 towards Barnstaple. At Parracombe ❸, leave the A39 and branch right through the village.

Parracombe Old Church (open, but no longer in use) is a remarkable specimen of medieval architecture. It is quite unrestored, and narrowly escaped demolition in the 19th century thanks to a spirited campaign led by the author and art critic John Ruskin in 1879. It has box pews, a simple screen, a flagstone floor and an ancient roof, but no stained glass or organ.

Return to the A39 to Blackmoor Gate and turn left on the A339 towards South Molton.

Detour to visit Arlington Court by turning right then left towards Barnstaple. After 3 miles (5km) turn left, signposted Arlington Court.

Arlington Court is an early 19th-century house crammed with eclectic bits and pieces gathered by Rosalie Chichester (step-aunt of yachtsman Sir Francis Chichester) up to her death in 1949. There are model ships, tapestries, stuffed birds, paperweights and other unrelated items. From May to the end of September you can also watch, via CCTV, the largest colony of lesser horseshoe bats in Devon. The stable block has a collection of 19th-century horse-drawn vehicles, some of which are used to take visitors around the grounds of the estate, which includes an ornamental Victorian garden, parkland grazed by sheep, and a lake with a bird hide.

Return to the A399, turn right towards South Molton, then left on the B3358 to Simonsbath ❹.

Simonsbath is the western-most settlement in Somerset. Although barely a hamlet, it does have an important place in the history of Exmoor, for it was the first farming estate carved out of the great royal hunting forest from the 17th century onwards. The Boevey family carried out stock-rearing experiments, improved many of the roads, enclosed land and introduced Cheviot sheep to the area.

From Simonsbath keep forward on the B3223, then fork right, keeping to the B3223 at the junction with the B3224. At a crossroads turn right to detour to Tarr Steps (signposted) ❺.

Spanning the River Barle is this ancient stone clapper bridge of 17 large granite slabs. It has certainly existed since medieval times (although the river has demolished it on many occasions), but its origins may be even earlier.

Return to the B3224 and take the lane opposite to descend to Winsford ❻.

Winsford is a village of many thatched roofs—the Royal Oak Inn has the most elaborate—as well as no fewer than eight bridges across the rivers Winn and Exe.

Turn left at Winsford and keep left at subsequent junctions to reach the B3224. Turn left to Exford ❼.

This village, with its large green overlooked by cottages and hotels, has been a crossing-point on the Exe since prehistoric times, although the opening of roads in the 19th century really put Exford on the map. Its church, up the hill, has an exceptional screen dating from the 15th century.

Turn right in Exford and fork right again on the road that leads northeast and over the west shoulder of Dunkery Hill towards Luccombe ❽. Just after you cross over the ridge at Dunkery Hill, a right turn gives access to the main parking area

OUT AND ABOUT

leading along the ridge to Dunkery Beacon.

The summit offers one of the best views in the West Country: South Wales is visible on a clear day, including two summits of the Brecon Beacons (▷ 284–285).

Continue through Luccombe to reach the A39. Turn left towards Lynton. A dead-end road on the right from the A39 leads to the National Trust village Selworthy, where the church is adorned with symbols of the Passion and angels. Continue on the A39 up Porlock Hill to return to Lynton.

Castle Rock can be climbed from the Valley of the Rocks

PLACE TO VISIT

Arlington Court
✉ Barnstaple EX31 4LP
☎ 01271 850296
🕐 Easter–end Oct Sun–Fri 11–5. House and carriage collection from 10.30. Grounds: Nov–end Mar daily dawn–dusk
💷 Adult £6.50, child £3.20, family £16.20

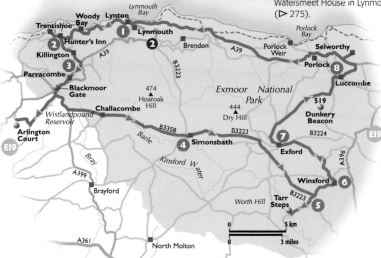

Poetic justice: Three of England's Romantic poets did their best to capture the magic of Exmoor's landscapes

WHERE TO EAT

The Royal Oak (tel: 01643 851 455), a thatched inn in Winsford. Watersmeet House in Lynmouth (▷ 275).

Arlington Court contains a cornucopia of 19th-century items, including stuffed birds and tapestries

OUT AND ABOUT

WATERSMEET AND THE LYNMOUTH FLOODS

The tranquil waters of Hoaroak Water and the East Lyn River once swelled up to biblical proportions in a catastrophic flood. They gouged out spectacularly deep ravines some 180m (600ft) beneath the moorland plateau and running closely parallel to the coast.

THE WALK

Length: 3 miles (4.5km)

Allow: At least 90 min

Start/end: National Trust parking area at Combe Park Hotel, Hillsford Bridge 1.5 miles (2.5km) south of Lynmouth map ref 429 E19

OS Landranger map: 180

OS Explorer map: OL9

Turn left out of the parking area, and then right to go over Hilsford Bridge ❶. Immediately pass through a gate on the left and proceed along the right bank of Hoaroak Water (signposted Watersmeet), descending slightly through a steep-sided, wooded valley, with the river rushing through the rocky ravine below. The route passes a waterfall and a viewing point on the left, and then reaches a flight of steps leading to the left to Watersmeet.

Continuing along the path veering to the right, the route proceeds up the right bank of the East Lyn River, past a junction with another path leading to Watersmeet and the remains of a lime kiln ❷.

The lime kiln was used to burn limestone shipped from South Wales and used as fertilizer. The view ahead extends to the high mass of Countisbury Common, which rises to 343m (1,125ft). In the early 18th century the English writer and adventurer Daniel Defoe (1660–1731) described Exmoor as a 'filthie barren waste', at a time when wild landscapes were not appreciated as they are today.

The route then leads through semi-natural oak woodland. At a junction, take the footpath ahead (signposted Rockford); the path drops through a beech glade to reach the riverbank. Carry on, and then cross Ash Bridge and turn left on the other side (signposted Fisherman's Path) ❸.

Red and roe deer frequent the moorlands and woodlands in

Hoaroak Water cut deep ravines into the rock, creating waterfalls

this area. The smaller roe deer are shy creatures, but they may be glimpsed occasionally at dawn or dusk. When a roe deer is startled and runs off, you may see the prominent white patch on its rump; the bucks have small antlers with short branches. The red deer is the largest native land animal in Britain. The fully grown stag is a formidable sight, standing as tall as 1.2m (4ft) at the shoulder, and with antlers up to 70cm (28in) long. Their main habitats are Exmoor and the Scottish highlands.

For an optional detour you can continue for 1 mile (1.5km) along the right bank to Rockford

Danger! The poisonous fly agaric toadstool is easily recognized

❹, where the Rockford Inn is a useful refreshment stop; you can then return via the path on the opposite bank.

To continue, carry on past Crook Pool, then along the narrow path that undulates above the river. Pass Watersmeet House ❺ and bear right around the garden fence.

A huge Monterey pine shades Watersmeet House itself; a younger replacement has been planted alongside. During the late 18th century such landscapes found favour with the Romantic movement. The Reverend W. S. Halliday purchased this site in 1829 and built Watersmeet as a hunting lodge and retreat. Today it is owned by the National Trust and has a café.

Carry on for a short distance along the right bank of the river and go over stone Chiselcombe Bridge.

The bridge was paid for by members of the public after an ancient bridge on the site was swept away in the notorious floods of 15 August 1952, when a 12m (40ft) wall of water rushed down into Lynmouth, killing 34 people and destroying several houses and bridges. The flood came after 228mm (9in) of rain fell within 24 hours—one of three heaviest periods of rainfall yet recorded in the British Isles. It is estimated that more than 13.6 billion litres (3 billion gallons) of water fell on the area that is drained by the two Lyn rivers.

On the other side of the bridge turn left and continue back up the riverbank. Cross back over Hoaroak Water by a wooden footbridge just above Watersmeet. Take the steps on the right, following signs to Hillsford Bridge, then bear right to retrace your steps upriver to the bridge and the parking area in Combe Park.

OUT AND ABOUT

Watersmeet House (below) was once a hunting lodge but now serves cups of tea. Pleasure-craft and working boats in Lynmouth harbour (right), scene of the catastrophic floods of 1952

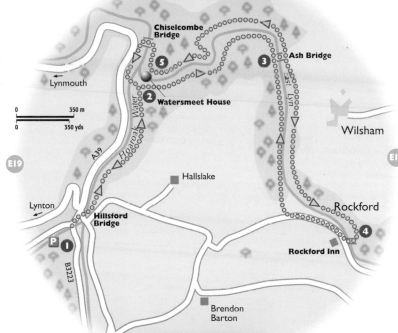

Chiselcombe Bridge

Ash Bridge

Lynmouth

2 Watersmeet House

Wilsham

0   350 m
0   350 yds

Hallslake

Lynton

Hillsford Bridge

Rockford

4

Rockford Inn

Brendon Barton

Watersmeet House is at the confluence of the East Lyn and Hoaroak Water (left)

WHERE TO EAT

Watersmeet House offers a selection of food and drink in a riverside setting. The Rockford Inn in Brendon, near Lynton (tel: 01598 741214) is a traditional country pub serving hot and cold meals, real ales and Devon cream teas.

PLACE TO VISIT

Watersmeet House
✉ Watersmeet Road, Lynmouth EX35 6NT
☎ 01598 753348
🕐 Easter–end Sep daily 10.30–5.30, Oct 10.30–4.30
🅿 Free. Pay-and-display parking

THE COTSWOLDS

Meandering country roads, enchanting villages and idyllic scenery make this area ideal for touring.

THE DRIVE

Distance: 77 miles (124km)	
Allow: One day	
Start/end: Winchcombe map ref 430 H17	
Tourist information office: Hollis House, The Square, Stow-on-the-Wold GL54 1AF, tel: 01451 831082	
www.cotswold.gov.uk	
OS Landranger maps: 150, 151, 163	

From Winchcombe ❶ take the B4632 northeast towards Broadway. At the roundabout turn right on the B4077, then left through Stanway and Stanton.

In the village of Stanway, Stanway Water Garden features a pyramid, a canal and cascade in the grounds of a 16th-century manor house. Stanton is another village seemingly unchanged over the years. A market cross and 17th-century sundial are in the main street.

From Stanton turn right on the B4632 to Broadway ❷. At Broadway turn right through the village and left up Broadway Hill to cross the A44.

The Long High Street beneath Broadway Hill has a range of architectural styles from centuries past, including Tudor (1485–1603), Stuart (1603–1714) and Georgian (1714–1830). Above the village is Broadway Tower, an eye-catching folly of 1798 built by the sixth Earl of Coventry.

Follow the B4632 and then turn right to Chipping Campden on the B4035.

Chipping Campden is arguably the ideal Cotswold town. Wool money helped build the 1627 market hall and the church.

Turn right just after entering Chipping Campden, then left through Broad Campden and Blockley ❸.

Blockley was a busy silk-milling village up to the late

19th century. To the east you can see one of Britain's largest collections of rare trees at Batsford Arboretum.

Turn right on the B4479, and left on the A44 through Bourton-on-the-Hill (the starting point for walk three, ▷ 278–279). Follow the A44 to Moreton-in-Marsh ❹. Southeast of this town, along the A44 and a signposted right turn, is Chastleton House.

Jacobean Chastleton House was occupied by the same family for 400 years and has been preserved by the National Trust since 1991. Elaborate topiary is a feature of the gardens, marking the birthplace of the modern form of croquet in 1865.

From Moreton-in-Marsh, turn right on the A429 into Stow-on-the-Wold.

Stow-on-the-Wold stands at the meeting of eight roads at a point where sheep markets used to be held.

Continue south on the A429, keeping right at the junction with the A424. Take the next left into architecturally interesting Lower Slaughter ❺. Return to the A429, turn right, and then left into Bourton-on-the-Water.

A series of stone bridges cross the River Windrush on its way across the village green of this bustling Cotswold village.

There's no shortage of tea rooms and the Cotswold Motor Museum and the Birdland Park and Gardens are notable attractions. Children will enjoy the Cotswold Farm Park.

Take minor roads through Great Rissington and Great Barrington to Burford ❻.

Burford has a fine sloping main street dropping down to a bridge over the River Windrush. Just south of town is the Cotswold Wildlife Park.

Turn right on the B4425, then turn right and immediately left on the A40 to Bibury.

Bibury ❼ is a showpiece Cotswold village; much of it was restored by the designer William Morris (1834–96).

Turn right to Ablington, then right to the A429. Turn right, then left. The next turning on the left is an optional detour to Chedworth Roman Villa ❽.

This Roman structure, excavated in 1864, has a hypocaust (underfloor heating system), bath-houses and mosaics.

Continue northwest from the A429, then turn left on to the A40. Turn right at the first crossroads. Cross the A436 and after Brockhampton turn right at the crossroads. Just before the descent into Winchcombe, a road signposted to the left leads to Belas Knap, an outstanding 4,000-year-old burial mound. Go back to Winchcombe.

Just outside the town is Sudeley Castle ❾. The 19th-century house includes the remains of the medieval castle where Catherine Parr (1512–48), the sixth wife of Henry VIII, was born.

Feeding time: Children enjoy meeting the animals at the Cotswold Farm Park at Bourton-on-the-Water

OUT AND ABOUT

PLACES TO VISIT

Batsford Arboretum
✉ Moreton-in-Marsh GL56 9QB
☎ 01386 701441
🕐 Feb to mid-Nov daily 10–5; rest of year Sat–Sun 10–4
💷 Adult £5, child £1

Birdland Park and Gardens
✉ Bourton-on-the-Water GL54 2BN
☎ 01451 820480
🕐 Apr–end Oct daily 10–6; Nov–end Mar daily 10–5
💷 Adult £4.95, child £3

Chastleton House
✉ Chastleton GL56 0SU
☎ 01608 674355; 01494 755585
(reservations); 01494 755560 (Infoline)
🕐 Late Mar–end Oct Wed–Sat pm; reservations necessary
💷 Adult £6, child £3, family £15

Chedworth Roman Villa
✉ Yanworth GL54 3LJ
☎ 01242 890256
🕐 Mar to mid-Nov Tue–Sun and holiday Mon 10–5
💷 Adult £5, child £2.50, family £12.50

Cotswold Motor Museum and Toy Collection
✉ Bourton-on-the-Water GL54 2BY
☎ 01451 821255
🕐 Daily 10–6
💷 Adult £2.95, child £1.95

Cotswold Wildlife Park
✉ Burford OX18 4JW
☎ 01993 823006
🕐 Daily 10–4.30 (Oct–end Feb 3.30)
💷 Adult £8.50, child £6

Sudeley Castle and Gardens
✉ Winchcombe GL54 5JD
☎ 01242 602308
🕐 Mar–end Oct daily 10.30–5.30
💷 Adult £7.20, child £4.20

WHERE TO EAT

Notable pubs in Cotswold villages include The Eagle and Child (tel: 01451 830670) in Stow-on-the-Wold, which is rated as one of Britain's best and serves excellent food. Entrance is through the reception of the Royalist Hotel, dating from AD947 and England's oldest inn. The Churchill Arms (tel: 01386 594000) in Chipping Campden is also recommended.

Lower Slaughter, on the banks of the River Windrush

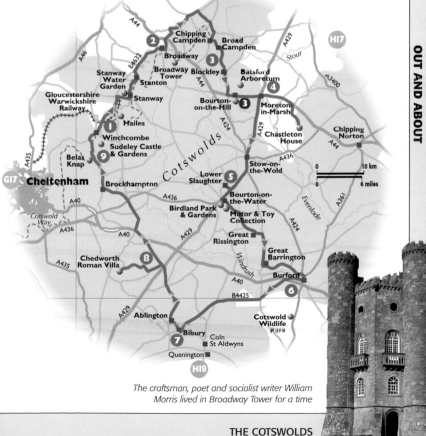

The craftsman, poet and socialist writer William Morris lived in Broadway Tower for a time

THE COTSWOLDS

BOURTON-ON-THE-HILL AND SEZINCOTE HOUSE

Beginning from the hillside village of Bourton-on-the-Hill, the less famous cousin of Bourton-on-the-Water, this short and mostly low-level walk explores well-defined paths through farmland near the extraordinary stately home of Sezincote House.

THE WALK	
Length: 3 miles (5km)	
Allow: 1.5 hours	
Start/end: Bourton-on-the-Hill map ref 430 H17	
OS Landranger map: 151	
OS Explorer map: OL45	

Follow the lane by the parking area that leads away from the main road. Turn left, and soon follow the waymarked track between walls leading to the right to a gate. Continue forward alongside a stone wall, and beyond the gate cross the field to another gate and continue through the next field to a stile in the fence. Continue in the same direction through a kissing gate, and pass through a belt of trees and through another gate. Walk across the field between spinneys (small areas of trees and bushes), with the cupola of Sezincote House ❶ drawing into view.

Sezincote House is a startling Indian fantasy that inspired the Prince Regent (later King George IV) to build the Royal Pavilion in Brighton (▷ 95). More striking from outside than inside, Sezincote dates back to the turn of the 19th century, when Charles Cockerell enlisted the help of his father and fellow architect Samuel Pepys Cockerell and Thomas Daniell, a well-known painter of exotic scenes. The bow-fronted and balconied main house is surmounted by an onion dome, a motif repeated elsewhere. The easily explored gardens, landscaped by Humphrey Repton (1752–1818), contain an exotic Oriental water garden, an Indian shrine and a large, semicircular orangery. There are also some very fine trees of an unusual size.

Go across an estate road and walk down a slope towards a wood ❷. At the bottom of the slope, keep to the right of a wooden fence, go through two gates in quick succession, and continue between two ponds and into a field. From here there is a good view of Sezincote House. Carry on across the field to a gate by a drinking trough, and continue up and slightly right to a gate in the top right-hand corner of the field ❸.

Turn left on a road, past a cottage and through two gateways, and then bear left and right towards Upper Rye Farm ❹. Go past the farm entrance on the left and head towards a black barn, keeping to the right of a fence to reach a gate, then turn sharp left to pass between the barn and a farmhouse.

Continue through a gate by a cattle grid then, just across a second cattle grid, take a stile on your left. Keep left alongside a ditch, cross a footbridge and bear sharp right along the edge of a field, with Bourton-on-the-Hill in view ahead.

At the top right-hand corner of the field ❺ climb a stile and continue on a path that leads through trees and alongside a stream and then bears left to reach a stile. Continue in the same direction across the next field to the stile ahead and on to a lane. Climb the stile opposite, and continue along the edge of the fields, then turn right at a tree along a path between hedges.

❻ Soon turn left alongside a hedge and proceed uphill through a series of gates and fields to reach the path used at the beginning of the walk. Retrace your steps to the parking area in Bourton-on-the-Hill.

Historic Bourton-on-the-Hill has a long, sloping High Street. Its church has Norman origins, and some of the pillars in the nave are from that time. Look for the Winchester bushel and peck—weight standards dating from the reign of Elizabeth I (1533–1603). Close by is a tithe barn bearing the name of Richard Palmer, who was linked by marriage to the Overbury family. Sir Thomas Overbury was murdered in the Tower of London in 1613 by the slow administration of poison. He had been imprisoned by Lady Essex because of his opposition to the marriage between her and Robert Carr, favourite of James I. He died after living in agony for some months, and it was only some years later that the truth of his manner of death emerged.

A terrace of stone cottages with immaculate gardens in Bourton-on-the-Hill

OUT AND ABOUT

Bourton-on-the-Hill meets Bombay at Sezincote House

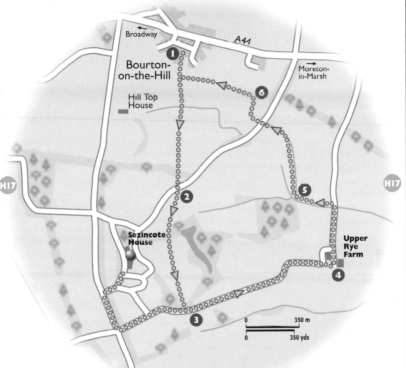

OUT AND ABOUT

Please close the gate: Many footpaths in the Cotswolds cross farmland

THE COTSWOLD WAY

This signposted path, leading 103 miles (166km) from Chipping Campden to Bath, takes a complicated route around some of the most satisfyingly varied Cotswold scenery—through hilly farmland and a sequence of classic villages and towns. The route has waymarks throughout, and is shown on OS maps. It can be joined at many points for some rewarding short walks. Easy strolls along it include across the fields from Stanway to Stanton, beneath the western escarpment, or to the ruins of Hailes Abbey from Winchcombe. A spectacular section north of the A436 from Crickley Hill Country Park passes the quarried pinnacle known as the Devil's Chimney, high above Cheltenham.

THE NEW FOREST

Bustling Lyndhurst makes an excellent base for touring the New Forest (▷ 108). This superb area of lowland heath, originally a Norman hunting forest, is renowned for its grazing wild ponies and red deer.

THE DRIVE	
Distance: 68 miles (108km)	
Allow: 3 hours	
Start/end: Lyndhurst, map ref 430 H2O	
Tourist information office: New Forest Visitor Information Centre, New Street, Lymington SO41 9BH, tel: 01590 689000	
www.thenewforest.co.uk	
OS Landranger maps: 184, 195, 196	

Lyndhurst ❶ is the unofficial 'capital' of the New Forest and busy with tourists in summer. In the churchyard is buried Alice Hargreaves (née Liddell), the original Alice of Lewis Carroll's *Alice's Adventures in Wonderland* (1865). The Verderers—the guardians of the forest since Norman times—employ agisters to patrol the forest daily, often on horseback, to supervise the animals grazing on the 36,423ha (90,000-acre) expanse of the forest. The New Forest Museum and Visitor Centre gives an insight into the area's history and traditions.

From Lyndhurst take the A337 north. After 2 miles (3.2km) turn left through Minstead, then left, left again and immediately right to cross the A31 to Brook, and follow the B3078 to Fordingbridge ❷.

The little town of Fordingbridge was originally called Forde, but had its name enlarged with the building of the 13th-century bridge, a seven-arched structure that has since been widened. South of the town, 13th-century St. Mary's Church has an imposing 15th-century porch and hammer-beam roof. The Avon is a renowned river for trout and pike. Northwest of town is Rockbourne, a village with an attractive group of Tudor and Georgian cottages alongside a stream, where tiny bridges connect the houses with the road. There's a wide variety of building materials, including tile, timber, flint, brick and thatch. South of

the village is the excavated site of Rockbourne Roman Villa, discovered in 1942 by a farmer digging out a ferret; it includes mosaic floors and underfloor heating systems.

Take the A338 south from Fordingbridge. Turn left at Ibsley on a minor road, turn right in 0.6 miles (1km) at Mockbeggar, then turn next left through Linwood, under the A31 and forking right to Bolderwood ❸.

At Bolderwood, in the heart of the forest, the Forestry Commission has created three walks of varying lengths through plantations of oak, beech and wellingtonia. The Bolderwood Deer Sanctuary gives the best opportunities for seeing the many deer that inhabit the New Forest, and there is an observation platform (bring binoculars). A memorial is dedicated to Canadian airmen, serving at nearby Stony Cross, who died in World War II. The route also passes the huge Knightwood Oak (▷ 282).

From Bolderwood follow an unclassified road southeast to cross the A35 to Rhinefield ❹.

Some of Britain's tallest trees tower above you on the Rhinefield Ornamental Drive, and include redwoods, spruces and Douglas firs. They were planted in 1859 as an approach to a long-vanished hunting lodge. Beyond the drive are mixed woodlands of beech, oak and pine, and there is also a Tall Trees nature trail. Rhinefield House, close by, is an exuberant Victorian building in the style of a castle, and a useful refreshment stop.

Continue from Rhinefield to Brockenhurst ❺.

Brockenhurst is a prosperous-looking village and one of the main locations in what was then the 'new' forest. Its

church dates from Norman times but the village is predominantly 19th- and 20th-century in character.

From Brockenhurst turn right on to the A337 to Lymington ❻.

The seaside town of Lymington made much of its money as a spa, salt town and sea port. Its Georgian and other buildings include Pressgang Cottage—headquarters in 1809 of the local press gang (men who forcibly enlisted others into the army or navy). Also of interest is 18th-century St. Thomas's Church on the High Street. Car ferries make a short crossing to Yarmouth on the Isle of Wight (▷ 102).

Leave Lymington by the B3054 (signposted Beaulieu). After 6 miles (10km) and just before Beaulieu, turn right for Bucklers Hard ❼.

Remarkably little has changed at the village of Bucklers Hard since 1800, when it was a shipbuilding hub. Three of the ships in Nelson's fleet at the Battle of Trafalgar (1805) were built here. Two rows of 18th-century shipbuilders' cottages slope towards the water. The Bucklers Hard Story reflects on the village's past. Boat trips are available in summer.

Return to the B3054 and turn right through Beaulieu. Then take the next right turn for Exbury ❽.

Late spring—when the rhododendrons and azaleas are blooming—brings a wealth of colour to Exbury Gardens (▷ 100). Lepe Country Park is an unspoiled stretch of coast overlooking the Isle of Wight—a good place for walks.

From Exbury head to Beaulieu, home of the National Motor Museum and Beaulieu Abbey (▷ 93), then take the B3056 back to Lyndhurst.

New Forest Museum and Visitor Centre
- ✉ High Street, Lyndhurst SO43 7NY
- ☎ 02380 283914
- 🕐 Daily 10–5, closed 25–26 Dec
- 💷 Adult £3, child £2.50, family £9

Rockbourne Roman Villa
- ✉ Rockbourne SP6 3PG
- ☎ 01725 518541
- 🕐 Apr–end Oct Mon–Sun 10.30–6
- 💷 Adult £2.25, child £1.25, family £6

The Bucklers Hard Story
- ✉ Beaulieu, Brockenhurst SO42 7XB
- ☎ 01590 614645
- 🕐 Easter–end Sep 10.30–5; Oct–Easter 11–4
- 💷 Adult £5.75, child £3.75, family £16

Stop at Rhinefield House (tel: 01590 622922) near Rhinefield, or have a picnic in Lepe Country Park, Exbury. There's also a café and restaurant at Beaulieu.

The wide main street of Bucklers Hard (left) was once used for rolling logs down to the shipyard. Today Lyndhurst's main street (above) attracts shoppers

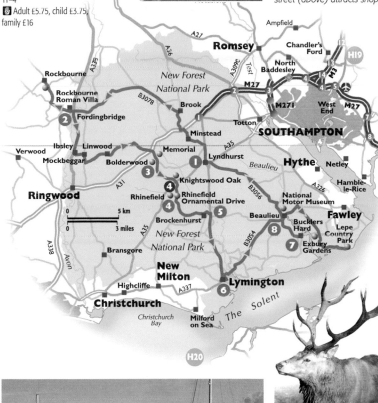

OUT AND ABOUT

Lymington (left) is a safe haven for yachts today, but press gangs once recruited in the town. Red deer (above) can be seen on quiet mornings in the New Forest

THE NEW FOREST **281**

THE KNIGHTWOOD OAK AND THE PORTUGUESE FIREPLACE

This circuit explores the contrasting landscapes of the New Forest (▷ 108), with its ancient woods of oak and beech typified by Bolderwood.

THE WALK

Length: 6 miles (9.5km)

Allow: 3 hours

Start/end: Brock Hill Forestry Commission parking area, off the A35 map ref 430 H20

OS Landranger map: 196

OS Explorer map: OL22

South of the starting point is the mid-19th-century conifer plantation of the Rhinefield Ornamental Drive, into which the walk can be extended.

Take the gravel path at the southern end of the parking area ❶ (beyond the information post), parallel with the road. After 90m (100 yards) turn right by a post and descend to reach a gravel track. Cross straight over and, where the path curves left, keep straight on to a gate and on to the A35. Cross over and take the gate opposite. Keep to the path as it leads uphill to a junction, where you turn right and follow the path to reach another road. Cross into the parking area for the Knightwood Oak and follow the sign to the Knightwood Oak ❷ itself.

The Knightwood Oak is the most famous in the forest, thought to be at least 350 years old. It owes its great age to pollarding (cutting back its branches) to encourage new growth to provide timber for fuel and charcoal. Its girth is a massive 7m (8 yards).

Return to the parking area, bear right and then right again into mixed woodland. Cross a stream and you soon reach a track. Bear left and keep to this trail, passing Reptile Trail markers, to reach a fork. Keep left until you reach a gate and road. Turn right to view the Portuguese Fireplace ❸.

The flint Portuguese Fireplace was used in the cookhouse of a Portuguese army unit, deployed during World War I to cut timber for pit props.

Return through Holidays Hill Inclosure to the fork of tracks.

The so-called 'inclosures' are areas of managed woodland where trees are protected from deer and ponies. These 17th-century plantations were used to produce large quantities of timber for the construction and shipbuilding industries. Holidays Hill Inclosure is one of the forest's oldest, and includes 300-year-old oak trees.

Bear left and follow the track to the New Forest Reptile Centre.

The New Forest Reptile Centre breeds rare species such as the smooth snake and sand lizard for re-release into the wild. On a sunny day you may be able to see adders, grass snakes and rare natterjack toads. Snake-catching was an important trade here in the 19th century. The most celebrated local catcher was Brusher Mills. It is believed he caught around 35,000 snakes, selling them to zoos and for medicine. He is buried in Brockenhurst churchyard.

The Knightwood Oak, which is probably the oldest tree in the New Forest

Walk along the access drive, passing Holiday Hills Cottage, then at the barrier on the left drop down to a path and follow it to cross a bridge ❹. Keep to the main path for 0.75 mile (1km), skirting the walls to Allum Green and several clearings ❺.

In this area you may see some of the 3,500 New Forest ponies grazing the lawns and trees. They are all owned by local 'commoners' and are descendants of a wild breed peculiar to the area. The owner places a brand mark on each pony, and during autumn they are rounded up and rebranded. It is illegal to feed the ponies.

The route climbs gently through the trees to a crossing and then turns right. Shortly, bear half right across the clearing and over a footbridge, then continue through the woodland edge to a telegraph pole. Bear right for 18m (20 yards), then left through a gate to the A35.

Turn left along the A35, then almost immediately right across the road to a gate. Carry on to a garden boundary and turn right, along a narrow path leading to a lane in Bank. Turn right, past the Oak Inn and walk through Bank. Just before a sharp left-hand bend by a cattle grid, bear right beside a barrier and walk straight on along a wide path.

Go through the trees ❻ and scrub to a fork on the edge of a clearing. Keep right along the path between an oak and a holly tree. Negotiate a boggy area, then keep left at a fork and follow the path to a surfaced lane at Gritnam.

Walk past Jessamine Cottage ❼. Where the lane bends right, go forward across rough grassland and into trees. Bear slightly right and walk alongside a thick birch copse. Take care to keep to the path, which is ill-defined in places, and eventually joins a wide grassy

OUT AND ABOUT

path. Turn left along this and continue along the path to a bridge.

Ignore the path to the left, but keep ahead through Brinken Wood **8**. The path enters a clearing and crosses a bridge and Warwickslade Cutting. At a gravel track turn right, then take the first path left and soon merge with the start of the Tall Trees Trail, opposite Brock Hill parking area, where you started.

PLACE TO VISIT

New Forest Reptile Centre
✉ Bournemouth Road, Lyndhurst SO34 7DP
☎ 023 8028 3141 (weekdays only)
🕑 Apr–end Sep daily 10–4.30
🅿 Free. Parking £2

WHERE TO EAT

The Oak Inn at Bank (tel: 02380 282350) is an 18th-century pub serving local ales and good food. It is just off the A35, southwest of Lyndhurst.

Don't feed the ponies: All 3,500 New Forest ponies are owned by locals and individually branded

You may see a harmless grass snake basking in sunshine, and other species at the Reptile Centre

OUT AND ABOUT

The Portuguese fireplace (above) dates from World War I. Wintry sunshine filters through beech glades (right) in the New Forest

THE KNIGHTWOOD OAK AND THE PORTUGUESE FIREPLACE **283**

BRECON BEACONS NATIONAL PARK

From the literary town of Hay-on-Wye this upland tour takes in some magnificent scenery around the Black Mountains, one of the national park's four distinct areas.

THE DRIVE

Distance: 91 miles (147km)
Allow: 4–5 hours
Start/end: Hay-on-Wye, map ref 434 F17
Tourist information office: The Craft Centre, Oxford Road, Hay-on-Wye HR3 5DF, tel: 01497 820144
www.breconbeacons.org
OS Landranger maps: 160, 161

Hay-on-Wye **1** stands high above the south bank of the River Wye. Welsh rebel leader Owain Glyndwr (c1350–1416) destroyed its castle during the 15th century, but the keep, parts of the walls and a gateway remain. The town's cinema has become the world's biggest second-hand bookshop; in fact the whole town seems to be taken up with second-hand books. Appropriately, Hay hosts a world-famous literary festival every summer.

From Hay drive southwest for 8 miles (13km) along the B4350 and A438 to Bronllys **2**.

From Bronllys there are clear views of the Brecon Beacons ahead and the Black Mountains, which dominate the scenery to the left. The 12th-century church here, now rebuilt, has a distinctive detached tower. Bronllys Castle (open access) is 0.5 mile (800m) along the A479.

From Bronllys continue along the A438 and A470. Turn right on to the B4602 to Brecon **3**.

At the confluence of the rivers Usk and Honddu, Brecon is a magnet for walkers. East of town is the terminus of the Monmouth and Brecon Canal, and to the south is the Brecon Beacons National Park. The city's cathedral dates mainly from the 13th and 14th centuries. The Brecon Cathedral Heritage Centre in the converted tithe barn traces the history of the priory. Brecon Castle is now in the grounds of the Castle Hotel.

The County Hall houses the Brecknock Museum of Local History and nearby the South Wales Borderers Museum has relics from the Zulu War of 1879 to World War II and later.

From Brecon continue southwards along the A470 towards Merthyr Tydfil and the heights of the Brecon Beacons. At Libanus, a right-hand dead-end turn leads up to the Brecon Beacons Mountain Centre **4**.

The Mountain Centre makes an ideal introduction to the park. There are easy walks around the common that surrounds the centre, with views of the highest parts of the park.

Before reaching Merthyr Tydfil turn on to an unclassified road north to Pontsticill **5**.

Walking and boating are major attractions in this area, as well as the Brecon Mountain Railway, which runs for 4 miles (6.5km) up the valley through unspoiled scenery.

Continue on unclassified roads past Talybont Reservoir to the village of Talybont-on-Usk **6**.

Talybont-on-Usk is now a base for walkers and outdoor activities, with the Outdoor Education Centre in the old train station. The 18th-century Monmouthshire and Brecon Canal, which passes through the village, was built to carry coal and iron ore. It eventually closed in 1962, but was

reopened by volunteers in 1970 for use by pleasure craft.

From Talybont-on-Usk, follow the B4558 to Llangynidr, then the B4560 and an unclassified road to Crickhowell **7**.

The name Crickhowell is derived from the Iron Age fort Crug Hywel ('Hywel's cairn'). The town grew up around Alisby's Castle, which was captured and destroyed by Owain Glyndwr in 1403 and is now a pretty ruin. The River Usk is crossed by an old bridge dating from the 17th century, which appears to have 13 arches on one side but only 12 on the other—the result of 19th-century alterations.

From Crickhowell take the A40 to Abergavenny **8**.

At the edge of the Brecon Beacons National Park, Abergavenny is overlooked by the Sugar Loaf mountain, 596m (1,955ft) high, and Ysgyryd (Skirrid) Fawr (488m/1,595ft). The castle, now in ruins, was founded in 1090.

From Abergavenny take the A465 northeast towards Pontrilas. At Llanvihangel Crucorney **9** turn left on an unclassified road to Hay-on-Wye via Llanthony.

This route leads up through the wild, remote scenery of the Black Mountains, past the ruins of Llanthony Priory (▷ 135), where a hotel occupies the former refectory and whose pub in a vaulted cellar is one of the most architecturally unusual in Wales. The road climbs to the top of Gospel Pass (542m/ 1,778ft) for a huge view into mid-Wales; you can get even higher by walking up the nearby summit of Hay Bluff (676m/2,221ft), to the right of the summit parking area.

Carry on down the steep gradient back to Hay-on-Wye.

PLACES TO VISIT

Abergavenny Castle
✉ Castle Street, Abergavenny NP7 5EE
☎ 01873 854282
🕙 Mar–end Oct daily 11–5; Nov–end Feb Mon–Sat
💷 Free

Brecknock Museum
✉ Captain's Walk, Brecon LD3 7DW
☎ 01874 624121
🕙 Apr–end Sep daily 10–5; rest of year Mon–Sat
💷 Adult £1, child (under 15) free

Brecon Cathedral Heritage Centre
✉ Cathedral Close, Brecon LD3 9DP
☎ 01874 625222
🕙 Mon–Sat 10.30–4, Sun 12.30–4
💷 Free

Brecon Mountain Railway
✉ Pant Station, Merthyr Tydfil CF48 2UP
☎ 01685 722988
🕙 Visit www.breconmountainrailway.co.uk for timetable
💷 Adult £8.50, child (3–15) £4.25

Choose your transport: A barge navigates the Monmouthshire and Brecon Canal (left) and the Brecon Mountain Railway (right) climbs past the Talybont Reservoir

South Wales Borderers Museum
✉ The Barracks, Brecon LD3 7EB
☎ 01874 613311
🕙 Daily 10–5, Sat–Sun 10–4
💷 Adult £3, child (under 16) free

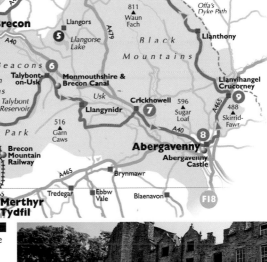

WHERE TO EAT

Oscar's, High Town, Hay-on-Wye (tel: 01497 821193) is a bistro with salad bar and home-made cakes. Both the White Swan Inn (tel: 01874 665276) and the Felin Fach Griffin (▷ 350) are outstanding pubs in Brecon.

There are impressive views from Bronnllys Castle (left). Hay-on-Wye is famous for its second-hand book trade—this outdoor book stall (right) is near the old castle walls

LLANGORSE LAKE

The crannog (artificial island) in Llangorse Lake is thought to be the ancient seat of the kings of Brycheiniog. This walk circumnavigates the lake before a modest ascent offers striking views of the Brecon Beacons (▷ 135).

THE WALK

Length: 8 miles (13km)

Allow: 4 hours

Start/end: Parking area beside public toilets, between caravan park and sailing club, map ref 434 F17

OS Landranger map: 160

OS Explorer map: OL13

From the parking area, aim for a concrete footbridge to the left of the caravan park on Llangorse Common ❶. Go diagonally left.

Soon you can see the crannog, the only known example in Wales, a few paces from the shore. Its access causeway has long since disappeared, and today there is (to the uninitiated) nothing to see—just a clump of reeds on a pile of stones. But it is rather more than that. The perimeter of this little island is made of pointed oak piles, hewn using a metal adze. The crannog is thought to have supported several early medieval dwellings. In 1925 a dugout canoe, dated at around AD800, was found nearby; it's now kept in the Brecknock Museum in Brecon (▷ 285).

When the Mercians (English) invaded parts of Wales from about AD850, this site—thought to be the heart of the kingdom of Brycheiniog ('land of Brychan')—did not escape their attention. These words are anglicized to Brecknock and Brecon; the name Brecon Beacons is still commonly used, while Brecknock is an alternative name for the old county of Breconshire. According to legend, the lake conceals an ancient city; its Welsh name, Llyn Syfaddan, means 'lake of the sunken island'.

Cross more fields, skirting the lake, to reach the church of St. Gastyn at Llangasty-Talyllyn ❷.

The 'llan' prefix, meaning church, is very common in Wales. This name translates as 'the church of St. Gastyn at the end of the lake'.

Turn right. After Llan (a house) take a waymarked footpath on the left. Soon walk with a hedge to your left. Turn right and cross two fields diagonally to a sunken lane, to the left of a farm. Turn right to a minor road ❸.

Go left. Take the first left turn, signed Cathedine 0.5 mile. Turn right beside Rectory Cottage. Take stiles through three fields; cross the fourth field diagonally to the B4560 (beware of traffic as you emerge on to this road). Turn right along it for 50m (55 yards), then take a rough track to the right of some farm buildings ❹.

Take a less distinct track (indicated by a blue waymarker arrow) before the ford, ascending along the left-hand side of a lightly wooded stream. In an eroded gully find a gate up to the left. Follow this sunken lane until it peters out ❺.

Turn left, above a fence and broken wall, then go through an old gate (blue waymarker) to pass a farmhouse ruin. Continue on a path, now through bracken, until 50m (55 yards) before the track descends to a gate ❻.

Turn sharp right, uphill, on a zigzagging green path. Turn left at a fence, then left again at a fence corner. Descend to a

Golden-ringed dragonflies, Britain's longest species of dragonfly, are common here

converted barn. Continue along the field's left edge. Go down to a gate among larches, beside a dilapidated wall ❼.

Walk through the forest, back into bracken. About 90m (100 yards) beyond a stream crossing, descend beside a farm track, taking the line of greatest slope down the field to the riding and climbing centre below ❽.

Turn right, then right again towards Cae-cottrel farm. Take a stile on the left. Skirt this field to the left. Pass into the next field through a gap in the hedgerow, skirting left again, to farm buildings and a track.

Turn right, following the lanes to Llangors ❾.

The village of Llangors consists of little more than a sinuous road, a church, chapel, shop and sub-post office, and a couple of pubs. At its heart is the church of St. Paulinus, on the site of a sixth-century building.

At a blind corner immediately before the churchyard, take a narrow signed footpath beside a house. Cross fields to return to the start of the walk.

OUT AND ABOUT

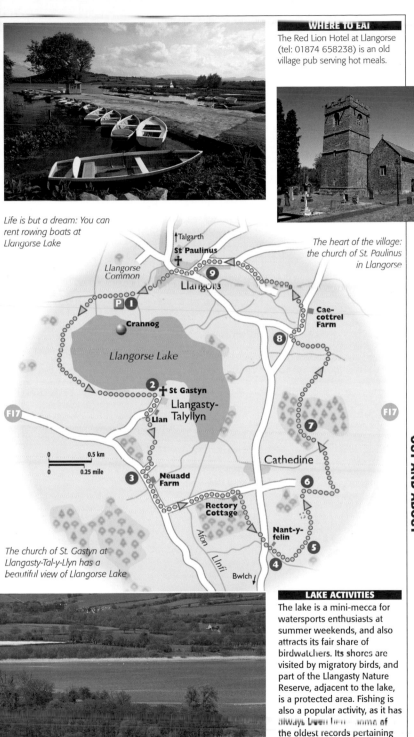

Life is but a dream: You can rent rowing boats at Llangorse Lake

The heart of the village: the church of St. Paulinus in Llangorse

↑Talgarth

St Paulinus
✝

Llangorse Common

Llangors

🅿 **1**

● Crannog

Cae-cottrel Farm

8

Llangorse Lake

2 ✝ **St Gastyn**

Llangasty-Talyllyn

Llan

F17

F17

0   0.5 km
0   0.25 mile

7

Cathedine

3

Neuadd Farm

6

Rectory Cottage

Afon Llnfi

Nant-y-felin

5

4

Bwlch ↓

The church of St. Gastyn at Llangasty-Tal-y-Llyn has a beautiful view of Llangorse Lake

OUT AND ABOUT

The lake is a mini-mecca for watersports enthusiasts at summer weekends, and also attracts its fair share of birdwatchers. Its shores are visited by migratory birds, and part of the Llangasty Nature Reserve, adjacent to the lake, is a protected area. Fishing is also a popular activity, as it has always been here... some of the oldest records pertaining to the lake commend its stock of fish.

PEMBROKESHIRE COAST NATIONAL PARK

The magnificent coastline of the Pembrokeshire Coast National Park can be elusive, as the roads tend to steer inland. This route glimpses some of the most scenic stretches, but the best way to explore is to walk a section of the Pembrokeshire Coast Path, which weaves along the seaboard. As you drive you'll see castles, historic small towns and the primeval-feeling Preseli Hills.

THE DRIVE
Distance: 108 miles (172km)
Allow: Half a day
Start/end: Tenby, map ref 428 D18
Visitor information office: National Park Visitor Centre, The Grove, St. David's SA62 6NW, tel: 01437 720392
www.visitpembrokeshire.com
www.pembrokeshirecoast.org.uk
OS Landranger maps: 145, 157, 158

Leave Tenby ❶ on the A4139, then turn left on to the B4585 to Manorbier ❷.

Manorbier was the birthplace of the medieval explorer and scholar Giraldus Cambrensis (c1146–1223)—locally known as Gerald of Wales—who described it as 'the pleasantest spot in Wales'. The castle gives an impressive view out to sea. The sandy beach is perfect for children.

Return to the A4139 for 5 miles (8km) to Lamphey.

The romantic ruins of a 13th-century bishop's palace lie to the northeast of Lamphey. The palace originated as a country retreat for the bishops of St. David's (▷ 145), and has ornate parapets, fish ponds and a 16th-century chapel.

Continue along the A4139 for another 2 miles (3km) to Pembroke ❸.

The ancient town of Pembroke was built around the 12th- to 13th-century Pembroke Castle (▷ 142), the birthplace of Henry VII (1457–1509). It still has its fine circular keep, and beneath it is a huge natural cavern known as The Wogan.

Head north towards Haverfordwest, picking up the A477 to cross the estuary ❹.

The estuary forms part of the huge natural harbour of Milford Haven, with its oil refineries. This part is the most industrialized stretch, but farther west there are some isolated headlands such as St. Ann's Head near Dale and Wooltack Point, overlooking the bird reserve of Skomer Island, west of Marloes.

On the far side of the bridge turn right on to an unclassified road, through Burton, Port Lion and Llangwm.

Along these quiet back roads you get glimpses of the wide rivers and the labyrinth of tidal creeks that drain into Milford Haven and form part of the national park. The Western and Eastern Cleddau rivers merge just above the village of Llangwm.

Carry on past Hook, along back roads, to Haverfordwest ❺. At the roundabout on the south side of town pick up signs for St. David's, leading northwest on the A487.

The 12th-century castle on the hill above Haverfordwest is now a ruin. There is more history close by at Castle House, the location of the town museum.

Continue on the A487 to Solva, where the road dips into a steep-sided valley. Solva, once a busy port from where steamships sailed as far as America, is a thriving sailing village today. Proceed along the A487 to St. David's ❻.

The smallest cathedral city in Britain, St. David's was founded by an early Christian community. The cathedral stands next to the ruins of the Bishop's Palace. West of St. David's, Whitesands Bay is an excellent bathing beach, and is the starting point for walks to St. David's Head, from where the Irish coast may sometimes be seen.

Take the A487 towards Fishguard but, before the edge of St. David's, turn left on the B4583 towards Whitesands Bay. At the first junction keep forward on an unclassified road heading past Trevine, and carry on through the tiny coastal village of Abercastle ❼.

Just west of Abercastle, at Longhouse Farm, Carreg Sampson is a 5,000-year-old burial chamber comprising massive stones.

At Abercastle follow the road as it turns right inland, carry on through Mathry and turn left on the A487 to Fishguard ❽.

Fishguard has two parts. Upper Fishguard stands back from the sea; from there the road falls steeply to Lower Fishguard, a quaint and largely unspoiled town. Ferries leave here for Rosslare in Ireland.

From Fishguard stick to the A487 and head east to Newport.

Just outside Newport is the Pembrokeshire Candle Centre, where you can see handmade candles being produced. The remains of Newport's 12th-century castle can still be seen behind the main street. Southeast of town, reached by back lanes, Pentre Ifan burial chamber is one of the finest Neolithic monuments of its type in Wales.

Continue along the A487. On the left, signposted from the road, is Castell Henllys.

At Iron Age Castell Henllys, reconstructed thatched circular huts show the life of the original residents. There are often costumed actors and craft demonstrations in the summer to entertain visitors.

Turn right on the B4329 towards Haverfordwest.

This road rises up on to the main ridge of the Preseli Hills **9**, another area with evidence of ancient settlers. It was from here that the stones of Stonehenge (▷ 87) originated, but how they were transported to the southwest of England remains uncertain.

Turn left on the B4313 to Narbeth.

Narbeth has a visitor office, museum and a 13th-century castle. Oakwood Theme Park, on the A4075, is the largest theme park in Wales, with white-knuckle rides and more.

From Narbeth head south on the A478, then turn right on the A4115 to Cross Hands and turn left on the A4075.

Carew is well worth a stop for its medieval castle, tide mill and ornately carved Celtic cross, placed above an inlet of the Carew River (next to the bridge by the castle).

South of Carew turn left on the A477 and then right on the B4318 back to Tenby.

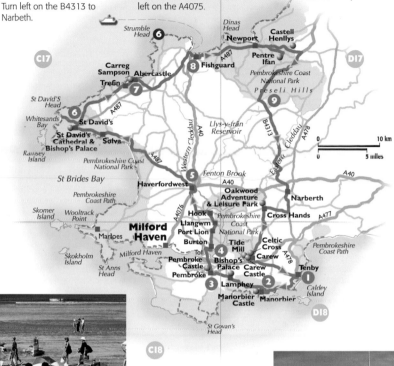

An outstanding family beach, Whitesands Bay is also one of Britain's best beaches for surfing

Impregnable in the 12th century, Haverfordwest Castle had crumbled by the 17th century, but it still commands spectacular views today

PLACES TO VISIT

Bishop's Palace
✉ Cathedral Close, St. David's SA62 6PE
☎ 01437 720517
🕐 Daily 9.30–6
💷 Adult £2.50, child (under 18) £2

Castell Henllys
✉ Pany Glas, Meline, Crymych SA41 3UT
☎ 01239 891319
🕐 Apr–end Oct daily 10–5
💷 Adult £3, child £2, family £0

Pembroke Castle
✉ Main Street, Pembroke SA71 4LA
☎ 01646 681510
🕐 Daily 9.30–6
💷 Adult £3, child £2, family £8

Pembrokeshire Candle Centre
✉ The Cilgwyn Candles, Trefelin, Cilgwyn, Newport SA42 0QN
☎ 01239 820470
🕐 Easter–end Oct daily 11–5; Nov–Dec 12–4
🆓 Free

Town Museum, Castle House
✉ The Castle, Haverfordwest SA61 2EF
☎ 01437 763087
🕐 Easter–end Oct Mon–Sat 10–4
💷 Adult £1, child (under 16) free

WHERE TO EAT
Blueberry's Restaurant at Wesley House, High Street, Tenby (tel: 01834 845785) serves all-day breakfasts, select coffees and teas, cakes, snacks, meals and drinks.

STRUMBLE HEAD AND THE FRENCH INVASION

This glorious stretch of coastline is so well endowed with heady scenery and the promise of seals and dolphins that the drama of its history seems superfluous. But this is the place where Britain confronted her last invaders.

THE WALK	
Length: 6 miles (10km)	
Allow: 3 hours	
Start/end: parking area opposite Strumble Head lighthouse, map ref 433 C17	
OS Landranger map: 157	
OS Explorer map: OL35	

From the parking area at Strumble Head, go right, away from the lighthouse and walk with the sea on your left ❶. When the road turns right, inland, cross a stile on the left-hand side to proceed along the signposted coast path. Descend almost to sea level at the bay of Porth Sychan ❷.

The French invasion of 1797 boasts its own tapestry, housed at Fishguard, but this is the only thing it has in common with the more successful venture at Hastings in 1066 (▷ 28). Led to believe that the Welsh peasants were ready to rise up against the English Crown, a company of 1,400 French troops landed in Pembrokeshire on 22 February 1797. They weren't crack troops, but mostly convicts under the leadership of an Irish-American colonel, and issued with four days' food and double rations of brandy.

Continue along the signposted coast path. It's important to ignore paths going inland on your right; they disappear into a muddy maze of farm tracks. Cross several footbridges, keeping the sea on your left. Climb to pass the site of St. Degan's Chapel. Ignore a signposted path going inland before crossing a footbridge at Penrhyn. Keep the sea on your left until the memorial to the French invasion is reached at Carregwastad Point ❸.

They landed at Carregwastad Point, on a calm, moonlit night, after the alarm had been raised at Fishguard, a little farther along the coast.

Bear right ❹ with the coast path and cross the first stile after the memorial. Turn right here to leave the coast path and take another signposted path which begins with the sea to your right, up through the gorse, then swings left inland to reach a way-mark post near a wall. Go right, keeping the wall on your left in a second field. Cross a stile beside a gate to follow a green lane. This bends left. Continue inland, ignoring another green lane on your right. Pass through a gate, ignoring another track signposted on your left, shortly before bearing right to Tre-Howel Farm ❺.

The invaders made their headquarters at Tre-Howel Farm and eagerly set about drinking Portuguese wine salvaged from a shipwreck the previous month. By the afternoon of 24 February most were helplessly drunk. And Lord Cawdor had already assembled 575 local men to save the kingdom. Tradition has it that it was the appearance of Jemima Nicholas and her cloaked and bonneted female companions that persuaded the French soldiers to surrender. The ladies circled the invaders from the hillsides; their red cloaks may have been mistaken for defenders' uniforms.

Take Tre-Howel's access drive through the yard and then turn left up a quiet road and turn right to enjoy sweeping views over the sea on your right.

The French lost 20 soldiers in early skirmishes and drownings. The only Welsh casualty was a woman killed accidentally when a pistol was being loaded. The centenary of the invasion was marked by a monument on Carregwastad Point. Strumble Head lighthouse was built on Ynys Meicel in 1908.

Bear right at a fork ❻ to follow the road down to Strumble Head's lighthouse. Ignore a drive for Llanwnwr Farm on your left. Return to the parking area to the left.

TIPS

● Avoid straying inland from the path before the memorial because there is a confusing network of paths through the muddy fields between the coast and the lane.
● If you lose the path inland, retrace your steps back to the coast path rather than try navigating to Tre-Howel farm.
● Strumble Head is signposted from the steep road up from Fishguard, but don't continue to the very end of the track as turning becomes difficult. Park opposite the lighthouse; you can walk across the causeway.

OUT AND ABOUT

Shine a light: Strumble Head lighthouse was built on a coastline that claimed 60 ships in the 19th century

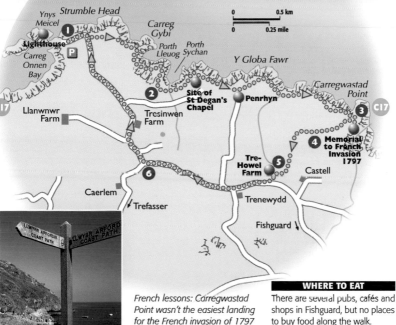

Ynys Meicel
Strumble Head
Lighthouse
Carreg Onnen Bay
Carreg Gybi
Porth Lleuog
Porth Sychan
Y Globa Fawr
Carregwastad Point
1
P
2
Site of St Degan's Chapel
Penrhyn
3
C17
C17
Llanwnwr Farm
Tresinwen Farm
4
Memorial to French Invasion 1797
Tre-Howel Farm
5
Castell
6
Caerlem
Trefasser
Trenewydd
Fishguard
0   0.5 km
0   0.25 mile

OUT AND ABOUT

French lessons: Carregwastad Point wasn't the easiest landing for the French invasion of 1797

The Pembrokeshire Coast Path is clearly signposted (above). The memorial at Carregwastad Point (left) marks the spot of the last hostile invasion of Britain

SNOWDONIA NATIONAL PARK

Although driving can be a little limited in Wales's largest and most dramatic national park (▷ 145), this tour of the principality's extensive mountainous region has plenty to offer.

THE DRIVE

Distance: 73 miles (117km)
Allow: 4 hours
Start/end: Snowdonia National Park Information Centre, Betws-y-Coed, map ref 434 E15
Tourist information office: Snowdon National Park Information Centre, tel: 01690 710426
www.eryri-npa.co.uk
OS Landranger maps: 115, 124

From the information office turn right on to the A5 and head north along this road through Betws-y-Coed ❶.

The route passes the entrance to Swallow Falls on the right. This waterfall has an attractive sylvan setting, making it one of the most frequented beauty spots in Snowdonia.

Continue along the A5, past the strange Tŷ Hyll (Ugly House), said to have been built overnight—traditionally a way of claiming freehold rights. Continue on the A5 past Capel Curig ❷ and Llyn (lake) Ogwen. From the parking area at the far end of Llyn Ogwen a short path leads to Llyn Idwal, beneath the vast crags of the Devil's Kitchen.

Llyn Idwal, a popular haunt of rock climbers, was where Idwal, son of the 12th-century Prince of Gwynedd, was pushed to a watery end by his jealous cousin.

Still on the A5, on entering Bethesda ❸ (after about 4 miles/6.5km) turn left on to the B4409. The road passes the spoil heaps of a slate quarry and continues through the village of Tregarth. Turn left (signed Caernarfon/Llanberis) on to the B4366 and continue to a roundabout. Take the first exit for Llanberis on the B4547 and presently turn left on to the A4086, which takes you in to Llanberis itself ❹.

Llanberis (▷ 141) is the site of the Welsh Slate Museum as well as the base station of the Snowdon Mountain Railway, which carries passengers to the summit of Snowdon.

From Llanberis, carry on along the A4086 up the Llanberis Pass.

As the road leaves Llanberis the grim, grey slateworks loom up over Llyn Peris, site of the Electric Mountain, which conducts underground tours into Dinorwig Power Station, built into Elidir mountain.

The route now winds through dramatic craggy scenery and over the Llanberis Pass for views of the valley below.

At the top of the Llanberis Pass, the Miners' Track and Pyg Track provide exciting ascents of the mountain. To get superb close-up views of Snowdon without making an ascent, walk the first section of the Miners' Track along a well-graded path, past two lakes and as far as Glaslyn lake, then return the same way.

Not long after crossing the pass the road reaches a T-junction ❺. Turn right on to the A498 for Beddgelert. There are more outstanding views as the road descends to pass Llyn Gwynant, a long lake at the foot of Y Lliwedd. Continue along the road to Beddgelert ❻, passing the Sygun Copper Mine on the left.

Beddgelert is a popular walkers' village crammed with hotels and eateries and always busy in high season.

From Beddgelert, turn left over the stone bridge by the Prince Llywelyn Pub and follow the road (A498) past the Royal Goat Hotel and along the Pass of Aberglaslyn, where the Afon (River) Glaslyn follows the road at the foot of Moel y Dyniewyd. Continue along the road as it twists higher above the river. Just as the landscape begins to open out take the left turning on to the B4410 (signed Llanfrothen/Garreg). Follow this road as it crosses the river and continues (with fine mountain views) to a crossroads. Turn right then left, following signs for Tan-y-Bwlch/Ffestiniog Railway and continuing on the B4410.

The road climbs through woodland with good views over Porthmadog before it reaches Rhyd ❼. From here the route winds over the craggy uplands, then drops through a pine forest and past Tan-y-Bwlch, a station on the Ffestiniog Railway.

At the A487 turn left (signed Dolgellau) and, after crossing the bridge, turn left again on to the A496 (signed Blaenau Ffestiniog). Fork left, staying on the A496 and following signs for Blaenau Ffestiniog. Soon Blaenau Ffestiniog comes into view and the road passes a left turning to the hydroelectric power station at Tanygrisiau. At the roundabout ❽ take the first exit (A470) for Betws-y-Coed.

The road leads past Llechwedd Slate Caverns and the flaky, grey heaps of quarried slate that dominate this area. To the left of the road there is access to Dolwyddelan Castle.

The A496 continues as a scenic mountain route. At the next major junction, take the left turn on to the A470 and keep left on the A5, crossing the bridge into Betws-y-Coed to return to the starting point of the drive.

PARC CENEDLAETHOL ERYRI

SNOWDONIA
NATIONAL PARK

OUT AND ABOUT

Sunset view of the 782m (2,566-ft) Moel Hebob across the long lake of Llyn Gwynant (left)

Take the easy way up on the Snowdon Mountain Railway, which leaves from Llanberis

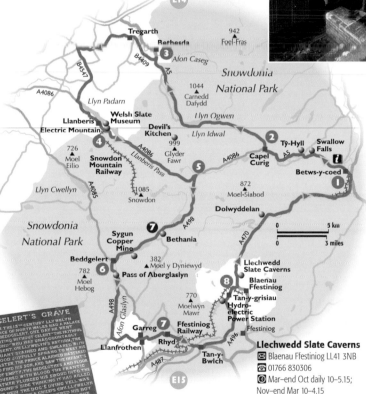

GELERT'S GRAVE

IN THE 13TH CENTURY LLYWELYN PRINCE OF NORTH WALES HAD A PALACE AT BEDDGELERT. ONE DAY HE WENT HUNTING WITHOUT GELERT "THE FAITHFUL HOUND" WHO WAS UNACCOUNTABLY ABSENT. ON LLYWELYN'S RETURN THE TRUANT STAINED AND SMEARED WITH BLOOD JOYFULLY SPRANG TO MEET HIS MASTER THE PRINCE ALARMED HASTENED TO FIND HIS SON AND SAW THE INFANT'S COT EMPTY THE BEDCLOTHES AND FLOOR COVERED WITH BLOOD THE FRANTIC FATHER PLUNGED HIS SWORD INTO THE HOUND'S SIDE THINKING IT HAD KILLED HIS HEIR THE DOG'S DYING YELL WAS ANSWERED BY A CHILD'S CRY LLYWELYN SEARCHED AND DISCOVERED HIS BOY UNHARMED BUT NEAR BY LAY THE BODY OF A MIGHTY WOLF WHICH GELERT HAD SLAIN. THE PRINCE FILLED WITH REMORSE IS SAID NEVER TO HAVE SMILED AGAIN. HE BURIED GELERT HERE THE SPOT IS CALLED

BEDDGELERT

Man's best friend: At Beddgelert you will find Gelert's Grave (left), the supposed final resting place of Prince Llywelyn's dog in the 13th century

PLACES TO VISIT

Dolwyddelan Castle
✉ Betws-y-Coed
☎ 01690 750366
🕐 Apr–end Nov daily 9.30–6.30; rest of year Mon–Sat 9.30–4, Sun 11–4
🎫 Adult £2, child £1.50

Electric Mountain
✉ Llanberis LL55 4UR
☎ 01286 870636
🕐 Jun–end Aug daily 9.30–5.30; Apr–end May, Sep–Oct 10.30–4.30; Oct–end Nov, Feb–end Mar Wed–Sun 10.30–4.30 🎫 Tours: adult £6.50, child £3.25, family £16

Llechwedd Slate Caverns
✉ Blaenau Ffestiniog LL41 3NB
☎ 01766 830306
🕐 Mar–end Oct daily 10–5.15; Nov–end Mar 10–4.15
🎫 Tours, adult £8.75, child £6.50

Snowdon Mountain Railway
✉ Llanberis LL55 4TY
☎ 0870 4580033
🕐 Mid-Mar to end Nov daily, every 30 min
www.snowdonrailway.co.uk
🎫 Return fare, adult £20, child £14

WHERE TO EAT
Plas Derwen, Holyhead Road, Betws-y-Coed (tel: 01690 710388) for snacks and meals.

SNOWDON AND THE WATKIN PATH

Even at its lower levels, this walk encounters some of the most varied and spectacular scenery in Snowdonia (▷ 145). It follows the path named after Sir Edward Watkin—a Victorian railway magnate and Liberal politician who gave the trail to the nation after his retirement.

Length: 4 miles (6.5km)

Allow: 2 hours

Start/end: Parking area at Pont Bethania, on A498 between Capel Curig and Beddgelert, map ref 433 E15

OS Explorer map: OL17

From the parking area cross the bridge and follow the road towards Beddgelert for 45m (50 yards), then cross it to reach a signed path. Cross the cattle grid and follow the tarmac lane **1** away from the road, with a river on the right and woodland on the left.

The ancient oak woods of Parc Hafod-y-Llan once stretched far up Cwm Llan, but were cleared for mining and sheep-rearing.

Leave the tarmac lane at the footpath sign, bearing left through a gate on a rough track, with a wall on the left. Go ahead through gates and follow the track as it curves and climbs to reach (eventually) a wooden gate above the waterfalls **2**.

After heavy rain these falls are among the best in the national park.

The wooden gate allows access to Snowdon National Nature Reserve. Within the reserve this track runs near the river. Continue past ruined copper mines and cross a bridge **3** of massive sleepers over the river. Pass more ruins and a tall cypress tree. Ahead now is the bulky rock outcrop of Gladstone Rock **4**.

This was where W. E. Gladstone gave an address to the people of Snowdonia on 13 September 1892, when he was 83 and prime minister for the fourth time. The event, held to commemorate the opening of the Watkin Path, took place in pouring rain, but Gladstone asked for an encore from the choir that Sir Edward Watkin had organized.

Past Gladstone's Rock, the track continues into Cwm Llan, eventually bearing right by old slate quarry buildings. Y Lliwedd, towering ahead, and Yr Aran, to the left, form the vast walls of the valley.

Above the quarry buildings 5 the track gives superb views of Snowdon to the left, and Y Lliwedd to the right, with Bwlch y Saethau and Bwlch Ciliau between them. Bwlch y Saethau (the Pass of the Arrows) is the legendary site of King Arthur's last battle against Mordred, his treacherous nephew.

If you are not ascending to the summit of Snowdon, retrace your steps at this point to return to the starting point.

If you wish to walk up to the summit, the path climbs steeply up to the left, eventually reaching a saddle and continuing northwest (even more steeply) to the summit. From the top there are several ways down, and you do not need to retrace your steps (frequent buses connect various trailheads around the mountain in summer; details are available at the local tourist information offices).

The easiest (but least interesting) way down is alongside the rail track to Llanberis. More spectacular are the Pyg Track and Miners' Track that head east to Pen-y-Pass parking area on the A4086. The Snowdon Ranger Path heads west from the summit to the A4085. The notoriously vertiginous Snowdon Horseshoe takes in knife-edge ridges and the ridge of Crib Goch, and is definitely not for the faint-hearted. Alternatively, you can take the Snowdon Mountain Railway down.

● This is the first part of one of the routes up Snowdon. You can turn round after point **5**, where the main ascent up Wales' highest mountain begins, or continue to the top.

● Although many people tackle Snowdon each weekend, it is full of dangers and you should only climb to the top if you have a good level of fitness, and are wearing walking boots with good, grippy soles. Part of the path involves clambering over boulders and is very uneven, and descending from the top needs great care (although the Snowdon Mountain Railway is an option when operating). Mobile phones may not have a signal and should not be relied upon to call for help.

● Check the weather forecast before venturing out, and be aware that the summit is often shrouded in cloud, and that weather conditions can change very suddenly.

● Take OS Explorer map OL17 and a compass, allow plenty of time, and carry spare clothing, food and drink.

Downhill all the way: walkers descending the Watkin Path on Snowdon

OUT AND ABOUT

Before setting out for a walk in Snowdonia make sure you are well prepared for all types of weather: Even on clear days conditions can change within minutes and clouds can reduce visibility rapidly

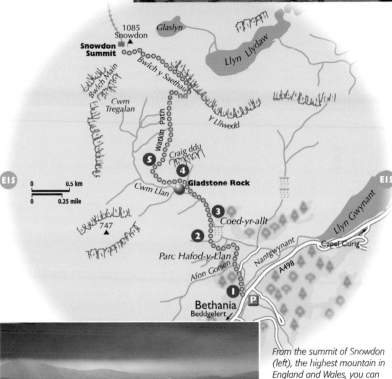

1085
Snowdon ▲

Glaslyn

Llyn Llydaw

Snowdon Summit

Bwlch y Saethau

Bwlch Main

Cwm Tregalan

Y Lliwedd

Watkin Path

Craig ddu

5

4 **Gladstone Rock**

Cwm Llan

3

Coed-yr-allt

2

Nantgwynant

Llyn Gwynant

Capel Curig

0   0.5 km

0   0.25 mile

747 ▲

Parc Hafod-y-Llan

Afon Gorsen

A498

1

Bethania
Beddgelert

E15

E15

P

From the summit of Snowdon (left), the highest mountain in England and Wales, you can see across half of Wales

Many people take the steam-powered Mountain Railway (below) up Snowdon, but walk back down from the top

WHERE TO EAT
No refreshment places on this route, but there is a café at the summit of Snowdon.

PLACE TO VISIT
Snowdon Mountain Railway
✉ Llanberis LL55 4TY
☎ 0870 4580033
🕐 Mid-Mar to end Nov daily, every 30 min, **www.**snowdonrailway.co.uk
💷 Return fare, adult £20, child £14

THE PEAK DISTRICT NATIONAL PARK

This drive explores the gentler southern White Peak, with its high, close-cropped sheep pasture, limestone dry walling and wooded valleys. It also offers a glimpse of the Dark Peak—bleaker moorland and angular outcrops of blackened millstone grit.

THE DRIVE

Distance: 57 miles (92km)

Allow: 2 hours

Start/end: Castleton, map ref 435 H14

Tourist information office: Old Market Hall, Bridge Street, Bakewell DE45 1DS, tel: 01629 813227

www.peakdistrict.org

OS Landranger maps: 110, 119

Perched above Castleton **1** is Peveril Castle, built by William Peveril—the illegitimate son of William the Conqueror—and immortalized in Sir Walter Scott's 1825 novel *Peveril of the Peak*. Castleton is surrounded by show caves (▷ 298), of which Peak Cavern has the best entrance.

From Castleton go east on the A625 through Hope, then turn right on to the B6049. Soon turn left on unclassified roads to Great Hucklow, via Foolow to Eyam **2**.

In 1665, the year of the Great Plague, a chest of infected cloth was sent from London to Eyam. Soon, four out of every five villagers were dead. The villagers resolved to isolate themselves and prevent the disease from wiping out other communities nearby. The churchyard graves reflect this sad story, and every August a service is held in a nearby dell, Cucklets Church.

Leave Eyam on the B6251, then go left on to the A623. At Baslow turn right on to the A619, then left on to the B6012. After 5 miles (8km) turn left at Edensor for Chatsworth **3**.

Chatsworth (▷ 152) is one of the grandest country houses in England, and is popularly known as the 'Palace of the Peak'. Edensor is its village.

Leave Chatsworth, then turn left on to the B6012. At Rowsley turn left on to the A6 for Matlock and carry on through Matlock Bath **4**.

Adjoining Matlock is Matlock Bath, the 19th-century spa town where tall Victorian villas scale the hillside. The spa pavilion now houses the Peak District Mining Museum, which includes access to the disused lead and fluorspar workings of Temple Mine. A cable-car takes you from the river at Matlock Bath to the 305m (1,000ft) Heights of Abraham, a park with zigzagging paths, a maze and a playground. At the top you can climb the Victoria Prospect Tower, and below ground there are two huge lead caverns to explore: Great Rutland and Great Masson.

Leave Matlock Bath on the A6 to reach Cromford **5**.

Cromford marks a significant point in the emergence of England as an industrial nation. It was here in 1771 that Sir Richard Arkwright (1732–92)—the inventor of mechanical spinning (▷ 34)—erected Cromford Mill, the world's first mechanized textile factory. Close by is the Cromford Canal, which once had a busy wharf, but now offers a tranquil towpath towards the old rail station. The defunct trackbed is now the High Peak Trail, a route for walkers and cyclists.

The National Tramway Museum at Crich, south of Cromford, has more than 40 trams from all over the world, built between 1873 and 1953. Volunteers keep the vehicles in pristine condition, and several trams run on any given day. The admission price allows unlimited rides along the 1-mile (1.5km) route.

From Cromford turn right on the A5012, signposted Buxton. Turn right on to the B5056, then left on the A6 to Bakewell **6**.

The fine, five-arched stone bridge, built in 1300 to span the River Wye, is the principal feature of this market town. The Romans came here for the warm springs. Most of the buildings are 17th- and 18th-century, but the Old House Museum, with wattle-and-daub walls, is at least 100 years older, with ancient objects. The town is the headquarters of the Peak District National Park (▷ 156), and its best-known shop is the Old Original Bakewell Pudding Shop. Bakewell puddings (never called Bakewell tarts here) originated in the kitchens of the Rutland Arms Hotel, when the cook accidentally poured egg on to the jam instead of the pastry. Just outside town is Haddon Hall, one of England's best medieval manor houses (▷ 153).

Go north on the A6 from Bakewell. At Ashford in the Water turn right on to the B6465 and, in 4 miles (6.5km) turn left on to the A623, then left into Tideswell **7**.

Tideswell expanded with the medieval wool trade, but over the years it has become a sleepy backwater, and little remains to indicate the town's heyday. One glorious exception is the 14th-century church of St. John the Baptist—known as 'the Cathedral of the Peak'—with a soaring tower. Tideswell is a venue for well-dressing, the local tradition of decorating wells with flowers, which takes place at the end of June or in early July.

From Tideswell follow the B6049 south, then the A6 to Buxton **8**.

Buxton is one of the highest towns in England, at 307m (1,007ft), and has plenty of reminders of its spa days (▷ 150).

Continue north on the A6 towards Chapel-en-le-Frith. Before reaching it, turn right on the A623, then left followed by a fork to the right on unclassified roads down the Winnats Pass and go back into Castleton.

OUT AND ABOUT

PLACES TO VISIT

Cromford Mill
✉ Cromford DE24 3RQ
☎ 01629 824297
🕐 Daily 9–5
🎟 Tours: adult £2, child £1.50

National Tramway Museum
✉ Matlock DE4 5DP
☎ 087075 87267
🕐 Mid-Mar to end Oct daily 10.30–5; rest of year 10.30–4
🎟 Adult £8.50, child £4.50

Old House Museum
✉ Heald Bank, The Yeld, Bakewell DE45 1FI I
☎ 01629 813165
🕐 Apr–end Oct daily 11–4
🎟 Adult £2.50, child £1

Peak District Mining Museum
✉ Pavilion, Matlock DE4 3NR
☎ 01629 583834
🕐 Summer daily 10–5; winter 11–4
🎟 Adult £3, child £2

Peveril Castle
✉ Castleton S33 8WQ
☎ 01433 620613
🕐 May–end Sep daily 10–6; Apr, Oct daily 10–5; rest of year Wed–Sun 10–4
🎟 Adult £3, child £1.50

Bakewell's historic five-arch stone bridge spans the River Wye

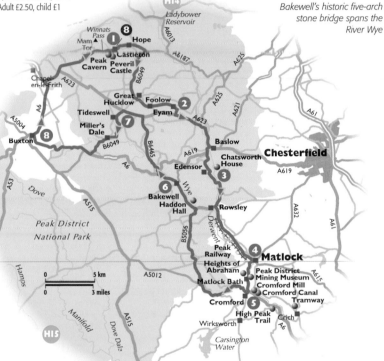

OUT AND ABOUT

Stone walls create a patchwork of fields in the Peak District National Park (left). Bakewell puddings (right) are a local treat

WHERE TO EAT
The French Renaissance Restaurant in Bath Street, Bakewell (tel: 01629 812687) is in a converted barn with stone walls and beamed ceiling, and would make a treat for lunch, with dishes such as pork fillet stuffed with black pudding. There are plenty of pubs and eateries in Castleton.

CAVE DALE AND THE CASTLETON CAVES

Castleton is where the shales and gritstone of the Dark Peak and the limestone plateau of the White Peak meet in the Peak District National Park (▷ 156). Here countless generations of miners have dug shafts and enlarged the natural caves that riddle the bedrock in search of ore. This route passes all the area's show caves and also takes in the hidden gorge of Cave Dale.

THE WALK

Length: 5 miles (8km)

Allow: 3 hours

Start/end: Castleton parking area, Derbyshire, map ref 435 H15

www.peakdistrict.org,

OS Landranger map: 110

OS Explorer map: OL1

From the parking area ❶ turn left down the main street, then right along Castle Street, passing the church and the youth hostel. On reaching the marketplace, turn left to Bar Gate, where a signpost points to Cave Dale. Go through a gate, and enter the limestone gorge of Cave Dale ❷.

Cave Dale has a narrow and dramatic entrance, with the ruined keep of Peveril Castle (▷ 296) crowning the cliff to the right. Geologists once thought that Cave Dale was a collapsed cavern, but now believe that it is a valley carved by glaciers in the last ice age. The path passes several cave entrances.

As you gain height the gorge shallows. The route crosses a stile in the right-hand wall, and then follows a well-defined track across pastureland. It then passes through a gate in another wall before merging into a path dropping from the grassy slope to the right. The track divides at a T-junction soon after: Take the left fork, leading uphill and slightly away from the wall on the right to reach the top corner of the field. Go through a gate at this point and follow a section of track between walls to reach a crossing of routes near the old Hazard Mine ❸. At this point turn right along a stony walled lane, which swings right to reach the B6061 near Oxlow House Farm. Take the path across the road to reach a disused quarry on Windy Knoll ❹.

The path directly opposite is an optional diversion to the windswept summit of Mam

Tor, known as the 'shivering mountain' because of its many landslips. This detour is well marked, as it crosses stiles, then the next road goes up a steep flight of steps on the right. **The summit is capped by the ramparts of an Iron Age hillfort, and there's an exhilarating ridge walk along the 2-mile (3.5km) path to Lose Hill.**

At the quarry, turn right on a footpath to the B6061. After turning left to the next road junction, take the old Mam Tor road straight ahead. The road was once the main A625, but huge landslides from Mam Tor have closed this section of it permanently and it no longer runs through to Castleton. After 370m (400 yards) turn right down the tarmac approach road to the Blue John Cavern ❺, then turn left by the ticket office.

The Blue John Cavern has some fine examples of the fluorspar known as Blue John which is fashioned into ornaments and jewellery. There are no natural stalagmites or stalactites, but the cave has excitingly deep vertical views.

Cross the stile in the fence and trace the path as it crosses a series of fields. Beyond a stile the path curves to the right, traversing the steep-sided, grassy slope of the hill. The path passes

the Treak Cliff Cavern ticket office ❻.

Treak Cliff Cavern is a small cavern that has been mined for Blue John and has the bonus of some attractive natural stalactite formations.

Go left down the concrete steps by the ticket office, then turn right on a concrete path with handrails. Just before reaching the road take a step stile on the right and follow a narrow path across a field by a collapsed wall. On the approach to Speedwell Cavern ❼ the path becomes indistinct, but there is an obvious stile straight ahead which leads on to the Winnats road.

A visit to Speedwell Cavern includes an underground boat trip through a level excavated by lead miners, forming a subterranean canal 500m (1,640ft) long. It took them 11 years, but low yields and high costs forced the early closure of the mine. The boat trip takes you down the canal to a landing stage just short of the 'bottomless pit', part of a natural cavern.

A path on the far side of the road takes the route through the National Trust's Longcliff Estate. This path follows roughly the line of a wall and veers left beneath the hill of Cow Low to reach Goosehill Farm. Here, follow the lane called Goosehill back into Castleton. Beyond Goosehill Bridge, turn left down a surfaced path alongside a stream and back to the parking area.

You can detour to Peak Cavern on the right, just before reaching the bridge; it's well worth a look just for the huge cave entrance, Britain's largest. There is still evidence here of the ropemakers who lived and worked in the cavern, and whose speciality was hangman's nooses.

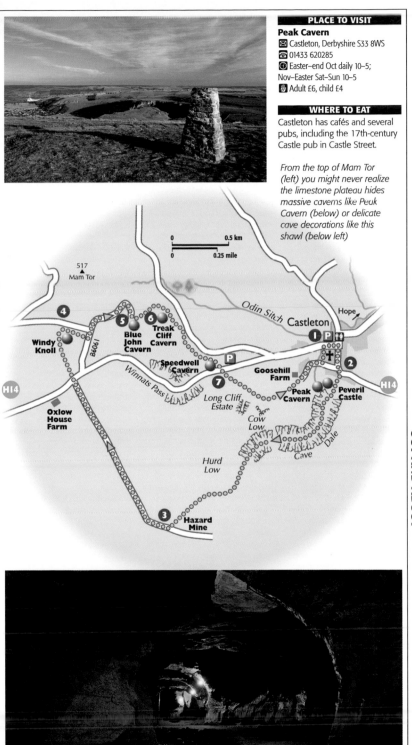

Peak Cavern
✉ Castleton, Derbyshire S33 8WS
☎ 01433 620285
🕐 Easter–end Oct daily 10–5;
Nov–Easter Sat–Sun 10–5
💷 Adult £6, child £4

WHERE TO EAT

Castleton has cafés and several pubs, including the 17th-century Castle pub in Castle Street.

From the top of Mam Tor (left) you might never realize the limestone plateau hides massive caverns like Peak Cavern (below) or delicate cave decorations like this shawl (below left)

OUT AND ABOUT

CAVE DALE AND THE CASTLETON CAVES **299**

THE LAKE DISTRICT NATIONAL PARK

This circuit takes in the best of the Lake District, from Wordsworth's Grasmere and the beautiful Langdale valley, to the spectacular high passes of Wrynose and Hardknott and the less-visited western areas of the national park (▷ 172).

THE DRIVE

Distance: 80 miles (129km)
Allow: One day
Start/end: Keswick, map ref 439 F11
www.lake-district.gov.uk
www.golakes.co.uk
OS Landranger maps: 89, 90, 96

Head south out of Keswick on the A591 (signposted Ambleside).

The road passes Thirlmere ❶, originally two small lakes, but both now dammed to form one large reservoir supplying Manchester with its water; you can take the unclassified road along the western shore (with paths along part of it). To the east, Helvellyn rises steeply.

Follow the A591 as far as Grasmere ❷.

At the edge of the village is Dove Cottage, the home of William Wordsworth (▷ 304).

Just beyond Dove Cottage the road twists and follows the lake of Grasmere before joining the banks of Rydal Water just before entering Rydal village ❸.

At St. Mary's Church in Rydal turn left and head up the steep hill to the parking area for Rydal Mount, the last of Wordsworth's homes in the Lakes (▷ 304).

After a visit to Rydal Mount, return to the A591 and continue south into Ambleside.

Ambleside is a popular spot, and busy at most times of the year. There are plenty of tea rooms and cafés here to make this a good lunchtime stop. Its most celebrated landmark is Bridge House, a tiny house over babbling Stock Ghyll, the trickle of a river that runs parallel to the main street. Legend has it that it was built like this so that the owner could avoid paying land taxes.

From Ambleside bear right at the mini roundabout along the A591. South of Ambleside turn right, following signs for the A593 to Coniston, and continue to Skelwith Bridge. Just before Skelwith Bridge, turn right on the B5343 to the valley of Langdale.

Langdale ❹ is dominated by the formidably craggy bulks of the Langdale Pikes, with the more distant summit of Bow Fell beyond.

At the end of the valley the road turns sharply left and passes a lone house before climbing steeply out of the valley over a cattle grid. At a T-junction turn right, following signs for the Wrynose and Hardknott passes.

At the top of the climb, the road drops steeply to Wrynose Bottom before crossing the River Duddon and climbing steeply again over Hardknott Pass. The ruins of Hardknott Roman Fort appear on the right as you drop down.

Carry on down into Eskdale ❺, a gentle ride due west along narrow country lanes. The road passes Dalegarth Station, terminus for the miniature Ravenglass and Eskdale Railway (steam and diesel services). At the T-junction bear right, following signs for Ravenglass and heading straight through Eskdale Green and up to Santon Bridge. At Santon Bridge, you can make a 4-mile (6.5km) detour along a right-hand turn following signs for Wasdale Head and Wast Water.

Here, England's highest mountain, Scafell Pike (978m/ 3,210ft), rises above its deepest lake.

From Santon Bridge, continue north, following signs to Gosforth ❻.

At Gosforth, outside St. Mary's Church, at the eastern end of the village, is a remarkable 10th-century wheel-head cross (signposted as the Viking Cross), richly carved with a fusion of pagan and Christian symbolism.

Continue straight on through Gosforth, following signs for the A595 to Whitehaven: turn left at the first T-junction, right at the mini roundabout and right again on to the A595.

You can detour (left) from here to the Sellafield Visitor Centre, which has plenty of interactive exhibits explaining the workings of the Sellafield nuclear reprocessing plant, around which tours are given.

Follow the A595 through New Mill to Calder Bridge ❼, then turn right on a minor road signposted Ennerdale. This road rises gently to gain views along the coast, where the surreal massiveness of Sellafield looms large. At the T-junction turn right to head into Ennerdale Bridge and straight on through the next village, Kirkland, to reach the A5086. Turn right on to this main road and into Lamplugh. In Lamplugh, take the first turning right, and follow signs to Loweswater ❽. Soon after Loweswater village, keep forward at a crossroads, then right at a T-junction with the B5289 (signposted Buttermere, but the sign may be obscured in the hedgerow on the left).

The B5289 drops down to follow the left bank of Crummock Water, then goes through Buttermere village and on past the banks of its lake before climbing up through Honister Pass, at the top of which is the working Honister Slate Mine ❾.

The road then drops from the top of the Honister Pass into rolling Borrowdale, via Rosthwaite and Grange, before following the bank of Derwentwater. The road leads back into Keswick. Bear left at the first roundabout and right at the second into the town.

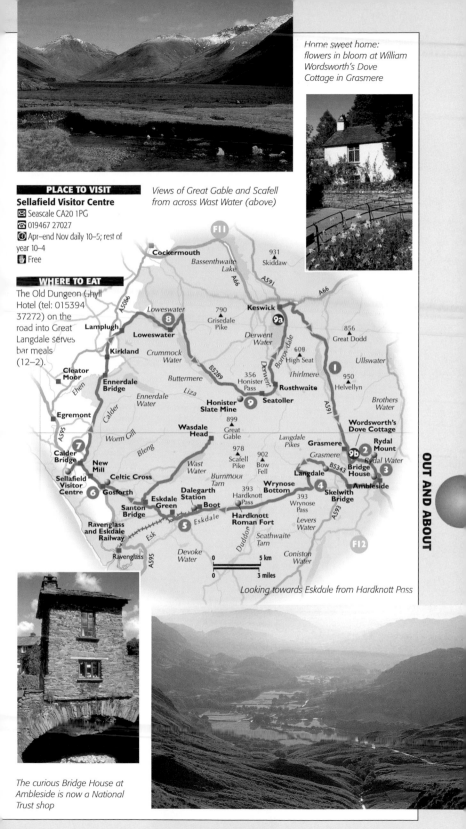

Home sweet home: flowers in bloom at William Wordsworth's Dove Cottage in Grasmere

PLACE TO VISIT

Sellafield Visitor Centre

✉ Seascale CA20 1PG

☎ 019467 27027

🕔 Apr–end Nov daily 10–5; rest of year 10–4

🎫 Free

WHERE TO EAT

The Old Dungeon Ghyll Hotel (tel: 015394 37272) on the road into Great Langdale serves bar meals (12–2).

Views of Great Gable and Scafell from across Wast Water (above)

Looking towards Eskdale from Hardknott Pass

The curious Bridge House at Ambleside is now a National Trust shop

OUT AND ABOUT

FRIAR'S CRAG AND CASTLERIGG STONE CIRCLE

The northeast shores of Derwentwater provide a magnificently varied walk, taking in some of the choicest views of this lake and the surrounding peaks. The later stages include the best-known prehistoric stone circle in the Lake District (▷ 172).

THE WALK

Length: 7 miles (11km)
Allow: 3–4 hours
Start/end: Parking area at Derwentwater, just south of Keswick and signposted off the B5289, map ref 439 F11
OS Landranger map: 89, 90
OS Explorer map: OL4

Take the lakeside road beside the Derwentwater landing stages ❶ and go along the tree-lined track to the end of Friar's Crag for a view of the lake.

Derwentwater is ringed by mountain peaks and dotted with mysterious little tree-clad islands. The writer John Ruskin (1819–1900) described this outlook from Friar's Crag as one of Europe's finest scenic viewpoints.

Retrace your steps to follow the path that swings right to a gate and proceed along the lake shore. Cross two footbridges, then go through a gate into a wood. Continue along the woodland fringe and across a footbridge, then bear right to go through a gate. Continue along a metalled road. Shortly before reaching the B5289, turn right on a path through the trees ❷.

Continue for about 350m (380 yards) parallel to the road then, at the end of the fence, bear right into the wood. Go over the first of the two wooden bridges and turn left up to the road. Cross into Great Wood parking area. Take the path from its right-hand corner and climb gently for about 270m (300 yards) to a track that comes down on your left. Turn up this and continue for 0.5 mile (800m) uphill through woodland. The path begins to level out: soon bear right to a T-junction, signposted Rakefoot and Walla Crag. Shortly the path ascends to a stile ❸.

Go over the stile, leave the woodland and go ahead between a wall and a fence. At a T-junction turn right through a gate signed Castle Rigg, Walla Crag. Continue along the edge of the ravine and through another gate. Keep ahead and, after 90m (100 yards) cross a footbridge on the left and keep ahead up steps, through a gate and turn left on to a metalled track. After 18m (20 yards) turn right through a gate signposted Castlerigg Stone Circle. Keep ahead on the left-hand edge of the field between a wall and a fence. Cross two stiles; turn left at the second stile following the sign for the stone circle. Follow the left-hand edge of the field, crossing further stiles to reach a gate in the A591 Keswick to Windermere road. Turn right, then take the first left on to a track passing houses (High Nest). Keep ahead through a field gate, then across stiles and fields to a lane next to a wood. Turn left on to a road ❹.

Castlerigg Stone Circle is in a field on your left. Dating from late Neolithic times to the early Bronze Age (c2500–2000BC), this is one of the most imposing prehistoric monuments in northern England. Its purpose remains a mystery, but it seems likely that its builders particularly valued the site's magnificent view of Derwentwater.

After viewing the stone circle, keep your back to the entrance

gate and cross the fields to the right by a stile (by a wall and fence junction) on to a lane. Turn left and continue for 0.5 mile (800m) back to the A591. Turn right along the footpath beside this often busy road.

After 0.5 mile (800m), take a minor road left, signposted to Rakefoot. Beyond a house on the right, turn right through a gate by a fingerpost, and follow a path that goes under a footbridge heading downhill through woodland to a stream. Cross a footbridge over the stream, turn right and follow the stream downhill to a gate. Continue past Springs Farm, and cross a bridge on a surfaced lane leading into Springs Road. After 0.5 mile (800m), passing houses on the way, bear left down a narrow path to a gate. Ascend some steps and continue uphill, bearing right through dense woodland. Towards the top, climb steeply left to the viewpoint of Castle Head ❺.

This low wooded hillock gives a surprisingly extensive view of Derwentwater, with the jagged outlines of Cat Bells and Causey Pike rising above the opposite shore. The largest of the lake's islands is St. Herbert's Island, named after its inhabitant from AD685. Lord's Island once had a house on it belonging to the Earl of Derwentwater, while Derwent Isle was home in the 16th century to a colony of German miners who came here to work in the nearby Goldscope Mine.

Return through the trees, bearing left to the lower slopes of the hill, to join up with a path that descends to the left to steps at a gap in the wall and the B5289. Cross over the road and bear left to steps and a ramp on the right. Descend the steps, then keep to the path ahead to reach a wood. Turn right to return to the parking area.

OUT AND ABOUT

WHERE TO EAT

Rembrandts in Station Road, Keswick (tel: 017687 72008) is a traditional, family-friendly English eating house, with panelled divisions between tables. It offers full English breakfast, soup-and-sandwich deals, and casseroles and fish suppers.

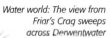

Water world: The view from Friar's Craq sweeps across Derwentwater

Cat Bells and Friar's Crag are reflected in the still waters of Derwentwater

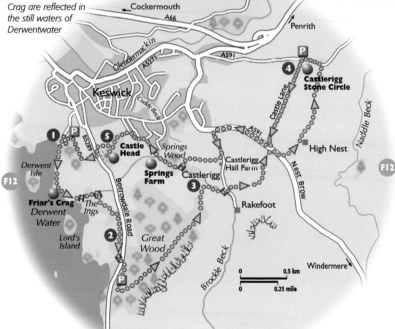

Cockermouth
A66
Penrith
Glendermackin
A271
A591
Keswick
Cuddy Beck
Castle Lane
Castlerigg Stone Circle
Naddle Beck
High Nest
A591
Nest Brow
Castle Head
Springs Wood
Castlerigg Hall Farm
Springs Farm
Castlerigg
Friar's Crag
Derwent Water
The Ings
Derwent Isle
Borrowdale Road
Lord's Island
Great Wood
Rakefoot
Brockle Beck
Windermere
0   0.5 km
0   0.25 mile
F12

OUT AND ABOUT

Castlerigg Stone Circle (below and left) near Keswick dates from the late Neolithic period

GRASMERE AND RYDAL WATER

This easy walk explores the countryside that inspired one of the most celebrated Romantic poets in the English language, William Wordsworth (1770–1850). Wordsworth called Grasmere 'the loveliest spot that man hath ever found'. The greater portion of his life was spent here.

THE WALK

Length: 3.5 miles (5.5km)

Allow: 2–3 hours

Start/end: Dove Cottage, by Grasmere, signposted on the A591, map ref 439 F12

OS Landranger map: 90

OS Explorer map: OL7

Facing Dove Cottage ❶, turn right and take the road leading uphill. The road levels and, just after a small pond on the left, curves right by Howe Top Farm. Bear left here, following the smaller road uphill. Keep to this path, known as the 'coffin route', disregarding the waymarked path leading to Alcock Tarn. The road passes a large garden behind a stone wall on the left. Soon Rydal Water comes into view to the right in the valley below. Ignore a path that forks downhill to the right, and keep ahead on the main track. At a right-hand bend ignore the uphill path on the left and keep to the level main path. Soon the path comes to a gate just past a cottage on the left. Go through into woods and proceed east. Then leave the woods behind to emerge into open countryside.

After about 30 minutes' walk, the path descends, passing behind Rydal Mount on the right. Beyond a gate, turn right downhill on to a road, passing the entrance to Rydal Mount ❷.

Enjoying an elevated position overlooking Windermere and Rydal Water, Rydal Mount was the family home of William Wordsworth from 1813 until his death. It contains family portraits, furniture, some of his personal possessions and some of the first editions of his work. During these years of his life, Wordsworth was a famous man, but his time at Rydal was not all happy. His sister Dorothy suffered a prolonged mental illness, and his daughter Dora died here. He produced far less poetry here than he did at Dove Cottage, and instead spent much of the time designing the garden.

Opposite Rydal Mount is the 18th-century Rydal Hall. The house is not open to the public, but you can walk around the grounds, which feature a grotto, waterfalls, formal gardens and a summer house that Wordsworth used to frequent.

Carry on down the road. After a few paces go through an iron gate on your right to Rydal church.

The Church of St. Mary is where William Wordsworth and his family worshipped, and the poet's pew is in front of the pulpit. Close by is Dora's Field (National Trust), a small plot which Wordsworth bought and later dedicated to his daughter. He planted it with daffodils in her memory.

Walk from the church to the main road, turn right and continue along the pavement for 90m (100 yards) to a waymarked footpath on the left. Follow this, cross a footbridge, then bear right at a fork, before passing through grassland above the river ❸.

From here the route is easy to follow, as the path enters woodland then emerges into the open beyond a gate. Continue on the lakeside path, eventually following it left, away from the lake, and uphill beside a wall. Go past a ruined barn and reach a narrow gate between slate gateposts in the wall on the right ❹.

Go through the gate into woodland. Follow the main path downhill, which soon bears left and levels, before continuing to a wooden bridge (ignore small paths branching off). Cross the bridge over the River Rothay and take the path ahead, which then bears to the right. Continue until, just before a ford and a bridge, a path branches to the left. Follow this left-hand path over a footbridge and pass National Trust toilets on the left to arrive at

the A591 opposite a post box ❺. Cross the road and take the waymarked path on the right of the post box. Enter woodland, with a stream on the left. Where the path branches by a waterfall take the right-hand path uphill and shortly go through the gate ahead (with another gate on the right). Climb the narrow stony track until it joins the outward route just below a stone cottage. Turn left and follow the route back to the start.

Finally, visit Dove Cottage and the Wordsworth Museum. The poet lived in this former pub, the Dove and Olive Bough (Wordsworth never knew it as Dove Cottage), with his family from 1799 to 1808. During that time he wrote much of his best-known poetry, including *The Daffodils, The Rainbow* and the ode *Intimations of Immortality*.

Although far from poor, the Wordsworth household of William, his wife Mary and his sister Dorothy imposed a rustic, spartan lifestyle on themselves. The rooms were dank and the walls were lined with newspapers to keep out the worst of the damp. William did the gardening and chopped wood, while Dorothy did the housework and Mary looked after the children. William and Dorothy roamed the fells for hours, and brought back plants for their garden. Dorothy recorded her thoughts in the now celebrated *Journals*. The house is kept in its original condition, and a museum displays his manuscripts, paintings and other items.

After the Wordsworths left, the poet Thomas de Quincey (1785–1859), a friend of Wordsworth and Samuel Taylor Coleridge (1772–1834), moved in with his wife. His best-known work is *Confessions of an English Opium Eater* (his opium scales are exhibited in Dove Cottage). De Quincey moved out in 1830.

GRASMERE VILLAGE

North of the walk in Grasmere village, the Church of St. Oswald dates from the 14th century and has a memorial to Wordsworth placed above the nave. He is buried alongside his wife and sister in the churchyard. Two other former Wordsworth homes (not open) are in the village: Opposite the church is the Old Parsonage, where they lived from 1811 to 1813, while at the north end of the village is a large white house known as Allan Bank, their home from 1808 to 1811. Near the church is Sarah Nelson's Gingerbread Shop, which has been in operation since the 1850s and sells virtually nothing else.

This portrait of Wordsworth (above), by Samuel Crosthwaite (1791–1868), is on display at Dove Cottage.

Rydal Water (right) was the inspiration for many of Wordsworth's poems

Keswick

Dockey Tarn

Dunney Beck

Dove Cottage & Wordsworth Museum ❶

How Top

White Moss Common

❺

Grasmere

Nab Scar

Rydal Mount Rydal Hall

A591

❷

Rydal

Heron Island

Rydal Water

Dora's Field

St Mary

Little Isle

❸

Jobson Close

Windermere

❹

Rough Intake

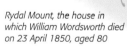
Loughrigg Terrace

Ewe Crag

0   0.25 km
0   0.25 mile

OUT AND ABOUT

Rydal Mount, the house in which William Wordsworth died on 23 April 1850, aged 80

The interior of Dove Cottage: Thomas de Quincey's opium scales are exhibited

NORTH YORK MOORS NATIONAL PARK

Exhilarating high moorland with superb views contrasts with fertile, green dales and stone-built villages in this tour of the North York Moors (▷ 176).

THE DRIVE

Distance: 55 miles (89km)

Allow: 3–4 hours

Start/end: Pickering, map ref 440 J12

Tourist information office: North York Moors National Park, The Old Vicarage, Bondgate, Helmsley, York YO62 5BP, tel: 01439 770657

www.northyorkmoors-npa.gov.uk

www.moors.uk.net

OS Landranger maps: 94, 100

Pickering ❶, the southern terminus of the North Yorkshire Moors Railway, is a market town on the northern edge of the vale. Of interest are the Beck Isle Museum of Rural Life and the 15th-century wall paintings in the Church of St. Peter and St. Paul.

From Pickering follow the A169 Whitby road, gradually climbing towards the moors. After 5 miles (8km) pass a turning on the left to Lockton.

A detour can be made to the attractive hilltop villages of Lockton and Levisham, on the edge of the Tabular Hills, before descending to the steep valley of Newton Dale.

Continue the main tour, climbing to 280m (920ft) on Lockton Low Moor. The road passes the Hole of Horcum (on the left), a spectacular natural hollow popular with hang-gliders. The road then drops. After 3 miles (5km), beyond the Saltersgate Inn, turn left on to an unclassified road, signed Goathland ❷.

To the right of the main road before the turning is the truncated triangular pyramid that houses the Fylingdales Ballistic Missile Early Warning Radar Station.

Cross Goathland Moor before descending to Goathland. Go right at the T-junction and pass the Mallyan Hotel to enter the village, which is close to Mallyan Spout waterfall (▷ 308).
  Follow signs for Whitby and cross the railway ❸. Climb

steeply on to the moors and after 2 miles (3km) turn left on to the A169. In another 0.5 mile (800m) turn left again on to an unclassified road, signposted Grosmont and Egton. The road crosses Sleights Moor. As you descend there are fine views along Esk Dale. The road drops steeply into Grosmont ❹.

Grosmont village developed in the 19th century to house miners for the local iron industry. The northern terminus of the North Yorkshire Moors Railway is here, running steam and diesel trains to Pickering.

Go over the level crossing and River Esk, then ascend steeply to Egton. In the village bear right (signed Whitby) and opposite the Wheatsheaf Inn turn left, signed Glaisdale. Follow the road that descends steeply into Glaisdale. From the higher part of Glaisdale follow the signs to Castleton, and after 1 mile (1.6km) bear right. In another 0.75 mile (1km), at the T-junction, turn right for Lealholm. Recross the River Esk then turn left, signed Danby. Continue through Esk Dale.

After 3.5 miles (5.5km) you reach the Moors Centre (Mar–end Dec daily; Jan–end Feb weekends only), which has local information and walks signposted from the grounds.

Keep left to Danby village ❺.

Here are remains of 14th-century Danby Castle, and the high-arched Duck Bridge over the River Esk, built in 1386.

Go over the staggered crossroads and continue to Castleton. Just beyond the village, bear left (signed Rosedale) to climb along the 348m (1,150ft) Castleton Rigg. After 4 miles (6.5km) turn left to Rosedale Abbey.
  Just before you turn, note Ralph Cross, the symbol of the national park, on your right. After the turn, another small medieval

white cross, known as Fat Betty (the shaft of which has disappeared), is to the left. From Ralph Cross ❻ go across the plateau of Rosedale Moor for 4 miles (6.5km) and then descend into Rosedale, before bearing left for Rosedale Abbey.

This quiet village became a busy mining centre after the discovery of ironstone in 1856. Next to the church are the remains of the 12th-century Cistercian nunnery after which the village was named.

At the end of the village turn right and ascend very steep Rosedale Chimney Bank. *To avoid this, continue straight ahead in Rosedale Abbey, turning right after 4.5 miles/7km, signed Lastingham; then follow the road though Lastingham and into Hutton-le-Hole.*

Rosedale Chimney Bank gets its name from a previous landmark, a 30m (100ft) high chimney. This remnant of the iron industry was demolished in 1972 for safety reasons, but the arches of iron kilns can be seen on the right. The summit of Rosedale Chimney Bank has far-ranging views. Lastingham church is worth a detour for its remarkably intact Norman crypt.

Cross Spaunton Moor. After 3 miles (5km), at the T-junction, turn right for Hutton-le-Hole ❼.

This streamside village has a large, hummocky central green and contains the Ryedale Folk Museum, with a variety of buildings of different ages erected from all over the area.

Turn left on to the Kirkbymoorside road. In 3 miles (5km), at a T-junction, turn left on to the A170, signed Scarborough. Return through the agricultural countryside of the Vale of Pickering, passing beside the village of Wrelton and through Aislaby and Middleton to return to Pickering.

OUT AND ABOUT

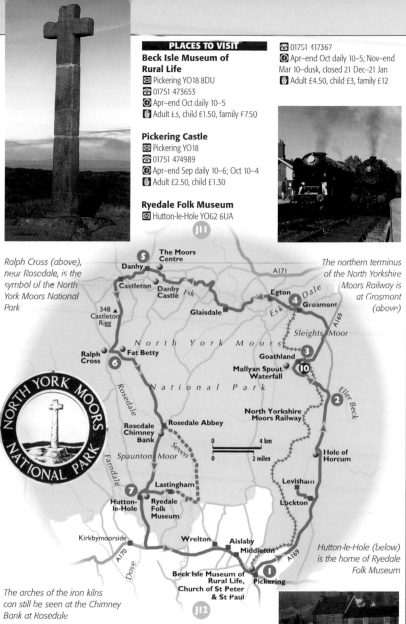

Ralph Cross (above), near Rosedale, is the symbol of the North York Moors National Park

PLACES TO VISIT

Beck Isle Museum of Rural Life
✉ Pickering YO18 8DU
☎ 01751 473653
🕐 Apr–end Oct daily 10–5
💷 Adult £3, child £1.50, family £7.50

Pickering Castle
✉ Pickering YO18
☎ 01751 474989
🕐 Apr–end Sep daily 10–6; Oct 10–4
💷 Adult £2.50, child £1.30

Ryedale Folk Museum
✉ Hutton-le-Hole YO62 6UA
☎ 01751 417367
🕐 Apr–end Oct daily 10–5; Nov–end Mar 10–dusk, closed 21 Dec–21 Jan
💷 Adult £4.50, child £3, family £12

The northern terminus of the North Yorkshire Moors Railway is at Grosmont (above)

Hutton-le-Hole (below) is the home of Ryedale Folk Museum

The arches of the iron kilns can still be seen at the Chimney Bank at Rosedale

WHERE TO EAT

There are plenty of tea shops in Pickering and Helmsley. For meals, the Star Inn (tel: 01439 770397) in Harome, near Helmsley, serves excellent food and local ales. It has three bedrooms.

OUT AND ABOUT

MALLYAN SPOUT AND WADE'S CAUSEWAY

Starting at a village set around a large open common this walk takes in some of the most stunning scenery in the North York Moors (▷ 176). A lush wooded ravine provides a view of Mallyan Spout waterfall, before you cross peaceful farmland.

THE WALK

Length: 4.5 miles (7km); extension to Wade's Causeway adds 1.5 miles (2.4km)

Allow: 2 hours (plus 30 min to Wade's Causeway)

Start/end: Goathland church, at west end of village, map ref 440 J12

OS Landranger map: 94

OS Explorer map: OL27

Goathland is a stop on the North Yorkshire Moors Railway, and the station is in the valley below the village. Running from Pickering to Grosmont, the line was laid out by rail pioneer George Stephenson (1781–1848) in 1836 for horse-drawn trains. It operated until 1957 and was reopened by enthusiasts in 1973. Most of its trains are steam-hauled. Part of the original route went up a steep incline between Goathland and Grosmont, but this proved to be too steep for horses or steam traction, and in 1865 a 'deviation line' was built by blasting away sections of bedrock. The original route is still open as a footpath, and passes a strangely incongruous terrace of railway cottages at Esk Valley between the two villages.

Opposite the church go through a kissing gate beside the Mallyan Spout Hotel, signposted Mallyan Spout. Follow the path to a streamside signpost and turn left. Continue past the waterfall, which tumbles down from a tributary stream to the left; take care here, as the rocks can be slippery.

In the valley of the West Beck, and especially near the waterfall of Mallyan Spout (21m/70ft) ❶, ferns grow prolifically. You may spot the male fern, with its pale green stems, the buckler fern, which has scales with a dark central stripe and pale edges, and the hartstongue fern with its distinctive strap-like fronds.

Follow the footpath signs over two footbridges, across a stile and up a flight of steps, to ascend a stile on to a road beside a bridge ❷.

Turn left along the road and climb the hill. Where the road bends left, go right along a bridleway through a gate. Turn left down a path to go over a bridge, then ahead between the buildings, through a gate and across the field.

Part of the way across the field ❸, go through a gate to the right into woodland. Ascend a stony track; go through a gate to reach a facing gate as you leave the wood. Do not go through this gate, but turn right up the field, going left at the top through a gateway. Continue with a wall on your right and go through a waymarked gateway in the wall and up the field, to emerge on to a metalled lane ❹.

Turn left along the lane, go through a gate and follow the sign for the Roman road. Go through another gate, still following the public bridleway signs as you join a track. Continue through a small gate to descend to another gate, and then carry on until you reach a ford. Cross the ford.

A highly recommended detour at this point is to turn right immediately over a footbridge, signposted Roman road. Go right at the end of the bridge and follow the path. Cross a stile and continue to the left, again signposted to the Roman road. Ascend to a wooden stile in the corner of the field and continue along the field edge with a wall on your left. Go through a gate to reach a sign giving details of the Roman road. From there, retrace your steps to return to the ford ❺.

At the ancient stony track, known as Wade's Causeway or Wheeldale Roman Road, you'll find out about the legend of giant Wade who was said to have built the road to take his cattle to market. You can still make out the ditches at each side of the road and the culverts (tunnels) still covered by stone capping in places. The road certainly took legionnaires from Malton to the signal station near Whitby, but its complete route has not been fully authenticated.

To continue the main walk, just after the route has crossed the ford go straight ahead along the track (but if you have come from the Roman road, do not recross the ford but turn right), eventually to reach a road by farm buildings. Turn right up to this road and, just before a wooden garage, turn left on a green track up the hillside ❻.

Go ahead at a crossing track, passing a small cairn (stone mound) and bending left along the ridge. The obvious path is marked by a series of little cairns, eventually taking a left fork where the path divides, to go down a small stream and join a clear track. Goathland church soon comes into sight. Pass the bridleway sign and descend the road near the church to return to the start.

TIP

● An optional extension takes in Wade's Causeway (also known as Wheeldale Roman Road), an exceptionally well-preserved stretch of ancient trackway crossing the moor.

OUT AND ABOUT

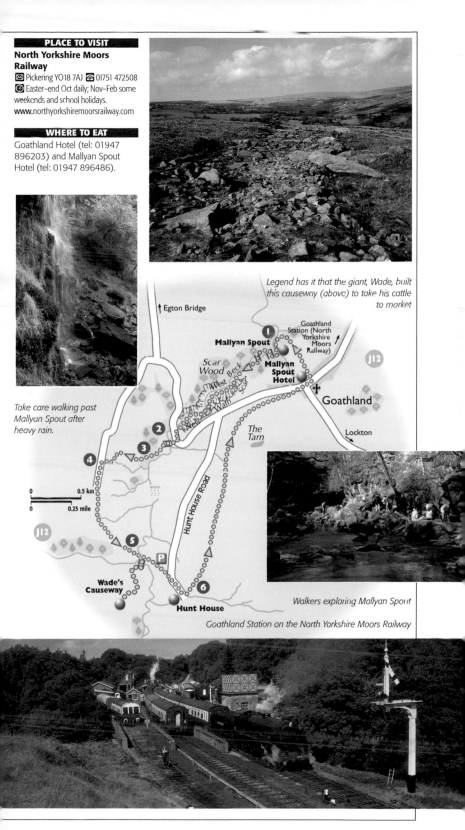

Legend has it that the giant, Wade, built this causeway (above) to take his cattle to market

Take care walking past Mallyan Spout after heavy rain.

↑ Egton Bridge

Mallyan Spout

Scar Wood

West Beck

Mallyan Spout Hotel

Goathland Station (North Yorkshire Moors Railway)

J12

Goathland

Lockton

The Tarn

Hunt House Road

0   0.5 km
0   0.25 mile

J12

Wade's Causeway

P

Hunt House

Walkers exploring Mallyan Spout

Goathland Station on the North Yorkshire Moors Railway

NORTHUMBERLAND NATIONAL PARK AND THE BORDER FOREST PARK

The remains of Hadrian's Wall, Britain's biggest Roman monument, can be seen at their best over the vast coniferous plantations and wild moorlands of the Kielder and Redesdale Forests. Forestry Commission roads allow motorists to enjoy this area right up to the Scottish border.

THE DRIVE

Length: 140 miles (225km)
Time: 4–5 hours
Start/end: Bellingham, map ref 439 G10
Tourist information office:
Northumberland National Park, Church House, Church Street, Rothbury NE65 7UP, tel: 01434 344396
www.nnpa.org.uk
OS Landranger maps: 80, 86, 87

In the small market town of Bellingham ❶, the church of St. Cuthbert has a unique barrel-vaulted roof with six-sided stone ribs to give added protection from fire. In the churchyard is a well whose waters are traditionally held to have healing powers.

Leave Bellingham on the B6320, signposted Hexham and, after 0.5 mile (800m), bear left and over a river. Take the next turning right, an unclassified road through North Tynedale. Continue for 4 miles (6.5km), cross a river bridge then turn right. At a T-junction turn left and continue past Stannersburn. After a while enter Kielder Forest and drive to Kielder Water.

Kielder Forest is a vast plantation of larch, spruce, Scots pine and lodgepole pine blanketing the Cheviot Hills. It forms part of the Border Forest Park, spanning the border into Scotland and creating the largest expanse of planted forestry in Britain. To the east its landscapes merge with the open moorland horizons of Northumberland National Park. Kielder Water, the largest reservoir in western Europe, offers a variety of activities.

Continue to Kielder village ❷.

This is one of several villages that developed with the area's forestry industry. Kielder Castle is an 18th-century shooting lodge that now serves as the Border Forest Park information

office and a Forest Museum. Continue for 3 miles (5km) and cross the Scottish border, then turn left on to the B6357, signposted Newcastleton. At a junction with the B6399 you can make a detour from the main route to Hermitage Castle ❸ by turning right for 4 miles (6.5km), then turning left on to an unclassified road.

Romantically associated with Mary, Queen of Scots (1542–87), brooding Hermitage Castle punctuates the desolate landscape. Its mighty towers and grim walls entirely suit their windswept situation. It was a stronghold of the Douglas family of Scottish nobles in the 14th century, and much later became the property of Mary's lover (and subsequently husband) James Bothwell (c1535–78).

On the main route, bear left on the B6357 to Newcastleton.

The village of Newcastleton was planned in the 18th century and was a flourishing weaving centre before forestry became important to local life in 1921.

Drive to the far end of the village and turn left on an unclassified road, signposted Roadhead. Cross a river bridge and turn right following signs for Roadhead. After 3 miles (4.8km) cross Kershope Burn to enter the English county of Cumbria. Ascend a winding road through Kershope Forest then continue to reach a white house. Turn left here, signposted Carlisle. After 4 miles (6.5km) bend right then left around another white house. Follow the road for 1.5 miles (2.5km) to reach the B6318. Turn left, and immediately left again on to an unclassified road and drive to Bewcastle ❹.

Several ancient remains can be seen in the bleak open

moorland that surrounds Bewcastle. Materials from a Roman fort that was once an outpost of Hadrian's Wall were used to build a castle here, but this too has succumbed to the ravages of time. In the village churchyard is the remarkable seventh-century AD Bewcastle Cross, intricately carved with runic inscriptions and patterns.

The road bears right to bypass the middle of Bewcastle and crosses a river bridge. After 5 miles (8km) cross the B6318, and after another 2.5 miles (4km) meet a T-junction. Turn left, signposted Birdoswald, and follow the line of Hadrian's Wall for 0.5 mile (800m) to Banks.

For details of Hadrian's Wall, ▷ 168. At Banks, a turret on the Roman wall was once manned by troops garrisoned at the nearest milecastle. A footpath leads east to the Pike Hill signal tower, part of a beacon system by which a warning of attack could be sent the length of the wall with surprising speed. One mile (1.6 km) southwest lies the Augustinian Lanercost Priory, which was founded in 1166. Its nave is still in use.

Continue from Banks to Birdoswald ❺.

At Birdoswald you can see the large and impressive outer defences of a Roman fort known as Camboglanna, and well-preserved sections of Hadrian's Wall extend east and west. Close by are the substantial remains of Harrow's Scar Milecastle.

Turn right on to the B6318, signposted Gilsland, and after 1 mile (1.6km) turn right to Gilsland ❻.

Hadrian's Wall runs south of this former spa and includes

OUT AND ABOUT

Poltross Burn Milecastle. Close to the village is an attractive waterfall.

From Gilsland turn left along the B6318, signposted Greenhead, and meet a junction; turn left to enter Greenhead **7**.

Close to Greenhead is a dramatic series of ravines known as the Nine Nicks of Thirlwall. Nearby are the ruins of 14th-century Thirlwall Castle.

From Greenhead, continue east on the B6318 to Chesters Fort, near which turn left on the B6320 to Bellingham.

Kielder Forest (right) and the Border Forest Park is the largest planted forest in Britain and more species are being planted to increase the forest's diversity

You pass the most famous features of Hadrian's Wall along this stretch, including Vindolanda, Housesteads Fort, the Temple of Mithras at Carrowburgh and Chesters Fort (▷ 168).

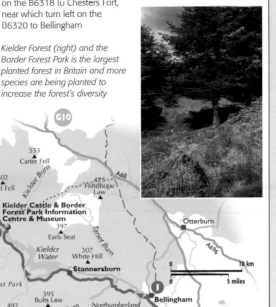

Bewcastle Cross (below) in the churchyard of St. Cuthbert in Bewcastle stands 4m (14ft) tall and dates from the seventh century. The Hadrian's Wall Study Centre overlooks Roman ruins at Birdoswald (right)

PLACES TO VISIT

Birdoswald Roman Fort
- ✉ Gilsland CA8 7DD
- ☎ 01697 747602
- 🕐 Mar–end Nov daily 10–5.30
- 💷 Adult £3.60, child £1.80, family £9

Forest Museum
- ✉ Kielder Castle NE48 1ER
- ☎ 01434 250209
- 🕐 Late Mar–end Oct, Dec daily 10–5; Nov weekends only

Hermitage Castle
- ✉ Newcastleton SY7 8AX
- ☎ 01387 376222
- 🕐 Apr–end Oct daily 9.30–6.30
- 💷 Adult £2.50, child £1

Lanercost Priory
- ✉ Lanercost CA8 2HQ
- ☎ 01697 73030
- 🕐 Apr–end Sep daily 10–6; Oct Thu–Mon 10–4
- 💷 Adult £2.60, child £1.30

HADRIAN'S WALL AND THIRLWALL CASTLE

A stretch of the Roman wall and a medieval castle are highlights of this varied walk.

THE WALK

Length:	4 miles (6.5km)
Allow:	2.5 hours
Start/end:	Parking area at Walltown, northwest of Haltwhistle, map ref 439 G10
OS Landranger map:	86
OS Explorer map:	OL43

From the car park ❶, follow the Pennine Way eastwards alongside the road for 0.5 mile (800m), and over a cattle grid. At a footpath sign for Walltown Crags turn left towards Hadrian's Wall.

Started by Emperor Hadrian in around AD122, the 76-mile (122km) barrier ran from the River Tyne to the Solway Firth, across the neck of northern England. One of the best surviving monuments of the Roman world, it separated Roman civilization from the 'barbarians' to the north. For much of its length it follows the Great Whin Sill, a natural barrier (▷ 168).

On reaching Hadrian's Wall the route goes right, but a short diversion to the left gives good views towards the Cumbrian hills. Returning to the wall, follow it along the top of Walltown Crags, past Turret 45a ❷.

There were originally nine gaps—the Nine Nicks of Thirlwall—along this stretch of the Great Whin Sill, but only five remain because of quarrying. Turret 45a was built before the rest of the wall and may have been a signal post used while the wall was being constructed.

From Turret 45a the route leaves the course of Hadrian's Wall after descending into the valley north of Walltown Farm ❸ and turning left along a track.

Walltown was once a village but is now no more than a farm. Close by was the site of a fortified tower once inhabited by John Ridley, whose brother Nicholas was a Protestant martyr burned at the stake in 1555.

Follow the track as it bends left and then right, go through a gateway and diagonally left past a waymark sign towards the roofs of High Old Shield. Go over a ladder stile in the wall, walk downhill across a footbridge and turn left on the metalled track ❹.

Turn right up the entrance to High Old Shield, signposted Cairny Croft. Where the track bends left, go over two stiles and follow the waymarked route behind the farm to go over another stile. Follow the stone wall and then descend to a stile. Cross another field, go over a stile in a stone wall and turn left. Follow a track to a further stile, and walk left of a wooden hut to a footpath sign ❺.

To avoid the stepping stones across a stream, Tipalt Burn, turn left towards Low Old Shield to join the metalled track in 0.5 mile (800m), turning right to Walltown parking area.
For the full route, continue straight ahead, then make towards the white cottage in the valley. Descend to cross a stile beside the stream, turn left and carefully go over the stepping stones.
Follow the road uphill ❻ for 400m (440 yards) to a footpath sign in the fence on the left. Go over the stile, cross a field to another stile and walk diagonally to a gate in the corner of the next field. On the road turn left to descend to Thirlwall Castle.

Built in the 14th century to defend a gap in the wall against the Scots, Thirlwall Castle is a grim tower built of

stones taken from Hadrian's Wall itself. Edward I (1239–1307) is said to have stayed here on his way to fight the Scots in 1306. Legend says a dwarf guards a solid gold table somewhere in the castle.

Take the farm track to the right of the castle, go over a footbridge and along the track by the buildings. After a right-hand bend, turn left up a track beyond a single stone gatepost. Where the track hairpins left, go straight ahead through a gate and uphill to the vallum ❼.

The earth rampart known as the vallum, 3m (10ft) wide at the bottom and 6m (20ft) wide at the top, was constructed parallel to the wall, at a distance of between 55m and 90m (180ft and 300ft). Crossed only at the forts, it was the result of new military ideas that came in around AD124.

Follow the vallum over two stiles and turn right on the metalled track to visit the Roman Army Museum.

Next to the fort of Magnis, the Roman Army Museum contains Roman excavation finds, life-size displays of army equipment and models, films evoking the harsh life of the Roman soldier, and a video showing representations of the wall and nearby Vindolanda as they were in Roman times.

From the museum carry on back to the parking area.

TIPS

● Waterproof footwear is needed at all times; crossing the Tipalt Burn on stepping-stones needs care and should not be attempted after heavy rain (a walking stick may help).
● A shorter, alternative route goes through Low Old Shield, missing out the stepping stones, Thirlwall Castle and the vallum.

OUT AND ABOUT

A ridge of hard rock called the Great Whin Sill made an ideal foundation for Hadrian's Wall

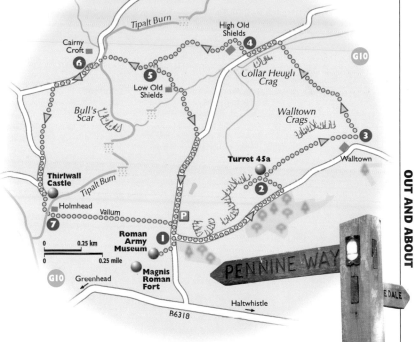

A signpost (above) for the Pennine Way, which runs beside this section of Hadrian's Wall (far left). You can visit a reconstructed Roman fort (left) at nearby Chesterholm, known to the Romans as Vindolanda

PLACES TO VISIT

Roman Army Museum
✉ Carrovan, Greenhead CA6 7SB
☎ 01697 747485
🕐 Mid–Feb to mid–Nov daily
💷 Adult £3.50, child (5–18) £2.20

Thirlwall Castle
✉ Northumberland National Park
☎ 01434 344777 (Ranger Service)
🕐 Daily
💷 Free

WHERE TO EAT

The Milecastle Inn (tel: 01434 321372) in Haltwhistle serves food daily, with sandwiches and home-made pies available at lunchtime.

YORKSHIRE DALES NATIONAL PARK

This tour takes in some of the subtle variety of the Yorkshire Dales (▷ 184), from remote Nidderdale to Richmond—one of the best-preserved market towns in northern England—to Swaledale, Wensleydale and the tranquil beauty of Wharfedale.

THE DRIVE

Length: 75 miles (120km)

Time: 3 hours

Start/end: Pateley Bridge, map ref 439 H12

Tourist information office: Yorkshire Dales National Park Authority, Colvend, Hebden Road, Grassington BD23 5LB, tel: 01756 752748

www.yorkshiredales.org.uk

OS Landranger maps: 98, 99, 104

From the heart of Pateley Bridge ❶ take a minor road from near the bridge itself that leads north into Nidderdale towards Ramsgill and Lofthouse ❷. Pass Gouthwaite Reservoir on your right.

Just west of Lofthouse is How Stean Gorge, a dramatic ravine edged by small cliffs and honeycombed with pot-holes, and with a footpath on its edge giving views along the gorge.

In Lofthouse turn right to take the steep road out of the village, over the moors towards Masham. Continue for about 6 miles (10km), passing two more reservoirs on the right. Take the third left turn, as you approach Healey, towards Ellingstring, turning left to the junction with the A6108, which you follow through Middleham to Leyburn.

On the way to Leyburn you pass the remains of Jervaulx Abbey on the right, near the village of Middleham (▷ 316–317). Leyburn ❸ is a busy Wensleydale town with many tea shops and a market on Friday. Tennants in Harmby Road is the largest antiques and house clearance auction room in Europe.

In Leyburn turn left then right, following the A6108 to the edge of Richmond. The route turns left just before the town centre. After passing a right turn to Catterick, turn immediately left up Hurgill Road, past a parking area on the left.

You can take a detour and continue into Richmond, with its formidable castle towering high over the river and, beyond the huge market-place, the remarkable Georgian Theatre Royal (▷ 177).

Hurgill Road takes you back along the River Swale, but climbs high above the river before dropping steeply down to Marske. Cross the bridge and turn right towards Reeth, then turn left on the B6270 to Grinton ❹.

Up to the 16th century the church at Grinton was the only one in Swaledale, and coffins had to be carried great distances over rough tracks on a route that became known as the Corpse Way. The church is called 'the Cathedral of the Dales', and was substantially rebuilt in the 15th century.

In Grinton turn right on to a minor road and take the right fork, following signs for Redmire along an impressive high moorland road passing disused lead mines. When the road finally descends, take the first turning on the right for Castle Bolton.

Castle Bolton is the estate village for the towering bulk of Bolton Castle, completed in 1399 and the former stronghold of the Scrope family. Mary, Queen of Scots (1542–87) was imprisoned here for six months. The castle was besieged and captured by Parliamentarian forces in 1645.

Turn right for Carperby. Turn left to the Aysgarth Falls ❺.

This is a very popular beauty spot. Although the falls consist of three different sections, only the Upper Falls are visible from the road. Nearby is a watermill, gift shop and tea room.

Beyond Aysgarth Falls turn left on to the A684, signposted Leyburn,

then take the second turning on the right on to the B6160 following the signs into West Burton.

This picture-book village has the largest village green in the Dales, with space for horses to graze. In the centre there is a pub and a pottery, but no church or market. At the north end of the village is a small waterfall.

Rejoin the B6160, which now takes you along the lesser-known Bishopdale and down through Wharfedale.

Buckden is a starting point for walks around northern Wharfedale. To walk the Dales Way follow the river northwest and join a lane past Hubberholme, a remote little hamlet with a rood loft of 1558—a rare survival of a decree by Elizabeth I that such adornments should be removed from churches. The drive then passes Kettlewell, once a hub of the lead-mining industry. Farther down Wharfedale look out for Kilnsey Crag on your right, easily identified as it juts out dramatically towards the main road. This is a popular target of climbers and is a haunt of peregrine falcons. Conistone is the start of walk 12b (▷ 318).

Carry on to Grassington .

This is a large village with narrow cobbled streets, 18th-century houses, pubs, the Yorkshire Dales National Park office and the Upper Wharfedale Folk Museum.

Go into Grassington and leave on the B6265 to return to Nidderdale and Pateley Bridge. Along this road you'll see a sign for the Stump Cross Caverns, lit show caves that you can walk around without a guide. Wolverine Cave has particularly fine stalactites and stalagmites.

PLACES TO VISIT

Bolton Castle

✉ Leyburn DL8 4ET
☎ 01969 623981
🕐 Apr–end Sep daily 10–5; Oct–end Mar 10–4
🎟 Adult £5, child £3.50, family £12

Upper Wharfedale Folk Museum

✉ The Square, Grassington
🕐 Apr–end Sep daily 11–1, 2–4.30; Sep–end Oct 2–4.30
🎟 Adult 75p, child 50p, family £2

WHERE TO EAT

Drinks and snacks are available at Yore Mill Visitor Centre (tel: 01969 663399) near the Aysgarth Falls.

Yorkshire Dales National Park

Richmond Castle, dating from 1071, was built on cliffs above the River Swale

The village of Kettlewell was established alongside the Dowber Gill Beck where it tumbles into the River Wharfe

MIDDLEHAM AND JERVAULX ABBEY

This is an easy walk by the riverside and through woodland, mostly on marked tracks, with the added historical interest of Middleham Castle and the substantial ruins of Jervaulx Abbey.

THE WALK

Length: 7.5 miles (12km)	
Allow: 3 hours	
Start/end: Middleham marketplace map ref 439 H12	
OS Landranger map: 99	
OS Explorer maps: OL30, 302	

From the marketplace walk to the side of Middleham Castle and go left into the cobbled alley by the Castle Keep Tea Rooms in Canaan Lane.

Middleham ❶ is a famous racehorse-training centre, sometimes called 'the Lambourn of the North'. Middleham Castle was a favourite place of Richard III (1452–85), who trained here as a knight. Edward IV (1442–83) and Henry VI (1421–71) were both imprisoned in the castle during the Wars of the Roses in the 15th century. The central keep, one of the largest in England, dates back to the 12th century.

Walk ahead, with Middleham Castle on your left. Continue through the gate and field. At the end of the field, go through the gate and continue in the same direction, but with the wall now on your left. Walk down to the River Cover ❷. Turn left over a stile in the fence and walk along the river. This woodland path is easy to follow. Continue along the riverbank. Go through the gate into a field and head to the right of the gate at the far side. Stay by the river to reach some stepping stones.

The track from Middleham to Jervaulx dates back to the 11th century, and these are believed to be the original stepping stones. They were thought to be lost until a few years ago when plans were made to reinstate the ancient path using concrete slabs, but workmen found these stones buried in the riverbed and replaced them.

Cross the river here, continue up the path, through the gate and turn left along the embankment. The path is clear, with occasional stiles and signposts leading to Cover Bridge ❸. Cross the road and pass through a gate marked 'public footpath, private fishing', and follow the wide embankment. Go through a gate and, after 0.5 mile (800m), go through another. The path continues for another 0.5 mile (800m) until you leave it through another gate, turning right along a track that leads to a road. Turn left on to the road and continue until you reach the entrance to Jervaulx Abbey ❹ on your left.

Founded in 1156 by Savigny monks who later became Cistercians, Jervaulx is known as the original home of Wensleydale cheese, and for the breeding of racehorses, the latter continued today in Middleham.

After visiting the abbey, retrace your steps to Cover Bridge and the Coverbridge Inn ❺.

Without this ancient, beamed inn there might be no Wensleydale cheese. Created at Jervaulx Abbey, the recipe for the cheese was passed to the landlord after the dissolution of Jervaulx in 1536. He sold the cheese for 40 years as Coverham cheese, before passing on the recipe—which then reverted to the famous name of Wensleydale.

Cross the bridge and turn left past the pub at the bungalow. Here a narrow gap in the wall leads you back to the River Cover, where you turn right to skirt the pasture. Go through a gate and follow the path along the riverbank. The path is well defined and after a few minutes' walking look for a stile in the wall on your right, which leads to another wall with a stile and two yellow arrows above it (beyond this wall are the stepping stones you crossed earlier).

Do not cross this stile but turn right up the field ❻, and go out through a gate. This leads into Straight Lane, a path that becomes a wider track. Some way beyond a house on your right, turn left through a tiny gap in the wall. Go up the field, turning left when you reach the wall at the far end and skirt round to a small stile to your right. Climb this and cross the field to another stile that takes you down a high-hedged path to rejoin Canaan Lane.

THE MIDDLEHAM JEWEL

The Middleham Jewel, a magnificent gold and sapphire pendant of the late 15th century, was unearthed close to Middleham Castle in 1985. It fetched £2.5 million at auction, when funds were raised to keep it in Britain. The original is now in the Yorkshire Museum in York (▷ 180–183), and there is a replica at Middleham Castle.

More than 500 horses train in Middleham under the watchful eyes of 15 trainers

OUT AND ABOUT

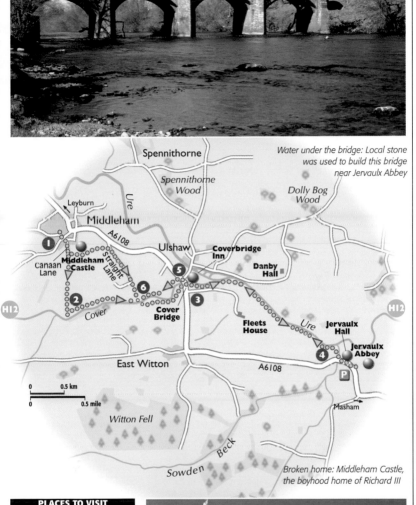

Spennithorne

Spennithorne
Wood

Dolly Bog
Wood

*Water under the bridge: Local stone
was used to build this bridge
near Jervaulx Abbey*

Leyburn

Ure

Middleham

A6108

Ulshaw

Coverbridge
Inn

Danby
Hall

Canaan
Lane

Middleham
Castle

Straight
Lane

❶

❷

❻

Cover

Cover
Bridge

❺

❸

Fleets
House

Ure

Jervaulx
Hall

Jervaulx
Abbey

❹

P

H12

H12

East Witton

A6108

0   0.5 km
0   0.5 mile

Masham

Witton Fell

Sowden

Beck

*Broken home: Middleham Castle,
the boyhood home of Richard III*

OUT AND ABOUT

PLACES TO VISIT

Jervaulx Abbey
✉ Jervaulx HG4 4PH
☎ 01677 460391
🕐 Dawn to dusk
💷 Adult £2, child £1.50

Middleham Castle
✉ Middleham DL8 4RJ
☎ 01969 623899
🕐 Mar–end Sep daily 10–6; Oct–end
Mar Mon, Thu–Sun 10–4
💷 Adult £3.30, child £1.70

WHERE TO EAT

There are several pubs and cafés
in Middleham itself and the
Coverbridge Inn. Tea room at
Jervaulx Abbey (mid-Mar to
end Oct).

WHARFEDALE AND KILNSEY CRAG

This is an easy stroll through Wharfedale fields, which are dominated by the imposing face of Kilnsey Crag.

THE WALK

Length: 2.5 miles (4km)

Allow: 1 hour

Start/end: Conistone, 3 miles (4.8km) south of Kettlewell off the B6160; park opposite Conistone Hostel and chapel map ref 439 G12

OS Landranger map: 98

OS Explorer map: OL2

Conistone village ❶ appears in the Domesday Book—the comprehensive inventory of English life compiled on the order of William I in 1086—as Cumestane, and its farmhouses date from the late 17th century. The attractive village houses are built of local limestone dressed with sandstone. The Church of St. Mary is well worth a visit. Inside the church gate on the left is a memorial stone to six young cavers whose bodies lie buried in Mossdale Caverns, where they were lost. The church itself is considered to be one of the oldest buildings in the area, with parts believed to date from Saxon times, though it is largely Norman and was restored in 1846.

From the parking area in Conistone turn left and follow the road out of the village towards the B6160. Cross Conistone Bridge then immediately turn off the road and take a footpath ❷ on the right, signposted Scar Lathe.

Dominating the landscape ahead and slightly to your left is the unmistakable sight of Kilnsey Crag. It is not particularly high—no match for Great Whernside farther up the dale—but its menacing shape reaching out towards the road is certainly eye-catching. The crag is popular with rock climbers, and is also the finishing point for the annual August public holiday Fell Race.

The path takes you almost straight ahead, veering slightly left to the point where the wall turns. Now go ahead with this

wall on your left. Scar Lathe ❸ is the solitary grey building visible below Kilnsey Crag. When the wall ends, head to the left, directly towards this building. Go over a stile in the fence and continue ahead on the path. Note the views of the wide open valley of Wharfedale up to the north.

When you reach the building, walk round the far side where, to the right, there is a gate and a stile. Cross the stile on to the B6160, turn left and continue a short distance to the Tennant Arms ❹. At the pub, take the right turn marked 'Unsuitable for Motors'. Another road joins from the left; pass this and keep on upwards through Kilnsey; the road swings left and continues uphill. As the road flattens there are views back towards Kilnsey and Conistone, and Wharfedale in all its glory. To visit Kilnsey Park keep on the B6160 for about 140m (150 yards).

Kilnsey belonged to Fountains Abbey in the 12th century, and subsequently became a comparatively industrial village of flour and textile mills. You can still see remains of some of the mills. Kilnsey Park is devoted to all aspects of rural life, particularly wildlife. Attractions include ducks and fish which children may feed, a museum, aquarium, adventure playground, accommodation and a restaurant. Trout smoked on the premises is on sale. There are displays of local crafts, such as drystone walling, and a collection of orchids, a conservation area containing red squirrels and two lakes for fly-fishing.

Bear left on to the wide bridleway, signposted Malham ❺. About 90m (100 yards) after going through a gate, the wall on

your left turns 90 degrees: Look for a small gate above the wall that leads over a stile, taking you almost back on yourself. Walk towards a derelict building, beside which is a little stone footbridge over a stream. Cross this and go through a gate to meet a track coming down from the right. Go over a stile on to the track leading down by a stream and back to the road, passing a farm and emerging alongside a house ❻. Turn left on to the B6160 and then take the first right to cross the bridge and return to Conistone. Take the right turn back to the parking area.

Catch of the day: A large trout fails to escape a fisherman at Kilnsey Trout Farm

ALTERNATIVE ROUTES

There are opportunities for extending the walk eastwards from Conistone, but you need to follow the OS Explorer map very carefully. An unmade track called Scot Gate Lane rises up on to the high ground, where you can turn right along the Dales Way, a route stretching 81 miles (130km) from Ilkley to Bowness in the Lake District, taking in the length of Wharfedale. This section of moor encounters sites of prehistoric settlements, shafts of abandoned lead mines and lumpy remnants of ancient field systems. Farther south, another track doubles back to the right to drop down to Conistone.

OUT AND ABOUT

WHEN TO GO

This walk is best done beneath clear blue skies in spring or summer.

WHERE TO EAT

Pub lunches and evening meals are available at the Tennant Arms, Kilnsey, but sandwiches are available all day.

PLACE TO VISIT

Kilnsey Park and Trout Farm
✉ Kilnsey, near Skipton BD23 5PS
☎ 01756 752150
🕐 Daily 9–5
💷 Admission free, charges for activities vary

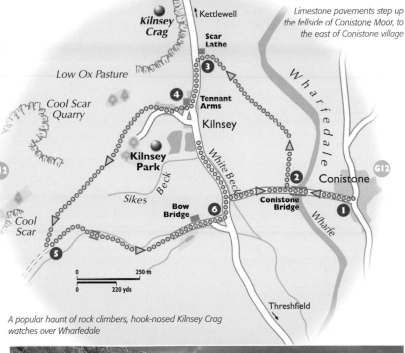

Limestone pavements step up the fellside of Conistone Moor, to the east of Conistone village

A popular haunt of rock climbers, hook-nosed Kilnsey Crag watches over Wharfedale

SCOTTISH BORDERS

This circular drive from Moffat takes in some of the loveliest landscapes of the Scottish Borders, chasing literary connections with novelists John Buchan (1875–1940) and Sir Walter Scott (1771–1832), and poets William Wordsworth (1770–1850) and James Hogg (1770–1835).

THE DRIVE

Distance:	120 miles (193km)
Allow:	1–2 days
Start/end:	Moffat, map ref 438 F10
Tourist information office:	Churchgate, Moffat DG10 9EG, tel: 01683 220620
OS Landranger map:	78

Leave the attractive 17th-century spa village of Moffat ❶ by the A701, which follows the Tweed valley. Turn right at the B712 to Dawyck Botanic Garden.

This is an outpost of the Royal Botanic Garden, Edinburgh. Established over 300 years ago, it is noted for its trees, with magnificent autumnal displays from beeches and maples.

Return along the B712, turn right at the A701, and follow this to Broughton ❷.

In a converted church in Broughton, the John Buchan Centre details the history of the master storyteller whose best-known novel is *The Thirty-nine Steps*. Buchan was also a historian, and wrote biographies of Sir Walter Scott and the 17th-century Scottish general James Montrose. Don't miss Broughton Gallery, set in a fairytale castle up the hill.

Continue on the A701 and turn right at the A72. Turn left at the A721 and right at the A702. Follow this into the narrow streets of West Linton ❸.

In the 17th century West Linton became famous for its stonemasons, who were the chief gravestone carvers in the area. Gifford's Stone, a well-worn bas relief on a wall in the main street, is by James Gifford. Opposite it is another of his works, the Lady Gifford Well, which he carved in 1666. The Cauld Stane Slap, an ancient road across the Pentland Hills, passes nearby.

Leave the village by the B7059. Turn right at the A701 and left at the B7059. Turn left at the A72 for Peebles. Pass the solid tower of Neidpath Castle on the right ❹, above the River Tweed, as you enter the town of Peebles. Leave the town on the A72, passing the Kailzie Gardens. After 6 miles (9.6km) reach Innerleithen.

This is Scotland's oldest spa. It boomed in the 19th century after Sir Walter Scott named one of his novels, *St. Ronan's Well* (1823), after the mineral wells in the town. In the High Street, Robert Smail's Printing Works is a tiny print shop started in 1840, when the press was powered by water. Historic Traquair House lies just over 1 mile (1.6km) to the south.

Stay on the A72 for 12 miles (19km) to reach the busy textile town of Galashiels ❺.

Galashiels is famous for its weaving. The story of the mills is told in the Lochcarron Cashmere Wool of Scotland Visitor Centre; entertaining factory tours show the entire process of tartan manufacture. Look for Old Gala House, founded around 1583. The nearby mercat (market) cross, which marks the centre of the old town, dates from 1695. It features in the Braw Lads Gathering, an annual festival dating from 1599, during which the boundaries of the town are

confirmed by being ridden on horseback.

Leave by the A7, signposted to Selkirk. Turn right at the B7060, then left at the A707 at Yair Bridge. Continue on this road, which becomes the A708 near Selkirk. Follow Ettrick Water and then Yarrow Water on the A708 to Yarrowford ❻, a distance of 13 miles (21km).

This scattered village lies on Yarrow Water, the river that inspired William Wordsworth to compose three poems in its praise. The former royal hunting lodge of Newark Tower lies downstream, and dates from 1423. Hunting took place in the hills of Ettrick Forest until the 16th century, when sheep farming was introduced.

The ruins of Foulshiels House also lie this way. It was the birthplace of explorer Mungo Park (1771–1806), who died in his search for the source of the Niger (▷ 322). Bowhill House, a 19th-century mansion with fine French furniture and a collection of paintings, is surrounded by a country park.

Continue on the A708, passing along the northwestern shore of St. Marys Loch.

At 3 miles (4.8km) long, this is one of the best places in southern Scotland for watersports. At the southern end of the loch, on a spit of land which separates it from the smaller Loch of the Lowes, a red sandstone monument recalls local poet James Hogg, known as the Ettrick Shepherd. Hogg spent many an evening in the nearby Tibbie Shiels Inn with his friend Sir Walter Scott.

Continue on the A708 for 9 miles (14.5km) and follow signs to the parking area at the Grey Mare's Tail waterfall. Stay on

A bronze ram tops the fountain at Moffat, prime sheep country

Broughton Gallery is in a mansion designed in 1937 by Sir Basil Spence

A stone bridge makes an eye-catching feature at Dawyck

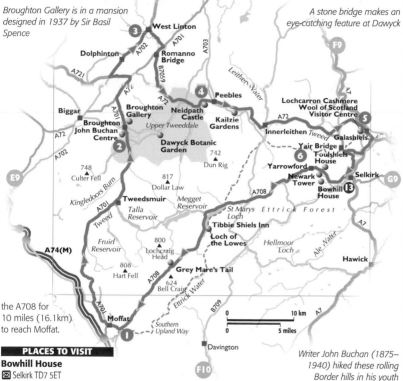

West Linton

Dolphinton

A702

A701

A703

Romanno Bridge

B7059

Leithen Water

F9

A72

Peebles

Biggar

A701

A72

Broughton Gallery

Neidpath Castle

Kailzie Gardens

A72

Lochcarron Cashmere Wool of Scotland Visitor Centre

5

Broughton John Buchan Centre

Upper Tweeddale

Innerleithen

Tweed

Galashiels

A72

A72

A702

2

Dawyck Botanic Garden

742

Dun Rig

Yair Bridge

6

Foulshiels House

Yarrowford

Selkirk

G9

E9

748

Culter Fell

817

Dollar Law

Newark Tower

Bowhill House

13

Kingledoors Burn

Tweedsmuir

Megget Reservoir

St Marys Loch

Ettrick Forest

Talla Reservoir

Tibbie Shiels Inn

A708

A7

Tweed

Fruid Reservoir

800

Lochcraig Head

Loch of the Lowes

Hellmoor Loch

Ale Water

A74(M)

808

Hart Fell

A708

Grey Mare's Tail

Hawick

624

Bell Craig

Ettrick Water

B709

0   10 km

0   5 miles

A7

the A708 for 10 miles (16.1km) to reach Moffat.

Moffat

1

Southern Upland Way

Davington

F10

Writer John Buchan (1875–1940) hiked these rolling Border hills in his youth

OUT AND ABOUT

PLACES TO VISIT

Bowhill House

✉ Selkirk TD7 5ET

☎ 01750 22204

🕐 Jul daily 1–4.30; park only: mid-Apr to end Aug Sat–Thu 11–5

🎫 House £6, park £2

Dawyck Botanic Garden

✉ Stobo EH45 9JU

☎ 01721 760254

🕐 Apr–end Sep daily 10–6; Mar and Oct 10–5; rest of year 10–4

🎫 Adult £3.30, child £1, family £8

Robert Smail's Printing Works

✉ 7–9 High Street, Innerleithen EH44

☎ 01896 830206

🕐 Easter and Jun–end Sep Thu–Mon 12–5, Sun 1–5

🎫 Adult £5, child £4, family £14

FROM SELKIRK TO
THE WILDS OF AFRICA

A gentle walk by Ettrick Water, laced with memories of the great explorer Mungo Park (1771–1806).

THE WALK

Length:	3 miles (4.8km)
Allow:	1 hour 40 min
Start/end:	West Port Car Park, Selkirk, map ref 443 F9
OS Explorer map:	338

The statue on Selkirk's High Street commemorates Mungo Park, the noted surgeon and explorer, who was born nearby at Foulshiels. Park was educated at Selkirk Grammar School, trained as a doctor and took a post as surgeon's mate on a ship bound for the East Indies. He returned from the voyage and promptly set off again, this time heading for Africa to map the River Niger. Park's journey lasted more than 2.5 years. He become desperately ill from fever and hunger, and was robbed many times. He was even captured and held prisoner by a tribal leader. He escaped after four months and continued his travels, following the River Niger to Sillis and only abandoning his journey when he became too ill to carry on. When Park returned to Scotland he published an account of his explorations, *Travels in the Interior Districts of Africa* (1799), which became a bestseller. Shortly afterwards he married and took a post as a doctor in Peebles. In 1805, Park set sail again for Africa, accompanied by his friend George Scott and brother-in-law Alexander Anderson, intending to complete the journey along the Niger. The intrepid explorers never came home. Scott, Andersen and others died from fever. Park refused to give up, writing 'I shall…discover the termination of the Niger or perish in the attempt.' He

The Selkirk bannock is a local delicacy—a sweet bread made with dried fruit

continued his journey with a few soldiers and bearers, but fate was against him. While trying to escape from hostile tribesmen who had attacked his party, he threw himself into the waters of the Niger and drowned. Tragedy struck again when his son followed in his footsteps some 20 years later, and also disappeared without trace.

From Park's statue in the High Street ❶ walk to the Market Place, go left down Ettrick Terrace, left at the church, then sharp right down Forest Road. Follow this downhill, cutting off the corners using the steps, to Mill Street. Go right, then left on to Buccleuch Road. Turn right following the signs for the riverside walk and walk across Victoria Park to join a tarmac track.

Turn left ❷, walk by the river, then join the road and continue to cross the bridge. Turn left along Ettrickhaugh Road, passing a row of cottages on your left. Just past them turn left, cross a tiny footbridge, then take the indistinct track on the left. Walk to

the riverbank and turn right ❸. Follow the path along the river margin; it's eroded in places so watch your feet. In spring and summer your way is sprinkled with wild flowers. Eventually join a wider track and bear left. Follow this to reach a weir and a salmon ladder. Turn right to cross the tiny bridge ❹.

Immediately after this go left and continue walking alongside the river until you reach a point at which Yarrow Water joins the Ettrick Water. Retrace your steps for about 91m (100 yards), then turn left at a crossing of tracks ❺.

Your route now takes you through the woods, until you cross over the little bridge by the weir again. Take the footpath to the left and follow the grassy track round the meadow until you come to the mill buildings ❻.

Bear right (but don't cross the bridge) and continue, walking with the mill lade (small canal) on your left. Where the path splits, take the track on the left to follow a straight, concrete path beside the water to reach the fish farm ❼ (you'll smell it).

Walk around the buildings, then bear left to continue following the mill lade. Go left over the footbridge, then right, passing the cottages again. At the main road go right to reach the bridge. Don't cross the bridge but join the footpath on the left ❽.

Follow this footpath as it goes past a sports ground, then skirts a housing estate. Continue walking until you reach the pedestrian footbridge on your right-hand side, where you cross over the river, bear right, then retrace your footsteps back over Victoria Park and uphill to the Market Place at the start of the walk.

OUT AND ABOUT

The Ettrick Valley is associated with James Hogg, best known for his novel Confessions of a Justified Sinner (1824)

A baronial tower adds distinctive Scottish character to an old house in Selkirk

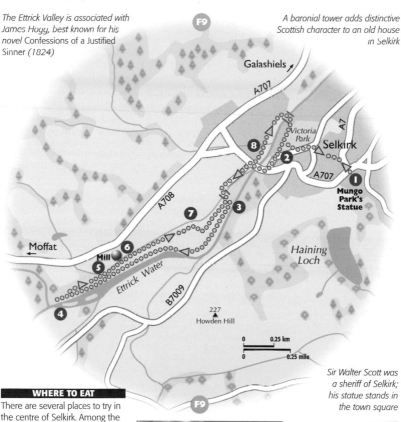

Sir Walter Scott was a sheriff of Selkirk; his statue stands in the town square

WHERE TO EAT

There are several places to try in the centre of Selkirk. Among the hotels offering bar meals is the Cross Keys by the Market Place, which serves toasted sandwiches and light snacks. There's also a small tea room. Look out for the famous Selkirk bannock on sale in the town bakeries.

PLACE TO VISIT

Sir Walter Scott's Courtroom
✉ Market Place, Selkirk TD7 4BT
☎ 01750 20761
🕐 Easter–end Sep Mon–Sat 10–4; Jun–end Aug Sun 10–2; Oct Mon–Sat 1–4
💷 Free

WESTERN HIGHLANDS

'The Road to the Isles', an old cattle drovers' road, leads into the western Highlands at the start of one of the most scenic routes in Scotland.

THE DRIVE
Distance: 205 miles (330km)
Allow: 2–3 days
Start/end: Fort William, map ref 442 D6
Tourist information offices: Cameron Centre, Cameron Square, Fort William PH33 6AJ, tel: 01397 703781 Main Street, Mallaig PH41 4QS, tel: 01687 462170; seasonal
OS Landranger map: 41

Leave Fort William **1** on the A82 towards Inverness, then turn left at the A830, signposted Mallaig. Turn right at the B8004 to Banavie, to admire Neptune's Staircase, the flight of locks on the Caledonian Canal (▷ 326–327). Return to the A830, then turn right and follow the road along Loch Eil to Glenfinnan **2**.

Glenfinnan, at the head of Loch Shiel, is famous for its links with the ill-fated Jacobite rebellion of 1745. Take the short path behind the National Trust for Scotland's visitor office to view the 21-arch Glenfinnan viaduct, by Sir Robert 'Concrete Bob' MacAlpine (1847–1934), which carries the scenic West Highland Railway to Mallaig. The railway runs parallel with the road for much of the way— look out for steam locomotives in summer.

Follow the A830, passing the shores of Loch nan Uamh.

A cairn marks the spot from where, after defeat at Culloden in 1746 and months in hiding in the Western Isles, Bonnie

Prince Charlie finally fled to exile in France. He was helped during this time by many ordinary people, and despite a well-publicized reward of £30,000, nobody betrayed him.

Continue on the A830, passing through woodland of beech, oak and birch to the village of Arisaig.

During World War II, agents of the Special Operation Executive (SOE) trained in this area, honing their fieldcraft skills before being dropped behind enemy lines in Europe. Their base was nearby Arisaig House, a manor house in a magnificent setting (private).

Continue on the A830 up the coast to Morar, with views out to the islands of Eigg and Skye.

Morar is famous for its silvery silica sands, and for its very own monster, Morag, who is believed to live in the murky depths of Loch Morar, 310m (1,017ft) down.

Continue on the A830 to Mallaig.

Mallaig's busy fishing harbour **3** faces the island of Skye across the Sound of Sleat, and is the mainland terminal for ferries to the Inner Hebrides, including the group of Rum, Eigg, Muck and Canna, known as the Small Isles. Mallaig rose to prominence after the arrival of the railway in 1901, which provided swift access south for

fishing catches. That was during the herring boom—now prawns are a mainstay. See them in Marine World, an aquarium on the harbour front. At the road's end, Mallaigvaig looks across to the hills of Knoydart, one of the remotest areas of Scotland.

Return along the A830 to Lochailort. Turn right at the A861 and follow it to Kinlochmoidart and Acharacle **4**.

Acharacle lies at the southwest tip of Loch Shiel. A detour on to the B8044 leads to the dramatic ruin of Castle Tioram, on Loch Moidart (free access). It lies on a rocky islet at the end of a sandy spit, and dates from the early 13th century, although the central keep is later. It was the seat of the Macdonalds of Clanranald, and was deliberately burned down when Allan, the 14th chief, set off in 1715 to join the Jacobite uprising, to prevent its use by Campbell enemies.

Continue on the A861 to Salen, then turn right at the B8007, to explore the Ardnamurchan peninsula. Continue on the B8007, passing through the scattered community of Kilchoan, to Ardnamurchan Point **5**.

The most westerly point on the British mainland, Ardnamurchan is marked with a lighthouse, and has superb views out to the islands of the Inner Hebrides, Barra and South Uist.

Return to Salen along the B8007, then turn right at the A861 to the Highland village of Strontian **6**.

Strontian gives its name to the element strontium, extracted from the mineral strontianite, discovered here in 1764. Strontium has a deep crimson flame when burned, and is used in fireworks. The area was extensively mined between 1722 and 1904 for lead, zinc

A stone cairn marks the spot on the shore of Loch nan Uamh where Bonnie Prince Charlie last set foot in Scotland

OUT AND ABOUT

Watching the sunset over Rum and Eigg, from the cliffs by Mallaig (left)

Mallaig's fishing has survived by changing tack, and prawns are now a staple catch

The Jacobite Express steam train pulls out of Glenfinnan (above)

The shell of Castle Tioram watches over Loch Moidart

and silver; it now supplies minerals for the lubrication of oil rigs. There are walks through the nearby Ariundel woods.

Continue on the A861, then turn right on to the A884. Follow this to Lochaline **7**.

Lochaline stands on the Sound of Mull, with a ferry service to Fishnish, and views to the ruins of Ardtornish Castle, and Duart Castle on Mull.

Return on the A884 to the junction (right) with the B8043. Follow this road to meet the A861. Turn right and follow this up Loch Linnhe to Ardgour. Take the Corran ferry across the loch at the Corran Narrows. At the other side turn left on to the A82 and return to Fort William.

PLACE TO VISIT

Mallaig Marine World

✉ Mallaig Harbour PH41 4XP

☎ 01687 462292

🕐 Jun–Aug Mon–Sat 9–6, Sun 11–6; Apr, May, Sep, Oct Mon–Sat 9–5, Sun 11–5; Nov–end Mar Mon–Sat 9–5

💷 Adult £2.75, child £1.50

OUT AND ABOUT

THE CALEDONIAN CANAL

A walk alongside—and underneath—Thomas Telford's masterpiece of civil engineering.

THE WALK	
Length: 4.5 miles (7.2km)	
Allow: 1 hour 45 min	
Start/end: Kilmallie Hall, Corpach, map ref 442 D6	
OS Explorer map: 392	

The first survey for a coast-to-coast canal across Scotland, linking the lochs of the Great Glen, was made by James Watt, inventor of the steam engine, in 1767. But it was the economic and military necessities of the Napoleonic Wars that finally sent the men with the wheelbarrows up to Fort William in 1803.

For this great enterprise, only one name was seriously considered: Thomas Telford (1757–1834). Apprenticed to a stonemason, Telford worked on a new bridge for his home town of Langholm, while educating himself in the poetry of Burns and Milton, and chemistry out of books lent by the local gentry. As well as the old-style stonework, Telford became a master of two entirely new techniques—the cast iron arch and the first suspension bridges. While working on the Caledonian Canal, he was also building

Going up: you'll have to climb 18 vertical metres (60ft) of ascent up Neptune's Staircase to complete this walk

nearly 600 miles (1,000km) of new roads and enlarging most of Scotland's harbours.

The canal was a tremendous feat of civil engineering. Some 200 million wheelbarrow-loads of earth were shifted over the next 19 years. Four aqueducts let streams and rivers pass below the waterway, and there was a dam on Loch Lochy and diversion of the rivers Oich and Lochy. Loch Oich needed to be deepened, and for this task a steam dredger had not only to be built, but invented and designed too.

After falling into a state of neglect in the 20th century, the canal was on the verge of closure when, in 1996, the government promised £20 million for a complete refurbishment.

From Kilmallie Hall ❶, go down past Corpach Station to the canal and cross the sea lock that separates salt water from fresh water.

Each of the 29 locks on the Caledonian Canal was designed to accommodate the width and length of a 40-gun frigate of Lord Nelson's navy.

Follow the canal (on your left) up past another lock, where a path on the right has a Great Glen Way marker. It passes under tall

sycamores to the shore. Follow the shoreline path past a soccer pitch and then turn left, across grass to a road sign that warns motorists of a nearby playground. A path ahead leads up a wooded bank to the tow path ❷.

Turn right along the tow path, for 0.5 mile (800m). Just before the Banavie swing bridge, a path down to the right has a Great Glen Way marker.

The Great Glen Way is a new National Trail that runs parallel to the tow path. It has been resurfaced as a cycleway running from the east coast to the west coast.

Follow waymarkers on street signs to a level crossing, then turn left towards the other swing bridge, the one with the road on it.

Just before the bridge ❸, turn right at signs for the Great Glen Way and the Great Glen Cycle Route and continue along the tow path to Neptune's Staircase ❹.

The fanciful name was given to the group of eight locks by Thomas Telford himself. It takes about 90 minutes for boats to work through the system. As each lock fills, slow roiling currents come up from

OUT AND ABOUT

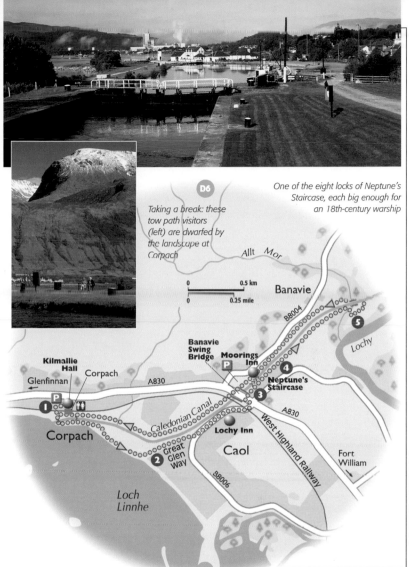

One of the eight locks of Neptune's Staircase, each big enough for an 18th-century warship

Taking a break: these tow path visitors (left) are dwarfed by the landscape at Corpach

underneath, and as each empties, water forced under pressure into the banks emerges from the masonry in little fountains. The 18m (60ft) of ascent alongside the locks is the serious uphill part of this walk.

A gate marks the top of the locks. About 183m (200 yards) later, a grey gate on the right leads to a dump for dead cars; ignore this one. Over the next 90m (100 yards) the canal crosses a little wooded valley, with a black fence on the right. Now comes a second grey gate. Go through, to a track turning back sharp right and descending to ford a small stream ⑤.

On the right, the stream passes right under the canal in an arched tunnel, and alongside is a second tunnel which provides a walkers' way to the other side. Water from the canal drips into the tunnel, which has a fairly spooky atmosphere. At the tunnel's end, a track runs up to join the canal's northern tow path. Turn right, back down the tow path. After passing Neptune's Staircase, cross the A830 to a level crossing without warning lights. Continue along the right-hand tow path. After a mile (1.6km) the tow path track leads back to the Corpach double lock.

WHERE TO EAT

The Moorings Inn at Banavie offers restaurant and bar meals. On the other side of both the A830 and canal, the unassuming Lochy family pub has picnic tables and promises 'massive portions'. At the walk start, a Spar shop sells hot pies, and Kilmallie Hall has a community garden with picnic tables to eat them at.

THE GREAT GLEN WAY

The Great Glen Way is a 75-mile (120km) coast-to-coast walking route between Fort William and Inverness. Cyclists can use the Great Glen Cycle Route which follows a similar route, sharing some of the trail.

Tours, whether day trips or longer, are easily reserved before or after you arrive in Britain. Guided walking and cycling trips—where you leave your luggage for somebody else to look after—are great ways to learn more about the countryside. There are also myriad themes for other excursions, with pivotal organizations such as English Heritage offering their own tours. The best place to look for ideas is a tourist information office or travel agent. Tour operators that are members of the Association of Independent Tour Operators (AITO) and the Association of British Travel Agents (ABTA) offer some assurances of quality. The Guild of Registered Tourist Guides represents 2,100 guides throughout Britain, including well-trained Blue Badge guides.

ABTA: 020 7637 2444; www.abta.com
AITO: 020 8744 9280; www.aito.co.uk
Guild of Registered Tourist Guides: 020 7403 1115; www.blue-badge.org.uk

WALKING

ADVENTURELINE WALKING HOLIDAYS
Tel: 01209 820847
www.adventureline.co.uk
Guided walking holidays in Cornwall, the Isles of Scilly and the Cotswolds.

BATH AND WEST COUNTRY WALKS
Tel: 01761 233807
www.bathwestwalks.com
Walks in Somerset and the Mendip Hills.

BYWAYS BREAKS
Tel: 0151 722 8050
www.byways-breaks.co.uk
Walking and cycling holidays in Shropshire, Cheshire and the Peak District.

CONTOURS WALKING HOLIDAYS
Tel: 01768 480451
www.contours.co.uk
Holidays throughout Britain.

COUNTRYWIDE HOLIDAYS
Tel: 01707 386800
www.countrywidewalking.com
Walking holidays across Britain.

FOOTPATH HOLIDAYS
Tel: 01985 840049
www.footpath-holidays.com
Britain-wide walking holidays.

FOOTPRINTS OF SUSSEX
Tel: 01903 813381
www.footprintsofsussex.co.uk
Walks along the South Downs Way.

HF HOLIDAYS
Tel: 020 8511 1500
www.hfholidays.co.uk
Variety of walking holidays across Britain.

HIGH TREK SNOWDONIA
Tel: 01286 871232
www.hightrek.co.uk
Walks in Snowdonia, including tough routes and scrambling.

HILLSCAPE
Tel: 01974 282640
www.wales-walking.co.uk
Walks in mid-Wales.

MOUNTAIN GOAT HOLIDAYS
Tel: 01539 445161
www.mountain-goat.com
Guided walks in the Lake District.

LIGHTFOOT
Tel: 01736 850715
www.lightfootwalkingholidays.co.uk
Unescorted walking holidays of the Cornish Coast Path.

MOUNTAIN INNOVATIONS
Tel: 01479 831331
www.scotmountain.co.uk
Guided walks in Scotland's Cairngorms, Ben Nevis, Speyside and the central Highlands.

NORTH WEST FRONTIERS
Tel: 01854 612628
www.nwfrontiers.com
Guided walks in Scotland's Highlands and Islands.

RAMBLERS HOLIDAYS
Tel: 01707 331133
www.ramblersholidays.co.uk
Independently run branch of the Ramblers' Association offering holidays in Britain.

SCOTWALK
Tel: 01896 830515
www.scotwalk.co.uk
Walking holidays in southern Scotland, Loch Lomond and the Trossachs.

SHERPA EXPEDITIONS
Tel: 020 8577 2717
www.sherpaexpeditions.com
Independently designed walks and cycle rides.

CYCLING

BICYCLE BEANO
Tel: 01982 560471
www.bicycle-beano.co.uk
Cycling holidays in Wales with emphasis on home-grown, organic vegetarian food.

COUNTRY LANES
Tel: 01425 655022
www.countrylanes.co.uk
Bicycle rental and tours from the New Forest, the Cotswolds and the Lake District.

CYCLE ACTIVE
Tel: 01768 840400
www.cycleactive.co.uk
Cycling holidays in Britain, including the Lake District and Scotland.

SADDLE SKEDADDLE
Tel: 0191 265 1110
www.skedaddle.co.uk
Cycling breaks in Scotland, Northumberland, the Lake District and the Cotswolds, and mountain biking in Scotland.

TOURING

BRIGHTWATER HOLIDAYS
Tel: 01334 657155
www.brightwaterholidays.com
Tours to famous gardens throughout Britain.

SPORTS TOURS
Tel: 01708 344001
www.sports-tours.co.uk
Tours based around soccer, rugby, hockey, netball and volleyball fixtures.

HOLT'S TOURS
Tel: 01293 455300
www.holts.co.uk
Guided tours to famous British battlefields and sites of historic interest.

NATURETREK
Tel: 01962 733051
www.naturetrek.co.uk
Guided botanical and bird-watching trips to Scotland and England.

OUT AND ABOUT

This chapter lists places to eat and places to stay alphabetically by town within Britain's regions.

Eating and Staying

EATING OUT IN BRITAIN

A number of clues betray Britain's improved attitude to food. Several TV chefs have become celebrities, for example, and supermarket aisles now have more fresh ingredients and fewer freezer cabinets. As a result, British palates are becoming more adventurous. Even small towns have a wide choice of cuisines. Continental café culture has infiltrated Britain and many pubs have finally picked up on the public's appetite for better food.

A huge range of international cuisines is on offer in Britain's restaurants

So is it goodbye overcooked meat and stodgy desserts? Not quite; you may still encounter restaurants—and especially pubs—resistant to progress, but more and more mediocre restaurants are being shown the door.

One result of this new enthusiasm is a style of restaurant cooking known as 'Modern British'. Modern British menus freely mix traditional and international flavours, ingredients and techniques. Traditional Scottish menus may include Aberdeen Angus beef, salmon and game such as venison; Traditional Welsh might use cockles, lamb or leeks.

Britain's colonial past has long spiced up the culinary scene. Indian curries are a particular favourite. But their popularity is challenged by Thai and Chinese cuisine. Larger towns and cities may have Turkish, Indonesian, Caribbean, Vietnamese, Hungarian, Russian, Mongolian or Mexican restaurants. Middle Eastern and North African restaurants are particularly strong in London. Some ethnic restaurants are entering epicurean territory with slick styling and fusion menus. Others depart from the familiar to offer authentic dishes from the sub-continent. The best destinations for ethnic cuisine are Bradford, Manchester's Curry Mile, Brick Lane in London, Bristol's East Side and Birmingham's Balti Triangle and Chinatown.

Another British favourite is Italian food. Many Italians emigrated to Britain in the 20th century, and Italian ice cream makers soon became local institutions; Italian-run cafés and restaurants are a sound choice if you want a good cup of coffee.

RESERVATIONS
In some restaurants, especially on quieter days, it is possible to walk in off the street and get a table, but if you want to dine in a particular place, it's always advisable to reserve a table in advance.

Less formal establishments may not take reservations, while top restaurants are reserved for weeks in advance. It's fairly common for a table reservation to last only a couple of hours; guests will then be expected to make way for the next sitting. Many restaurants stop serving surprisingly early, so don't turn up at 10.30pm and expect a seat without checking in advance.

DRESS CODE
Restaurant etiquette is more relaxed these days but it's unwise to turn up at a chic restaurant wearing jeans and a T-shirt. Our guide indicates which establishments prefer jacket and tie, but if in doubt simply telephone and ask.

SMOKING
Almost every establishment (barring some pubs) has a no-smoking section. Smoking will be banned in all pubs and restaurants in England from summer 2007 (▷ 407).

LICENSING LAWS
Britain's licensing laws have historically been restrictive compared to the rest of Europe. The majority of pubs still close at 11pm, although many have taken advantage of recent changes in the law and now close an hour or two later. Children aged 16–18 can drink alcohol with a meal. Restaurants with a 'bring your own' policy may charge a corkage fee.

VEGETARIAN
Most menus include some meat-free options, but these choices are often limited, so it's advisable to check in advance what's available. Some restaurants do not include vegetarian options on the menu but will prepare one if requested.

EATING

A GUIDE TO BRITISH FOOD

BREAKFAST

The traditional English breakfast is filling, fatty and enormously comforting. A typical 'fry up' is based around fried egg and bacon, but common accompaniments include sausages, mushrooms, toast, fried bread, grilled tomatoes, baked beans and black pudding (made from barley, oats and pigs' blood). In Wales it is traditional to include cockles and laverbread (a type of seaweed) in a breakfast fry up, while Scotland favours kippers (smoked herring).

MEAT

The roast is the cornerstone of British cuisine. Done well (but not over done) it's a satisfying and social meal. The meat at the heart of the meal is usually a whole bird (chicken is the most common, and turkeys and geese are traditional at Christmas) or a leg, joint or other cut of lamb, beef or pork. This is accompanied by roast potatoes, vegetables and gravy made from the roasting juices.

Pigs have been part of the British diet for thousands of years and are the source of black pudding, bacon and sausages (bangers). Britain has plenty of game, though this varies with the country's geography: Grouse are shot in the uplands, pheasants in the wooded valleys and rabbits in the fields. In Scotland, venison is a favourite.

SANDWICHES AND PICNICS

Probably the most typically English sandwich is the dainty cucumber variety that sometimes forms part of afternoon tea, but these are generally confined to upscale hotels, and countrywide, you're more likely to encounter hearty baguettes or rustic slices of bread with a filling of cheese, meat or salad.

The British have a romantic view of picnics. These days a picnic lunch can mean anything from a packet of sandwiches eaten in the park to an elaborate exercise with wicker hampers, tablecloths, snacks and portable crockery.

FISH

Britain's fishermen provide a steady flow of fish for the country, but for the freshest seafood head for the coast. Cornwall has an excellent reputation and Scotland is another area of excellence—look out for Loch Fyne oysters, Arbroath smokies, lobster and salmon. Other seafood hotspots include East Anglia (for oysters and Cromer crab), Northumbria for Craster kippers, South Wales for cockles and Morecambe Bay for potted shrimps. London is historically linked with whitebait and jellied eels, and the latter are still widely available from the street stalls and pie and mash shops of the East End.

One of Britain's favourite dishes is fish and chips (French fries): white fish—usually cod or haddock—is coated in batter then deep fried and served with chips. Fish and chip shops can be found throughout the country but these, too, are at their best near the coast.

ALCOHOLIC DRINKS

A little-known fact about Britain is that it has numerous wine producers. The most traditional of these make fruit wines such as elderflower and damson but there are also some flourishing vineyards, especially in the south of the country.

Cider remains a popular English drink, as it has been for thousands of years. Most pubs will sell clear, commercial varieties but you can track down stronger ciders made by independent producers in counties such as Somerset and Herefordshire. Cider produced in small quantities on farms is often called scrumpy.

Traditional British ale has a stronger taste and is less fizzy than lagers and European beers. There are hundreds of independent brewers in Britain, each one producing a distinctive style of ale. Well-established brewers include Shepherd Neame in Kent (the country's oldest brewery), which produces a hoppy, tawny-coloured bitter, and Marston's Pedigree, which comes from the famous brewing town of Burton-on-Trent.

AFTERNOON TEA

A great British institution, afternoon tea remains hugely popular and is widely available in hotels and tea rooms across the country from 2 or 3pm onwards. There are numerous regional variations, but the most widely known is probably the 'cream tea' (scones served with jam and clotted cream) traditionally associated with the West Country. Tea is thought to have arrived in Britain in the 17th century with Catherine of Braganza, the Portuguese wife of Charles II. By the 19th century, it was a fashionable drink and many merchants blended teas according to the recipes of customers, such as Earl Grey, whose bergamot-scented blend is sold in most tea shops.

EATING

PUB

Is it a pub? Is it a restaurant? The new breed of 'gastro pub' is both. The trend started in London several years ago and can be summed up as restaurant-quality food served in a pub environment. The gastro pub menu is more adventurous than typical pub food, frequently influenced by Mediterranean countries and Asian flavours. The pub part of the equation means that you can expect an interesting selection of beers, as well as a fully-fledged wine list. Gastro

CAFÉS, BRASSERIES AND BISTROS

Nowadays, the word café refers to the stylish Continental-style establishments increasingly found in small towns as well as the cities, bridging the gap between pubs, restaurants and coffee bars. Workmen's cafés–affectionately called 'greasy spoons'–sell teas, snacks and meals, usually of the fried variety. Bistros and brasseries often stay open all day. The emphasis in each–and the terms seem interchangeable–is on a simpler style of cooking.

The quality of food in Britain's pubs has greatly improved in recent years

pubs are found all over the country–the stripped pine interiors and the prices (up to £16 for a main dish) are the giveaways.

The quintessential country pub has bare stone walls, open fires and low beams. The features are sometimes copied by the mock 'olde worlde' chain pubs. Some pubs in cities survive from the Victorian period; look for enamelled tiles and lots of glass and mirrors. Other traditional customs, such as a ban on children in the bar area and restricted opening hours, are gradually being left behind. These days, most (but not all) pubs welcome families and many stay open throughout the day, though food is often only available from 12 to 2 and from 6 until 9.

Pub menus have traditionally included 'bar snacks'–lighter, cheaper meals including sandwiches and filled baked potatoes–but these days most will also serve substantial dishes such as steak and ale pie or bangers and mash.

FAST FOOD

Fast food often means take-away food, and in many cases it's possible to buy a meal for under £4.50. American fast food chains now grace every corner of Britain. Other fast food outlets include sandwich bars, fish and chip shops and a wide variety of take-aways offering food from international cuisine, particularly in the larger cities where the kebab shop might stand a few doors down from African, Chinese or Indian establishments.

TEA SHOP

A delightfully English tradition, tea shops usually open from mid-morning until 4 or 5pm. They specialize in teas, cakes and light meals and are particularly common in areas popular with tourists, such as the West Country and rural Yorkshire. They are a splendid place to relax after a day's sightseeing.

SAVOURY DISHES

Bangers and Mash: Fried sausages and mashed potato
Cottage Pie: Minced beef and vegetables topped with mashed potato
Fish and Chips: Fish, typically cod or haddock, deep fried in batter, served with chips
Lancashire Hotpot: Casserole of lamb and onions topped with sliced potato
Scotch Egg: Hard-boiled egg covered with sausage meat; eaten cold
Shepherd's Pie: Minced lamb and vegetables topped with mashed potato
Toad in the Hole: Sausages baked in batter

Welsh Rarebit: Thick cheese sauce spread on toast then grilled

PUDDINGS

Bakewell Tart: An almond-flavoured flan, with jam, on a pastry base
Bread and Butter Pudding: Slices of buttered bread baked with dried fruit, milk and eggs
Fruit Crumble: Stewed fruit, such as apple or rhubarb, with a topping of flour and butter
Queen of Puddings: A baked pudding of milk, sugar and eggs, topped with jam and meringue
Spotted Dick: A once-famous pudding made with suet pastry with currants

EATING

ROSETTE AWARDS

The AA's restaurant inspectors award ❀ rosettes to restaurants annually on a rising scale from one to five. These awards are based purely on the quality of food.

❀ Excellent local restaurants serving food prepared with care, understanding and skill, using good-quality ingredients.

❀❀ The best local restaurants, with higher standards, better consistency and obvious attention to the selection of quality ingredients.

❀❀❀ Outstanding restaurants that demand recognition beyond their local area. The cooking will be underpinned by the selection and sympathetic treatment of highest quality ingredients. Timing, seasoning and the judgement of flavour combinations will be consistently excellent, supported by other elements such as intelligent service and a good wine list.

❀❀❀❀ Among the very best restaurants in Britain. These restaurants exhibit ambition, excellence, superb technical skills and remarkable consistency. They combine appreciation of culinary traditions with a desire for further exploration and improvement.

❀❀❀❀❀ The finest restaurants in Britain, where the cooking stands comparison with the best in the world. These restaurants will have highly individual voices, exceptional culinary skills and set standards to which others aspire.

In some popular towns and cities, we have mentioned extra places to get something to eat, from delicatessens to small restaurants. Although these establishments may not have been awarded rosettes, standards are high.

MAJOR RESTAURANT CHAINS

Britain is a good place for eclectic and unusual eating, but there are also plenty of tried and tested chains, where you know exactly what you're getting and how much you'll have to pay.

	Price range (£-£££)	Alcohol	Child Menu	Take-away	Phone number	Website
RESTAURANTS						
Ask Pizza and Pasta	££	✔	✔	✔	01727 735800	www.askcentral.co.uk
Beefeater	£££	✔	✔	✗	01582 844300	www.beefeater.co.uk
Belgo	£££	✔	✗	✗	020 7557 6333	www.belgo-restaurants.com
Bella Italia	££	✔	✔	✔	020 7121 3200	www.bellaitalia.co.uk
Browns	£££	✔	✔	✗	020 7845 7100	www.browns-restaurants.co.uk
Café Rouge	££	✔	✔	✗	020 7121 3200	www.caferouge.co.uk
Caffè Uno	££	✔	✔	✗	0845 612 5236	www.caffeuno.co.uk
Carluccio's	££	✔	✗	✗	020 7580 3050	www.carluccios.com
Chez Gérard	£££	✔	✗	✔	020 7881 8870	www.chezgerard.com
Digby Trout	££	✔	✔	✔	020 7370 8352	www.digbytrout.co.uk
Garfunkel's	££	✔	✔	✗	020 7643 9000	www.garfunkels.co.uk
Loch Fyne	£££	✔	✗	✔	020 8404 6686	www.lochfyne.com
Nando's	££	✔	✔	✔	0800 975 8181	www.nandos.co.uk
Pizza Express	££	✔	✗	✔	01895 618618	www.pizzaexpress.co.uk
Pizza Hut	££	✔	✔	✔	020 8732 9000	www.pizzahut.co.uk
TGI Friday's	££	✔	✔	✔	01582 424200	www.tgifridays.co.uk
Wagamama	££	✔	✔	✔	020 7631 3140	www.wagamama.com
SANDWICHES AND FAST FOOD						
Burger King	£	✗	✔	✔	01095 206000	www.burgerking.co.uk
Domino's Pizza	££	✗	✔	✔	01908 580000	www.dominos.co.uk
Gourmet Burger Kitchen	££	✗	✔	✔	020 7585 1372	www.gbkinfo.co.uk
KFC	£	✗	✔	✔	01483 717000	www.kfc.co.uk
McDonald's	£	✗	✔	✔	0870 241 3300	www.mcdonalds.co.uk
Pret à Manger	££	✗	✔	✔	020 7827 8888	www.pret-a-manger.co.uk
Subway	£	✗	✔	✔	01823 550020	www.subway.co.uk
Yo Sushi	££	✔	✔	✔	020 7841 0700	www.yosushi.co.uk
COFFEE SHOPS						
Caffè Nero	£	✗	✔	✔	020 7520 5150	www.caffenero.co.uk
Coffee Republic	£	✗	✗	✔	020 7033 0600	www.coffeerepublic.co.uk
Costa Coffee	£	✗	✗	✔	01582 424200	www.costa.co.uk
Starbucks	££	✗	✗	✔	020 7731 4599	www.starbucks.co.uk

EATING

THE WEST COUNTRY

There's much more to West Country cuisine than Cornish pasties and cream teas—but it would be a shame to visit the region and not sample either. Pasties are envelopes of pastry filled with meat and vegetables. They were traditionally hand-held lunches for miners.

Cornish teas are a high-calorie combination of clotted Cornish cream and Devon butter. For those who take cream teas seriously, regional etiquette dictates that in Cornwall the jam is put on to the scone before the cream, while in Devon the cream is applied first.

Other regional produce includes Cheddar cheese—once matured in the caves of Cheddar Gorge—Somerset cider, fudge and fresh seafood.

Cornish restaurants have gradually shaken off a questionable reputation, to the extent that Padstow, on the north coast, is now one of the country's gastronomic centres. This is due in part to the TV chef and seafood specialist Rick Stein and his local empire: The Seafood Restaurant, St. Petroc's Bistro and his café draw visitors to Padstow all year round. Stein has not only put Cornwall on the culinary map, he has also campaigned for locally produced foods.

EATING

BATH

THE MOODY GOOSE RESTAURANT ❀ ❀

7A Kingsmead Square, Bath BA1 2AB
Tel: 01225 466688
www.moody-goose.com
This basement restaurant is located in an elegant Georgian terrace. The modern British cooking is solid and reassuring, though it veers from a classical approach to a more contemporary stance. Starters may include a wonderful galantine of Gressingham duck with quince and sage, with main courses such as a very

tender and flavourful roast saddle of venison with an orange and coriander (cilantro) crust. Service is notably friendly. No children under eight.

🕐 Mon–Sat 12–2, 6–10; closed two weeks Jan and public holidays (except Good Friday)

🍴 L from £13, D from £25, Wine from £14

🚭

🛁 Bath Spa

THE WINDSOR HOTEL ❀

69 Great Pulteney Street, Bath BA2 4DL
Tel: 01225 422100
www.bathwindsorhotel.com
The Sakura restaurant in the Windsor Hotel (▷ 372) is authentically Japanese down to the basic wooden seats, the music and a Japanese garden. Choose from traditional styles of Japanese cooking—sukiyaki or shabu-shabu—and watch your meal take shape in a cooking pot built into the table. Green tea is served, and sake, Japanese lagers and wine

PRICES AND SYMBOLS

The restaurants are listed alphabetically within each town. The prices are for a two-course lunch (L) and a three-course à la carte dinner (D). The prices in pubs are for a two-course lunchtime bar meal and a two-course dinner in the restaurant, unless specified otherwise.

For a key to the symbols, ▷ 2.

are also available. No children under 12.

🕒 Tue–Sat 6–11; closed L

🍴 D from £25, Wine from £12.50

🚫

🚗 M4 junction 18 onto A4, turn left onto A36, then turn right at next mini roundabout and take second turning on left for Great Pulteney Street

🚇 Bath Spa

BOURNEMOUTH

BISTRO ON THE BEACH ❀

Solent Promenade, Southbourne Coast Road, Southbourne, Bournemouth BH6 4BE

Tel: 01202 431473

www.bistroonthebeach.co.uk

This colourful, buzzing bistro offers great sea views, plenty of friendly spirit and good value, no-nonsense cooking. Food is Modern British, with a comprehensive selection of specials.

🕒 Tue–Sat 6.30–12

🍴 D from £18.95, Wine from £12.50

🚫

🚗 From Bournemouth take coast road to East Cliff. At lights turn right then right again to join overcliff. In 1 mile (1.5km) at mini roundabout take second exit; 400m (1,300ft) to parking area. Path leads to bistro

🚇 Bournemouth

BRADFORD-ON-AVON

THE KINGS ARMS

Monkton Farleigh BA15 2QH

Tel: 01225 858705

www.kingsarm-bath.co.uk

This 11th-century Bath stone building, with a pantiled roof, was originally a monks' retreat.

Converted into a pub in the 17th century, the bar food includes home-cooked ham, egg and chips.

🕒 Mon–Fri 12–3, 5.30–11; Sat and Sun 12–11

🍴 L from £12.90, D from £23.50, Wine from £11.75

🚗 Follow A4 from Bath to Bradford-on-Avon. At Bathford join A363, turning left to Monkton Farleigh

BRISTOL

HOWARDS RESTAURANT ❀

1A–2A Avon Crescent, Hotwells, Bristol BS1 6XQ

Tel: 0117 926 2921

An enduring Bristol institution, bistro dining with great views. This unpretentious and

Bath's Moody Goose Restaurant was once a Chinese laundry

consistent eatery is a cosy cocoon from the hustle and bustle of the city. The food is solidly traditional, with the emphasis on meat and classically based sauces. Unbeatable lunchtime value.

🕒 Mon–Fri 12–4, 5.30–10.30, Sat 12–11, Sun 12–9.30; closed public holidays

🍴 L from £10, D from £20.15, Wine from £12..50

🚗 Five minutes from the city centre following signs for M5/Avonmouth. On dockside, over small bridge

🚇 Bristol Temple Meads

CHELTENHAM

CAFÉ PARADISO ❀

Bayshill Road, Montpellier, Cheltenham GL50 3AS

Tel: 01242 527788

www.aliaskandinsky.com

Café Paradiso in Alias Hotel Kandinsky (▷ 373) is bright and welcoming. Very much in the Italian mould but with modern European influences. Try the 'Paradiso Pronto' menu for quick lunches or linger over Sunday lunch.

🕒 12–2.30, 7–9.45 (Fri–Sat 6.30–10.15, Sun 7–9)

🍴 L from £13.50, D from £18.50, Wine from £13.25

🚫

🚗 From junction 11 of M5 take A40 to town centre. Right at second roundabout, second exit at third roundabout into Bayshill Road. Hotel on corner of Bayshill and Parabola roads

🚇 Cheltenham Spa

LE CHAMPIGNON SAUVAGE ❀❀❀❀❀

24 Suffolk Road, Cheltenham GL50 2AQ

Tel: 01242 573449

www.lechampignonsauvage.com

The understated exterior of Le Champignon Sauvage belies the excitement to be found within. David Everitt-Matthias' cooking style is often startling, earning him a peerless reputation for hard work and dedication. Pressed skate, potato and leek terrine, with oyster and leek emulsion is a technical tour de force, exquisitely layered, and subtly flavoured. Equally impressive desserts include a hot fig tart with a honey spice bread ice cream. Vegetarian by request only.

🕒 Tue–Sat 12.30–1.30, 7.30–9. Closed Easter, three weeks in Jun and 10 days at Christmas

🍴 L from £18, D from £23, Wine from £11

🚫

🚗 South of town centre near Boys' College on A40 (Oxford). Call for exact details

🚇 Cheltenham Spa

DORCHESTER

YALBURY COTTAGE & RESTAURANT ✿✿
Lower Bockhampton DT2 8PZ
Tel: 01305 262382
The short set-price menu at this charming bed-and-breakfast (▷ 374) offers a range of unpretentious modern British dishes with clear international influences. Fillet of beef, cooked to a turn and retaining all its succulence and flavour, is served on a bed of crushed potato with Madeira sauce. But the real show-stealer is a pineapple tarte tatin with beautifully caramelized fruit, and crisp, light, buttery pastry.
🕐 7–9; closed L
🍴 D from £30, Wine from £13.50
🚫
🚗 2 miles (3km) east of Dorchester off A35, past Hardy's Cottage, straight over crossroads, then 400m (440 yards) on left, past red telephone box, opposite village pump
🚉 Dorchester South

EXETER

MICHAEL CAINES AT THE ROYAL CLARENCE ✿✿
Cathedral Yard, Exeter EX1 1HD
Tel: 01392 310031
www.michaelcaines.com
Talented chef Michael Caines has now firmly established this smart restaurant at the Royal Clarence (▷ 374). Modern British is the theme for some skilful, unfussy dishes such as pan-fried monkfish and scallops accompanied by a leek fondue. Service is slick and efficient. Vegetarian and children's menus are available. Reserve ahead at weekends.
🕐 12–2.30, 7–10; closed Sun and D 25 Dec
🍴 L from £16.50, D from £28, Wine from £16
🚫 No pipes, no cigars
🚗 From junction 30 of the M5, towards the A379. Follow signs to the city centre and the hotel is opposite the cathedral behind High Street
🚉 Exeter Central

FOWEY

FOWEY HALL ✿✿
Hanson Drive, Fowey PL23 1ET
Tel: 01726 833866
www.foweyhall.com
The dining room at this fine hotel (▷ 374) offers a dazzling modern British menu packed with luxury local produce. A tip—stick to the simple dishes and you'll be blown away.
🕐 12–2.15, 7–10
🍴 L from £12, D from £32.50, Wine from £10.25
🚫
🚗 Arriving in Fowey cross mini roundabout into town centre. Pass school on right after 400m (440 yards) turn right into Hanson Drive
🅿 Par

Michael Caines at the Royal Clarence is an Exeter landmark

ISLES OF SCILLY

THE ISLAND ✿✿
Tresco TR24 0PU
Tel: 01720 422883
www.tresco.co.uk/holidays/island_hotel
.asp
The dining room of this hotel (▷ 374) offers Modern British food with the emphasis on excellent fish and seafood. You may wish to finish off a meal with the lightest, most succulent sticky toffee pudding you've ever tasted.
🕐 12–2, 6.30–9.15; closed Nov–end Feb
🍴 L from £10, D from £37.50, Wine from £15.50
🚫
🚁 Helicopter service from Penzance to Tresco; hotel in north east of island

LYME REGIS

ALEXANDRA ✿
Pound Street, Lyme Regis DT7 3HZ
Tel: 01297 442010
www.lymeregis.co.uk
This elegant restaurant in the welcoming Alexandra hotel (▷ 375) serves up imaginative dishes including pan-fried crab cakes with saffron sauce and horseradish potato cake, with locally made ice cream for dessert. No children under ten.
🕐 12.30–1.30, 7–8.30; closed Jan and Christmas
🍴 L from £14.75, D from £23.95, Wine from £13.95
🚫
🚫
🚗 From A30 turn on to A35, A358, then take A3052 to Lyme Regis

MARAZION

GODOLPHIN ARMS
Marazion, near Penzance TR17 0EN
Tel: 01736 710202
www.godolpinarms.co.uk
Family-run, with a friendly welcome and good service, the restaurant in this hotel (▷ 375) offers plenty of seafood, including moules marinière, alongside pub favourites such as chargrilled steaks. Less familiar options might include roasted avocado and goats' cheese served with apple and a tomato and basil sauce. There's a family room and garden terrace.
🕐 Mon–Sat 10.30am–11pm, Sun 12–10.30
🍴 Bar L from £12, D from £25, Wine from £11
🚭 In restaurant
🚗 From A30 follow signs for Marazion for 1 mile (1.6km) to the hotel/pub, at the end of the causeway to St. Michael's Mount

MOUSEHOLE

OLD COASTGUARD HOTEL ✿
The Parade TR19 6PR
Tel: 01736 731222
www.oldcoastguardhotel.co.uk
Those in the know come to this hotel (▷ 375) to enjoy fresh regional produce, meats and cheeses prepared and presented in a variety of

contemporary and traditional ways, with plenty of vegetarian and seafood options. Expect ceviche of mixed fish, or grilled Cornish goats' cheese, followed perhaps by Newlyn crab salad, grilled salmon, rib-eye steak or pan-fried duck. Round off your meal with Cornish ices.

🕐 12–2.30, 6–9.30; closed 25 Dec
🍷 L from £17, D from £22.50, Wine from £13
🚭
🚗 A30 to Penzance, take coast road through Newlyn to Mousehole, inn is first building on left

NETTLECOMBE

MARQUIS OF LORNE
Nettlecombe DT6 3SY
Tel: 01308 485236
www.marquisoflorne.com
This cosy inn (▷ 376) provides an ideal setting in which to enjoy home-cooked food and real ales. The daily changing blackboard menus offer tasty dishes based on fresh local produce, whether you choose a light snack or à la carte dinner in the separate dining room—but be warned, the portions are generous. The proprietors have joined the Campaign for Real Food, and even the children's menu provides wholesome cooking.

🕐 Mon–Sat 11.30–2.30. 6.30–11, Sun 12–3, 6.30–11
🍷 L from £13.20, D from £17.15, Wine from £13.95
🚗 North from Bridport on A3066, after 1.5 miles (2.5km) at mini-roundabout turn right, through West Milton, straight over junction (signposted Powerstock), pub 500m (550 yards) on left

PADSTOW

THE SEAFOOD RESTAURANT 🌸🌸🌸
Riverside, Padstow PL28 8BY
Tel: 01841 532700
www.rickstein.com
The success of chef/proprietor Rick Stein's TV programmes and books might be relied upon to fill the tables here, but

this restaurant is rightly popular on its own merits. Passion, care and attention to detail are apparent throughout. Main courses such as sea bass with tomato, butter and vanilla vinaigrette rely on the exemplary quality of the fish and accurate cooking. No children under three. Accommodation is also available (▷ 376).

🕐 12–2, 7–10; closed 1 May and one week at Christmas
🍷 L from £25.50, D from £34, Wine from £20
🚗 Take A389 towards Padstow, after 3 miles (5km) turn right at T-junction. At signs for Padstow town centre turn right to centre; restaurant on riverside

Seawater splashes the windows at Marazion's Godolphin Arms

ST. PETROC'S HOTEL AND BISTRO 🌸
4 New Street, Padstow PL28 8EA
Tel: 01841 532700
www.rickstein.com
This hotel (▷ 376) has an unpretentious eaterie. A European menu strong on Mediterranean flavours specializes in sea-fresh fish. Booking is essential in summer.

🕐 12–2, 7–10; closed 1 May and one week at Christmas
🍷 L from £18.50, D from £24.50, Wine from £16.50
🚭 No pipes, no cigars
🚗 Take A30, A38 and A389 towards Padstow. Continue 3 miles (5km), turn right at T-junction and follow signs to Padstow town centre

PENZANCE

THE SUMMERHOUSE 🌸🌸
Cornwall Terrace, Penzance TR18 4HL
Tel: 01736 363744
www.summerhouse-cornwall.com
The food is Mediterranean using the freshest of local and Cornish produce. The tropical walled garden is perfect for summer drinks and dining. No children under eight.

🕐 Wed–Sun 7–9.30; closed Mon–Tue, L all week and Dec–end Feb
🍷 D from £26, Wine from £12
🚗 Enter Penzance on A30 and drive along harbour past open-air bathing pool. Follow promenade and turn right immediately after Queen's Hotel; Summerhouse 30m (100ft) on left
🚉 Penzance

PLYMOUTH

TANNERS RESTAURANT 🌸🌸
Prysten House, Finewell Street, Plymouth PL1 2AE
Tel: 01752 252001
www.tannersrestaurant.co.uk
Tanners is housed in one of Plymouth's oldest domestic buildings, the 15th-century house where the Pilgrim Fathers ate their final meal in England. The restaurant offers a modern menu with daily specials acknowledging French, British and American influences—scallops in champagne sauce, and waffles with caramel sauce and vanilla ice cream.

🕐 Tue–Sat 12–2.30, 7–9.30, closed first week in Jan, 25 and 31 Dec
🍷 L from £12.50, D from £31, Wine from £12.95
🚭
🚗 Town centre, behind St. Andrews Church, on Royal Parade
🚉 Plymouth

PORLOCK

THE OAKS HOTEL ❀
Porlock TA24 8ES
Tel: 01643 862265
www.oakshotel.co.uk
The use of superior ingredients is evident in the traditional British cuisine at this hotel's (▷ 376) restaurant. The appealing four-course dinner menu ends with home-made chocolates. Vegetarian menu by request. No children under eight.

🕐 7–8.30, closed Nov–end Mar
🍽 D from £30, Wine from £12.50
🚭
🚌 At bottom of Dunstersteepe Road, on left after entering Porlock from Minehead

ST. IVES

PORTHMINSTER BEACH RESTAURANT ❀
Porthminster, St. Ives TR26 2EB
Tel: 01736 795352
www.porthminstercafe.co.uk
A large but intriguing menu of predominantly Mediterranean-style dishes, with a dash of the Orient. Reserve a window table.

🕐 12–3.30, 6–10; closed early Nov–end Mar
🍽 L from £15, D from £19, Wine from £11.50
🚭 No pipes, no cigars
🚌 On Porthminster Beach, behind St. Ives train station
🚉 St. Ives

ST. MAWES

HOTEL TRESANTON ❀ ❀
27 Lower Castle Road, St. Mawes TR2 5DR
Tel: 01326 270055
www.tresanton.com
The restaurant acknowledges the great French brasseries and ocean-going liners of the 1930s. The cooking is simple; fish and meat is either pan-fried, seared or roasted.

🕐 12–2.30, 7–9.30
🍽 L from £20, D from £35, Wine from £13.50
🚭 No pipes, no cigars
🚌 From St. Austell take A390 towards Truro. After 4 miles (6.5km) turn on to B3287 to St. Mawes. Hotel is in the town centre, on the waterfront

TORQUAY

ORESTONE MANOR HOTEL RESTAURANT ❀ ❀
Rockhouse Lane, Maidencombe TQ1 4SX
Tel: 01803 328098
www.orestone.co.uk
The cuisine is highly regarded, contemporary English, making use of locally landed seafood. Friendly and intelligent service is a strength. No children under seven.

🕐 12–2.30, 7–9
🍽 L from £14.95, D from £25.50, Wine from £14.75
🚭 No pipes, no cigars
🚌 From Teignmouth take A379, through Shaldon towards Torquay. In 3 miles (5km) take sharp left into Rockhouse Lane. Hotel is signed

Well's Fountain Inn is popular with the cathedral choir

TOTNES

EFFINGS ❀
50 Fore Street, Totnes TQ9 5RP
Tel: 01803 863435
www.effings.co.uk
It may be just a few wooden tables behind a delicatessen, but Michael Kann and Jacqueline Williams' quirky set-up hits the spot. Fine local ingredients are cleverly used in modern and classic recipes, yielding strong flavours in asparagus and wild mushroom salad with summer truffles. You can also buy home-made meals to go.

🕐 9.30–5.30, closed D all week, Sun and public holidays

SPECIAL IN ST. IVES

ALBA RESTAURANT ❀ ❀
Old Lifeboat House, Wharf Road, St. Ives TR26 1LF
Tel: 01736 797222
www.alba-restaurant.co.uk
The skilful and well-chosen combinations (stir-fried squid with olive oil, garlic, parsley and chilli or an Oriental-style salmon broth) show imagination and simplicity on a menu with a natural bias towards fresh seafood and Cornish produce. Oriental dishes are a speciality. Reserve ahead for a window table.

🕐 12–3, 6–10; closed D Sun–Mon (Nov–end Mar, excluding Christmas) and 25–26 Dec
🍽 L from £14.50, D from £22.85, Wine from £11.95
🚭
🚭
🚌 First building on St. Ives harbour front, opposite new Lifeboat House
🚉 St. Ives

🍽 L from £18.20, Wine from £13.75
🚭
🚌 From A38 follow signs for Totnes, then town centre, restaurant close to Eastgate Arch
🚉 Totnes

WELLS

THE FOUNTAIN INN
1 St. Thomas Street, Wells BA5 2UU
Tel: 01749 672317
www.fountaininn.co.uk
This 16th-century inn close to the cathedral has earned a reputation for good food and drinks. An extensive range of home-cooked bar food includes beef, ale and mushroom pie, plus a separate menu upstairs in Boxer's Restaurant—seared carpaccio of beef followed by baked guinea fowl.

🕐 Mon–Sat 10.30–2.30, 6–11, Sun 12–3, 7–10.30; closed 25–26 Dec
🍽 L from £7.50, D from £16, Wine from £9.95
🚌 City centre at junction of A371 and B3139

EATING

THE SOUTH EAST AND EAST ANGLIA

As the most developed and densely populated region of Britain, there is ever-decreasing space for regional food producers in the south east. But there are still specialities to look out for, such as small, succulent crabs from Cromer in Norfolk, oysters from Whitstable in Kent and Colman's mustard from Norwich.

Kent, with its abundant orchards, is known as the 'Garden of England'. The county also produces hops for beer and is home to Britain's oldest brewery, Shepherd Neame, which produced its first beer in 1698. Tours of the Faversham-based brewery cost £5.80 (adult) and must be reserved in advance (tel: 01795 542016; www.shepherd-neame.co.uk).

The south east has two outstanding international chefs: In Oxfordshire Raymond Blanc runs the world-renowned Le Manoir Aux Quat' Saisons in Great Milton (▷ 341) and a brasserie, Le Petit Blanc, in Oxford city centre. And adventurous eaters queue to eat at The Fat Duck (▷ 340), Heston Blumenthal's restaurant in Bray, Berkshire.

EATING

ARUNDEL

GEORGE & DRAGON 🏵
Burpham BN18 9RR
Tel: 01903 883131
Standards are consistently high at this charming pub, with good-quality ingredients handled with confident simplicity. Reserve ahead. No children under eight.
🕐 7.15–9.15; closed Sun, D Mon, 25 Dec, public holidays
🍴 D from £26.95, Wine from £12.95
🚫
🚗 2.5 miles (4km) along no-through road signed Burpham, off A27, 1 mile (1.6km) east of Arundel
🚉 Arundel

BRANCASTER STAITHE

THE WHITE HORSE 🏵
Brancaster Staithe PE31 8BY
Tel: 01485 210262
www.whitehorsebrancaster.co.uk
The beautiful views from the bistro at this hotel (▷ 378) are complemented by consistently well-prepared, home-cooked, Modern European food, with plenty of fresh fish and vegetarian options. Staff are informal and friendly.
🕐 Daily 12–2.30, 7–9.30
🍴 L from £12.35, D from £16.30, Wine from £12.50
🚗 On A149 coast road between Hunstanton and Wells-next-the-Sea

BRAY

THE FAT DUCK ✿✿✿✿✿✿
High Street, Bray SL6 2AQ
Tel: 01628 580333
www.fatduck.co.uk
Two small cottages in an English village seem an unlikely location for an international destination restaurant. Chef Heston Blumenthal is the leading exponent in the scientific approach to cuisine. After a palate-cleansing froth of green tea, vodka and lime juice, starters might include quail jelly with pea purée and langoustine cream. The main courses feel more conventional by comparison, but there is nothing ordinary about the slow-cooked pork belly on braised cabbage with a gratin of macaroni with pig's trotter and truffle. Desserts include chocolate coulant with blue cheese and coffee. Lunch is a bargain, given what's on offer. Children are especially welcome here.
🕐 12–2.30, 7–9.30; closed Mon, D Sun, two weeks at Christmas
🍴 L from £32.50, D from £60, Wine from £17.50
🚗 From M4 junction 8/9 (Maidenhead) take A308 towards Windsor, turn left into Bray; restaurant in centre of village on right

BRIGHTON

THE GINGERMAN RESTAURANT ✿✿
21A Norfolk Square, Brighton BN1 2PD
Tel: 01273 326688
The Gingerman is a popular place so reserving is essential. There is a two- or three-course fixed-price dinner menu and a simple lunch with two choices at each course. The Modern British menu offers lots of seasonal flavours in food such as English asparagus, summer vegetables and spring lamb.
🕐 Tue–Sat 12.30–2, 7.30–10; closed two weeks summer, two weeks winter
🍴 L from £12.95, D from £25, Wine from £12.50
🚭 No cigars, no pipes
🚫
🚉 Brighton

TERRE À TERRE ✿✿
71 East Street, Brighton BN1 1HQ
Tel: 01273 729051
www.terreaterre.co.uk
This exciting vegetarian and vegan restaurant has a loyal following. The innovative, flavour-packed Modern British dishes might include arepas mojo, corn cakes in chermoula cornmeal, or saltimbocca funghi—a wild mushroom confit wrapped in creamed polenta and encased in sunblushed tomatoes. The wine list places a strong emphasis on organic wines with some beers too.
🕐 Tue 6–10.30, Wed–Fri 12–3, 6–10.30, Sat–Sun 12–10.30; closed Mon and L Tue

Innovative vegetarian cuisine at Brighton's Terre à Terre

🍴 L from £15, D from £20, Wine from £15.95
🚫
🚉 Brighton

BROCKENHURST

SIMPLY POUSSIN ✿✿
The Courtyard, Brookley Road, Brockenhurst SO42 7RB
Tel: 01590 623063
www.simplypoussin.co.uk
This conservatory and dining room is a pillar of quality, offering excellent and often local ingredients and fine French technique. Examples from the Modern British menu include goat's cheese melted in a wafer-thin ravioli coat on balsamic beans, and an orange

sauce with pink breast of duck that is smooth, glossy and rich with flavour. Desserts might include passion fruit soufflé or trio of chocolate. No children under seven. Call ahead to reserve and check location.
🕐 12–2, 7–10; closed Sun–Mon and 25–26 Dec
🍴 L from £10, D from £35, Wine from £13 🚫 In restaurant
🚗 Village centre through an archway between two shops

CAMBRIDGE

ANATOLIES
30 Bridge Street, Cambridge CB2 1UJ
Tel: 01223 312412
Turkish restaurant set in the basement of the building with a charcoal grill and—sometimes—belly dancing entertainment.

CANTERBURY

AUGUSTINE'S RESTAURANT ✿
1–2 Longport, Canterbury CT1 1PE
Tel: 01227 453063
Fine Georgian townhouse where modern European cuisine is the order of the day. A simple lunch menu featuring good-value fixed-price meals aims to please, while dinner is more daring. Mains might include Barbary duck with polenta and black olive sauce, or Swiss cheese soufflé with buttered spinach.
🕐 From 12 and from 6.30; closed Mon, D Sun and two weeks in Jan
🍴 L from £10.95, D from £19, Wine from £14.90
🚫
🚗 Follow signs to St Augustine's Abbey
🚉 Canterbury East or West

DOVE INN ✿
Plumpudding Lane, Dargate ME13 9HB
Tel: 01227 751360
www.shepherdneame.co.uk
This splendid pub offers astonishingly good food. Blackboard menus feature fresh fish from Hythe and local game. Lunchtime snacks include pan-fried crevettes with fresh garden herbs and pickled ginger. Main courses range from confit duck leg

EATING

MIDSUMMER HOUSE

✿✿✿

Midsummer Common, Cambridge
CB4 1HA
Tel: 01223 369299
www.midsummerhouse.co.uk

This large conservatory restaurant overlooks a pretty walled garden, and is Cambridge's finest restaurant. The menu covers much of rural France, with five choices at each level à la carte, and a short fixed-price lunch offering similar dishes. Deep-fried snails with a lemon, bacon and artichoke risotto is a typical starter, while sauté salmon with a white chocolate and caviar sauce shows some unexpected twists. Expect well-executed desserts such as pistachio soufflé, and caramelized popcorn parfait.

🕐 Tue–Sun 12–2, 6–11; closed 20–29 Mar, 14–30 Aug and 18 Dec–3 Jan
🍴 L from £26, D from £48.50, Wine from £20
🚭
🔧
🚗 Park in Pretoria Road then cross footbridge, restaurant on left
🚉 Cambridge

with braised red cabbage to roast monkfish wrapped in Bayonne ham and basil, with desserts such as lemon tart. Splendid sheltered garden for summer meals.

🕐 Wed–Sat 12–2, 7–9, Sun 12–2
🍴 L from £17, D from £21.50, Wine from £13
🚗 Off A299, 5 miles (8km) northwest of Canterbury. Phone for directions

ELY

THE ANCHOR INN ✿

Sutton Gault, Sutton CB6 2BD
Tel: 01353 778537
www.anchor-inn-restaurant.co.uk

Characterized by simple, Modern British cooking using quality fresh ingredients, typical dishes at this inn (▷ 379) might be wild boar sausages with mashed potato,

green beans and cider sauce, or smoked haddock risotto with leeks and herb crème fraîche. Look out for a good sticky toffee pudding.

🕐 12–2, 7–9; closed 26 Dec
🍴 L from £16.50, D from £20.40, Wine from £11.95
🚭 No smoking area, no pipes
🚗 Signposted off B1381 in Sutton village, 7 miles (11km) west of Ely via A142

GREAT MILTON

LE MANOIR AUX QUAT' SAISONS ✿✿✿✿✿

Church Road, Great Milton OX44 7PD
Tel: 01844 278881
www.manoir.com

Little is left to chance at Raymond Blanc's ever-evolving

Midsummer House Restaurant is Cambridge's finest

hotel masterpiece (▷ 379). Its vegetable gardens deliver a harvest of organic produce for the kitchen. The dining room is composed of three parts, the most contemporary in style being the conservatory. Service is polished but without pretension. Rooted in French classics, the menu offers à la carte, alongside a list of specialities and a tasting menu for the whole table. Luxurious ingredients abound with foie gras, caviar, oysters and langoustines all featuring in the hors d'oeuvres. Desserts are beautifully crafted and the terrific wine list has an expected French bias; make

use of the excellent half-bottle selection. No jeans, shorts or trainers.

🕐 Daily 12.15–3, 7.15–10
🍴 L from £45, D from £82, Wine from £30
🚭
🚗 From junction 7 of M40 follow A329 towards Wallingford. After 1 mile (1.6km) turn right, signposted Great Milton Manor

ISLE OF WIGHT

PRIORY BAY HOTEL ✿✿

Priory Drive, Seaview PO34 5BU
Tel: 01983 613146
www.priorybay.co.uk

A marine-themed dining room is found in this peaceful hotel (▷ 379), with beautiful views out to sea (reserve a window table). The seasonally changing menu offers unusual combinations on a classical theme.

🕐 Daily 12.30–2.15, 7–9
🍴 L from £15.45, D from £27.50, Wine from £12.50
🚭
🚗 On B3330 to Nettlestone

THE RED LION

Church Place, Freshwater PO40 9BP
Tel: 01983 754925
www.redlion-wight.co.uk

This civilized inn attracts the yachting fraternity, who are drawn by the interesting food as much as the picturesque setting. Order early to guarantee your chosen dishes from the blackboard as demand is intense. Everything is freshly made from tried and tested recipes, such as spicy-coated sardines followed by Red Lion fish pie. Puddings include lemon meringue pie and citrus cheesecake.

🕐 Mon–Sat 11.30–3, 5.30–11; Sun 12–3, 7–10.30
🍴 L from £15, D from £22, Wine from £12
🚗 In Freshwater follow signs for parish church

EATING

KING'S LYNN

ROSE & CROWN ❀
Old Church Road, Snettisham PE31 7LX
Tel: 01485 541382
www.roseandcrownsnettisham.co.uk
Dining at this historic inn
(▷ 379) has an international
flavour. Try red mullet and king
prawn tom yam or confit duck
leg with hash browns and
pomegranate molasses. The
less adventurous may prefer
fish and chips washed down
by a fine East Anglian ale.
🕐 12–2, 6.30–9; closed 25 Dec
🍴 L from £14, D from £18.50, Wine
from £11.50
🚭
🚌 North from King's Lynn on A149
signed to Hunstanton; hotel in centre of
Snettisham between market square and
church 🚉 King's Lynn

NORWICH

ADLARD'S RESTAURANT ❀❀
79 Upper St. Giles Street, Norwich
NR2 1AB
Tel: 01603 633522
www.adlards.co.uk
Adlard's is a high-class
favourite. The short, well-
balanced British/French menu
might offer a simple seafood
theme to start, such as
smoked salmon or oysters,
then progress to a robust roast
leg of partridge with
sweetcorn galette. Vegetarian
options are available. Desserts
might include poached figs
with burnt honey parfait and
spiced red wine mousse. There
is an impressive wine list.
🕐 12.30–1.45, 7.30–10.30; closed Sun,
L Mon, one week after Christmas
🍴 L from £17, D from £31.50,
Wine from £15.50
🚭 Smoking allowed, but no pipes or
cigars
♿
🚌 In city centre, 200m (650ft) behind
City Hall
🚉 Norwich

TATLERS ❀❀
21 Tombland, Norwich NR3 1RF
Tel: 01603 766670
www.tatlers.com
Brasserie-style restaurant. The
atmosphere is friendly and

low-key, with relaxed but
attentive service. Dishes are
Modern British with classical
French undertones—black
pudding with truffle oil
dressing and braised red
cabbage and Puy lentils—and
local produce features
strongly. There's a good wine
list too, with half-bottles
available.
🕐 12–2, 6.30–10; closed Sun, 2–3 Jan,
24, 28 Dec and public holidays
🍴 L from £14, D from £21, Wine from
£11.75
🚭 No cigars, no pipes
🚉 Norwich

*The Red Lion is an Isle of Wight
gem*

OXFORD

GEE'S RESTAURANT ❀
61 Banbury Road, Oxford OX2 6PE
Tel: 01865 553540
www.gees-restaurant.co.uk
This beautiful conservatory is
airy by day and romantic by
night. Dishes are a mix of
English and French cuisine,
using mostly organic produce.
🕐 12–2.30, 6–10.30; closed 25–26 Dec
🍴 L from £12.95, D from £22, Wine
from £13.50
🚭
♿
🚌 From M40, junction 8 take northern
ring road and follow signs to city centre
through Summertown. Gee's opposite
Parktown on Banbury Road
🚉 Oxford

LE PETIT BLANC BRASSERIE
❀❀❀
71–71 Walton Street, Oxford OX2 6AG
Tel: 01865 510999
www.lepetitblanc.co.uk
At this busy yet relaxed French-
style brasserie, the food
clings to its Gallic roots but
substitutes British ingredients
wherever possible, offering
satisfying brasserie favourites.
🕐 Mon–Sat 12–11, Sun 12–10; closed
25 Dec
🍴 L from £12, D from £14.50, Wine
from £12.95
🚭
♿
🚌 From city centre, north along St.
Giles, left into Little Clarendon Street
and right at end of Walton Street
🚉 Oxford

ST. ALBANS

ST. MICHAEL'S MANOR ❀❀
Fishpool Street, St. Albans AL3 4RY
Tel: 01727 864444
www.stmichaelsmanor.com
A traditional vein runs through
a mainly contemporary menu
at this hotel (▷ 380), with
imaginative touches such as
chilled grilled prawns with
Bloody Mary sauce and
avocado mousse.
🕐 12.30–2.30, 7–9.30; closed D
25 Dec and 1 Jan
🍴 L from £22.50, D from £37.50, Wine
from £17.50
🚭
♿
🚌 From St. Albans Abbey follow
Fishpool Street towards St. Michael's
village. Hotel is 0.5 mile (0.8 km) on left
🚉 St. Albans

SOUTHWOLD

THE CROWN ❀❀
90 High Street, Southwold IP18 6DP
Tel: 01502 722275
www.adnams.co.uk
Both restaurant and bar food
at this inn (▷ 381) are of
good quality and British in
style with European accents.
Fresh, local ingredients are
prepared and cooked using
classical methods. The daily
changing fixed-priced menu
specializes in local fish. No
children under five.

🕐 12–2, 7–9.30
🍴 L from £18.50, D from £29, Wine from £13.75
🚭
🚗 Off A12, take A1095 to Southwold and stay on main road into town centre; hotel on left in High Street
🚉 Darsham

STADHAMPTON

THE CRAZY BEAR ❀ ❀
Bear Lane, Stadhampton OX44 7UR
Tel: 01865 890714
www.crazybeargroup.co.uk
A flamboyant refurbishment has resulted in this rural 16th-century hotel (▷ 381) having two separate dining rooms, one embracing fine English dining, the other offering a Thai-style brasserie. Menus from both restaurants are also available in the bar along with open Swiss sandwiches. Modern dishes in the restaurant might include combinations like Moroccan spiced partridge terrine. The Thai dishes, some of the finest in the country, are best sampled from good-value set menus. No Thai desserts, but classic English offerings might include chocolate marquise.
🕐 12–3, 7–10
🍴 L from £12.50, D from £15, Wine from £14
🚭 No-smoking area, no pipes
🚗 From junction 7 of the M40 turn left at end of slip road into Stadhampton village. Over mini roundabout, left at petrol station. Hotel is second on left

WELLS-NEXT-THE-SEA

THE CROWN RESTAURANT ❀
The Buttlands NR23 1EX
Tel: 01328 710209
www.thecrownhotelwells.co.uk
Local seafood features on the forward-looking menu—Wells crab with roasted pepper parfait, for example, while meat dishes are robust but sensitively treated. Finish with almond and apricot tart.
🕐 7–9; closed D Sun–Mon (low season)
🍴 D from £29.50, Wine from £12.90
🚭
🚗 9 miles (14km) from Fakenham on B1105. At the top of Buttlands Green

WINDSOR

THE CASTLE HOTEL ❀
18 High Street, Windsor SL4 1LJ
Tel: 0870 400 8300
www.macdonald-hotels.co.uk
This 16th-century former coaching inn's restaurant creates an intimate atmosphere while more informal dining is available in the lounge. The two- or three-course menu offers classical French cuisine with game featuring strongly.
🕐 7am–9.45pm
🍴 L from £19.95, D from £29.50, Wine from £15.75
🚭
🚗 From M4 junction 6/M25 junction 15 follow signs to Windsor town centre

St Albans' St. Michael's Manor is in splendid grounds

and Castle. Hotel at top of hill by the castle, opposite Guildhall
🚉 Windsor & Eton Central or Riverside

SIR CHRISTOPHER WREN'S HOUSE HOTEL & SPA ❀ ❀
Thames Street, Windsor
Tel: 01753 861354
www.sirchristopherwren.co.uk
Formal décor is the setting for accomplished cooking designed to please a classy clientele. Traditional favourites get a modern British twist and fixed-price lunch and children's menus are available.
🕐 12.30–2.30, 6.30–10
🍴 L from £9.95, D from £29.50, Wine from £16.50
🚭
🚗

SPECIAL IN WINCHESTER

HOTEL DU VIN & BISTRO ❀ ❀
14 Southgate Street, Winchester SO23 9EF
Tel: 01962 841414
www.hotelduvin.com
The bistro at this branch of the hotel chain harnesses French chic while friendly and knowledgeable staff provide good service. France is the main source of inspiration for the food but British and Mediterranean influences are also welcomed while the wine list commands respect.
🕐 12–1.45, 7–9.45
🍴 L from £21, D from £27, Wine from £13
🚭 Smoking allowed but no pipes and no cigars
🚗 M3 junction 11 towards Winchester, follow signs. Hotel is 2 miles (3km) from junction 11 on left-hand side just past cinema
🚉 Winchester

🚗 From M4 junction 6 take first exit from relief road, follow signs to Windsor, take first major exit on left, turn left at lights
🚉 Windsor & Eton Central or Riverside

WOODSTOCK

FEATHERS HOTEL ❀
Market Street, Woodstock OX20 1SX
Tel: 01993 812291
www.feathers.co.uk
Cooking is in the classic modern Mediterranean vein at the Feathers Hotel, with a mosaic of guinea fowl and sweetbreads with sauce gribiche being followed, for example, by a timbale of pommes lyonnaise and desserts such as an accomplished pineapple tatin.
🕐 12.30–2.30, 7–9.30
🍴 L from £16.50, D from £35, Wine from £13.50
🚭
🚗 From Oxford take A44 to Woodstock, take first left after lights; hotel on left

EATING

LONDON

London, more so than anywhere else in the country, is the domain of the celebrity chef and the destination restaurant. At the top of the list is Gordon Ramsay and his eponymous temple to gastronomy in Chelsea. But there are also places run by Alastair Little (Alastair Little Restaurant), Antonio Carluccio (Neal Street Restaurant), Jamie Oliver (Fifteen) and John Torode (Smiths of Smithfield). Prices in London restaurants seem high, but in terms of standards the capital is competing successfully at the very top of the market with other European cities. And there's a place for every occasion and palate, from superlative traditional British cooking at St. John to Asian flavours at Champor Champor.

For marginally more economical eating try a gastro pub, a trend pioneered in London by pubs such as The Eagle. A hybrid of pub and restaurant, gastro pubs serve robust meals that are a step up from typical pub food. The best will focus on one or two styles, such as Thai, Spanish or northern Italian. It'll be a bit more expensive than the average pub but more relaxed than a bistro.

London's restaurant industry is notoriously fast-moving, with chefs moving and places opening and closing at a steady pace. You might want to check reviews in the papers for the next hotly tipped restaurant–Fay Maschler writing in the *Evening Standard* is highly regarded. Note that even the hottest restaurants can offer very reasonably priced lunchtime menus.

**ALASTAIR LITTLE
RESTAURANT** ✸✸
49 Frith Street W1V 5TE
Tel: 020 7734 5183
The fixed-price menu runs on Mediterranean lines with a nod to Italy. Superb breads precede a starter of, say, pappardelle with game sauce or potato pancake with smoked eel. Follow up with bacon braised in red wine. Finally don't miss roasted black figs with honey and mascarpone.

🕐 12–3, 6–11.30; closed Sun, L Sat, Christmas, public holidays
🍷 L from £29, D from £38, Wine from £17.50
🚭 No pipes, no cigars
♿
🚇 Tottenham Court Road

AL DUCA ✸
4–5 Duke of York Street SW1Y 6LA
Tel: 020 7839 3090
www.alduca-restaurant.co.uk
Reasonably priced but classy restaurant. First-rate fish

(roasted cod with lentils and parsley sauce, perhaps) and pasta dishes (such as ravioli with woodpigeon and rosemary jus). The 130 or so Italian wines are evenly spread in terms of price.

🕐 12–2.30, 6–11; closed Sun, Christmas, New Year, public holidays
🍷 L from £17.50, D from £24, Wine from £16
🚭 No pipes, no cigars
♿
🚇 Piccadilly

The restaurants are listed alphabetically within each town. The prices are for a two-course lunch (L) and a three-course à la carte dinner (D). Prices in pubs are for a two-course lunchtime bar meal and a two-course dinner in the restaurant, unless specified otherwise.

For a key to the symbols, ▷ 2.

ASSAGGI ❀❀
39 Chepstow Place W2 4TS
Tel: 020 7792 5501
A relaxed Italian restaurant with bare floorboards, wooden tables and plenty of yellow and terracotta. The cooking is traditional Italian, with an emphasis on fine flavours and quality ingredients. Starters may include *fregola con arselle* (fregula pasta with clams) or *calamari ripieni* (stuffed squid). Main courses include pasta and dishes such as *quaglia ripiena* (stuffed roasted quail) or *filetto di vitello al rosmarino* (pan-roasted fillet of white veal, rosemary and glazed baby onions).
⊙ 12.30–2.30, 7.30–11; closed Sun, two weeks at Christmas, public holidays
🍴 L from £23.90, D from £30.15, Wine from £13.95
🚭 No pipes, no cigars
💳
🚇 Notting Hill Gate, Bayswater

BLUEPRINT CAFÉ ❀
The Design Museum, 28 Shad Thames SE1 2YD
Tel: 020 7378 7031
www.conran.com
A bustling, stylish restaurant on the first floor of the Design Museum with views to die for. The menu is sophisticated yet simple. Changed twice daily, Modern British dishes with Middle Eastern and Asian influences, such as rabbit cooked with peppers and black olives, are presented in a straightforward manner.

⊙ 12–3, 6–11, closed D Sun, 25–28 Dec, 1 Jan
🍴 L from £17.50, D from £22.50, Wine from £15
🚇 Tower Hill, London Bridge

CHAMPOR CHAMPOR ❀
62 Weston Street SE1 3QJ
Tel: 020 7403 4600
www.champor-champor.com
A small, South East Asian restaurant. Roughly translated, champor champor means 'mix and match' in Malay, and this is reflected in the fusion of Asian cuisines with its roots in Malaysia. A two-course fixed-price meal might include tofu, courgette (zucchini) and lychee satay followed by spicy

Mediterranean flavours at Soho's Alastair Little Restaurant

stingray baked in banana leaf with mushroom curry.
⊙ 6.15–10.15 (times may vary—check); closed Sun, seven days at Easter, 14 days Christmas–New Year
🍴 D from £24.90, Wine from £13
🚭 No pipes, no cigars
🚇 London Bridge

LE CAPRICE RESTAURANT ❀❀
Arlington House, Arlington Street SW1A 1RT
Tel: 020 7629 2239
The menu at this unashamedly glamorous, retro-chic restaurant offers a tireless repertoire of uncomplicated, well-presented staples: eggs Benedict, deep-fried haddock with minted pea purée and chips, and comfort puds like

banana sticky toffee pudding. Reserve in advance.
⊙ 12–3, 5.30–12; closed 1 Jan, Aug public holiday, D 24 Dec, 25–26 Dec, L 27 Dec
🍴 L from £14.50, D from £20.25, Wine from £13.25
🚭 No pipes
💳
🚇 Green Park

CHUTNEY MARY ❀❀
535 King's Road, Chelsea SW10 0SZ
Tel: 020 7351 3113
www.chutneymary.com
This completely revamped, popular Indian restaurant has acquired a menu that combines old favourites with exciting new specialities, such as the buttered crab popular in Bombay's seafood restaurants or Chutney Mary's own creation, an Indian foie gras dish with seared mango and mild chilli marsala jelly.
⊙ 12.30–3, 6.30–11.30; closed L Mon–Fri, D Christmas
🍴 L from £16.50, D from £27.50, Wine from £17
💳
🚇 Fulham Broadway

THE DUKE OF CAMBRIDGE
30 St. Peter's Street N1 8JT
Tel: 020 7359 3066
This was one of London's first pubs to specialize in organic food, wines and beers. Blackboard menus feature seasonal Modern European dishes and change twice a day. Dishes might include pumpkin and sage soup, grilled asparagus with anchovies, capers and poached egg, pan-fried sea trout, slow roast pork belly and baked aubergine with tomato, onion and parsley. Leave space for rhubarb fool with shortbread. All dishes are available as children's portions. There is a garden and a patio.
⊙ 12–11 (Sun 12–10.30). Restaurant: 12.30–3, 6.30–10.30 (Sun 12.30–3, 7–10); closed 25–26 Dec, 1 Jan
🍴 L from £13.50, D from £19, Wine from £13
🚇 Angel

EATING

THE EAGLE

159 Farringdon Road, Clerkenwell EC1R 3AL

Tel: 020 7837 1353

The Eagle helped create the gastro pub. Expect big flavours. The straightforward, rustic blackboard-driven menu leans towards Iberia.

🕐 12–11; closed D Sun, one week at Christmas, public holidays

🍴 Bar meals from £5, Wine from £11

🚇 Angel, Farringdon

FIFTEEN ❀❀

13 Westland Place N1 7LP

Tel: 0871 330 1515

www.fifteenrestaurant.com

This venture from celebrity chef Jamie Oliver can be reserved for months in advance. But don't let that put you off—Fifteen offer simple but creative cooking. This is food to be enjoyed. 'Please use your fingers—don't be English', says the menu after a description of a juicy partridge dish.

🕐 12–2.15, 6.30–9.30; closed D Sun, public holidays

🍴 L from £22, D (6 courses) from £60, Wine from £16

🚭 In restaurant

🚇 Old Street

FRENCH HOUSE

49 Dean Street, Soho W1D 5BG

Tel: 020 7437 2799

Weekly changing menus at this small bar might feature navarin of lamb, roast monkfish with Parma ham, confit of duck with braised lentils and red cabbage, or risotto of roast pumpkin. No children under 18 or dogs allowed.

🕐 11–11 (Sun 12–10.30). Restaurant: Mon–Sat 12–3, 5.30–11; closed 25 Dec

🍴 L (3 courses) from £20, D from £20, Wine from £12.50

🚇 Leicester Square

THE GLASSHOUSE ❀❀

14 Station Road, Kew TW9 3PZ

Tel: 020 8940 6777

This chic restaurant is modern and airy, with extremely hospitable and knowledgeable service. Uncomplicated dishes—perhaps a ragout of mussels

and monkfish or slow-roast belly of pork—are accompanied by something from the extensive and globally diverse wine list. Reserving is advised.

🕐 12–2.30, 7–10.30; closed Christmas, 1 Jan

🍴 L from £20, D from £32.50, Wine from £15

🚭

🚇 Kew Gardens

J SHEEKEY ❀❀

28–32 St. Martin's Court WC2N 4AL

Tel: 020 7240 2565

This much-loved seafood establishment is in a class of its own when it comes to fish dishes. Menus can include

The celebrated Eagle is the quintessential gastro pub

seared tuna with fennel and Sicilian tomato salad, along with a smoked anchovy dish with slow-baked beetroot and horseradish cream. Reserving is essential.

🕐 12–3, 5.30–midnight; closed D 24 Dec, 25–26 Dec, D 31 Dec, 1 Jan, public holidays

🍴 L from £15.50, D from £20.75, Wine from £15

🚭 No pipes, no cigars

🚇 Leicester Square

THE LANSDOWNE

90 Gloucester Avenue, Primrose Hill NW1 8HX

Tel: 020 7483 0409

One of the earlier dining pubs in Primrose Hill, The

Lansdowne blends an airy bar and outdoor seating with a slightly more formal upper dining toom. Here you'll find waiter service, and it's worth reserving your table. All food is freshly prepared on the premises, using organic or free-range ingredients wherever possible. The seasonal menu offers such dishes as home-made pizzas and sausages, chicken and chorizo stew and grilled sea bass with purple-sprouting broccoli. Children welcome.

🕐 12–11 (Sun 12–4, 7–10.30). Restaurant Tue–Sat 7–10, Sun 1–3; closed 25–26 Dec

🍴 Bar L from £8, D from £23.50, Wine from £13.50

🚇 Chalk Farm

LINDSAY HOUSE RESTAURANT ❀❀❀

21 Romilly Street W1V 5AF

Tel: 020 7439 0450

www.lindsayhouse.co.uk

Ring the bell for admission to this quirky Soho success story and succumb to the twin temptations of cutting-edge cooking and sheer indulgence. Chef Richard Corrigan and his team rarely put a foot wrong and their well-judged experiments ensure a heady journey for the diner. Adventurous starters like pink slices of veal kidney with harissa sauce and couscous might be followed by a perfectly balanced ensemble of tender pigeon breasts, pork rillette and soft foie gras, served with creamy mash. Sliced poached pear in Sauternes jelly with a quenelle of piquant blue cheese bavarois is a sensational dessert. A tasting menu offers further inventive choices for the whole table. Jacket and tie preferred but children welcome.

🕐 12–2.30, 6–11; closed Sun, L Sat, one week Christmas, one week Easter

🍴 L from £19.50, D from £48, Wine from £26

🚭 No pipes, no cigars

🚇 Leicester Square

MORO ✿✿
34–36 Exmouth Market, Clerkenwell
EC1R 4QE
Tel: 020 7833 8336
www.moro.co.uk
Packed Spanish/North African eatery with good-value meals. Many dishes are inspired by the wood-fired oven, and range from the simple grilled chicory with jamon and sherry vinegar to the more complex wood-roasted turbot with roast beetroot lentils and churrasco sauce. A warm goat's curd with pine nuts, raisins and orange blossom water in filo pastry provides an unusual end to the meal. The wine list is biased towards Spain and reasonably priced.
🕐 12.30–2.30, 7–10.30; closed Sun, L Sat, Christmas, New Year, public holidays
🍴 L from £22, D from £27, Wine from £12
🚭 No pipes or cigars
Ⓔ Farringdon Road, Angel

NEAL STREET RESTAURANT ✿✿
26 Neal Street WC2H 9QW
Tel: 020 7836 8368
www.carluccios.com
Antonio Carluccio's passions–mushrooms and truffles–are showcased on the authentic menu of this Covent Garden landmark. Succulent veal sweetbreads cooked with lemon and butter make a delicious main course or try ribbon pasta with black truffle sauce or pappardelle with wild mushroom sauce. You can expect excellent ice cream for dessert. And, typically for an Italian restaurant, children are always welcome.
🕐 12–2.30, 6–11; closed Sun, Easter Mon, 25 Dec–2 Jan, public holidays
🍴 L from £21, D from £25, Wine from £18.50
♿
Ⓔ Covent Garden

THE OXO TOWER RESTAURANT ✿✿
8th Floor, Oxo Tower Wharf, Barge House Street SE1 9PH
Tel: 020 7803 3888
www.harveynichols.co.uk
With its amazing view through floor-to-ceiling windows overlooking the river and City beyond, this cubed tower cannot fail to impress. Cooking is modern in style but not outlandish, in dishes such as lobster, tomato and basil jelly with Sevruga caviar and pan-fried veal sweetbreads with a sauce of ceps, parsley and lemon oil. Desserts might include coconut rice

Enjoy fabulous views at the Oxo Tower Restaurant

pudding with spiced ice cream.
🕐 12–3, 6–11.30; closed 25–26 Dec
🍴 L (3 courses) from £30, D from £35, Wine from £15
🚭 No pipes
Ⓔ Blackfriars

THE PERSEVERANCE
63 Lambs Conduit Street WC1N 3NB
Tel: 020 7405 8278
A central London haven of good food, fine wine and conviviality. The elegant, candlelit dining room upstairs offers six starters: home-made gnocchi, courgettes (zucchini) and mussels, maybe, while main dishes might include gilt-head sea bream with globe artichokes, confit potatoes and

red wine sauce, or daube of pork with cep casserole. Sunday lunch requires reserving.
🕐 12–11. Restaurant: Mon–Fri 12.30–3, 7–10, Sat 7–10, Sun 12.30–3; closed Christmas
🍴 L from £18, D from £23, Wine from £12
Ⓔ Holborn, Russell Square

THE REAL GREEK ✿✿
15 Hoxton Market N1 6HG
Tel: 020 7739 8212
www.therealgreek.co.uk
This Victorian pub has been transformed into an urban-fashionable bistro. You enter it via the adjoining sister venture, Mezedopolio, a wine and medezes bar. Look for salt cod in batter or salad of lump-fish roe to start with followed by lamb kebab served with sweetbreads and rice, or pan-fried fish with macaroni. Reservation advised.
🕐 12–3, 5.30–10.30; closed Sun, 23–27 Dec, public holidays
🍴 L from £20.95, D from £22.30, Wine from £13.25
Ⓔ Old Street

THE RED FORT ✿✿
77 Dean Street W1D 3SH
Tel: 020 7437 2525
www.redfort.co.uk
This long-established Indian consists of a busy basement bar and a more formal ground-floor restaurant. The latter specializes in cuisine from the New Delhi region and offers diners both an à la carte and a two-course set menu. You might start with tandoori sweet potato, pear, guava and avocado marinated in tandoori spices–and follow with *murgh makhanwala*, corn-fed chicken cooked in a creamy tomato and fenugreek sauce. Children welcome.
🕐 12–2.15, 5.45–11; closed L Sat, Sun, 24–26 Dec
🍴 L from £12, D from £16, Wine from £16
🚭 Section, no pipes
♿
Ⓔ Leicester Square

THE RIVER CAFÉ ✿✿✿
Thames Wharf, Rainville Road W6 9HA
Tel: 020 7386 4200
www.rivercafe.co.uk
The River Café is still serving some of the best Italian food around. The emphasis is on the finest raw materials lovingly prepared. The twice-daily-changing menu might include plump whole pigeon roasted in the wood oven, tender to the bone and accompanied by mouthwatering roasted pumpkin, fennel, celeriac and carrots. Desserts are typically Italian and fairly simple.
🕐 12.30–3, 7–11; closed D Sun, Easter, 22 Dec–3 Jan, public holidays
🍴 L from £30, D from £36, Wine from £12
🚭 No pipes, no cigars
♿
Ⓜ Hammersmith

ST. JOHN ✿✿
26 St. John Street EC1M 4AY
Tel: 020 7251 0848
www.stjohnrestaurant.co.uk
This restaurant has a menu that nods at traditional British cooking. There's plenty of offal—salted kid's liver, pressed pork and gizzard, tiny, tender rabbit's heart, kidneys and liver—and unusal ingredients such as smoked eel with bacon and mash, roast bone marrow and tripe, sausage and chick peas. More cautious diners might opt for langoustine with mayonnaise or cod and chips.
🕐 12–3, 6–11; closed Sun, L Sat, Easter, Christmas, New Year
🍴 L from £20, D from £25, Wine from £14
Ⓜ Farringdon

SIMPLY NICO ✿
48a Rochester Row SW1P 1JU
Tel: 020 7630 8061
www.trpplc.com
Among this famous restaurant's strengths is a romantic Parisian atmosphere. *Terrine de campagne*, salmon and crab fishcakes and pear and almond tart all pass muster without the forceful rustic flavours that

you might expect of a true French bistro.
🕐 12–2.30, 6.30–10.30; closed L Sat, Sun, Easter, Christmas
🍴 L from £17, D from £21.50, Wine from £13.95
🚭 No pipes, no cigars
♿
Ⓜ Victoria

SMITHS OF SMITHFIELD ✿✿
Top Floor, 66–67 Charterhouse Street EC1M 6HJ
Tel: 020 7251 7950
www.smithsofsmithfield.co.uk
The food at this large restaurant is organic and additive-free and includes pumpkin tortellini with oregano and Parmesan crisps

Gordon Ramsay's flagship restaurant is in Chelsea

and Welsh chicken with mushroom ravioli, tarragon and mustard sauce.
🕐 12–3.30, 6.30–12; closed L Sat, 25–26 Dec, 1 Jan
🍴 L from £12.50, D from £18, Wine from £13.75
♿
Ⓜ Farringdon, Barbican, Chancery Lane

TAMARIND ✿✿
20 Queen Street, Mayfair W1J 5PR
Tel: 020 7629 3561
www.tamarindrestaurant.com
Tamarind serves exquisite Indian food at affordable prices. Dishes include tandoori prawns and scallops on a salad of sour grapes. The braised lamb with onions, spinach and five-spice sauce

RESTAURANT GORDON RAMSAY ✿✿✿✿✿
68 Royal Hospital Road SW3 4HP
Tel: 020 7352 4441
www.gordonramsay.com
Gordon Ramsay is probably the most acclaimed chef in Britain today and Royal Hospital Road is the foundation of his empire. For somewhere with such a huge reputation, it's surprisingly intimate. Service is as good as it gets, with every dish accurately explained and plenty of help when navigating the wine list. Simplicity, integrity and lightness of touch are Ramsay hallmarks, along with determination and consistency. The quality of ingredients is irreproachable in, for example, a pan-fried fillet of wild sea bass with crushed new potatoes, braised baby pak-choi, langoustines and Hermitage sauce, while timing is dead-on. Desserts are a delight. Prices, for the food, are decidedly reasonable.
🕐 12–2.30, 6.45–11; closed Sat–Sun, two weeks Christmas, public holidays
🍴 L from £35, D from £65, Wine from £12
♿
♿
Ⓜ Sloane Square

is outstanding. Choices of dessert are a little bizarre, featuring dumplings of milk and semolina and *gajar ka halwa*, which can be best described as exotic carrot cake. No children under 10.
🕐 12–2.45, 6–11; closed L Sat, 25–26 Dec, 1 Jan
🍴 L from £14.50, D from £34, Wine from £19
🚭 No pipes, no cigars
♿
Ⓜ Green Park

WALES

Wales has a strong suit of edible specialities. Laver bread, made from seaweed and oatmeal, and bara brith, a rich tea bread, are two of the most localized, while Welsh lamb is prized all over Britain. Cawl is a stew of lamb or mutton and vegetables—including leeks, Wales' national emblem. White, crumbly Caerphilly cheese is an ingredient of Welsh rarebit, which is essentially grilled cheese on toast.

Many restaurants benefit from having fresh, locally grown produce on their doorsteps, and some, such as the Walnut Tree (▷ below) have reputations for excellence that stretch beyond the Welsh border. The gastro pub has also reached Wales, and the Felin Fach Griffin (▷ 350) in Brecon is an especially successful example.

ABERGAVENNY

WALNUT TREE INN ❀❀
Abergavenny NP7 8AW
Tel: 01873 852797
Freshness and seasonal availability dictate the content of the menu, which offers honest and satisfying Italian cooking along the lines of braised lamb and potato tortino with rosemary and grilled leeks, or fillet of cod with a soft herb crust, and spinach, cockle and tomato sauce.

⊙ 12–2.30, 7–9.30 Tue–Sun, closed D Sun, Mon public holidays, 24 Dec–1 Jan
🍷 L from £16.50, D from £23, Wine from £13.50
🚌 3 miles (5km) northeast of Abergavenny on B4521

ABERYSTWYTH

CONRAH HOTEL ❀❀
Ffosrhydygaled, Chancery, Aberystwyth SY23 4DF
Tel: 01970 617941
www.conrah.co.uk
You'll find the cream of Welsh produce at this country house hotel (▷ 385), where quality classical and modern international dishes with strong Welsh influences are served in the luxurious Victorian/Edwardian restaurant. From the fixed-price menu expect medallions of Welsh black beef, and desserts such as pear and dark chocolate tart with pistachio Anglaise.

⊙ Closed 22–30 Dec, D Sun in low season
🍷 L from £12, D from £16, Wine from £12
🍴 In restaurant
🚌 On A487, 3 miles (5km) south of Aberystwyth
🚂 Aberystwyth

PRICES AND SYMBOLS

The restaurants are listed alphabetically within each town. The prices are for a two-course lunch (L) and a three-course à la carte dinner (D). Prices in pubs are for a two-course lunchtime bar meal and a two-course dinner in the restaurant, unless specified otherwise.

For a key to the symbols, ▷ 2.

EATING

ANGLESEY

YE OLDE BULLS HEAD INN
❀ ❀

Castle Street, Beaumaris LL58 8AP
Tel: 01248 810329

This central inn now includes a thoroughly modern restaurant decorated in chic, minimalist style. It has acquired a loyal following for its equally up-to-date British cooking, underpinned by good-quality produce. A meal might include steamed fillet of bream with crab noodles and fresh oyster sauce, followed by medallions of venison and pigeon breast with Puy lentils and morel jus. No children under seven.

⏱ 7–9.30; closed L Mon–Sat, Sun, 1 Jan and 25–26 Dec
🍴 L from £9.50, D from £16.95, Wine from £12.50
🅂 In restaurant

BRECON

THE FELIN FACH GRIFFIN ❀ ❀

Felin Fach, Brecon LD3 0UB
Tel: 01874 620111
www.eatdrinksleep.ltd.uk

Staff at this bright-red pub are positive, and the food, while familiar, is consistent and carefully conceived. Smoked haddock rarebit is light and full flavoured, while calves' liver with bacon and mash is perfectly cooked. Puddings include a great, zingy lemon tart with top-notch pastry. The wine list is short but well-chosen.

⏱ 12.30–2.30, 7–9.30; closed L Mon and two weeks late Jan–early Feb
🍴 Bar L from £12, D from £38, Wine from £10.95 🅂
🚌 4.5 miles (7km) north of Brecon on A470

CARDIFF

IZAKAYA JAPANESE TAVERN ❀

Mermaid Quay, Cardiff Bay CF10 5BW
Tel: 029 2049 2939

In the style of a traditional rural Japanese tavern, Izakaya serves the kind of authentic food the Japanese enjoy every day. Five different types of seating arrangement each create a slightly different mood. Don't be put off by the laminated menu

picturing the huge range of dishes–it aids accessibility and the food is good.

⏱ 12–2.30, 6–11; closed 23–26, 31 Dec, 1 Jan
🍴 L from £5.90, D from £17, Wine from £14
🚌 Leave M4 at junction 33 for A4232. Restaurant on first floor Mermaid Quay

THE ST. DAVID'S HOTEL AND SPA ❀ ❀

Havannah Street, Cardiff CF10 5SD
Tel: 029 2045 4045
www.rfhotels.com

Tides Restaurant is adjacent to this hotel's (▷ 386) stylish cocktail bar. The menu features the best of Welsh ingredients, such as braised

Fresh wholesome fare at Creigiau's Caesars Arms

shank of lamb, and is supplemented by a daily market menu focusing on in-season produce.

⏱ 12.30–2.15, 6.30–10.15
🍴 L from £13.95, D from £20, Wine from £15
🅂 In restaurant
🚌 M4 junction 33/A4232 for 9 miles (15km) for Techniquest at top exit slip road; first left at roundabout then first right 🅿 Cardiff Central

CREIGIAU

CAESARS ARMS ❀

Cardiff Road, Creigiau CF15 9NN
Tel: 029 2089 0486

This Victorian pub has a large restaurant extension. The menu is written on a blackboard over the counter,

where foods are attractively displayed and orders taken. Farther into the restaurant is a kitchen area where customers can see their food being prepared. The accent is on freshness and plain cooking, with dishes such as crispy laver balls with mushrooms and lemon, and strawberry millefeuille.

⏱ 12–2.30, 6.30–12; closed 25 Dec, D Sun
🍴 L from £11.95, D from £18, Wine from £12.95
🚌 3 miles (5km) from M4 junction 34 take A411 (Cardiff) and turn left at Creigiau

DOLGELLAU

GEORGE III HOTEL

Penmaenpool, Dolgellau LL40 1YD
Tel: 01341 422525

The waterside Cellar Bar in this pub is ideal for families, cyclists and walkers, while the upper-level Dresser Bar and the main dining rooms are more genteel. Noted for local salmon and sea trout, pheasant and wild duck in season, meals are home-cooked by the landlord. These include soups, chicken liver pâté or steak and Stilton baps, while the restaurant contributes rack of Welsh mountain lamb, sticky toffee pudding and cheeses from Harlech and Caws Llyn.

⏱ Daily 11–11
🍴 L from £12, D from £16, Wine from £10
🅂 In restaurant
🚌 2 miles (3km) west of A493 beyond RSPB Centre

HAY-ON-WYE

OLD BLACK LION ❀

26 Lion Street, Hay-on-Wye HR3 5AD
Tel: 01497 820841
www.oldblacklion.co.uk

This fine old coaching inn (▷ 387) has charm and character. Service is friendly, and a wide range of competently prepared food is provided. The impressive Modern European menu includes wild boar on a bed of lyonnaise potatoes, and

EATING

rack of lamb with sweet potato mash and rosemary jus. No children under five.
🕐 8am–11pm
🍴 L from £15, D from 20, Wine from £12.95
🚫 In restaurant
🚗 From tourist information office parking area turn right along Oxford Road, pass NatWest bank and take next left (Lion Street); hotel soon on right

LLANBERIS

Y BISTRO ❀
Glandwr, 43 45 Stryd Fawr (High Street), Llanberis LL55 4EU
Tel: 01286 871278
www.ybistro.co.uk
Y Bistro is a well-established, spacious, period restaurant in the heart of Llanberis, run by a husband-and-wife team. The modern Welsh menu of simple dishes (described in English and Welsh) includes unfussy main courses such as Welsh lamb with red wine and rosemary sauce on potato rosti. A good opportunity to try one of the three Welsh wines on the approachable list.
🕐 7.30–10
🍴 D from £24, Wine from £10.50
🚫
🚗 In village centre at foot of Mount Snowdon by Lake Padarn

LLANWRTYD WELLS

CARLTON HOUSE ❀ ❀ ❀
Dolycoed Road LD5 4RA
Tel: 01591 610248
Considered to be something of a treasure in this beautiful area of Wales, with food remaining at the heart of the operation. Mary Ann Gilchrist's cooking is imaginatively biased towards local Welsh ingredients and she bakes excellent breads (rosemary and garlic, gruyère and cheddar) that quickly vanish. The menus offer plenty to delight with a daily changing menu. Inspired cooking from one of Wales' best.
🕐 D 7–8.30; closed Sun
🍴 L from £19.50 (by arrangement only), D from £24.50, Wine from £11.50
🚗 In town centre

MONTGOMERY

DRAGON HOTEL ❀
Market Square SY15 6PA
Tel: 01686 668359
This is a historic black-fronted coaching inn with a homely interior. The menu makes good use of Welsh ingredients, offering traditional dishes with an occasional modern twist. Close to Montgomery Castle.
🕐 12–2, 7–9
🍴 D from £20.75, Wine from £10
🚗 Behind town hall

NEWPORT

THE INN AT THE ELM TREE ❀
St. Brides, Wentlooge, Newport NP10 8SQ
Tel: 01633 680225

Newport's Inn at the Elm Tree is a stylish choice

Fresh local produce is the key to the menu's success at this modern, stylish restaurant: organic pork from just across the road, Welsh lamb, Welsh Black beef, game in season from local estates, as well as lobsters and oysters from Cardigan Bay. No children under 12.
🕐 12–2.30, 5.30–9.30; closed D Sun, in winter
🍴 L from £10, D from £12.50, Wine from £11
🚫 In restaurant
🚗 From M4 junction 28 take A48 towards Castleton. At first roundabout turn left; continue 1.5 miles (2.4km) right on to Morgan Way. Turn right at T-junction on to B4239 for 2.5 miles (4km)

PWLLHELI

PLAS BODEGROES ❀ ❀
Nefyn Road, Pwllheli LL53 5TH
Tel: 01758 612363
This Georgian manor house restaurant's distinctly contemporary, both in décor and cuisine. Local produce is used imaginatively, as in a rosemary kebab of mountain lamb with griddled baby courgettes (zucchini) and garlic cream. Other dishes might include roast fillet of sea bream with crab, spinach, ginger and a coconut sauce. For pudding look out for the popular chocolate soufflé with white chocolate ice cream.
🕐 12–2, 7–9; closed Mon, L Tue–Sat and Dec–end Feb
🍴 L from £17.50, D from £40, Wine from £14
🚫
🚗 On A497 1 mile (1.6km) west of Pwllheli

ST. ASAPH

THE PLOUGH INN
The Roe, St. Asaph LL17 0LU
Tel: 01745 585080
This 18th-century former coaching inn on the original Holyhead–London road buzzes throughout the day and has become a notable dining venue by night. With horse racing as its principal theme, the Paddock Bar offers a snack menu to accompany your beer. The chic Racecourse Bistro features a fresh fish display and specialities such as cod in beer batter with real chips. Meanwhile, the art deco restaurant Graffiti Italiano offers pizzas and pasta in many guises, in addition to such dishes as veal medallions with mushrooms, cream and herb risotto.
🕐 Daily 12–11 (10.30 Sun)
🍴 L from £10.95, D from £20, Wine from £11.95
🚫 In restaurant
🍷 Wine shop
🚗 Rhyl and St. Asaph turning from A55 left at roundabout; pub 180m (600ft) on left

EATING

SKENFRITH

THE BELL AT SKENFRITH ❀❀
Skenfrith NP7 8UH
Tel: 01600 750235
Normally two fish courses are available in the bar, and one in the restaurant, at this 17th-century coaching inn. Often available are confit of duck with celeriac mash and orange, onion and coriander (cilantro) marmalade, and Welsh rack of lamb with smoked garlic polenta and rosemary jus. Try the real ales or hand-pumped scrumpy. The AA Pub of the Year for Wales 2003.
🕐 12–2.30, 7–9.30; closed first two weeks of Feb
🍽 L from £18, D from £30, Wine from £12

SWANSEA

FAIRYHILL ❀❀❀
Reynoldston, Swansea SA3 1BS
Tel: 01792 390139
Fairyhill (▷ 388) is a beacon for all that's good about Welsh produce and dedicated cooking. On the menu are modern twists of traditional dishes using the best local produce, such as pristine baked sea bass with a soft herb crust and butter sauce. All complemented by one of Wales' most comprehensive wine lists and excellent service. No children under eight.
🕐 12–2.30, 7.30–9; closed 1–16 Jan and 26 Dec
🍽 L from £15.95, D from £37.50, Wine from £14.50
🍷 In restaurant
🚗 Just outside Reynoldston off A4118 from Swansea

TALYBONT-ON-USK

THE USK INN
LD3 7JE
Tel: 01874 676251
This refurbished free house has long been welcoming travellers with a good range of real ales. Food is taken seriously with imaginative menus that make the most of fresh local produce. Expect twice-cooked lamb shank with minted red wine sauce, beef

fillet with goats' cheese or roast monkfish on lemon balm. There are several vegetarian choices. Children and dogs welcome.
🕐 8am–11pm; closed 25–26 Dec
🍽 L from £10, D from £25, Wine from £12.95
🚗 6 miles (10km) east of Brecon, just off the A40 to Abergavenny, if coming through Talybont turn onto Station Road alongside rail bridge, pub on right

TENBY

PANORAMA HOTEL AND RESTAURANT ❀
The Esplanade, Tenby SA70 7DU
Tel: 01834 844976
This is romantic candlelit dinner territory: well dressed

Enjoy local produce at Talybont-on-Usk's inn

and with sea views. Where possible, the food is sourced from Pembrokeshire to produce an understated but tempting international menu unsurprisingly featuring seafood. Examples include poached salmon rolls with dill and honey mayonnaise dressing, and interesting combinations such as pan-fried fillet of pork with grain mustard, fresh herbs, woodland mushrooms, vermouth and cream.
🕐 7–9, D only; closed Sun and 25 Dec
🍽 D from £25, Wine from £9.95
🍷 In restaurant
🚉 Tenby

THE NEWBRIDGE ❀❀
Tredunnock NP15 1LY
Tel: 01633 451000
www.thenewbridge.co.uk
The AA's Welsh Restaurant of the Year in 2005 has a faintly Tuscan look to its bar/bistro-style interior. Although the Newbridge is tucked away in rural Monmouthshire, its menu draws extensively on the Mediterranean side of modern British food, using local produce to good effect in daily changing pork and beef dishes as well as excellent changing fish choices.
🕐 12–3, 6.30–10; closed 26 Dec, 1 Jan
🍽 L from £12, D from £28, Wine from £12.50
🚗 South of Usk, drive through Tredunnock village and inn is by River Usk

WOLF'S CASTLE

THE WOLFE INN
Wolf's Castle SA62 5LS
Tel: 01437 741662
This stone, oak-beamed inn consists of four distinctive rooms, which, together with a secluded patio garden, offer a relaxed atmosphere. The freshest local produce is used to create the fine cuisine in the restaurant and the simplest of dishes in the brasserie. These range from cutlet of wild boar with forest fruits and nut seasoning served with a rich port wine and blackberry sauce to butcher's bangers (sausages) with mash and onion gravy. There's always a monthly guest beer, and a wide selection of coffees and teas.
🕐 Mon–Sat 11–3, 6–11, Sun 11–3
🍽 L from £15, D from £25, Wine from £8.95
🍷 In restaurant
🚗 On A40 halfway between Haverfordwest and Fishguard

EATING

THE MIDLANDS

Many people are surprised to learn that the town with the most celebrated restaurants outside London isn't another major city but sleepy little Ludlow in Shropshire. With two of the country's top restaurants—Mr. Underhills and Hibiscus (▷ 356)—for 9,000 inhabitants, Ludlow has become a foodie phenomenon. By London standards the establishments are small; Mr. Underhills has just 24 covers and weekends are reserved a long time in advance. However, weekday reservations are more easily available. In addition, Britain's best food festival (▷ 253) sets up its stalls in the town every September. In Birmingham there's food-related evidence of the region's industrial heritage, as chocolate and custard were both produced in the city: Cadbury World (▷ 150) is a popular attraction next to the chocolate factory, while the Bird's Custard Factory is now an arts centre (▷ 249).

One notable speciality of the region is often overlooked: spring water. Malvern, Ashbourne and Buxton in the Peak District all produce bottled water from underground springs.

EATING

ALDERLEY EDGE

ALDERLEY EDGE HOTEL ※ ※
Macclesfield Road, Alderley Edge
SK9 7BJ
Tel: 01625 583033
www.alderleyedgehotel.com
The air-conditioned, split-level conservatory restaurant at this country-house hotel (▷ 389) has a comprehensive, Modern European à la carte menu—including a mosaic of local game birds served with pickled young turnips, foie gras beignet and damson chutney—and also fixed-price meals. Home-grown herbs, fish from Fleetwood and a

dizzying array of breads also feature. There is an impressive wine list.
🕐 12–2, 7–10; closed D 25–26 Dec, 1 Jan
🍴 L from £17.95, D from £29.50, Wine from £11.50
🚭 Section, no pipes
🚗 Off A34 in Alderley Edge on to B5087 towards Macclesfield. Hotel 200m (650ft) on right

BAKEWELL

RUTLAND ARMS HOTEL ※
The Square, Bakewell DE45 1BT
Tel: 01629 812812
www.bakewell.demon.co.uk

In this hotel's (▷ 389) restaurant local ingredients are to the fore and cooking is traditional but with a modern influence. An accurate wild mushroom risotto, and well-constructed roast summer quail on crushed pea mash are typical of the fixed-price menu.
🕐 Daily 12–2, 7–9
🍴 L from £13.95, D from £28.50, Wine from £12.50
🚭
🚗 On A6 in centre of Bakewell, opposite war memorial
🚉 Bakewell

The restaurants are listed alphabetically within each town. The prices are for a two-course lunch (L) and a three-course à la carte dinner (D). Prices in pubs are for a two-course lunchtime bar meal and a two-course dinner in the restaurant, unless specified otherwise.

For a key to the symbols, ▷ 2.

BAMFORD

YORKSHIRE BRIDGE INN

Ashopton Road, Hope Valley S33 0AZ
Tel: 01433 651361
www.yorkshire-bridge.co.uk
Food is available in the bar or dining room of this historic inn (▷ 389). Dishes may include pork and leek sausages and prosciutto ravioli, or traditional favourites such as steak and kidney pie. Grills, baked potatoes, sandwiches and salads make filling snacks. Food can be served in the garden.
🕐 11–11. Restaurant 12–2, 6–9.30
🍴 L from £16, D from £30, Wine from £10.50
🚭 In restaurant
🚗 A57 (Sheffield–Glossop road), at Ladybower Reservoir take A6013 Bamford road, inn 1 mile (1.6km) on right

BASLOW

FISCHER'S BASLOW HALL

❀ ❀ ❀
Calver Road, Baslow DE45 1RR
Tel: 01246 583259
www.fischers-baslowhall.co.uk
Baslow Hall (▷ 390) has all the trademarks of a 17th-century manor—built in 1907, it is in fact a clever architectural fake. There is however nothing fake about Max Fischer's cooking, a lifetime's dedication to food means that he, and his dedicated team, deliver sophisticated, elegant fare that is pricey for the area but well worth it. No children under 12.
🕐 12–2, 7–10; closed L Mon, D Sun (except hotel residents), 25–26 Dec

🍴 L from £17.50, D from £59, Wine from £18.50
🚭
🚗 On A623 between Baslow and Calver

BIRMINGHAM

JESSICA'S ❀ ❀

1 Montague Road, Edgbaston B16 9HN
Tel: 0121 455 0999
www.jessicasrestaurant.co.uk
One of the city's most modish eateries. Jessica's takes food seriously and delivers a tempting menu with innovative cooking. If you're not sure, try the seven-course tasting menu; the fixed-price lunch is also good value. Jessica's was the AA Restaurant of the Year for England in 2005.

Max Fischer offers outstanding cuisine in Baslow

🕐 12.30–2.30, 7–10.30; closed Sun, L Mon, L Sat, one week Easter, last two weeks Jul, one week Christmas
🍴 L from £15, D from £29.95, Wine from £15.95
🚭
🚭
🚗 Off Hagley Road
🚉 Birmingham New Street

BROADWAY

THE LYGON ARMS ❀ ❀ ❀

High Street, Broadway WR12 7DU
Tel: 01386 852255
www.thelygonarms.co.uk
The choice and range of menus are the strengths of this historic hotel (▷ 390). The Modern British dishes produce gutsy flavours from the simple use of quality ingredients, notably a

starter of pigeon breast with beetroot, mustard seed relish, salad leaves and cranberry and orange dressing. Oliver's Brasserie is the alternative dining venue for a less formal setting. No children under six. Smart casual dress preferred.
🕐 12–2, 7–9.30; closed L Mon–Fri
🍴 L from £25, D from £25, Wine from £11.20
🚭
🚗 Turn off A44, signed Broadway, hotel on High Street

CASTLE DONINGTON

THE NAG'S HEAD

Hilltop, Castle Donington DE74 2PR
Tel: 01332 850652
www.caledonian-brewery.co.uk
The extensive menu at this old-fashioned pub features tempting starters and snacks, including seared scallops with balsamic vinegar. Unusual and inventive main dishes include sliced beef fillet in Cajun sauce with tsatziki dressing. Traditional homemade puddings round off the menu.
🕐 Mon–Sat 11.30–2.30, 5.30–11, Sun 12–3, 7–10.30. Restaurant Mon–Sat 12–2, 5.30–9.30; closed 26 Dec–4 Jan
🍴 L from £8.95, D from £30, Wine from £11
🚉 Long Eaton 4.5 miles (7km)
🚗 From A42 take A453 to Castle Donnington, this leads to Hilltop and the pub.

CHACOMBE

GEORGE AND DRAGON

Silver Street, Chacombe, near Banbury OX17 2JR
Tel: 01295 711500
This is an attractive, honey-stoned, 16th-century pub tucked away in a pretty village. Blackboards list the interesting choice of food, from sandwiches and out-of-the-ordinary pasta dishes to crispy duck breast with chilli and cranberry sauce. Highchairs available.
🕐 12–11. Restaurant 12–2, 7–9.30
🍴 L from £10, D from £13.50, Wine from £10.95
🚭 In restaurant
🚗 From junction 11 of M40 take A361

to Daventry, then first right to Chacombe and second left in village
🚗 Banbury 3 miles (4.5km)

CHESTER

OLD HARKERS ARMS

1 Russell Street, Chester CH1 5AL
Tel: 01244 344525
www.harkersarms.chester.co.uk
There's a good selection of sandwiches and paninis in the restaurant at lunchtime at this canalside pub, and an interesting range of dishes that might include Caribbean-style chicken, salmon and smoked haddock fishcakes, and leek and apricot sausages. All wines are available by the glass. No children.
🕐 11.30–11. Restaurant Mon–Fri 11.30–2.30, 5.30–9.30, Sat–Sun 12–9.30; closed 26 Dec–2 Jan
🍽 L from £11.90, D from £15.85, Wine from £11.50
🚭 No-smoking area in restaurant
🚃 Down the steps off City Road on the banks of the canal.
🚗 Bache 2 miles (3km)

CLIPSHAM

THE OLIVE BRANCH ❀❀

Main Street, Clipsham LE15 7SH
Tel: 01780 410355
Don't be fooled by the laid-back atmosphere at this popular restaurant—food is taken very seriously here, and the casual approach is due simply to a lack of pretension. Starters tend to be simple combinations of high-quality ingredients (whitebait with garlic and lemon mayonnaise), while main courses might include honey-glazed ham hock with poached egg and bubble and squeak, or a sublime bouillabaisse.
🕐 12–2, 7–9.30; closed D Sun, 26 Dec, 1 Jan
🍽 L from £10.50, D from £18.50, Wine from £9.95
🚭 Section
🚃 9 miles (15km) north of Stamford on A1

GRINDLEFORD

MAYNARD ARMS

Main Road, Grindleford S32 2HE
Tel: 01433 630321
www.maynardarms.co.uk
The modern interior of this 1898 coaching inn (▷ 390) is matched by the contemporary British menus in the Longshore Bar and Padley Restaurant. Local produce features strongly in dishes such as roast rack of Derbyshire pork glazed with mozzarella and served with sautéed greens and charcuterie sauce. For a traditional finish, go for the original Bakewell pudding and custard.

Lincoln's Wig & Mitre has a historic interior

🕐 Mon–Sat 11–3, 5.30–11, Sun 12–10.30. Restaurant 12–2, 7–9.30 (closed L Sat)
🍽 L from £8.95, D (4 courses) from £27.95, Wine from £13
🚭 In restaurant
🚃 From Sheffield take A625 to Castleton. Left into Grindleford on B6521. After Fox House, hotel on left
🚗 Grindleford

HEREFORD

CASTLE HOUSE ❀❀❀

Castle Street, Hereford HR1 2NW
Tel: 01432 356321
www.castlehse.co.uk
The cuisine at this Victorian mansion (▷ 391) is exceptionally good. Canapes indicate what is to come with a selection that might feature

quails' eggs on toast, lemon fishcake or tempura. There is a lightness of touch in dishes such as fennel and Ricard cappucino with mackerel *escabèche*.
🕐 12.30–1.30, 7–9.30
🍽 L from £19.60, D from £31.65, Wine from £16.95
🚭
🚃 Follow signs to City Centre East. At junction of Commercial Road and Union Street, follow Castle House hotel signs
🚗 Hereford

LEDBURY

FEATHERS HOTEL ❀

High Street, Ledbury HR8 1DS
Tel: 01531 635266
www.feathersledbury.co.uk
Dinner is served in this hotel's (▷ 391) sedate Quills Restaurant, or in Fuggles, the friendly bar/brasserie. The menu includes steaks alongside more complex dishes such as duck with Chinese spices, brandied kumquats and pommes boulangère.
🕐 12–2, 7–9.30
🍽 L from £16, D from £20.50, Wine from £11.95
🚭 No smoking area, no pipes, no cigars
🚭
🚃 South from Worcester on A449; east from Hereford on A438; north from Gloucester on A417
🚗 Ledbury

LINCOLN

WIG & MITRE

30–32 Steep Hill, Lincoln LN2 1TL
Tel: 01522 535190
www.wigandmitre.com
This pub restaurant is justifiably popular. Among the noteworthy dishes are spiced crab risotto and steamed plum jam sponge. Many decent wines are available by the glass.
🕐 8am–midnight. Restaurant 8am–11pm
🍽 L from £15, D from £19.95, Wine from £12.45
🚭 In restaurant
🚃 In town centre next to Lincoln Castle car park, at the top of Steep Hill
🚗 Lincoln

LUDLOW

HIBISCUS ❀❀❀❀
17 Corve Street, Ludlow SY8 1DA
Tel: 01584 872325
Claude Bosi may have been resident in Ludlow for some time but his French roots are obvious. An apprenticeship served in some of France's best restaurants has born fruit in this small restaurant. Among the starters, foie gras comes pan fried and skewered on a fresh liquorice stick. Fricassée of Hereford snails with wild garlic broth, black olive and lemon has breathtaking flavours and roast rabbit with raisin sauce, spicy quince purée, gratin of cauliflower and citrus is similarly intense.
🕐 12.30–1.30, 7–10, closed Sun–Mon, L Tue, two weeks Jan, one week Aug
🍴 L from £19.50, D from £45, Wine from £14.75
🚭
🚗 Town centre, bottom of hill, below Feathers Hotel
🚉 Ludlow

MR. UNDERHILLS ❀❀❀
Dinham Weir, Ludlow SY8 1EH
Tel: 01584 874431
www.mr-underhills.co.uk
Dinner at this smart-looking restaurant is a set three courses, consisting of skilfully prepared Modern British dishes that emphasize the freshness of the excellent produce. A typical dinner menu might be fillet of brill on savoy cabbage and apple with lime-scented cardamon, followed by new season's lamb poached with spring vegetables and mint, then dessert and cheeses. Wines come from a comprehensive Euro-centric list, with a good range of half bottles. Children welcome; vegetarian by request only.
🕐 D only, 7.30–8.30; closed Tue, one week Jan, one week Jul
🍴 D from £32, Wine from £13
🚗 From Castle Square, facing castle, turn left around castle; turn right before bridge, restaurant on left

NORTON

THE HUNDRED HOUSE HOTEL ❀❀
Bridgnorth Road, Norton, Shifnal TF11 9EE
Tel: 01952 730353
www.hundredhouse.co.uk
The 'hundred herb house' might be a more fitting name for this comfortable inn (▷ 391), given the huge variety of aromatic plants flourishing both indoors and out. Bowls of fresh herbs on the tables invite diners to flavour their own food, while bunches of drying herbs dangle from the wooden rafters. The home-grown herbs also bring a terrific aroma to the Modern

Home-grown herbs are essential at The Hundred House Hotel

British dishes that celebrate the local produce, such as rack of Shropshire spring lamb, while desserts include apricot and almond flan.
🕐 12–2.30, 6–9.30
🍴 L from £25, D from £30, Wine from £14.95
🚭 Section, no pipes, no cigars
🚗 Midway between Telford and Bridgnorth on A442, in centre of village

NOTTINGHAM

HART'S HOTEL ❀❀
Standard Hill, Park Row, Nottingham NG1 6FN
Tel: 0115 988 1900
www.hartsnottingham.co.uk
This Modern British brasserie offers creatively conceived dishes that really pack in the flavours. Serrano ham and deep-fried mozzarella with a pear relish could be followed by a souffléd haddock omelette with an Emmental glaze, accompanied by a glass of wine from the reasonably priced list.
🕐 12–2, 7–10.30; closed D 25 Dec, 26 Dec, 1 Jan
🍴 L from £11.95, D from £22.25, Wine from £12.50
🚭 Section, no pipes, no cigars
🚗 From junction 24 of M1, take A453 to city centre. Hotel at junction of Park Row and Rope Walk, close to city centre

ROSS-ON-WYE

THE MOODY COW
Upton Bishop, Ross-on-Wye HR9 7TT
Tel: 01989 780470
This old stone inn has been popular since the early 1990s for its good, homemade food. The extensive, imaginative menu includes pan-fried duck breast with a sweet raspberry compote, and desserts such as lavender crème brûlée. The friendly, farmhouse-style bar serves meals and real ales. Children's meals available.
🕐 Tue–Sat 12–2.30, 6.30–11, Sun 12–3, 6.30–11. Restaurant Tue–Sat 12–2, 6.30–9.30, Sun 12–2
🍴 L from £16, D from £21, Wine from £11.95
🚭 In restaurant
🚗 Off junction 3 of M50, then 2 miles (3km) into Upton Bishop

STAMFORD

THE GEORGE OF STAMFORD ❀
71 St. Martins, Stamford PE9 2LB
Tel: 01780 750750
www.georgehotelofstamford.com
A beautiful 16th-century coaching inn (▷ 392) in the heart of the stone-built town of Stamford. The bars offer light snacks such as filled ciabatta, sausage and mashed potatoes. More elaborate dishes are served in the candlelit restaurant, or sample a lighter menu in the garden lounge or in the ivy-clad courtyard. No children under 10.

EATING

Mon–Fri 11–2.30, 6–11, Sat–Sun 11–11. Restaurant 12.30-2.30, 7.30-10.30

L from £17.50, D from £27, Wine from £13.50

Smoking in restaurant after 10pm only, no pipes, no cigars

Turn off A1, 15 miles (24km) north of Peterborough on to B1081, 1 mile (1.6km) on left

Stamford

STOW-ON-THE-WOLD

THE EAGLE AND CHILD
The Royalist Hotel, Digbeth Street, Stow-on-the-Wold GL54 1BN
Tel: 01451 830670
www.theroyalisthotel.co.uk
This excellent pub is a relaxing place in which to sample real ales and excellent food from the hotel kitchen, including first-class Cotswold lamb hotpot with champ mash and sautéed greens. Reserving in advance is advisable.

11–11 (12–11 in winter). Restaurant Tue–Sat 12–3, 7–10, Sun 12–3

L from £12.75, D from £17.25, Wine from £11.95

From junction 8 of M40 follow A40 to Burford. Join A424 to Stow-on-the-Wold. Turn right on to A436 downhill and hotel is on left of green

Moreton-in-Marsh

947AD AT THE ROYALIST HOTEL ❀ ❀ ❀
Digbeth Street, Stow-on-the-Wold GL54 1BN
Tel: 01451 830670
www.theroyalisthotel.co.uk
The restaurant in this ancient inn (▷ 392) offers high-quality cooking with a seasonal menu ranging from roast scallops with apple purée, artichoke crisps and scrumpy sauce, to roast venison with pear and juniper berry tatin.
For dessert try '947AD' Grande Assiette, or a selection of English cheeses with home-made caraway water biscuits.

Tue–Sat 12–2, 7–9

L from £12.75, Dinner from £34.50, Wine from £11.95

See Eagle and Child above

Moreton-in-Marsh

STRATFORD-UPON-AVON

FOX AND GOOSE INN ❀
Armscote, near Stratford-upon-Avon CV37 8DD
Tel: 01608 682293
www.foxandgoose.co.uk
Matching the décor and ambience of this stylish pub/restaurant is a daily-changing menu from a team of talented young chefs—a mix of traditional dishes and more à la mode offerings, such as coconut and saffron risotto with caramelized pineapple.

11–3, 6–11. Restaurant 12–2.30, 7–9.30; closed 25–26 Dec, 1 Jan

L from £12.70, D from £16.20, Wine from £11.95

Section

Stow-on-the-Wold's Eagle and Child is an exceptional pub

From Stratford-upon-Avon take A3400 south for 7 miles (11km). After Newbold-on-Stour turn right towards Armscote (signed), then 1 mile (1.6km) to village

Stratford-upon-Avon

STRATFORD VICTORIA ❀
Arden Street, Stratford-upon-Avon CV37 6QQ
Tel: 01789 271000
www.marstonhotels.com
The spacious restaurant at this eye-catching, modern hotel (▷ 392) features European-themed dishes. Pan-seared scallops with home-made noodles are a signature dish, or you may like to try peppered duck breast accompanied by a red onion

tatin and orange, ginger thyme reduction.

12.30–2, 6–9.45 (Sun 7–9.45)

L from £15.50, D from £27, Wine from £15.95

A439 into Stratford town then follow A3400 (Birmingham). At traffic lights turn left into Arden Street and hotel is 150m (300ft) on right

Stratford-upon-Avon

WARWICK

THE TILTED WIG
11 Market Place, Warwick CV34 4SA
Tel: 01926 410466
This attractive pub was originally a coaching inn and is now a Grade II listed (landmark) building. Its solid menu offers quality, home-cooked dishes, which might include cottage pie, tuna steak, chilli con carne or tagliatelle. Food can be served outside.

11–11 (Sun 12–10.30); closed 25 Dec

L from £10, D from £13.25, Wine from £10.50

From M40 junction 15 take A429 into Warwick, after 1.5 miles (2.5km) turn left into Brook Street and on to Market Place

Warwick

WORCESTER

BROWN'S RESTAURANT ❀
The Old Cornmill, South Quay, Worcester WR1 2JJ
Tel: 01905 26263
This former warehouse and foundry is today a welcoming restaurant on the riverbank opposite Worcestershire County Cricket ground. A sample fixed-price dinner menu takes in pheasant, calves' liver, roast duck, beef fillet, quails, a fish dish and a vegetarian option. Smart casual dress preferred.

12.30–1.45, 7.30–9.45; closed Mon, L Sat, D Sun and one week at Christmas

L from £21.50, D from £38.50, Wine from £15.95

From M5 junction 7 follow signs to city centre. At traffic lights turn into Copenhagen Street parking area, next to restaurant

Worcester

EATING

THE NORTH

Lancashire staples include black pudding, a sausage made from pork, blood and suet, and hotpot—a stew of potatoes, onion and lamb. Meanwhile, Yorkshire puddings—made from a simple batter and now traditionally served with roast beef—were once eaten before the meat course to fill workers up.

Cumbrian food is distinguished by its use of ginger and rum—a reflection of its one-time prominence in trade with the West Indies. One independent Yorkshire brewery, the Black Sheep Brewery in Masham, offers tours by arrangement (tel: 01765 680100; www. blacksheepbrewery.com). Although it only produced its first barrel of beer in 1992, its founder was Paul Theakston, a member of five generations of Masham's famous brewing family.

In recent years immigration has added immeasurably to the dining options in the north of England. The city of Bradford now has the highest concentration of Asian restaurants in the country, and Curry Mile in Manchester is a neon-lit strip of curry houses.

Modern European cooking is also going from strength to strength in Manchester with the opening of hip eateries Juniper in Altrincham (▷ below) and Marco Pierre White's River Room in the stylish Lowry Hotel (▷ 395). Look out too for seafood fresh from the North Sea fishing boats based at Whitby on the east coast.

ALTRINCHAM

JUNIPER ❀❀❀
21 The Downs WA14 2QD
Tel: 0161 9294008
This hip restaurant has transformed itself visually to favour a classic look. There are also exciting changes to the Modern French food, with boundlessly creative, idiosyncratic combinations of superbly sourced ingredients. By comparison, the desserts sound almost banal, with classics such as tarte tatin.

Service is slick, and the wine list is good.
🕐 12–2.30, 7–10; closed L Sat, Sun–Mon
🍴 L from £20, D from £35, Wine from £18 🚫
🚌 A556 Chester to Manchester road

APPLEBY-IN-WESTMORLAND

THE ROYAL OAK INN
Bongate CA16 6UN
Tel: 017683 51463
The interior of this historic pub consists of a classic tap room with blackened beams, oak panelling and open fire, a comfortable lounge and two dining rooms. Ingredients are sourced locally wherever possible and menus change regularly. Options include home-made soups, Sunday lunches and vegetarian meals.
🕐 Mon–Sat 11–11 (10.30 Sun)
🍴 L from £15, D from £20, Wine from £10
🚌 Take A66 east from M6 junction 38, village on B6542 to right

EATING

BERWICK-UPON-TWEED

MARSHALL MEADOWS COUNTRY HOUSE HOTEL ❀
Berwick-upon-Tweed TD15 1UT
Tel: 01289 331133
Pleasant, attentive staff complement the chef's fine Modern British creations to make dining here an enjoyable occasion. An unusual curry and raisin dinner roll is a tasty introduction to a refreshingly light salmon, langoustine and prawn mousse, followed maybe by moist rack of lamb and a smooth crème brûlée.
🕔 Closed Christmas week
🍴 L from £14.95 (by arrangement only), D from £26, Wine from £13.50
🚭 In dining room
🚗 Just off A1 about 1 mile (1.6km) from Berwick-upon-Tweed

BEVERLEY

THE MANOR HOUSE ❀ ❀
Northlands, Walkington HU17 8RT
Tel: 01482 881645
In the restaurant of this popular country house a delightful cheese soufflé prepares you for the pleasure of selecting from the extensive menu, featuring Modern British cuisine with Asian and Pacific Rim influences. Seared calves' liver and lambs' kidneys with colcannon offers a satisfying lead into dessert, especially delicious pastry encasing a selection of fresh fruits, but any number of well-presented alternatives will satisfy. No children under 12.

🕔 Closed Sun, 24 Dec–2 Jan and public holidays
🍴 L from £10, D from £14, Wine from £13.50
🚭 In restaurant
🚗 4 miles (6.5km) southwest of Beverley off B1230.

BLACKBURN

MILLSTONE AT MELLOR ❀ ❀
Church Lane, Mellor BB2 7JR
Tel: 01254 813333
www.shireinns.co.uk
This old coaching inn in the beautiful Ribble Valley retains a feel of period authenticity while conjuring up surprisingly sophisticated Modern British food. There is a healthy nod to local traditions and local

A touch of Gallic elegance at Altrincham's Juniper

produce still features in dishes like chicken and black pudding terrine, or braised Pendle lamb shank in a port wine jus.
🕔 12–2.15, 6.30–9.15
🍴 L from £16.95, D from £25.95, Wine from £13.95
🚭 No smoking in dining room
🚗 Call for directions

BOLTON ABBEY

DEVONSHIRE ARMS COUNTRY HOUSE HOTEL ❀ ❀ ❀
Bolton Abbey BD23 6AJ
Tel: 01756 710441
There is nothing starchy about the elegant Burlington Restaurant at this beautiful hotel (▷ 393), nor indeed its modern Anglo-French cuisine. You can glide effortlessly from pan-seared langoustine with artichoke pannacotta and a shellfish dressing, to pumpkin and truffle risotto, before lingering over a tantalizing dessert menu.
🕔 12–2.30, 7–10; closed L Mon–Sat
🍴 L from £15, D from £25, Wine from £11.95 (in Brasserie). D from £58 in restaurant
🚭 In restaurant
🚗 On B6160 to Bolton Abbey 230m (250 yards) north of junction with A59 roundabout junction
🚆 Ilkley 4.5 miles (7km)

DURHAM

BISTRO 21 ❀
Aykley Heads House, Aykley Heads DH1 5TS
Tel: 0191 3844354
Bistro 21 is an intimate, laidback dining experience in a restored farmhouse with a loyal, local following. The list of daily specials is announced on a blackboard. A modern take on traditional English cooking, using simple combinations of fresh flavours. Children are welcome.
🕔 12–2, 7–10.25; closed Sun, 25 Dec
🍴 L from £13, D from £25, Wine from £12.50
🚭 In restaurant
🚗 Off B6532 from Durham centre; pass County Hall on right, turn right at double roundabout into Aykley Heads
🚆 Durham

SEVEN STARS INN
High Street, North Shincliffe DH1 2NU
Tel: 0191 3848454
A little gem tucked away on the edge of picturesque Shincliffe, this quaint inn remains virtually unaltered since 1724. Expect imaginative British cuisine with exotic influences: typically, open ravioli of monkfish rounded off with mixed summer fruit crumble. No children.
🕔 Mon–Sat 11.30–11, Sun 12–10.30
🍴 L from £12, D from £18, Wine from £10
🚭 In restaurant
🚗 Telephone for directions

EATING

EAST WITTON

THE BLUE LION
East Witton, near Leyburn DL8 4SN
Tel: 01969 624273
www.thebluelion.co.uk
There is excellent food available in the bar of this traditional pub, but serious diners reserve ahead for the dining room, where dishes include duck and Toulouse sausage served with pancetta and mashed potato.
🕐 11–11 Mon–Sat , 12–10.30 Sun
🍴 L from £16, D from £25, Wine from £11.50
🚭
🚗 Telephone for directions

HALIFAX

SHIBDEN MILL INN ❀❀
Shibden Mill Fold HX3 7UL
Tel: 01422 365840
This 17th-century inn retains much charm and character. A cosy bar and candlelit restaurant attract plenty of drinkers and diners and the chef offers a wide selection of dishes. Interesting starters may be followed by grilled calves' liver, seared salmon fillet with a cider sauce or braised shin of beef with celeriac mash. Lighter meals include scrambled eggs with smoked salmon and baby capers and poached egg and glazed buck rarebit on sun-dried tomato bread. Food can be served outside in the garden.
🕐 12–2, 6–9.30
🍴 L from £8.95, D from £18, Wine from £10.50
🚗 Halifax

HARROGATE

THE BOAR'S HEAD HOTEL ❀❀
Ripley Castle Estate HG3 3AY
Tel: 01423 771888
This converted coaching inn is part of the Ripley Castle estate, owned by the Ingilby family for over 27 generations. By all accounts Lady Ingilby is a rigorous taskmaster and taster, taking a personal interest in the inventive, reliable Modern British menu,

while her husband, Sir Thomas, shows the same interest in assembling the 200-bin wine list. Main courses encompass grilled fillet steak and a selection of vegetarian alternatives, while desserts include steamed Black Forest sponge with sozzled cherries.
🕐 12–2, 7–9.30
🍴 L from £15, D from £30, Wine from £12.95
🚗 On A61 Harrogate–Ripley road, in village centre

HAWORTH

WEAVERS RESTAURANT ❀
15 West Lane BD22 8DU
Tel: 01535 643822

East Witton's Blue Lion offers top-quality pub food

Occupying three village cottages is this restaurant serving traditional but modern British food in this famous literary town (▷ 169). The à la carte and blackboard menus typically include warm shredded duck, venison sausage and black pudding salad, slow-cooked shoulder of Yorkshire lamb (plus vegetarian options), and almond and apricot tart with vanilla ice cream.
🕐 11.30–2.30, 6.30–9; closed L Tue and Sat, D Sun, Mon
🍴 L from £12.95, D from £16.95, Wine from £12.50
🚭 In restaurant
🚗 From A629 take B6142 to Haworth centre by Brontë Museum parking area

HELMSLEY

STAR INN
Harome, Helmsley YO6 5JE
Tel: 01439 770397
Unpretentious, hearty British food cooked with great skill from fine fresh ingredients (much of it home-grown or produced locally to order) is the winning formula here. The thatched 14th-century restaurant/pub off the tourist track serves the same food in a small bar and cosy dining room, each with open fires. A refreshing degree of simplicity is evident in the beetroot and spinach risotto, and well-made puddings include a classic glazed lemon tart with tayberry sauce.
🕐 11.30–3, 6.30–11, dinner Tue–Sun; closed two weeks Jan
🍴 L from £25, D from £35, Wine from £13
🚭 In dining room
🚗 From Helmsley take A170 towards Kirkbymoorside. After 1.5 miles (2.5km) turn right towards Harome. After another 1.5 miles (2.5km) Star Inn is first building on right

KESWICK

THE HORSE AND FARRIER INN
Threlkeld Village CA12 4SQ
Tel: 01768 779688
Popular with fell walkers, this 300-year-old stone inn has traditional bars and dining room. Imaginative dinners include chicken breast with mushroom, bacon and sherry cream sauce on herb risotto. Food is also served on the patio.
🕐 Mon–Sat 11–11, Sun 12–10.30
🍴 L from £13, D from £20, Wine from £9.95
🚭 In dining room
🚗 Telephone for directions

LEEDS

BRASSERIE FORTY FOUR ❀❀
44 The Calls LS2 7EW
Tel: 0113 2343232
This riverside restaurant in a converted grain store attracts interest in its slick, contemporary Mediterranean

EATING

menus. Busy and buzzy Forty Four attracts loyal legions of foodies, but the lunchtime menu also provides a budget option for shoppers. There's a growing global influence on the food as crispy duck won tons vie with mulligatawny or Scottish mussels. Main courses include roasted skate wing with a crust of crab, Parmesan and lemon, a delicate balance of complementary flavours illustrating the skill of the chef.

🕐 12–2, 6–11; closed L Sat, Sun
🍴 L from £12.50, D from £19.95, Wine from £11.20
🚭 No pipes, no cigars
🚗 From Crown Point Bridge turn left past church and left into High Court Road; on river
🚆 Leeds

LIVERPOOL
SIMPLY HEATHCOTES ❀
Beetham Plaza, 25 The Strand L2 0XL
Tel: 0151 2363536
Opposite Liverpool's pier head is this stylish and sophisticated, minimalist designer eaterie serving Modern British cuisine with plenty of twists and specialities from the north of England. Typical dishes might include a starter of goat's cheese hash brown followed by a main course of honey-roast ham served with mustard mash, butter and broad beans and a herb butter sauce. Vegetarian options are available.

🕐 12–2.30, 7–10; closed 25–26 Dec, 1–2 Jan
🍴 L from £27, D from £31, Wine from £12 🚭
🚗 Opposite pier head

MANCHESTER
SIMPLY HEATHCOTES ❀
Jacksons Row, Deansgate M2 5WD
Tel: 0161 8353536
Tucked away in a narrow side street, this modern and spacious restaurant is reached via a sweeping staircase. Keeping to the format of his other brasseries, Paul Heathcote flirts with a menu that includes his signature Modern British dishes such

as black pudding and Goosnargh duckling, along with more contemporary touches. Main courses include a lovely fillet of cod with crispy bacon and red wine reduction, perhaps followed by superb melt-in-the-mouth iced pear parfait with hazelnut wafers and dark chocolate ice cream. A number of starters are also available as main courses.

🕐 12–2.30, 7–10; closed 25–26 Dec, 1–2 Jan
🍴 L from £14, D from £20, Wine from £13.95
🚭
🚗 M62 junction 17. Restaurant at top of Deansgate
🚆 Manchester Victoria

Café 21 brings a French-café style to Newcastle upon Tyne

NEWCASTLE UPON TYNE
CAFÉ 21 ❀
Queen Street, Newcastle Quayside
NE1 3UG
Tel: 0191 2220755
This stylish eaterie with French café service is located underneath the Tyne Bridge. Blackboards list the day's menu of Modern British dishes and special wine offers, and well-trained staff give informed advice on both food and drink. It is busy day and night offering fishcakes with buttered spinach, parsley cream and chips, or baked fillet of pork with sage and onion mousse and black pudding fritters.

🕐 12–2.30, 6–10.30; closed Christmas
🍴 L from £14, D from £25, Wine from £13
🚗 Telephone for directions

PICKERING
FOX AND HOUNDS COUNTRY INN ❀
Main Street, Sinnington, York YO62 6SQ
Tel: 01751 431577
It always inspires confidence to see a restaurant that is used by local people for both eating and drinking. The welcoming atmosphere of the bar extends into the more formal dining area, where you can experience not just good, hearty cooking (including vegetarian options), but also some delicate intricacies of flavours and styles. Modern and traditional British dishes are at ease side by side on this menu.

🕐 12–2, 6.30–9
🍴 L from £13, D from £25, Wine from £11.75
🚗 In centre of Sinnington, 274m (900ft) off A170 between Pickering and Helmsley

ROSEDALE ABBEY
THE MILBURN ARMS HOTEL ❀
Rosedale Abbey, Pickering YO18 8RA
Tel: 01751 417312
www.milburnarms.co.uk
The Priory Restaurant in this charming country-house hotel (▷ 396) is known for its quality cuisine. Pan-fried duck's livers and a medley of seafood sharpen the palate for local roast pheasant, grilled halibut steak and roast rack of Yorkshire lamb. Food can be served outside in the garden.

🕐 11.30–3, 6.30–11; closed 25 Dec
🍴 L from £15, D from £25, Wine from £13.50
🚗 A170 west from Pickering, right at Rosedale sign then 7 miles (11km) north

EATING

SHEFFIELD

THE FAT CAT
23 Alma Street S3 8SA
Tel: 0114 2494801
This consistently top-rated pub is a place of quiet relaxation free from music and slot machines, with good home-cooked food and fine beers. The food always includes a variety of vegetarian and gluten-free fare as well as daily specials. Typical dishes include tikka mushrooms with rice and nutty parsnip pie, followed by jam roly-poly.

🕐 Mon–Sat 12–3, 5.30–11, Sun 12–3, 7–10.30; closed 25–26 Dec
🍽 L from £3.50, D from £3.50, Wine from £8.20
🚉 Sheffield

WARENFORD

WARENFORD LODGE
Warenford, Belford NE70 7HY
Tel: 01668 213453
This 200-year-old coaching inn is a popular venue for both visitors and locals who enjoy the country atmosphere and notable Northumbrian dishes. You can expect main courses ranging from fillet of beef with Lindisfarne oyster dumplings to a vegetarian option of leek roly-poly with vegetable casserole. Baked lemon pudding served with thick cream is a house speciality, and the Northumberland cheese platter is also noteworthy.

🕐 Tue–Sun 7–11 (10.30 Sun); closed 1 Jan and 25–26 Dec
🍽 D from £16, Wine from £10.80
🚗 Just east off the A1 10 miles (16km) north of Alnwick

WINDERMERE

HOLBECK GHYLL ✿✿✿
Holbeck Lane LA23 1LU
Tel: 01539 432375
www.holbeckghyll.com
Dining is an integral part of the experience at this hotel overlooking Windermere and Langdale Fells. Both the formal and traditional restaurant and the more contemporary terrace provide diners with stunning views. The latter has French doors which open out onto a heated patio. Food is a mixture of classic French and English cooked with skill and precision to create fresh, unfussy dishes with an intense clarity of flavours. Start with roast quail served with onion compote and truffle jus, followed by a fillet of turbot on a beautifully balanced ragout of girolles, bacon, lettuce, potato and celery. Meals are served in a professional manner but without stuffiness. An extensive wine list includes some serious French and Italian heavyweights. A jacket and tie is preferred in the restaurant. No children under eight.

Dine in Georgian surroundings at York Pavilion Hotel

🕐 12.30–2, 7–9.30; closed 5–25 Jan
🍽 L from £22.50, D from £49, Wine from £19.50
🚭 In restaurant
🚗 3 miles (5km) north of Windermere on A591, turn right into Holbeck Lane

THE SAMLING ✿✿✿
Ambleside Road, LA23 1LR
Tel: 015394 31922
www.thesamling.com
Tucked away in a 28ha (70-acre) estate of woodland, meadow and landscaped garden, the Samling is a chic oasis of contemporary cuisine above one of England's loveliest lakes. The ambitious menus ooze creativity with the occasional slice of traditional French cooking. The three-course fixed-price menu is a good place to start, but aspiring gourmets will enjoy the eight-course extravaganza.

🕐 12.30–2, 7–10
🍽 L from £48, D from £48, Wine from £30
🚗 On A591 towards Ambleside, first right after Low Wood Hotel, 2 miles (3.2km) from Windermere town.

YORK

MELTON'S RESTAURANT ✿✿
7 Scarcroft Road YO23 1ND
Tel: 01904 634341
The Modern British cooking at this inviting shop-fronted restaurant has influences from Europe, Asia and North America—buckwheat blinis with beetroot gravadlax and crème fraiche—from the à la carte or set-price lunch/early evening menu. It is a family-run establishment (rather than part of an impersonal chain). Details are impressive, from the varied canapés to the homemade cheese biscuits, and the warm service shows pride in the food.

🕐 12–2, 5.30–10; closed L Mon, Sun, three weeks at Christmas, one week in Aug
🍽 L from £16.50, D from £27, Wine from £13.50
🚭 No pipes, no cigars
🚗 South from city centre across Skeldergate Bridge, opposite Bishopthorpe Road parking area

YORK PAVILION HOTEL ✿✿
45 Main Street, Fulford YO10 4PJ
Tel: 01904 622099
www.yorkpavilionhotel.com
Langton's brasserie, known for its seafood, occupies half a dozen rooms of this hotel. A rustic starter such as grilled peppered goats' cheese with dressed leaves and tapenade oil might be followed by a main of fillet of red mullet with chive and crayfish risotto. The wine list is admirable. Children are welcome.

🕐 12–2, 6.30–9.30
🍽 L from £15, D from £25, Wine from £14
🚗 South from city centre on A19 (Selby), hotel 2 miles (3km) on left

EATING

SCOTLAND

Scotland's high rate of heart disease hides the fact that much of the national cuisine is as healthy as it is tasty. Seafood–shellfish, halibut, cod, herring and haddock–is landed at many fishing towns and villages, although the best-known fish is salmon. Farmed salmon have superseded wild salmon and are of varying quality. Go for the less intensively farmed specimens.

On land, beef from grass-fed Aberdeen Angus cattle is highly prized, and game, including venison (both wild and farmed), grouse, partridge and pheasant, is widely available during the shooting season. Grouse shooting opens on 12 August, the 'Glorious Twelfth'.

The Scottish diet has typically made the most of sometimes meagre ingredients: haggis, after all, is a sheep's stomach stuffed with offal, oatmeal and onion and served with mashed turnips (neeps) and potatoes (tatties).

Bakeries produce shortbread, oatcakes, Dundee cake and drop scones, which all accompany a cup of tea successfully.

The best restaurants serving dishes prepared with local Scottish ingredients may be accredited by the Taste of Scotland organization (www.taste-of-scotland.com).

EATING

PRICES AND SYMBOLS

The restaurants are listed alphabetically within each town. The prices are for a two-course lunch (L) and a three-course à la carte dinner (D). Prices in pubs are for a two-course lunchtime bar meal and a two-course dinner in the restaurant, unless specified otherwise.

For a key to the symbols, ▷ 2.

ACHILTIBUIE

THE SUMMER ISLES HOTEL
❀ ❀

Ullapool IV26 2YG
Tel: 01854 622282

In summer, long daylight hours afford excellent views of the islands late into the evening from this spectacularly located hotel. The style is broadly European, so a meal from the daily changing five-course menu could include goats' cheese crouton on black olive tapenade followed by Summer Isles langoustine and spiny

lobsters with hollandaise sauce. After this, roast rib of Aberdeen Angus beef with mushrooms, red onion and red wine sauce then a selection from the sweet trolley. No children under six.

⏰ 12.30–2, D at 8; closed mid-Oct to Easter

🍴 L from £26 D from £47, Wine from £15

🚭 In dining room

🚌 10 miles (16km) north of Ullapool. Turn left off A835 on to single-track road. 15 miles (24km) to Achiltibuie. Hotel 90m (100 yards) after post office on left

APPLECROSS

APPLECROSS INN
Shore Street IV54 8LR
Tel: 01520 744262
A traditional white-painted inn on the shore of Applecross Bay. The lively kitchen staff have the pick of the rich local produce to create some stunning dishes, including seafood, Aberdeen Angus steaks and game. Favourites include king scallops in garlic butter with crispy bacon on rice, and fresh monkfish and squat lobster in a rich prawn sauce on home-made tagliatelle. Meat-eaters will relish the Applecross venison casserole with braised red cabbage on apple and wholegrain mustard mash, and to finish try raspberry cranachan or cardamom pannacotta.
🕐 11–11 Mon–Sat , 2.30–11 Sun (12.30–7, Sun, Dec–end Jan)
🍴 L from £12, D from £18, Wine from £10
🪑 In dining room
🚗 From Lochcarron to Kishorn, then left on to unclassifed road to Applecross over 'Bealach Na Ba'

BANCHORY

BANCHORY LODGE HOTEL ❀
AB31 5HS
Tel: 01330 822625
Cooking is traditional and sound at this 16th-century coaching inn (▷ 399), relying on quality ingredients, such as Aberdeen Angus beef, with complementary saucing and garnishing.
🕐 12–2, 6–9
🍴 Bar L from £6, D from £50, Wine from £12.50
🪑 In dining room
🚗 Off A93 18 miles (29km) west of Aberdeen

EDINBURGH

BLUE BAR CAFÉ ❀
10 Cambridge Street EH1 2ED
Tel: 0131 2211222
This modern brasserie goes from strength to strength with a menu that is flexible, good value and imaginative. Lunch could be as simple as a crayfish sandwich or a bowl of white bean and chorizo soup. A more substantial meal would be carpaccio of beef with Parmesan followed by corn-fed chicken with aromatic leek risotto and bacon dressing. Deftly prepared desserts such as chocolate tart with caramelized oranges also feature.
🕐 12–3, 6–11; closed Sun, 25–26 Dec
🍴 L from £9.95, D from £18, Wine from £12.95
🪑 Section
🚗 From Princes Street turn into Lothian Road second left, first right, above the Traverse Theatre

Andrew Fairlie at Gleneagles enjoys a prestigious setting

OFF THE WALL RESTAURANT ❀❀
105 High Street, Royal Mile EH1 1SG
Tel: 0131 558 1497
This Royal Mile restaurant has an uncomplicated approach to cuisine: no fussiness or unnecessary flourishes, just perfectly prepared food that speaks for itself. The décor's based on the same mantra of simplicity. Expect modern cooking made from the finest Scottish ingredients: Beef fillet, perhaps, with red cabbage, port sauce and buttery truffle mash; or venison with celeriac and a chocolate sauce. And as befits its name, Off the Wall delivers a few unexpected combinations—squab pigeon with black

SPECIAL IN AUCHTERARDER

ANDREW FAIRLIE AT GLENEAGLES ❀❀❀
Gleneagles PH3 1NF
Tel: 01764 694267
www.gleneagles.com
Applaud Andrew Fairlie's bold move in taking his talents to such a revered institution as Gleneagles. He created a totally new restaurant in an area of the hotel previously used as a champagne bar. This is an evenings-only venue with pitch-black walls punctuated by paintings and dramatic lighting. There is an element of theatre at work with an earthy dish of pan-fried langoustines and shellfish cappucino having the cloche removed at the table to reveal a rich, aromatic foam. Staff are young, knowledgeable and quick to enthuse about the cooking, which is neat, unpretentious and often inspired.
🕐 7–10 D only; closed Sun, Jan
🍴 D from £60, Wine from £25
🪑 In dining room
🚗 Signposted from A9
🚗 Gleneagles

pudding and orange sauce, for instance. Vegetarian options available on request.
🕐 12–2, 6–10; closed Sun, 25–26 Dec, 1–2 Jan
🍴 L from £16.50, D from £38, Wine from £13.95
🪑 Section
🚗 On Royal Mile near John Knox House. Entrance via stairway next to Baillie Fyfes (first floor)

STAC POLLY ❀
8–10 Grindlay Street EH3 9AS
Tel: 0131 229 5405
Two low-ceilinged rooms make for an intimate atmosphere in this charming restaurant in the heart of the city with its cream parchment walls, red carpet and tartan-covered chairs. Modern Scottish cuisine dominates the menu, for example baked

RESTAURANT MARTIN WISHART ※※※
54 The Shore, Leith EH6 6RA
Tel: 0131 553 3557

Serious French staff are intent on communicating their passion for food and wine. This is sophisticated territory. There's a juggernaut of a carte with enough eye-catching flair, luxury and creativity to compete with any national restaurant. Terrine of confit duck, foie gras with sweet and sour pear, duck bonbon and walnut toast is a flawlessly executed dish, while fillet of Buccleuch beef, confit of bone marrow, celeriac puree, beignets of salsify and *marchand de vin* sauce is similarly precise. Smart dress is preferred.

🕐 12–2, 7–10; closed L Sat, Sun–Mon, 25 Dec
🍽 L from £20.50, D from £45, Wine from £19.50
🚗 Telephone for directions

supreme of Scottish salmon served with braised leeks, bacon dumplings and a lemon butter sauce. Desserts, and the wine list, are appealing.

🕐 12–2, 6–11; closed L Sat and Sun
🍽 L from £14.95, D from £30, Wine from £14.95
🚭 No pipes, no cigars
🚗 In town centre, beneath Castle, near Lyceum

GLASGOW

THE BUTTERY ※※
652 Argyle Street G3 8UF
Tel: 0141 221 8188

The Buttery is something of a hidden gem. The menu features wild boar with creamed, apple-scented barley, iced fudge and marshmallow parfait. Check directions before you set off.

🕐 12–2, 7–10
🍽 L £16, D £38, Wine from £16
🚗 From roundabout at end of Elderslie Street, take left. 600m (620 yards) on left down Argyle Street.

SHISH MAHAL ※
60–68 Park Road G4 9JF
Tel: 0141 339 8256

Fast and friendly restaurant cooking meals in the classic Pakistani tradition. Black-clad waiters serve a selection of lamb favourites like kashmiri, rogan josh and bhoona, along with baltis in cast-iron bowls, a wonderful pakora medley featuring fish, chicken and vegetable, a delicious tarka daal, and freshly baked naan bread. Reservation essential.

🕐 12–2, 5–11; closed L Sun
🍽 L from £5.50, D from £12.95, Wine from £9.95
🍴 In dining room
🚇 Glasgow Charing Cross

Modern Scottish cuisine in the heart of Edinburgh at Stac Polly

UBIQUITOUS CHIP ※※
12 Ashton Lane G12 8SJ
Tel: 0141 334 5007

No trip to Glasgow would be complete without a visit to this city institution to sample some fine, Modern Scottish cuisine, which applies a modern slant to original and traditional recipes. Just stepping inside the glass-roofed, green leafy courtyard provides a special experience after the busy streets of Glasgow. Diners can choose from several menu options, all of which successfully pay homage to Scotland's fine fresh produce and national specialities. So expect to find such things as free-range Perthshire pork,

braised for 36 hours with truffle oil and served with leeks and basil mashed potatoes.

🕐 12–2.30, 6.30–11; closed 25 Dec, 1 Jan
🍽 L from £22, D from £39, Wine from £14.95
🚇 In the West End of Glasgow off Byres Road. Beside Hillhead underground station

INNERLEITHEN

TRAQUAIR ARMS HOTEL
Traquair Road EH44 6PD
Tel: 01896 830229

The food at this traditional inn (▷ 401) has a distinctive Scottish flavour with dishes of Finnan savoury, salmon with ginger and coriander (cilantro), and fillet of beef Traquair. A selection of omelettes, salads and baked potatoes is also available.

🕐 Daily 11am–midnight; closed 25–26 Dec, 1 Jan. Restaurant: daily 12–9
🍽 L from £12, D from £20, Wine from £11
🍴 In restaurant
🚗 6 miles (9.5km) east of Peebles on A72. Hotel 90m (100 yards) from junction with B709

INVERNESS

BUNCHREW HOUSE HOTEL ※※
Bunchrew IV3 8TA
Tel: 01463 234917

This hotel's (▷ 401) well-proportioned Classical dining room looks out across the Beauly Firth. Despite the romantic location, there is nothing whimsical about the food or the dedication to combining quality produce with sound cooking practices. Expect west coast crab cake with braised scallops, roast loin of west Highland lamb, and caramelized lemon tart with an Armagnac sauce.

🍽 12.30–1.45, 7–9.15; closed 24–26 Dec
🍽 L from £20, D from £35.50, Wine from £13.50
🍴 In dining room
🚗 2.5 miles (4.5km) from Inverness on A862 towards Beauly

EATING

ISLAY, ISLE OF

THE HARBOUR INN ❀ ❀
The Square, Bowmore PA43 7JR
Tel: 01496 810330
This lovely old hotel (▷ 401) overlooks Loch Indall and houses an elegant restaurant specializing in 'Tastes of Islay'. These might include pheasant, partridge and woodcock in various guises along with the finest local fish—Loch Gruinart oysters, perhaps, or a special recipe fish chowder. Many dishes are paired with whiskies from the distilleries on the island.

🕐 12–2.30, 6–9; closed L Sun, 25 Dec, 1 Jan
🍽 L £12.50, D from £25, Wine from £11.65
🚫 In dining room
🚌 Bowmore is situated 8 miles (13km) from the ports of Port Ellen and Port Askaig

KILCHRENAN

ARDANAISEIG HOTEL ❀ ❀
PA35 1HE
Tel: 01866 833333
www.ardanaiseig.com
This old country house hotel (▷ 401) has its own herb garden, helping to enhance the predominantly Scottish-led ingredients and flavours, particularly seafood, in the restaurant. A set menu might feature Inverawe smoked trout with potato salad, trout caviar and herb oil, to be followed by mains such as herb crusted saddle of lamb with Provençale vegetables and tomato and cumin sauce. The wine list is impressive. No children under seven.

🕐 12.30–2, 7–9; closed 2 Jan–10 Feb
🍽 L from £12, D (6 courses) from £42, Wine from £18
🚫 In dining room
🚌 Take A85 to Oban. At Taynuilt turn left on to B845 towards Kilchrenan. In Kilchrenan turn left by pub. Hotel in 3 miles (5km)

KIRKCUDBRIGHT

SELKIRK ARMS HOTEL ❀ ❀
Old High Street DG6 4JG
Tel: 01557 330402
www.selkirkarmshotel.co.uk
The restaurant in this comfortable hotel (▷ 401) conjures up some innovative, Modern British cooking with creative flavour combinations such as gateaux of prawns and cream cheese on a pear salad with a red pepper sauce and saddle of venison on a confit of vegetables served with a juniper reduction to follow. Local produce, particularly seafood, puts in a regular appearance on the menu, and there's a good-value selection

Fine local seafood at the Isle of Islay's Harbour Inn

of wines as well as an extensive range of malt whiskies to sample.

🕐 7–9.30
🍽 L from £12, D from £25, Wine from £12.50
🚫 In dining room
🚌 5 miles (8km) south of A75 junction with A711

ORKNEY ISLANDS

CREEL RESTAURANT ❀ ❀
Front Road, St. Margaret's Hope KW17 2SL
Tel: 01856 831311
There's a warm welcome at this waterfront restaurant. Simple use of fresh local produce, particularly fish and seafood, ensures honest, flavoursome fare. Begin with

velvet crab bisque or maybe steamed lemon sole. Sea scallops and roasted monkfish tails served with leeks, fresh ginger and beans or grilled chicken fillet with roasted red pepper marmalade could follow. Strawberry shortcake, pannacotta, or possibly chocolate mascarpone torte will leave you happily satisfied with just enough room for coffee with handmade chocolates and fudge.

🕐 D only, 6.45–9; closed Jan–end Mar, Nov
🍽 D from £30, Wine from £11
🚫 In dining room
🚌 13 miles (20km) south of Kirkwall. On A961 on waterfront in village

PEAT INN

THE PEAT INN ❀ ❀ ❀
Peat Inn, KY15 5LH
Tel: 01334 840206
www.thepeatinn.co.uk
Using the very best Scottish produce, this country inn serves up the highest-quality French-infused cuisine. There's a great tasting menu and the à la carte is of a manageable size to try cassoulet of lamb, pork and duck, or fillet of halibut on a lobster risotto. The fixed-price lunch is very good value and the wine list is like a taster's guide to French wine.

🕐 12.30–2, 7–10; closed Sun–Mon, 25 Dec, 1 Jan
🍽 L (3 courses fixed price) £22, D fixed price £32, Wine from £18
🚌 At junction of B940/B941, 6 miles (9.2km) Southwest of St. Andrews.

PERTH

LET'S EAT ❀ ❀
77–79 Kinnoull Street PH1 5EZ
Tel: 01738 643377
Close to the River Tay in the centre of town, this comfortable establishment appeals to a wide audience and has built up a good reputation for its light, modern bistro food. A team of competent staff provide polite, understated service of dishes like a simply prepared and

EATING

well-balanced fillet of halibut with Skye langoustines, Glamis sea kale, asparagus and a prawn essence, and a divine dessert of Valrhona chocolate tart with a white chocolate sorbet. The wine list offers plenty of choice from new and old world regions, as well as good-value house wines.

🕐 12–2, 6.30–9.45; closed Sun, Mon; two weeks Jan, two weeks Jul

🍽 L from £13.95, D from £22.50, Wine from £12.50

🪑 In dining room

🚗 On corner of Kinnoull Street and Atholl Street, close to North Inch

ST. ANDREWS

THE INN AT LATHONES ❀ ❀
Largoward KY9 1JE
Tel: 01334 840494

Full of character and individuality, this lovely country inn has a colourful, cosy restaurant. Select from one of three menus—including a seven-course delicacy option—all offering Modern Scottish and European cuisine. Good quality raw ingredients tell in the tartare of salmon starter and again in the rib-eye of mature Glenfarg Angus beef with a Lagavulin, smoked bacon and wild mushroom sauce. Thick chips cooked in beef dripping deserve a mention too. Balance your cholesterol intake with a simple red berry soup to finish.

🕐 12–2.30, 6–9.30; closed Christmas, two weeks Jan

🍽 L from £14.50, D from £27.50, Wine from £12.50

🪑 In dining room

🚗 5 miles (8km) south of St. Andrews on A915. In 0.5 mile (800m) before Largoward on left just after hidden dip

ST. MONANS

THE SEAFOOD RESTAURANT ❀ ❀
16 West End KY10 2BX
Tel: 01333 730327
www.theseafoodrestaurant.com

So modest is the entrance to this restaurant that you could easily miss it, but let the sea

wall be your guide and you won't go wrong. The cooking style is fashionably modern, and a penchant for contrasting flavours and textures results in some dazzling collaborations: A starter salad of lobster, langoustine and mango with radish shoots, mizuna, basil purée and gazpacho avoids going an ingredient too far, as does baked fillet of halibut with shiitake mushrooms, asparagus, crushed potatoes and a garlic and herb butter. Adding immeasurably to the dining experience are the great sea views from this simple yet elegant restaurant. There are no vegetarian dishes available.

Cutting-edge cuisine at
St. Monans' Seafood Restaurant

The restaurant was the AA's Scottish Seafood Restaurant of the Year for 2003.

🕐 12–2.30, 6–9.30; closed Mon, D Sun, 25–26 Dec, 1–2 Jan

🍽 L from £16, D from £30, Wine from £18

🪑 In dining room

🚗 Take A959 from St. Andrews to Anstruther then head west on A917 through Pittenweem. In St. Monans go to harbour, then right

SKYE, ISLE OF

THE THREE CHIMNEYS ❀ ❀ ❀
Colbost IV55 8ZT
Tel: 01470 511258

Situated at the end of the island, overlooking Loch Dunvegan. Fish and shellfish naturally feature heavily but

they don't dominate a menu that is defined by the use of quality produce. Starters include Loch Dunvegan langoustines with salad leaves and herbs from Glendale and pan-fried pigeon breast on pearl barley risotto. Lobster bisque could serve as the definitive version of the dish with fathom-deep flavours and satisfying chunks of lobster meat. Much praise is also due for west coast halibut, startlingly white with an accompanying lobster ravioli and basil butter sauce. Desserts hold their own with accomplished efforts like brioche bread-and-butter pudding with Seville orange anglaise. A very special place.

🕐 12.30–2, 6.30–9.30; closed L Sun; three weeks Jan

🍽 L from £18.50, D from £45, Wine from £18

🪑 In dining room

🚗 From Dunvegan take B884 to Glendale

SWINTON

WHEATSHEAF ❀ ❀
Main Street TD11 3JJ
Tel: 01890 860257
www.wheatsheaf-swinton.co.uk

Overlooking the village green, this country inn serves above-average food. There are two dining areas—the original dining room and a pine sun lounge. Service is relaxed, but efficient and Modern British cuisine uses fresh local produce cooked to order. The lunch menu changes daily and offers very good choice and value. The dinner menu is equally appealing, with breast of wild wood pigeon on a medallion of Scotch beef fillet with black pudding in madeira sauce, for instance, or fillet of salmon on a crayfish, tomato and coriander (cilantro) sauce.

🕐 12–2.15, 6–9; closed Mon (except residents), D Sun

🍽 L from £10, D from £20, Wine from £11.95

🪑 In dining room

🚗 On A6112, halfway between Duns and Coldstream

EATING

STAYING IN BRITAIN

If you've ever wanted to stay in a castle, a beachside cottage or on a working farm, then Britain is the place to do it. The variety is staggering, with something for every budget. We've selected some of the country's best hotels, inns and bed-and-breakfast guesthouses. Below is a guide to further options. Most local Tourist Information Centres will have a bed-booking service–useful for last-minute hunts for rooms. The VisitBritain organization makes lists of accommodation widely available.

BED-AND-BREAKFAST

Bed-and-breakfast seems to be a particularly British arrangement: you stay overnight in somebody's house in your own room, with breakfast included in the price. There are thousands of bed-and-breakfasts across the country. Small guesthouses may have just one room for guests, others up to six or seven rooms. Prices compare favourably with hotels, but the real advantage of bed-and-breakfast is that guests enjoy an intimate hospitality that hotels cannot match. They are a good way of getting inside knowledge on a place and are especially useful in more remote areas. Remember that even if you have reserved accommodation for several days, hosts will usually expect you to be out of the house for most of the day. Prices range from £30 per night to more than £100. We've selected some of the best bed-and-breakfasts in all price brackets, but a local Tourist Information Centre will have a complete list. You will need to reserve in advance during peak periods and local events. Look out for quirky properties such as Lavenham Priory (▷ 379); chapels, windmills, barns and listed (landmark) buildings have all been converted to bed-and-breakfast properties.

BOTHIES

Out in the hills of Scotland, northern England and Wales, there is a network of small buildings (about 100)–called bothies–available to hillwalkers. Few are mapped or signposted and they are maintained by volunteers from the Mountain Bothies Association (www.mountainbothies.org.uk) so some may be on the verge of collapse while others may have beds and a fireplace. Walkers can stay the night for free, although a small donation is appreciated. If you're planning to do some walking in Scotland, northern England or Wales, it is a good idea to ask about bothies close to your route in a local Tourist Information Centre.

CAMPING

Since most land is privately owned in Britain, you cannot pitch a tent just anywhere. And it is illegal to camp in national parks and nature reserves. Instead, there are designated campsites, most with facilities such as running water, some with shops and laundries. These are often signposted from roads. Expect to spend between £2 and £10 per night. Investing in a camping stove (available from outdoor activity shops) is a good idea since open fires are not permitted. You may have to share the site with caravans (trailer houses). The Camping and Caravanning Club (tel: 024 7669 4995; www.campingandcaravanningclub. co.uk) recommends camp (and caravan) sites and can provide advice on camping (and caravanning).

CARAVANNING

Caravans and camper vans (RVs) remain a widespread feature of Britain's roads in summer, to the chagrin of some other motorists. There are numerous caravan parks, often close to seaside resorts. The Caravan Club (tel: 0800 521161, www.caravanclub.co.uk) recommends certain caravan sites and offers advice on travelling in Britain with a caravan.

FARM STAYS

Staying on a farm is an increasingly popular form of accommodation with several advantages. Food is often fresh, filling and wholesome, the rural location gives an insight into life in Britain's countryside and children often find farms more interesting than hotels. Many farms have diversified and will also offer activities to guests. Accommodation may be either on a bed-and-breakfast basis, or self-catering. Farms accredited by VisitBritain are found at Farm Stay UK (tel: 01271 336141; www.farmstayuk.co.uk).

STAYING

HOME EXCHANGE AGENCIES

Homeowners in Britain interested in swapping houses with families abroad for holidays register with home exchange agencies. They are predominantly internet-based and the leading agencies include: www.gti-home-exchange.com, www.homelink.org.uk and www.homebase-hols.com. It may be a cost-effective system, but it requires careful research.

HOSTELLING

There are more than 300 youth hostels in Britain.

where hotels have extra facilities or activities available, such as a spa, gym, swimming pool or sports.

Most hotels will serve meals throughout the day. In fact, some hotels are better known as restaurants rather than hotels. There are also 'restaurants with rooms.' As the name suggests, these are restaurants which also have a handful of rooms available for guests. They are usually found outside cities, and mean that diners don't have to drive home after their meals. A good example is Raymond Blanc's Le Manoir Aux Quat' Saisons (▷ 379).

If you are doing a lot of travel by car, you are

Those that are members of the Youth Hostels Association (YHA; tel: 0870 770 8868, www.yha.org.uk) and the Scottish Youth Hostels Association (SYHA; tel: 01786 891400, www.syha.org.uk) will be affiliated to Hostelling International (HI), but there are also independent hostels. For people living in Britain annual membership of the YHA is £15.50 (under 26s £10); for the SYHA £6 (under 18s £2.50). For all ages for those from outside Britain annual membership of Hostelling International is £10. You don't have to be a member of the YHA or SYHA to stay at their hostels—for £3 extra per night you can stay at a YHA hostel and for £1 extra you can stay at a SYHA hostel, or you can become a member at the hotel. Prices are usually lower than £20 per night and standards are generally good but hostels remain the domain of the budget traveller.

HOTELS

Britain has an enormous choice of hotels: stylish town houses, grand country houses, old coaching inns, modern conversions, roadside lodges, five-star international hotel chains and more. It's a competitive business so look out for late deals on accommodation. Some hotels, especially the big chains in cities, rely on business guests during the week and may offer discounted rooms at the weekend to fill the establishment.

Hoteliers are also well informed on ways of parting guests from their money. It is common for hotels to charge extra for items from the mini-bar; prices are often significantly higher than they might be from the bar downstairs. Similarly, if you use the phone line in your room, for calls or internet access, expect to pay higher charges. Check in advance what the rates are, rather than have an expensive surprise when you check out. Food ordered by room service also attracts a supplement. Porters and chambermaids in hotels should be tipped about £1. We have indicated

likely to use the chain hotels beside roads and in motorway service areas. They may be impersonal and bland, but are also, usually, clean, convenient and economical.

PUBS

If you can tolerate the possibility of a little late-night noise, pubs can be a convenient source of accommodation. Many of the pubs in our listings, especially those in the countryside, will have one or more bedrooms available to travellers. Rates are generally reasonable, typically £30 per night, and accommodation is often, but not always, on a bed-and-breakfast basis.

SELF-CATERING

Many British holidaymakers prefer staying in a cottage, house or apartment and catering for themselves. It is often less expensive than staying at a hotel.

There are thousands of properties available, but the best of those in holiday hotspots, such as Cornwall and the Lake District, are often reserved very far ahead. Reservations are usually taken by the week, although in the low season shorter stays may be possible. VisitBritain approves many properties and local Tourist Information Centres will have lists of available properties. Several specialist agencies manage self-catering properties. A travel agent will have brochures for reliable companies, such as Rural Retreats (tel: 01386 701177, www.ruralretreats.co.uk), managing self-catering properties in Britain.

Both The National Trust (tel: 0070 458 4422 www.nationaltrustcottages.co.uk) and The Landmark Trust (tel: 01628 825928, www.landmarktrust.co.uk) offer interesting properties for let. The Landmark Trust specializes in conversions of historic buildings such as forts. The National Trust has holiday cottages at many of its sites, as well as less expensive properties elsewhere.

MAJOR HOTEL CHAINS

Company logo	Company statement	Number of hotels	Telephone number and website
Best Western	Britain's largest group has around 350 independently owned and managed hotels. Buildings may be modern or traditional and many have leisure facilities and rosette awards	350	08457 737373 www.bestwestern.co.uk
Campanile	Campanile offers modern accommodation for the budget market	17	020 8326 1500 www.campanile.fr
COPTHORNE	Part of the Millennium and Copthorne group, comprising 11 four-star hotels in provincial locations and London	11	0800 414741 www.millenniumhotels.com
	A large group of three-star hotels ranging from rural to city centre locations across the UK	72	0845 300 2000 www.corushotels.co.uk
DE VERE HOTELS Hotels of character, run with pride	De Vere comprises 21 four- and five-star hotels, which specialize in leisure stays, golf and conferences	21	0870 606 3606 www.devereonline.co.uk
Express by Holiday Inn	Express by Holiday Inn offers superior budget accommodation with complimentary breakfast at over 80 modern hotels in the UK	80	0800 434040 www.ichotelsgroup.com
Holiday Inn HOTELS · RESORTS	The internationally known group offers a wide range of hotels throughout the UK	80	0800 405060 www.ichotelsgroup.com
ibis Accor hotels	Ibis is a growing chain of modern travel accommodation with properties across the UK	43	0870 609 0963 www.ibishotel.com
Innkeeper's Lodge	Travel accommodation from Bass Leisure Retail, featuring comfortable rooms and complimentary breakfast	80	0870 243 0500 www.innkeeperslodge.com
Leisureplex	A group of two-star hotels located in seaside resorts	14	08451 305888 www.alfatravel.co.uk
MACDONALD HOTELS	A large group of predominantly four-star hotels, traditional and modern in style, located across the UK	61	0870 400 9090 www.macdonald-hotels.co.uk
Malmaison HOTELS	A growing brand of three-star city centre hotels	5	020 7479 9512 www.malmaison.com
Marriott HOTELS · RESORTS · SUITES	This international brand offers four-star hotels in primary locations. Most are modern and have leisure facilities; some have a focus on golf	70	0800 221 222 0800 699 996 www.marriott.co.uk
MARSTON HOTELS	A quality independent group of mainly four-star hotels with leisure facilities in primary locations across the UK	11	0845 1300 700 www.marstonhotels.com
NOVOTEL	Part of French group Accor, Novotel provides modern three-star hotels in key locations throughout the UK	29	020 8283 4500 www.novotel.com
premier travel inn	Good quality, modern, budget accommodation. Every Premier Travel Inn has an adjacent licensed family restaurant, often a Barest, Beefeater, Brewer's Fayre, Chef & Brewer, Millers Kitchen or TGI Fridays	450	0870 242 8000 www.premiertravelinn.co.uk
Radisson EDWARDIAN	This high-quality London-based group offers mainly four-star hotels in key locations throughout the capital	11	0800 374411 www.radissonedwardian.com
RELAIS & CHATEAUX	An international consortium of rural, privately owned hotels, mainly in the country house style	23	00 33 1 45 72 96 50 www.relaischateaux.com
Travelodge	Good-quality, modern budget accommodation across the UK. Almost every lodge has an adjacent family restaurant, often a Little Chef, Harry Ramsden's or Burger King	275	08700 850950 www.travelodge.co.uk

STAYING

HOTEL CLASSIFICATION

The Automobile Association (AA) is Britain's leading organization for the classification of hotels and restaurants. All hotels recognized by the AA should have the highest standards of cleanliness, proper records of reservations, give professional service, assist with luggage on request, accept and deliver messages, provide a designated area for dinner (if available) and breakfast with drinks available in a bar or lounge, and provide an early morning call on request.

A guide to some of the general expectations for each star classification is as follows:

★ star: A relatively informal yet competent style of service and an adequate range of facilities, including a television. The majority of bedrooms have a private bath. At least one designated eating area for breakfast and dinner (if available).

★★ stars: As above plus professional management, with at least one restaurant or dining room for breakfast and dinner. Last orders for dinner no earlier than 7pm.

★★★ stars: As above plus direct dial telephones, remote control television, private bath or shower and WC, a wide selection of drinks in the bar and last orders for dinner no earlier than 8pm.

★★★★ stars: As above plus a range of high-quality toiletries and private bath with fixed overhead shower and WC. Uniformed, well-trained staff with additional services, a night porter and a serious approach to cuisine. Well-appointed public areas. Last orders for dinner no earlier than 9pm.

★★★★★ stars: These are the most luxurious hotels, offering extra facilities and services, top-quality rooms and a full concierge service. A wide selection of drinks, including cocktails, is available in the bar, and the restaurant's menu and food should reflect the quality of the hotel. Last orders for dinner no earlier than 10pm.

THE TOP HOTELS

These hotels, identified by open stars (☆), stand out as the very best hotels in Britain and range from large luxury hotels to small country inns.

DIAMOND RATING ◆

Bed-and-breakfast and guesthouse accommodation in the UK is rated for the quality of its operation. This quality is rated with diamond symbols on a rising scale from one to five. The criteria for a higher rating are guest care and quality rather than the choice of extra facilities.

At all grades, guests can expect:

● a prompt and professional check in and out
● comfortable accommodation equipped to modern standards
● regularly changed bedding and towels
● a sufficient hot water supply at all times
● adequate storage, heating and lighting and comfortable seating
● a full English or Continental breakfast

Evening meals may or may not be available.

OPEN DIAMOND RATING ◇

To help readers seek accommodation, the very best establishments in each of the top three quality ratings (five, four and three diamonds) are identified with open diamonds.

The Angel Hotel is one of many in the historic Suffolk town of Lavenham

STAYING

THE WEST COUNTRY

Accommodation in the West Country is evolving, with the arrival of boutique hotels such as the Hotel Barcelona in Exeter (▷ 374) and, due to the downturn in Britain's farming economy, with more farms offering bed-and-breakfast and farm holidays. Accommodation can be reserved long in advance for the school summer holidays in July and August, so make reservations early. Festivals, including the Bath International Music Festival in May and June, the Glastonbury Festival in June and the Cheltenham Festival of Literature in October, can also cause shortages in accommodation.

PRICES AND SYMBOLS

Prices are the starting price for a double room for one night, unless otherwise stated. Breakfast is included unless noted otherwise. All the hotels listed accept credit cards unless otherwise stated. Note that rates vary widely throughout the year.

For a key to the symbols ▷ 2.

BATH

APSLEY HOUSE HOTEL
◆◆◆◆◆

Newbridge Hill, Bath BA1 3PT
Tel: 01225 336966
www.apsley-house.co.uk
Apsley House bed-and-breakfast is conveniently located within walking distance of the heart of the

city. The house is extremely stylish and elegant, and the spacious bedrooms (one with a king-size four-poster bed) have fine views. There's also a bar, lounge and garden. Light suppers are served by prior arrangement. No dogs.

🕑 Closed one week at Christmas
💷 £70
🛏 10 🚭
🚌 On A431, 1 mile (1.6km) west of city
🚇 Bath Spa

THE QUEENSBERRY HOTEL
☆☆☆

Russel Street, Bath BA1 2QF
Tel: 01225 447928
www.thequeensberry.co.uk
This delightful hotel in four town houses is on a quiet street near the city centre. Spacious bedrooms are tastefully furnished, and deep

armchairs, fresh flowers and marble bathrooms add to their appeal. There are comfortable lounges, a small bar and a courtyard garden. The Olive Tree restaurant offers rustic but modern food. Valet parking service. No dogs.

💷 £100
🛏 29 🚭 In restaurant
🚇 Bath Spa

THE WINDSOR HOTEL
★★★★

69 Great Pulteney Street, Bath BA2 4DL
Tel: 01225 422100
www.bathwindsorhotel.com
This Georgian town house is a short, level walk from the heart of town. The historic terraced house has been refurbished to a high standard and furnished with antiques. The restaurant Sakura (▷ 334)

serves authentic Japanese cuisine. No children under 12. No dogs.

🌀 Closed one week at Christmas

💷 £135

🛏 14 🚭

🚗 M4 junction 18 onto A4, turn left onto A36, then turn right at next mini roundabout and take second turning on left for Great Pulteney Street

🚉 Bath Spa

BOURNEMOUTH

HOTEL MIRAMAR ★★★

East Overcliff Drive, East Cliff, Bournemouth BH1 3AL
Tel: 01202 556581
www.miramar-bournemouth.com

This Edwardian hotel has superb views of the sea. Friendly staff provide a relaxing environment. The public areas offer a choice of lounges and there is also a croquet lawn.

💷 £120

🛏 43 🚭 In 10 rooms and in restaurant

🚗 At Wessex Way roundabout turn into St. Pauls Road. Turn right at next roundabout, take third exit at the next, and 2nd exit at next roundabout into Grove Road. Hotel parking 50m (165ft) on right

🚉 Bournemouth

BRADFORD-ON-AVON

BRADFORD OLD WINDMILL

◇◇◇◇◇

4 Masons Lane, Bradford-on-Avon BA15 1QN
Tel: 01225 866842
www.bradfordoldwindmill.co.uk

A unique bed-and-breakfast property, sympathetically restored to retain many original features. Bedrooms are individually decorated and include a number of interesting choices such as a suite with a minstrels' gallery. There's also a comfortable lounge. No children under six, or dogs

🌀 Closed Jan–end Feb and Christmas

💷 £79

🛏 3 🚭

🚗 Enter Bradford on A363; at mini roundabout at Castle pub turn towards town centre. After 50m (55 yards) turn left into private drive immediately beside first roadside house (no sign or number)

BRISTOL

HOTEL DU VIN & BISTRO
★★★★

The Sugar House, Narrow Lewins Mead, Bristol BS1 2NU
Tel: 0117 925 5577
www.hotelduvin.com

The third property in one of Britain's most innovative hotel groups extends the high standards for which the chain is renowned. The hotel is housed in a converted 18th-century sugar refinery. Bedrooms are exceptionally well designed and the hotel provides great facilities with a modern minimalist feel.

💷 £125

🛏 40

Apsley House Hotel, Bath was built for the Duke of Wellington

🚗 From A4 follow signs for city centre. After 400m (450 yards) pass Rupert Street parking (NCP) on right. Hotel on opposite side of road

🚉 Bristol Temple Meads

CALNE

CHILVESTER HILL HOUSE
◆◆◆◆◆

Calne SN11 0LP
Tel: 01249 813981
www.chilvesterhillhouse.co.uk

This elegant Victorian house stands in well-kept grounds. Dr. and Mrs Dilley ensure a warm welcome to their bed-and-breakfast, where bedrooms are spacious and comfortable. A set dinner is available by arrangement. Stables and golf course

available locally. No children under 12. No dogs.

💷 £80

🛏 3 🚭 In dining room

🚗 A4 from Calne towards Chippenham; after 0.5 miles (1km) turn right, marked Bremhill. House immediately on right

🚉 Chippenham

CHELTENHAM

ALIAS HOTEL KANDINSKY
★★★★

Bayshill Road, Montpellier, Cheltenham GL50 3AS
Tel: 01242 527788
www.aliaskandinsky.com

A large, white, Regency villa that blends modern comfort with quirky eclectic decoration. Stylish bedrooms vary in size and have additional facilities such as CD and video players. There are various lounges, a conservatory and the bright Café Paradiso restaurant (▷ 335). Hidden in the cellars is U-bahn, a wonderful 1950s-style cocktail bar.

💷 £95

🛏 48 🚭 4 bedrooms and in restaurant

🚗 From junction 11 of M5 take A40 to town centre. Right at second roundabout, second exit at third roundabout into Bayshill Road. Hotel on corner of Bayshill and Parabola roads

🚉 Cheltenham Spa

CLOVELLY

RED LION HOTEL ★★

The Quay, Clovelly EX39 5TF
Tel: 01237 431237
www.clovelly.co.uk

A charming 18th-century inn enjoying an idyllic location in this historic fishing village. Bedrooms are sizeable and stylish with spectacular views. Fresh local fish, landed alongside the hotel, features on the daily changing menu. The friendly and attentive service contributes to a relaxing and memorable stay.

💷 £93.50

🛏 11 🚭 In restaurant

🚗 Turn off A39 at Clovelly Cross on to B3237. Proceed to bottom of hill, take first turn on left by white rails to harbour

STAYING

DORCHESTER

YALBURY COTTAGE & RESTAURANT ◆◆◆◆◆
Lower Bockhampton DT2 8PZ
Tel: 01305 262382
In the hamlet of Lower Bockhampton, this delightfully attractive 300-year-old thatched property is a charming bed-and-breakfast. Oak-beam ceilings, inglenook fireplaces and stone walls are features of the lounge and restaurant (▷ 336). Comfortable, well-equipped bedrooms overlook either the vivid gardens or adjacent fields.
🌡 £94
🛈 8 🅢
🚗 2 miles (3km) east of Dorchester off A35, past Hardy's Cottage, straight over crossroads, then 400m (450 yards) on left, past red telephone box, opposite village pump
🚉 Dorchester South

EXETER

HOTEL BARCELONA ★★★★
Magdalen Street, Exeter EX2 4HY
Tel: 01392 281000
www.aliasbarcelona.com
Within walking distance of the city centre, the Barcelona provides stylish accommodation with a glamorous atmosphere. Public areas include Café Paradiso, an informal eatery with a varied menu, a nightclub, a range of meeting rooms and a pretty garden terrace ideal for alfresco dining.
🌡 £95
🛈 46 🅢 In restaurant
🚗 From A30 Okehampton follow city centre signs. At Exe Bridges roundabout turn right for city centre up hill over traffic lights. Parking and hotel on right
🚉 Exeter St. David's

THE ROYAL CLARENCE HOTEL ★★★
Cathedral Yard, Exeter EX1 1HD
Tel: 01392 319955
www.royalclarencehotel.co.uk
This hotel is a much-loved Exeter landmark. Bedrooms are characterful, ranging from compact to grand, some with views over the cathedral green. The hotel is known for

the stylish Michael Caines restaurant (▷ 336); for more informal dining, try the café bar or Well House Tavern.
🌡 £130
🛈 55
🅢 In 28 bedrooms and in the restaurant
🚗 From junction 30 of the M5, towards the A379. Follow signs to the city centre and the hotel is opposite the cathedral behind High Street
🚉 Exeter Central

FALMOUTH

DOLVEAN HOTEL ◆◆◆◆◆
50 Melvill Road, Falmouth TR11 4DQ
Tel: 01326 313658
www.dolvean.co.uk
The attractive bedrooms of this bed-and-breakfast are

Dorchester's Yalbury Cottage is in a delightful village setting

individually decorated, with comfortable beds. There is an inviting lounge, and delicious home-cooked breakfasts are served at individual tables in the dining room. No children under 12. No dogs.
🌡 £72
🛈 11 🅢
🚗 On main road to Pendennis Castle and National Maritime Museum

FOWEY

FOWEY HALL ★★★
Hanson Drive, Fowey PL23 1ET
Tel: 01726 833866
www.foweyhall.com
This mansion looks out on to the English Channel from its wonderful setting high above the estuary. The imaginatively

designed bedrooms offer charm, individuality and sumptuous comfort, while beautifully appointed public rooms include the wood-panelled dining room where accomplished cuisine is served (▷ 336). Families are very much a priority here with a range of facilities to entertain children of all ages. Enjoying glorious views, the well-kept grounds have a covered pool and sunbathing area. Also children's play area and table tennis. Bicycle rental available.
🌡 £160
🛈 24 🅢 In restaurant 🚭
🚗 Arriving in Fowey cross mini roundabout into town centre. Pass school on right after 400m (450 yds) turn right into Hanson Drive
🚉 Par

FROME

THE TALBOT 15TH-CENTURY COACHING INN ◆◆◆◆
Selwood Street, Mells BA11 3PN
Tel: 01373 812254
www.talbotinn.com
Located in the peaceful village of Mells near Bath, this 15th-century inn retains many original features. Careful renovation has resulted in well equipped bedrooms (all with private bathroom) and the rustic public areas are full of character and offer a relaxed, informal setting for the enjoyment of good food and real ales.
🌡 £95
🛈 8 🅢
🚗 A36 Bath to Warminster road, right into Frome, A362 to Radstock and follow signs for Mells
🚉 Frome

ISLES OF SCILLY

THE ISLAND ☆☆☆
Tresco TR24 0PU
Tel: 01720 422883
www.tresco.co.uk/holidays/island_hotel.asp
Staff provide a warm welcome and attentive service at this hotel with sea views from most bedrooms and public areas. Bedrooms, some in separate

buildings in the grounds, are brightly furnished and many have a private balcony. There's a fine restaurant (▷ 336), heated outdoor pool, tennis courts, croquet and sea fishing. No dogs.

🕙 Closed Nov–end Feb

💷 £117 including breakfast and dinner

🛏 48 🍴 In restaurant 🛥

🚗 Helicopter service from Penzance to Tresco; hotel in north east of island

LAUNCESTON

STENHILL COUNTRY HOUSE
♦♦♦♦♦

Stenhill Farm, North Petherwin PL15 8NN
Tel: 01566 785686
www.stenhill.com
The perfect place for a relaxing break, Stenhill bed and breakfast is set in extensive grounds, gardens and farmland. This 500-year-old Devon longhouse has been lovingly restored, with authentic features expertly retained. Bedrooms are beautifully decorated, and some feature four-poster beds. When possible, home-grown and local ingredients are included in breakfast (and dinner, by arrangement). Activities include croquet, putting and private fishing. No children or dogs.

💷 £60

🛏 3 🍴

🚗 Leave A30 from Exeter at exit for Launceston, go three-quarters round roundabout to go under A30 bridge. Follow signs for Bude & Tamar Otter Park; Stenhill 0.5 miles (800m) before Otter Park on left

LYME REGIS

ALEXANDRA ★★★

Pound Street, Lyme Regis DT7 3HZ
Tel: 01297 442010
www.lymeregis.co.uk
This welcoming, family-run hotel dates back to 1735. Public areas have ample sitting areas to relax, unwind and enjoy the magnificent views. Imaginative, innovative dishes are served in the elegant restaurant (▷ 336). Bedrooms, which vary in size, have attractive furniture.

🕙 Closed Jan and Christmas

💷 £70

🛏 26 🍴 In restaurant

🚗 From A30 turn on to A35, A358, then take A3052 to Lyme Regis

LYNMOUTH

RISING SUN HOTEL ★★

Harbourside EX35 6EG
Tel: 01598 753223
www.risingsunlynmouth.co.uk
Impossibly romantic smugglers inn. The building is all you'd expect of a 14th-century construction—thatched roof, panelled walls and oak floors—and the location, overlooking the harbour and East Lyn river, is charming. The individually designed

Sleep in a four-poster bed at the Talbot near Frome

bedrooms are located within the inn or in adjoining cottages and have modern facilities. No children under eight. No dogs.

💷 £108

🛏 16

🍴 In 11 bedrooms and in restaurant

🚗 Leave M5 at junction 23, take A39 to Lynmouth, hotel opposite harbour

MARAZION

GODOLPHIN ARMS ★★

Marazion, near Penzance TR17 0EN
Tel: 01736 710202
www.godolphinarms.co.uk
This 170-year-old hotel is right on the water's edge opposite St. Michael's Mount. Stunning views of the Mount are on offer from most of the

bedrooms, which themselves are colourful, comfortable and spacious. There is a good restaurant (▷ 336), and even direct access to a large beach.

🕙 Closed 24–25 Dec

💷 £70

🛏 10 🍴 In restaurant

🚗 From A30 follow signs for Marazion for 1 mile (1.6km) to the hotel, at the end of the causeway to St. Michael's Mount

MOUSEHOLE

OLD COASTGUARD HOTEL
▲ ▲

The Parade TR19 6PR
Tel: 01736 731222
www.oldcoastguardhotel.co.uk
With its stylish bar, brasserie (▷ 336) and sun lounge, this is the perfect base to explore this part of west Cornwall. Above the village, the hotel is set in subtropical gardens leading down to the sea, and most of the bedrooms (21 in all) enjoys spectacular views over Mounts Bay. No dogs.

🕙 Closed 25 Dec

💷 £75

🛏 21 🍴 In restaurant

🚗 A30 to Penzance, take coast road through Newlyn to Mousehole, hotel is first building on left

MULLION

POLURRIAN ★★★

Mullion TR12 7EN
Tel: 01326 240421
www.polurrianhotel.com
This long-established hotel is set in landscaped gardens, 100m (300ft) above the sea. Public areas are spacious and comfortable, and the bedrooms are individually styled. There are well-equipped leisure facilities with sauna, solarium, Jacuzzi, gym, squash and tennis courts, cricket net, and two heated pools (one outdoors). Use of the croquet lawn, putting green, mountain bikes, surf and body boards is welcomed.

💷 £130

🛏 39 🍴 In restaurant 🛥 🎾

🚗 From A30 take A3076 to Truro. Follow signs for Helston on A39 then A394 to The Lizard and Mullion

STAYING

NETHER STOWEY

APPLE TREE ★★
Keenthorne, Nether Stowey, Bridgwater
TA5 1HZ
Tel: 01278 733238
www.appletreehotel.com
This is a convenient and
popular place. Bedrooms have
plenty of character, with
several situated in an adjoining
wing, overlooking the garden.
The friendly owners make
every effort to ensure that
guests have an enjoyable stay.
No dogs.
📳 £68
🛏 14 🚭 In restaurant
🚗 From Bridgwater follow A39
towards Minehead; hotel on left 2 miles
(3km) past Cannington
🚉 Bridgwater

NETTLECOMBE

MARQUIS OF LORNE ◆◆◆◆
Nettlecombe DT6 3SY
Tel: 01308 485236
www.marquisoflorne.com
The Marquis is a 16th-century
farmhouse, set amid lovely
countryside. It's a good base
for exploring the Isle of
Purbeck and the West Dorset
Heritage Coast, and serves
excellent food (▷ 337). There
are seven bedrooms with
private bathrooms. No children
under ten. No dogs.
📳 £70
🛏 7
🚭 In one lounge and in the dining room
🚗 North from Bridport on A3066, after
1.5 miles (2.5km) after mini-roundabout
turn right, through West Milton, straight
over junction (signposted Powerstock),
pub 500m (550 yards) on left

PADSTOW

THE SEAFOOD RESTAURANT
Riverside, Padstow PL28 8BY
Tel: 01841 532700
www.rickstein.com
Rick Stein's Seafood
Restaurant (▷ 337) enjoys an
enviable reputation, and it is
no surprise to discover that
high standards are maintained
in the accommodation here.
Bedrooms are spacious and
comfortable with fine-quality
fixtures and fittings. Additional

rooms are housed close by in
St. Edmunds, where
refurbishment has resulted in
luxurious standards with
much style.
🅲 Closed 1 May and 24–26 Dec
📳 £60
🛏 32 🚭
🚗 Take A389 towards Padstow, after
3 miles (5km) turn right at T-junction. At
signs for Padstow town centre turn right
to centre; restaurant on riverside

ST. PETROC'S HOTEL AND BISTRO ◆◆◆◆◆
4 New Street, Padstow PL28 8EA
Tel: 01841 532700
www.rickstein.com
One of the oldest buildings in
town, this charming bed-and-

*Porlock's Oaks Hotel offers
splendid sea views*

breakfast establishment is
located just up the hill from
the picturesque harbour. Style,
comfort and individuality are
all great strengths here. The
bistro (▷ 337) is very popular.
🅲 Closed 1 May and 24–26 Dec
📳 £115
🛏 10 🚭 In dining room
🚗 Take A30, A38 and A389 towards
Padstow. Continue 3 miles (5km), turn
right at T-junction and follow signs to
Padstow town centre

PORLOCK

THE OAKS HOTEL ☆☆
Porlock TA24 8ES
Tel: 01643 862265
www.oakshotel.co.uk
A charming Edwardian house,
quietly located and in

attractive grounds, with
elevated views across the
village towards the sea.
Bedrooms are thoughtfully
furnished and comfortable,
and the public rooms include
a charming bar and peaceful
drawing room. The dining
room (▷ 338) features a daily
changing menu. No children
under eight.
🅲 Closed Nov–end Mar (except
Christmas and New Year)
📳 £160 (including breakfast and
dinner)
🛏 8 🚭 In bedrooms and in restaurant
🚗 At bottom of Dunstersteepe Road,
on left after entering Porlock from
Minehead

ST. MAWES

IDLE ROCKS ★★★
Harbour Side, St. Mawes TR2 5AN
Tel: 01326 270771
www.richardsonhotels.co.uk
Superbly situated on the
waterside overlooking the
attractive fishing port with
excellent sea views and an
outdoor terrace for use in the
summer. Bedrooms are
individually styled and
furnished to a high standard.
📳 £118
🛏 33 🚭 In restaurant
🚗 Off A390, onto A3078, and 14 miles
(22.5km) to St. Mawes. Hotel on left

TORQUAY

COLINDALE HOTEL ◆◆◆◆◆
20 Rathmore Road, Chelston, Torquay
TQ2 6NY
Tel: 01803 293947
www.colindalehotel.co.uk
This friendly bed-and-
breakfast, set in attractive
gardens, is stylish and elegant,
and service is attentive. Guest
rooms, some of which have
views over Torbay, are well
appointed. Excellent, freshly
cooked dinner (by prior
arrangement, high season
only) and breakfast feature
interesting dishes. No children
under 11. No dogs.
📳 £54
🛏 8
🚭 In bedrooms and in dining room
🚉 Torquay

STAYING

THE SOUTH EAST AND EAST ANGLIA

Cambridge and Oxford are the most popular bases for visitors and it's advisable to reserve accommodation early in these cities. Unsurprisingly they are also the most expensive places to stay. Meanwhile Aldeburgh and Southwold on the east coast have become fashionable destinations for weekending Londoners.

STAYING

ALBURY

THE DRUMMOND ARMS
♦♦♦
The Street, Albury GU5 9AG
Tel: 01483 202039
The old inn is centrally located in this picturesque village, with attractive gardens running down to a small river. Well-appointed and comfortable bedrooms—all with private facilities, and one with a sauna and spa bath—are strengths, while the separate restaurant offers an extensive menu; a good selection of traditional pub food is also available in the popular bar. No children under 14. No dogs.
💷 £65
ⓘ 11 Ⓢ In restaurant
🚗 Off A25 between Guildford and Dorking. Take A248 signed Albury, Godalming; Drummond 1 mile (1.6km) on right

ARUNDEL

NORFOLK ARMS ★★★
High Street, Arundel BN18 9AD
Tel: 01903 882101
www.forestdale.com
This Georgian coaching inn enjoys a superb setting beneath the battlements of Arundel Castle. Bedrooms come in a variety of sizes and styles and all are well equipped. Public areas include two bars, a comfortable lounge and a traditional English restaurant.
💷 £120
ⓘ 34
Ⓢ In 6 bedrooms and in restaurant
🚗 Arundel

BOSHAM

THE MILLSTREAM HOTEL
★★★
Bosham Lane, Bosham PO18 8HL
Tel: 01243 573234
www.millstream-hotel.co.uk

Lying in the idyllic village of Bosham, this attractive hotel provides comfortable, well-equipped and tastefully decorated bedrooms. Many guests regularly return here for the relaxed ambience created by the notably efficient and friendly staff. Public rooms include a cocktail bar opening out onto the garden and a pleasant restaurant where freshly prepared food can be enjoyed. The hotel is close to Chichester harbour and sailing trips can be arranged. No dogs.
💷 £135
ⓘ 35
Ⓢ In bedrooms and in restaurant
🚗 4 miles (6km) west of Chichester on A259, left at Bosham roundabout. After 1 mile (1.6km) turn right at T-junction to church and quay, hotel 0.5 mile (800m) on right

BRANCASTER STAITHE

THE WHITE HORSE ★★

Brancaster Staithe PE31 8BY
Tel: 01485 210262
www.whitehorsebrancaster.co.uk
Charming hotel on the north Norfolk coast with glorious views over the tidal marshes. Contemporary bedrooms, in two wings, are attractively decorated and thoughtfully equipped. A large bar and lounge area lead to the conservatory restaurant (▷ 339) with its wide-sweeping views.

🍽 £104
🛏 15 🍴 In restaurant
🚗 On A149 coast road between Hunstanton and Wells-next-the-Sea

BRIGHTON

PASKINS TOWN HOUSE ◆◆◆◆

18–19 Charlotte Street, Brighton BN2 1AG
Tel: 01273 601203
www.paskins.co.uk
This environmentally friendly town house bed-and-breakfast offers individually designed bedrooms. But breakfast is the speciality and includes home-made vegetarian sausages.

🍽 £40
🛏 19 🍴 In dining room
🚉 Brighton

CAMBRIDGE

CENTENNIAL HOTEL ★★

63–71 Hills Road, Cambridge CB2 1PG
Tel: 01223 314652
www.centennialhotel.co.uk
This friendly hotel has well-presented public areas that include a quiet, welcoming

lounge and a relaxing bar and restaurant. Bedrooms are generally quite spacious, clean and have a good range of facilities; several rooms are available on the ground floor.

🕐 Closed 23 Dec–1 Jan
🍽 £88
🛏 39
🍴 In 26 bedrooms and in restaurant
🚉 Cambridge

GONVILLE HOTEL ★★★

Gonville Place, Cambridge CB1 1LY
Tel: 01223 366611
www.gonvillehotel.co.uk
Well established, with regular guests and very experienced staff, the Gonville is popular for its informality. The air-

East Tytherley's Star Inn overlooks the village cricket ground

conditioned public areas are cheerfully furnished, and bedrooms are well appointed.

🍽 £99
🛏 78
🍴 In 38 bedrooms and in restaurant
🚗 From M11 junction 11 take A1309 and follow city centre signs. At second mini roundabout turn right into Lensfield Road over junction with traffic lights; hotel soon on right
🚉 Cambridge

CANTERBURY

THE COUNTY ★★★★

High Street, Canterbury CT1 2RX
Tel: 01227 766266
www.macdonald-hotels.co.uk
This historic hotel has cellars that date back to the 12th century. It offers warm

hospitality and comfortable accommodation in the heart of the city. Public areas include the tea room, serving traditional cream teas, and Sully's Restaurant.

🍽 £85
🛏 74
🍴 In 33 bedrooms and in restaurant
🚗 From M2 junction 7 follow Canterbury signs on to ring road. At Wincheap roundabout turn into city. Left into Rosemary Lane and into Stour Street; hotel at end
🚉 Canterbury East or West

MAGNOLIA HOUSE ◆◆◆◆◆

36 St. Dunstan's Terrace, Canterbury CT2 8AX
Tel: 01227 765121
Magnolia House is an attractive guesthouse, combining a warm welcome with superbly appointed bedrooms. The pleasant lounge looks out over the front garden. Evening meals can be arranged and a wide choice is offered at breakfast. No children under 12. No dogs

🍽 £85
🛏 7 🍴
🚗 From A2 take turn for Canterbury, left at first roundabout approaching city (signposted University), then third turn on right

EAST TYTHERLEY

STAR INN ◆◆◆◆

East Tytherley, near Romsey SO15 0LW
Tel: 01794 340225
www.starinn-uk.com
A charming 16th-century coaching inn adjoining the village cricket ground in a quiet backwater between Salisbury and Romsey. Accommodation is provided in a purpose-built block separate from the main pub—three spacious bedrooms with high levels of quality and comfort. Award-winning food is a particular attraction. An outdoor children's play area is also available. No dogs.

🕐 Closed Mon (except public holiday Mon) and 25–26 Dec
🍽 £70
🛏 3

In bedrooms and in dining room
5 miles (8km) north of Romsey off A3057, take left turn onto B3084 then left for Awbridge and Lockerley; follow road past Lockerley for 1 mile (1.6km)

ELY

THE ANCHOR INN
Sutton Gault, Sutton CB6 2BD
Tel: 01353 778537
www.anchor-inn-restaurant.co.uk
With stunning country views, this 17th-century inn retains many original features and is enhanced by period furniture. Bedrooms are spacious, comfortable and equipped with a host of thoughtful extras. Excellent Modern British cuisine is available (▷ 341). No children and no dogs.
Closed 26 Dec
£75
2
Signposted off B1381 in Sutton village, 7 miles (11km) west of Ely via A142
Ely

FARNINGHAM

BEESFIELD FARM ◇◇◇◇◇
Beesfield Lane, Farningham DA4 0LA
Tel: 01322 863900
www.beesfieldfarm.co.uk
This attractive farmhouse bed-and-breakfast is surrounded by open farmland. The individually decorated bedrooms are beautifully appointed and have many thoughtful touches. No children under 12. No dogs. Credit cards are not accepted.
Closed 8 Dec–end Jan
£80
3
Turn off A20 to A225, then left to Beesfield Lane; farm is 0.5 mile (800m) on left
Eynsford or Swanley

GREAT MILTON

LE MANOIR AUX QUAT' SAISONS ☆☆☆☆
Church Road, Great Milton OX44 7PD
Tel: 01844 278881
www.manoir.com
This renowned hotel, set in beautiful grounds and gardens, epitomizes luxury. Bedrooms, either in the main house or the garden courtyard, are individually styled and offer the highest levels of comfort and quality. Stylish public areas feature wonderful artwork and include the main reason for any visit to Le Manoir, the conservatory restaurant (▷ 341).
£275
32 In restaurant
From junction 7 of M40 follow A329 towards Wallingford. After 1 mile (1.6km) turn right, signposted Great Milton Manor

Beesfield Farm in Farningham is set around mature gardens

ISLE OF WIGHT

AQUA HOTEL ◆◆◆◆
17 The Esplanade, Shanklin PO37 6BN
Tel: 01983 863024
www.aquahotel.co.uk
Public rooms and many of the bedrooms at this friendly, family-run hotel enjoy fine sea views. The bedrooms are well equipped and some have the added bonus of a balcony. The sea views can also be enjoyed from the gardens. No dogs.
£52
22
Off Arthurs Hill/North Road; at Fiveways junction into Hope Road and follow to Esplanade
Shanklin

PRIORY BAY HOTEL ★★★
Priory Drive, Seaview PO34 5BU
Tel: 01983 613146
www.priorybay.co.uk
This peacefully located hotel has its own stretch of sand and a nine-hole golf course, tennis, croquet and an outdoor pool. There are also woodland lawns and formal gardens. The well-equipped and mostly spacious bedrooms are very comfortable, and there is a fine dining room (▷ 341).
£110
31 In restaurant
On B3330 to Nettlestone

KING'S LYNN

ROSE & CROWN ★★
Old Church Road, Snettisham PE31 7LX
Tel: 01485 541382
www.roseandcrownsnettisham.co.uk
This 14th-century inn is close to some of west Norfolk's most beautiful beaches. Public rooms include a choice of dining areas (▷ 342) as well as a family room and non-smoking bar. A walled garden is available on sunny days, as is a children's play area.
Double up to £70
11 In bedrooms and in restaurant
North from King's Lynn on A149 signed to Hunstanton; hotel in centre of Snettisham between market square and church King's Lynn

LAVENHAM

LAVENHAM PRIORY ◇◇◇◇◇
Water Street, Lavenham CO10 9RW
Tel: 01787 247404
www.lavenhampriory.co.uk
This superb property dates back to the 13th century. It has been carefully restored, maintaining much of its original character. Breakfast is served in the spectacular Merchant's Room or in the sheltered courtyard herb garden. Guests also have use of the Great Hall. No children under 10 and no dogs.
Closed 21 Dec–2 Jan
£95
6
A1141 to Lavenham, turn by side of Swan Hotel into Water Street and then right after 50m (160ft) into private drive

STAYING

MILFORD-ON-SEA

WESTOVER HALL HOTEL
☆☆☆
Park Lane, Milford on Sea SO41 0PT
Tel: 01590 643044
www.westoverhallhotel.com
This late-Victorian mansion has uninterrupted views across to the Isle of Wight and is just a few moments' walk from the beach. Dramatic stained-glass windows, oak panelling and a galleried entrance hall add to the interior décor, and the bedrooms display panache and originality.
🍴 £165
ⓘ 12 ⓢ
🚗 Follow M3 and M27 onto A337 to Lymington and signs to Milford-on-Sea on to B3058. Hotel outside village centre, towards cliff

NORWICH

THE GEORGIAN HOUSE HOTEL ★★★
32–34 Unthank Road, Norwich NR2 2RB
Tel: 01603 615655
www.georgian-hotel.co.uk
Close to the cathedral, two Victorian houses have been restored to create this hotel. Public areas include a comfortable bar, TV lounge and an elegant restaurant offering a daily changing menu.
🍴 £90
ⓘ 28
ⓢ In 20 bedrooms and in restaurant
🚗 Follow cathedral signs from city; hotel off inner ring road
🚉 Norwich

OXFORD

BURLINGTON HOUSE
◆◆◆◆◆
374 Banbury Road, Summertown, Oxford OX2 7PP
Tel: 01865 513513
www.burlington-house.co.uk
A warm welcome is assured at this immaculately maintained Victorian bed-and-breakfast. The attractive furnishing schemes complement the original features, and two of the bedrooms overlook a pretty patio garden. Memorable breakfasts are served in a

homey dining room. No children under 12. No dogs.
🍴 £85
ⓘ 11 ⓢ
🚗 At Peartree roundabout follow signs to Oxford. At next roundabout take second exit A40. After about 0.5 mile (800m) at next roundabout take third exit. Hotel on corner of fourth road on left
🚉 Oxford

THE OLD BANK HOTEL
★★★★
92–94 High Street, Oxford OX1 4BN
Tel: 01865 799599
www.oxford-hotels-restaurants.co.uk
This former bank has been converted into a very stylish and comfortable hotel. Bedrooms are smart and have

Portsmouth's Seacrest Hotel has an excellent waterfront location

CD players and air conditioning. Public areas include the vibrant all-day Quod Bar and Restaurant, a separate residents' bar, and an outside courtyard.
🅖 Closed 25–27 Dec
🍴 £160
ⓘ 42 ⓢ
🚉 Oxford

PORTSMOUTH

SEACREST HOTEL ★★
11–12 South Parade, Southsea PO5 2JB
Tel: 023 9273 3192
www.seacresthotel.co.uk
This smart hotel provides the ideal base for exploring the town. Bedrooms, many benefiting from sea views, are decorated to a high standard.

🍴 £60
ⓘ 28
ⓢ In 20 bedrooms and in restaurant
🚗 From M27/M275 follow signs for seafront, Pyramids and Sea Life Centre; hotel opposite Rock Gardens and Pyramids
🚉 Portsmouth & Southsea

RYE

JEAKE'S HOUSE ◆◆◆◆◆
Mermaid Street, Rye TN31 7ET
Tel: 01797 222828
www.jeakeshouse.com
This bed-and-breakfast is in one of the most beautiful parts of town. The individually decorated bedrooms combine traditional elegance and comfort with modern facilities. No children under 12.
🍴 £86
ⓘ 11 ⓢ In dining room
🚉 Rye

ST. ALBANS

ST. MICHAEL'S MANOR ★★★
Fishpool Street, St. Albans AL3 4RY
Tel: 01727 864444
www.stmichaelsmanor.com
This hotel, set in extensive grounds, is furnished and decorated to a luxurious standard throughout, and offers excellent dining opportunities (▷ 342). Staff combine warmth with informality.
🍴 £175
ⓘ 22
ⓢ In 3 bedrooms and in restaurant
🚗 From St. Albans Abbey follow Fishpool Street towards St. Michael's village. Hotel is 0.5 mile (800m) on left
🚉 St. Albans

SALISBURY

NEWTON FARMHOUSE
◆◆◆◆◆
Southampton Road, Whiteparish SP5 2QL
Tel: 01794 884416
www.newtonfarmhouse.co.uk
This farmhouse bed-and-breakfast on the fringe of the New Forest dates from the 16th century. The house has been thoughtfully restored, and five of the eight bedrooms have four-poster beds. Delicious home-cooked meals

STAYING

are available by prior arrangement. No dogs. Credit cards not accepted.

🛏 £50

ⓘ 8 🚭 🏊

🚗 Just south of Salisbury: 6 miles (10km) on A36, 1 mile (1.6km) south of junction with A27

🚉 Salisbury

SEVENOAKS

DONNINGTON MANOR ★★★

London Road, Dunton Green, Sevenoaks TN13 2TD
Tel: 01732 462681
www.donningtonmanorhotel.co.uk

This extended 15th-century manor house is on the outskirts of Sevenoaks. The original part of the building boasts public rooms with a wealth of character including an attractive oak-beamed restaurant, a comfortable lounge and an intimate bar.

🛏 £110 (room only, English breakfast £9.95 extra, Continental breakfast £6.95 extra)

ⓘ 60

🚭 In 20 bedrooms and in restaurant

🏊

🚗 From M25 junction 4 follow signs for Bromley/Orpington to roundabout. Turn left on to A224 (Dunton Green), left at second roundabout, left at Rose and Crown, hotel is 300m (330 yards) on right

SHERINGHAM

ROMAN CAMP INN ★★

Holt Road, Aylmerton NR11 8QD
Tel: 01263 838291
www.romancampinn.co.uk

Ideally placed for touring the north Norfolk coastline, this hotel provides spacious bedrooms that are pleasantly decorated and come with a good range of useful extras. Public rooms include a smart conservatory-style restaurant, comfortable lounge, smart bar and dining room.

ⓒ Closed 25 Dec

🛏 £88

ⓘ 15

🚭 In 2 bedrooms and in restaurant

🚗 On A148 between Sheringham and Cromer

🚉 Cromer (1.5 miles/2.5km)

SOUTHWOLD

THE CROWN ★★

90 High Street, Southwold IP18 6DP
Tel: 01502 722275
www.adnams.co.uk/hotels/crown

This old posting inn in the heart of the town combines a pub, wine bar and an intimate restaurant (▷ 342) with superb accommodation. The bedrooms are tastefully decorated. Public rooms feature a back-room bar and an elegant lounge.

ⓒ Closed first or second week in Jan

🛏 £116

ⓘ 13 🚭 In restaurant

🚗 Off A12, take A1095 to Southwold and stay on main road into town centre; hotel on left in High Street

🚉 Darsham

The Newton Farmhouse was owned by Lord Nelson's family

STADHAMPTON

THE CRAZY BEAR

Bear Lane, Stadhampton OX44 7UR
Tel: 01865 890714
www.crazybearhotel.co.uk

This unusual small hotel combines modern chic with old-world character. The art deco bedrooms and extravagant suites are presented and equipped to a very high standard. The hotel features two popular and attractive restaurants (▷ 343).

🛏 £110

ⓘ 12

🚗 From junction 7 of the M40 turn left at end of slip road into Stadhampton village. Over mini roundabout, left at petrol station. Hotel is second on left

WINCHESTER

THE WINCHESTER ROYAL ★★★

Saint Peter Street, Winchester SO23 8BS
Tel: 01962 840840
www.marstonhotels.com

Situated in the heart of the city, this friendly hotel, dating back in parts to the 16th century, has seen recent improvements to its ground floor areas.

🛏 £138

ⓘ 75

🚭 In 48 bedrooms and in restaurant

🚗 From M3 junction 9 to Winnal Trading Estate. Follow road to city centre, cross river, turn left, then first right. On to one-way system and turn second right. Hotel immediately on right

🚉 Winchester

WINDSOR

AURORA GARDEN ★★

Bolton Avenue, Windsor SL4 3JF
Tel: 01753 868686
www.auroragarden.co.uk

A warm welcome is assured at this hotel in a quiet part of town. Bedrooms are spacious.

ⓒ Closed 25 Dec

🛏 £100

ⓘ 19 🚭 In restaurant

🚗 From M4 junction 6 take A332 (Windsor). At first roundabout take second exit towards Staines. At third roundabout, take third exit for 500m (550 yards) to hotel on right

🚉 Windsor & Eton Central

WOODSTOCK

THE BEAR HOTEL ★★★

Park Street, Woodstock OX20 1SZ
Tel: 0870 400 8202
www.macdonald-hotels.co.uk

This 13th-century coaching inn exudes charm and comfort. Modern facilities in the hotel's bedrooms do nothing to detract from their character. Public rooms include an intimate bar and restaurant.

🛏 £118

ⓘ 52

🚭 In 20 bedrooms and in restaurant

🚗 From Oxford, reached from M40 or A34 to the south of the city, take A44 into Woodstock and left to town centre; hotel on left opposite town hall

LONDON

Inexpensive accommodation in London is hard to find and often inconveniently located. The best bet is to budget for a little more and pick a hotel closer to the centre. Since there is no shortage of mid-market hotels, off-peak periods can be excellent hunting times for bargains, with reduced rates and special offers. Check hotels' websites for late deals. Weekends are often cheaper than midweek accommodation, with fewer business guests.

STAYING

PRICES AND SYMBOLS

Prices are the starting price for a double room for one night, unless otherwise stated. Breakfast is included unless noted otherwise. All the hotels listed accept credit cards unless otherwise stated. Note that rates vary widely throughout the year.

For a key to the symbols ▷ 2.

THE BERKELEY ☆☆☆☆☆

Wilton Place, Knightsbridge SW1X 7RL
Tel: 020 7235 6000
www.the-berkeley.com
The Berkeley never fails to impress. Having undergone refurbishment there is an excellent range of bedrooms, each one furnished with care and attention to detail. The striking Blue Bar enhances the reception rooms. The health spa offers a range of treatment rooms and includes an open-air rooftop pool. Two restaurants provide a contrast of style: modern snack-style at the Boxwood Café and French cuisine at Pétrus. There is a sauna and spa.

🛏 £369
ⓘ 214 ⓢ In 32 bedrooms 🔇 🏊 📺
🚇 Knightsbridge

BYRON HOTEL ◆◆◆◆

36–38 Queensborough Terrace W2 3SH
Tel: 020 7243 0987
www.capricornhotels.co.uk
This terraced house retains a number of original features. Bedrooms vary in size but all are well furnished and equipped with modern facilities. There's a dining room, for breakfast, and a guest lounge.

🛏 £85
ⓘ 45 ⓢ In dining room
🚇 Bayswater

CLARIDGE'S ☆☆☆☆☆

Brook Street W1A 2JQ
Tel: 020 7629 8860
www.claridges.co.uk
Impressive standards of luxury, style and service are upheld at this iconic bastion of British hospitality. Sumptuously decorated, air-conditioned bedrooms have Victorian or art deco themes to reflect the architecture of the building. Excellent service and dishes at the restaurant, Gordon Ramsay at Claridge's, run by Mark Sargeant, a protégé of Gordon Ramsay. Reservations are advised.

🛏 £306
ⓘ 203 ⓢ In 34 bedrooms
🔇 🏊 Use of sister hotel's pool 📺
🚇 Bond Street

THE DORCHESTER ☆☆☆☆☆
Park Lane W1A 2HJ
Tel: 020 7629 8888
www.dorchesterhotel.com
One of London's finest hotels, The Dorchester is sumptuously decorated. Bedrooms have individual design schemes, are beautifully furnished and have huge, luxurious baths. The Promenade is ideal for afternoon tea or drinks. In the evenings you can relax to the sound of live jazz in the bar, and enjoy a cocktail or an Italian meal. Other dining options include the traditional The Grill and The Oriental. There is a spa, gym, sauna, solarium and Jacuzzi.
🍴 £417
🛏 250 🔲 🍸
🚇 Hyde Park Corner

EURO HOTEL ◆◆◆
51–53 Cartwright Gardens, Russell Square WC1H 9EL
Tel: 020 7387 4321
www.eurohotel.co.uk
This friendly bed-and-breakfast enjoys an ideal location in a leafy Georgian crescent. Many of the bedrooms have private bathrooms.
🍴 £75
🛏 34 🔲 In dining room
🚇 Russell Square

FOUR SEASONS HOTEL LONDON ☆☆☆☆☆
Hamilton Place, Park Lane W1A 1AZ
Tel: 020 7499 0888
www.fourseasons.com
This long-established hotel is in the heart of Mayfair. Service is superlative. The large bedrooms are elegant and the conservatory rooms are particularly special.
🍴 £423
🛏 220 🔲 In 96 bedrooms 🔲 🍸
🚇 Hyde Park Corner

THE GAINSBOROUGH ◆◆◆◆
7–11 Queensberry Place, South Kensington SW7 2DL
Tel: 020 7957 0000
www.eeh.co.uk
This smart mid-Georgian town house is located in a quiet street near the Natural History Museum. Bedrooms are individually designed and decorated in fine fabrics, with quality furnishings. There is a small lounge and 24-hour room service.
🍴 £182
🛏 49
🔲 In dining room
🚇 South Kensington

GALLERY ◇◇◇◇
8–10 Queensberry Place, South Kensington SW7 2EA
Tel: 020 7915 0000
www.eeh.co.uk
This stylish property offers friendly hospitality, attentive service and sumptuously

The Gainsborough is an ideal choice for South Kensington

furnished bedrooms, some with a private terrace. Public areas include a choice of lounges (one with internet access) and an elegant bar. Room service is available 24 hours a day.
🍴 £188
🛏 36 🔲 In dining room
🚇 South Kensington

GRANGE BLOOMS ★★★★
7 Montague Street WC1B 5BP
Tel: 020 7323 1717
www.bloomshotel.com
Part of an 18th-century terrace, this elegant town house is just around the corner from the British Museum. Bedrooms are furnished in Regency style and day rooms consist of a lobby lounge, a garden terrace, a breakfast room and cocktail bar, all graced with antique pieces, paintings and flowers. There is 24-hour room service.
🍴 £195
🛏 26 🔲 In 12 bedrooms
🚇 Russell Square

GREAT EASTERN HOTEL
☆☆☆☆☆
Liverpool Street EC2M 7QN
Tel: 020 7618 5000
www.great-eastern-hotel.co.uk
A modern minimalist hotel with a prime location in the heart of the City. Air-conditioned bedrooms are simple yet stylish, and equipped with DVD and CD players. The impressive array of restaurants includes the elegant Aurora, offering fine dining, Fishmarket, a fish restaurant with champagne bar, Terminus offering all day meals and snacks and Miyabi, a Japanese restaurant. There is a gym complete with treatment rooms, a steam room and personal trainers.
🍴 £311
🛏 267 🔲 In 74 bedrooms 🔲 🍸
🚇 Liverpool Street

THE HALKIN HOTEL ☆☆☆☆
Halkin Street, Belgravia SW1X 7DJ
Tel: 020 7333 1000
www.halkin.como.bz
Contemporary in design, this individual hotel is in a peaceful area just a stroll away from Hyde Park. The stylish, fully air-conditioned bedrooms combine comfort and practicality and many include state-of-the-art facilities. You'd expect impressive food from this chic hotel, and it delivers. The restaurant, Nahm, is run by chef David Thompson, an expert on Thai cuisine.
🍴 £176
🛏 41 🔲 In 9 bedrooms 🔲
🚇 Hyde Park Corner

HART HOUSE HOTEL ♦♦♦♦
51 Gloucester Place, Portman Square
W1U 8JF
Tel: 020 7935 2288
www.harthouse.co.uk
This elegant Georgian house
enjoys a prime location. Both
bedrooms and public areas are
smartly furnished and stylishly
decorated and retain much of
the original character of the
house.
🍴 £105
🛏 16 🅂
🚇 Baker Street, Marble Arch

LANGORF HOTEL ♦♦♦♦
20 Frognal, Hampstead NW3 6AG
Tel: 020 7794 4483
www.langorfhotel.com
This elegant Edwardian
building has been tastefully
furnished throughout. The
bedrooms are smartly
presented. Public areas
include a small reception
lounge and a dining room.
🍴 £85
🛏 31
🅂 In dining room
🚇 Finchley Road

LINCOLN HOUSE HOTEL ♦♦
33 Gloucester Place W1U 8HY
Tel: 020 7486 7630
www.lincoln-house-hotel.co.uk
Friendly, family-run Georgian
town house which has been
impressively renovated.
🍴 £69
🛏 23 🅂 In dining room
🚇 Marble Arch

MANDARIN ORIENTAL HYDE PARK ☆☆☆☆☆
66 Knightsbridge SW1X 7LA
Tel: 020 7235 2000
www.mandarinoriental.com
Bedrooms and suites are
decorated to a high standard
in this stylish hotel, and many
have superb views. There's a
choice of dining options: The
Park Restaurant, offering light
brasserie-style dishes; the
sophisticated Foliage, serving
the highest standard of
cuisine; and the fashionable
Mandarin Bar serving light
snacks and exotic cocktails.

🍴 £425
🛏 200 🅂 In 106 bedrooms 🅂 🖂
🚇 Knightsbridge

MENTONE HOTEL ♦♦♦
54–56 Cartwright Gardens, Bloomsbury
WC1H 9EL
Tel: 020 7387 3927
www.mentonehotel.com
This bed-and-breakfast in a
Victorian terrace overlooking
pleasant gardens is close to
many central London
attractions. Bedrooms have
private bathrooms. Tennis
courts.
🍴 £75
🛏 43
🅂 In dining room
🚇 King's Cross, Russell Square, Euston

*The Millennium Gloucester is
popular with international visitors*

MILLENNIUM GLOUCESTER HOTEL LONDON KENSINGTON ★★★★
4–18 Harrington Gardens SW7 4LH
Tel: 020 7373 6030
www.millenniumhotels.com/gloucester
Air-conditioned bedrooms are
furnished in a variety of
contemporary styles.
Additional amenities are
provided in club rooms, which
have a dedicated lounge.
Eating options include
Singaporean cuisine and more
formal Italian food.
🍴 £250
🛏 610 🅂 In 439 bedrooms 🅂 🖂
🚇 Gloucester Road

MILESTONE HOTEL AND APARTMENTS ☆☆☆☆☆
1 Kensington Court W8 5DL
Tel: 020 7917 1000
www.milestonehotel.com
This town house has been
carefully restored and the
themed bedrooms are of a
very high standard; facilities
include DVD players in each.
There are superb suites and
some duplexes. A snug bar has
a conservatory extension and
there's also a luxurious lounge.
🍴 £305
🛏 57 🅂 In 22 bedrooms 🅂 🖂
🚇 High Street Kensington

ST. GEORGE HOTEL ♦♦♦♦
9 Gloucester Place W1U 3JH
Tel: 020 7486 8586
www.stgeorge-hotel.net
A Grade II listed (landmark)
house in the West End.
Bedrooms are well furnished.
Breakfast is served in a smart
breakfast room and the staff
offer a warm welcome.
🍴 £75
🛏 19
🅂 In 6 bedrooms and in breakfast
room
🚇 Baker Street

THE SAVOY ☆☆☆☆☆
Strand WC2R 0EU
Tel: 020 7836 4343
www.the-savoy.co.uk
Service is impeccable at this
renowned hotel and
bedrooms and suites offer
excellent levels of comfort. The
choice of dining areas presents
a predicament; whether to opt
for the Grill run by chef Marcus
Wareing, an alumnus of
Gordon Ramsay's restaurant,
the River Restaurant or La
Banquette. Jackets and ties are
preferred. No visit would be
complete without afternoon
tea in the Thames Foyer,
perhaps enjoying the regular
Sunday afternoon tea dance.
🍴 £395
🛏 263 🅂 🖂 🏊 Indoor
🅂 In 55 bedrooms
🚇 Charing Cross

STAYING

WALES

Accommodation in Wales may not be as chic as in London, but it's also not as expensive. Instead of luxury hotels, expect to find friendly, family-run bed-and-breakfasts, farm stays and small local hotels in peaceful surroundings. Several spots serve as bases for tourists and walkers: Brecon in the Brecon Beacons National Park, Betws-y-Coed in Snowdonia National Park and Britain's smallest city, St. David's, in the Pembrokeshire Coast National Park. They attract the most visitors but also have the highest concentration of hotels. Out of season some generous deals may be available.

ABERYSTWYTH

CONRAH HOTEL ★★★

Ffosrhydygaled, Chancery, Aberystwyth SY23 4DF
Tel: 01970 617941
www.conrah.co.uk
The elegant public rooms at this country-house hotel include a choice of comfortable lounges with open fires. Bedrooms are located in both the main house and a nearby wing. There is an excellent restaurant (▷ 349). No children under five.
🄲 Closed 22–30 Dec, D Sun in low season
🛏 £125
🛈 17 🔲 In restaurant ☒
🚗 On A487, 3 miles (5km) south of Aberystwyth
🚉 Aberystwyth

BETWS-Y-COED

TY GWYN

Betws-y-Coed LL24 0SG
Tel: 01690 710383
www.tygwynhotel.co.uk
Situated on the edge of the village, close to Waterloo Bridge, this historic coaching inn retains many original features, and quality furnishings and memorabilia throughout enhance the intrinsic charm of the property.
🄲 Closed Jan
🛏 £34; discount for under-16s
🛈 12 🔲 In dining room
🚗 Junction of A5/A470 by Waterloo Bridge
🚉 Betws-y-Coed

CARDIFF

THE BIG SLEEP HOTEL ◆◆◆◆

Bute Terrace, Cardiff CF10 2FE
Tel: 029 2063 6363
www.thebigsleephotel.com
Part of Cardiff's skyline, this city centre bed-and-breakfast hotel opposite Cardiff International Arena offers well-equipped bedrooms ranging from standard to penthouse, with spectacular views over the city towards the bay. Continental breakfast is served or 'breakfast to go' is an alternative for the visitor wishing to make an early start. There is a bar on the ground floor and secure parking. No dogs.
🛏 £45; discount for under-12s
🛈 81
🚉 Cardiff Central

TAN Y FOEL COUNTRY HOUSE ☆☆

Capel Garmon, Betws-y-Coed
LL26 0RE
Tel: 01690 710507
www.tyfhotel.co.uk

A refreshing small hotel in many respects, this 16th-century stone-built house offers fine views along the Conwy valley from its elevated position. The lounge and breakfast room are decorated in a modern style with a slight Eastern influence, while the conservatory restaurant is more traditional and warmed by a wood-burning stove. Dinner, using local organic produce where possible, is a highlight of any stay. Individually furnished bedrooms, including the imaginative use of an old hayloft, are designed for comfort and relaxation. No children under seven. No dogs.

🟢 Closed Dec–end Jan
🖐 £141
🛈 6 🚭
🚗 Off A5 at Betws-y-Coed on to A470, travel 2 miles (3km) north, signed Capel Garmon on right; turn towards Capel Garmon for 1.5 miles (2.5km), hotel sign on left

---

PRICES AND SYMBOLS

Prices are the starting price for a double room for one night, unless otherwise stated. Breakfast is included unless noted otherwise. All the hotels listed accept credit cards unless otherwise stated. Note that rates vary widely throughout the year.

For a key to the symbols ▷ 2.

MARLBOROUGH GUEST HOUSE ◆◆◆◆

98 Newport Road, Cardiff CF24 1DG
Tel: 029 2049 2385

This family-run guesthouse is just a few minutes from the city centre and has a warm

---

and friendly atmosphere. Not all the bedrooms are spacious but the bathrooms are particularly well fitted. A comfortably furnished lounge is available for residents, and hearty breakfasts are served in the pleasant breakfast room. No dogs.

🖐 £45; discount for under-10s
🛈 8 🚭
🚉 Cardiff Queen Street

THE ST. DAVID'S HOTEL AND SPA ★★★★★

Havannah Street, Cardiff CF10 5SD
Tel: 029 2045 4045
www.thestdavidshotel.com

This imposing contemporary building sits in a prime

Relaxing at Dolgellau's Fronoleu Country Hotel

position on Cardiff Bay. A seven-storey atrium provides a dramatic first impression on entering, and leads to the practically laid out and comfortable bedrooms. A quiet lounge on the first floor suits guests seeking a place for relaxation. There is a good restaurant (▷ 350).

🖐 £200
🛈 132 🚭 In restaurant 🏊 📶
🚗 M4 junction 33/A4232 for 9 miles (15km) for Techniquest at top exit slip road; first left at roundabout then first right
🚉 Cardiff Central

CHEPSTOW

BEAUFORT HOTEL ★★

Beaufort Square, Chepstow NP6 5EP
Tel: 01291 622497
www.beauforthotelchepstow.com

This 16th-century coaching inn is centrally located in town. The bedrooms are brightly decorated, and the public areas include a friendly bar and a pleasant restaurant where well-prepared meals are served. A large meeting and function room is also available.

🖐 £59; discount for under-14s
🛈 22
🚉 Chepstow

CONWY

BRYN DERWEN ◆◆◆

Woodlands, Conwy LL32 8LT
Tel: 01492 596134

Sympathetically restored and retaining many of its original Victorian features, Bryn Derwen is in an elevated position near the castle with views over the town. The brightly furnished bedrooms offer modern facilities. The breakfast room overlooks the garden, and guests also have use of the period-style lounge. No dogs.

🖐 £45; discount for under-15s
🛈 6 🚭 In dining room
🚉 Llandudno

GROES INN ★★★

Tyn-y-Groes, LL32 8TN
Tel: 01492 650545
www.groesinn.com

With its comfortable, well-equipped bedrooms in a separate building, this 16th-century inn has managed to retain many of its traditional features. But the modern additions complement it well, notably the conservatory extension to the restaurant, which opens out on to the lovely rear garden. Some bedrooms also have private terraces or balconies.

🟢 Closed 24, 25, 26 Dec
🖐 £95
🛈 14 🚭 In restaurant
🚗 2 miles (3.2km) out of Conwy town on B5106 towards Trefriw

DOLGELLAU

FRONOLEU COUNTRY HOTEL ★★

Tabor, Dolgellau LL40 2PS
Tel: 01341 422361
www.fronleu.co.uk
This 16th-century farmhouse, carefully extended to retain many original features, lies in the shadow of Cader Idris mountain. The bar and lounge are located in the old building where there are exposed timbers and open fires. Most of the bedrooms are in the modern extension. The restaurant attracts a large local following. Private fishing available.

🛏 £50; discount for under-16s
🍴 11 🍽 In restaurant
🅿 Junction of A487/A470 towards Tabor opposite Cross Foxes and continue for 1.25 miles (2km). From Dolgellau take road for hospital and continue another 1.25 miles up the hill
🚉 Fairbourne

HAVERFORDWEST

LOWER HAYTHOG FARM ◆◆◆◆

Spittal, Haverfordwest SA62 5QL
Tel: 01437 731279
www.lowerhaythogfarm.co.uk
Located in an expanse of unspoiled countryside, this 14th-century farmhouse provides high standards of comfort and good facilities. Bedrooms, some of which are in former farm buildings, are filled with thoughtful extras, and an elegant oak-beamed dining room is the perfect setting for imaginative home-cooked dinners. Private fishing and pony rides available. Credit cards not accepted.

🛏 £50; discount for under-12s
🍴 6 🍽
🅿 5 miles (8km) north of Haverfordwest off B4329, continue along this road until rail bridge; entrance on right
🚉 Haverfordwest

HAY-ON-WYE

OLD BLACK LION ★★

26 Lion Street, Hay-on-Wye HR3 5AD
Tel: 01497 820841
www.oldblacklion.co.uk
This fine old coaching inn, with a history stretching back several centuries—it was occupied by Oliver Cromwell (1599–1658) during the siege of Hay Castle, then a loyalist stronghold—has charm and character. Privately owned and personally run, it offers comfortable and well-equipped bedrooms, some of which are in a building next door. Excellent food is available (▷ 350). No children under five. No dogs (except guide dogs).

The Wild Pheasant in Llangollen is a leafy retreat

🛏 £80
🍴 6 🍽 In restaurant
🅿 From tourist information office parking area turn right along Oxford Road, pass NatWest bank and take next left (Lion Street); hotel soon on right

LLANBERIS

QUALITY HOTEL SNOWDONIA ★★★

Llanberis LL55 4TY
Tel: 01286 870253
www.hotels-snowdonia.com
This hotel sits near the foot of Snowdon, between the Peris and Padarn lakes. Pretty gardens and grounds make an attractive backdrop for the many weddings held here. The refurbished bedrooms are well equipped, and there are spacious lounges and bars, plus a large dining room with conservatory overlooking the lakes. Activities include mountaineering, cycling and walking.

🛏 £100; discount for under-15s
🍴 106 🍽 In restaurant
🅿 On A4086 Caernarfon to Llanberis road directly opposite Snowdon Mountain Railway 🚉 Bangor

LLANDRINDOD WELLS

HOTEL METROPOLE ★★★

Temple Street, Llandrindod Wells
LD1 5DY
Tel: 01597 823700
www.metropole.co.uk
The centre of this famous spa town is dominated by this Victorian hotel, which has been personally run by the same family for over 100 years. The lobby leads to a choice of bars and an elegant lounge. Bedrooms vary in style, but all are moderately spacious and well equipped. Leisure facilities include a sauna and beauty salon.

🛏 £98; discount for under-16s
🍴 120 🍽 In restaurant 🏊 🧖
🚉 Llandrindod Wells

LLANGOLLEN

THE WILD PHEASANT HOTEL AND RESTAURANT ★★★

Berwyn Road, Llangollen LL20 8AD
Tel: 01978 860629
www.wildpheasanthotel.co.uk
Some bedrooms at this friendly hotel have four-poster beds; guests can also request non-smoking rooms and rooms on the ground floor. There is a reception area (resembling an old village square) and a large function suite. The fixed-price menu in the formal restaurant changes daily.

🛏 £84; discount for under-15s
🍴 40 🍽
🚉 Ruabon

MERTHYR TYDFIL

NANT DDU LODGE HOTEL
★★★
Cwm Taf, Nant Ddu, Merthyr Tydfil
CF48 2HY
Tel: 01685 379111
www.nant-ddu-lodge.co.uk
Close to the Brecon Beacons
and with origins stretching back
200 years, this delightful hotel
has seen many improvements
in the caring hands of the
present owners. Décor
throughout is contemporary
and the bedrooms are
thoughtfully furnished.
🛏 £80; discount for under-12s
🛈 28 ⓢ In restaurant
🚗 On main A470, 6 miles (10km)
north of Merthyr Tydfil and 12 miles
(19km) south of Brecon
🚆 Merthyr Tydfil

PORTMEIRION

THE HOTEL PORTMEIRION
★★★
Portmeirion LL48 6ET
Tel: 01766 770000
www.portmeirion-village.com
Saved from dereliction in the
1920s, this elegant hotel enjoys
one of the finest settings in
Wales, nestling beneath the
wooded slopes of the village,
overlooking the sandy estuary
towards Snowdonia. Many
rooms have private sitting
rooms and balconies with
spectacular views. The mostly
Welsh-speaking staff offer
warm hospitality. Facilities
include beauty salon and
tennis courts.
🛏 £175
🛈 51 ⓢ In restaurant 🏊
🚗 2 miles (3km) west of Portmeirion
village, which is south off A487

SWANSEA

FAIRYHILL ★★
Reynoldston, Swansea SA3 1BS
Tel: 01792 390139
www.fairyhill.net
Not so many years ago this
fine 18th-century house had
foliage poking through the
roof and wild ponies running
amok on its untended
pastures. To stay here today is
a delight, deep in the heart of

the Gower Peninsula. Relaxing
day rooms, leading out to the
front patio, are a perfect
setting to picking at the
mandatory deep-fried
Penclawdd cockles and laver
bread before dinner (▷ 352).
🕙 Closed 1–16 Jan and 26 Dec
🛏 £140
🛈 8
ⓢ In restaurant
🚗 Just outside Reynoldston off A4118
from Swansea

THE GROSVENOR HOUSE
◆◆◆◆
Mirador Crescent, Uplands, Swansea
SA2 0QX
Tel: 01792 461522
www.grosvenor-guesthouse.co.uk

*The Fairyhill in Swansea has
been wonderfully restored*

This immaculate house is in
the fashionable Uplands
district, convenient for touring
the Gower Peninsula and the
Mumbles. After a warm
welcome from the hosts,
guests are shown to their
pleasant bedrooms. Guests
also have access to secure
parking, a lounge and the
dining room at this bed-and-
breakfast. No children under
four.
🕙 Closed 18 Dec–2 Jan
🛏 £54; discount for under-16s
🛈 7 ⓢ
🚗 Off A4118 in the Uplands area of
town
🚆 Swansea

TALSARNAU

MAES Y NEUADD
COUNTRY HOUSE ☆☆
LL47 6YA
Tel: 01766 780200
This 14th-century hotel enjoys
stunning views over the
Snowdonian mountains and
across the bay to the Lleyn
Peninsula. The team here are
committed to highlighting
and restoring some of the
hidden features of the house.
Bedrooms, some in an
adjacent coach house, are
individually furnished and
many have fine antique pieces.
Public areas display a similar
welcoming character, including
the restaurant which serves
locally sourced and home-
grown ingredients. Activities,
such as clay pigeon shooting,
croquet and cooking lessons,
can be arranged.
🛏 £141 including breakfast and dinner
🛈 16 ⓢ In restaurant
🚗 3 miles (5km) northeast of Harlech,
signposted on an unclassified road off
B4573

TENBY

ATLANTIC HOTEL ★★★
The Esplanade, Tenby SA70 7DU
Tel: 01834 842881
www.atlantic-hotel.uk.com
This hotel has an enviable
position looking out over
South Beach and Caldy Island.
Inside there is a traditional feel
and the bedrooms have
homely touches. Guests can
relax in the comfortable
lounge or enjoy a drink in the
cocktail bar before taking
dinner in one of two
restaurants. Other facilities
include a heated indoor
swimming pool, solarium, spa
and sauna.
🕙 Closed 19–28 Dec
🛏 £94; discount for under-16s
🛈 42 ⓢ 🏊
🚆 Tenby

THE MIDLANDS

Buxton and Bakewell (where the eponymous pastry-based jam and sponge cake pudding originates) are the Peak District's two tourism centres, but it is Stratford-upon-Avon that attracts by far the most people in the region. As a consequence it is essential to reserve accommodation ahead, and expect to pay higher prices than elsewhere in the Midlands. Accommodation can be reserved through the tourist information centre's booking service (tel: 0870 160 7930).

PRICES AND SYMBOLS

Prices are the starting price for a double room for one night, unless otherwise stated. Breakfast is included unless noted otherwise. All the hotels listed accept credit cards unless otherwise stated. Note that rates vary widely throughout the year.

For a key to the symbols ▷ 2.

ALDERLEY EDGE

ALDERLEY EDGE HOTEL ★★★
Macclesfield Road, Alderley Edge SK9 7BJ
Tel: 01625 583033
www.alderleyedgehotel.com
This well-furnished hotel, with charming grounds, was built in 1850. The attractive bedrooms and suites offer excellent quality and comfort. The bar and adjacent lounge lead into

the split-level conservatory restaurant (▷ 353).
🍴 £140
🛏 52
🚭 In 19 bedrooms and in the restaurant
🚗 Off A34 in Alderley Edge on to B5087 towards Macclesfield. Hotel 200m (650ft) on right

BAKEWELL

RUTLAND ARMS HOTEL
The Square, Bakewell DE45 1BT
Tel: 01629 812812
www.bakewell.demon.co.uk
The antique furniture, comfortable chairs and open fires of the public rooms in this 19th-century hotel create a homely ambience of bygone times, while the friendly staff are attentive and welcoming. There is a good restaurant (▷ 353).

🍴 £81
🛏 35
🚭 In 12 bedrooms and in restaurant
🚗 On A6 in centre of Bakewell, opposite war memorial
🚉 Matlock

BAMFORD

YORKSHIRE BRIDGE INN ★★
Ashopton Road, Hope Valley S33 0AZ
Tel: 01433 651361
www.yorkshirebridge.co.uk
Despite the name, this 19th-century inn is in Derbyshire and surrounded by majestic Peak District scenery. Excellent food is available (▷ 354). Bedrooms are attractively furnished, comfortable and well equipped.
🍴 £64
🛏 14
🚭 In 10 bedrooms and in restaurant
🚗 A57 (Sheffield–Glossop road), at Ladybower Reservoir take A6013 Bamford road, inn 1mile (1.6km) on right

BASLOW

FISCHER'S BASLOW HALL ☆☆
Calver Road, Baslow DE45 1RR
Tel: 01246 583259
www.fischers-baslowhall.co.uk
Located at the end of a
chestnut tree-lined drive on
the edge of the Chatsworth
estate is this beautiful manor
house. It offers sumptuous
accommodation and facilities
throughout. Staff provide very
friendly and attentive service.
The main house contains
traditional and individually
themed rooms, while the
Garden House has spacious,
more contemporary rooms
with Italian marble bathrooms.
The memorable cuisine in the
restaurant (▷ 354) is a
highlight of any stay.
Ⓒ Closed 25–26 Dec
🅿 £120
ⓘ 11 Ⓢ
🚌 On A623 between Baslow and Calver

BIRMINGHAM

WESTBOURNE LODGE
♦♦♦♦♦
25–31 Fountain Road, Edgbaston
B17 8NJ
Tel: 0121 429 1003
www.westbournelodge.co.uk
This bed-and-breakfast has 24
bedrooms, including family
rooms on the ground floor.
Facilities include a comfortable
lounge, a bar with access to
the patio and garden, and a
pleasant dining room.
Ⓒ Closed 24 Dec–1 Jan
🅿 £65
ⓘ 24 Ⓢ
🚌 50m (150ft) from A456, 1.25 miles
(2km) from Five Ways
🚉 Birmingham University

BROADWAY

BOWERS HILL FARM ◇◇◇◇
Bowers Hill, Willersley WR11 5HG
Tel: 01386 834585
www.bowershillfarm.com
Located in immaculate
farmhouse gardens, this
Victorian house has been
sympathetically renovated to
provide comfortable bedrooms
and modern bathrooms.
Breakfast can be taken in the

dining room or conservatory,
and a guest lounge with open
fire is also available.
🅿 £50
ⓘ 3 Ⓢ
🚌 From A44 Broadway to Evesham,
follow signs to Willersley. At village
follow signs to Badsey industrial estate
from mini roundabout, farm 2 miles
(3km) on right by postbox

THE LYGON ARMS ★★★★
High Street, Broadway WR12 7DU
Tel: 01386 852255
www.thelygonarms.co.uk
A hotel with a wealth of
historic charm and character in
the heart of the Cotswolds.
Dating back to the 16th
century, it offers comfortable

*The Chester Crabwall Manor
Hotel is set in fine woodland*

bedrooms with modern
facilities and some fine antique
furniture. Public rooms include
a variety of lounge areas and a
choice of dining options
(▷ 354)—the Great Hall, with
award-winning cuisine by
Martin Blunos, or the more
informal Oliver's Brasserie.
There is a health spa that
includes a heated swimming
pool, gym, sauna, steam room
and beauty treatments, plus
there are tennis facilities, a
croquet lawn, bicycle hire and
the possibility for horseback
riding nearby.
🅿 £179
ⓘ 69 Ⓢ In restaurant 🚭 🖥
🚌 Turn off A44, signed Broadway,
hotel on High Street

BUXTON

ROSELEIGH HOTEL ♦♦♦♦
19 Broad Walk, Buxton SK17 6JR
Tel: 01298 24904
www.roseleighhotel.co.uk
This impressive stone building
overlooking the Pavilion
Gardens provides clean and
spacious bedrooms. The public
rooms are comfortable, while
the resident owners of this
bed-and-breakfast
establishment offer excellent
hospitality. No dogs.
Ⓒ Closed 16 Dec–10 Jan
🅿 £60
ⓘ 14 Ⓢ
🚌 A6 to Safeway roundabout, turn on
to Dale Road, right at lights. In 100m
(300ft) turn left by Swan pub downhill
and right into Hartington Road
🚉 Buxton

CHESTER

THE CHESTER CRABWALL
MANOR HOTEL ☆☆☆☆
Parkgate Road, Mollington CH1 6NE
Tel: 01244 851666
www.marstonhotels.com
This manor house dates from
the mid-17th century. Today it
stands in 4ha (11 acres) of
immaculate, mature gardens
and woodland. The individual
bedrooms are generally
spacious, and traditional in
style. Facilities include a super
leisure club with sauna,
solarium and gym, jacuzzi,
heated indoor pool, several
comfortable lounges and a
stylish conservatory restaurant.
There's also a croquet lawn
and helipad.
🅿 £181
ⓘ 48
Ⓢ In 2 bedrooms and in restaurant
🚭 🖥
🚌 Northwest off A540 from Chester
🚉 Bache 2 miles (3km)

GRINDLEFORD

MAYNARD ARMS ★★★
Main Road, Grindleford S32 2HE
Tel: 01433 630321
www.maynardarms.co.uk
In the heart of the Peak District
National Park, a delightful
country hotel set in
immaculately kept gardens

with views of the Derwent Valley and beyond. Bedrooms are tastefully furnished and decorated, some with four-poster beds and two with separate sitting rooms. A lounge on the first floor overlooks the garden. Excellent bar food and restaurant (▷ 355).

£105
🛏 10 🚭 In restaurant
🚗 From Sheffield take A625 to Castleton. Left into Grindelford on B6521. After Fox House, hotel on left
🚉 Grindleford

HEREFORD

CASTLE HOUSE ☆☆☆
Castle Street, Hereford HR1 2NW
Tel: 01432 356321
www.castlehse.co.uk
This Georgian town house hotel is just a short stroll from the cathedral. Unashamedly plush, it is the epitome of elegance and sophistication. The character bedrooms are equipped with every luxury to ensure a memorable stay and are complemented by the well-proportioned and restful lounge and bar. The experience is completed by award-winning cuisine in the restaurant (▷ 355).
£175
🛏 15 🚭 In restaurant
🚗 Follow signs to City Centre East. At junction of Commercial Road and Union Street, follow Castle House hotel signs
🚉 Hereford

LEDBURY

FEATHERS HOTEL ★ ★ ★
High Street, Ledbury HR8 1DS
Tel: 01531 635266
www.feathersledbury.co.uk
This historic, timber-framed hotel in the middle of Ledbury has a king-sized helping of old-fashioned charm. The bedrooms don't disappoint and excellent meals can be enjoyed in the rustic brasserie (▷ 355), with its adjoining bar. Facilities include a leisure centre with solarium, Jacuzzi, steam room and a heated indoor pool.

£100
🛏 19 🚭 In 2 bedrooms
🚗 South from Worcester on A449; east from Hereford on A438; north from Gloucester on A417. Hotel in centre of town in High Street
🚉 Ledbury

LINCOLN

EDWARD KING HOUSE ◆◆
The Old Palace, Minster Yard, Lincoln LN2 1PU
Tel: 01522 528778
www.ekhs.org.uk
Once the residence of the bishops of Lincoln, this historic house lies in the lea of the cathedral and next to the old palace. The public areas include a television lounge and a

Lincoln's historic Edward King House

spacious dining room where a hearty breakfast is served.
🔘 Closed Christmas and New Year
£48
🛏 17 🚭
🚗 Follow local directions to cathedral, then through archway in southeast corner of Minster Yard 🚉 Lincoln

LUDLOW

BROMLEY COURT B&B ◆◆◆◆◆
73 Lower Broad Street, Ludlow SY8 1PH
Tel: 01584 876996
www.ludlowhotels.com
Situated in the Georgian/early Victorian area of this historic town, this smart little bed-and-breakfast hotel is a combination of separate houses, all retaining original

features and enhanced by period furnishings. A relaxed and friendly atmosphere prevails and a freshly prepared breakfast, which relies heavily on local produce, is served in the comfortable dining room.
£95
🛏 3 🚭
🚗 Just off B4361; over Ludford Street, forward 20m (60ft) on right
🚉 Ludlow

MUCH WENLOCK

RAVEN HOTEL ★ ★ ★
Barrow Street, Much Wenlock TF13 6EN
Tel: 01952 727251
www.ravenhotel.com
This town centre hotel is made up of several historic buildings with a 17th-century coaching inn at the centre. Accommodation includes some rooms on the ground floor, and all are well furnished and equipped to a high standard. There's also a restaurant and a beauty salon.
£85
🛏 15 🚭 In restaurant
🚗 From M54 junction 4 or 5 take A442 south then A4169 to Much Wenlock 🚉 Telford Central

NORTON

THE HUNDRED HOUSE HOTEL ★ ★
Bridgnorth Road, Norton, Shifnal TF11 9EE
Tel: 01952 730353
www.hundredhouse.co.uk
Primarily Georgian, but with parts dating back to the 14th century, this one-time coaching inn and courthouse is now a friendly, family-owned hotel. It offers individually styled, well-equipped bedrooms which have period furniture and attractive soft furnishings. Public areas include intimate bars and dining areas (▷ 356).
🔘 Closed 25 Dec night and 26 Dec night
£99
🛏 10
🚗 Midway between Telford and Bridgnorth on A442, in centre of village

NOTTINGHAM

LACE MARKET HOTEL ★★★★
29–31 High Pavement, Nottingham
NG1 1HE
Tel: 0115 852 3232
www.lacemarkethotel.co.uk
This smart building—a conversion of two Georgian town houses opposite the Galleries of Justice—is located in the trendy Lace Market area of the city, once famous for Nottingham's prime industry. The stylish, contemporary bedrooms include a selection of spacious superior rooms and split-level suites. Equipment includes CD players and mini bars. Public areas include the popular Merchants Restaurant and Saints Bar. There's also complimentary use of the nearby health club.
🍴 £110
🛏 42 🚭
🅿 Follow tourist signs for Galleries of Justice which is opposite hotel
🚉 Nottingham

STAMFORD

THE GEORGE OF STAMFORD ★★★
71 St. Martins, Stamford PE9 2LB
Tel: 01780 750750
www.georgehotelofstamford.com
Steeped in hundreds of years of history, this delightful coaching inn provides spacious public areas including a choice of dining options (▷ 356), comfortable lounges, a business centre and a range of quality shops. Bedrooms are stylishly appointed, ranging from traditional to contemporary in design. A highlight is afternoon tea, taken in the brightly planted courtyard, weather permitting.
🍴 £110
🛏 47 🚭 In 3 bedrooms
🅿 Turn off A1, 15 miles (24km) north of Peterborough on to B1081, 1 mile (1.6km) on left
🚉 Stamford

STOW-ON-THE-WOLD

THE ROYALIST HOTEL ★★★
Digbeth Street, Stow-on-the-Wold
GL54 1BN
Tel: 01451 830670
www.theroyalisthotel.co.uk
Dating from AD947 and certified as the oldest inn in England, this superb hotel has a wealth of history and character. The public areas and bedrooms (some with Jacuzzi) of the hotel and adjoining pub. The 947AD restaurant (▷ 357) is excellent.
🍴 £70
🛏 8 🚭
🅿 From junction 8 of M40 follow A40 to Burford. Join A424 to Stow-on-the-

The Royalist Hotel in Stow-on-the-Wold

Wold. Turn right on to A436 downhill and hotel is on left of green
🚉 Moreton-in-Marsh

STRATFORD-UPON-AVON

SEQUOIA HOUSE PRIVATE HOTEL ◆◆◆◆
51–53 Shipston Road, Stratford-upon-Avon CV37 7LN
Tel: 01789 268852
www.sequoiahotel.co.uk
This elegant Victorian house retains many original features, highlighted by the quality furnishing and décor throughout. The bedrooms of this smart bed-and-breakfast, some of which are in a sympathetic conversion of former outbuildings, are equipped with practical extras.

A spacious, modern restaurant overlooks the gardens from which guests have direct access to the river and town centre. No children under five or dogs.
🕐 Closed 21–27 Dec
🍴 £69
🛏 23 🚭
🅿 On A3400 close to Clopton Bridge
🚉 Stratford-upon-Avon

STRATFORD VICTORIA ★★★★
Arden Street, Stratford-upon-Avon
CV37 6QQ
Tel: 01789 271000
www.marstonhotels.com
This eye-catching modern hotel, with its red-brick façade, is within walking distance of the town centre. The open-plan public areas include a lounge, a small bar and a larger restaurant (▷ 357) with exposed beams and ornately carved furniture. Other facilities include gym, jacuzzi and beauty salon.
🍴 £149
🛏 100
🚭 In 40 bedrooms and in restaurant
💆
🅿 A439 into Stratford town then follow A3400 (Birmingham). At traffic lights turn left into Arden Street and hotel is 150m (500ft) on right
🚉 Stratford-upon-Avon

WORCESTER

BURGAGE HOUSE ◆◆◆◆
4 College Precincts, Worcester WR1 2LG
Tel: 01905 25396
Ideally located adjacent to the cathedral and many historical attractions, this impressive Georgian house retains many original features. Bedrooms, one of which is located on the ground floor, are large and homely and the elegant dining room is the setting for a full English breakfast. No dogs.
🕐 Closed 23–30 Dec
🍴 £55
🛏 4 🚭
🅿 From M5 junction 7 head for city centre, at seventh traffic lights turn left into Edgar Street, College Precinct is pedestrian-only street on right

THE NORTH

The 2002 Commonwealth Games in Manchester revitalized the city's hotel scene and visitors rarely have problems finding a place to stay. York also has plenty of accommodation although, as the north's most popular destination, the best places fill quickly in the summer. York's tourist information centre can make reservations (tel: 01904 621756).

PRICES AND SYMBOLS

Prices are the starting price for a double room for one night, unless otherwise stated. Breakfast is included unless noted otherwise. All the hotels listed accept credit cards unless otherwise stated. Note that rates vary widely throughout the year.

For a key to the symbols ▷ 2.

ALTRINCHAM

ASH FARM COUNTRY HOUSE
♦♦♦♦♦
Park Lane, Little Bollington WA14 4TJ
Tel: 0161 9299290
www.ashfarm.co.uk
This 18th-century farmhouse bed-and-breakfast is peacefully located on a country lane. The bedrooms boast handmade furniture. The many personal touches include homemade biscuits, fresh fruit, bathrobes and hot-water bottles for cooler nights. There is a large lounge and separate breakfast area with beautiful views over the Cheshire countryside. No children under 12 or dogs.
⊙ Closed 5 Jan–15 Jan
🛏 £63
① 3 🚭
🚗 Turn off A56 beside Stamford Arms

BAMBURGH

VICTORIA HOTEL ★★
Front Street NE69 7DP
Tel: 01668 214431
www.victoriahotel.net
In the centre of town overlooking the village green, this hotel has been sympathetically upgraded and offers an interesting blend of tradition and modernity. The bedrooms, some with views to Bamburgh Castle and Holy Island, are elegantly furnished. The bar is popular with locals. There's also a restaurant.
🛏 £94
① 29 🚭 In restaurant
🚗 Off A1 north of Alnwick turn on to B1342 near Belford and follow signs to Bamburgh
🚉 Chathill

BOLTON ABBEY

DEVONSHIRE ARMS COUNTRY HOUSE HOTEL ☆☆☆
Bolton Abbey BD23 6AJ
Tel: 01756 710441
This beautiful hotel dates back to the 17th century and has the feel of a country house. There are log fires in the sitting rooms and the rooms in the older part of the house have four-poster beds. There is an excellent restaurant (▷ 360).
🛏 £230
① 40
🚭 In restaurant and reception area
🚗 On B6160 to Bolton Abbey 230m (250 yards) north of junction with A59 roundabout junction
🚉 Ilkley 5 miles (7km)

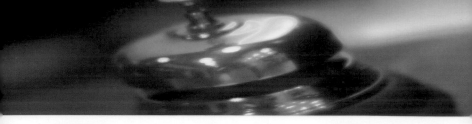

CARLISLE

BESSIESTOWN FARM ◆◆◆◆◆

Catlowdy CA6 5QP
Tel: 01228 577219
www.bessiestown.co.uk

This delightful farmhouse is a useful place to break a journey to or from Scotland. Bedrooms are stylish and include family rooms and a luxury suite with spa bath. There's also a heated indoor swimming pool. Freshly prepared dinners and hearty breakfasts with home-made bread set travellers up for the day. No dogs.

🍴 £65
🛏 5 🚭
🚗 From Bush Hotel in Longtown, 6.5 miles (10km) to Bridge Inn, turn right onto B6318, 1.5 miles (2km) to Catlowdy, farm first left

CONISTON

CONISTON LODGE HOTEL ◆◆◆◆◆

Station Road LA21 8HH
Tel: 01539 441201
www.coniston-lodge.com

Coniston Lodge bed-and-breakfast is ideally situated for exploring the Lake District. All six bedrooms are attractively decorated. Ambitious cooking, which might include homemade pâté, local game and fish, can be sampled in the dining room. No dogs.

🍴 £90
🛏 6 🚭
🚗 At crossroads on A593 close to filling station; turn uphill at crossroads into Station Road
🚉 Windermere

DURHAM

KINGSLODGE HOTEL AND RESTAURANT ★★★

Flass Vale DH1 4BG
Tel: 0191 3709977
www.kingslodge-info.co.uk

With the illusion of a secluded setting, this stylish modern hotel is popular with both business and leisure guests. Accommodation is provided in compact but well-designed rooms. For meals, Knights is a contemporary restaurant and champagne bar, and there is

also a less formal bar and beer terrace, and a bright and comfortable lounge.

🍴 £100
🛏 21 🚭 In restaurant
🚗 A1 junction 62 over first three roundabouts, then right at fourth. Take first left then first right; hotel is at end of road
🚉 Durham

GRASSINGTON

ASHFIELD HOUSE HOTEL ◆◆◆◆◆

Summers Fold, Grassington, Skipton BD23 5AE
Tel: 01756 752584
www.ashfieldhouse.co.uk

Guests are greeted like old friends at this beautifully

The Kingslodge provides a haven in the centre of Durham

maintained 17th-century house, peacefully tucked away a few paces from the village square. The bedrooms of this luxury bed-and-breakfast are attractively decorated. The smart lounges offer a high level of comfort where guests can relax or enjoy pre-dinner drinks from an honesty bar. A freshly prepared four-course dinner is available by arrangement (except Saturday). No children under 12. No dogs.

🕐 Closed 25 Dec, one week in Mar
🍴 £80
🛏 7 🚭
🚗 Take B6265 to village centre then turn left off Main Street into Summers Fold
🚉 Skipton

HARROGATE

RUSKIN HOTEL ◆◆◆◆◆

1 Swan Road HG1 2SS
Tel: 01423 502045
www.ruskinhotel.co.uk

This popular bed-and-breakfast has bedrooms that are stylishly decorated and furnished with Victorian pine; one has a beautiful four-poster bed and another its own separate entrance. The drawing room looks out over the neatly maintained garden and the elegant dining room opens out on to the terrace. Delicious light suppers are available by prior arrangement. Guests can also use the local leisure centre by arrangement.

🍴 £85
🛏 7 🚭
🚗 Off A61 Ripon road; turn left opposite The Majestic 🚉 Harrogate

HAWKSHEAD

QUEEN'S HEAD HOTEL ❀❀

Main Street LA22 0NS
Tel: 01539 436271

In this prettiest of Lakeland villages, the Queen's Head pub doesn't spoil the show. The 16th-century building stands in Hawkshead's traffic-free centre festooned with hanging baskets and window boxes. The interior has bare beams, a real fire and plenty of curios. Bedrooms are decorated in a country style.

🍴 £90
🛏 14
🚗 A590 to Newby Bridge, take first right to Hawkshead

HAWORTH

OLD WHITE LION HOTEL ★★

Main Street, Haworth, Keighley BD22 8DU
Tel: 01535 642313
www.oldwhitelionhotel.com

Over 300 years old and steeped in history, this delightful hotel is at the top of an old cobbled street, just 0.5 mile (800m) from Haworth station. There is an oak-panelled lounge and a choice of homey bars serving a range of meals. Formal dining is

available in the popular restaurant. The comfortably furnished bedrooms are well equipped and vary in size and style.

🛏 £69.50

🛈 15

🚗 Turn off A629 on to B6142 into Haworth

🚉 Haworth, Keighley

HELMSLEY

FEVERSHAM ARMS HOTEL ★★★

1 High Street YO62 5AG
Tel: 01439 770766

The bedrooms in this comfortable hotel are furnished to a high standard and there is a comprehensively equipped leisure centre with a gym. Tennis courts and a heated swimming pool can be found in the pleasant grounds. Diners have a choice of formal or informal styles of eating, and menus offer a wide choice.

🛏 £140

🛈 19

🍽 In restaurant 🍷 📺

🚗 From junction 49 of A1 take A168 to Thirsk then A170 to Helmsley. From York take B1363 north, turn left on to B1257 and then A170. Hotel is 125m (140 yards) from Market Place

🚉 Malton

ISLE OF MAN

BALLACALLIN HOUSE ★★

Dalby Village, Patrick, Isle of Man IM5 3BT
Tel: 01624 841100

This small, privately owned hotel in Dalby is personally run and offers well-equipped, modern accommodation. Bedrooms with four-posters and a two-bedroom suite are available. Some enjoy sea views, as do the bright restaurant and the spacious lounge bar.

🛏 £70

🛈 10 🍽

🚗 A27 Peel to Port Erin road at south end of Dalby

KESWICK

DERWENTWATER HOTEL ★★★

Portinscale CA12 5RE
Tel: 01768 772538
www.derwentwater-hotel.co.uk

This is a popular and friendly holiday hotel with gardens that stretch down to the shores of Derwentwater. Some of the bedrooms have good views of the lake. Inviting public areas include a conservatory, lounge and shop, and a restaurant. Outdoor facilities include a croquet lawn and putting green, private fishing, and access to local leisure facilities, including free use of a nearby health spa.

Enjoy all mod cons at the Liverpool Marriott

🛏 £140; discount for under-15s

🛈 46 🍽 In restaurant

🚗 Off A66 turn into Portinscale and through village then when road turns right take left turn as signposted

🚉 Penrith

LEEDS

MALMAISON HOTEL ★★★

Sovereign Quay LS1 1DQ
Tel: 0113 3981000
www.malmaison.com

Close to the waterfront, this stylish property offers striking bedrooms with CD players. The bar leads into a brasserie, where guests can choose between a full three-course meal or a substantial snack. Service is both enthusiastic and friendly. A small fitness centre and impressive meeting rooms complete the package.

🛏 £79

🛈 100 🍽 In 70 bedrooms 🍷 📺

🚗 From M621/M1 junction 3 follow signs to Leeds city centre. At KPMG building turn right into Sovereign Street; Malmaison is at end of street on right 🚉 Leeds City

LIVERPOOL

LIVERPOOL MARRIOTT HOTEL CITY CENTRE ★★★★

1 Queen Square L1 1RH
Tel: 0151 476 8000

The Marriott is a large, impressive modern hotel located in the heart of the city. The elegant public rooms include a café bar, cocktail bar and Oliver's Restaurant, for dining in stylish surroundings. The bedrooms benefit from many facilities. The hotel also has a well-equipped health club with heated indoor pool, plus sauna, solarium and Jacuzzi.

🛏 £140; discount for under-16s

🛈 146 🍽 In restaurant 🍷 📺

🚗 From city centre follow signs for Queen Square parking, hotel is adjacent

🚉 Liverpool Lime Street

MANCHESTER

THE LOWRY HOTEL ★★★★★

50 Dearmans Place, Chapel Wharf, Salford M3 5LH
Tel: 0161 827 4000
www.roccofortehotels.com

Rocco Forte's superbly located city centre hotel is part of the Chapel Wharf development on the banks of the River Irwell, and this forms the backdrop for the hotel. The decorative style throughout is contemporary, with good use made of light and space to create an environment that is modern yet welcoming. Marco Pierre White's River Room restaurant is justly renowned. Facilities include a sauna and gym, with spa and swimming pool available offsite.

🛏 £230; discount for under-12s

🛈 165 📺

🚉 Manchester Piccadilly or Victoria

MALMAISON ★★★

Piccadilly M1 3AQ
Tel: 0161 2781000
www.malmaison.com
Even more chic and stylish following substantial building work, the well-presented Malmaison now offers extra comfort, including some additional air-conditioned bedrooms. Good meals are served in the busy brasserie, and other facilities include a small but exclusive spa, plus sauna, solarium, jacuzzi and gym.

🍴 £129
🛏 167 ⚐
🚗 Follow city centre signs then signs to Piccadilly station to find hotel opposite at bottom of station approach
🚉 Manchester Piccadilly

MASHAM

SWINTON PARK ★

Masham, Ripon HG4 4JH
Tel: 01765 680900
www.swintonpark.com
The original part of this imposing castle dates from the 17th century, and it was extended during the Victorian and Edwardian eras. The bedrooms are tastefully furnished and come with features such as CD players, and there is also a gym and Jacuzzi. Samuel's restaurant features local produce, much of it from the Swinton estate. A superb range of activities and outdoor facilities includes private fishing, croquet, putting, shooting, falconry and horseback riding. There's also a golf course nearby.

🍴 £140; discount for under-12s
🛏 30 🚭 In restaurant ⚐
🚗 Turn off A1 left (west) on to B6267 to Masham. Follow signs through Masham town centre and turn right on to Swinton Terrace. Follow road 1 mile (1.6km) over bridge and up hill. Swinton Park is on right
🚉 Northallerton

MORECAMBE

CLARENDON HOTEL ★★★

76 Marine Road West, West End Promenade LA4 4EP
Tel: 01524 410180
www.mitchellshotels.co.uk
This well-maintained seafront hotel was been completely refurbished to offer bright, cheerful public areas and smartly appointed bedrooms, all with fully tiled bathrooms. Its position offers fine views over Morecambe Bay and the mountains of the Lake District beyond. There is a restaurant, and afternoon teas and bar meals are also available. The Davy Jones Locker bar is in the cellar.

Swinton Park in Masham offers many sporting facilities

🍴 £90; discount for under-14s
🛏 29
🚗 From M6 junction 34 follow Morecambe signs. At roundabout with The Shrimp on corner take first exit to Westgate and follow to waterfront. Turn right at traffic lights and hotel is third block along Central Promenade
🚉 Morecambe

NEWCASTLE UPON TYNE

MALMAISON QUAYSIDE ★★★

Newcastle upon Tyne NE1 3DX
Tel: 0191 245 5000
www.malmaison.com
Overlooking the river and the new Millennium Bridge, this hotel has a prime position in the new up-and-coming redeveloped quayside district.

Bedrooms are spacious and contemporary in style, offering large beds, music and communications systems as standard. Public areas include spa, sauna, solarium and gym facilities, some meeting rooms and the popular riverside brasserie.

🍴 £135
🛏 120 ⚐
🚗 Follow signs for Newcastle city centre and take road for Quayside/Law Courts. Hotel is 100m (300ft) past Law Courts 🚉 Newcastle Central

ROSEDALE ABBEY

THE MILBURN ARMS HOTEL ★★

Rosedale Abbey, Pickering YO18 8RA
Tel: 01751 417312
www.milburnarms.co.uk
Hidden deep in the folds of the North York Moors National Park, this charming country-house hotel acts as a perfect retreat from the modern world. Dating back to 1776, the family-run hotel offers 13 beautifully furnished bedrooms with a welcoming bar and log fires in the public rooms. The hotel's Priory restaurant (▷ 361) is well regarded.

🕐 Closed 25 Dec
🍴 £80
🛏 11
🚗 A170 west from Pickering, right at Rosedale sign then 7 miles (11km) north

SCARBOROUGH

OX PASTURE HALL COUNTRY HOTEL ★★★

Lady Ediths Drive, Raincliffe Woods YO12 5TD
Tel: 01723 365295
This delightful country hotel is a lovely conversion of a farmhouse, set in the North Riding Forest Park. Six of the bedrooms are in the main house and the others around an attractive garden courtyard. Public areas include a split-level bar, a quiet lounge and attractive restaurant offering à la carte and fixed-price menus. Outside is a croquet lawn and

LINTHWAITE HOUSE HOTEL AND RESTAURANT ☆☆☆

Crook Road, Windermere LA23 3JA
Tel: 01539 488600
www.linthwaite.com

Linthwaite House is set in 6ha (14 acres) of hilltop grounds that include its own fishing tarn, and enjoys stunning views of Windermere lake—particularly from its bright, attractive conservatory. Other public rooms include a comfortable lounge, a smokers' bar and a restaurant serving carefully prepared meals. The bedrooms, which are individually decorated in both contemporary and traditional styles, are thoughtfully equipped. Service and hospitality are real strengths at this hotel. There's also a croquet lawn, putting green, private fishing and free use of the nearby leisure spa.

🛏 £99; discount for under-12s
🍴 26 🚭 In restaurant
🚗 Take A591 towards the lakes for 8 miles (13km) to large roundabout. Take first exit (B5284) and continue for 6 miles (10km). Hotel is on left, 1 mile (1.6km) past Windermere golf club
🚆 Windermere

putting green, and private fishing is available.

🛏 £115; discount for under-12s
🍴 23 🚭 In restaurant
🚗 Take A171 out of Scarborough. After passing hospital follow tourist sign for Forge Valley and Raincliffe Woods. Turn left and hotel is 1.5 miles (2.5km) on right
🚆 Scarborough

WHITBY

STAKESBY MANOR HOTEL ★★

Manor Close, High Stakesby YO21 1HL
Tel: 01947 602773
www.stakesby-manor.co.uk

Situated in a residential area, this Georgian mansion attracts many regulars. The bedrooms are impressively furnished, and the management very professional.

🚭 Closed 24–30 Dec
🛏 £88; discount for under-15s
🍴 13 🚭 In restaurant
🚗 At roundabout junction of A171/B1416 take road for West Cliff; third turning on right

WINDERMERE

CEDAR MANOR COUNTRY LODGE ◇◇◇◇◇

Ambleside Road LA23 1AX
Tel: 015394 43192

This neat hotel is set in large gardens on the edge of town. Some of the bedrooms are in a former coach house, all are smartly presented and have private bathrooms. Public areas include a lounge and split-level breakfast room.

Linthwaite House offers superb views of Windermere

Guests have use of the facilities at Windermere Marina.

🛏 £74
🍴 9 🚭
🚗 From M6 junction 36 stay on A591 beyond Windermere turning, hotel is on left past St. Mary's Church

YORK

ALEXANDER HOUSE ◆◆◆◆◆

94 Bishopthorpe Road YO23 1JS
Tel: 01904 625016
www.alexanderhouseyork.co.uk

Guests are made to feel very much at home at this Victorian terraced house, just a short walk from the city centre. The owners of this stylish bed-and-breakfast delight in sharing their home with guests, and have created four superbly

HAZELWOOD ◆◆◆◆

24–25 Portland Street, Gillygate
YO31 7EH
Tel: 01904 626548
www.thehazelwoodyork.com

The Hazelwood bed-and-breakfast is an elegant Victorian town house quietly situated in the heart of the ancient city, only 350m (400 yards) from York Minster. The bedrooms are individually styled and tastefully fitted to very high standards using designer fabrics. There's a wide choice of breakfasts. No children under eight. No dogs.

🛏 £75
🍴 14 🚭
🚗 Approaching York from north on A19 turn left before City Gate and take first turning left
🚆 York

equipped rooms. Delicious breakfasts featuring quality local produce are served in the well-appointed dining room. No children under 12.

🚭 Closed 25 Dec–1 Jan
🛏 £59
🍴 4 🚭
🚗 From A64 take A1036 York road west into city centre. Turn right at Scarcroft Road, at the end turn right and Alexander House is 100m (300ft) on left
🚆 York

THE GRANGE HOTEL ☆☆☆

1 Clifton, York YO30 6AA
Tel: 01904 644744
www.grangehotel.co.uk

This bustling Regency town house is conveniently placed. The bedrooms have been thoughtfully equipped, and the public rooms are comfortable and stylish. There are two dining options—The Brasserie in the cellar, which has an informal atmosphere, and The Ivy, which is lavishly decorated and offers a fine dining menu.

🛏 £135; discount for under-12s
🍴 30
🚗 On A19 York–Thirsk road about 500m (550 yards) from city centre
🚆 York

STAYING

SCOTLAND

Unless you've reserved well in advance there's one time of year when you'll not find an empty room in Edinburgh, and that's Festival time from late August. Also wildly popular is celebrating Hogmanay–New Year's Eve–in Edinburgh. Advance reservation is essential for both occasions.

Scotland's National Tourist Board (www.visitscotland.com) provides a room-booking service during these peak periods.

ABERDEEN

ARDOE HOUSE ★★★★
South Deeside Road, Blairs AB12 5YP
Tel: 01224 860600
www.macdonald-hotels.co.uk
This Scots baronial-style mansion stands in an elevated position above the beautiful countryside of the Dee Valley. In the main house the rooms are tastefully furnished to retain the ambience of a country house hotel, with a more modern feel to those in the extension. There is a leisure club with sauna, gym, supervised pool and solarium, and an impressive cocktail lounge serving over 180 different malt whiskies.
💷 £105
🛏 117 🍴 In restaurant 🏊
🚗 3 miles (5km) west of city off B9077

ARDUAINE

LOCH MELFORT ★★★
PA34 4XG
Tel: 01852 200233
www.lochmelfort.co.uk
Enjoying one of the finest locations on the west coast, this popular, family-run hotel has outstanding views across Asknish Bay towards the islands of Jura, Scarba and Shuna.
💷 £78; discount for under-14s
🛏 27
🚗 On the A816, midway between Oban and Lochgilphead 🚉 Oban

AVIEMORE

THE OLD MINISTER'S HOUSE ◆◆◆◆◆
Rothiemurchus PH22 1QH
Tel: 01479 812181
www.theoldministershouse.co.uk
The Old Minister's House is beautifully furnished and immaculately maintained while the bedrooms are spacious and equipped to a high standard. There is a lounge and a dining room where hearty breakfasts are served. No children under four.
💷 £60
🛏 4 🍴
🚗 From Aviemore take B970, signed Glenmore and Coylumbridge.

Establishment is 0.75 miles (1km) from Aviemore at Inverdruie

🏧 Aviemore

BALLATER
BALGONIE COUNTRY HOUSE ★★
Braemar Place AB3 5NQ
Tel: 013397 55482
www.royaldeesidehotels.com
This Edwardian house is set in neatly tended gardens. There is a homey bar and lounge, and carefully prepared meals are served in the dining room. Bedrooms and public areas offer good levels of comfort. The proprietors ensure a friendly welcome.

🅲 Closed 6 Jan end Feb
💷 £100; discount for under-14s
ⓘ 9
🚗 Off A93 Aberdeen–Perth road, on the western outskirts of village of Ballater. Hotel is signed
🏧 Aberdeen

BANCHORY
BANCHORY LODGE HOTEL
AB31 5HS
Tel: 01330 822625
This tranquil hotel offers the added attraction of the River Dee, famed for its salmon, running through its grounds. Victorian furnishings accentuate the sense of comfort, and traditional dining is on offer (▷ 364). Fishing is possible from March to the end of September.

💷 £130
ⓘ 22 🚭 In dining room
🚗 Off A93 18 miles (29km) west of Aberdeen

DALBEATTIE
AUCHENSKEOCH LODGE ◆◆◆◆◆
Southwick, Dalbeattie DG5 4PG
Tel: 01387 780277
www.auchenskeoch.co.uk
A former Victorian shooting lodge set in 8ha (20 acres) of stunning grounds with woodland and a small loch. The house is full of charm, and traditional furnishings, log fires and artwork help preserve the original character

of the house. A set four-course dinner is served in the stylish dining room. No children under 12. Private fishing is available.

🅲 Closed Nov–Easter
💷 £60
ⓘ 3
🚗 5 miles (8km) southeast of Dalbeattie, off B793
🏧 Dumfries

DUNDEE
SANDFORD COUNTRY HOUSE HOTEL ★★★
Newton Hill, Wormit DD6 8RG
Tel: 01382 541802
www.sandfordhotelfife.com
The Sandford offers glorious views of the Fife countryside,

Banchory Lodge Hotel was originally a coaching inn

log fires, local antiques and a kitchen that samples the best of the region's cuisine. A variety of bedroom sizes are available, all tastefully modern and well equipped.

💷 £70
ⓘ 16 🚭 In dining room
🚗 4 miles (6.5km) south of Tay Bridge near junction of A92 and B946

DUNKELD
KINNAIRD ★★★
Kinnaird Estate PH8 0LB
Tel: 01796 482440
www.kinnairdestate.com
This striking Edwardian mansion stands in a majestic countryside estate. Public rooms are furnished with antiques and beautiful

paintings. Sitting rooms are warm and inviting with deep-cushioned sofas and open fires. Bedrooms are furnished with luxurious fabrics. Cooking is creative. No children under 12. Tennis courts, private fishing and shooting are available.

💷 £275, including breakfast and dinner.
ⓘ 9
🚗 From Perth, take A9 north. Keep on A9 past Dunkeld and continue for 2 miles (3km), then take B898 on the left
🏧 Dunkeld or Birnam

EDINBURGH
BONNINGTON GUEST HOUSE ◆◆◆◆◆
202 Ferry Road EH6 4NW
Tel 0131 554 7610
This Georgian house offers individually furnished bedrooms that retain many of the property's original features. The homely lounge is complemented by an attractive dining room, where a fine Scottish breakfast is served. There is a particularly warm welcome here.

💷 £50; discount for under-11s
ⓘ 6
🚗 On A902
🏧 Edinburgh Waverley

MALMAISON ★★★
One Tower Place EH6 7DB
Tel: 0131 468 5000
www.malmaison.com
The stylish Malmaison overlooks the port of Leith. Bedrooms have striking décor, CD players, mini bars and a number of individual touches. Food and drink are equally important here, with brasserie-style dining and a café-bar.

💷 £99
ⓘ 101 🚻
🚗 A900 from city centre towards Leith. At end of Leith Walk continue over lights, through two more sets of lights, then left into Tower Street; hotel on right

THE SCOTSMAN ★★★★★

20 North Bridge EH1 1YT
Tel: 0131 556 5565
www.thescotsmanhotel.co.uk
The former head office of *The Scotsman* newspaper has been transformed into this state-of-the-art boutique hotel, where traditional elegance blends seamlessly with cutting-edge technology and friendly, attentive service. Bedrooms are all smartly furnished and very well equipped. The galleried Brasserie restaurant offers an informal dining option.
🅦 £250
ⓘ 68 ⛵ 🐕
🚗 A8 to city centre, left on to Charlotte Street. Right into Queen Street, right at roundabout on to Leith Street. Keep straight on, left on to North Bridge, hotel on right
🚉 Edinburgh Waverley

FORT WILLIAM

ASHBURN HOUSE ◆◆◆◆◆

8 Achintore Road PH33 6RQ
Tel: 01397 706000
www.highland5star.co.uk
This elegant Victorian villa, which enjoys wonderful views overlooking Loch Linnhe and the Ardgour Hills, is just five minutes from the town centre. The bedrooms are spacious, with an extensive range of amenities. No dogs.
Ⓒ Closed Dec–end Jan
🅦 £70, discount for under-14s
ⓘ 7 🚭
🚗 At the junction of A82 and Ashburn Lane, 500m (550 yards) from the large roundabout at the southern end of the High Street; or 400m (440 yards) on the right after entering 30mph zone from the south
🚉 Fort William

GAIRLOCH

THE OLD INN

Gairloch IV21 2BD
Tel: 01445 712006
The oldest hotel in Gairloch, dating from around 1792, with views across Gairloch harbour. The Inn has been sympathetically restored. There is an excellent range of real ales and plenty of accommodation.

The Old Inn was the AA Pub of the Year for Scotland 2003.
🅦 £45
ⓘ 14
🚗 Just off main A832, near harbour at southern end of village

GLAMIS

CASTLETON HOUSE ☆☆☆

Castleton of Eassie DD8 1SJ
Tel: 01307 840340
www.castletonglamis.co.uk
Exemplary levels of guest care by enthusiastic owners and their young team are features of this Victorian house set in its own grounds. Bedrooms are noted for their comfortable beds. Lunches are also served here, but it is dinner that will

Castleton House in Glamis provides exceptional service

provide a particularly memorable experience.
🅦 £140, discount for under-14s
ⓘ 6
🚗 On A94 midway between Forfar and Cupar Angus, 3 miles (5km) west of Glamis
🚉 Dundee

GLASGOW

KELVINGROVE HOTEL ◆◆◆

944 Sauchiehall Street G3 7TH
Tel: 0141 339 5011
www.kelvingrove-hotel.co.uk
This well-maintained, friendly hotel lies just west of the city centre. Bedrooms, including several rooms suitable for families, are particularly well equipped and have fully tiled private bathrooms. There is a

bright breakfast room and a reception lounge that is manned 24 hours.
🅦 £50
ⓘ 22 🚭
🚗 0.25 miles (400m) west of Charing Cross. From M8 junction 18 follow signs for Kelvingrove
🚉 Kelvinhall or Glasgow Central

ONE DEVONSHIRE GARDENS ☆☆☆☆

5 Devonshire Gardens G12 0UX
Tel: 0141 339 2001
www.onedevonshiregardens.com
One Devonshire Gardens is one of the city's most stylish hotels. The sumptuously furnished drawing room is the focal point of the day rooms, with all the elegance and comfort expected in such a grand house. An imaginatively prepared Scottish menu is served in the small dining room and there is 24-hour room service.
🅦 £145; discount for under-14s
ⓘ 14
🚗 From M8 junction 17 turn right at slip road lights (A82). Continue 1.5 miles (2.5km). Go over first traffic lights, left at second. Take first right at mini roundabout. Hotel is at end of road
🚉 Glasgow Central

GLENELG

GLENELG INN

IV40 8JR
Tel: 01599 522273
This characterful old village inn commands stunning views across the Glenelg Bay. From here the little summer-only ferry chugs across the Sound of Sleat to Skye. As well as a bar where fiddlers often play and an excellent dining room noted for local cuisine, there are comfortable bedrooms with magnificent views.
🅦 £100 including dinner
ⓘ 7 🚭 In dining room
🚗 From Shiel Bridge (A87) take unclassified road to Glenelg

GRANTOWN-ON-SPEY

THE PINES ★★

Woodside Avenue PH26 3JR
Tel: 01479 872092
www.thepinesgrantown.co.uk

This impressive Victorian house is set in well-tended gardens, a short walk from the heart of town. Bedrooms are generally spacious and many have views of the beautiful Speyside scenery. No children under 12.

🕐 Closed Nov–end Feb
💷 £100
ℹ️ 8 🚭
🚉 Aviemore

INNERLEITHEN

TRAQUAIR ARMS HOTEL ◊◊◊
Traquair Road EH44 6PD
Tel: 01896 830229
This traditional inn is in a village setting close to the River Tweed, surrounded by lovely countryside and with a dining room (▷ 365) and homey bar.

🕐 Closed Dec 25, 26, 1–3 Jan
💷 £58
ℹ️ 15 🚭 In restaurant
🚉 6 miles (9.5km) east of Peebles on A72. Hotel 90m (100 yards) from junction with B709

INVERNESS

BUNCHREW HOUSE HOTEL
Bunchrew IV3 8TA
Tel: 01463 234917
www.bunchrew-inverness.co.uk
This beautifully located 17th-century mansion retains much of its original character. The dining room (▷ 365) has marvellous views.

🕐 Closed 24–27 Dec
💷 £130
ℹ️ 14 🚭 In dining room
🚉 2.5 miles (4.5km) from Inverness on A862 towards Beauly

ISLAY, ISLE OF

THE HARBOUR INN
The Square, Bowmore PA43 7JR
Tel: 01496 810330
The bedrooms in this charming old hotel are stylishly furnished and the public rooms have wonderful views of the surrounding bay. There is a fine restaurant (▷ 366).

🕐 Closed 25 Dec, 1 Jan
💷 £90
ℹ️ 7 🚭 In dining room
🚉 Bowmore is situated 8 miles (13km) from the ports of Port Ellen and Port Askaig

JEDBURGH

JEDFOREST HOTEL ★★★
Camptown TD8 6PJ
Tel: 01835 840222
www.jedforesthotel.com
This country house hotel is set in 14ha (35 acres) of woodland and pasture. Jedforest provides a stylish haven. Immaculately presented throughout, it offers an attractive dining room, a brasserie and a lounge. The bedrooms are very smart, with the larger ones being particularly impressive.

💷 £140 including dinner; discount for under-13s
ℹ️ 12 🚭
🚉 3 miles (5km) south of Jedburgh, off A68

Jedforest Hotel is a fine base for the Central Borders

KELSO

THE ROXBURGHE HOTEL AND GOLF COURSE ★★★
Heiton TD5 8JZ
Tel: 01573 450331
www.roxburghe.net
This impressive Jacobean mansion is set in 200ha (500 acres) of mature wood and parkland. Sporting pursuits are popular, with many guests enjoying shooting, fishing and golf. Bedrooms are individually designed and a number have real fires. Comfortably furnished lounges are a perfect setting for lavish afternoon teas.

💷 £140; discount for under-12s
ℹ️ 22

🚉 3 miles (5km) south of Kelso off A698
🚉 Berwick-upon-Tweed

KILCHRENAN

THE ARDANAISEIG HOTEL ★★★
By Loch Awe PA35 1HE
Tel: 01866 833333
Idyllic and tranquil, this old country house hotel sits in a striking location on the shores of Loch Awe. Grand in every sense with a good restaurant (▷ 366). No children under seven.

🕐 Closed 2 Jan–10 Feb
💷 £103
ℹ️ 16 🚭 In dining room
🚉 Take A85 to Oban. At Taynuilt turn left on to B845 towards Kilchrenan. In Kilchrenan turn left by pub. Hotel in 3 miles (5km)

KIRKCUDBRIGHT

SELKIRK ARMS HOTEL ★★★
Old High Street DG6 4JG
Tel: 01557 330402
www.selkirkarmshotel.co.uk
This modern hotel has well-equipped rooms and a creative restaurant (▷ 366).

💷 £97.50
ℹ️ 16 🚭 In dining room
🚉 5 miles (8km) south of A75 junction with A711

MELROSE

FAUHOPE HOUSE ◆◆◆◆◆
Gattonside TD6 9LU
Tel: 01896 823184
Here you'll find first-class hospitality and excellent breakfasts, plus a chance to savour the splendid interior of a delightful country house. Public areas are elegantly furnished; the dining room is particularly stunning. Bedrooms are a haven of luxury, all individual in style and superbly equipped. No dogs.

💷 £70
ℹ️ 5 🚭
🚉 Turn right off A68 on to B6360 to Gattonside. At the 30mph sign turn right, then right again and go up a long drive leading to Fauhope

MOFFAT

WELL VIEW ☆
Ballplay Road DG10 9JU
Tel: 01683 220184
www.wellview.co.uk
Well View still retains many
original Victorian features. The
individually furnished
bedrooms are comfortable and
thoughtfully equipped. Dinner
is the highlight of a stay; the
six-course tasting menu focuses
on fine, fresh ingredients,
which are locally sourced
where possible. The bar meals
are excellent value.
🕒 Closed two weeks Feb, two
weeks Oct
💷 £110; discount for under-11s
🛏 6
🚗 On A708 from Moffat, pass fire
station and take first left

MULL, ISLE OF

HIGHLAND COTTAGE ☆☆
Breadalbane Street, Tobermory
PA75 6PD
Tel: 01688 302030
www.highlandcottage.co.uk
Visitors are assured of a
personal welcome at this
charming cottage-style hotel.
Bedrooms are appointed to a
high standard and feature
antique beds and a range of
thoughtful extras. Public areas
include a relaxing lounge, an
honesty bar and an elegant
dining room.
🕒 Closed four weeks mid-Oct to
mid-Nov
💷 £120
🛏 6
🚗 A848 Craignure/Fishnish ferry
terminal, pass Tobermory signs, go
ahead at mini roundabout across
narrow bridge, turn right. Hotel on the
right opposite the fire station
🚉 Oban

PERTH

HUNTINGTOWER ★★★
Crieff Road, PH1 3JT
Tel: 01738 583771
www.huntingtowerhotel.co.uk
An Edwardian-era house in a
delightful country setting has
been refurbished to provide
excellent accommodation.
Lunches are served in a

pleasant conservatory while
more formal dining is available
in the Oak Room. The spacious
bedrooms have a full
complement of modern
facilities.
💷 £100
🛏 34 🍽 In restaurant
🚗 3 miles (5km) west of Perth off A85

ST. ANDREWS

ST. ANDREWS GOLF HOTEL
☆☆☆
40 The Scores KY16 9AS
Tel: 01334 472611
www.standrews-golf.co.uk
Friendly attentive service is a
particular feature of this hotel,
which overlooks the bay and
enjoys fine views of the

*Glen Orchy House offers some
excellent views*

coastline and links. The
bedrooms have a crisp, clean,
contemporary design. There is
a choice of bars and a wood-
panelled restaurant. Lunch is
very good value and the wine
list has global appeal.
💷 £170; discount for under-12s
🛏 22
🚗 Follow signs 'Golf Course' into Golf
Place and in 180m (200 yards) turn
right into The Scores
🚉 Leuchars

SHETLAND ISLANDS

GLEN ORCHY HOUSE ◊◊◊◊
20 Knab Road, Lerwick ZE1 0AX
Tel: 01595 692031
www.guesthouselerwick.com
This welcoming and well-
presented hotel is within easy

POOL HOUSE HOTEL ★★★
IV22 2LD
Tel: 01445 781272
www.poolhousehotel.co.uk
Where the sparkling river Ewe
tumbles out into Loch Ewe,
this externally modest hotel
conceals a magnificent
country-house interior. There
are delightful views along the
coast and bay.
💷 £165
🛏 5 🍽
🚗 In village 9.6km (6 miles) N of
Gairloch on A832

walking distance of the town
centre. Bedrooms are modern
in design. Breakfasts, as
substantial as dinner, are
chosen from the daily-changing
menu.
💷 £69; discount for under-12s
🛏 22
🚗 Next to the coastguard station

SKYE, ISLE OF

HOTEL EILEAN IARMAIN ★★
Isle Ornsay, Sleat IV43 8QR
Tel: 01471 833332
www.eilean-iarmain.co.uk
This 19th-century hotel
overlooking Isle Ornsay
harbour enjoys spectacular sea
views. Rooms are on the
simple side (not all have TVs),
but the cuisine is breathtaking.
💷 £80
🛏 12
🚗 Take A851 to Isle Ornsay harbour
front

STIRLING

STIRLING HIGHLAND ★★★★
Spittal Street FK8 1DU
Tel: 01786 272727
Set high above the town the
hotel occupies what was once
the old high-school building.
The Scholars Restaurant and
adjoining Headmaster's Study
Bar are housed in original
classrooms. Bedrooms are
modern and well-equipped.
💷 £115
🛏 96
🚗 On road leading to Stirling Castle;
follow Castle signs

STAYING

Planning

WEATHER

CLIMATE

Being an island, Britain's climate is naturally determined by its surrounding seas. Weather fronts move in from the west across the Atlantic—low pressure brings wind, rain and changeable conditions, and high pressure brings more settled weather. Most weather fronts that affect Britain intersect with the Atlantic's warm Gulf Stream, explaining why Britain's climate is milder than countries such as Canada and Russia on the same latitude. When this water-laden sea air meets land, rain falls. As a result the wettest areas of Britain are to the west: Cornwall and Wales. These cloudy depressions are punctuated by anti-cyclones that bring fine weather. Prevailing winds are from the southwest, but cold winds from the northeast (Scandinavia) and warm winds from the southeast (Africa) sometimes affect the country.

Winter (December to late February) is chilly, but snow is rare in southern Britain. However, it is more widespread in the hills of northern England, Wales and Scotland; Scotland's Highlands have skiable snow most winters.

Edinburgh 41m 135ft

York 8m 27ft

Bath 181m 595ft

LONDON 69m 203ft

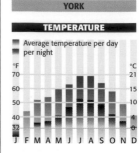

YORK

TEMPERATURE

Average temperature per day
per night

RAINFALL

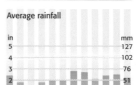

Average rainfall

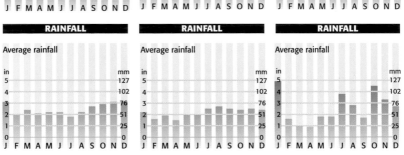

LONDON

TEMPERATURE

Average temperature per day
per night

RAINFALL

Average rainfall

EDINBURGH

TEMPERATURE

Average temperature per day
per night

RAINFALL

Average rainfall

BATH

TEMPERATURE

Average temperature per day
per night

RAINFALL

Average rainfall

WEATHER SITES			
Organization	Notes	Telephone/Fax	Website
The Met Office (UK)	Highly informative site, with inshore marine forecasts and specialist forecasts for leisure activities, including images from webcams at several locations for mountain pursuits.	Tel: 0870 900 0100 Fax: 0870 900 5050	www.metoffice.gov.uk enquiries@metoffice.gov.uk
BBC	Comprehensive online information, UK and world weather reports, plus many related topics. Includes satellite imagery and five-day and regional forecasts.		www.bbc.co.uk/weather
Countryfile	Television show on Sunday morning on BBC1, also gives a five-day forecast		www.bbc.co.uk/nature/ environment/programmes/ countryfile

PLANNING

MET OFFICE FORECASTS FOR MOUNTAINOUS REGIONS		MetCALL (60p per minute)	MetFAX (£1 per minute)
Region			
West Highlands	Trossachs, Argyll, Lochaber, northwest Highlands, Skye	09068 500441	09060 100405
East Highlands	Grampians east of Rannoch Moor, Cairngorms	09068 500442	09060 100406
The Lake District	North of England	09068 500484	09060 100407
Snowdonia	North of Wales	09068 500449	09060 100408

WEATHER REPORTS

The Meteorological (Met) Office, founded in 1854, is the government agency responsible for weather forecasting and supplying information to broadcasters such as the BBC. It is a global service and its website is an excellent place to start with any weather-related query. Daily forecasts are given at the end of television and radio news programmes, and are also available by phone, fax, text messaging or on the internet. The Met Office also provides detailed vital shipping and other marine forecasts.

Regional forecasts

For regional forecasts from the Met Office for the next hour, day, five or ten days, by telephone or fax, see their website: www.metoffice.gov.uk for a full list of numbers to dial.

Regional variations

Despite the small size of the United Kingdom, there are considerable regional variations in its weather. The moderating influence of the sea affects the coastal climate for up 20 miles (32km) inland. In winter the coast is often warmer than inland areas and in summer it is often cooler. Mountainous areas (see below) are notoriously unpredictable and the weather is often harsh. The coldest areas of the country in winter are the Grampian and Tayside regions of Scotland, with average daily temperatures in January as low as –5°C (23°F). The sunniest parts tend to be flat areas near the coast, such as the Isle of Wight with up to 1,800 hours of sunshine out of 4,000 daylight hours annually. South-facing slopes receive more sunshine than north-facing slopes. The wettest areas are in the south and west of the country, while much of the east, including Cambridgeshire and East Anglia, is in a rain shadow. Cities will also have their own micro-climates and are often drier and warmer than surrounding land.

MOUNTAINOUS AREAS

The weather in Britain's mountain regions (parts of Scotland, Wales and the Lake District) can often be more changeable and dramatic than in low-lying areas, regardless of season. British mountains may not be high but in winter they can be dangerous for the unprepared. Expect temperatures to drop by about two degrees per 300m (985ft) of ascent and wind speeds to double with every 900m (about 3,000ft) of altitude. The Met Office provides twice-daily forecasts for those going into the mountains, with information such as weather hazards, wind speeds, cloud cover, temperatures at altitude and the freezing level.

FLOOD-PRONE AREAS

Several areas of Britain can be susceptible to flooding, usually in flat flood basins, such as the Vale of York, close to rivers. Flooding is more of a risk to property than life, and should not be more than

DAYLIGHT HOURS

January	8
February	9
March	11
April	13
May	15
June	17
July	16
August	15
September	13
October	11
November	10
December	8

a very infrequent inconvenience to visitors. Warnings are issued on television and radio, or you can call the national Floodline (tel: 0845 988 1188) or log on to the Environment Agency's website (www.environment-agency.gov.uk) for the latest news.

WHEN TO GO

May and June have the bonus of long daylight hours, when it stays light until well after 9pm—and after 11pm in northern Scotland.

June to the end of August is the warmest and busiest period, especially during school holidays (late July to end August). Rural and coastal areas—such as the West Country, the national parks and the Scottish Highlands—as well as major tourist cities are very busy at Easter and in July and August. Spring and September are appreciably quieter, although the weather is less reliable.

Autumn and early spring often have the windiest conditions of the year. Global warming appears to have made winter start later and end earlier, with frosty conditions often not arriving until November. On average January is the coldest month. The winter months can be a good time for visiting cities; accommodation is often less expensive and sights are less crowded. But note that some attractions close in winter (November to Easter), including most National Trust properties. However, major city museums stay open year round.

TIME ZONES

Britain is on Greenwich Mean Time (GMT)—also known as Universal Time (UTC)—during winter. In summer (late March to late October) clocks go forward one hour to British Summer Time (BST).
The chart below shows time differences from GMT in principal cities around the world.

City	Time difference	Time at 12 noon GMT
Amsterdam	+1	1pm
Auckland	+10	10pm
Berlin	+1	1pm
Brussels	+1	1pm
Chicago	-6	6am
Dublin	0	12pm
Johannesburg	+2	2pm
Madrid	+1	1pm
Montréal	-6	6am
New York	-5	7am
Paris	+1	1pm
Perth, Australia	+8	8pm
Rome	+1	1pm
San Francisco	-8	4am
Sydney	+10	10pm
Tokyo	+9	9pm

PLANNING

Britain's National Health Service (the NHS) was set up in 1948 to provide healthcare for the nation's citizens based on need not the ability to pay. It is funded by taxpayers—to the tune of £70 billion per year in England alone—and managed by a government department. While NHS care for British citizens is free, private healthcare can also be bought from organizations such as BUPA. Visitors from the European Union (EU) are entitled to free NHS treatment (see below) but people of many other nationalities will have to pay for medical treatment.

BEFORE YOU DEPART
Consult your doctor at least 6–8 weeks before leaving. Free medical treatment is available for visitors from EU countries and Switzerland: Pick up a form from your local post office to apply for a free European Health Insurance Card (EHIC). Several countries have reciprocal healthcare agreements with the UK. In most cases a passport is sufficient identification for hospital treatment. But most countries, including the US and Canada, do not have agreements with Britain, and a comprehensive insurance policy is advisable.
● No inoculations are required to enter Britain. However, it is advisable to have a tetanus booster before departure. And check with your doctor whether you need immunization or health advice for: meningococcal meningitis; hepatitis B; diphtheria; and measles/MMR (measles, mumps, rubella).

WHAT TO BRING
Visitors from the EU and Switzerland should bring their European Health Insurance Card (EHIC, see above). Those from outside the EU should bring their travel insurance policy and a photocopy. Travel insurance is recommended. While emergency medical care is provided free of charge at Accident and Emergency departments of NHS hospitals, the cost of further medical treatment and repatriation is usually covered by a travel insurance policy.

HEALTHY FLYING
● Visitors to Britain from as far as the US, Australia or New Zealand may be concerned about the effect of long-haul flights on their health. The most widely publicized concern is deep vein thrombosis (DVT). Misleadingly labelled 'economy-class syndrome' DVT is the formation of a blood clot in the body's deep veins, particularly in the legs. The clot can be deadly as it moves around the bloodstream.
● People most at risk include the elderly, smokers, the overweight, pregnant women and those using the contraceptive pill. If you are at increased risk of DVT see your doctor before departing. Flying increases the likelihood of DVT because passengers are often seated in a cramped position for long periods of time and may become dehydrated.

To minimize risk:
drink water (not alcohol)
don't stay immobile for hours at a time
stretch and exercise your legs periodically
do wear elastic flight socks, which support veins and reduce the chances of a clot forming

EXERCISES

| 1 ANKLE ROTATIONS | 2 CALF STRETCHES | 3 KNEE LIFTS |

Lift feet off the floor. Draw a circle with the toes, moving one foot clockwise and the other counterclockwise

Start with heel on the floor and point foot upward as high as you can. Then lift heel high keeping ball of foot on the floor

Lift leg with knee bent while contracting your thigh muscle. Then staighten leg, pressing foot flat to the floor

Other health hazards for flyers are airborne diseases and bugs spread by the plane's air-conditioning system. These are largely unavoidable but if you have a serious medical condition seek advice from a doctor before flying.

● Visitors with existing medical conditions and allergies, for example to commonly used drugs, should wear a warning bracelet or tag. Take a first-aid kit with you. This should include: assorted adhesive plasters (Band Aids); sterile dressings; a bandage with safety pins; cotton wool; insect repellent; antiseptic cream; painkillers; remedies for constipation and for diarrhoea; antihistamine tablets; sunscreen; personal medicines.

STAYING HEALTHY
Tap water is safe to drink if it is from the mains. Drinking water that comes from a tank, for example in a train toilet or in the upstairs rooms of a house, will be less fresh.

Between May and September the sun can be strong and a high-factor sunscreen (factor 15 or above) is recommended. Apply it every couple of hours and more often if you are swimming or sweating. Remember that it is also possible to burn on a cloudy day.

PLANNING

MAJOR PHARMACIES		
Name	**Telephone**	**Website**
Boots the Chemist	0115 950 6111	www.boots.com
Co-op Pharmacy	0161 654 4488	www.co-oppharmacy.co.uk
Lloyds Pharmacy	024 7643 2400	www.lloydspharmacy.co.uk
Moss Pharmacy	020 8890 9333	www.mosspharmacy.co.uk
Superdrug	020 8684 7000	www.superdrug.com
Sainsbury Pharmacy	020 7695 6000	www.sainsburys.com
Tesco Pharmacy	01992 632222	www.tesco.com

HOSPITAL EMERGENCY DEPARTMENTS IN KEY CITIES		
Name	**Address**	**Telephone**
Charing Cross Hospital	Fulham Palace Road, London W6 8RF	020 8846 1234
Royal United Hospital	Coombe Park, Bath BA1 3NG	01225 428331
Royal Infirmary of Edinburgh	51 Little France Crescent EH16 4SU	0131 536 1000
John Radcliffe Hospital	Headley Way, Oxford OX3 9DU	01865 741166
York Hospital	Wigginton Road, York YO31 8HE	01904 631313

Call 999 or 112 for an ambulance

• There are no malaria-carrying mosquitoes in Britain, but in the warmer months biting insects can be an annoyance, especially near water, so insect repellent is advisable. In Scotland tiny biting insects known as midges are a particular problem by the lochs and sea during May to late September.

• Major chemists (pharmacies) and larger supermarkets have a wide range of medicines that you can buy over the counter, although items such as antibiotics require a prescription from a doctor.

• Chemists maintain opening rotas in many areas, with times of the duty chemist displayed in pharmacy windows and in local newspapers.

HOW TO GET A DOCTOR

If you are injured you should dial 999 or 112 for an ambulance or go to the casualty (emergency) department of a hospital. If you fall ill or require medication and a doctor, make an appointment with any doctor's surgery; local surgeries are listed in the *Yellow Pages* or log on to the NHS website. There are also more than 40 NHS walk-in centres nationally, giving fast access to health advice and treatment; these are open to everyone seven days a week.

• Free 24-hour medical advice from a qualified nurse is available through the government service NHS Direct (tel: 0845 4647; www.nhsdirect.nhs.uk).

• If you are staying at a hotel or bed-and-breakfast the staff should be able to help you contact a doctor urgently. In many cases emergency telephone numbers will be displayed in a central area or in your room. You can also log on to www.nhs.uk and click on 'Looking for local NHS services' for details about the nearest doctor, dentist, optician or pharmacy.

DENTAL TREATMENT

Patients over 16 have to pay for dental treatment, either through private practices or (slightly cheaper) through the NHS. It is sensible to go for a dental check-up before you leave home. Dentists are listed in telephone directories or you can use the British Dental Association's online service at www.bda-findadentist.org.uk.

OPTICIANS

Wearers of spectacles and contact lenses should bring their prescription, or a spare pair, with them in case of loss or breakage. Opticians can quickly make a replacement pair of spectacles.

SMOKING

Passive smoking (inhaling others' cigarette smoke) has become a major issue in Britain.

• Smoking is banned on buses, trains and on the London Underground. From summer 2007, smoking will be banned in pubs, clubs, restaurants, cinemas, offices, all forms of public transport and all other enclosed public spaces in England. An equivalent ban is already in place in Scotland, and Wales is expected to follow suit.

• The website of Action on Smoking and Health (ASH; www.ash.org) is a useful resource.

OPTICIANS		
Name	**Telephone**	**Website**
Boots Opticians	0845 070 8090	www.boots.com/opticians
David Clulow (London)	020 8515 6700	www.davidclulow.com
Dollond & Aitchison	0121 706 6133	www.danda.co.uk
Specsavers	01481 236000	www.specsavers.co.uk
Vision Express	0115 986 5225	www.visionexpress.com

ALTERNATIVE MEDICAL TREATMENTS		
A wide range of alternative treatments is available in the UK. These treatments are not free for visitors. The listings below are a starting point; local telephone directories will have more details.		
Name	**Telephone**	**Website**
British Osteopathic Association	01582 488455	www.osteopathy.org enquiries@osteopathy.org
British Chiropractic Association	0118 950 5950	www.chiropractic.uk.co.uk enquiries@chiropractic-uk.co.uk
The Society of Homeopaths	0845 450 6622	www.homeopathy-soh.org info@homeopathy-soh.org
Physiotherapists: Use a telephone directory and choose a chartered therapist		

DOCUMENTATION AND CUSTOMS

PASSPORTS

Foreign visitors must have a passport valid for at least six months when entering the UK.

The United Kingdom (England, Wales, Scotland and Northern Ireland), the Channel Islands, the Isle of Man and the Republic of Ireland form a common travel

area. Once you have entered this area, passing through immigration control at any point of entry, you are free to travel within it. However, to take an internal flight, you should carry a passport as identification.

Loss of passport

If you lose your passport, contact your embassy in the UK. It helps if you have details of your passport number; either carry a photocopy of the relevant pages of your passport, or scan them and email them to yourself at an account that you can access anywhere in case of emergency (such as www.hotmail.com).

Visas

Citizens of any one of the European Economic Area (EEA) countries—the EU, plus Switzerland, Norway and Iceland—can enter the UK on leisure or business for any length of stay without a visa. Visitors from the US, Australia, Canada or New Zealand do not require a visa for stays of up to six months. But, you must have enough money to support yourself without working or receiving money from public funds.

Those wishing to stay longer than six months, and nationals of certain other countries, require a visa.

You are usually allowed to enter and leave the UK as many times as you like during the validity of your visa. On arrival you must be able to produce documentation establishing your identity and nationality. For details see www.ukvisas.gov.uk.

CUSTOMS

Goods you buy in the EU

If you bring in large quantities of alcohol or tobacco, a Customs Officer is likely to ask about the purposes for which you hold the goods. This particularly applies if you have with you more than the following amounts:

- 3,200 cigarettes
- 400 cigarillos
- 200 cigars
- 3kg (7lb) of smoking tobacco

- 110 litres of beer
- 10 litres of spirits
- 20 litres of fortified wine (such as port or sherry)
- 90 litres of wine (of which only 60 litres can be sparkling wine)

There are limits on the amount of tobacco products you can bring into the UK from some EU countries. From the Czech Republic: 200 cigarettes or 50 cigars or 100 cigarillos or 250g (9oz) of smoking tobacco. From Estonia: 200 cigarettes or 250g (9oz) of smoking tobacco (no limit on other tobacco products). From Hungary, Latvia, Lithuania, Poland, Slovakia or Slovenia: 200 cigarettes (no limit on other tobacco products).

The EU countries are: Austria, Belgium, Cyprus*, Czech Republic, Denmark, Estonia, Finland, France, Germany, Greece, Hungary, Italy, Latvia, Lithuania, Luxembourg, Malta, Netherlands, Poland, Portugal, Republic of Ireland, Slovakia, Slovenia, Spain (but not the Canary Islands), Sweden, the UK (but not the Channel Islands). *Though Cyprus is part of the EU, goods from any area of Cyprus not under control of the Government of the Republic of Cyprus are treated as non-EU imports.

Travelling to the UK from outside the EU

You are entitled to the allowances shown below only if you travel with the goods and do not plan to sell them. For further information see HM Revenue and Customs website: www.hmrc.gov.uk and click on Travel Information.

- 200 cigarettes; or
- 100 cigarillos; or
- 50 cigars; or
- 250g (9oz) of tobacco

- 60cc/ml of perfume
- 250cc/ml of toilet water

- 1 litre of spirits or strong liqueurs over 22 per cent volume; or
- 2 litres of fortified wine, sparkling wine or other liqueurs
- 2 litres of still table wine

- £145 worth of all other goods including gifts and souvenirs.

Visa regulations can change at short notice, so always check before you travel.

CUSTOMS

Entrants to the UK will have to pass through Customs. Arrivals with 'nothing to declare' should pass through the green channel; those with 'goods to declare' should go to the red channel and arrivals from other EU countries with nothing to declare should pass through the blue channel.

VAT refunds

See page 411.

WORK PERMITS

These permits enable employers based in the UK to employ people who are not nationals of EEA countries and who are not entitled to work. Applications are made by the employer. Citizens of the Commonwealth, British Dependent Territories or British Overseas citizens between 17 and 27 can work part-time or casually for up to two years, as long as work is not the main reason for the visit.

TRAVEL INSURANCE

Insurance is recommended for personal possessions, legal liability and medical costs. See Health (▷ 406–407) for information on what the NHS provides. An annual policy may be best value for frequent overseas travellers.

PLANNING

PACKING AND PRACTICALITIES

There is very little that cannot be acquired in Britain if you have forgotten anything or need to replace something.

CLOTHES AND LUGGAGE
Bring a selection of clothing for a wide range of weather conditions. Rainwear is essential, and also recommended are a lightweight waterproof jacket for summer and a small shoulder bag or rucksack for daily use when sightseeing and walking around town. Avoid expensive-looking, cumbersome luggage if you intend moving around the country a lot.

ADAPTORS
Britain uses 240 volts AC and three-pin plugs, so you'll need an electrical adaptor or converter. Small appliances such as razors and laptops can run on a 50-watt converter, while irons and hairdryers require a 1,600-watt converter. Combination converters cover both types. An adaptor is also required for telephone sockets.

OTHER ITEMS TO PACK
● Details of emergency contacts and friends.
● Your driving licence or permit. An International Driving Permit may be useful if your licence is not in English.
● First aid kit with sticking plasters (adhesive tape), antiseptic cream, cream for insect stings, diarrhoea medicine, laxatives, painkillers, plus any personal medication.
● Glasses or contact lenses and solution, and prescription details.
● Photocopies of passport and travel insurance (or send scanned versions to a secure email account that you can access while you are away).
● Traveller's cheques and/or credit cards (preferably more than one card), and a small amount of cash in sterling (£).
● Numbers of credit/debit cards, registration numbers of mobile phones, cameras and other expensive items (in case of loss).
● Compass (for finding your way in unfamiliar cities).

MEASUREMENTS
Britain officially uses the metric system, with fuel sold in litres,

CLOTHING SIZES
The chart below shows how British, European and US clothes sizes differ.

UK	Europe	US	
36	46	36	SUITS
38	48	38	
40	50	40	
42	52	42	
44	54	44	
46	56	46	
48	58	48	
7	41	8	SHOES
7.5	42	8.5	
8.5	43	9.5	
9.5	44	10.5	
10.5	45	11.5	
11	46	12	
14.5	37	14.5	SHIRTS
15	38	15	
15.5	39/40	15.5	
16	41	16	
16.5	42	16.5	
17	43	17	
8	36	6	DRESSES
10	38	8	
12	40	10	
14	42	12	
16	44	14	
18	46	16	
20	48	18	
4.5	37.5	6	SHOES
5	38	6.5	
5.5	38.5	7	
6	39	7.5	
6.5	40	8	
7	41	8.5	

and food in grams and kilograms. However, imperial measurements are used widely in everyday life. Beer in pubs is still sold in pints (just under 0.5 litres), and road distances and speed limits are given in miles and miles per hour (mph) respectively. The British gallon (4.5460 litres) is larger than the US gallon (3.7854 litres).

PUBLIC TOILETS
Although some unpleasant facilities survive, most public toilets are modern and well maintained. They are generally plentiful and free in built-up areas. In some city locations smart, self-cleaning, stainless-steel cubicles (superloos) have been installed, and these normally cost 30p to use; there

CONVERSION CHART

From	To	Multiply by
Inches	Centimetres	2.54
Centimetres	Inches	0.3937
Feet	Metres	0.3048
Metres	Feet	3.2810
Yards	Metres	0.9144
Metres	Yards	1.0940
Miles	Kilometres	1.6090
Kilometres	Miles	0.6214
Acres	Hectares	0.4047
Hectares	Acres	2.4710
Gallons	Litres	4.5460
Litres	Gallons	0.2200
Ounces	Grams	28.35
Grams	Ounces	0.0353
Pounds	Grams	453.6
Grams	Pounds	0.0022
Pounds	Kilograms	0.4536
Kilograms	Pounds	2.205
Tons	Tonnes	1.0160
Tonnes	Tons	0.9842

is a similar charge to use toilets at certain large rail stations. Major department stores, large supermarkets and all motorway service stations and filling stations have free toilets. In rural areas toilets can sometimes be found at some roadside lay-bys and in parking areas. It is considered unacceptable for non-customers to use the toilets in pubs, cafés and restaurants.
● Some public toilets for visitors with wheelchairs (for example at train stations) are opened with a special 'RADAR key' available to those with registered disabilities. If you do not have a key, ask the station staff for help.
● Toilets for people with disabilities are unisex, and often also contain baby-changing facilities.

LAUNDRY
When you book accommodation you may like to check whether there are laundry facilities. Telephone directories list launderettes and dry cleaners. Some launderettes offer 'service washes', where the washing and drying are done for you (the typical cost is £5–£6 for a small bag), either on the same day or within 24–48 hours. Dry cleaning is expensive (around £4 per jacket or skirt), but widely available. Some dry cleaners also offer clothing repairs such as zip replacements.

PLANNING

PACKING AND PRACTICALITIES 409

Britain can be an expensive country for visitors, so it's a good idea to explore your options for carrying and changing money.

● Expect to spend a minimum of about £40 per day, if you're travelling independently. It's not hard to spend more than £100 in a day.

● The best idea is to carry money in a range of forms—cash, at least one credit card, bank card/charge/Maestro card and traveller's cheques. The last of these are the safest, as you will be refunded in the event of loss (keep the counterfoil separate from the cheques themselves), usually within 24 hours.

CREDIT CARDS
Credit cards are widely accepted; Visa and MasterCard are the most popular. These can also be used for withdrawing currency at cashpoinst (ATMs), where you pay a fixed withdrawal fee, making it more economical the larger the amount you withdraw, and avoiding the commission

LOST/STOLEN CREDIT CARDS
American Express
01273 696933
Diners Club
01252 513500/0800 460800
MasterCard/Eurocard
0800 964767
Maestro
0113 277 8899
Visa/Connect
0800 895082

charged for changing foreign banknotes and cashing traveller's cheques. If your credit cards or traveller's cheques are stolen call the issuer immediately, then

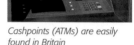

Cashpoints (ATMs) are easily found in Britain

report the loss to the police; you'll need a reference number for insurance purposes.

CASHPOINTS (ATMS)
These are widely available across the country. Check with your bank if you are uncertain whether you will be charged for using another bank's cash machines.

LINK is the UK's only branded network of self-service cash machines. Use of LINK machines is free, except for credit, charge and store cards, for which you pay a cash advance fee. You are also charged for the use of 'convenience' machines installed by cash-machine-owners in certain private locations (such as petrol (gas) stations and convenience stores); charge rates are clearly displayed, and are usually around £1.25–£1.75.

BANKS AND POST OFFICES
● Most banks open Mon–Fri, 9.30–4.30pm, some also open on Sat morning and a few on Sun morning.

CASH

There are 100 pence (p) to the pound (£). Coins are in denominations of **1p, 2p, 5p, 10p, 20p, 50p, £1** and **£2**. Banknotes are in denominations of **£5, £10, £20** and **£50**. Banknotes issued in Scotland look different, but are generally accepted in England and Wales.

2 pounds – £2   1 pound – £1   50 pence – 50p   20 pence – 20p

10 pence – 10p   5 pence – 5p   2 pence – 2p   1 penny – 1p

CHEQUEPOINT
CHANGECAMBIO

Chequepoint
548 Oxford Street W1C 1LU
Tel: 020 7723 1005
Marble Arch Underground

71 Gloucester Road SW7 4SS
Tel: 020 7373 9682
Gloucester Road Underground

2 Queensway (first floor) W2 3RX
Tel: 020 7229 0093
Website: www.chequepoint.com
Bayswater or Queensway Underground

● It pays to shop around for the best exchange and commission rates on currency. You do not pay commission on sterling traveller's cheques if you cash them at a bank affiliated with the issuing bank.
● You need to present ID (usually passport) when cashing traveller's cheques.
● About 1,700 post offices offer commission-free bureau de change services (tel: 08458 500900), with an online ordering service available through www.postoffice.co.uk. Payment is in cash, or by cheque, banker's draft, Visa, MasterCard, Maestro, Delta, Solo or Electron.
● Most post offices are open Mon–Fri, 9–5.30, Sat 9–12.30.

BUREAUX DE CHANGE

● These operate in most major streets in towns and cities in Britain, as well as at airports, rail stations and Underground stations in central London. They are mostly open 8am–10pm. Rates may be higher than at banks; it pays to shop around. Commission rates for currency and traveller's cheques should be clearly displayed.
● 'Commission free' bureaux often offer very poor rates, and should be used only for small amounts.

CONCESSIONS

Reduced fares on buses, trains and Underground services are available for the under-16s. Over-60s can purchase a Senior Railcard for £20, giving a one-third reduction on off-peak rail services. For concessions on public transport, ▷ 46, 47 and 54. For discount passes, ▷ 417.

MAJOR BANKS

There are four main clearing banks in the UK and they each have hundreds of branches. All have foreign exchange facilities.

Name	Head Office Address	Telephone
Barclays	54 Lombard Street EC3P 3AH	020 7699 5000
LloydsTSB	25 Gresham Street EC2V 7HN	020 7626 1500
NatWest	135 Bishopsgate EC2M 3UR	0800 505050
HSBC	8 Canada Square E14 5HQ	020 7991 8888

THE EURO (€)

Britain may not have committed itself to the euro currency yet, but it is possible to spend euros in Britain. The problem is knowing where.
● Many major chain stores, including the Body Shop, Clarks, Debenhams, Dixons, Habitat, HMV, Marks & Spencer, Miss Selfridge, Topman, Topshop, Virgin and Waterstone's accept euros in some or all of their branches.
● Some pubs owned by J. D. Wetherspoon, Scottish and Newcastle and Shepherd Neame take euros, as do some BP and TotalFinaElf petrol (gas) stations.
● Train tickets on the Gatwick Express, Heathrow Express, Stansted Express and Virgin trains can also be paid in euros.
● Some phoneboxes in London accept euro coins.
● Outside London, generally, the bigger the city, the more places will accept euros. Some of the chain stores that accept euros will display a sticker to advertise the fact, otherwise the best advice is to ask before you shop.

WIRING MONEY

In an emergency money can be wired to visitors from their home countries, but this can be expensive and time-consuming. Money can be wired from bank to bank, which takes up to two working days, or to agents such as Travelex (tel: 01733 318922, www.travelex.co.uk) or Western Union (tel: 0800 833 833, www.westernunion.com).

VAT REFUNDS

● Value Added Tax (VAT) of 17.5 per cent is added to certain purchases, including consumer durables and antiques.
● If you are a visitor from a non-EU country you can claim VAT back for large purchases from shops that operate the Global Refund scheme. When you make your purchase you can request a tax refund form, which you present to the customs officer on leaving the UK. Alternatively you can post the form back to the shop when you have returned home or collect an immediate cash refund at 339 Oxford Street, London W1 (tel: 020 8222 0101; www.globalrefund.com).
● Refunds can be made up to three months after an item has been purchased.

Exchange rates at time of publication		
£1= unit value in £ sterling		
US $	$1	£0.57
Canadian $	$1	£0.50
Australian $	$1	£0.42
New Zealand $	$1	£0.37
Euro €	€1	£0.69
For up-to-date exchange rates use an online currency converter such as www.xe.com/ucc/		

TIPPING	
Restaurants (where service is not included)	10%
Tour guides	£1–£2
Hairdressers	10%
Taxis	10%
Chambermaids	50p–£1 per day
Porters	50p–£1 per bag

10 EVERYDAY ITEMS AND HOW MUCH THEY COST	
Takeaway sandwich	£2.50
Bottle of water	£1.00
Cup of tea or coffee	90p–£1.75
Pint of beer	£2.20
Glass of house wine	£2.50
British national daily newspaper	30p–65p (Mon–Fri), more at weekends (Sun, up to £1.50)
Roll of camera film	£5
20 cigarettes	£5
Ice cream	£1
Litre of petrol	92p–95p

COMMUNICATION

With technology rapidly changing the way we communicate, the humble postcard is in danger of looking old-fashioned. But however you want to keep in touch with friends and family, there is a multitude of generally swift, convenient and reliable options in Britain.

TELEPHONES

The main public phone company is British Telecom (BT), which operates 70,000 payphones throughout the UK.

AREA CODES, COUNTRY CODES AND TELEPHONE DIRECTORIES

● When making a local call omit the initial area code.
● When making an international call dial the international code, the country code, followed by the telephone number minus the initial 0.
● Most area codes are four- or five-digit numbers beginning with 01.
● For London the code is 020. Telephone directories (phone books) and *Yellow Pages* show the code in brackets for each telephone number.
● There is a full list of area codes and country codes in every phone book.

PUBLIC PHONEBOXES

● Boxes are generally silver or red and are found at all main line stations, Underground stations and on the streets in towns and cities throughout the country.
● You can use credit and debit cards to make calls from BT payphones (75p setup charge, other calls for instance to mobiles £1; then 20p per minute all times).

COUNTRY CODES FROM THE UK	
Australia	00 61
Belgium	00 32
Canada	00 1
France	00 33
Germany	00 49
Ireland	00 353
Italy	00 39
Netherlands	00 31
New Zealand	00 64
Spain	00 34
Sweden	00 46
US	00 1

● Payphones accept 10p, 20p, 50p and £1 coins; some also accept £2 coins. Only unused coins are returned, so avoid using high denomination coins for short calls.
● Some establishments, such as hotels and pubs, have their own payphones, for which they set their own profit margin. These can be exorbitant, and are recommended only in an emergency. Similarly, phone calls made from hotel rooms often incur high charges.

USING A MOBILE PHONE

Britain has wholeheartedly embraced mobile phone technology, although mobiles are sometimes discouraged in pubs and elsewhere, and some train carriages (cars) have dedicated 'quiet areas'. There's a proliferation of mobile phone shops in almost every town.
● If you're visiting from overseas and already have a mobile phone, you can purchase a SIM card for between £10 and £20 which gives you access to one of the main networks such as O_2, Orange or Vodafone.

DIALLING CODE PREFIXES	
00	international codes
01	area codes
02	area codes
07	calls charged at mobile rates
080	free calls
084	calls charged at local rates
087	calls charged at national rates
09	calls charged at premium rates

For details of charges, call the operator on 100

When dialling Britain from abroad, dial 0044 and omit the first 0 of the area code.

USEFUL TELEPHONE NUMBERS

Directory enquiries: competing services from several companies: try **118500** (BT) or **118111** (One.Tel)

International directory enquiries: competing services from several companies: try **118505** (BT) or **118211** (One.Tel)

International operator: 155

Operator: 100

Time: 123

● A 'pay as you go' option allows you to top up your account at supermarkets and other shops when necessary. You are usually given a choice of accounts, depending on how much and when you are likely to make calls. A subscription-type account is more useful if you are staying in the country for a substantial period.
● It is also possible to use your own phone and SIM card, depending on what sort of phone you have. You need to know whether your phone operates on a GSM (Global System for Mobile Communications) frequency. Single band GSM phones, which work on 900MHz freqency, can be used in more than 100 countries, but not in the US or Canada. Most phones sold in the US work on 1900MHz and require a new SIM card for use in

CALL CHARGES	
Minimum charge	30p
All UK calls to numbers beginning 01 and 02	30p for up to 15 minutes (10p for every 7.5 minutes thereafter)
Calls to mobile phones	63p per minute Mon–Fri 6am–6pm; 37.5p per minute Mon–Fri 6pm–6am and weekends.
Belgium, France, Germany, Italy, Netherlands, Sweden, US, Canada, Australia and New Zealand	£1 per minute at all times
Call Charges	Local calls and long-distance calls within Britain are the same price irrespective of time of day. Calls to mobile phones are generally more expensive than other calls.

PLANNING

Britain. Dual (900 and 1900MHz) and tri band phones can be used in most countries around the world without alteration.

● Note that there are still 'black holes' where you cannot get a mobile phone signal, and that these vary for each network.

● Remember to pack an adaptor for the charger.

USING THE INTERNET

● A major network of multimedia Web phones is being installed by BT in high streets, stations, airports and motorway service stations across the country. These enable users to surf the internet and send emails and text messages. Internet access costs £1 for 15 minutes, and 10p for each 90 seconds thereafter. The cost of sending an instant email is 20p. Text messages cost 10p a message. Additionally 1,450 payphones allow you to send text messages and emails.

● Some public libraries have free internet access; for details see www.peoplesnetwork.gov.uk. They may threaten the future of some internet cafés (charges typically £1–£2 per hour), which are currently found in major cities and towns.

WIRELESS BRITAIN

In addition to internet cafés and web phones, BT has introduced more than 2,000 wireless 'hotspots' in locations such as airports, hotels, cafés and service stations across the country (to find the location of your nearest wireless hotspot in the UK go to www.wifinder.com). The hubs allow laptop and pocket PC users within a 100m (109 yards)

With new mobile technology it is easy to stay in touch on the move

radius broadband access to the internet using wireless technology known as 'Wi-Fi'. You need a laptop or pocket PC PDA running Microsoft Windows XP, 2000 or Microsoft Pocket PC 2002, and a wireless LAN card. Any 'Wi-Fi' approved card should work with BT Openzone. Note that the service remains an expensive, if convenient, way of surfing the internet.

USING A LAPTOP

If you intend to use your own laptop in the UK remember to bring a power converter to recharge it and a plug socket adaptor. A surge protector is also a good idea. To connect to the internet you need an adaptor for the phone socket, available (in the UK) from companies such as Teleadapt (www.teleadapt.com). If you use an international service provider, such as Compuserve or AOL, it's cheaper to dial up a local node rather than the number in your home country. Wireless technology, such as Bluetooth, allows you to connect to the internet using a mobile phone; check beforehand what the charges will be. Dial tone frequencies vary from country to country so set your modem to ignore dial tones.

POST

● For all post office information, call the customer helpline, tel: 0845 722 3344.

● Post boxes are painted bright red (except some in post offices) and are either set into walls or are freestanding circular pillar boxes. Collection times are shown on each post box.

● Stamps are available from newsstands and supermarkets in addition to post offices.

● Generally airmail is preferable for mail sent outside Europe; for

Look for the Post Office sign or a post box to send a letter home

bulky items surface mail is substantially cheaper but typically takes around eight weeks. Airmail to North America takes about four days, to Europe around three days and to Australasia about five days.

● Large post offices have poste restante services, where items may be collected.

● To send items inland for next-day delivery, use Special Delivery. Through this service you can insure the items for various amounts, and also insure in case of loss.

VIDEOS AND DVDS

Videos, DVDs and console games purchased in Britain will be formatted to the PAL standard prevalent in Europe and Asia. They will not work in Canada or the US, where TV and video equipment is formatted to the NTSC standard.

POSTAGE RATES		
First class within UK	Up to 60g (2oz)	30p
	(usually arrives next day, but not guaranteed)	
Second class within UK	Up to 60g (2oz)	21p
	(usually two to three days)	
Proof of posting	Free	
Airmail Rates		
Americas, Middle East, Africa,	Letter (100g/3.5oz)	£2.16
India, Southeast Asia	Postcard	47p
Europe	Letter (100g/3.5oz)	£1.14
	Postcard	42p
Australasia	Letter (100g/3.5oz)	£2.44
	Postcard	47p

PERSONAL SECURITY

Levels of violent crime remain relatively low in Britain, but there are crime hotspots to avoid in certain larger cities. In most tourist areas, however, the main danger is petty theft. Be particularly wary of thieves on the London Underground, and in crowded places such as airports and main train stations. Avoid unlit urban areas at night, and carry bags close to you. If someone tries to grab your bag never fight and let go at once.

If you are going out late, arrange a lift home or a taxi. Use only reputable and licensed minicab firms or black cabs, and make sure that you get out of the car in a well-lit area. If you are driving alone take a mobile phone with you so that you can stay in your car in case of breakdown. Lock the doors when stationary, particularly at night, and don't pick up hitchhikers.

Lone women should not have problems, but should exercise caution, particularly at night. Never hitch, and use your common sense on public transport: Sit near the driver or conductor on buses and avoid empty carriages (cars) on trains and on the Underground.

LOST PROPERTY

If you lose something contact the nearest police station and complete a lost-property form in as much detail as possible. Airports have dedicated lost-property offices, but contact individual airlines if you lose belongings on board the aircraft.

Within London, items found on buses, Underground trains and in taxis are usually handed into a local police station and logged. They are then forwarded to the

---

EMERGENCY NUMBERS

Police, ambulance, fire services, coastguard, mountain rescue or cave rescue

999 or 112

Transport for London Lost Property Office at 200 Baker Street, London NW1 5RT (tel: 0845 330 9882); open Mon–Fri 8.30–4). You are advised to provide a stamped addressed envelope, and a finder's fee based on its value is payable.

EMERGENCY PHONE NUMBERS

Telephone 999 or 112 for the police, ambulance, fire service, coastguard and mountain rescue. Tell the operator which service you require, where you are, the number of the phone you are using, what the problem is and where it has happened.

For non-emergency police matters contact the nearest police station—the phone book has details, or call directory enquiries. Similarly if you have non-urgent health concerns contact NHS Direct (tel: 0845 4647), whose trained medical staff can advise you or direct you to the nearest doctor (▷ 407).

POLICE

Britain's 141,000-plus policemen are approachable and, if asked, give information and directions. The British Transport Police work on the railways and the Tube. Call 0800 405040 to report non-emergency crimes on these services. If you are the victim of a crime you can call Victim Support (tel: 0845 3030 900) for support and legal advice.

Traffic wardens issue parking tickets and deal with traffic issues

---

but have limited powers. Security guards are not endorsed by or part of the police force, and have no more powers of arrest than a normal member of the public.

What to do if you are arrested

Try to remain calm and polite, even if you know a mistake has been made. You cannot be arrested for minor offences such as speeding unless you add to the offence. In motoring incidents you are obliged to give your name and address.

On-the-spot fines (starting at about £40) can be issued for offences such as being drunk and/or disorderly. Fixed penalties are also given out for motoring offences. If the police just want your help, they may ask you to accompany them to the station. Ask if you can return the next day with a lawyer.

You can be arrested if the police suspect you of a serious offence. You will then receive a formally worded caution advising you of your rights. You can ask for legal representation before answering police questions. A free duty solicitor (lawyer) is available. You are entitled to toilet facilities, reasonable refreshment and one phone call.

Regional police	Telephone
Bath	0845 4567000
Birmingham	0845 1135000
Bristol	0845 4567000
Edinburgh	0131 3113131
Glasgow	0141 5323000
Leeds	0845 6060606
Liverpool	0151 7096010
London	020 7230 1212
Manchester	0161 8725050
Newcastle	01661 872555
Oxford	0845 8505505
York	0845 6060247

EMBASSIES IN LONDON

Contacting your embassy

If you lose your passport or are arrested, you should contact your embassy or high commission in London.

Country	Address	Website
Australian High Commission	Australia House, Strand WC2B 4LA, tel: 020 7379 4334	www.australia.org.uk
Canadian High Commission	Macdonald House, 1 Grosvenor Square W1K 4AB, tel: 020 7258 6600	www.dfait-maeci.gc.ca/canadaeuropa/united_kingdom/
New Zealand High Commission	New Zealand House, 80 The Haymarket SW1Y 4TQ, tel: 020 7930 8422	www.nzembassy.com
South African High Commission	South Africa House, Trafalgar Square WC2N 5DP, tel: 020 7451 7299	www.southafricahouse.com
American Embassy	24 Grosvenor Square W1A 1AE, tel: 020 7499 9000	www.usembassy.org.uk

PLANNING

MEDIA

Britain has a lively media culture, with some of the world's oldest newspapers and the global presence of the BBC's (British Broadcasting Corporation) radio and television productions.

TELEVISION

Excluding satellite, cable and digital, there are five main national terrestrial channels (see panel opposite). Most hotels have satellite or cable channels. There is no advertising on the BBC channels, which are funded by a licence fee from all viewers.

RADIO

The viewers' television licence funds BBC radio. There are also several independent and commercial stations nationwide. Analogue FM and AM stations are also available digitally; more information can be found at www.digitalradionow.com.

Radio 1: 97.6–99.8FM
Broadcasts the latest pop and rock with brief news bulletins.
www.bbc.co.uk/radio1

Radio 2: 88–90.2FM
Features classic rock, pop, country, folk, reggae and soul hits interspersed with chat, news bulletins and music documentaries.
www.bbc.co.uk/radio2

Radio 3: 90.2–92.4FM
Broadcasts music from classical and jazz to world music with cultural and drama programmes.
www.bbc.co.uk/radio3

Radio 4: 92.4–94.6FM or 198LW
Broadcasts topical and political news, comedy, art, drama and quiz shows, with radio plays and documentaries.
www.bbc.co.uk/radio4

Radio Five Live: 909/693AM
A news and sports station with chat and current affairs debates between callers and guests.
www.bbc.co.uk/fivelive

Classic FM: 100–102FM
An advertising-funded station broadcasting classical music.
www.classicfm.com

Virgin Radio: 105.8FM in London, 1215AM elsewhere
A national commercial radio station transmitting rock and new music, along with sports and music news.
www.virginradio.co.uk

TERRESTRIAL CHANNELS

BBC1 Shows soaps, chat shows, children's shows, documentaries and drama. News and weather: 6am–9.15am, 1pm, 6pm, 10pm weekdays and BBC News 24 from early morning to 6am. Regional news is shown after national news broadcasts.

BBC2 Specializes in comedy, natural history, history and cultural shows. News: Newsnight 10.30pm weekdays

ITV Shows a variety of mainstream shows including soaps, dramas and films. News and weather: 12.30pm, 6.30pm, 10.30pm weekdays. Regional news updates are shown before the national news broadcasts at 6pm. ITV is split into regional companies, which take national shows at peak times then broadcast their own regional schedules.

Channel 4 Broadcasts include quality films, documentaries and comedy. In Wales, Channel 4 is replaced by Welsh-language channel S4C. News and weather: 12pm and 7pm weekdays

Five Not every area of the country can receive Five. News and weather: 11.30am, 5.30pm and 7pm weekdays

NEWSPAPERS AND MAGAZINES

National newspapers in Britain have traditionally been divided into quality papers in a broadsheet format and smaller tabloids. Confusingly, most 'broadsheets' have now switched to a tabloid format. Broadsheets (costing from 50p) focus on serious news reporting while tabloids (costing from 30p) cover celebrity gossip and human-interest stories. Bulky weekend newspapers are more expensive, with sections on travel, finance, sport and the arts. International and foreign-language newspapers are sold at airports and larger train stations. Some bookshops and newsstands also stock foreign papers.

Newsstands, supermarkets and some bookshops sell magazines. Current affairs magazines include *The Week*, *The Spectator*, *The New Statesman* and the satirical *Private Eye*.

NATIONAL NEWSPAPERS

'Broadsheets'

The Daily Telegraph (1855) and The Sunday Telegraph (1961)	Britain's most popular daily broadsheet with a right-of-centre political point of view www.telegraph.co.uk
The Times (1785) and The Sunday Times (1822)	In depth national and international news, politics, arts, finance. Sunday edition is huge www.thetimes.co.uk
Financial Times (1888)	Predominantly financial news, with sober analysis of international news. Good Saturday edition www.ft.com
The Guardian (1821) and The Observer (1791)	Left-of-centre daily and Britain's oldest Sunday paper, *The Observer*. Excellent website www.guardian.co.uk
The Independent (1986) and The Independent on Sunday (1990)	Relatively young papers with a mainly urban readership, and left-of-centre agenda. Good arts and sport coverage www.independent.co.uk

'Tabloids'

The Daily Mail (1896) and The Mail on Sunday (1982)	Strident tabloids selling more than two million copies with mix of news and gossip www.dailymail.co.uk
Daily Express (1900) and Sunday Express	National news, entertainment, gossip, sport www.express.co.uk
The Sun (1969) and The News of the World (1843)	With 3.5 million readers, Britain's most popular paper. Thrives on sensationalism www.thesun.co.uk
The Daily Mirror (1903) and The Sunday Mirror (1963)	Left-wing rival to *The Sun* with fewer titillating stories and lower sales www.mirror.co.uk
The Daily Star (1978) and The Daily Star Sunday (2002)	Sensationalism and gossip in low-budget tabloid www.dailystar.co.uk
The People (1881)	Sunday-only newspaper which thrives on sensationalism www.thepeople.co.uk
Sunday Sport (2002)	A Sunday-only niche paper aimed at 'lads' with a frivolous sex- and sports-based approach.

USEFUL WEBSITES

A vast amount of information can be found on the internet, with thousands of websites originating in Britain. Those listed below are good places to start.

GENERAL INFORMATION
www.metoffice.gov.uk
Met Office, the official weather service with detailed forecasts.
www.fco.gov.uk
Foreign and Commonwealth Office advice.
www.visitbritain.com
VisitBritain
www.ordnancesurvey.co.uk
Ordnance Survey, the government mapping agency.
www.multimap.co.uk
UK street maps at a range of scales by postcode or location (which you can print off for free).
www.yell.com
Yellow Pages telephone directory.
www.bt.com/directory-enquiries
Directory Enquiries for free.

NEWS AND SPORT
www.bbc.co.uk
News as it happens from the BBC, plus weather, sport, TV.

RAIL TRAVEL
www.thetrainline.com
Reserve tickets and find out fares and journey times.
www.nationalrail.co.uk
General information on rail travel and train times.

Transport timetables
www.pti.org.uk
National and local transport timetables, including bus, coach, rail, air and ferry services.

ROAD TRAVEL
www.highways.gov.uk
The offical website of the government's Highways Agency, providing real-time traffic news and information about roadworks and local conditions on roads.
www.theaa.com
Use the Automobile Association's website to plan your route.

AIRPORTS
www.a2bairports.com
Information on airports in the UK and Republic of Ireland.
www.baa.co.uk
British Airports Authority.

THE GOVERNMENT AND THE MONARCHY
www.direct.gov.uk
Links to government departments and services.
www.pm.gov.uk
Find out about Number 10 Downing Street, the home of the Prime Minister.
www.parliament.uk
This site explains how Britain is governed from the House of Commons.
www.scottish.parliament.uk
www.wales.gov.uk
www.ni-assembly.gov.uk
Information on the regional parliaments and assemblies in Scotland, Wales and Northern Ireland.
www.royal.gov.uk
The official website of the British monarchy is informative and interesting.

HERITAGE
www.english-heritage.org.uk
English Heritage.
www.cadw.wales.gov.uk
CADW (Welsh Historic Monuments).
www.historic-scotland.gov.uk
Historic Scotland.
www.thenationaltrust.org.uk
The National Trust.
www.nts.org.uk
National Trust for Scotland.
www.bbc.co.uk/history
Coverage of historical documentaries on the BBC.
www.sealedknot.org
A battle re-enactment society.

COUNTRYSIDE
www.forestry.gov.uk
The Forestry Commission, manages forests, including recreation facilities.
www.defence-estates.mod.uk
The Defence Estates manages Ministry of Defence (MoD) land and gives information on access.

NATIONAL CONSERVATION
www.english-nature.org.uk
English Nature, responsible for 200 national nature reserves.
www.snh.org.uk
Scottish Natural Heritage.
www.countrysideaccess.co.uk
Countryside Agency.
www.landmarktrust.org.uk
Landmark Trust, restores architecturally interesting buildings and lets them for self-catering holidays.

www.woodland-trust.org.uk
Woodland Trust, woodland conservation charity offering free access to 1,100 sites.

NATIONAL PARKS
www.breconbeacons.org
Brecon Beacons National Park.
www.broads-authority.gov.uk
Norfolk and Suffolk Broads.
www.cairngorms.co.uk
Cairngorms National Park.
www.dartmoor-npa.gov.uk
Dartmoor National Park.
www.exmoor-nationalpark.gov.uk
Exmoor National Park.
www.lake-district.gov.uk
Lake District National Park.
www.lochlomond-trossachs.org
Loch Lomond and the Trossachs National Park.
www.newforestnpa.gov.uk
New Forest National Park.
www.northyorkmoors-npa.gov.uk
North York Moors National Park.
www.nnpa.org.uk
Northumberland National Park.
www.peakdistrict.org
Peak District National Park.
www.pembrokeshirecoast.org.uk
Pembrokeshire Coast National Park.
www.cyri-npa.co.uk
Snowdonia National Park.
www.yorkshiredales.org.uk
Yorkshire Dales National Park.

WALKING
www.ramblers.org.uk
The Ramblers' Association, with extensive coverage of walking in Britain.
www.nationaltrail.co.uk
The official site for Britain's long-distance footpaths.

BEACHES
www.blueflag.org
Blue Flag, a symbol of high environmental standards and good sanitary and safety facilities awarded to more than 3,000 beaches and marinas in 33 countries across Europe, South Africa, Canada and the Caribbean.
www.seasideawards.org.uk
Yellow and blue flag award given to beaches that are safe, well managed and have water quality meeting European legislation.
www.goodbeachguide.co.uk
The Good Beach Guide by the Marine Conservation Society, lists beaches with the highest water-quality standards.

OPENING TIMES AND ENTRANCE FEES

Most businesses open Monday to Friday, and some open on Saturday. Sunday is distinctly quieter, as shops can open for only six hours. Some smaller shops, particularly in smaller towns, may close early one day in midweek (often Wednesday).

The following is a rough guide to opening times, although there are many variations.

PUBLIC HOLIDAYS
Known as **bank holidays** in the UK, as these are periods when banks and many shops close. Many tourist sites now stay open (and some open specifically on these days), but virtually everything (including public transport) shuts down on 25–26 Dec. Summer bank holidays can cause major traffic delays, especially on roads to popular areas such as Cornwall and the Lake District; accommodation over holiday weekends is often fully booked in advance.

ENTRANCE FEES
Most museums, houses, galleries, gardens, cinemas, theatres and other attractions have reduced entrance fees for under-16s, holders of student cards, the unemployed and those aged 60 and over. Season tickets are often available and can be good value.

Membership of the **National Trust** (NT, tel: 0870 458 4000)

NATIONAL HOLIDAYS
Although banks and businesses close on public (bank) holidays, most tourist attractions and shops remain open, except on 25 and 26 Dec and 1 Jan. If any of these days falls on a Saturday or Sunday, the next weekday is a holiday.

New Year's Day (1 January)
Good Friday
Easter Monday
First Monday in May
Last Monday in May
Last Monday in August
Christmas Day (25 December)
Boxing Day (26 December)

gives free admission to all NT and **National Trust for Scotland** (NTS, tel: 0131 243 9300) properties and gardens. You can join at any NT property.

English Heritage (EH, tel: 0870 333 1181), its Welsh counterpart **Cadw** (tel: 029 2050 0200) and its Scottish counterpart **Historic Scotland** (HS, tel: 0131 668 8999) manage hundreds of historic properties in Britain. Most of them are castles, archaeological sites and ruined monasteries, plus a few stately homes and industrial monuments.

● English Heritage members get free admission to EH properties, and half-price admission to Cadw and HS properties (free after first year of membership). You can join at any EH, Cadw or HS property.

DISCOUNT PASSES
Serious sightseers can save money with a choice of discount cards available from the Britain and London Visitor Centre in Lower Regent Street, London, major tourist offices and most airports. For travel concessions ▷ 411.

London Pass (**www.londonpass.com**): Gives admission to over 60 attractions in and around London (with an option of free travel on public transport) and a pocket guide. Valid for one, two, three or six days, and costs from £27.

York Pass (www.yorkpass.com): Gives admission to over 30 attractions in the city for one, two or three days, and costs from £19.

Bath Pass (**www.bathpass.com**): Costing from £19, passes for one, two, three or seven days give admission to over 30 attractions.

Great British Heritage Pass (www.gbheritagepass.com): Allows free entry to 600 historic properties and gardens, including those not run by English Heritage or the National Trust (▷ left). Passes (available only to non-UK residents) are for four, seven or 15 days or one month, with prices from £28. Contact VisitBritain (▷ 418) in your home country for details on where you can purchase this pass.

OPENING TIMES		
Opening hours can vary considerably.		
Banks	Mon–Fri 9.30–4.30	Some large branches also open Sat morning and a few on Sun morning.
Pharmacies	Most pharmacies open Mon–Sat 9–5 or 5.30	Notices in the window and in local newspapers indicate extended-hour rosters of local pharmacies. You should always be able to find at least one that is open.
Galleries, Houses and Museums	These vary widely. Many open Mon–Sat 10–5, Sun 12–5	Some do not admit visitors who arrive fewer than 30 min before closing time.
Post Offices	Mon–Fri 9–5.30, Sat 9–12.30	
Pubs	Changes in licensing laws mean that pubs now negotiate their own individual opening hours	However, most still maintain the traditional hours, which are 11–11. Some close around 3–6pm. In England and Wales pubs open Sun 12–10.30pm.
Restaurants	No hard and fast rule. Typically around 12–2.30pm and 6–9pm or 6–11pm	Take-aways may stay open later than 11pm.
Shops	Smaller shops Mon–Sat 9–5 or 5.30	Department stores are open until 6pm, and on Wed or Thu until 7 or 8pm. Larger shops in cities and major towns open Sun 10am to 4pm or 11am to 5pm. Some convenience stores open longer hours—8am–10pm or 11pm, seven days a week.
Supermarkets	8am–9pm or later Mon–Sat and for six hours (such as 10–4) on Sun	Some are open 24 hours.

PLANNING

TOURIST OFFICES

TOURIST INFORMATION

There are 800 Tourist Information Centres (TICs) across Britain, with national and regional tourist boards for England, Wales and Scotland. TICs are a useful source of maps, brochures and information on places to stay, where to eat and local events. Many supply free local area street maps.

Many TICs have accommodation services, and most will also book rooms in the local area free of charge. For bookings outside the area, you may be charged a small fee (in the region of £2.50).

VisitBritain is the body responsible for promoting British tourism. Its website, www.visitbritain.com is very useful, especially for pre-departure planning.

TOURIST INFORMATION OFFICES

NATIONAL TOURIST BOARDS

VisitBritain:
Britain and London Visitor Centre, 1 Lower Regent Street, London SW1Y 4XT. Personal callers only: Mon 9.30–6.30, Tue–Fri 9–6.30, Sat–Sun 10–4 (Sat 9–5, Jun–end Oct), www.visitbritain.com

Visit Scotland:
Visit Scotland Centre, PO BOX 705, Edinburgh EH4 3EU, tel: 0845 2255 121, fax: 01506 832121, www.visitscotland.com

Visit Wales:
VisitWales Centre, Brunel House, 2 Fitzalan Road, Cardiff CF24 0UY, tel: 08701 211251, fax: 08701 211259, www.visitwales.com

REGIONAL TOURIST BOARDS

Cheshire & Warrington Tourism Board:
Grosvenor Park Lodge, Grosvenor Park Road, Chester, Cheshire CH1 1QQ, tel: 01244 346543, fax: 01244 343127, www.visit-cheshire.com

Lancashire & Blackpool Tourist Board:
St. George's House, St. George's Street, Chorley, Lancashire PR7 2AA, tel: 01257 226600, fax: 01257 469016, www.lancashiretourism.com

South West Tourism:
Tourism House, Pynes Hill, Exeter EX2 5WT, tel: 08704 420880, fax: 08704 420881, www.visitsouthwest.co.uk

Cumbria Tourist Board:
Ashleigh, Holly Road, Windermere LA23 2AQ, tel: 01539 444444, fax: 01539 444041, www.golakes.co.uk

Marketing Manchester:
Churchgate House, 56 Oxford Street, Manchester M1 6EU, tel: 0161 237 1010, fax: 0161 228 2960, www.destinationmanchester.com

Tourism South East:
40 Chamberlayne Road, Eastleigh, Hampshire SO50 5JH, tel: 023 8062 5400, fax: 01892 511008, www.southeastengland.uk.com

East of England Tourist Board:
Toppesfield Hall, Market Place, Hadleigh, Ipswich IP7 5DN, tel: 08702 254800, fax: 08702 254890, www.visiteastofengland.com

The Mersey Partnership:
12 Princes Dock, Princes Parade, Liverpool, Merseyside L3 1BG, tel: 0151 227 2727, fax: 0151 227 2325, www.visitliverpool.com

Visit London:
See Britain and London Visitor Centre (above), tel: 08701 566366, www.visitlondon.com

East Midlands Tourism:
Apex Court, City Link, Nottingham NG2 4LA, tel: 0115 988 8546, fax: 0115 853 3666, www.eastmidlands.com

One North East Tourism:
Stella House, Goldcrest Way, Newburn Riverside, Newcastle upon Tyne NE15 8NY, tel: 0191 229 6200, fax: 0191 229 6201, www.visitnorthumbria.com

Yorkshire Tourist Board:
312 Tadcaster Road, York YO24 1GS, tel: 01904 707961, fax: 01904 701414, www.yorkshirevisitor.com

Heart of England Tourism:
Woodside, Larkhill Road, Worcester WR5 2EZ, tel: 01905 761100, fax: 01905 763450, www.visitheartofengland.com

---

VISITBRITAIN OFFICES OVERSEAS

Australia:
Level 2, 15 Blue Street, North Sydney NSW 2060, tel: 02 9021 4400, fax: 02 9021 4499, www.visitbritain.com/au

Ireland:
18/19 College Green, Dublin 2, tel: 01 670 8000, fax: 01 670 8244, www.visitbritain.com/ie

South Africa:
Lancaster Gate, Hyde Park Lane, Hyde Lane, Hyde Park, Sandton 2196 (visitors); PO Box 41896, Craighall 2024 (mail), tel: 011 325 0342/3, fax: 011 325 0344, www.visitbritain.com/za

Canada:
5915 Airport Road, Suite 120, Mississauga, Ontario L4V 1T1, tel: 905 405 1840/1 888 VISIT UK, fax: 905 405 1835, www.visitbritain.com/ca

New Zealand:
Level 17, IAG House, 151 Queen Street, PO Box 105-652, Auckland 1, tel: 09 309 1899/0800 700 741, fax: 09 377 6965, www.visitbritain.com/nz

USA:
551 Fifth Avenue, Suite 701, New York NY 10176-0799, tel: 212 986 2266/1 800 462 2748, fax: 212 986 1188, www.visitbritain.com/usa

PLANNING

BOOKS, FILMS AND MAPS

Britain's long-established love affair with the arts has produced some of the best-known authors and film-makers in the world and an enviable reputation as a leading light in the arts world.

BOOKS

For a general overview of the country, look no further than Simon Schama's three-volume **A History of Britain** (2001), covering events from 3000BC to AD2001. Other areas of Britain's rich history are explored in Will Hutton's **The State We're In** (2003), and **The World We're In** (1996), an economic and political survey of modern-day Britain; **The Queen's Story** (2003) by Marcus Kiggell, following the monarch's 50 years on the throne; Jeremy Paxman's **The English: a Portrait of a People** (1999), the psyche of a nation through the eyes of one of Britain's most vociferous broadcasters; and **The Buildings of England** (1951–74), a series by Nikolaus Pevsner.

Fiction writers have been no less prolific, with some of the most famous names in literature writing about and based in Britain. Eighteenth-century fiction includes **Sense and Sensibility** (1811), **Pride and Prejudice** (1813) and **Persuasion** (1815) by Jane Austen, some of the seminal works on society of the time; the Brontë sisters' **Jane Eyre** (1847, by Charlotte) and **Wuthering Heights** (1847, by Emily), capturing the angst of romance and obsession in Victorian Britain; several classics by Charles Dickens, including **Bleak House** (1853), **David Copperfield** (1850) and **Oliver Twist** (1837), all set in different parts of the country; and **Middlemarch** (1872), by George Eliot (pseudonym of Mary Ann Evans), in which the characters try to overcome the dogma of the past and embrace a burgeoning new society.

More recent fiction includes **England, England** (1999) by Julian Barnes, a sharp-edged satire on Englishness, **Jamaica Inn** (1936) by Daphne du Maurier, a dramatic romance set in the author's beloved Cornwall, and E. M. Forster's **Howard's End** (1910), a study of society

angst in Hertfordshire and Shropshire. **Brighton Rock** (1938), by Graham Greene, is a dark depiction of a man taken over by greed, guilt and Brighton's criminal underworld, while D. H. Lawrence's **Sons and Lovers** (1913) is about a mother's obsessive love for her sons. Virginia Woolf's **Mrs Dalloway** (1925) is set in a single day in 1923 and tells the story of society hostess Clarissa Dalloway; Laurie Lee's **Cider with Rosie** (1959) is a rural romp through the Cotswolds during the 1920s.

FILMS

From a successful and well-regarded state in the 1930s, the British film industry went into a decline for several decades. In recent years it has strived to return to its former health, supplying independent productions that can hold their own against the Hollywood studios, with global successes such as the James Bond movies, **Bridget Jones's Diary** (2001) and **Love Actually** (2003).

Classic movies from the British school encompass **Brief Encounter** (1945), with Trevor Howard and Celia Johnson resisting extramarital temptation in a British railway station, **Kind Hearts and Coronets** (1949), a savage comedy on Britain's class system, with Sir Alec Guinness playing several characters in the same family, and Alfred Hitchcock's **The Thirty-Nine Steps** (1935), in which innocent Richard Hannay gets caught up in a spy ring and ends up fleeing across the Scottish countryside.

The 1960s brought a rash of movies exploring the British class system, either through comedy or tragedy, including **If** (1968), a study of the restricted world of the English public school, the highly praised **Kes** (1969), the story of a lonely Yorkshire schoolboy who finds happiness with his kestrel, and **This Sporting Life** (1963), where the late Richard Harris acts out his frustrations at becoming a star rugby player through violence.

Several smaller-budget British films may not have made the international stage but are nonetheless memorable. **Local Hero** (1983) tells the story of a

Texan oil baron who wants to buy up a remote Scottish village, until the villagers win him over. **Withnail and I** (1986) depicts the lives of two out-of-work actors in the sixties and has a devoted cult following.

With the influx of independent production companies in the 1980s and 1990s, some famous titles have been produced in recent years, including Robert Altman's **Gosford Park** (2001), yet another study of the British class system, with an all-star cast showing the British country house in all its glory, **Billy Elliot** (2000), in which the hero, a young boy played by Oscar-winner Jamie Bell, battles his northern mining background and the desire to become a ballet dancer, **The Full Monty** (1997), with its scenes of Robert Carlyle and his cohorts practising the striptease, and **Notting Hill** (1999), written by Richard Curtis, who brought the world **Four Weddings and a Funeral**, where the west London enclave is the background of the romance between bumbling bookshop owner Hugh Grant and movie star Julia Roberts.

GUIDEBOOKS

AA City Pack London
Pocket book and map in transparent wallet. £6.99
London: A City Revealed
A visual tribute to London, with over 350 large colour photographs. £30
The AA Days Out Guide
Over 2,000 places to visit, with opening times and prices. £11.99
The AA Hotel Guide £16.99
The AA Restaurant Guide
Reviews of more than 1,800 restaurants in Britain. £16.99

MAPS

AA Street by Street London
17 maps and atlases in a variety of sizes and scales. £3.99 to £30
Street by Street Z-Maps £1.50
Stanfords at 12–14 Long Acre, London (tel: 020 7836 1321, www.stanfords.co.uk) is a specialist map shop with maps for all regions of the British Isles.

The website www.multimap.co.uk displays UK street maps at a range of scales by postcode or location that can be printed from the internet free of charge.

A BRIEF GUIDE TO ARCHITECTURAL PERIODS

Roman

The Romans invaded Britain in AD43 and by AD57 they controlled most of the country. Their legacy can be seen in London (▷ 117–132), Bath (▷ 68–71), Chester (▷ 151), Cirencester (▷ 76), York (▷ 180–183) and the grand Roman villas at Fishbourne (▷ 98), Lullingstone (▷ 103) and Bignor (▷ 93). Britain's most striking Roman structure is Hadrian's Wall in the north of England (▷ 168).

Anglo-Saxon

During the Anglo-Saxon period (886–1066) Churches were built of stone and characterized by their simple arched windows with thick central supports. The first St. Paul's Cathedral (▷ 127) was founded in AD604 and Edward the Confessor had Westminster Abbey (▷ 132) finished in 1066.

Norman

In the late 11th and 12th centuries the Norman conquerors brought new styles and craftsmen from Normandy. Massive fortified buildings and churches were thrown up in the wake of the Norman invasion, recognizable by their rounded arches, heavy masonry and highly decorated walls and doorways.
Examples include: Westminster Hall (▷ 132), the oldest remaining part of the medieval Palace of Westminster, erected in 1097 (but renovated in the 14th century); The White Tower, at the heart of the Tower of London (▷ 130); the keep at Dover Castle (▷ 99); Restormel Castle (▷ 85).

Early English and Decorated

Architecture of the late 12th and 13th centuries became lighter, using pointed rather than rounded arches, especially in lancet windows This period marked the move towards the long, vertical lines of the Gothic style and an increasing focus on window space. As windows became bigger, buttresses were added to transfer the outward thrust of the roof to the ground. Increasingly elaborate tracery and decoration were employed on

arches, doorways and especially windows in buildings of the later 13th and 14th centuries.
Examples: Westminster Abbey, rebuilt 1245, (▷ 132); York Minster (▷ 181); the magnificent ruins of Rievaulx Abbey ▷ 177).

Perpendicular Gothic

Evolving from the Decorated style, simpler lines and more uniform tracery on windows and walls emerged during the late 14th and 15th centuries, with much use of fan-vaulting and four-centred arches. Designs became lighter, using greater areas of glass.
Examples: Henry VII Chapel, Westminster Abbey (▷ 132); the nave of Winchester Cathedral (▷ 116).

Tudor and Early Stuart

Named after the royal families, these architectural styles from the late 15th and 16th centuries marked a shift from the Gothic to the Renaissance styles, with the emphasis on domestic architecture for the expanding aristocracy and gentry. Brick and wood-panelling became popular.
Examples: Hampton Court Palace (▷ 100); Shakespeare's Globe Theatre (▷ 128), a modern reconstruction of the 16th-century original; Blenheim Palace (▷ 94); Cotehele House (▷ 77).

Late Stuart

The Palladian style, recalling the work of 16th-century Italian architect Andrea Palladio, reflected Roman classical influences in porticoes and symmetrical façades. Classical styles merged in the 18th century with baroque ornamentation and rich detail.
Major Architects: **Inigo Jones** (1573–1652): designed the Queen's House, Greenwich and London's Banqueting Hall. Made the Palladian style fashionable.
Sir Christopher Wren (1632–1723): designed St. Paul's Cathedral (▷ 127), Greenwich Hospital and many of London's City churches following the Great Fire of 1666.
Nicholas Hawksmoor (1661–1736): Wren's assistant, who preferred monumental classicism. Designed many of

London's churches, including St. George's Bloomsbury and Christchurch, Spitalfields.
Sir John Vanbrugh (1664–1726): designed Castle Howard (▷ 166) and Blenheim Palace (▷ 94).

Georgian and Regency

During the Georgian period (1714–1830) architects turned back to the Palladian style, and in the late 18th and early 19th centuries Greek Classical influences came to the fore, prompting an emphasis on simplicity and symmetry, especially in the new terraced town houses. The Regency period (named after the Prince Regent) saw the advent of floor-to-roof bow windows and wrought ironwork in staircases and balconies.
Major Architects: **Robert Adam** (1728–92): designed London's Osterley House and Syon House, Culzean Castle (▷ 189) and Edinburgh's Charlotte Square.
William Kent (1675–1748): advocated the return to Palladianism. Designed Chiswick House and Kensington Palace (▷ 125).
John Nash (1752–1835): known for his Regency houses and responsible for London's Regent's Park terraces and Brighton's Royal Pavilion (▷ 95).
Sir John Soane (1753–1837): liked austere Classical designs. Responsible for London's Bank of England and Dulwich Art Gallery.
Decimus Burton (1800–81): a leader in the Regency style, who worked with Nash on the Regent's Park terraces and designed London's Athenaeum Club.
John Wood the Elder (1704–54): designed Queen Square and The Circus in Bath (▷ 71).
John Wood the Younger (1728–81): designed the Royal Crescent and the Assembly Rooms in Bath (▷ 70).
Isambard Kingdom Brunel (1806–59): was responsible for the Clifton Suspension Bridge (▷ 73).
Lancelot 'Capability' Brown (1716–83): English landscape gardener who designed the gardens at Blenheim Palace (▷ 94), Kew Gardens (▷ 126); Stowe in Buckinghamshire.

PLANNING

Victorian

Architecture of the period from 1837 to 1901 called on a mish-mash of influences as new public buildings such as train stations and municipal offices sprang up. These were notable for their neo-Gothic designs, romanticized medieval motifs, rich details and extensive use of steel, iron and glass. In contrast, mass housing was built for industrial workers.
Examples: London's Houses of Parliament (▷ 132), Natural History Museum (▷ 126), Albert Memorial (▷ 125), St Pancras station, Tower Bridge (▷ 129); Glasgow City Chambers; National Gallery of Scotland, Edinburgh (▷ 192); Truro Cathedral (▷ 90).
Major Architects: **Sir Charles Barry** (1795–1860): designed the Houses of Parliament (▷ 132) after their destruction by fire in 1834 and Manchester Athenaeum.
Sir George Gilbert Scott (1811–78): designed London's St. Pancras station and the Foreign Office; Glasgow University.
Augustus Welby Northmore Pugin (1812–52): led the neo-Gothic movement, working on the Houses of Parliament.
Alfred Waterhouse (1830–1905): designed the Natural History Museum (▷ 126); Manchester Town Hall.
Sir Aston Webb (1849–1930): a president of the Royal Academy, who designed London's Admiralty Arch, Buckingham Palace's east façade (▷ 119), and the Victoria & Albert Museum (▷ 131).
Alexander 'Greek' Thompson (1817–75): designed churches, warehouses and tenements in Glasgow (▷ 198–200).

Late Victorian and Edwardian

In the late 19th century the Arts and Crafts Movement was promoted by William Morris as a reaction against mass production, with the aim of making hand-made objects and fine art a part of daily life. Its influence extended to architecture as suburban brick houses, with terracotta panelling, balconies and large gardens. The organic motifs of art nouveau were popular until about 1914.
Examples: Red House, Bexley Heath; Holy Trinity Church, Chelsea.

Major Architects: **Philip Webb** (1831–1915): an exponent of a simple, domestic style, designing furniture and metalwork with Morris, as well as the Red House.
Sir Edwin Lutyens (1869–1944): designed the Cenotaph in Whitehall (▷ 132) and many country houses outside London.
Sir Herbert Baker (1862–1946): worked with Lutyens. Best known for his controversial reconstruction of the Bank of England.
Charles Rennie Mackintosh (1868–1928): designed the Glasgow School of Art and other buildings mainly in Glasgow.

Inter-War

Public and domestic buildings made use of art deco's geometric lines, bold colours and exotic motifs, often using Egyptian themes, marking the huge public interest in archaeologist Howard Carter's discovery of the tomb of Tutankhamun. Traditional materials such as tiles and stained glass were paired with modern chromium plating.
Examples: Metropolitan Catholic Cathedral of Christ the King, Liverpool (▷ 173); BBC Broadcasting House.
Major Architects: **Berthold Lubetkin** (1901–90): prolific Russian architect who designed the Penguin Pool in London Zoo (▷ 242).
Sir Giles Gilbert Scott (1880–1960): grandson of Sir George Gilbert Scott, designed the Bodleian Library, Oxford (▷ 106).

Post World War II

After 1945 designs became increasingly stark and massive, using materials such as concrete, especially in the high-rises of the 1960s. The high-tech style of the 1970s and 1980s exposed the inner workings of buildings. Stainless steel and glass were popular materials. An emphasis on lightness combined with elegant, unconventional lines is seen in Britain's newest structures.
Examples: London's South Bank Centre; Millennium Bridge.
Major Architects: **Sir Richard Rodgers** (1933–): designed the Lloyds Building, with its 'inside-out' display of pipes and lifts.
Sir Norman Foster (1935–): responsible for London's Millennium Bridge.

PLANNING

GLOSSARY FOR US VISITORS

anticlockwise	counterclockwise
aubergine	eggplant
bank holiday	a public holiday that falls on a Monday; there are two in May and one in August
banknote	bill (paper money)
bill	check (at restaurant)
biscuit	cookie
bonnet	hood (car)
boot	trunk (car)
busker	street musician
caravan	house trailer or RV
car park	parking lot
carriage	car (on a train)
casualty	emergency room (hospital department)
chemist	pharmacy
chips	french fries
coach	long-distance bus
coaching inn	pubs or hotels dating from 17th–19th centuries, located on main travel routes
concessions	reduced fees for tickets, often available to students, children and elderly people
courgette	zucchini
crèche	day care
crisps	potato chips
directory enquiries	directory assistance
dual carriageway	two-lane highway
en suite	a bedroom with its own private bathroom; may also just refer to the bathroom
football	soccer
full board	a hotel tariff that includes all meals
garage	gas station
garden	yard (residential)
GP	doctor
half board	hotel tariff that includes breakfast and either lunch or dinner
high street	main street
hire	rent
inland	within the UK
jelly	Jello™
jumper, jersey	sweater
junction	intersection
layby	rest stop, pull-off
level crossing	grade crossing
lorry	truck
licensed	a café or restaurant that has a licence to serve alcohol (beer and wine only unless it's 'fully' licensed)
lift	elevator
main line station	a train station as opposed to an underground or subway station (although it may be served by the underground/subway)
nappy	diaper
off-licence	liquor store
pants	underpants (men's)
pavement	sidewalk
petrol	gas

plaster	Band-Aid or bandage
post	mail
public school	private school
pudding	dessert
purse	change purse
pushchair	stroller
return ticket	roundtrip ticket
rocket	arugula
roundabout	traffic circle or rotary
self-catering	accommodation including a kitchen
single ticket	one-way ticket
stalls	orchestra seats (in theatre)
subway	underpass
surgery	doctor's office
tailback	traffic jam
takeaway	takeout
taxi rank	taxi stand
ten-pin bowling	bowling
tights	panty-hose
T-junction	an intersection where one road meets another at right angles (making a T shape)
toilets	restrooms
torch	flashlight
trolley	cart
trousers	pants
way out	exit

COMMON SCOTTISH WORDS

ben	hill
bonny	pretty
burn	stream
cairn	stones forming a landmark
ceilidh	gathering, party, dance
croft	small-holding of farm land
dram	measure of whisky
gae	go
glen	valley
kirk	church
loch	lake
wee	small

BRITISH FLOOR NUMBERING

In Britain the first floor of a building is called the ground floor, and the floor above it is the first floor. So a British second floor is a US third floor, and so on. This is something to watch for in museums and galleries in particular.

BRITISH LISTED BUILDINGS

'Listed' buildings in Britain are those that merit protection as part of the nation's architectural heritage. The list of protected buildings is compiled by the Department of Culture, Media and Sport and buildings have to meet certain criteria to be listed. Generally, they have to be architecturally or historically interesting, or have a close historical association with important events or have value as part of a group of buildings. There are three grades of listing (Grade I, Grade II* and Grade II) and buildings are graded according to their importance to the nation. All surviving buildings constructed before 1700, for example, are listed. Those in the highest grades, Grade I and II*, are eligible for grants. There are about 370,000 listed buildings.

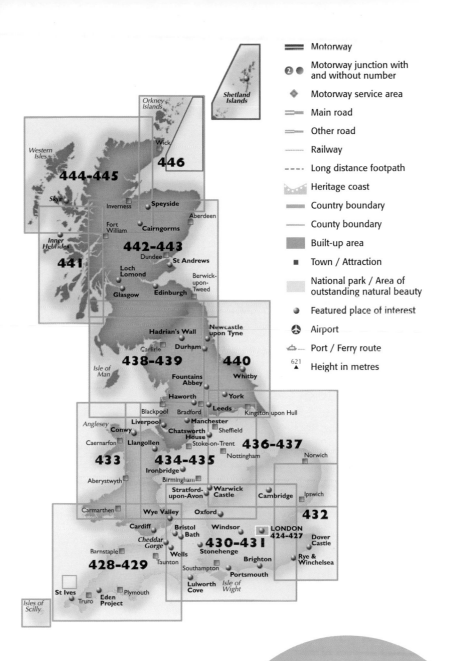

	Motorway
② ●	Motorway junction with and without number
◆	Motorway service area
	Main road
	Other road
	Railway
----	Long distance footpath
	Heritage coast
	Country boundary
	County boundary
	Built-up area
■	Town / Attraction
	National park / Area of outstanding natural beauty
●	Featured place of interest
✈	Airport
⚓	Port / Ferry route
621 ▲	Height in metres

Shetland Islands

Orkney Islands

Wick

446

Western Isles

444-445

Skye

Inner Hebrides

441

Inverness

Speyside

Fort William

Cairngorms

Aberdeen

442-443

Dundee

St Andrews

Loch Lomond

Berwick-upon-Tweed

Glasgow

Edinburgh

Newcastle upon Tyne

Hadrian's Wall

Durham

Carlisle

438-439

440

Isle of Man

Fountains Abbey

Whitby

Haworth

York

Blackpool

Bradford

Leeds

Kingston upon Hull

Anglesey

Liverpool

Manchester

Conwy

Chatsworth House

Sheffield

Caernarfon

Llangollen

Stoke-on-Trent

436-437

433

434-435

Nottingham

Norwich

Aberystwyth

Ironbridge

Birmingham

Stratford-upon-Avon

Warwick Castle

Cambridge

Ipswich

Carmarthen

Wye Valley

Oxford

432

Cardiff

Bristol

Windsor

LONDON 424-427

Cheddar Gorge

Bath

430-431

Dover Castle

Barnstaple

Wells

Stonehenge

Brighton

Rye & Winchelsea

428-429

Taunton

Southampton

Portsmouth

Isles of Scilly

St Ives

Truro

Eden Project

Plymouth

Lulworth Cove

Isle of Wight

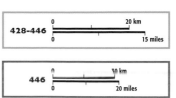

428-446	0 ———————— 20 km	
	0 ———————— 15 miles	

446	0 ———————— 30 km	
	0 ———————— 20 miles	

Maps

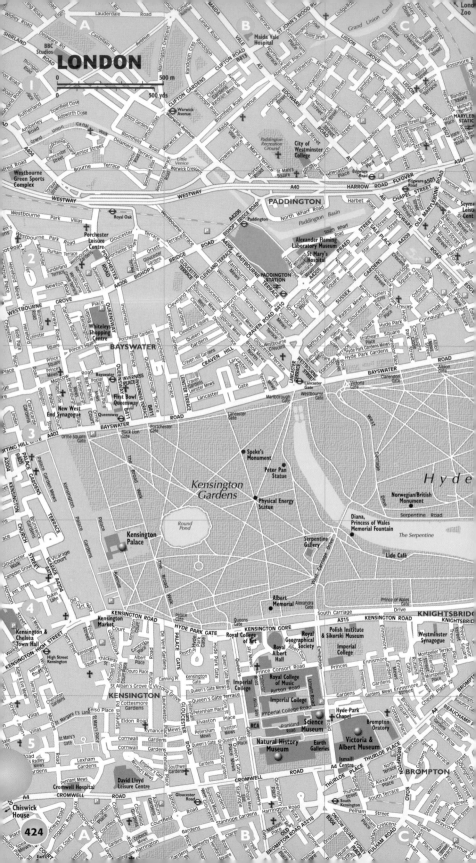

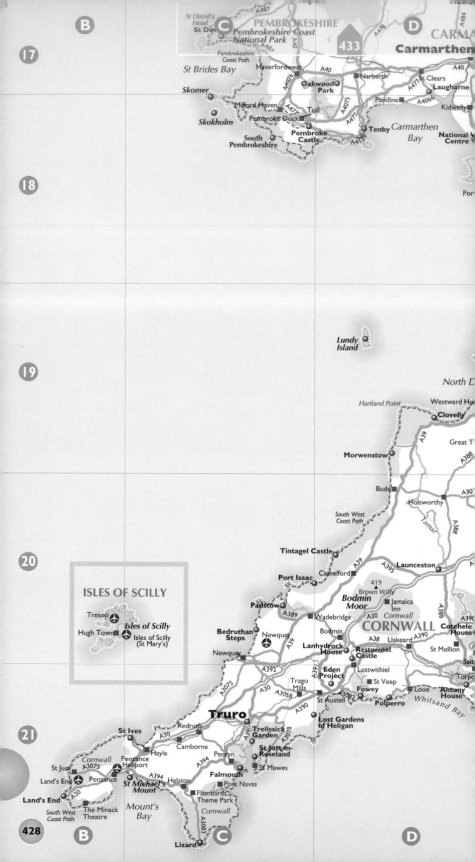

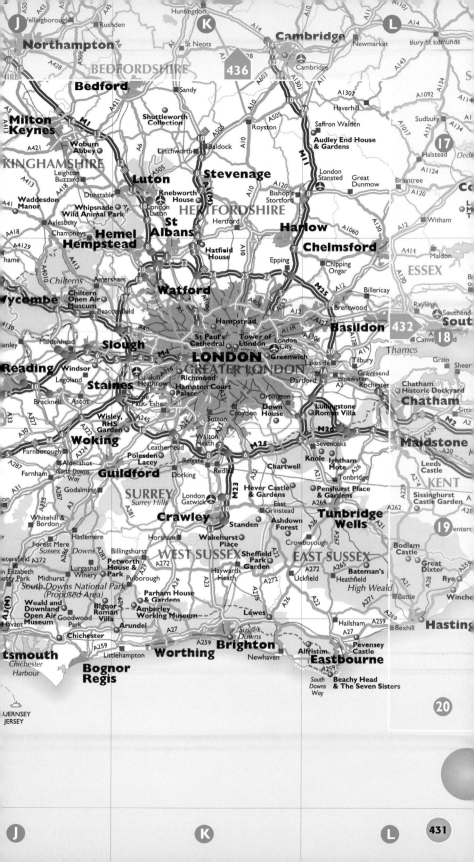

Amlwch

ISLE OF ANGLESEY
A5025

Holyhead   *Anglesey*

Holy Island   Benllech

Rhosneigr   Llangefni   Beaumaris

A4080   Menai   Bangor   A55
Bridge

Greenwood   **Penrhyn**
Forest Park   **Castle**
Bethesda

Caernarfon   Llanberis   1062
▲ Carnedd
Llewelyn

Caernarfon   **Snowdonia**   999
Bay   **National**   Glyder Fawr
Park   Capel
1085   Curig
▲ Snowdon

A4085

Peninsula   Blaenau   *Gwydyr Forest Park*
Ffestiniog

Nefyn   Criccieth   Porthmadog   Ffestiniog
A497   A497   **Portmeirion**   A4212

Lleyn   Pwllheli   **Harlech**   **GWYNEDD**
Castle
Abersoch   *Snowdonia*
A496   Coed-y-Brenin
Forest Park

Bardsey Island   Dolgellau
Barmouth   892   A470
▲ Cader   A487   *Dyfi*
A493   Idris

Centre of
Alternative
Technology   **434**

Tywyn   Machynlleth
A493   **Celtica**   752
▲ Ply   **16**   Llanid

Ynyslas   A44   Llangurig
Aberystwyth   A4120

CEREDIGION   Elan
A487   *Valley*

Aberaeron   Tregaron

A485
A482   *Teifi*
A475   Lampeter   A483
North Pembrokeshire   Cardigan   A486   A482   Llanw
& the Preseli Hills   Castell   A484   Llandysul
Henllys   **Welsh**   A475   **Dolaucothi**
Wildlife   Newcastle   **Gold Mines**
Strumble   **Centre**   Emlyn   Llando
Head   Newport   **National Wool**
A487   **Museum**   Llandovery
Fishguard   A40   A40   A4069

St   **PEMBROKESHIRE**   A478   A484   A40   A4069
David's
Head
St David's   **Pembrokeshire Coast**   **CARMARTHENSHIRE**
National Park   A40   Llandeilo   **Dan-Yr-Ogof**
A487   **Carmarthen**   *Towy*   **National**
Pembrokeshire   A40   **National**   Carreg   Showca
Coast Path   Haverfordwest   A40   **Botanic Garden**   Cennen
Brides Bay   **of Wales**   **Castle**
Narberth   **428**   A40   A4067
omer   C   Oakwood   D   A471   A40   E   **433**
Park   Laugharne   Ammanford   A109
Pendine   A4066   A4109

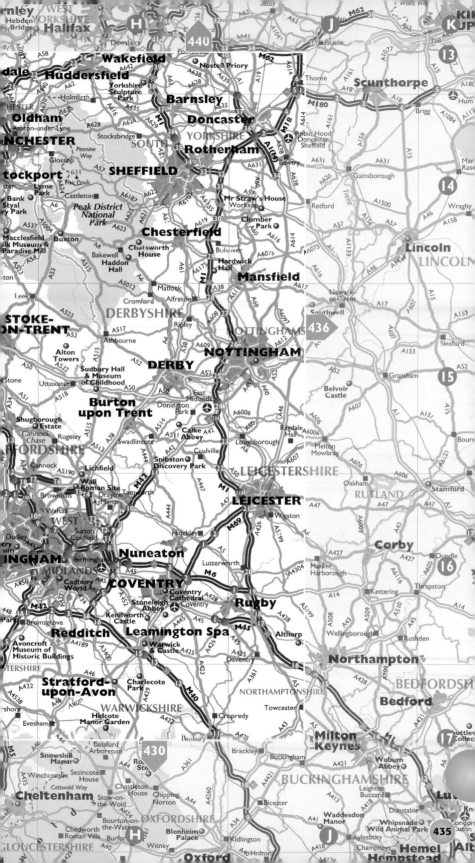

ablethorpe

Skegness

The
Wash

Hunstanton

The
Burnhams

Wells-next-
the-Sea

A149

Norfolk Coast

Holkham
Hall

Peddars Way &
Norfolk Coast Path

Sheringham

Cromer

Holt

Felbrigg
Hall

A149

North
Walsham

Sandringham

A149

Houghton
Hall

Castle
Rising

King's Lynn

A148

Peddars Way &
Norfolk Coast Path

A148

A1065

Fakenham

A148

Aylsham

A1067

A140

A1151

A149

A47

A10

A47

Dereham

A47

A1122

NORFOLK

Swaffham

Norwich

Norwich

Acle

The
Broads

Caister-on-Sea

A47

Great
Yarmouth

Downham
Market

Watton

Wymondham

A11

A1075

A140

A146

A143

A12

Lowestoft

1122

A10

A134

Thetford
Forest Park

Attleborough

Otter Trust

Bungay

A143

Beccles

A146

16

Littleport

A1101

A1065

Thetford

A11

A1066

Diss

Harleston

A145

A144

Ely

A142

Mildenhall

A1088

A143

Halesworth

Southwold

A1101

A11

Eye

A1120

A12

A14

432

ridge

A14

A143

Newmarket

Bury St Edmunds

A11

A140

Framlingham

Saxmundham

A1094

Suffolk Coast

A1302

Haverhill

Stowmarket

A134

SUFFOLK

A14

Wickham
Market

A12

Snape
Maltings
& Heaths

Aldeburgh

A1092

A1141

Woodbridge

Sutton
Hoo

Orford
Orford Ness

Saffron Walden

Sudbury

A131

A1071

Hadleigh

A134

A12

Ipswich

A137

A14

Audley End House
& Gardens

Felixstowe

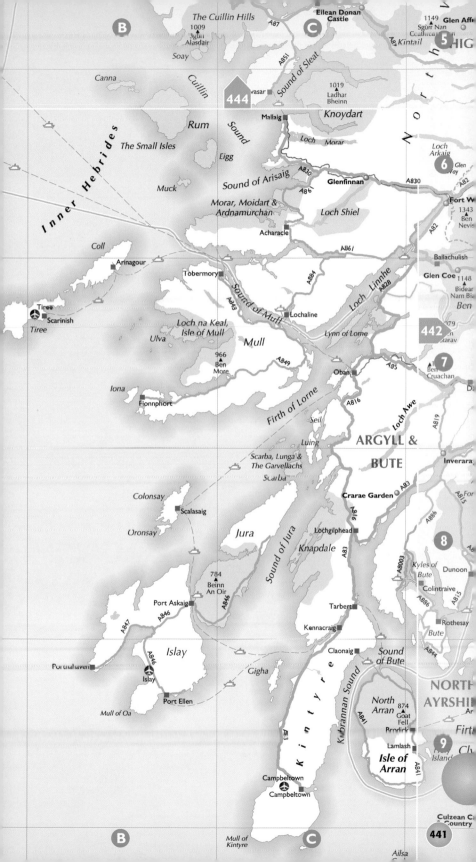

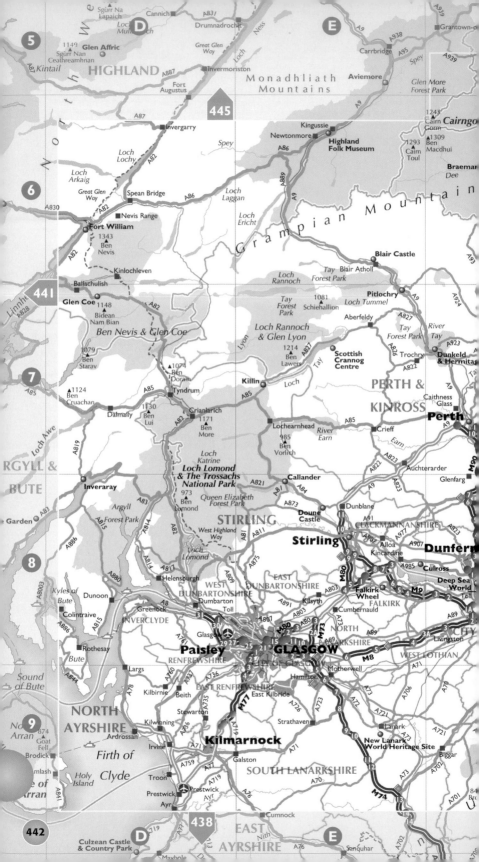

17

A

B

C

Butt of Lewis

Port of Ness
(Port Nis)

A857

Oiseval
Gallery

A858

Carloway (Carlabhagh)

Stornoway
(Steornabhagh)

A857

A858

A866

Stornoway

Lewis (Leodhais)

A859

Broad Bay

The Minch

WESTERN ISLES

Outer Hebrides

Scarp

South Lewis,
Harris &
North Uist

A859

Taransay

Tarbert
(Tairbeart)

Shiant
Islands

A859

Harris
(Hearadh)

Pabbay

Berneray

Sound of Harris

Inverewe
Gardens

A83?

Gairlo

North Uist
(Uibhist a Tuath)

Lochmaddy
(Loch nam Madadh)

The Little Minch

A865

A867

Trotternish

Uig

Rona

Weste

Benbecula

A87

A855

Benbecula
(Beinn Na Faoghla)

A850

Sound of Raasay

Inner Sound

Dunvegan

A863

Skye

Portree

Raasay

A865

South Uist
(Uibhist a Deas)

Scalpay

Kyle of Lochalsh

South Uist
Machair

A863

Drynoch

Eilean Dona
Castle

A

South Uist
Machair

Lochboisdale
(Loch Baghasdail)

The Cuillin Hills

A87

1009
Sgurr
Alasdair

Eriskay
(Eiriosgaigh)

Soay

A851

Barra

Sound of Barra

Canna

Cuillin

Ardvasar

Sound of Sleat

1019
Ladhar
Bheinn

Barra
(Barraigh)

Castlebay
(Bagh a Chaisteil)

Mallaig

Knoyda

Sandray

441

Rum

The Small Isles

Sound

Loch

Morar

Eigg

Hebrides

Muck

Sound of Arisaig

A830

Glenfinr

A86

Morar, Moidart &

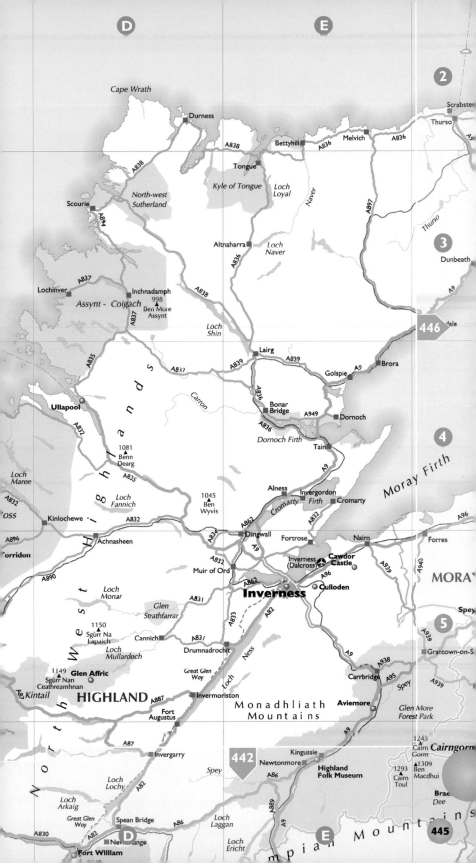

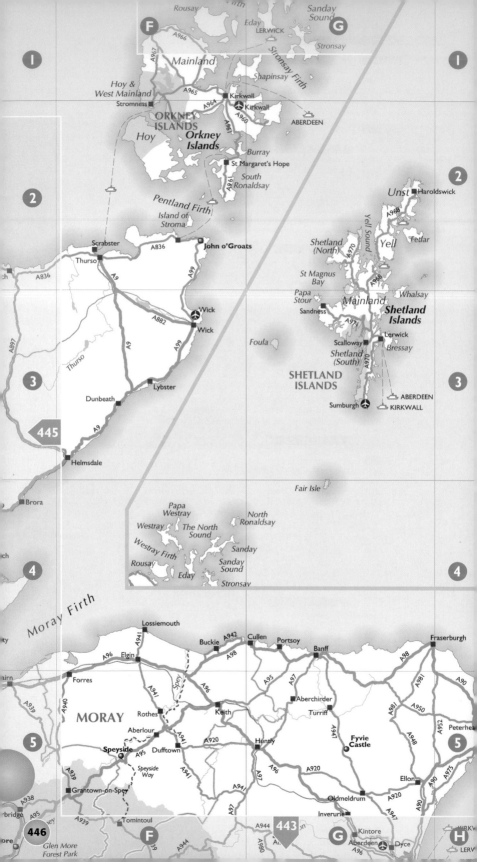

ACKNOWLEDGMENTS

Abbreviations for the credits are as follows:
AA = AA World Travel Library, **t** (top), **b** (bottom), **c** (centre), **l** (left), **r** (right)

UNDERSTANDING BRITAIN

4l AA/A Baker: 4c Britain On View; 4r AA/S J Whitehorne; 5r AA/E Meacher; 5b AA/M Jourdan; 6l AA/L Whitwam; 6c AA/J Tims; 6r AA/T Mackie; 8tr Britain On View; 8l AA/W Voysey; 8tcr Britain On View, 8cr AA/C Lees; 8bcr AA/S & O Mathews; 8br AA/M Jourdan; 9tl Britain On View; 9ctl AA/W Voysey; 9cbl AA/J Beazley; 9bl AA; 9cr AA/D Forss; 9br AA/M Birkitt; 10tl Britain On View; 10cl AA/M Jourdan; 10bl Britain On View; 10tr AA/R Moss; 10tcr AA/M Jourdan; 10bcr Britain On View; 10br Britain On View; 10b Britain On View.

LIVING BRITAIN

11 AA/C Lees; 12/13bg Britain On View; 12tl Guards Polo Club; 12cl Royal Collection © 2003 Her Majesty Queen Elizabeth II/Derry Moore; 12c Getty Images; 12cr Rex Features; 12/13bg Rex Features; 13tl AA/L Allen; 13tr M Moody; 13cl Britain On View; 13cr Getty Images; 14/15bg AA/W Voysey; 14tl AA; 14tcl House of Commons Information Office; 14tcr Britain On View; 14tr Britain On View; 14bl AA/M Jourdan; 15tl Rex Features; 15tr AA/M Jourdan; 15cl A Gooch; 15cr Getty Images; 16/17bg AA/J Miller; 16tl AA/W Voysey, 16cl Britain On View; 16r Britain On View; 16bl AA/K Doran; 17tl AA/S McBride; 17tr Leicester Promotions; 17cl AA/M Jourdan; 17cr Britain On View; 17r AA; 18/19bg AA/T Mackie; 18tl AA/C Coe; 18tr AA/D Tarn; 18bl AA/C Sawyer; 18cr AA/R Moss; 19tl AA/J Gregory; 19tr AA/P Wilson; 19cl AA/M Jourdan; 19c Britain On View; 19cr AA/R Strange; 20/21bg AA; 20tl AA/M Hayward; 20tr AA/C Jones; 20cl AA/W Voysey; 20cr Empics Ltd; 20br AA/M Jourdan; 21tl Empics Ltd; 21cl Britain On View; 21cr AA/M Birkitt; 22/23bg Doug Hall, Bonneys, courtesy of Gateshead County Council; 22tl AA/C Sawyer; 22cl AA/C Lees; 22tr Terry Frost/Royal Academy of Arts; 22tcr Birmingham Hippodrome Theatre; 22bcr AA/M Jourdan; 22br Topham Picturepoint; 23tl Eden Project; 23cl Tom Howard; 23c Topham Picturepoint; 23r courtesy of Gateshead County Council; 24bg Stockbyte; 24tl Topham Picturepoint; 24cl The Roslin Institute; 24r Alfred Pasieka/Science Photo Library.

THE STORY OF BRITAIN

25 AA/W Voysey; 26/7bg AA/I Burgum; 26/7 AA/I Burgum; 26cl AA/T Souter; 26c AA/S L Day; 26bl AA/R Tenison; 27cl AA; 27c AA; 27cr AA; 27cb Mary Evans Picture Library; 27b AA/W Voysey; 27br Britain On View; 28/9bg AA/C Jones; 28/9 AA/W Voysey; 28cl Mary Evans Picture Library; 28bl AA/S L Day; 29cl Mary Evans Picture Library; 29c Mary Evans Picture Library; 29cr AA; 29bl Mary Evans Picture Library; 29br Mary Evans Picture Library; 30/1bg AA/J Beazley; 30/1 AA/J Beazley; 30cl AA/M Alexander; 30bl Mary Evans Picture Library; 30cr AA; 31cl AA; 31c Mary Evans Picture Library; 31cr AA; 31bl AA; 31bc AA; 31br AA; 32/3bg Mary Evans Picture Library; 32/3b Mary Evans Picture Library; 32cl AA; 32/3c AA; 32bl AA; 33cl AA; 33cr Mary Evans Picture Library; 33bl AA/S McBride; 33br AA/R Strange; 34/5bg AA/C Jones; 34/5 AA/C Jones; 34cl AA/J Welsh; 34cr AA; 34bl AA; 35cl Illustrated London News; 35c AA; 35bcl AA; 35bc AA/R Weir; 35br AA; 36/7bg AA/C Molyneux, 36/7 AA/C Molyneux; 36cl Illustrated London News; 36cr Illustrated London News; 36bl AA/L Whitwam; 37cl Illustrated London News; 37c Britain On View; 37cb AA/J Tims; 37bl Illustrated London News; 37br Illustrated London News; 38/9bg Hulton Archives/Getty Images; 38/9 Hulton Archives/Getty Images; 38cl Hulton Archives/Getty Images; 38cr Illustrated London News; 38bl Illustrated London News; 39cl Hulton Archives/Getty Images;

39c Hulton Archives/Getty Images; 39cr Rex Features; 39bl Hulton Archives/Getty Images; 39br AA/W Voysey; 40bg AA/M Jourdan; 40bl Rex Features; 40cr Rex Features; 40br Rex Features.

ON THE MOVE

41 AA/M Jourdan; 42/3 Digital Vision; 43 AA/J Miller; 44/5 Digital Vision; 44 AA/J Smith; 45 Digital Vision; 46/7 AA/B Smith; 46c AA/J Tims; 46l AA/M Jourdan; 46b Reproduced with kind permission of London's Transport Museum; 48/9 Digital Vision; 50/1 Digital Vision; 52/3 Digital Vision; 52 AA/W Voysey; 54/5 Digital Vision; 54 AA/S McBride; 55tr AA/C Jones; 55bl Britain On View; 56t Stagecoach UK Bus; 56c National Express Group PLC; 56b National Express Group PLC; 57 AA/M Jourdan; 58t AA/W Voysey; 58r AA/S McBride; 59 Digital Vision; 60t Digital Vision; 60l Britain On View; 60b EasyJet Company Limited; 61t AA/M Jourdan; 61r AA/M.Jourdan; 62t AA/M Jourdan 62r AA/M Jourdan; 62b AA/W Voysey; 63t AA/S McBride; 63r First Great Western; 64 AA/S McBride.

THE SIGHTS

65 AA/V Bates; 67tl AA/M Jourdan; 67tc AA; 67tr AA/C Jones; 68 AA/S L Day; 69t AA/E Meacher; 69cl AA/E Meacher; 69c AA/E Meacher; 69cr AA/M Birkitt; 69b AA/E Meacher; 70t AA/E Meacher; 70b AA/S L Day; 70/1 AA/E Meacher; 71 Britain On View; 72tl AA/R Moss; 72tr AA/C Jones; 73t AA/C Jones; 73r AA/T Souter; 74tl AA/C Jones; 74tc AA/C Jones; 74tr AA/P Baker; 75t AA/R Tenison; 75c Eden Project; 75b Eden Project; 76t AA/K Doran; 76b Britain On View; 77tl AA/M Jourdan; 77tc AA/C Jones; 77tr Britain On View; 77b AA/P Baker, 78tl AA/C Jones; 78tc AA/R Moss; 78tr AA/R Moss; 79tl Fleet Air Arm Museum; 79tc AA/C Jones; 79tr AA/S L Day; 79c AA/S L Day; 80t AA/R Ireland; 80l AA/M Jourdan; 81tl AA/S L Day; 81tc Britain On View; 81tr AA/C Jones; 82tl Britain On View; 82tc AA/C Jones; 82tr AA/C Jones; 83tl AA/C Jones; 83tr AA/M Jourdan; 83b AA/R Moss; 84tl AA/C Jones, 84tr AA/S L Day; 84b AA/C Jones; 85tl AA/C Jones; 85tc AA/R Tenison; 85tr AA/S & O Mathews; 86t AA/A W Besley; 86b AA/C Jones; 87tl AA; 87tr AA/E Meacher; 88tl AA/W Voysey; 88tr AA/C Jones; 88b AA/R Moss; 89tl AA/C Jones; 89tr AA/R Newton; 90tl AA/C Jones; 90tc AA/H Palmer; 90tr AA/M Jourdan; 92tl AA; 92tc AA/P Brown; 92tr AA/M Birkitt; 92b AA/C Jones; 93tl AA/J Miller; 93tc AA/P Baker; 93tr AA/T Souter; 94tl AA/C Jones; 94tr AA/A Baker; 95tl AA/P Baker; 95tr AA/J Miller; 96t AA/C Coe; 96cl AA/M Birkitt; 96c AA/C Coe; 96cr AA/L Whitwam; 96b AA/L Whitwam; 97 Britain On View; 98tl AA/D Noble; 98tc AA/J Miller; 98tr AA/T Souter; 98tl AA/W Voysey; 98tr AA/C Jones; 100tl AA/M Birkitt; 100tc AA/D Forss; 100tr AA/D Forss; 100tl Britain On View; 101tc AA/M Birkitt; 101tr Britain On View; 102tl Britain On View; 102tc AA/S McBride; 102tr AA/W Voysey; 103tl AA/C Jones; 103tr AA/M Birkitt; 104 AA; 105t AA/A Lawson; 105cl AA/A Lawson; 105c AA/A Lawson; 105cr AA/A Lawson; 105b AA/C Jones; 106tl AA/S L Day; 106tr AA/A Lawson; 106b AA/A Lawson; 108tl AA/W Voysey; 108tc AA/R Ireland; 100tr The Otter Trust; 109t AA/W Voysey; 109cr AA/W Voysey; 109b AA/S & O Mathews; 110tl AA/D Forss; 110tr AA/S & O Mathews; 111tl AA/P Baker; 111tr AA/J Miller; 112tl AA/J Miller; 112cl Britain On View; 112b AA/W Voysey; 113t AA/W Voysey (by permission on the Dean and Canons of Windsor); 112/3 AA/W Voysey; 114tl Shuttleworth Collection; 114tc AA/W Voysey; 114tr AA/S L Day; 115tl AA/C Jones; 115tr AA/W Voysey; 116tl AA/M Birkitt; 116tc AA/S L

Abbreviations for the credits are as follows:
AA = AA World Travel Library, t (top), b (bottom), c (centre), l (left), r (right)

Day; 116tr AA/W Voysey; 118 AA/M Jourdan; 119t AA/S McBride 119r Royal Collection/Derry Moore; 120tl AA/R Strange; 120tr AA/J Tims; 120b AA/R Strange; 121tl Dali Universe; 121tc AA/D Ireland; 121tr AA/R Strange; 121b AA/M Jourdan; 122t AA/R Strange; 122cl AA; 123t ©British Museum; 123l AA/G Wrona; 124tl AA/S McBride; 124tc AA/B Smith; 124tr Britain On View; 125tl AA/M Jourdan; 125tr AA/R Strange; 126tl AA; 126tr AA/M Jourdan; 127t AA/J Tims; 127r AA/P Kenward; 128tl Science Museum; 128tc AA/P Kenward; 128tr AA/M Jourdan; 129tl AA/M Jourdan; 129tr AA/M Jourdan; 130 AA/S McBride; 131t Victoria & Albert Museum; 131bl Victoria & Albert Museum; 131br AA/J McMillan; 132tl AA; 132tr AA/J McMillan; 134tl AA/C Jones; 134tc AA/N Jenkins; 134tr AA/G Matthews; 135tl AA/N Jenkins; 135tr AA/P Aithie; 136t Britain On View; 136l AA; 137tl AA/I Burgum; 137tc AA/I Burgum; 137tr AA/I Burgum; 137b AA/I Burgum; 138tl AA/I Burgum; 138tc Dan-Yr-Ogof National Show Caves; 138tr AA/C Molyneux; 139t AA/N Jenkins; 139r AA/G Matthews; 140tl AA/I Burgum; 140tr AA/I Burgum; 141tl AA/C Jones; 141tc AA/I Burgum; 141tr Britain On View; 142tl National Botanic Garden of Wales; 142tr Britain On View; 142b Photodisc; 143t AA/C Jones; 143cr AA/R Newton; 143br Britain On View; 144tl AA/N Jenkins; 144tr AA/T D Timms; 144tl AA/I Burgum; 145tc AA/C Jones; 145tr AA/N Jenkins; 146tl M Moody; 146tc Trefriw Woollen Mills; 146tr Welsh Wildlife Centre; 147t AA/A J Hopkins; 147cr AA; 147br Britain On View; 149tl Alton Towers; 149tr Britain On View; 150tl Black Country Living Museum; 150tc Cadbury World; 150tr Britain On View; 151tl AA/C Jones; 151tr M Hayward; 151b Britain On View; 152t AA/P Baker; 152b AA/A Midgley; 153tl AA/C Jones; 153tr AA/H Palmer; 154tl AA/C Jones; 154tr AA/M Hayward; 154b AA/M Allwood-Coppin; 155tl AA/H Palmer; 155tr AA/J Mottershaw; 156tl AA/P Baker; 156tc AA/A J Hopkins; 156tr AA/C Jones; 157tl AA/P Baker; 157tc Snibston Discovery Centre; 157tr Britain on View; 158t Britain On View; 158cl AA/H Palmer; 158/9 AA/H Palmer; 158b AA/M Short 159 AA/H Palmer; 160tl AA/S L Day; 160tr Warwick Castle; 161tl West Midlands Safari Park; 161tc AA/H Palmer; 161tr AA/H Palmer; 163tl Britain On View; 163tr AA/C Lees; 164tl AA/J Beazley; 164tr AA/S L Day; 165tl Britain On View; 165tr AA/D Tarn; 166tl AA; 166tr AA/L Whitwam; 167tl Catalyst Museum; 167tc AA/C Lees; 167tr AA; 168t AA/J Beazley; 168l AA/C Lees; 169t AA/L Whitwam; 169r AA/A Baker; 170tl AA/L Whitwam; 170tc Britain On View; 170tr AA/L Whitwam; 171tl AA; 171tr AA/P Sharpe; 172tl AA/T Mackie; 172tr AA/S L Day; 172b © The Board of Trustees of the Armouries; 173t AA/S L Day; 173r Britain On View; 174tl AA/C Lees; 174tr picturesofmanchester.com/Len Grant; 175tl AA/D Tarn; 175tr AA/C Lees; 175cl AA; 176tl AA/J Morrison; 176tc AA/C Lees; 176tr AA/P Wilson; 177tl AA/L Whitwam; 177tc AA/P Baker; 177tr AA/L Whitwam; 178tl AA/J Mottershaw; 178tc AA/J Beazley; 178tr AA/E A Bowness; 179tl AA/M Trelawny; 179b AA/L Whitwam; 180 Ian Leonard/Alamy; 180r AA/P Bennett; 181t AA/P Bennett; 181cr AA/P Wilson; 181br AA/R Newton; 182tl Britain On View; 182cb AA/P Bennett; 183 AA/P Bennett; 184tl AA/D Tarn; 184tr Yorkshire Sculpture Park; 184b AA/P Wilson; 186tl AA/M Alexander; 186tr AA/E Ellington; 187tl AA/M Alexander; 187tr Steve Austin/Stockscotland; 187b Photodisc; 188tl AA/S L Day; 188tc AA/J Beazley; 188tr AA/R Weir; 189tl AA/R Weir; 189tc AA/J Smith; 189tr Deep Sea World; 190 Britain On View; 191t AA/K Paterson; 191r AA; 193tr AA/K Paterson; 193cr AA/J Smith; 193br AA/K Paterson; 194tl AA/J Smith; 194tc AA/S L Day; 194tr AA/S Whitehorne; 195tl AA/S L Day;

195tr AA/S L Day; 196tl Britain On View; 196tr AA; 197tl AA/P Sharpe; 197tr AA/E Ellington; 198t AA/S Whitehorne; 198l Greater Glasgow and Clyde Valley Tourist Board; 198/9 Greater Glasgow and Clyde Valley Tourist Board; 199t Greater Glasgow and Clyde Valley Tourist Board; 199r AA/S Whitehorne; 200tl AA/S Gibson; 200cl AA/M Alexander; 200c AA/S J Whitehorne; 200r AA/R Newton; 201tl AA/J Beazley; 201r AA/J Henderson; 202t AA/S Whitehorne; 202l Britain On View; 203tl AA/R G Elliott; 203br AA/A Baker; 204tl AA/S Anderson; 204tc AA/D Corrance; 204tr AA/S Whitehorne; 205tl AA/S L Day; 205tr AA/S L Day; 206tl AA/R Weir; 206br AA/ E Ellington; 207tl Britain On View; 207tr AA/J Henderson; 208tl AA/S L Day; 208tc Britain On View; 208tr Britain On View.

WHAT TO DO
209 Photodisc; 210–213t McArthur Glen Designer Outlets; 210l A Stonehouse; 210r A Stonehouse; 211l AA/R Moss; 211r AA/M Hayward; 213c AA/C Sawyer; 214–5t Bournemouth International Centre; 214l Bournemouth International Centre; 214r Ludlow Assembly Rooms; 215l The Ocean Rooms; 215r Fridge; 216t The Ocean Rooms; 216l AA/C Sawyer; 216cr Britain On View; 217–219t AA/C Jones; 217l Britain On View; 217r C Jones; 218/9 AA/C Jones; 218l AA/C Jones; 218r AA; 221–227t Digital Vision; 221 AA/C Jones; 222c C Jones; 223c Broadmead, Bristol; 224c AA/C Jones; 225c AA/S&O Mathews; 226c Shore Surf School; 228–233t Digital Vision; 228c AA/C Jones; 229c Komedia; 230c Lakeside Shopping Centre; 231c Phoenix Picture House; 232c AA/C Jones; 234–242t Selfridges; 234c AA/R Strange; 235c AA/P Kenward; 236c Britain On View; 237c Odeon Leicester Square; 238c Gautier Deblonde; 239c Fridge; 240c Britain On View; 241c Photodisc; 243–247t Britain On View; 243c Britain On View; 244c New Theatre Cardiff; 245c Britain On View; 246c AA/ N Jenkins; 248–253t Profile Nottingham; 248c AA/M Hayward; 249c Jinney Ring Craft Centre; 250c Britain On View; 251c Jonathan Harris Studio Glass Ltd; 252c AA/I Burgum; 254–259t AA/T Mackie; 254c Jan Chlebik/Old Trafford Football Ground; 255c Betty's; 256c Harvey Nichols; 257c The Mersey Partnership (TMP); 258c Stephen Joseph Theatre; 260–266t AA/J Smith; 260c AA/J Carnie; 261c Alan Richardson; 262c Jenners; 263c Johnston's of Elgin; 264c Greater Glasgow & Clyde Valley Tourist Board; 265c AA/J Henderson.

OUT AND ABOUT
267 AA/P Baker; 269tr AA/P Baker; 269br AA/C Jones; 270 AA/C Jones; 271tr Britain On View; 271cr AA/C Jones; 271b AA/R Moss; 273tr AA/C Jones; 273tl AA; 273b AA/P Baker; 274t AA/S & O Mathews; 274b AA/K Paterson; 275tl AA; 275tr AA/R Moss; 275b AA/K Doran; 276 AA/K Doran; 277c Britain On View; 277br AA/K Doran; 278b AA; 279t AA; 279b AA/W Voysey; 281tc AA/D Forss; 281tr AA/W Voysey; 281bl AA/W Voysey; 281br AA/W Voysey; 282 AA/W Voysey; 283tr AA/W Voysey; 283cr AA/W Voysey; 283bl AA/W Voysey; 283br AA/W Voysey; 284 AA/C Molyneux; 285tl AA/N Jenkins; 285tr AA/C Molyneux; 285b AA/I Burgum; 286 AA/N Jenkins; 287tl AA/C Molyneux; 287tr AA/C Molyneux; 286/7 AA/C Jones; 289l AA/I Burgum; 289r AA/I Burgum; 290 AA/N Jenkins; 291t AA/I Burgum; 291bl AA/I Burgum; 291br AA/N Jenkins; 291t AA/I Burgum; 293tl AA/A Grierley; 293tr AA/R Newton; 293bl AA/D Croucher; 294 AA/N Jenkins; 295tl Britain On View/Steve Lew; 295bl Britain On View; 295br Britain On View; 297tl AA/P Baker; 297bl AA/M Birkitt; 297br

AA/R Newton; **298** AA/M Birkitt; **299** AA/M Hayward; **299b** AA/M Birkitt; **301tl** AA/E A Bowness; **301tr** AA/E A Bowness; **301bl** AA/E A Bowness; **301br** AA/S L Day; **302** Britain On View; **303tl** AA/T Mackie; **303tr** Britain On View; **303b** AA/T Mackie; **305t** Britain On View; **305cr** AA; **305bl** AA/E A Bowness; **305br** Britain On View; **307tl** AA; **307tr** AA/J Mottershaw; **307cl** AA; **307bl** AA/L Whitwam; **307br** AA/J Morrison; **309tl** AA; **309tr** AA/S Gregory; **309cr** AA/S Gregory; **309b** AA; **311tl** AA; **311tr** AA/J Beazley; **311bl** AA; **311br** AA/E A Bowness; **312** AA/A J Hopkins; **313t** AA/C Lees; **313br** AA/J Beazley; **313bc** AA/C Lees; **315tr** AA/P Baker; **315cl** AA/H Williams; **315b** AA/D Tarn; **316** AA/S & O Mathews; **317t** AA/L Whitwam; **317b** AA/D Tarn; **318** AA; **319t** AA/R Czaja; **319b** AA/J Morrison; **320** AA/C Lees; **321tl** AA/C Lees; **312tr** AA/C Lees; **321b** Britain On View; **322** Scottish Borders Tourist Board; **323tl** Scottish Borders Tourist Board; **323tr** AA/C Lees; **323b** AA/C Lees; **324** AA/J Carnie; **325tl** AA/J Carnie; **325tr** AA/J Carnie; **325bl** AA/S L Day; **325bc** AA/S L Day; **326** AA/S L Day; **327t** AA/J Henderson; **327cl** Christine Spreiter.

EATING AND STAYING

329 AA/C Sawyer; **330l** Photodisc; **330cl** Photodisc; **330cr** Britain On View; **330r** Britain On View; **331t** Britain On View; **331b** Britain On View; **332l** AA/M Jourdan; **332cl** Britain On View; **332cr** Britain On View; **332r** AA/M Jourdan; **334–367t** AA/C Sawyer; **334c** AA/P Baker; **339c** AA/I Miller; **344c** AA/M Jourdan; **345c** AA/W Voysey; **346c** AA/W Voysey; **348c** AA/W Voysey; **349c** AA/I Burgum; **353c** AA/C Molyneux; **358c** AA/P Bennett; **363c** AA/S Day; **365c** J Edmanson; **368l** Britain On View; **368cl** Britain On View; **368cr** Britain On View; **368r** AA/R Mort; **369l** Britain On View; **369cl** Britain On View; **369cr** Britain On View; **369r** Britain On View; **371t** AA; **371b** AA/C Sawyer; **372–402t** AA/C Sawyer; **372c** AA/S Day; **377c** AA/John Miller; **382c** AA/R Turpin; **385c** AA/Rich Newton; **389c** AA/M Birkitt; **393c** AA/S Gregory; **398c** AA/S Whitehorne.

PLANNING

403 AA/C Sawyer; **407** AA/J A Tims; **410c** AA/R Strange; **411** AA/R Strange; **413bl** AA/A Kouprianoff; **413tr** AA/J A Tims; **413cr** AA/R Strange.

Every effort has been made to trace the copyright holders, and we apologise in advance for any accidental errors. We would be happy to apply the corrections in the following edition of this publication.

Project editor
Robin Barton

AA Travel Guides design team
David Austin, Glyn Barlow, Alan Gooch, Kate Harling, Bob Johnson,
Nick Otway, Carole Philp, Keith Russell

Picture research
Carol Walker

Internal repro work
Susan Crowhurst, Ian Little, Michael Moody

Production
Lyn Kirby, Helen Sweeney

Mapping
Maps produced by the Cartography Department of AA Publishing

Main contributors
Judith Bamber, Oliver Bennett, Colin Follet, Mike Gerrard, Tim Locke,
Jackie Staddon, Hilary Weston, Jenny White, Nia Williams, David Winpenny

Copy editor
Maria Morgan

Updaters
Chris Bagshaw, Colin Follett, Tim Locke

Revision management
Cambridge Publishing Management Ltd

Published by AA Publishing, a trading name of Automobile Association Developments Limited, whose
registered office is Fanum House, Basing View, Basingstoke, RG21 4EA. Registered number 1878835.

A CIP catalogue record for this book is available from the British Library.

ISBN-10: 0-7495-4002-8
ISBN-13: 978-0-7495-4002-9

Key Guide is a registered trademark in Australia and is used under license.
Binding style with plastic section dividers by permission of AA Publishing.

Colour separation by Keenes
Printed and bound by Leo, China

Find out more about AA Publishing and the wide range of travel publications and services the AA
provides by visiting our website at www.theAA.com/travel

We believe the contents of this book are correct at the time of printing.
However, some details, particularly prices, opening times and telephone numbers do change.
We do not accept responsibility for any consequences arising from the use of this book.
This does not affect your statutory rights. We would be grateful if readers would advise us of
any inaccuracies they may encounter, or any suggestions they might like to make to improve
the book. There is a form provided at the back of the book for this purpose, or you can
email us at Keyguides@theaa.com

COVER PICTURE CREDITS
Front Cover, top to bottom: AA/S L Day; AA M Jourdan; AA M Birkitt; AA M Jourdan
Back Cover, top to bottom: AA/C Lees; AA/C Jones; Photodisc; AA. Spine: AA/S L Day

Dear Key Guide Reader

●

Thank you for buying this Key Guide. Your comments and opinions are very important to us, so please help us to improve our travel guides by taking a few minutes to complete this questionnaire.

You do not need a stamp (unless posted outside the UK). If you do not want to cut this page from your guide, then photocopy it or write your answers on a plain sheet of paper.

Send to: Key Guide Editor, AA World Travel Guides
FREEPOST SCE 4598, Basingstoke RG21 4GY

Find out more about AA Publishing and the wide range of travel publications the AA provides by visiting our website at
www.theAA.com/bookshop

ABOUT THIS GUIDE

Which Key Guide did you buy? _____

Where did you buy it?_____

When? _ _ month/ _ _ year

Why did you choose this AA Key Guide?
❑ Price ❑ AA Publication
❑ Used this series before; title _____
❑ Cover ❑ Other (please state) _____

Please let us know how helpful the following features of the guide were to you by circling the appropriate category: very helpful (**VH**), helpful (**H**) or little help (**LH**)

Size	**VH**	**H**	**LH**
Layout	**VH**	**H**	**LH**
Photos	**VH**	**H**	**LH**
Excursions	**VH**	**H**	**LH**
Entertainment	**VH**	**H**	**LH**
Hotels	**VH**	**H**	**LH**
Maps	**VH**	**H**	**LH**
Practical info	**VH**	**H**	**LH**
Restaurants	**VH**	**H**	**LH**
Shopping	**VH**	**H**	**LH**
Walks	**VH**	**H**	**LH**
Sights	**VH**	**H**	**LH**
Transport info	**VH**	**H**	**LH**

What was your favourite sight, attraction or feature listed in the guide?

Page _____ Please give your reason _____

_____

Which features in the guide could be changed or improved? Or are there any other comments you would like to make?

_____

_____

ABOUT YOU

Name (Mr/Mrs/Ms) _____

Address _____

_____

Postcode _____ Daytime tel nos _____

Email _____
Please *only* give us your mobile phone number/email if you wish to hear from us about other products and services from the AA and partners by text or mms.

Which age group are you in?
Under 25 ❑   25–34 ❑   35–44 ❑   45–54 ❑   55+ ❑

How many trips do you make a year?
Less than 1 ❑   1 ❑   2 ❑   3 or more ❑

ABOUT YOUR TRIP

Are you an AA member?   Yes ❑ No ❑

When did you book?   _ _ month/_ _ year

When did you travel?   _ _ month/_ _ year

Reason for your trip?   Business ❑ Leisure ❑

How many nights did you stay? _____

How did you travel?   Individual ❑ Couple ❑ Family ❑ Group ❑

Did you buy any other travel guides for your trip? _____

If yes, which ones? _____

_____

Thank you for taking the time to complete this questionnaire. Please send it to us as soon as possible, and remember, you do not need a stamp (*unless posted outside the UK*).

AA Travel Insurance call 0800 072 4168 or visit www.theaa.com

---

Titles in the Key Guide series:
Australia, Barcelona, Britain, Brittany, Canada, Costa Rica, Florence and Tuscany, France, Germany, Ireland, Italy, London, Mallorca, Mexico, New York, New Zealand, Normandy, Paris, Portugal, Prague, Provence and the Côte d'Azur, Rome, Scotland, South Africa, Spain, Thailand, Venice, Vietnam.
Published in May 2007: Croatia   **Published in October 2007:** China

---